Handbook of Generative Approaches to Language Acquisition

STUDIES IN THEORETICAL PSYCHOLINGUISTICS
VOLUME 41

Managing Editors

Lyn Frazier, *Dept. of Linguistics, University of Massachusetts at Amherst*
Thomas Roeper, *Dept. of Linguistics, University of Massachusetts at Amherst*
Kenneth Wexler, *Dept. of Brain and Cognitive Science, MIT, Cambridge, Mass.*

Editorial Board

Robert Berwick, *Artificial Intelligence Laboratory, MIT, Cambridge, Mass.*
Matthew Crocker, *Saarland University, Germany*
Janet Dean Fodor, *City University of New York, New York*
Angela Friederici, *Max Planck Institute of Human Cognitive and Brain Sciences, Germany*
Merrill Garrett, *University of Arizona, Tucson*
Lila Gleitman, *School of Education, University of Pennsylvania*
Chris Kennedy, *Northwestern University, Illinois*
Manfred Krifka, *Humboldt University, Berlin, Germany*
Howard Lasnik, *University of Maryland*
Yukio Otsu, *Keio University, Tokyo*
Andrew Radford, *University of Essex, U.K.*

For further volumes:
http://www.springer.com/series/6555

Jill de Villiers • Tom Roeper
Editors

Handbook of Generative Approaches to Language Acquisition

Editors
Jill de Villiers
Department of Psychology
Smith College
Bass Hall 401
Northampton, MA 01063
USA
jdevilli@email.smith.edu

Tom Roeper
Linguistics Department
University of Massachusetts at Amherst
226 South College
150 Hicks Way
Amherst, MA 01003
USA
roeper@linguist.umass.edu

ISSN 1873-0043
ISBN 978-94-007-1687-2   e-ISBN 978-94-007-1688-9
DOI 10.1007/978-94-007-1688-9
Springer Dordrecht Heidelberg London New York

Library of Congress Control Number: 2011935733

© Springer Science+Business Media B.V. 2011
No part of this work may be reproduced, stored in a retrieval system, or transmitted in any form or by any means, electronic, mechanical, photocopying, microfilming, recording or otherwise, without written permission from the Publisher, with the exception of any material supplied specifically for the purpose of being entered and executed on a computer system, for exclusive use by the purchaser of the work

Printed on acid-free paper

Springer is part of Springer Science+Business Media (www.springer.com)

Contents

Introduction 1
Jill de Villiers and Tom Roeper

Missing Subjects in Early Child Language 13
Nina Hyams

Grammatical Computation in the Optional Infinitive Stage 53
Ken Wexler

Computational Models of Language Acquisition 119
Charles Yang

The Acquisition of the Passive 155
Kamil Ud Deen

The Acquisition Path for Wh-Questions 189
Tom Roeper and Jill de Villiers

Binding and Coreference: Views from Child Language 247
Cornelia Hamann

Universal Grammar and the Acquisition of Japanese Syntax ... 291
Koji Sugisaki and Yukio Otsu

Studying Language Acquisition Through the Prism of Isomorphism 319
Julien Musolino

Acquiring Knowledge of Universal Quantification 351
William Philip

Index 395

Contributors

Jill de Villiers Departments of Psychology and Philosophy, Smith College, Bass Hall 401, Northampton, MA, USA, jdevil@smith.edu

Kamil Ud Deen Linguistics Department, University of Hawaii, 1890 East-West Road, Moore Hall #559, Honolulu HI 96822, USA, kamil@hawaii.edu

Cornelia Hamann Carl von Ossietzky Universität Oldenburg Fakultät III, Institut für Fremdsprachenphilologien, Seminar für Anglistik/Amerikanistik D-26111, Oldenburg, Germany, cornelia.hamann@uni-oldenburg.de

Nina Hyams Linguistics Department, UCLA, 3125 Campbell Hall, Los Angeles CA 90095-1543, USA, hyams@humnet.ucla.edu

Julien Musolino Psychology Department, Rutgers University, Busch Campus 152 Frelinghuysen Road, Piscataway, NJ 08854-8020, USA, julienm@ruccs.rutgers.edu

Yukio Otsu Linguistics, Keio University, Kanagawa-ken, Japan Minato, Tokyo, Japan, oyukio@sfc.keio.ac.jp

William Philip Linguistics, University of Utrecht, Utrecht, The Netherlands, W.C.H.Philip@uu.nl

Tom Roeper Linguistics Department, 226 South College, University of Massachusetts at Amherst, 150 Hicks Way, Amherst, MA, USA, roeper@linguist.umass.edu

Koji Sugisaki Mie University, Tsu, Mie, Japan, sugisaki@human.mie-u.ac.jp

Ken Wexler MIT Brain & Cognitive Sciences, 77 Massachusetts Avenue, 46-2005, Cambridge, MA 02139, USA, wexler@mit.edu

Charles Yang Department of Linguistics & Computer Science, University of Pennsylvania, Philadelphia, USA, charles.yang@ling.upenn.edu

Introduction

Jill de Villiers and Tom Roeper

1 Some History

The volume represents the paradigm of *generative* approaches to language acquisition, and does so unabashedly. There are shared assumptions about universal grammar as a guide to acquisition, about the formal nature of syntax, and of the child's biological preparedness for learning. Working within the shared paradigm allows researchers to pursue exquisite details in both empirical and theoretical work. But that does not hold the authors back from addressing and sometimes questioning foundational assumptions in many of the papers. There are many theories of acquisition beyond generative grammar and many new theories will arrive in the future. What is unquestionably clear is that work in the generative paradigm has produced an enormous amount of empirical data relevant to any future theory. This volume summarizes a great deal of it.

Where did the study of language acquisition begin? One of our goals in this handbook is not only to assemble a compendium of knowledge gained, but enable the reader to step back and see what kinds of progress have been made, what new challenges arise, and what directions are most promising for the future. We have invited various authors most of whom have had a central role in the exploration of core constructions in grammar to summarize their field from their perspective.

J. de Villiers (✉)
Departments of Psychology and Philosophy, Smith College, Bass
Hall 401, Northampton, MA, USA
e-mail: jdevil@smith.edu

T. Roeper
Linguistics Department, 226 South College, University of Massachusetts at Amherst,
150 Hicks Way, Amherst, MA, USA
e-mail: roeper@linguist.umass.edu

Our goal was to elicit a succinct and coherent view of a major domain in acquisition, via the authors' deep personal knowledge and historical overview of developments. In this introduction we will summarize the core points of view expressed. But first, we make some broad comments about changes in linguistic theory relevant to acquisition perspectives.

At the beginning, linguistic theory in the generative tradition offered to science the promise of a unique form of biological explanation: an explanation of how a child acquired language that began from innate mental assumptions that were given in a mathematical representation. The concepts were so abstract that the set of combinations was inherently unlimited, and therefore the set of possible grammars was infinite. Then how could a child solve the problem outlined in the Aspects model (Chomsky 1965), to select the grammar of his community from an infinite set?

Several unusual concepts underlay the claim: rules, hierarchies, and transformations were, by hypothesis, pertinent to what a child's mind did when speech was heard. These psychological constructs had been regarded as late features of an instructed cognition, for example, geometry and rules were learned in school, not something wielded innately. Reference had seemed inevitably to be at the heart of language, yet unlike every previous theory, Chomsky (1976: Rules and Representations) claimed that reference was almost irrelevant to the building of grammar.

Two inherent capacities were proposed to govern acquisition, the first being the autonomy of syntax. If syntax is autonomous, then it could possibly be recognized just by observing variation in surface order of words, as a hard skeleton might be revealed to underpin the movements of a soft body. If such "distributional" evidence were the key, and meaning played no role, then one could, in principle, learn grammar by listening to the radio. Furthermore, the goal of communication could be a completely external motivation with no obvious connection to the organization of structures undergoing acquisition, that is, no point by point mapping of function onto form.

The second property was a Grammar Evaluation Metric, a separate biological capacity which could determine by mathematical methods which grammar was best if several could capture the data. The Evaluation metric would then generate a set of possible grammars and choose the shortest, in an early version of representational economy. This separate acquisition device might, as a biological entity, be subject also to a critical time period. These mathematical representations gave birth to learnability theory which for instance, suggested that all rules should first be obligatory, then optional, because an obligatory rule has immediate counter-evidence, but an optional one does not, allowing a grammar to be acquired as a logical object with minimal data.

In the evolution of the field linking theoretical linguistics and language acquisition, several things occurred: the grammar expanded to include a set of modules that were not completely "syntactic" in character, going beyond what word-order captures: thematic roles, case-assignment, and binding relations (**Chomsky 1981: introduction of Principles and Parameters**) No role, for instance, had been given to the paradigms of case-marking, so a case-module was posited. The syntactic trees were expanded to include other systems whose primitives were inherently different (a set of thematic roles and case), from which a <u>modular</u> grammar emerged. But without <u>constrained links</u> (ultimately interfaces, see below) between modules, these new dimensions lead, again, to an even greater explosion of possible grammars from a strict learnability perspective. The set of case-markings, thematic roles, and structures could all vary, producing more possible grammars. Since the primitives are inherently diverse, it is not easy to imagine an evaluation against a single mathematical standard of simplicity (like length of grammar). For instance, if a language can be captured with a grammar that has either simplicity in the movement system (just a single feature moves) or simplicity in Logical form (LF and surface structure coincide via Pied-piping of more than a single feature), how does the child decide?[1] The diversity of grammar called for a different conceptualization of how to constrain possible grammars so that a child can acquire them.

2 Parameters

The first answer to that question was a theory of parameters: a finite set of grammars with fixed decision points (Chomsky 1981; Roeper and Williams 1987). The parameters were deductively linked to assist in learning: e.g. Does a language have empty expletives? If so, then subjects are obligatory. It was a substantive theory of biological connections that might cross modular boundaries, for example one could imagine a parameter that linked empty categories, intonation, and case.

The theory of parameters has undergone revisions, challenges, and reformulations. One important development has been the notion of micro-parameters advanced by Kayne (2000), suggesting that hundreds of small parametric options, often lexically linked, are possible. A second suggestion is that they are partially subject to indirect negative evidence [which correlates generally with claims from Bayesian theory in which absence of statistical support leads to rejection, but see the more refined view of grammar competition from Yang (2002) and Roeper (2000)]. A third kind of argument (Boeckx 2008) is linked to recent claims by Chomsky (2005) introducing interface theory and a new angle on acquisition theory. Acquisition is accomplished by (1) a small component of UG, (2) Experience and (3) so-called "3rd Factors" of biological design that ensure computational efficiency. Boeckx (2008) observes, at an abstract level, that this perspective might allow the elimination of parameters. This logical possibility remains highly programmatic, but may have some promise.

In sum, while it is clear that the notion of parameter-setting is a controversial one and that the theories are in considerable flux, it is nonetheless remarkable how early children's grammars reflect the particular properties of their language, a fact noted in all of the chapters.

---

[1] See Roeper (2003) for discussion of how a child copes with a shift in grammar where making one module simpler makes another more complex.

3 Interfaces

A second shift is on the horizon under modern conceptions of minimalism: Interface theory. Minimalism radically limits UG to recursive operations of Merge and a tight theory of Label projection (Chomsky 2010). Then we expect that **grammar development will be constrained and coordinated by Interface principles** whose character is partially determined by the other mental systems that are engaged. This conceptualization immediately alters the acquisition problem as well. The relevance of these diverse dimensions is, however, only the beginning: they cannot apply helter-skelter. There must be a coordinating mechanism that will dictate how the child carries out a sequential mapping of interface factors for a new sentence as yet unintegrated in the grammar. It leads to this claim:

Interface principles guide the acquisition process in connecting modules.

It is natural that researchers are increasingly making reference to the role of other aspects of language and their connection to other aspects of the mind in the child's acquisition of grammar, but the mechanisms of the interface with, for instance, the intentional conceptual system remain obscure. **It maybe that acquisition will reveal those interface mechanisms more directly than grammaticality judgments.**

There are two ways, not mutually exclusive, that acquisition researchers have taken to this question of how discourse considerations apply. Appropriately many ideas which began as experimental design features have become theoretical issues themselves and now motivate interesting work on the relationship between discourse and grammar. Experiments must be carefully designed to maximize the appropriateness of the discourse for the syntactic (or semantic) phenomenon in question, and once this is done, the child can be shown to have precocious understanding of the form or not. Such concerns have formed the heart of much dispute over the merits of different empirical investigations, and form the basis for the modern debates about competence and performance, reflected in several of the chapters (particularly those by Philip, Musolino, Hamann, Sugisaki & Otsu, Deen).

A second approach reflects the new interest in interfaces, and acknowledges that aspects of discourse too, might be subject to development. In particular, the range of options for movement to positions in the "left periphery" of the syntactic hierarchy, the presence of Focus and Topic projections and their variation across languages, leads to the recognition that the child must achieve a complex integration of several factors to set some syntactic parameters. Some of these decisions may await development in other cognitive domains: the development of perspectives on others' knowledge, or Point of View, or Theory of Mind are the most often invoked (see chapters by de Villiers and Roeper, Hamann, Sugisaki and Otsu, Deen).

In general, what these chapters repeatedly show is that the child simultaneously draws on many modules from the outset. Hyams discusses the relevance of Discourse representation and pragmatics, saying, "it is clear from the newest work on early grammars that children have to integrate their language-particular grammars with the discourse-pragmatic constraints that come from universal Information Structure".

In their treatment of parameters, Wexler and Yang discuss the relevance of Tense -a semantic representation of time- to early decisions about what moves. Hamann discusses several dimensions of discourse representation such as logical presuppositions and the semantics of "guises" that seem to be relevant to the acquisition of binding. Roeper & de Villiers discuss the relevance of discourse representation and how it must be integrated to solve Superiority cross-linguistically.

Acquisition work reflects developments in linguistic theory, but it must also provoke new conceptions. That it is a lively field in its own right is richly evidenced in the chapters in this volume.

4 The Papers

The paper by Nina Hyams provides a succinct historical introduction to the use of generative grammar as an explanatory theory for language acquisition. However, the early work did not imagine the introduction of parameter theory, which, she argues, not only explains how acquisition can proceed despite an impoverished input, but how it in fact proceeds given the differences between languages. The great strength of the parametric approach is that it allows child grammars to be essentially adult-like (Continuity) and proposes a deductive path by which children arrive at their grammar. The main point of the paper is to account for the missing subjects seen so frequently in child language, even when the input does not allow dropped subjects.

How early is the pro-drop parameter set, and if it is early, why do children continue to drop subjects? The history of the topic is a clash between the rival accounts of generative grammar, on the one hand, and ideas about processing/production limitations on the other. Hyams leads us expertly along that path revealing a rich set of arguments that undergird the representations of children's earliest grammars and provide a model of how linguistic theories interact with acquisition data.

After discussing early accounts of mis-setting parameters such as the subset principle and morphological uniformity, Hyams' paper moves to consider more contemporary accounts such as competing grammars (see Yang's chapter), and Rizzi's (1994) truncation hypothesis, in which null subjects are to be found at the edge of root clauses, a position in which they are accessible to *discourse* identification. The motivation for truncation nicely connects to the intuition that there is a production constraint on early sentences. The paper ends with an interesting study that finally brings children's comprehension into the picture of null subjects, and uses it to bolster the claim that the phenomenon is ultimately grammatical, not performance-based.

Like Hyams' chapter, the central concern of the chapter by Ken Wexler is the very early stages of grammar, and the work therein is almost exclusively based not on experimental work but on detailed and quantitative analyses of early child transcripts. The chapter by Wexler considers the facts about children's early omission of Tense, or the Optional Infinitive stage. He makes the case that the phenomenon is central to discussions of how early parameters are set, and how Universal grammar constrains early production. First, the broad array of facts about the OI stage are brought out. The puzzle is that there are languages in which children do not show this OI stage, so there is an important distinction to be made linguistically, and that set of facts belies any simplistic account of the results, say, in English.

After discussion of theories that attempt to deal with the phenomenon at a more superficial level, Wexler addresses three theoretical accounts that provide a broader perspective. Truncation theory (Rizzi 1994) receives a thorough analysis, as does the Unique Checking Constraint, both of which require positing that the child has fewer resources available at the beginning and that the OI is a product of that, rather than an incomplete grammar. The UCC is a computational account, not a structural account, so it makes different predictions than does the truncation account, for example about embedded clauses, some of which remain to be fully tested. Nevertheless, an astonishing array of empirical phenomena has been well accommodated under this framework. An essential part of the reasoning is that biological maturation is needed to transition the child to an adult grammar: that language acquisition is to be seen as growth, rather than learning. Increasingly, evidence of language as a biological "organ" can be found, for example in studies of families with language impairments, or in heritability studies, though the distance between these facts and the linguistic phenomena is wide at present.

Wexler's chapter discusses in detail a rival notion stemming from a more empirically based approach, namely, the learning-theoretic model of Legate and Yang (2007) (see Yang, this volume). The difference of opinion here concerns the adequacy of specification of the parameters around Tense, and the extent to which there could be unambiguous "triggers" to set those parameters. Yang's work depends on the assumption of probabilistic, stochastic processes, based on positive input, even though it is set in a UG framework. In Wexler's view, the OI stage is characterized by the child's "brilliant" knowledge of parameters, with the exception of finiteness, so any slow, input-dependent procedures are fundamentally mistaken.

Charles Yang's chapter takes the reader on a journey into computational modeling of the process of change in grammar, with one eye on the linguistics – which must be universal and particular enough at the same time – and another on plausible psychological mechanisms. He demonstrates that generalization is still the fundamental requirement, and that is not significantly challenged by the construction of item-based grammars as models of acquisition. Yang describes the major results of learnability approaches: how the language acquisition device can achieve a plausible, human-type, grammar in a finite time from a finite sample of input. A variety of solutions have been tried, such as constraints on the class of grammars, but distributional approaches are considered closely. Yang argues that these should not be considered antithetical to generative accounts, as they seem needed for any model of how grammatical categories arise, for instance. But learning syntactic distributions, such as transitional probabilities between adjacent words, is still fraught with difficulties. The learning-as-selection approach is connected to the notion of parameter setting and asks: what are the cues or triggers that allow one parameter to be chosen over another? Are these cues preprogrammed? The most extreme version of this is the grammar-selection model of Yang, (see also Multiple Grammars, Roeper 1999) in which entire grammars are evaluated for their fit to a particular input sentence and rise and fall in probability as a consequence. Central to this model is the notion of a parameter signature: a particular linguistic property – such as the relative position of adverbs and tensed verbs – that is the sign that verbs raise to Tense. Yang is optimistic that such signatures can be found, but argues that the learnability models have to incorporate data and realistic assumptions from acquisition evidence.

Parametric theory has been challenged on three fronts:

1. The parameters do not work cleanly and deliver absolute decisions. For instance, the Head parameter for German OX works for verbs, but not prepositions. Therefore it is clear that some subtler decisions should be made.
2. Input frequencies make a difference. For instance, Yang shows that the amount of information available to a child will correlate with when all the dimensions of a parameter are finally set.
3. Micro-parameters, as proposed by Kayne (2000), which suggests that there are hundreds of small parameters.

The last hypothesis has not really been explored in the acquisition domain and offers an important new perspective on both of the other critiques. We discuss one example which pertains to the different perspectives offered by Wexler and Yang.

The Scandinavian languages are known to exhibit enormous subtle variation in what structures allow V2 (see Westergaard 2009). In actuality, English does the same, since both quotation and stylistic inversion allow V2 (Roeper 1999):

"nothing" said Bill
in the room ran John

This means that there may be many small decisions with respect to V2 that require separate evidential settings. In effect, the child will choose narrow lexical or lexical class, or pragmatic properties as a condition for V2 before they decide that it is all forms of V that move, and not just transitive, quotative, or auxiliaries ("residual V2") that are allowed to move. Early forms of V2 will then show some sensitivity to this parametric direction, but the full generality of the parametric decision will not be evident until later because in fact the parameter reduces to a series of implicational micro-parameters which require independent evidence.

Thus it is not the larger amount of total evidence that is critical, but exactly what kinds of evidence arise. Yang shows that OVS sentences are rare in German and children use them late. This indicates that while many early forms of V2 arise early, such as Locative-verb-subject (da geht er), the child waits for specific evidence before applying later forms, such as OVS, and a particular grammar could include one but not the other.

Thus, if V2 is a set of micro-parameters, it is neither correct to say that it is set early nor that it is set late, but rather that we need a more articulated vision of what the options in the parametric space are, as Kayne (2000) suggests.

This approach fits what we have seen elsewhere: the child is very sensitive to subdivisions in the language – verb-classes, adverb-types – from the outset which is the fundamental reason why we do not see wildly unexpected overgeneralizations at early points.

It also allows us to see that grammars may not be fully resolved into a single grammatical type, but rather carry evidence of Multiple Grammars within them: English retains some V2 properties while it has moved, over 500 years, from an SOV to an SVO structure.

Kamil Ud Deen's chapter addresses the development of the passive construction in children, long held to be an area of difficulty both in comprehension and in production. The passive involves movement rules, so the child must attend to the morphological and lexical cues that reveal the structure is not the standard canonical order. The chapter reviews the consistent findings in the empirical literature about what factors make the passive hard or easier for children, and then turns to the various theoretical accounts of the difficulty. The bold claim was that children have difficulty with A-chains in general, and maturation is the source of the chane in the child's ability, which occurs around age 5 years. Deen points to the clarity and testability of the claim about A-chains, and reviews the empirical work that has extended the claim to other A-chain constructions, especially drawing on other languages, and extending the theory into modern terms using the Minimalist notion of a Phase. A different model concerning a difficulty with Theta transmission is also tested against the standard empirical data. But are the traditional data trustworthy, or might the methods traditionally used somehow underestimate children's ability with the passive by failing to set the right conditions for its use? These are difficult questions that must always be addressed carefully in the field of acquisition, because they lie at the heart of the competence-performance distinction. But the greatest challenge to the ideas that the passive is late may come from a group of languages whose acquisition has been relatively neglected, namely Bantu languages, a matter on which Deen is well-placed to address, given his work on Swahili. Sugisaki and Otsu argue that the passive in Japanese provides a very interesting test of the idea that A-chains are delayed maturationally, and of whether success on them may be subject to other conditions, perhaps involving the interface with Theory of Mind.

Wh-questions provide a rich arena for the testing of generative ideas about acquisition, since their analysis has been at the heart of linguistic theory for 40 years. In the chapter on wh-questions, Tom Roeper & Jill de Villiers translate theoretical ideas into a series of proposals that make predictions about acquisition steps and stages. One such idea is the modularity of linguistic systems, which translates into a proposal that a child will seek to achieve an analysis that calls upon a single module first. A second is that Merge should be preferred over Move. These lead to potential explanations of stages in the development of questions in which children depart from adult grammar, such as in the case of *why*, and also why they might show a preference for e.g. subject questions before object questions.

The chapter considers empirical evidence and theoretical accounts of phenomena such as the order of questions in development, subject-auxiliary inversion and constraints on long distance movement. But it is the analysis of "partial movement" and the peculiar failure of children to provide the appropriate point of view on opaque clauses that attracts new attention. It is here that considerations of the semantic and pragmatic interfaces with syntax arise, as it is proposed that children prefer to ship off the grammatical parse to semantic interpretation one Phase at a time.

Introduction

The chapter considers other interfaces of syntax of questions with semantics and pragmatics, namely, the set or variable properties of a wh-question: when do they arise, how do they interact in multiple questions, and what constraints apply?

The paper by Cornelia Hamann begins with the core problem: if the binding principles are such a central part of UG, why do children have difficulty for so long with the interpretation of pronouns in object position? The paper reviews the evidence on behalf of two positions: first, the children do know Principle B but certain other performance factors could mask it, and second, that there is a real problem with pronoun interpretation that may require integrating syntax and pragmatics. Work across multiple languages is necessary in determining the grammatical nature of the problem: why do children in some languages show no difficulty? Hamann provides a summary of recent theoretical work on binding that makes it clear that there is more involved in interpretation of pronouns than the simple binding principles. Various theorists have proposed *coreference* rules that require consideration of pragmatics in one way or another, either as Rule P (Chien and Wexler 1990), Intrasentential coreference (Grodzinsky and Reinhart 1993) or most recently, subtler syntactic facts linked to scalar implicatures (Verbuk and Roeper 2010), needed to explain why both adults and children allow apparent violations of Principle B (Adam, 3;69 "he's taking it home with him"). The most radical idea (Chomsky 1995) is that interpretation of pronouns and anaphors involves the interface between semantics and pragmatics, and that binding principles are not part of S-structure/spellout.

The data on acquisition are striking in the asymmetries that generally appear: that pronouns are understood much more poorly than reflexives, that quantified NPs are usually better than non-quantified antecedents, and that production is much better than comprehension. The theoretical positions on these findings are multiple and distinct, but despite the variation there is some convergence on a combination of a pragmatic failure and an underspecification of the features of the pronoun.

Cross-linguistically, the data are perplexing. Pronominal clitics are better understood than non-clitic pronouns, but oddly, there is a delay of interpretation in the case of *clitic climbing* environments. A variety of proposals have been made to explain these effects, but the case of German, which does not have clitic pronouns, but does not show a delay of Principle B effect, stands out as a puzzle. The data are rich and mysterious in this domain, and clearly many opportunities exist for more research. It seems necessary in the future to pay attention to other environments in which children must attend to the *guise* of an NP, perhaps in referential opacity environments, to fully explore the role this plays in the delays in acquisition.

The chapter by Koji Sugisaki and Yukio Otsu beautifully sets out the central problem, "Plato's Problem", summarizes the central tenets of UG approaches, and then asks what about Japanese syntax acquisition can illuminate that account. Their first illustration is with the knowledge that SOV is the unmarked order, despite input that might suggest both are possible. Japanese children know that SVO sentences are conditioned by complex factors, and that OSV orders occur from a movement operation. Further clever experiments reveal that children are sensitive to the hierarchical, configurational, properties of Japanese, and to c-command. The results of work on wh questions provide striking confirmation that even in a language that has wh-in-situ, children are sensitive to the constraints on interpretation of those questions (see de Roeper & de Villiers' chapter). The special properties of the long-distance reflexive, *zibun*, are also shown to be present a surprisingly early age, complicating the picture of how binding relations are established (see also chapter by Hamann).

The final two chapters in the volume consider quantifiers: the interaction of syntax with quantification, and whether there are UG linguistic constraints on quantifier meaning. Julien Musolino in his chapter addresses the central question of quantifier scope, fundamentally, how does the syntax of the sentence interact with the meanings of the quantifiers inside it? A central observation is that children prefer to interpret quantifiers and negation in their surface order, showing *isomorphism*. The preferred methodology has been the experimental Truth-Value-Judgment task, in which children watch an event and then decide if a puppet described it correctly or not. Musolino addresses the variety of proposals that have been made to account for this departure from adult grammar, beginning with a grammatical account entailing the subset principle and a proposed typology of quantified noun phrases (QNPs). The claim was that children had difficulty accessing the principles involved in dealing with certain QNPs, but further empirical work made that claim less plausible: adults make the mistake (of failing to recognize non-isomorphic interpretations) in certain circumstances, and children do not make the mistake in others. In particular, the felicity conditions of the negation, a pragmatic manipulation, make a difference. An alternative explanation resides in the parsing domain: that revising an isomorphic interpretation is harder for children. More radically, a further account proposed by Guilin (the QAR, or Question-Answer Requirement) regards children's choice of isomorphism as a pragmatic epiphenomenon.

The move from a purely grammatical account to a parsing account, and then to consideration of pragmatics and context, is a theme throughout several of the chapters in this book, as considerations have broadened to consider the interface of syntax with other, often much less specified, modules. But in the course of exploring what can and what cannot be explained by each approach, the chapter on isomorphism provides a glimpse into the detailed and intertwined experimental and theoretical work in the field of language acquisition. The opportunity arises for more work that broadens the methodology used to explore how quantifiers and negation interact: there is nothing explored in spontaneous or elicited production, for example, and in other areas (see Hamann, Roeper & de Villiers, Philips, Deen, Wexler), sometimes insights are gained from the results from multiple approaches.

Bill Philip's chapter takes on the challenge of accounting for how children acquire the meanings of quantifiers, and the linguistic constraints that shape those meanings. He argues that UG may offer very little guidance about scopal ambiguity, or even about the mapping between sentence forms and types of quantification. Yet children show knowledge of basic universal quantification at an early age. The real acquisition problem lies in how the child discovers the semantic restrictions on how universal quantifiers apply to objects. Philip argues that the grammatical restrictions on the relevant NPs must be acquired from positive evidence, not from UG or from parametric variation.

Since the earliest work on the subject, it has been noticed that children exhibit a strange error, variously known as "spreading" or "exhaustive pairing". The phenomenon occurs over a wide variety of environments and in different kinds of methodological contexts, and Philip reviews evidence that counters claims that it is a methodological artifact. As is familiar from the papers in this volume, there are two potential classes of explanation: one that posits a knowledge difference between children and adults, and the second that suggests a problem in processing. The event quantificational hypothesis is a proposal that children misapply the semantic restriction, and rely instead on pragmatic principles. Crucially, Philip proposes that the pragmatic principles used by children are not constrained in the same way as those of adults faced with similar ambiguities, and that children lack the processing resources to bring the right knowledge to bear. In this way, Philip carves an interesting and convoluted path for a child to the achievement of full competence in quantification, bringing together innate knowledge, underdeveloped knowledge, and processing restrictions. These factors are carefully specified, and then put to the test in three new studies of Dutch children, filtered to include only certain participants at the right stage.

The novelty in Philip's provocative piece is the disentangling of what is innately known from what may be innately specified but acquired late, and from that which is acquired without the help of UG, from positive evidence. In an area like quantification it is extraordinarily difficult to differentiate the contributions made by these factors, and Philip lays out a significant empirical and theoretical challenge to the field to test these ideas.

5 Conclusion

Linguistic theory has become ever more refined, leaning on ever more subtle data. And yet first language acquisition, exposed to an increasingly sharper microscope, shows that the subtle detail of modern theory is reflected in the earliest data we can find. Moreover there is astonishing consistency across children in the manner in which they honor abstract principles, although their everyday experience is utterly diverse.

References

Boeckx, C. 2008. *Bare syntax*. Oxford: Oxford University Press.
Chien, Y.-C., and K. Wexler. 1990. Children's knowledge of locality conditions in binding as evidence for the modularity of syntax and pragmatics. *Language Acquisition* 1: 225–295.
Chomsky, N. 1965. *Aspects of the theory of syntax*. Cambridge, MA: MIT Press.
Chomsky, N. 1976. *Rules and representations*. Oxford: Blackwell.
Chomsky, N. 1981. *Lectures on government and binding*. Dordrecht: Foris.
Chomsky, N. 1995. *The minimalist program*. Cambridge, MA: MIT Press.

Chomsky, N. 2005. Three factors in language design. *Linguistic Inquiry* 36: 1–22.
Chomsky, N. 2010. *MIT lectures fall.*
Grodzinsky, Y., and T. Reinhart. 1993. The innateness of binding and coreference. *Linguistic Inquiry* 24: 69–102.
Kayne, R. 2000. *Parameters and universals*. Oxford/New York: Oxford University Press.
Legate, J.A., and C. Yang. 2007. Morphosyntactic learning and the development of tense. *Language Acquisition* 14: 315–344.
Rizzi, L. 1994. Early null subjects and root null subjects. In *Language acquisition studies in generative grammar*, ed. T. Hoekstra and B. Schwartz. Amsterdam: Benjamins.
Roeper, T. 2000. Universal bilingualism. *Bilingual Language Cognition* 2: 169–186.
Roeper, T. 2003. Multiple grammars, feature-attraction, pied-piping, and the question: Is AGR inside TP? In *Vulnerable domains in multilingualism*, ed. N. Müller. Amsterdam: Benjamins.
Roeper, T., and E. Williams. 1987. *Parameter-setting*. Dordrecht: Kluwer.
Verbuk, A., and T. Roeper. 2010. How pragmatics and syntax make principle B acquirable. *Language Acquisition* 17: 51–65.
Westergaard, M. 2009. *The acquisition of word order: Input cues, information structure and economy*, Linguistik Aktuell/Linguistics Today, vol. 145. Amsterdam: John Benjamins.
Yang, C. 2002. *Knowledge and learning in natural language*. Oxford: Oxford University Press.

Missing Subjects in Early Child Language

Nina Hyams

1 Language Acquisition and Linguistic Theory

The marriage of linguistic theory and language acquisition is approaching its golden anniversary. In her 1966 dissertation Ursula Bellugi provided a transformational analysis of the development of negation in English-speaking children. On the model of the Standard Theory of Generative Grammar (Chomsky 1965), she proposed a system of phrase structure and transformational rules to describe the various stages of negation and the transitions from one stage to the next. Following Bellugi's seminal work, various studies provided transformational analyses of other aspects of child grammar (Bloom 1970; Klima and Bellugi 1966; Brown and Fraser 1964; Brown et al. 1964; Brown 1973 among others). In keeping with the goals of generative grammar, these studies attempted to provide an explicit procedure for generating all and only the utterances produced by children in a specific age range or with respect to a specific aspect of grammar. While acknowledging that children's early utterances were more or less reduced versions of the adult target – "telegraphic" as characterized by Brown and Fraser (1964)—the descriptive focus was on the categories and combinations that the child reliably produced, rather than what he failed to produce or produced only probabilistically.

Fast forward 20 some odd years, it had become increasingly apparent that the "telegraphic" child's two and three word utterances belie a far richer and more abstract grammatical system. His language shows grammatical dependencies such as agreement (Hyams 1983, 1986; Guasti 1993/1994; Poeppel and Wexler 1993), case (Babyonyshev 1993; Schütze 1996), and verb movement (Pierce 1992; Verrips and Weissenborn 1992 among others), hence a sensitivity to the grammatical function of nouns and to the tense and aspect of verbs. The focus of generative acquisition research into early development shifted from the description of what

N. Hyams (✉)
Linguistics Department, UCLA, 3125 Campbell Hall, Los Angeles, CA 90095-1543, USA
e-mail: hyams@humnet.ucla.edu

children produce to investigation of what they seem to know, but fail to systematically produce. This includes, in particular, the various missing elements that give early language its telegraphic look – dropped pronouns, auxiliaries, inflections, determiners, and the functional architecture that supports these elements.

Much of the shift in focus was prompted by the publication of Chomsky's Lectures on Government and Binding (LGB) (1982). The principles and parameters model of Universal Grammar (UG) outlined in LGB ushered in a new era of syntactic research, but also a renewed interest and excitement in childhood grammatical development. The view of grammar acquisition as a system of parameter setting seemed ideally suited to address the logical problem of language acquisition – how human speakers come to know as much as we do based on limited language experience. The parameters more clearly defined the boundary conditions on the child's task – to choose among competing values (ideally binary) along an array of parameters. They also offered a new perspective on the role that input plays in the acquisition process, viz. the primary linguistic data act as "triggers" to set each parameter at one or another of its predetermined values. On this view, much of the child's linguistic knowledge is "imprinted" rather than learned in the classical sense.

Parameter theory also provided a more tractable framework for understanding and describing grammatical development – the temporal unfolding of language in the child. Within this framework, what we descriptively refer to as a "stage" represents the instantiation of a particular parameter value (or values), either correct or incorrect vis-à-vis the target grammar. If incorrect, the parameter must be reset at some point on the basis of relevant input data, and this resetting would give rise to a new "stage" or grammar. Conceived in this way, each stage in the acquisition sequence is constrained by the parameter space of UG much in the way we understand grammatical variation across adult languages to be so constrained.

Parameter theory thus offers not only a model of how language acquisition could proceed in principle under the boundary conditions set by an impoverished linguistic environment (impoverished with respect to abstract linguistic rules and representations) and UG, it also provides a model of how development proceeds in fact. It is fair to say that parameter theory considerably broadened the application and explanatory potential of linguistic theory to acquisition research. As example, the development of children's negative sentences from an external Neg element (*No the sun shining*) to a clause internal position (*The sun not shining*), as posited by Bellugi, was reformulated by Pierce (1992) as movement of the verb from its base-generated VP internal position to a higher functional head (INFL) over negation, a rule not specifically designed to capture a shift in the child's language, but a well-worn rule of many adult languages, a parametric option of UG.[1]

Among the abstract elements in child language that received heightened attention post-LGB were missing subjects in non-null subject languages such as English, illustrated in (1)–(3) below. Earlier studies had remarked upon missing subjects

---

[1] But see Stromswold (1990) and Drozd (1995) for criticism of the parameter-setting model of "external negation."

(e.g. Greenfield and Smith 1976), but it is fair to say that missing subjects were not a central area of research.

In this paper I will discuss early grammatical development through the prism of missing subjects in child language. I will review some of the central work on this topic, and attempt to draw out the more general implications of missing subjects for parameter-setting models of development and maturational models. I will also discuss more recent analytical directions, which focus on the informational context of missing subjects. I begin by discussing grammatical approaches to missing subjects, including parameter setting and maturational analyses (Sect. 2). I then turn to performance-based accounts (Sect. 3), especially those that focus on production constraints in young children. The review of findings from spontaneous production and imitation studies leads to a discussion of the converging results of the different methodologies used to explore null subjects in early language. In this context, I present the results of a recent comprehension study on null subjects in English (Orfitelli 2008; Orfitelli and Hyams 2008, 2010) and the implications of those results for competence and performance models (Sect. 4). Finally, I discuss some recent (and not so recent) findings illustrating children's pragmatic knowledge in choosing specific subject types (null, pronominal, lexical), how early sensitivity to information structure (IS) interacts with grammatical knowledge (and potentially production output), and how pragmatic principles may in fact account for certain results that have thus far been attributed to processing limitations in early language.

2 Missing Subjects and Parameter Missettings

Once we assume that UG consists of a system of parameters and that the child's task is to set these parameters at the appropriate values for the target language, it is a small step to imagine that children could misset these parameters, or that the parameters might come preset at a universal value, correct for some languages, but not for others. The parameter missetting hypothesis provides a framework to directly address the question of why the child makes certain "errors" but not others, and shows a particular developmental sequence rather than another logically possible one.

2.1 The Pro-drop Hypothesis

The parameter missetting idea was developed in Hyams (1983, 1986), where I argued that children's missing subjects are the result of a positive setting along the pro-drop (or null subject) parameter, the parameter responsible for licensing null subjects by "rich" inflection in languages like Italian and Spanish. The subject drop phenomenon is illustrated in (1)–(3) in English, French and Danish, languages that do not license null subjects in their adult version, the examples in (1) are from Bloom et al. (1975a, b) and Brown (1973); the Danish and French examples, in (2) and (3) respectively, are from Hamann and Plunkett (1998).

(1) a. Want more apple.
    b. Tickles me.
    c. No play matches.
    d. Show Mommy that.
(2) a. Ikke kore traktor.
      Not drive tractor
      '(I, you, he) doesn't drive the tractor.'
    b. Se, blomster har.
      Look, flowers have.
      'Look, (I, you, he, she, etc.) have/s flowers.'
(3) a. A tout tout tout mangé
      has all all all eaten
      '(He) has eaten everything.'
    b. Oter tout ta.
      empty all that
      '(I) empty all that.'

According to Hyams (1983, 1986), all children start out speaking 'Italian' with respect to the null subject option. The formulation of the pro-drop parameter I adopted was inspired by Rizzi (1982), who argued that in some languages (e.g. Italian, Spanish) Agr is essentially a subject pronoun making the overt expression of the subject DP optional; in other languages (e.g. English, French) Agr is not pronominal and null subjects are therefore not licensed. The particular parameter I suggested, as distinct from Rizzi's, clustered the null subject property together with several other properties of (early) grammar, including the lack of lexical expletives (e.g. in weather and raising constructions) and modals as a distinct verbal category. The developmental prediction of such a system was that children would show all the characteristics of the [+pronominal] Agr setting at the same time. And those children for whom the target is not a pro-drop grammar, for example English and German-speaking children, would lose all these properties at roughly the same time at the point at which the parameter was reset to a [−pronominal] Agr. Two developmental stages are therefore predicted with respect to null subjects (and other properties), Italian, then English (or German).

This particular implementation of a developmental or "real time" parameter setting model turned out to be empirically flawed in a number of respects (which I return to below), but the logic seemed, and still seems to me to be correct. There are, in particular, three noteworthy features. First, the parameter setting model provides a narrowly constrained, and hence more explanatory model of acquisition than earlier standard theory, rule-based models. The "rules" of early grammar and the "errors" that children make are not random, nor do they arise from principles not otherwise motivated. Deviations from the target, though "target-inconsistent," to use Rizzi's (2005b) terminology, are still UG-consistent. Thus, as I noted in Hyams (1983, 1986), parameter theory gives a precise sense to the claim that child grammars are not fundamentally different from adult grammars (cf. also Klein 1982 and White 1981), a hypothesis that is now known as the continuity hypothesis, a term coined by Pinker (1984). Second, the deductive structure of the parameters, subsuming what would otherwise be disparate grammatical properties that would have to be individually learned, goes some distance towards accounting for the speed and ease of acquisition – the logical problem of language acquisition. Third, parameter (re-)setting provides a partial solution to what Felix (1987) called the 'stage-transition question', viz., what accounts for the transition from one stage (i.e., grammar) to the next?

Despite satisfying these desiderata of a generative theory of language development, there were problems with the pro-drop hypothesis, some of which were apparent almost immediately. First, the hypothesis is inconsistent with certain aspects of learnability theory, in particular, a developmental interpretation of the subset principle (Berwick 1982), according to which any parameter that is incorrectly set in development should generate a language that is a subset of the target. In the case of the pro-drop parameter, the [−pronominal] setting, i.e. English, which allows only overt subjects, is a subset of the [+pronominal] setting, Italian, which allows both null and overt subjects. It therefore seemed counterintuitive that Italian should be the initial setting (cf. also Lillo-Martin 1994). In Hyams (1983, 1986) I finessed this problem by showing that because of the expletive pronoun and modal properties subsumed by the parameter, the languages generated by the two values do not really fall into a subset relation. For example, though Italian is a superset of English with respect to referential subjects, as just shown, English allows lexical expletives (*It's cold outside*) and Italian does not, reversing the subset relations. Moreover, in English modals constitute a separate verbal category that undergoes inversion (*Can/have you dance?*) and can be stranded under ellipsis, as in tags (*You can't sing, can you?*), etc., while Italian has neither of these properties. So in these respects as well, English is a superset of Italian.[2] The combined effects are that English and Italian are not in a subset-superset relationship, but rather form intersecting sets. The subset principle is therefore vacuous. The only relevant requirement – that there be positive evidence to tell the English (and German, etc.)-speaking child that she is not in a pro-drop language – is satisfied by lexical expletives and the broader distribution of modals.

---

[2] A third trigger suggested in Hyams (1983, 1986) is the appearance of overt pronominal subjects in contexts that would be infelicitous in an adult NS language, for example, a 3rd person pronoun whose antecedent is well established in the discourse situation, as in (i):

(i) Mario ha mangiato troppo. Adesso (*lui) si sente male.

   Mario ate too much. Now he feels sick.

As I will discuss below children have early knowledge of the pragmatic constraints on pronouns and null subject use.

The hypothesis that modals and expletives constitute triggering data immediately brought to the fore a second problem. Surely, children hear lexical expletives, questions, and tags at a very early age. So why don't these data, if they are indeed triggers, have any effect until age 3 or so, the point at which children seem to stop dropping subjects? Parameter resetting sets limits on the range and direction of the transitions between stages, but it does not explain the timing. Borer and Wexler (1987) labeled this the "triggering problem", the solution to which, they argued, is to assume that principles (and perhaps parameters) of UG undergo maturation. On this view the pro-drop parameter becomes available for setting during the 3rd year, and so the triggers are irrelevant until that point.

Elaborating somewhat on the parameter maturation idea just mentioned, we might assume that parameters are not all available to be fixed at the initial state, but rather come "on-line" according to some sort of developmental schedule. A priori there is nothing implausible about this suggestion. However, Borer and Wexler (1992) were at pains to argue that maturation does not entail discontinuity in development, discontinuity in the specific sense of being unconstrained by UG. They thus proposed that maturation is "UG-constrained." For example, regarding A-chain maturation, the focus of their 1987 paper, during the pre-A-chain stage children's grammars generate a smaller set of representations than the adult grammar, but do not generate impermissible structures.

With respect to parameters, however, the situation is rather different. To say that the pro-drop parameter is off-line, hence unset, during the first 3 years of life means that the grammatical representation of subjects in the child's grammar is not UG-constrained as there is no specification of either the obligatoriness (as in English) or optionality (as in Italian) of overt subjects. We would therefore expect haphazard or random behavior in this domain. But this is not the case. As data from Valian (1990), Lorusso (2007) and Serratrice (2005) has shown, null subjects in child Italian have roughly the same frequency and distribution as in the adult grammar: Approximately 70% of subjects are null and they occur in both root and subordinate clauses.[3] This target-like behavior suggests that Italian-speaking children have an early and correct setting of the pro-drop parameter, as argued by Valian. The same can be said for children acquiring other pro-drop languages such as European Portuguese (Valian and Eisenberg 1996). If the pro-drop parameter emerges maturationally, then it should come on-line for the English-speaking child at the same time as the Italian- or Portuguese-speaking child, which is to say, well before age 3. Moreover, according to Borer and Wexler's proposal, it must be immediately set to English at that point. Otherwise, we run up against the triggering problem again. Thus, the triggering problem associated with the pro-drop hypothesis is not solved by maturation unless we assume Italian and English-speaking children mature at different rates, which seems implausible on its face.

---

[3] Valian (1991) puts the rate of null subjects in adult Italian at 50% (following Bates 1976) while Lorusso (2007) and Serratrice (2005) place it close to the 70% child null subject rate.

I noted above that the pro-drop hypothesis avoids the subset problem because the parameter clusters together various properties that alter the standardly assumed subset-superset relations of this parameter. But this strategy only works to the extent that the developmental predictions of the model are empirically supported.

The corpora initially investigated seemed to support the co-occurrence of these different properties in real time, but later studies, in particular Valian (1991), showed that this clustering effect was not reliable. For example, Valian found in her cross-sectional study that the English-speaking children produced modals and expletive subjects while still dropping referential subjects.[4] Moreover, as noted above, in comparing Italian and English-speaking children matched for grammatical level, Valian found that they behaved differently with respect to null subjects and also overt pronouns; the English-speaking children showed far fewer null subjects (30% vs. 70% for Italian children) and far more overt pronouns than would be expected if they were speaking a true pro-drop language. Similar differences were found between English-speaking and (European) Portuguese-speaking children (Valian and Eisenberg 1996), casting further doubt on the hypothesis that English null subjects were equivalent to those of a true pro-drop language. Finally, Valian (1991) (see also Roeper and Weissenborn 1990) also noted that in English null subjects did not occur in subordinate clauses, or in post-*wh* environments, in marked contrast to Italian child language (Guasti 1996).[5] Similar root clause effects were found for French children (Crisma 1992; Levow 1995; Hamann 2000), for Dutch children (Haegeman 1995, 1996) and for German children (Clahsen et al. 1995). I return to these effects below.

2.2 *Morphological Uniformity*

Several other versions of the parameter missetting hypothesis followed. Jaeggli and Hyams (1988) proposed an analysis in terms of morphological uniformity. This account was based on the 'morphological uniformity principle' (Jaeggli and Safir 1989), according to which null subjects are licensed in languages with uniformly inflected or uniformly uninflected verbal paradigms. Jaeggli and Hyams suggested that while Italian children correctly assume a uniformly inflected (and hence null subject) language, English-speaking children incorrectly assume English is a uniformly uninflected (hence also null subject) language. Thus, children acquiring both types of language have null subjects as a grammatical option, but with different identification properties. Null subjects in Italian are identified by

---

[4] Wang et al. (1992) also found that the English-speaking children in their study used expletive subjects during the NS stage.

[5] Valian's observation of limited null subjects in post-*wh* environments is refined in Roeper and Rohrbacher (2000) who observe that 95% of post-*wh* null subjects occur in non-finite (bare verb) sentences (e.g. *Where___ go/going?*) while only 5% occur in finite contexts (e.g. *Where __ goes/went/is going?*). See also Bromberg and Wexler (1995) who replicate these results.

person/number inflection on the verb, while null subjects in English are identified by a (possibly null) topic, as in discourse-oriented languages such as Chinese and Japanese (Huang 1984).

The morphological uniformity hypothesis still assumed a universal initial setting, viz., [+uniform], but this setting could be satisfied in two different ways depending on whether the input language was richly inflected (e.g. Italian) or not (e.g. English). In this sense it improved upon the original pro-drop idea because it allowed for some early influence of target language input. It also resolved a problem inherent in the pro-drop hypothesis, which is, how are early null subjects identified (or recovered) in languages like English, French and Danish which do not have "rich" agreement. The morphological uniformity hypothesis predicted that children exit the null subject stage once they "realize" that English does have some verbal inflection (in line with earlier proposals of Guilfoyle 1984 and Lebeaux 1987). This prediction was not confirmed. Most English-speaking children begin using present and past tense morphology before exiting the null subject stage (cf. Hyams and Jaeggli 1986; Sano and Hyams 1994; Valian et al. 1996; Ingham 1998). Similar results were observed for French (Rasetti et al. 2000) and Dutch (Hamann and Plunkett 1998), which, like English, were predicted to be uniformly uninflected during the null subject stage.

2.3 The Topic Drop Hypothesis

Other topic drop accounts of null subjects fared no better than the morphological uniformity hypothesis. The proposal that children start out with a discourse-oriented null subject grammar of the Chinese or Korean sort (Hyams 1991) cannot account for the differences in the frequency and distribution of missing subjects in English vs. Chinese-speaking children. In particular, English-speaking children show a huge subject-object asymmetry in the rate of argument drop while Chinese-speaking children drop both subjects and objects at roughly target-like rates from the earliest stage (Wang et al. 1992; cf. also Kim 1997 on argument drop in Korean child language.) Similar considerations hold for an analysis of early English as a topic drop grammar of the Germanic sort (Hyams and Wexler 1993), languages that typically license both subject and object drop provided the argument is fronted to Topic position.

2.4 Competing Grammars Hypothesis

The parameter setting models discussed above all involve the assumption of a default or initial parameter setting which may or may not be correct for the target language. In contrast to this, Valian (1991) proposed that multiple parameter settings (viz. grammars) may be initially available to the child (see also Fodor 1998 and Roeper 2000 for similar suggestions). Thus with respect to the null subject phenomenon, she suggested that children initially entertain both the pro-drop and non-pro-drop options on an equal footing, wavering between the two grammars until sufficient evidence accrues to favor one over the other. Valian's rationale for this model is based on her assumptions about the child's parser. The child's parser, she observes, being parasitic on his grammar, cannot analyze input not generated by that grammar. Therefore, it cannot in principle analyze the triggers necessary to induce a parameter resetting. So, if the initial setting of the parameter is a pro-drop grammar, the English-speaking child would be unable to analyze the lexical expletives or first position modals, etc., which do not occur in true pro-drop languages, and, according to Hyams (1983, 1986) are necessary to reset to the correct non-pro-drop grammar. Because the assumption is that the child cannot use as triggering data any input that is not generated by her current grammar, that is, any input that results in a failed parse, she must necessarily have access to both parameter values. Armed with both grammars/parsers, the child is able to parse all of the relevant input. Elsewhere (Hyams 1994) I have defended the pro-drop analysis against this particular criticism. On a parameter setting model grammatical development is generally conceived of as a 'failure-driven process' (Wexler and Culicover 1980; Clark and Roberts 1991). The child moves from one grammar or parameter value to another as she encounters input data that are unanalyzable (or unparsable) under her current grammar. Under the triggering assumption, the parsing paradox described by Valian does not block development. Rather it drives it, as it is precisely the assumption of a failed parse under some parameter value that triggers the resetting to the other value.[6]

More recently, Yang (2002) has proposed a formal version of the multiple grammars model, which also incorporates a statistical component. According to his 'variational' model, the learner has available multiple grammars to analyze the input. When a particular grammar succeeds in assigning an analysis it is rewarded (given more weight in the hypothesis space), it if fails it is punished. As learning proceeds, the more successful grammar becomes stronger, eventually pushing out the competitors. The speed with which the learner eliminates an incorrect grammar is a function of the frequency of the disconfirming evidence in the input for that grammar.

With respect to the null subject phenomenon, Yang proposes that the child's initial hypothesis space is defined by three grammar types: an Italian pro-drop grammar, a Chinese topic drop grammar, and an English non-null subject grammar. The high frequency of null objects in the Chinese input allows the Chinese-speaking

---

[6] There are a number of questions raised by this model. For example, how does the parser "know" which parameter is misset? A case in point, discussed at length in Gibson and Wexler (1994), is the German/Dutch child faced with a verb second sentence. This data could in principle trigger a (re)setting of the head-direction parameter to head first VO order (which would be incorrect according to many analyses of V2 languages), or it could trigger the verb second parameter to a (correct) positive value. For further discussion of this issue and related matters, see Clark and Roberts (1991) and also Gibson and Wexler (1994).

child to quickly eliminate the English and Italian grammars, neither of which permits null objects. The Italian-speaking child can also quickly converge on the target, eliminating the English grammar on the basis of frequent null subjects in the Italian input, and the Chinese grammar on the basis of argument *wh* questions with null subjects, as in (4a).[7] Yang observes that Chinese does not permit null subjects with argument topics, only with adjunct topics (cf. 4b,c).[8]

(4) a. Chi$_i$ __ha bacciato t$_i$?
 Who has (he) kissed?'
 who __has kissed
 b. Zai gongyuan-li $_i$ [da-le ren]
 In park-loc beat-asp people
 'It is in the park (but not at school) that (he) beat people up.'
 c. Sue$_i$ [xihuan t$_i$]
 Sue likes
 'It is Sue (but not Mary) that (he) likes.'

As for the English-speaking child, she eliminates the Italian grammar on morphological grounds; the English input does not contain unambiguous agreement (a necessary feature of the pro-drop option on Yang's assumption). Given that uninflected forms are very frequent in the English input, the Italian pro-drop grammar should disappear from the competition quickly. On the other hand, the Chinese option is harder to eliminate. This is because the only relevant disconfirming evidence, according to Yang, is expletive *there* sentences (not possible in topic drop grammars), which occur infrequently in the input (under 1% by Yang's estimation).[9] The English- speaking child therefore maintains both an English non-null subject grammar and a Chinese topic drop grammar (until roughly age 3 – the end of the NS stage)

The co-existing Chinese and English grammars explain several properties of the early English NS stage. First, we expect null subjects, but not at the frequency that they occur in a true topic drop language because English-speaking children access the Chinese grammar only probabilistically, unlike Chinese children who do so 100% of the time.[10] Most interestingly, the variational model also predicts that

---

[7] Yang estimates that the frequency of sentences such as (5a) in the input to Italian children at about 15% He does not provide any information about the basis for that estimate.

[8] Yang assumes, as is standard since Chomksy (1977), that *wh* fronting and topicalization are essentially the same process, both involving movement to Spec CP. Chinese does not have overt *wh* movement.

[9] Yang does not say why he does not include expletive *it* as disconfirming evidence since it is also not possible in Chinese (Wang et al. 1992).

[10] According to Wang et al. (1992) 2-year old Chinese-speaking children drop subjects at a rate of about 55.7 while the English-speaking children in their study had a drop rate of about 26%.

English-speaking will drop objects and that the ratio of null subjects to null objects (NO) will be the same as for Chinese-speaking children (when the English data are scaled up to 100%, as if they were monolingual Chinese-speaking children). This prediction is confirmed when tested against data in Wang et al. (1992). The null object (NO)/null subject (NS) ratio for the Chinese-speaking children is 36% (56%NS/20%NO) and the ratio for the English-speaking children is 32% (26% NS/8% NO).[11]

Another prediction of the variational account of NSs is that English-speaking children will drop subjects in adjunct *wh* questions, but not in object *wh* questions, paralleling the argument/adjunct asymmetry in Chinese topicalization discussed in the text (cf. 5b,c). Yang reports that this asymmetry is confirmed in Adam's data (Brown 1973).[12]

Despite these very interesting results, the variational model also suffers from some serious empirical shortcomings, the most important of which is that NSs in non-null subject languages are heavily skewed towards non-finite contexts, especially root infinitives (Guilfoyle 1984; Kramer 1993; O'Grady et al. 1989; Poeppel and Wexler 1993; Sano and Hyams 1994; Phillips 1995 among others). With respect to English specifically this non-finiteness effect shows up in several grammatical contingencies. First, as Valian (1991) observes, null subjects do not occur with modals (which are inherently finite in English). Nor do they occur with finite forms of the copulas (*is, am, are*) of the copula (Sano and Hyams 1994).[13] Additionally, as observed in Roeper and Rohrbacher (2000) and Bromberg and Wexler (1995), NSs in *wh* questions virtually never occur in questions with finite verbs (e.g. *Where __ goes/went?*), but are restricted to bare verb contexts (e.g. *Where __ go?*) (see note 5). Finally, they do not occur in embedded contexts (Valian 1991; Roeper and Weissenborn 1990). Yang (2002) does not discuss these contingencies and it is difficult to see how the variational model can account for them, the restriction to root contexts in particular, given that Chinese NSs are not constrained in this way. In this respect it fares no better than previous parameter setting models, as I will discuss in the following section.

---

[11] The ratio of NS to NO in other English-speaking children is considerably lower. Valian's (1991) Group 1 children have a NS/NO ratio of 20% (36% NS excluding *wh* questions and 8% NO). The ratio of NS/NO for Adam, Eve and Sarah (based on Bloom 1991) is 16% (55% NS/8% NO). It is possible that the discrepancies are due to different coders and coding procedures.

[12] It is difficult to evaluate this result, first because it is based on only one child. Also, studies that track children's early production of *wh* questions (e.g. Tyack and Ingram 1977) have shown that *where* questions are the most frequent early on. It is therefore possible that Adam uses disproportionately more *where* questions in the earlier files when he is also using more null subjects, but that these are independent factors.

[13] Hamann and Plunkett (1998) find a similar asymmetry in missing subjects in Danish-speaking children. Missing subjects are significantly more frequent with finite lexical verbs than with the finite copula.

2.5 Null Subjects and RIs: The PRO Hypothesis

As just noted, another extremely important finding that directly challenges the parameter missetting accounts of early missing subjects is the finding that in the acquisition of many non-null subject languages there is a close association between missing subjects and absence of finiteness on the verb (Guilfoyle 1984; Kramer 1993; O'Grady et al. 1989; Poeppel and Wexler 1993; Sano and Hyams 1994; Phillips 1995). Sano and Hyams proposed that the null subject phenomenon is not due to a missetting of the null subject parameter, but rather to the fact that an underspecified Infl (responsible for non-finite root clauses) licenses a PRO in subject position. While Sano and Hyams focused on early English, Kramer (1993) reached similar conclusions based on data from German and Dutch.[14] The PRO hypothesis explains why in Dutch, German and other non pro-drop languages, null subjects seem to occur disproportionately more often in non-finite root clauses (see Hoekstra and Hyams 1998 for summary of cross-linguistic findings). This is in marked contrast to the situation in Italian and other true pro-drop languages where the null subject *pro*, is licensed in finite contexts like a lexical pronoun. It is also unlike Germanic topic drop in which the dropped topic (subject or object) (arguably licensed by verb movement to C (V2)) is also restricted to finite contexts.

The association between missing subjects and RIs thus constitutes further evidence against the parameter account – at least as regards null subjects in non-finite clauses. However, as observed in Hamann and Plunkett (1998) and Rasetti et al. (2000), there remains a significant number of null subjects in finite contexts – ranging from 10% to 55% across different children and languages (see Rasetti et al. 2000 for summary of statistics; also Hoekstra and Hyams 1998). Of particular interest are the null subjects in finite clauses in English, French, and Danish, languages that do not have a pro-drop or topic drop option. Thus as Rizzi (2000, 2005a, b) observes, a parameter missetting account may still be valid for these cases. In what follows I restrict my discussion to null subjects in finite clauses and I will assume that the missing subjects in non-finite clauses are licensed by whatever mechanisms license PRO in infinitival contexts in adult grammars (the PRO theorem, null case, etc.).[15]

2.6 Null Subjects in Finite Clauses

Restricting our attention to finite clauses, as already noted, an accumulation of cross-linguistic data has shown that the distribution of null subjects in Italian child language is like adult Italian (Guasti 1996; Rizzi 2005a, b). Similarly, Chinese and

---

[14] To my knowledge, Weverink (1989) was the first to note the strong relationship between null subjects and RIs, based on Dutch child language. She proposed a more pragmatic type of analysis according to which RIs are topic-comment structures in which the topic is optional.

[15] It is also possible that the RI phenomenon itself results from a parameterized system, for example, Rizzi's (2005a, b) proposal that RIs result from VP truncation.

Korean children drop both subjects and objects like adult speakers (Wang et al. 1992; Kim 1997) and Dutch/German-speaking children omit subjects and object in first, that is topic position, like their parents (de Haan and Tuijman 1988). It seems that the parameters responsible for null arguments – the pro-drop parameter and null argument parameters of both the Chinese and Germanic sort – take their place among other well-studied parameters such as V to I and V2, that appear to be correctly set from the earliest observable point (Pierce 1992; Poeppel and Wexler 1993).[16] If children acquiring these various languages show early morphosyntactic convergence (EMC) (Hoekstra and Hyams 1998) (or 'very early parameter setting' (VEPS) – Wexler 1998), it stands to reason that English (and French and Danish)-speaking children do too.[17]

So, let us assume in fact that English/French/Danish-speaking children also have correct, i.e. negative, settings of the pro-drop and topic drop parameters. Nonetheless, these children omit subjects at high rates (see Hoekstra and Hyams 1998 for summary of statistics). One possibility is that subject drop is due to performance factors, as first suggested in L. Bloom (1970) and more recently, in Bloom (1991), Valian (1990) and Gerken (1991) among others. I return to this proposal below. Alternatively, children may drop subjects under a parametric option that is different from the parameters discussed thus far, as has been suggested by Rizzi (2005a, b).

2.7 *Root Subject Drop and Truncation*

Rizzi (2005a, b) proposes that subject drop in early English (and French) is an instance of 'root subject drop' (RSD), a principle according to which a subject may be null in the specifier of the root. These null subjects at the edge of the root are accessible to discourse identification. His idea is that children initially assume a positive value of this parameter under pressure from a limited production system, in accordance with a formal strategy as in (5).

---

[16] Yang (2002) challenges the claim that the V2 parameter is set early based on the observation that many of children's early finite utterances are V1. However, it has long been established that V2 is the surface manifestation of verb movement to Comp (den Besten and Hans 1977; Koster 2003), and is associated with topicalization of some XP to Spec CP. Children (like adults) drop the XP in topic position (subject, object or adverb) yielding a verb initial sentence (Haegeman 1994). V2 (like all rules) is a structural, not linear notion. What is relevant to determining if the child has set the V2 parameter is whether there is V to C movement, which includes both V1 and V2 utterances. By this correct, structural criterion the evidence overwhelmingly supports the claim that children set the V2 parameter very early in development (Verrips and Weissenborn 1992; Wexler 1994; Poeppel and Wexler 1993; Hyams 1992).

[17] See Yang (2002) for an alternative view, according to which a parameter may be at different times in different languages depending on the frequency of disconfirming evidence in the input. See Sect. 2.4.

(5) Adopt parametric values which reduce the computational load on the production system and are not contradicted by positive evidence" (Rizzi 2005b, (7)).

Rizzi suggests that the computational strategy in (5) is a temporary competitor to the subset principle, allowing an initial superset language, in this case a null subject language. The "unlearning" of this superset value happens maturationally. As the production system matures, the child, under pressure from the subset principle, abandons this strategy unless supported by positive evidence. Thus, children born into languages that have no pro-drop or topic drop options will nevertheless drop subjects in root contexts and only in root contexts.

RSD receives support from a number of adult languages. Rizzi reports on various languages, such as Levantine Arabic (Kenstowicz 1989), Corsican, and certain varieties of Brazilian Portuguese in which subject drop is limited to main clauses, in contrast to what occurs in "true" NS languages like Italian. A similar pattern is observed in Gruyère Franco Provençal (De Crousaz and Schlonsky 2003), in which subject omission is possible only from initial position, hence neither in *wh* contexts or with preposed adjuncts. Rizzi also proposes that Germanic topic drop is an instance of RSD.

RSD is heavily dependent on an assumption of clausal truncation (Rizzi 1993/1994) and, by hypothesis, on the variation that languages show with respect to the level at which truncation is possible. Rizzi's original truncation hypothesis (Rizzi 1993/1994) held that young children (roughly to age 3) lack the grammatical axiom that the root clause = CP (or Force P in more recent proposals). Accordingly, they may have 'minimal projections' where the adult may not, terminating, for example, at the VP or IP (FinP) level. In more recent work, Rizzi (2005b) observes that adult languages also vary in the choice of categories that can be taken as the root. He proposes the structure of the left periphery as in (6) with Force as the universal default root category while other layers can be taken as root by specific languages.

(6)   Force ... Top ... Foc ... Fin ... AgrS ... T ...

Thus, "pure" topic drop languages, such as German and Dutch, have the option of truncating at TopP, making the specifier of TopP a target of omission, while Levantine Arabic, Corsican, and certain varieties of Brazilian Portuguese allow truncation at the FinP level, and hence license omission in the specifier of FinP. Other possibilities exist as well. Truncation at the VP level gives rise to root infinitives (RIs) (Rizzi 1993/1994); truncation at FocP gives rise to systems allowing null *wh* operators, and truncation below ForceP would license null complementizers in declarative (as opposed to interrogative) clauses. (See Rizzi 2005b for further details.) UG makes available various truncation options, as exhibited by the range of adult languages just noted (and perhaps others yet to be discovered), and children set (and may misset) the "point of truncation" value for their language. Thus, RSD is not a parameter per se, but rather, the parametric options derive from the different truncation loci.

The RSD model accounts for a number of important properties of early subject drop. Central among these are the root/first position effects discussed earlier (Valian 1991; Roeper and Weissenborn 1990). It also dissociates subject drop in English/French/Danish from null subjects in Italian and other true pro-drop languages, a desirable result given the empirical difficulties faced by the pro-drop hypothesis, and it allows for the omission of both referential subjects and expletives (not possible on a topic drop analysis because Top does not house expletives). Additionally, it explains the similar trajectories of RIs and null subjects in finite contexts in Danish. French and Dutch (Hamann and Plunkett 1998; Rasetti et al. 2000; Haegeman 1995) if both RIs and NSs result from truncation, of VP and IP, respectively (see note 15). Finally, it provides an answer to the important question of why some parameters (e.g. head direction, V to I, V2) are fixed early in development (according to VEPS or EMC) while others (e.g. root null subjects, RIs) are delayed much longer: The solution to this puzzle is that parameters with the potential to ease the computational load on the production system by licensing null elements (e.g. null arguments, null tense/Aux as in RIs), and which are not contradicted by positive evidence, are likely to be set later in development.[18] In all these respects, then, the root subject drop as an account of NSs in finite clauses specifically, is superior to previous parameter setting models of early null subjects.

The RSD hypothesis does raise a few questions, however. The first concerns the trajectory of subject omission in non-pro drop languages and the second, the interaction of RSD with other argument omission parameters in languages such as Italian or Dutch. Finally, there is the question to what extent the empirical evidence really supports the claim that null subjects are (in part) a performance effect. I will now discuss the first two of these points, and return to the performance question below.

We noted earlier that the pro-drop and topic drop parameters are fixed early in development (either positively in the case of Italian, and German/Dutch children respectively, or negatively as by English/French/Danish-speaking children). But adult English (and other non-pro drop languages such as French) also have a restricted subject drop option, so-called 'diary drop', discussed in Thrasher (1977) and Haegeman (1990, 1992) and illustrated in (7). Diary drop adheres to certain well-defined structural conditions. Subjects may drop, but objects may not. More generally, subjects may be omitted only from first position, as in (7a, b), so not following *wh* phrases or preposed adjuncts, as in (7b, c) (from Haegeman 1990, 2000).

---

[18] Although the pro-drop parameter also licenses null subjects, it is set early in development because there is positive evidence in the form of rich inflection, i.e. a highly differentiated agreement system in languages like Italian (Rizzi 2005a, b; Yang 2002). We return to the question of whether and how pro-drop and RSD might interact below.

(7) a. Wonder what they're doing.
  b. Could do better. (from school report)
  c. *When will come back?
  d. *That book, don't like.
  e. M'accompagne au Mercure, puis a la gare.
   '(he) takes me to Mercure, then to the station...'

   (Paul Léautaud, Le Fleau, Journal Particulier, 1917–1930, pp. 69–70)

The observation that English/French-speaking children's null subjects are restricted to root clauses, and more specifically, to first position (Valian 1991; Roeper and Weissenborn 1990) is quite consistent with diary drop. So it seems logical to assume that the mechanisms that allow for diary drop in adult English also operate on children's grammars. But if so, then children's initial option to truncate at FinP (making RSD possible) is a correct target setting and English/French-speaking children show early morphosyntactic convergence with respect to this parameter (as with many other parameters). Indeed, Rizzi (2005a, b) takes diary drop to be an instance of RSD. On his analysis (see also Haegeman 1994) diary drop results from truncation at the FinP level (see 6) – an option realized by English and French-speaking adults. So, assuming children are showing early convergence on the adult target, what then accounts for the higher frequency and broader application of RSD by children, who clearly are not restricting subject drop to contexts that are acceptable in the adult language? And how do children gradually reduce the frequency and distribution of RSD to adult norms under the reasonable assumption of no negative evidence? I return to this question in Sect. 6. Additionally, if RSD is diary drop, it is not obvious how to account for the virtual absence of NSs with modals (1991) and finite forms of the copula (Sano and Hyams 1994) in early English, as these are possible under adult diary drop (e.g. 7b).

On the other hand, it is possible that children give up RSD as their production capacities mature, in accordance with the subset principle. On this view, the RSD option would then have be reactivated at some later point to account for adult diary drop. That is, children would learn on the basis of positive evidence that subjects can be omitted in specific registers, but not otherwise. Assuming this is the case, we would expect a trajectory of missing subjects of the following sort: an initial period of frequent missing subjects, followed by a period of no subject drop at all, and then a later introduction of subject drop in diary and contexts. Conversely, if children's early RSD is effectively diary drop and they never reset the relevant parameter, we might expect a gradual decrease in null subjects ending with a frequency and distribution that matches the adult's. In one case we would see a strong discontinuity and in the other case we would not.

I know of no detailed longitudinal study of subject drop in English that would answer this question at this time. Rasetti et al. (2000) traces the frequency of null subjects in several French-speaking children over several months. There we see a gradual decline in subject drop in finite contexts ending at a frequency of between

10% and 30% depending on the child. However, the periods of observations are quite early (ending at 1;11 to 2;9 depending on the child) and therefore, it is impossible to know whether these children would subsequently stop dropping subjects completely and only later begin adult-like diary drop.[19]

A second question concerns the interaction of RSD with other argument omission options, in particular the pro-drop and topic drop parameters. The English case seems clear. Children have negative settings on the pro-drop and topic drop parameters, and a positive setting for RSD, that is, FinP truncation. But what of, say, Italian children, who correctly set the pro-drop parameter to a positive setting on the basis of rich verbal agreement in their input language, as proposed in Yang (2002) and Rizzi (2005a, b). If RSD is an initial "unmarked" option, is it also the case for children acquiring pro-drop languages? Presumably so, unless there is some blocking mechanism according to which RSD is turned off as pro-drop is activated. Perhaps the pro-drop option is a valve that reduces performance pressures on the child and thus allows an earlier abandonment of the RSD option. On the empirical front, if children assume both pro drop and RSD, we might expect a higher frequency of null subjects earlier on, dropping to adult rates at the RSD option disappears. There are conflicting data on this point. Valian (1991), following Bates (1976), reports that Italian adults drop subjects at a rate of approximately 50%, while Italian children drop at 70%. Similarly, Valian and Eisenberg (1996) report that Portuguese-speaking children drop subjects at higher rates than adults. These results would support the hypothesis that both RSD and pro drop operate initially. However, other studies show a similar null subject rate in Italian children and adults (Serratrice 2005; Lorusso et al. 2004) and in Spanish-speaking (Bel 2003) and Catalan-speaking children (Cabré Sans and Gavarró 2006) suggesting continuity of pro-drop and a blocking of RSD.

Similar questions arise in connection with topic drop languages if we assume that object topic drop (or V2) is the trigger for topic drop or TopP truncation, on Rizzi's model Dutch and German-speaking children have evidence for a positive value along the relevant parameter (while English/French/Danish-speaking children do not have such evidence).[20] But if RSD is also an initial option – and one that is not blocked by topic drop – then we would expect subject topic drop to occur at higher rates in children than in adult speakers (the effect of both IP and TopP truncation), while object drop should remain constant (only TopP truncation). I know of no relevant longitudinal data, but this would be an interesting issue to pursue. If there is an asymmetry between subject and object drop along the lines just mentioned, it may be that topic drop blocks diary drop because they both instantiate the RSD/truncation parameter, while pro drop is a separate parameter that acts independently.

---

[19] Hamann and Plunkett (1998) provide month by month frequencies of null subjects in two Danish-speaking children, but it is difficult to determine from their graphs whether there is a steady decline or a more discontinuous type of development. We leave this issue open for now.

[20] Hamann and Plunkett (1998) show that Danish, though it is a V2/topicalization language, does not readily allow topic drop. Under 1% of adult utterances have dropped topics.

In short, although a great deal is known about the overall frequency and distribution of null subjects in various child languages, it would be useful to have a more detailed accounting of the trajectory of null subjects (and objects) over time. This would provide a clearer picture of the interaction among different parameters, and also between the grammar and whatever effects might arise from an immature production system, or as will be discussed in more detail below (Sect. 5), in interaction with the pragmatic/discourse system.

3 Grammar-External Accounts

The RSD hypothesis is motivated in part by considerations of grammar-external production constraints; the formal mechanisms of subject drop fall squarely within the grammar, but children adopt RSD under pressure from a constrained production system.

Other proposals claim that subject omission is purely an effect of production limitations, and is not grammatically licensed (Bloom 1970, 1991; Valian 1990, 1991). Still other proposals hold that missing subjects depend on aspects of information structure, viz. that omission is permitted under certain situational and discourse conditions. In this section I will review the empirical basis for the claim that null subjects result from an overworked production system. Later, in Sect. 5, I will return to the effects of discourse conditions on subject omission.

3.1 Processing Limitations

Pure processing accounts of the null subject phenomenon in child language (e.g. Bloom 1991; Valian 1991) make several important claims. The first is that null subjects are not a grammatical option for young English-speaking children and so do not appear in the grammatical representation of the sentence. Instead, subjects are grammatically represented as either full lexical NPs such as *John*, *the bo*y*s*, or as pronouns, and are subsequently dropped during the production of the sentence because of a constraint on output. This claim prompted Hyams and Wexler (1993) to refer to this model as the output omission model (OOM). A second claim, made specifically in Bloom (1991), is that lexical subjects such as *John* impose a greater processing load than pronouns, and that omitting the subject completely imposes the lightest load. Thus, the probability of omission is a function of the "heaviness" of the subject, with lexical subjects more likely to be omitted than pronoun subjects. A third claim is that processing load is greatest at the beginning of a sentence. According to Bloom (1991), "the processing load at every point is proportional to the number of yet-to-be expanded nodes that must be kept in working memory" (Bloom, p. 501), so that elements at the onset of an utterance are more likely to be dropped than elements at the end. This last claim is intended to account for the most salient fact about subject drop, which is that it occurs at a far higher frequency than object drop, in early English.

Prima facie, the grammatical contingencies between missing subjects and other parts of the sentence structure seem to argue strongly against a pure processing account. For example, the NS-finiteness relationship discussed earlier is unexpected if the "heaviness" of the subject affects the structural complexity of the VP: a finite VP (including finite verb/copula or modal) presumably recruits more processing resources than the infinitive and so should occur more frequently with null subjects than do RIs, contrary to fact. In addition, subjects in English can drop in post-*wh* contexts (with non-finite verbs, see note 5). This is also unexpected. In these cases, it is the first position *wh* phrase that should drop rather than the subject. And as with the RI-null subject contingency, the fact that the subject drops in *wh* questions with non-finite (bare) verb is unexpected as these are presumably less complex than finite verbs.

Other findings seem to support the OOM. Bloom (1991) observed that in the spontaneous corpora of Adam, Eve, and Sarah that VP length (measured in terms of words) decreases as a function of the heaviness of the subject: VPs are shortest in sentences with lexical subjects, longer with pronouns, and longest when the subject is omitted.[21] The intuitive explanation for this effect is that the more resources the child takes up in producing the subject, the less are available for expanding in the VP. The VP length effect is replicated by Valian in both spontaneous speech (Valian 1991) and elicited imitation (Valian et al. 1996) in English-speaking children and in Hamann and Plunkett's (1998) study of the spontaneous productions of two Danish-speaking children.

Interestingly, while finding that VP length decreases as a function of subject "heaviness", Hamann and Plunkett also find that overall the MLU of subjectless sentences is shorter than in sentences with subjects, meaning that on average, processing resources, as measured by utterance length, do not determine subject omission. How can we reconcile these apparently conflicting results?

Hyams and Wexler (1993) ran the same VP length analysis on the spontaneous speech of several Italian adults, that is, adult speakers of a null subject language. Strikingly, we found the same VP length effect as a function of subject heaviness as was found for the children, although the overall MLUs for adults are obviously longer. The similarity between Italian adults and the English/Danish-speaking children strongly suggests that the VP length effect has little to do with production constraints (as presumably Italian adults are not so constrained), but rather, is associated with some – possibly pragmatic – factor associated with argument omission. I will elaborate on this idea in Sect. 5.

The claim that full NP subjects are more likely to be dropped than pronouns is also directly contradicted by experimental evidence. Both Gerken (1991) and

---

[21] A similar result was found many years earlier in Bloom (1970) who looked at the expression of subjects as a function of VP length in sentence with the verb *make*.

Valian et al. (1996) have found that in elicited imitation young English-speaking children are less likely to repeat pronominal subjects than lexical NP subjects. In other words, pronouns are more likely to drop than full NPs.[22] Valian et al. (1996) also found that children were less likely (though not significantly so) to repeat an expletive pronominal subject (e.g. *it, there*) than a referential one (e.g. *I, we*) and also that children were more likely to omit a pronominal subject when it followed a topic-introducing sentence, (e.g. *See the three frogs. They catch flies*) than when it did not have such an introduction. Both of these findings are unexpected on a production limitation model because the length of the experimental sentences is held constant across these conditions.

A second major statistical fact offered in support of the OOM is the finding that Italian children omit subjects at a rate of 70% whereas English-speaking children omit subjects at a rate of roughly 30% (Valian 1991). Valian explains this difference under the hypothesis that English-speaking children are dropping subjects for performance reasons, whereas Italian children are taking advantage of a grammatical pro-drop option. But this argument based on frequency differences is a spurious one; there is no theoretical reason why a performance constraint should yield fewer null subjects than a grammatical option or vice versa. The frequency differences suggest that there is some difference between Italian- and English-speaking children with respect to the use of null subjects, but it does not speak to the question of where the difference lies. For example, it is equally consistent with the idea that RSD (for whatever reason) is less frequent than pro-drop.

Hyams and Wexler (1993) developed a formal model incorporating two of the central claims of the OOM; first, that null subjects are not a grammatical option for the child, but result from the dropping of a lexical NP or pronoun in production, and second, that lexical NPs are heavier, hence more likely to drop than pronominal subjects (Bloom 1991). This model predicts that missing subjects are more likely to result from the dropping of a lexical subject than from the dropping of a pronoun. Therefore, as children grow out of the performance limitation and subject omission ceases, the proportion of lexical subjects should increase. We found that this prediction was in no way confirmed. For both Adam and Eve there is a steady increase in the proportion of pronouns over time whereas the proportion of lexical subjects remains roughly constant. As Hyams and Wexler note, this "trade-off" between null subjects and pronominal subjects with the proportion of lexical subjects remaining constant is exactly what would be predicted if subject omission has a grammatical basis. In adult NS languages null subjects serve the same pragmatic function as pronouns in a non-null subject language (i.e. to refer to contextually specified information). The hypothesis that children's missing subjects are a grammatical option predicts that as English-speaking children abandon this grammar

---

[22] In Valian's study, this result held only for the lower MLU group. Children with an MLU<3 produced repeated 76% of pronouns and 90% of lexical subjects 90%. The older group with MLU>3 repeated pronominal and lexical subjects equally often (92% vs. 95%).

(whatever its precise characterization), there will be a marked increase in the proportion of pronominal subjects.[23]

The trade-off between null subjects and pronouns is also confirmed in Valian's (1996) imitation study, as well as in Hughes and Allen's (2008) study of the pragmatic/discourse conditions on missing subjects. (I discuss these conditions further in Sect. 5.) These results are not predicted by the processing account of subject omission.

3.2 Metrical Effects

The production limitations account of missing subjects argues that processing difficulties increase as a function of the sentence length. Gerken (1991) proposes, instead, that children's productions are constrained by a metrical template favoring trochaic feet, that is, a phonological unit consisting of a strong syllable followed by a weak one (S-W). Children apply this template to their output and drop weak syllables that do not align with the trochaic template. This template applies to words, favoring omission of the weak syllable in words like *gi-raffe*, which reduces to the strong syllable *raff* whereas a word such as *ze-bra,* which has an S-W structure, is less likely to reduce (Gerken 1994).

More relevant to the current discussion is the fact that the metrical template also applies at the sentence level, favoring omission of pronominal subjects in sentences such as (8).

(8)   He loves her
      W   S   W

In (8) *he* is a weak syllable that does not fit the trochaic template. On the other hand, the pronominal object *her* does not drop because it forms a trochaic unit with the verb. In this way the metrical hypothesis is able to account for the subject-object asymmetry in English. It is also consistent with the formal results in Hyams and Wexler just discussed (1993) that show that pronominal subjects are more likely to drop than full NP subjects; on the metrical analysis this is because pronouns are prosodically weak.

---

[23] It is also not possible to explain the trade-off between null and pronominal subjects by some independent factor having to do with the general difficulty of pronouns (relative to NPs) that makes them less likely to be used at the earlier ages. If this were the case, we would expect to see the same trends in object position that we see in subject position; that is, we should see an increase in pronominal objects over time. Hyams and Wexler (1993) showed that this is not the case. The proportion of pronominal to lexical objects remains roughly constant over time. This finding also casts doubt on Yang's (2002) hypothesis that null objects in early English result from a Chinese-like topic drop grammar. If this were the case, we should also see a rise in object pronouns over time as null objects decrease.

However, like the production limitations model, the metrical analysis does not explain the syntactic contingencies, for example, why subjects are more likely to be omitted in RIs than in finite clauses in many languages. Also, as noted by Hamann and Plunkett (1998), the metrical account does not generalize easily to other languages. For example, in German post-verbal subjects are omitted to a much higher degree than in situ objects though the metrical structure is the same (Hamann 1996), and in French object clitics are dropped from both iambic and trochaic feet (Hamann et al. 1996; Jakubowicz et al. 1996). Finally, as Valian (1996) observes, the metrical account also fails to account for her imitation findings that expletive subjects are omitted more than referential subjects, and also that pronominal subjects following topic sentences are dropped more often. In both these cases metrical factors are held constant. I discuss Valian's imitation study further in the next section.

3.3 Spontaneous Production and Imitation

Valian (1996) argues in support of a processing account of early missing subjects on the basis of an elicited imitation study with 19 children (ages 1;10 to 2;8). Her argument centers on a comparison of English-speaking children in two MLU groups, one with MLUs greater than 3 (MLU >3), the other less than 3 (MLU < 3). According to Valian, the higher MLU group is adult-like with respect to the null subject option. In other words, the children in this group know that sentences require overt subjects. They imitate subjects at an overall rate of 87%. The children in the lower MLU group, on the other hand, still drop subjects to a significant degree. They imitate subjects at an overall rate of 63%.

Despite the difference in the overall rate of subject omission, the two MLU groups behave similarly with respect to factors that have been argued to indicate a pro-drop or Chinese-like topic-oriented NS grammar. Higher omission of expletive over referential subjects is indicative of a pro-drop grammar, and omission of subjects following topics, indicative of a Chinese-type topic drop grammar. As noted above, both the lower and higher MLU groups show more omission of expletive subjects over referential pronoun subjects (consistent with the pro-drop account), and both groups drop pronominal subjects more after a sentence introducing a topic (consistent with a Chinese-type topic drop account). On the other hand, the two groups differed with respect to the VP length effect: the lower MLU group showed shorter VPs as a function of subject type (NP< pronoun< null subject, as in Bloom 1991), while the higher MLU group showed no such effect. Because the two groups differed in their overall rate of missing subjects, but showed similar effects with expletive vs. referential subjects as well as topic establishment, Valian concludes that they do not have different grammars. Therefore, she argues, subject omission in the lower MLU group is not a grammatical effect, but rather due to limited processing resources, as shown by the difference in VP length results.[24] Valian also found that missing subjects do not correlate with a systematic lack of inflection, as would be predicted, for example, by the morphological uniformity hypothesis, or other accounts that tie subject drop to an underspecified or missing Infl.[25]

Valian's results are quite interesting. They argue against a pro-drop account of the sort proposed in Hyams (1983, 1986), and also against the idea that children start out with a Chinese-type topic drop grammar (Hyams 1991; Yang 2002). But they do not bear on Rizzi's RSD hypothesis which does not predict more expletive drop than referential pronoun drop (early English is explicitly not Italian on this analysis). Nor does it predict more subject drop following topic establishment (early English is also not Chinese according to RSD). Moreover, on the RSD hypothesis null subjects are licensed in finite contexts (Spec of FinP). So, the RSD hypothesis is not challenged by Valian's morphological results.

But what of the VP length results? Following Bloom (1991), Valian takes this result (which she found for MLU <3 group, but not for the MLU >3 group) as support for a processing account of missing subjects. However, the VP length effect is not problematic for the RSD account. Indeed, Rizzi's model specifically appeals to processing limitations as the reason children initially choose the "more economical" [+RSD] parametric value. I will return to the VP length results in Sect. 5 where I offer an alternative, pragmatic explanation for this effect, as originally suggested in Hyams and Wexler (1993).

4 Converging Methodologies

It is important to bear in mind that Valian's results are based on children's imitative language, in contrast to most of the earlier studies of missing subjects which are based on spontaneous production. That children's elicited imitation should resemble their spontaneous language is not surprising. As early as 1964, Ervin-Tripp and also Brown and Fraser showed that the imitations of "telegraphic" children mirrored their spontaneous productions; children drop subjects, auxiliaries, determiners, and so on in both cases. The usual assumption for why this happens has been that there is an underlying mechanism common to all linguistic performance, namely, the grammar. On this view, the child's imitations are

---

[24] Valian's explanation for the expletive and topic effects is that they are input driven, viz. that expletives can be more easily dropped in adult language. Even if this is true – as an instance of diary drop – it only pushes the interesting question back a generation. Why can adults drop expletives more easily? It is possible that for both children and adults expletives carry less informational content and hence, are more easily omitted according to pragmatic principles.

[25] I have in mind analyses such as Radford's (1990) very influential small clause hypothesis and the Clahsen et al.'s (1994) proposal that children lack Agr projections. There has been a great deal of discussion about the empirical problems associated with such accounts (particularly in languages other than English), which, for reasons of space, I will not review here.

filtered through his grammar and the same grammatical rules (parameter settings, etc.) are therefore in play (Ervin-Tripp 1964; Brown and Fraser 1964; Lust et al. 1986, 1987).

The notion that imitation reflects competence has also been the rationale for the frequent use of imitation tasks to tap grammatical knowledge in areas as diverse as relative clauses, backwards and forwards anaphor, coordination, and head direction (see Lust et al. 1987 for review). As Lust et al. point out, the crucial point of these imitation studies is that they are designed to test a precise *grammatical* factor and other, performance-related factors, such as sentence length and complexity, are controlled for. Thus, if children respond differently with respect to the various conditions, this is a reflection of their grammatical competence. For example, Lust et al. (1986) showed that children are better at imitating postposed adverbial clauses which coincide with the right-branching structure of English(e.g. *John rode the bike when he was at school*), than preposed ones (e.g. *When he was at school, John rode the bike*) even though length is held constant. In fact, in a number of imitation studies the results go in the opposite direction of what is predicted by a performance account. For example, children are more successful at imitating sentence coordination (e.g. *Push the truck and push the car*) than reduced or phrasal coordination (e.g. *Push the truck and the car*), even though the former is longer than the latter. Similarly, English-speaking children do better when the reduction site is in a forward position (e.g. *Push the truck and __ the car*) than in a backwards position (e.g. *Push ___ and pull the trunk*), where again, the length factor would predict the opposite result. Children acquiring languages with a left-branching structure show the opposite results.

Though it seems likely that different cognitive resources are recruited in spontaneous production and elicited imitation, it is possible that they are subject to some similar production constraint (as suggested by Brown and Fraser 1964).[26] After all, both behaviors involve the *production* of an utterance. But suppose we eliminate the production component entirely. We might then expect different results if, indeed, production limitations are responsible for missing subjects. On the other hand, if we also find that children accept null subjects in comprehension, we can attribute this to the underlying grammar.[27] In the next section I report the results of a comprehension study on null subjects.

---

[26] Brown and Fraser (1964) state "a basic factor causing the child's reduction of adult sentences is surely an upper limit on some kind of immediate memory span for the situation in which the child is imitating and a similar limit of programming span for the situation in which the child is constructing sentences" (p. 76).

[27] Valian (1991, 1996) in her discussion of VP length effects in imitation says that the results show the length of sentences that "children are hearing can also have an effect on their use of subjects" and that "the processing limitations begin their influence during the comprehension phase of the task and continue through production" (p. 162). It is not obvious that the effect found in imitation is due to a *comprehension* problem, as Valian implies, given that similar effects are found in spontaneous speech which has no obvious comprehension component.

4.1 *Null Subjects in Comprehension*

Orfitelli (2008) conducted comprehension experiments to see if English-speaking children (who are productively in the missing subject stage) also understand and accept null subject sentences in comprehension (cf. also Orfitelli and Hyams 2007). Our hypothesis is straightforward: when children show the same (non-)adult behavior in comprehension and production (and imitation), this is due to the effects of the grammar – common to all linguistic performance. On the other hand, if the effect is strictly due to constraints on production (due to sentence length or metrical structure), then it should not show up in comprehension.

The experimental task is based on the truth value judgment (TVJ) methodology of Crain and McKee (1985). The design of the experiment exploits the fact that in English, null subjects are licensed in imperative, but not typically in declarative contexts (diary drop contexts excepted, as noted above). The children in the study see a scenario and then hear a comment made by an observing puppet, Mr. Bear. They are asked to be Mr. Bear's teacher for the day, and to tell him if his statements matched the scenario or not, and why. Thirty children (13 boys, 17 girls) were tested, ten children in each 6-month interval between 2½ and 4 years (2.54–3.97 years, mean age 3.25).

There were four different scenarios in the task, each consisting of a story and an accompanying pair of pictures. The first of the pair was always a picture of two "big kids" named Mary and Billy, while the second picture was always of two "little kids" named Emma and Ben. In the "big kid" scenarios, the children are engaged in a particular activity, such as drawing a picture or playing with blocks, while in the "little kid" scenarios the children are shown next to the props (i.e. paper and crayons or blocks) but not using or playing with them. Each subject was told that the "big kids" are old enough to engage in these activities without being given permission, and, moreover, they do these activities every day. On the other hand, the "little kids" have to wait for their babysitter – Mr. Bear – to tell them that it's okay to play with the blocks, crayons, etc.

Before the experiment began, subjects were told that Mr. Bear's comments would either describe what the children were doing, or would tell them to do something. It was then established that it would be silly for Mr. Bear to tell the older children to do an activity they were already doing. It would, however, be appropriate for him to describe their actions. Conversely, it would be silly for Mr. Bear to describe the younger children performing an action they were not doing, but it would be appropriate for him to tell them to do the activity, because they were waiting for his permission. So the "big kid" scenarios provide the declarative context while the "little kid" scenarios provide the imperative context. Table 1 gives examples of the test sentences with adult judgments.

The declarative (a) and imperative (b) conditions serve as controls. High performance on these conditions indicates that the child comprehends declarative and imperative clauses in an adult manner, and understands the scenario and the task. Children who performed badly (less than seven out of eight items correct) on either

Table 1 Example items with adult judgments[a]

		"Big kid"/declarative scenario	"Little kid"/imperative scenario
a.	They always play with blocks	Match	No match
b.	Please play with blocks	No match	Match
c.	Play with blocks	No match	Match

[a]Playing with blocks was one of four scenarios. The other scenarios involved eating a cookie, drawing a picture, and putting on socks

Table 2 Individual performance on the null subject condition

	2;6-2;11	3;0-3;5	3;6-3;11
AC (7–8 correct)	1	2	7
C (2–6 correct)	0	0	1
BC (0–1 correct)	9	8	2

the declarative or imperative condition were not included in any subsequent analyses. The sentence in (c) is the experimental null subject condition. The subjects were tested on whether they accept this sentence in declarative and imperative contexts. If children are adult-like they will give the responses in Table 1, they will accept the sentence (=match) for the "little kid" scenario, allowing an imperative meaning, and they will reject (= no match) for the "big kid" scenario, disallowing a declarative meaning. On the other hand, if children have a null subject grammar, they will accept the null subject sentence in the 'big kid' scenario, where the interpretation is declarative and also presumably allow it in the "little kid" scenario, assuming they also allow an imperative reading for NS sentences.

In addition, a 10-min audio recording was made of all children who participated in the judgment task. These transcripts provided information on the child's spontaneous production of null subject sentences. Children who showed a proportion of null subjects (in non-imperative contexts) greater than 30% were considered to be in the NS stage. This proportion of null subject utterances is roughly what has been observed in the natural production of English-speaking children in the NS stage (Valian 1991). If the NS stage is the result of a non-adult grammar, viz. one that that license null subjects, then we should see a high correspondence between an individual child's production of NS sentences and that same child's assignment of a declarative reading to the sentences in the null subject experimental condition.

The results were as follows: 30 of the 35 children tested performed well on declarative and imperative controls, and were thus included in the analysis of the null subject sentences. Children's individual performance on the null subject condition is shown in Table 2. Most of the children in the two youngest groups performed below chance (BC). Below chance means they got 0 or 1 item correct out of 8 in the null subject condition. By contrast, 7 out of 10 children in the oldest group performed above chance (AC), as compared to only two children in the younger age groups. Interestingly, only one child performed at chance (C). The consistent BC performance of the younger groups indicates that they have a consistent analysis of the null subject sentences. All but two of the children in the youngest age groups accepted null subject sentences in declarative contexts, as is expected if they have a NS grammar. Ten of the children, 7 of whom were in the oldest group, showed adult-like performance. In contrast to the younger groups, the oldest children tested performed well above chance as a group. This increase in adult-like comprehension at 3½ years mirrors the decrease in production of NS sentences that occurs at this age.

This behavior in comprehension is predicted by grammatical accounts, but not by processing accounts, which hold that children's do not grammatically represent NSs, but rather drop phonological subjects in production because of limitations in the planning and/or executing of the sentence.

In addition, an individual subject analysis that compared each child's performance on the null subject condition of the judgment task to the proportion of NS sentences she produced in the recording showed a 100% correspondence. Children who were classified as being in the NS stage by the recording task were also classified as being in the NS by the comprehension task. This perfect correspondence again supports the grammatical account according to which children have a NS grammar that underlies both production and comprehension.

There was one unexpected result in Experiment 1. In NS languages, null subjects are licensed in both declarative and imperative contexts, and thus it is expected that children in the NS stage would accept the experimental NS sentences in both the declarative and imperative scenarios. This was not the case. While the younger children overwhelmingly allowed NS sentences in a declarative context, they unanimously rejected them in the imperative situations. A possible explanation for this result is that the NS children, for whom a subjectless sentence is ambiguous between an imperative and declarative structure, are being pushed toward the declarative reading because all of the control imperative sentences began with 'please'. If the children adopt a strategy according to which imperative usage requires 'please', this would induce them to interpret subjectless sentences lacking 'please' as declarative. To test this hypothesis, we did a follow up study. In the second experiment, we included vocative imperatives (e.g. *Hey kids, play with blocks*) to neutralize a potential 'please' strategy. We found the same overall pattern of results, i.e. one adult-like group that allowed only an imperative reading of NS sentences, and a second group that allowed declarative meaning (the NS group). In Experiment 2, however, the NS group allow *both* the imperative and declarative readings in equal measure. This supports the hypothesis that in Experiment 1 the children were using a 'please' strategy to disambiguate the otherwise ambiguous NS sentences (see Orfitelli and Hyams for further discussion). More generally, the results of the comprehension study strongly favor a grammatical account according to which missing subjects are a grammatical option in early language (to roughly age 31/2), and not simply the output of an overwrought production system.

To sum up the discussion thus far, while children are certainly more limited than adults in their productive abilities, the statistical and empirical evidence does not lend strong support to the hypothesis that children drop subjects because of constraints on sentence length or on metrical structure. The convergence of evidence from different methodologies – that children omit subjects in elicited imitation, in spontaneous production, and also accept them in comprehension – strongly supports the hypothesis that omission is due to a common underlying system, the grammar.

It is, of course, still possible that that the grammatical option to omit subjects is determined under pressure from limited processing capacity, as proposed by Rizzi (2005b). The strongest support to date for processing effects in subject omission is the VP length result obtained by Bloom (1991) and Valian (1991, 1996). In the following section I will propose that VP length is in fact a pragmatic effect, as originally suggested in Hyams and Wexler (1993). Before returning to the VP length results, however, I first discuss the approach to argument realization that is assumed within most syntactic theories (since Chomsky 1982). I then provide a brief overview of studies that have investigated children's knowledge of the information structure principles that govern the distribution of null and overt arguments. As we will see, many of these studies replicate Hyams and Wexler's finding of a trade-off over time between null subject and overt pronouns, discussed above (Sect. 3.1), a result that is consistent with a modular grammatical/pragmatic account of subject omission, but at odds with a processing account.

5 Information Structure and Null Subjects

Grammatical accounts of null subjects are necessarily modular in structure (Chomsky 1982). The grammar (e.g. Italian, Chinese, etc.) allows the occurrence of a null element (pro, PRO, null topics and so on) under certain structural conditions of licensing and identification. But the syntax does not legislate when a particular subject will be omitted. This is a function of the information structure (IS) of the sentence, considerations such as the preceding discourse, situational context including speaker/hearer, the informational value of the subject, among other factors.[28] All languages that permit argument omission, whether Italian-like pro drop languages, German-like topic drop, Chinese-like topic drop languages (Huang 1984), or mixed systems such as American Sign Language (Lillo-Martin 1994), have strict conditions on when the argument can, or must be omitted.

Conversely, discourse conditions alone cannot sanction missing arguments. For example, there is no discourse or situational factor that explains why languages require expletive subjects (e.g. 'it is raining, it seems that ....'), which are by definition void of informational content.[29] This is a purely grammatical requirement. Moreover, there exist syntactic properties that covary with the NS phenomenon and which do not lend themselves to an obvious pragmatic explanation. For example,

---

[28] As pointed out by Sorace et al. (2009), pronoun realization also involves an understanding of the listener's mental state and perspective.

[29] My thanks to Tom Roeper for pointing this out.

NS languages allow *wh*-extraction over a complementizer, as in Italian *Chi pensi che __ sia partita?* ('Who do you think that __ left?'), an extraction that is blocked in non-null subject languages, such as English. Indeed, one of the strongest pieces of evidence for a grammatical basis to null subjects comes from language development. Children acquiring Dutch, German, French and other non-null subject languages use far more null subjects with root infinitives than with finite verbs (see Hoekstra and Hyams (1998) for summary of statistics). Quite the contrary is predicted on informational grounds; children should be more likely to omit subjects when agreement features are specified on the verb. So the modular view of null arguments implicates both the grammar and information structure. In the next section I discuss the role of informational factors on children's NS use.

5.1 Is Effects on Null Subjects in Child Language

Early work on children missing subjects focused on the possible licensing mechanisms for null subjects in early grammar (e.g. pronominal Agr, morphological uniformity, etc.). And the empirical results reviewed above clearly support a grammatical model of early null subjects. But this does not exclude that children are sensitive to discourse factors and that these factors affect their use of null subjects, just as grammatical analyses of adult NS languages do not preempt the role of pragmatic factors in how null subjects are deployed. It is an empirical question to what extent children – both those acquiring NS languages and also those acquiring languages in which the target is not a null subject or topic drop language – adhere to discourse conditions on argument omission.

The earliest work addressing these questions is Greenfield and Smith (1976) who attributed subject omission to a pragmatic tendency in children to drop old information, elements that are well established in discourse and/or non-linguistic context, and to produce those elements that provide new, focal information (possibly under pressure from an immature production system). Because subjects express old or given information more often than objects, they are frequently omitted while objects are not, giving rise to a subject-object asymmetry in argument drop. As Rizzi (2005b) observes, however, a purely informational account of this sort is at odds with the finding that in many languages, including German, French, Dutch, Flemish, children do not drop subjects in post-*wh* contexts even though it is the *wh*-phrase that is focalized while the subject is old information.[30]

More recently, a number of studies have investigated pragmatic/discourse effects in children acquiring null subject languages. Clancy (1993, 1997) shows that children acquiring Korean (age 1;8-2;10) are more likely to drop arguments that are more prominent in discourse (according to a range of features, including newness, contrast, query, absence, person and animacy) and express those arguments that are

---

[30] In English this restriction holds in finite *wh*-clauses (Roeper and Rohrbacher 2000 – see note 5).

less prominent and hence less recoverable from context. Similarly, in a study of four Inuktitut-speaking children (aged 2;0-3;6), Allen (2000) shows the argument omission can be significantly predicted by the degree of 'informativeness' of an argument (as measured by several variables including newness, contrast, absence, differentiation in context, and person). Serratrice and Sorace (2003), using the same principles introduced by Clancy and Allen, also find significant discourse/pragmatic effects in the distribution of overt versus null subjects in six Italian-speaking children (ages 1;8 and 3;3), reflecting the distribution of the adult language. Serratrice and Sorace are explicit in assuming that the pragmatic principles operate within the boundaries imposed by the grammar, in this case a pro-drop grammar.

If children acquiring NS languages are sensitive to IS features governing argument realization, is the same true of subject drop in non-null subject grammars such as English? Guerriero et al. (2001) compare the effects of IS on the distribution of null, pronominal, and lexical subjects in the spontaneous speech of 3-year old English-speaking and Japanese-speaking children. They find that both groups of children tend to represent arguments that are new to discourse with lexical NPs and given arguments as either null or pronominal. They also find convergence with the adult targets in that Japanese children tend to omit arguments that represent given information while the English-speaking children pronominalize such arguments. Guerriero et al. note that the English-speaking children are old enough (3 years) to have exited the NS stage, and thus show an adult-like preference for pronouns over null arguments.

These results lead us to wonder what would happen if these children had been observed 6 months to a year earlier, while still in the NS stage. If the distribution of null, pronominal, and lexical arguments in NS languages has its basis in universal principles of information structure, as is generally assumed (e.g. Du Bois 1987; Guerriero et al. 2001, among others), and if young English-speaking children have a grammar that permits null subjects (e.g. a RSD grammar), we predict (a) that they would show a distribution of null and overt arguments similar to that of children acquiring 'real' NS languages, and (b) that there would be a trade-off over time between null arguments and pronouns, as Hyams and Wexler (1993) found. In other words, they would show continuity with respect to the discourse principles and the representation of new versus given information, but the grammatical representation of this information would shift over time from null to pronominal arguments as they move from a NS grammar to a non-NS grammar. This contrasts with a processing account (Bloom 1991; Valian 1991; Valian et al. 1996), which predicts a trade-off between null subjects and lexical NPs.[31] Interestingly, Guerriero et al. (2001) note that a separate longitudinal study of English-speaking children that they conducted "nicely shows the developmental changes in which null forms become pronominal" (p. 328). Similarly, Hughes and Allen (2008), who investigate the role of discourse-pragmatic information in the distribution of referential forms in 4-English-speaking children (aged 2;0-3;1), also find a trade-off over time between null subjects and pronouns. These results parallel those observed in Hyams and Wexler (1993).

---

[31] And which also do not predict any particular effect of discourse conditions.

Hughes and Allen examine the effects of various 'accessibility features' (factors that render the referent of an NP more or less transparent), such as animacy, contextual disambiguation, physical presence, prior mention, linguistic disambiguation and joint attention. In addition to the trade-off between null subjects and pronouns, they also find that lexical forms decrease over time, which also contributes to the rise in pronouns. This result contrasts with Hyams and Wexler (1993), who found that NPs remain constant. The decrease in NPs is unexpected on an IS account as lexical NPs typically constitute new information, and therefore, unlike null subjects, which are presupposed, should not be replaced by pronouns. Hughes and Allen explain this result as an effect of motherese. They note that a prominent feature of child-directed language is the "overuse" of lexical NPs in cases where the referent is highly accessible, such as when the referent is either speaker or addressee, as illustrated in (9a,b) or has already been clearly established in discourse, as in (9d,e). (Examples are from Hughes and Allen).[32]

(9) a. MOT: Mommy doesn't want any sugar [mom about herself]
    b. MOT: How old is Brian last week [speaking to child]
       CHI: Brian got a big job to do.
    d. CH: Butterfly has gone.
       MOT: Where has the butterfly gone?
    e. MOT: Where does the crocodile go.
       CH: The crocodile go there.

Hughes and Allen suggest that redundant NPs in the input may be responsible for the higher than anticipated number of lexical NPs in highly accessible contexts in the children's language. These lexical forms are later replaced (appropriately) by pronouns as the motherese effect diminishes.[33] Thus, the decrease in lexical NPs over time is very likely due to an independent motherese effect, and thus consistent with the hypothesis that English-speaking children initially use null subjects, and later pronouns, in discourse appropriate ways.[34]

Valian (1996) also finds that English-speaking children drop (or fail to imitate) pronouns more frequently than lexical NPs. Again, this is a direct consequence of the relative informational value of pronouns, which are redundant, and NPs, which introduce new information. Moreover, Valian (1996) and Hughes and Allen (2006)

---

[32] This phenomenon is also discussed in Hyams (2008) where I refer to examples such as (9a,b) as 'Mommy deixis'.

[33] Hughes and Allen (2008) also note that discourse/pragmatics effects are "cumulative" in that the degree of accessibility of a referent, as measured by the number of accessibility features it has, is also a factor in explaining the distribution of null, pronominal, and lexical forms. See their paper for details.

[34] The children studied by Hughes and Allen are somewhat older than the children studied by Hyams and Wexler (who looked at Adam and Eve's data, Childes, Brown 1973; MacWhinney and Snow 1985). It is possible that that the age differences are the source of the different results we found with respect to lexical NPsif children stop using lexical forms to refer to speaker/addressee (*mommy* deixis) at a somewhat older age.

find that the rate of subject omission is substantially higher for 1st and 2nd person pronouns than for 3rd person, again an obvious contextual effect. This avoidance of pronouns is expected if the children's grammar licenses another option, namely the null subject option. According to Valian's measures, the children in her lower MLU group drop subjects and they are also the ones who show an 'avoid pronoun' strategy (Chomsky 1982). The higher MLU children, who have passed out of the NS stage, again by Valian's measures, imitate both pronouns and full NPs to the same degree. Finally, it is the lower MLU group that shows the VP length effect. This, I will suggest follows from pragmatic principles that can also be identified across adult NS languages. I turn to the VP length effect directly.

5.2 An Information Structure Account of the VP Length Effect

Hyams and Wexler (1993) suggested a pragmatic analysis of the VP length effect found in young English-speaking children (Bloom 1991). Our proposal was prompted by the finding that adult Italians also show this same result: VPs of null subject sentences tend to be longer than VPs in sentence with overt subjects, and there is also a difference in the predicted direction between sentences with pronominal subjects vs. lexical subjects.

Hyams and Wexler proposed that a VP in a NS language like Italian is more likely to contain new, focal information (hence be longer) when the subject is presupposed (i.e. null), while the use of a lexical NP subject signals new information (e.g. change of topic) and so will have a non-focalized (hence shorter) VP. In a NS language a pronoun subject is neither new information nor strictly presupposed, as it is used only when pragmatically warranted for contrast, disambiguation or emphasis and so on. Hence VP length in sentences with pronominal subjects falls somewhere in between. Although our proposal lacked much in the way of precision, there are some additional findings that lend plausibility to a pragmatic explanation of the VP length result. Du Bois (1987, 2003) observes that cross-linguistically, subjects of transitive verbs are associated with given information, and so show up as null or pronominal forms. Conversely, subjects of intransitive verbs and objects of transitive verbs are both associated with new information, and are therefore usually lexically realized.[35] Assuming that children are sensitive to these principles (and various studies show that they are, as I will discuss below), the expectation is that children will drop subjects of transitive verbs more than subjects of intransitive verbs. This would clearly contribute to making the VPs of null subject sentences

---

[35] Du Bois (1987) explains this distribution in terms of 'informativeness' in the following way: because the subject of a transitive verb acts on the object or controls the events expressed by the verb, its presence is recoverable from the object which is acted upon (hence *given*). Intransitive verbs, on the other hand, denote events that are not controlled by the subject, rather the subject is affected, as is the object of a transitive verb and therefore, these arguments are not recoverable (hence *new*).

(typically transitive) "longer" than the VPs of sentences with expressed subjects (typically intransitive) – not for processing reasons, but because of the information structure of the two types of VPs.

Indeed, Clancy (1993), Allen and Schroeder (2003) and Gürkanli et al. (2007) find that verb transitivity (as it relates to informativeness- see note 36) plays a role in argument realization in children acquiring Korean, Inuktitut, and Turkish (all NS languages); subjects of intransitives and objects of transitives tend to be lexically realized, while subjects of transitive verbs are omitted. Guerriero et al. (2001) find this same result for both their English and Japanese-speaking children. Thus, these studies all replicate Dubois' crosslinguistic finding for adults in children, consistent with the hypothesis that the VP length effect is a pragmatic one.

If VP length is a pragmatic effect and not a processing one, this would explain why Hyams and Wexler (1993) found the same result with adult Italian speakers. It would also clarify the seemingly contradictory results in Hamann and Plunkett's (1998) Danish-speaking children. Recall that they find that VP length decreases as a function of subject "heaviness" (null > pronoun > NP), but they also find that the MLUs for subjectless sentences are lower overall than for sentences with subjects, a result that they interpret to mean that, on average, processing resources do not determine subject omission.

6 Some Concluding Remarks

It would be misleading to suggest that children adhere perfectly to adult principles of information structure. Children do sometimes drop arguments when the referent is not easily accessible (Hughes and Allen 2008, among others). This may be partially responsible for the observation that children acquiring NS languages drop subjects more than adults (though, as noted earlier, there are conflicting findings in this regard). On the other hand, children may show a higher NS rate than adults because their language is more narrowly confined to the immediate discourse situation, and also because in adult-child interactions, it is typically adults who initiate topic changes (Serratrice 2005). These factors would inflate adult use of overt subjects relative to children's. If the latter speculation is correct, we would expect that as the child's discourse abilities develop such that she initiates more topic changes and is also less tightly tied to the immediate discourse situation, her NS rate will converge on that of the adult speaker.[36]

How the child acquiring a non-NS language such as English comes to match adult norms with respect to NS use, viz. diary drop is less clear. In Sect. 2.4, I considered two possible subject drop trajectories, one discontinuous, the other continuous.

---

[36] Hamann and Plunkett (1998) did not find an effect of discourse on subject omission in child Danish. However, as they acknowledge, they looked only at previous mention and not at any of the other IS variables that have been found to influence null subject use.

A discontinuous trajectory would be consistent with a parametric shift (from RSD to non-RSD and then the learning of diary drop contexts by positive evidence). A continuous trajectory would instead be consistent with the idea that children maintain RSD into adulthood where it then manifests itself as 'diary drop'. In this instance there must be a developmental shift in the child's frame of reference (or discourse world) from a deictic one (based on immediate discourse/situational context) to a much stricter diary context.[37] Exactly how that shift occurs is not obvious.

It seems clear that young children are more limited in their productive capacities than adults, due to shorter memory and attention spans, less planning capacity, and so on, Thus far, however, there is little compelling evidence that performance factors are sufficient to explain the missing subject phenomenon. Given the grammatical contingencies associated with null subjects, especially the interaction with finiteness and *wh* questions, the most plausible explanation is that whatever production constraints exist, they operate within the parameters of the grammatical system, as proposed in Rizzi (2005a, b).

However, a mixed processing-competence account is supported only to the extent that there is indeed evidence pointing to specific performance effects on subject omission. The strongest evidence to date is the VP length effect (Bloom 1970, 1991). Hyams and Wexler (1993) replicate this result in Italian adults, making a processing explanation unlikely. Moreover, various studies of both adults and children have shown that new information is more often represented in subject of transitive verbs (Du Bois 1987, 2003; Clancy 1993; Allen and Schroeder 2003; Gürkanli et al. 2007). This would mimic the VP length effect, but for pragmatic reasons, as suggested in Hyams and Wexler, without recourse to processing constraints in children that are neither well understood nor precisely formulated.

There is now substantial evidence from children acquiring null subject languages of different types that general principles of information structure influence the distribution of null and overt subjects in languages where argument omission is a grammatical option. However, such principles alone cannot license null arguments in languages in which this is not a grammatical option. Rather, the IS principles operate within the constraints of the grammatical system.

There is also increasing evidence that English-speaking children are sensitive to such informational principles, first with respect to null subjects and then with respect to the (almost) functionally equivalent pronouns that eventually supplant null arguments. This array of pragmatic data lends additional support to the hypothesis that null subjects are a grammatical, and likely parametric option for young children.

Various parameter setting models of the NS phenomenon have been proposed over the years, some suggesting a fixed initial setting, others multiple, competing settings.

---

[37] In Hyams (1996) I suggest that children drop pronouns, determiners and tense (during the RI stage) because they have an option to interpret these functions deictically, that is, through situational anchoring. This idea is further developed in Hyams (2007) where I look at the interpretations associated with different non-finite verbs (e.g. RIs, bare participles, bare verbs, etc.) in various child languages.

There are also different analyses of how parameter resetting is determined—maturation, processing load, or statistical factors, or some combination of these. There is a range of empirical findings many of which are handled by one or the other of these accounts, but it does not seem that any one account covers the full range of facts. Also, some of the empirical predictions made by the various hypotheses discussed in this overview have yet to be tested in detail. I think it is fair to say that the jury is still out on the correct analysis of early null subjects, but it is clear that the phenomenon is vastly more complex than was initially assumed.

Acknowledgments I would like to thank Robyn Orfitelli and Kamil Ud Deen for their helpful comments on an earlier draft of this paper. I am grateful also to Jill de Villiers and Tom Roeper for inviting me to contribute to this volume, and for carefully reading and critiquing this paper.

References

Allen, S. 2000. A discourse-pragmatic explanation for argument representation in child Inuktitut. *Linguistics* 38(3): 483–521.
Allen, S., and H. Schroeder. 2003. Preferred argument structure in early Inuktitut spontaneous speech data. In *Preferred argument structure: Grammar as architecture for function*, ed. J. Du Bois, L. Kumpf, and W. Ashby, 301–338. Amsterdam: Benjamins.
Babyonyshev, M. 1993. Acquisition of the Russian case system. In *Papers on case & agreement II*, ed. C. Phillips. MIT Working Papers in Linguistics 19: 1–43.
Bates, E. 1976. *Language and context: The acquisition of pragmatics*. New York: Academic.
Bel, A. 2003. The syntax of subjects in the acquisition of Spanish and Catalan. *Probus: International Journal of Latin and Romance Linguistics* 15(81): 1–26.
Berwick, R.C. 1982. Locality principles and the acquisition of syntactic knowledge. PhD diss., MIT, Department of Computer Science, Cambridge, MA.
Bloom, L. 1970. *Language development: Form and function in emerging grammars*. Cambridge, MA: MIT Press.
Bloom, P. 1991. Subjectless sentences in child language. *Linguistic Inquiry* 21: 491–504.
Bloom, L., P. Lightbown, and L. Hood. 1975a. Structure and variation in child language. *Monographs of the Society for Research in Child Development* 40(2): 1–79.
Bloom, L., P. Miller, and L. Hood. 1975b. Variation and reduction as aspects of competence in language development. In *Millllesota symposia 011 child psychology*, vol. 9, ed. A. Pick, 3–55. Minneapolis: University of Minnesota Press.
Borer, H., and K. Wexler. 1987. The maturation of syntax. In *Parameter setting*, ed. T. Roeper and E. Williams, 123–172. Dordrecht: Reidel.
Borer, H., and K. Wexler. 1992. Bi-unique relations and the maturation of grammatical principles. *Natural Linguistics and Linguistic Theory* 10: 147–189.
Bromberg, H., and K. Wexler. 1995. Null subjects in Wh questions. *MIT WPL* 26: 221–248.
Brown, R. 1973. *A first language*. Cambridge, MA: Harvard University Press.
Brown, R., and C. Fraser. 1964. The acquisition of syntax. In *The acquisition of language*, ed. U. Bellugi and R. Brown, 43–78. Chicago: University of Chicago Press.
Brown, R., C. Fraser, and U. Bellugi. 1964. Explorations in grammar evaluation. In *The acquisition of language*, ed. U. Bellugi and R. Brown, 79–91. Chicago: University of Chicago Press.
Cabré Sans, Y., and Gavarró, A. 2006. Subject distribution and verb classes in child Catalan. In *Proceedings of the 2nd Conference of GALANA*, 51–60. Somerville: Cascadilla Press.
Chomsky, N. 1965. *Aspects of the theory of syntax*. Cambridge, MA: MIT Press.

Chomksy, N. 1977. On Wh movement. In *Formal Syntax*, eds. P. Culicover, P. T. Wasow, and A. Akmajian, New York: Academic Press.
Chomsky, N. 1982. *Some concepts and consequences of the theory of government and binding*. Cambridge, MA: MIT Press.
Clahsen, H., S. Eisenbeiss, and M. Penke. 1994. Lexical learning and early syntactic development. In *Language learning and language disorders*, ed. H. Clahsen. Amsterdam: John Benjamins Publishing Co.
Clahsen, H., C. Kursawe, and M. Penke. 1995. Introducing CP: Wh-questions and subordinate clauses in German child language. *Essex Research Reports in Linguistics* 7: 1–28. Essex: University of Essex, Department of Linguistics.
Clancy, P. 1993. Preferred argument structure in Korean acquisition. In *Proceedings of the 25th Annual Child Language Research Forum*, ed. E. Clark, 307–314. Stanford: CSLI.
Clancy, P. 1997. Discourse motivations of referential choice in Korean acquisition. In *Japanese/Korean linguistics*, vol. 6, ed. H. Sohn and J. Haig, 639–659. Stanford: CSLI.
Clark, R., and I. Roberts. 1991. A computational model of language learnability and language change. Unpublished manuscript, Geneva: University of Geneva.
Crain, S., and C. McKee. 1985. The acquisition of structural restrictions on anaphora. In *Proceedings of NELS 15*, 94–110. Amherst: University of Massachusetts, GLSA.
Crisma, P. 1992. On the acquisition of wh-questions in French. *GenGenP*, 115–122. Geneva: University of Geneva.
Crousaz, D., and U. Schlonsky. 2003. The distribution of a subject clitic pronoun in a Franco-Provençal dialect. *Linguistic Inquiry* 34: 413–442.
de Haan, G., and K. Tuijman. 1988. Missing subjects and objects in child grammar. In *Language development*, ed. P. Jordens and J. Lalleman, 101–122. Dordrecht: Foris.
den Besten, Hans. 1977/1983. On the interaction of root transformations and lexial deletive rules. In *On the formal syntax of Westgermania*, ed. W. Abraham, 7–131. Amsterdam: J. Behjamins.
Drozd, K. 1995. Child English pre-sentential negation as metalinguistic exclamatory sentence negation. *Journal of Child Language* 22: 583–610.
Du Bois, J. 1987. The discourse basis of ergativity. *Language* 63: 805–855.
Du Bois, J. 2003. Argument structure: Grammar in use. In *Preferred argument structure: Grammar as architecture for function*, ed. J. Du Bois, L. Kumpf, and W. Ashby, 81–108. Amsterdam: Benjamins.
Ervin-Tripp, S. 1964. Imitation and structural change in children's language. In *New directions in the study of language*, ed. E. Lenneberg. Cambridge, MA: MIT Press.
Felix, S. 1987. *Cognition and language growth*. Dordrecht: Foris.
Fodor, J.D. 1998. Unambiguous triggers. *Linguistic Inquiry* 29: 1–36.
Gerken, L. 1991. The metrical basis for children's subjectless sentences. *Journal of Memory and Language* 30(4): 431–451.
Gerken, L. 1994. Young children's representation of prosodic phonology: Evidence from English-speakers' weak syllable productions. *Journal of Memory and Language* 33(1): 19–38.
Gibson, E., and K. Wexler. 1994. Triggers. *Linguistic Inquiry* 25(3): 407–454.
Greenfield, P., and J. Smith. 1976. *The structure of communication in early language development*. New York: Academic.
Guasti, M.-T. 1993/1994. Verb syntax in Italian child grammar: Finite and non-finite verbs. *Language Acquisition* 3(1): 1–40.
Guasti, T. 1996. The acquisition of Italian interrogatives. In *Generative perspectives on language acquisition*, ed. H. Clahsen, 241–270. Amsterdam: Benjamins.
Guerriero, A., A. Cooper, Y. Oshima-Takane, and Y. Kuriyama. 2001. A discourse-pragmatic explanation for argument realization and omission in English and Japanese children's speech. In *Proceedings of the 25th Annual BUCLD*, vol. 1, 319–330. Somerville: Cascadilla Press.
Guilfoyle, E. 1984. The acquisition of tense and the emergence of lexical subjects. McGill Working Papers in Linguistics. McGill University, Montreal, Canada.
Gürkanli, O., M. Nakupoglu, and A. Özyürek. 2007. Shared information and zrgument omission in Turkish. In *Proceedings of the 31st Annual BUCLD*, vol. 2, 262–273. Somerville: Cascadilla Press.

Haegeman, L. 1990. Non-overt subjects in diary contexts. In *Grammar in progress*, ed. J. Mascaro and M. Nespor, 167–179. Dordrecht: Foris.
Haegeman, L. 1992. *Generative syntax: Theory and description. A case study of West Flemish*. Cambridge: CUP.
Haegeman, L. 1994. Root infinitives, tense and truncated structures. *Language Acquisition* 4(3): 205–255.
Haegeman, L. 1995. Root null subjects and root infinitives in early Dutch. In *Proceedings of the GALA 1995*, ed. C. Koster and F. Wijnen. Groningen: Center for Language and Cognition.
Haegeman, L. 1996. Root infinitives, clitics and truncated structures. In *Generative perspectives on language acquisition*, ed. H. Clahsen, 271–309. Amsterdam: Benjamins.
Haegeman, L. 2000. Adult null subjects in non pro-drop languages. In *The acquisition of syntax*, ed. M.A. Friedman and L. Rizzi, 329–346. Harlow: Longman.
Hamann, C. 1996. Null arguments in German child language. *Language Acquisition* 5: 155–208.
Hamann, C. 2000. The acquisition of constituent questions and the requirements of interpretation. In *The acquisition of syntax*, ed. M. Friedemann and L. Rizzi, 190–201. Harlow: Longman.
Hamann, C., and K. Plunkett. 1998. Subjectless sentences in child Danish. *Cognition* 69: 35–72.
Hamann, C., L. Rizzi, and U. Frauenfelder. 1996. The acquisition of subject and object clitics in French. In *Generative perspectives on acquisition*, ed. H. Clahsen, 309–334. Amsterdam: Benjamins.
Hoekstra, T., and N. Hyams. 1998. Aspects of root infinitives. *Lingua* 106: 81–112.
Huang, C.-T.J. 1984. On the distribution and reference of empty pronouns. *Linguistic Inquiry* 15: 531–574.
Hughes, M., and S. Allen. 2006. A discourse-pragmatic analysis of subject omission in child English. In *Proceedings of the 30th Annual BUCLD*, vol. 1, 293–304. Somerville: Cascadilla Press.
Hughes, M., and S. Allen. 2008. Child-directed speech and the development of referential choice in child English. Talk presented at the *International Association for the Study of Child Language Conference*, Edinburgh, Scotland.
Hyams, N. 1983. The acquisition of parameterized grammars. PhD diss., MIT Department of Linguistics, Cambridge, MA.
Hyams, N. 1986. *Language acquisition and the theory of parameters*. Dordrecht: Reidel.
Hyams, N. 1991. A reanalysis of null subjects in child language. In *Theoretical issues in language acquisiton*, ed. J. Weissenborn, H. Goodluck, and T. Roeper. New Jersey: Lawrence Erlbaum Associates, Inc.
Hyams, N. 1992. The genesis of clausal structure. In *The acquisition of verb placement; functional categories and V2 phenomena in language development*, ed. J. Meisel, 371–400. Dordrecht: Kluwer.
Hyams, N. 1994. V2, null arguments and C projections. In *Language acquisition studies in generative grammar*, ed. T. Hoekstra and B. Schwartz, 1–55. Philadelphia: Benjamins.
Hyams, N. 1996. The underspecification of functional categories in early grammar. In *Generative Perspectives on Language Acquisition*, ed. H. Clahsen. John Benjamins: Amsterdam.
Hyams, N. 2007. Aspectual effects on interpretation. *Language Acquisition* 14(3): 231–268.
Hyams, N. 2008. Reflections on Motherese. In *An Enterprise in the Cognitve Science of Language*, eds. T. Sano, M. Endo, M. Isobe, K. Otaki, K. Sugisaki, and T. Suzuki, 1–12. Tokyo: Hituzi Syobe Publishing.
Hyams, N., and O. Jaeggli. 1986. Null subjects and morphological development in child language. Unpublished manuscript.
Hyams, N., and K. Wexler. 1993. On the grammatical basis of null subjects in child language. *Linguistic Inquiry* 24(3): 421–459.
Ingham, R. 1998. Tense without agreement in early clause structures. *Language Acquisition* 7: 51–81.
Jaeggli, O. and N. Hyams. 1988. Morphological uniformity and the setting of the null subject parameter. In *Proceedings of the NELS* 18, 239–253. University of Massachusetts, Amherst: GLSA.

Jaeggli, O., and K. Safir. 1989. The null subject parameter and parametric theory. In *The null subject parameter*, ed. O. Jaeggli and K. Safir, 1–44. Dordrecht: Kluwer.

Jakubowicz, C., N. Müller, B. Riemer, and C. Rigaut. 1996. The case of subject and object omission in French and German. In *Proceedings of the 21st Annual BUCLD*, vol. 1, 331–342. Somerville: Cascadilla Press.

Kenstowicz, M. 1989. The null subject parameter in modern Arabic dialects. In *The null subject parameter*, ed. O. Jaeggli and K. Safir, 263–342. Dordrecht: Kluwer.

Kim, Y.-J. 1997. The acquisition of Korean. In *The cross-linguistic study of language acquisition*, vol. 4, ed. D.I. Slobin, 335–435. Hillsdale: Lawrence Erlbaum.

Klein, S.M. 1982. Syntactic theory and the developing grammar: reestablishing the relationship between linguistic theory and data from language acquisition. PhD diss., UCLA, Los Angeles, California.

Klima, E., and U. Bellugi. 1966. Syntactic regularities in the speech of children. In *Psycholinguistic papers*, ed. J. Lyons and R. Wales, 183–208. Edinburgh: Edinburgh University Press.

Koster, J. 2003. All languages are Tense second. In *Germania et alia: A linguistics Webschrift for Hans den Besten*, eds. J. Koster and Henk van Riemdijk: www.let.rug.nl/~koster/DenBesten/Koster.pdf.

Kramer, I. 1993. The licensing of subjects in early child language. *MIT WPL* 19, 197–212

Lebeaux, D. 1987. Comments on Hyams. In *Parameter setting*, ed. T. Roeper and E. Williams, 23–39. Dordrecht: Foris.

Levow, G. 1995. Tense and subject position in interrogatives and negatives in child French. *MIT WPL* 26, 281–304.

Lillo-Martin, D. 1994. Setting the null argument parameters: Evidence from American sign language. In *Syntactic theory and first language acquisition: Cross-linguistic perspectives. Vol. 2, Binding, Dependencies, and Learnability*, ed. B. Lust, G. Hermon, and J. Kornfilt, 301–318. Hillsdale: Lawrence Erlbaum.

Lorusso, P. 2007. The acquisition of aspect in L1 Italian. In *Proceedings of the 2nd Conference of GALANA*, 253–264. Somerville: Cascadilla Press.

Lorusso, P., C. Coprin, and M. T. Guasti. 2004. Overt subject distribution in early Italian children. Online. Available: http://www.bu.edu/linguistics/APPLIED/BUCLD/supp29.html.

Lust, B., L. Solan, S. Flynn, C. Cross, and E. Schuetz. 1986. A comparison of null and pronoun anaphora in first language acquisition. In *Studies in the acquisition of anaphora. Vol. I, Defining the Constraints*, ed. B. Lust, 245–278. Dordrecht: Reidel.

Lust, B., Y. Chien, and S. Flynn. 1987. What children know: Methods for the study of first language acquisition. In *Studies in the acquisition of anaphora. Vol. II, Applying the constraints*, ed. B. Lust, 271–356. Dordrecht: Reidel.

MacWhinney, B., and C. Snow. 1985. The child language data exchange system. *Journal of Child Language* 12: 271–296.

O'Grady, W., A.M. Peters, and D. Masterson. 1989. The transition from optional to require subjects. *Journal of Child Language* 16: 513–529.

Orfitelli, R. 2008. Null subjects in child language: The competing roles of competence and performance. Master's thesis, UCLA, Los Angeles, California.

Orfitelli, R., and N. Hyams. 2008. An experimental study of children's comprehension of null subjects: Implications for grammatical/performance accounts. In *Proceedings of the 32nd Annual BUCLD*, vol. 2, 335–346. Somerville: Cascadilla Press.

Orfitelli, R., and N. Hyams. 2010. Null subjects in child language: The competing roles of competence and performance. UCLA manuscript, Los Angeles, California.

Phillips, C. 1995. Syntax at age 2. Crosslinguistic differences. *MIT WPL* 26, 325–382.

Pierce, A. 1992. *Language acquisition and syntactic theory: A comparative analysis of French and English child grammars*. Dordrecht: Kluwer.

Pinker, S. 1984. *Language learnability and language development*. Cambridge, MA: Harvard University Press.

Poeppel, D., and K. Wexler. 1993. The full competence hypothesis of clause structure. *Language* 69(1): 1–33.

Radford, A. 1990. *Syntactic theory and the acquisition of English syntax.* Cambridge, MA: Blackwell.
Rasetti, L., M. Friedemann, and L. Rizzi. 2000. Null subjects and root infinitives in child grammar of French. In *The acquisition of syntax,* 236–268. Harlow: Longman.
Rizzi, L. 1982. *Issues in italian syntax.* Dordrecht: Foris.
Rizzi, L. 1993/1994. Some notes on linguistic theory and language development: The case of root infinitives. *Language Acquisition* 3: 371–393.
Rizzi, L. 2000. Remarks on early null subjects. In *The acquisition of syntax,* ed. M. Friedemann and L. Rizzi, 269–292. Harlow: Longman.
Rizzi, L. 2005a. On the grammatical basis of language development: A case study. In *The Oxford handbook of comparative syntax,* ed. G. Cinque and R. Kayne, 70–109. New York: Oxford University Press.
Rizzi, L. 2005b. Grammatically-based target-inconsistencies in child language. In *Proceedings of the Inaugural Conference of GALANA.* Cambridge, MA: UCONN/MIT Working papers in Linguistics.
Roeper, T. 2000. Universal bilingualism. *Bilingual Language Cognition* 2: 169–186.
Roeper, T., and B. Rohrbacher. 2000. True Pro-drop in child English and the principle of economy or projection. In *The acquisition of scrambling and cliticization,* eds. S. Powers and C. Hamann, 345–396. Dordrecht: Kluwer.
Roeper, T., and J. Weissenborn. 1990. How to make parameters work: Comments on Valian. In *Language processing and language acquisition,* ed. L. Frazier and J. de Villiers, 147–162. Dordrecht: Kluwer.
Sano T. and Hyams, N. 1994. Agreement, finiteness, and the development of null arguments. In Acquisition of scrambling and cliticization, eds. S. Powers and C. Hamann, 345–396. Dordrecht: Kluwer. *Proceedings of NELS* 24, ed. M. Gonzales, 543–548. University of Massachusetts, Amherst: GLSA.
Schütze, C. 1996. Evidence of case-related functional projections in early German. In *The Proceedings of the Fourteenth West Coast Conference on Formal Linguistics,* 447–462. Stanford: CSLI.
Serratrice, L. 2005. The role of discourse pragmatics in the acquisition of subjects in Italian. *Applied Psycholinguistics* 26: 437–462.
Serratrice, L., and A. Sorace. 2003. Overt and null subjects in Monolingual and Bilingual Italian acquisition. In *Proceedings of the 27th Annual BUCLD,* vol. 2, 739–750. Somerville: Cascadilla Press.
Sorace, A., L. Serratrice, F. Filaci, and M. Baldo. 2009. Discourse conditions on subject pronoun realization: Testing the linguistic intuitions of older bilingual children. *Lingua* 119: 460–477.
Stromswold, K. 1990. Learnability and the acquisition of auxiliaries. MIT PhD diss.
Thrasher, R. 1977. *One way to say more by saying less. A study of so-called subjectless sentences.* Kwansei Gakuin University Monograph Series, vol. 11. Tokyo: The Eihosha Ltd.
Tyack, D., and D. Ingram. 1977. Children's production and comprehension of questions. *Journal of Child Language* 4: 211–224.
Valian, V. 1990. A problem for parameter-setting models of language acquisition. *Cognition* 35(2): 105–122.
Valian, V. 1991. Syntactic subjects in the early speech of American and Italian children. *Cognition* 40: 21–81.
Valian, V., and Z. Eisenberg. 1996. Syntactic subjects in the spontaneous speech of Portuguese-speaking children. *Journal of Child Language* 23: 103–128.
Valian, V., J. Hoeffner, and S. Aubry. 1996. Young children's imitation of sentence subjects: Evidence of processing limitations. *Developmental Psychology* 32(1): 153–164.
Verrips, M., and J. Weissenborn. 1992. Routes to verb placement in early German and French. The independence of finiteness and agreement. In *The acquisition of verb placement. Functional categories and V2 phenomena in language acquisition,* ed. J. Meisel, 283–331. Dordrecht: Kluwer.
Wang, Q., D. Lillo-Martin, C. Best, and A. Levitt. 1992. Null subject versus null object: Some evidence from the acquisition of Chinese and English. *Language Acquisition* 2: 221–254.

Weverink, M. 1989. The subject in relation to inflection in child language. MA thesis, University of Utrecht, The Netherlands.

Wexler, K. 1994. Optional infinitives, head movement and economy of derivation. In *Verb movement*, ed. N. Hornstein and D. Lightfoot. Cambridge: Cambridge University Press.

Wexler, K. 1998. Very early parameter setting and the unique checking constraint: A new explanation of the optional infinitive stage. *Lingua* 106(1–4): 23–79.

Wexler, K., and P. Culicover. 1980. *Formal principles of language acquisition*. Cambridge, MA: MIT Press.

White, L. 1981. Grammatical theory and language acquisition. PhD diss., McGill University, Montreal, Canada.

Yang, C. 2002. *Knowledge and learning in natural language*. Oxford: Oxford University Press.

Grammatical Computation in the Optional Infinitive Stage

Ken Wexler

This paper gives a survey of some of the major properties of and approaches to the Optional Infinitive stage of linguistic development. After a brief account of its first discovery, we turn to an account of some of the major properties, including rates of OI production and how they change over time and vary cross-linguistically. We consider "surfacy" accounts of the stage (for example, the possibility that the use of the root infinitival where it doesn't belong is a kind of phonological simplification) and then turn to other approaches. Some attention is devoted to the possibility that the OI stage arises from the omission of an auxiliary. Again, evidence argues against this approach. We conclude that radical omission models, in which the features of Tense (and possibly other inflectional elements) are totally missing from the phrase-marker for an OI, are on the right track. We turn to the relations of subject case and OI's and formulate the ATOM model to describe the stage. We give empirical evidence in support of the Null Subject/OI correlation, including a detailed discussion of a recent paper on Italian development that we compare to another paper on Dutch. Both papers investigate large numbers of children. We consider two major contenders for the best approach to the OI stage, the Truncation model and the Unique Checking Constraint (UCC) model. The empirical evidence favors the UCC, including its ability to explain NS/OI but also some direct empirical evidence such as the omission of *to*, an inflectional element in embedded clauses. We give a fairly detailed summary of the *to*-omission data. If the UCC is the best theory, how does it go away so that children become linguistic adults? We argue that only a biologically based maturation theory can account for the data, assessing the arguments and briefly summarizing some genetic results. To illustrate the subtle detail that OI stage analysis is now capable of, we consider the problem of *be*-omission in some detail and give a recent analysis that explains the data in a perspicuous way. The paper then turns to quite radically different

K. Wexler (✉)
MIT Brain & Cognitive Sciences, 77 Massachusetts Avenue, 46-2005,
Cambridge, MA 02139, USA
e-mail: wexler@mit.edu

accounts, briefly discussing the empiricist approach. For more detailed attention we turn to a recent paper which tries to explain the existence of the OI stage as arising from difficulties in a child's learning that his/her language has Tense. We conclude that approach fails to predict the central phenomena of the OI stage. The paper then briefly mentions some important issues that have not been dealt with.

Like so much in science, the existence of an "Optional Infinitive" stage in child grammar was an accidental discovery. But a discovery made by a prepared mind (Beveridge 1949). In the fall of 1988, having newly arrived, I was teaching my first graduate course in language acquisition at MIT. I was lecturing according to my preferred framework for the field of generative grammar on the development of linguistic objects, in particular of different kinds of chains. With Hagit Borer, I had earlier proposed (Borer and Wexler 1987) that Argument-chains (A-chains), for example verbal passives, were late in development, and that A-bar chains, for example wh-movement, were much earlier. Both of these syntactic objects involved movement of whole phrases. In the mid-1980s a third type of object was introduced into syntax, Xo chains, or head movement. The head of the phrase moved, not the full phrase. Mark Baker's work was very important in this regard, studying incorporation and other phenomena. I was curious about how head movement fit into the developmental picture. Was it a kind of A-movement (an idea that was around at that time)? If so, on the A-chain deficit account of Borer and Wexler, it should be late. The developmental facts would be important not only for language acquisition, but also for the study of syntax itself.

Around that time, following up on earlier ideas of Emonds, Pollock (1989) had introduced head-movement as a mechanism to account for some curious facts about verbs in French. In particular, finite (tensed) verbs always appear before the main negative morpheme, *pas*. Nonfinite (untensed) verbs, on the other hand, always appear *after pas*. See (1).

(1) a. Jean (n') aime PAS Henri
  John   likes not Henry
  'John doesn't like Henry'
 b. Ne PAS sembler heureux...
  Not   to seem happy...
  'To not seem happy'

Since child French data was relatively available, I proposed to the class that we could perhaps discover something about the status of Xo-chains (head movement) in children by discovering whether they knew that the position of *pas* depended on the finiteness of the verb. We could look at child productions with *pas* to see whether the appropriate word order variation illustrated in (1) occurred. I also pointed out that perhaps we would not learn much from looking at production data at a very young age, because children do not produce many embedded sentences until they are about 3. We would need at least a finite embedding verb and an infinitival complement to observe the pattern. (Note that the examples of *pas infinitive* in (1), as in all relevant examples in the adult language (e.g. in Pollock's paper), involve embedded infinitivals.)

Amy Pierce was in the class. She had several transcripts of French children (provided by Patsy Lightbowm; cf. Lightbowm 1977). She decided to look at her data, despite my suggestions that perhaps it would not be telling (another lesson of science is that stubborn graduate students are valuable). She came back soon enough with the answer: 3 or 4 young children (in their 2's) got the word order/finiteness correlation pretty much perfectly in their productions! How could this be? Were they using lots of infinitivals that demonstrated the effect? No, Amy replied, one could see the effect in their root sentences. Many of these sentences had infinitival main verbs. When *pas* also appeared, it appeared before the infinitival form. But finite verbs also appeared, in the productions of the same child. In that case, *pas* appeared after the verb.

Juergen Weissenborn, visiting from Germany, was also in the class. He had French child data also, though (so far as I remember) not nearly as extensive as the Lightbowm corpus. He confirmed exactly the same finding in his data.

Here are some examples from Pierce (1992a,b):

(2) Untensed verbs: Tensed verbs
  a. Pas manger la poupee   c. Patsy est pas la-bas
     Not to eat the doll   Patsy is not down there
  b. Pas attraper une fleur   d. March pas
     Not to catch a flower   Walks not

Infinitives in the root? The standard thought in pretty much all approaches to language acquisition, from generative to empiricist, was that young children were very bad at inflectional morphemes, that it took them forever to learn the morphemes, that we expect odd forms of the verb in funny positions because children can't learn inflection.[1] So the existence of a root verb with what looked like an infinitival ending wasn't so surprising.[2] Standard thought would simply have had it that children didn't know the syntax or semantics of the verbal inflections, they just confused them. One mostly thought that what looked like an infinitive on the verb

---

[1] One voice against that was Hyams (1992), who argued, against much opposition, that young Italian children knew much about inflectional morphology. Hyams hadn't observed root infinitives, however. The fact that her arguments were about Italian would have made these observations difficult, as we will see.

[2] The verbs were considered infinitival because they had the form/phonetics of an infinitive, not a finite form, e.g. *attraper* in (2b). In French, the infinitive of 1st conjugation verbs like *attraper* has the same phonetic form as the past participle, so it might be thought that the verb was a participle with the auxiliary missing. Even if this were true, the word order facts that are predicted will be the same. That is, the participle (like the infinitive, but unlike the finite form) comes after *pas*. Many languages have infinitives that are phonetically different than the participle, so this issue won't arise. Even in French, Wexler (1993) shows that there are many 2nd and 3rd conjugation French root infinitives in Pierce's data, despite that fact that they are phonetically different from participles (e.g. *dormir*, where the participle is *dormi* or *voir* where the participle is *vu*). Levow (1995) does a careful analysis of French corpora and concludes that even for the 1st conjugation verbs, there are many infinitives as well as many participles.

was just the child's (deficient) way of marking the finite form. It was all about learning morphology, a very slow and tedious process, (almost) everybody thought.

But these data didn't seem to admit of such an easy dismissive answer. If children thought the infinitival verbs were forms of finite verbs, why did they so systematically produce finite and nonfinite verbs on different sides of *pas*? No, the infinitival-appearing verbs must be *infinitival*! The finite-appearing verbs must be *finite*! Thus was born the *Optional Infinitival* stage. Children sometimes produced finite main verbs and sometimes produced nonfinite main verbs. (Thus the "optional" infinitive stage.[3])

Wexler (1990, 1992, 1993) were the first papers to propose an "Optional Infinitive" stage in child grammar. These papers also were the first to argue that the OI stage was a cross-linguistic phenomenon, providing evidence from several languages. The evidence involved quantitative studies of verb form (finite or nonfinite) and, crucially, quantitative studies of verb placement correlated with morphological form (finite or nonfinite) of the verb. An even richer example will be given soon. The definition of the stage involves a set of interrelated phenomena. In general, in those languages that mark tense[4] on the verb, root declarative clauses show obligatory tense marking. Yet children appear to often omit tense from their verb in root clauses. Infinitives appear instead of tensed verbs. For the most part, these root infinitival sentences are ungrammatical (at least in their intended meaning, often

---

[3] The OI stage is equally known as the *Root Infinitive* stage. This distinction is purely terminological, depending on whether one wishes to emphasize the possible simultaneous existence of finite verbs or the fact that the relevant verbs are in the root. One might even name the stage the *Optional Root Infinitive* stage, another piece of terminology. In fact, as Wexler (1993) suggested might exist, and as Wijnen (1998) has since argued for very early Dutch, there might even be early periods in which *only* non-finite verbs appeared in the corpus. On the other hand, there is good evidence, to be discussed later, that child tense omission occurs in embedded sentences, sentences that should be finite for adults, showing OI phenomena in non-roots. The general property that clearly holds is that the child uses non-finite verbs in constructions where the adult must use a finite verb. The OI stage is the simple name for this phenomenon.

[4] And even in those that don't. See Cable (2005) for evidence for the OI stage in Afrikaans, a language with extremely little overt agreement or tense marking on the main verb. Cable argues on the basis of the OI stage in Afrikaans that Tense and Agreement exist syntactically in that language. He writes, "Afrikaans is well-known for being the least inflected of the Germanic languages … [T]here exists no marking of agreement in number or person on Afrikaans verbs or adjectives …. Whatever number or person the subject of an Afrikaans sentence has, the verb assumes the same, invariant form. Afrikaans also possesses a relatively reduced system of tense morphology. All main verbs have a past participial form, which is used in conjunction with the past auxiliary *het* to express past tense. Furthermore, there are only two verbs in Afrikaans that have a distinct form in the infinitive: "wees" (to be) and "hê" (to have; main verb). All other verbs in Afrikaans possess a single invariant form, used for both non-finite and finite present tense clauses." After going through the evidence for an OI stage in Afrikaans, Cable concludes, "At a more basic level, the existence of the OI-Stage in child Afrikaans solidifies the general conclusion that the OI-Stage is rooted in abstract, syntactic properties of a language, and not in its superficial morphological details."

completely ungrammatical⁵) in the adult language. Yet children produce them often. Wexler's definition of the OI stage is:

(3) The properties of the OI stage are the following:

  a. Root infinitives (non-finite verbs) are possible grammatical sentences for children in this stage
  b. These infinitives co-exist with finite forms
  c. The children nevertheless know the relevant grammatical Principles and have set the relevant parameters correctly

One of the major results of Wexler's papers in the early 1990s was the linking of the early development of French and the early development of Germanic V2 (verb-second) languages.[6] A V2 language moves the main verb (i.e. the primary, "first" verb, it might be an auxiliary, for example) of the main clause to "second" position, in particular to the head of CP (C the "complementizer").[7] An XP from the main clause moves to first position (Specifier, CP), thus placing the verb in 2nd position in the sentence. This is most dramatic in languages like Dutch and German in which the basic position (in embedded clauses, for example) of the verb is as verb-final, so that the verb in the root clause appears in quite a distinct position with respect to most elements of the sentence. Examples[8] from Dutch are in (4).

(4) a. (Marieke zegt) dat Saskia een boek leest
          S   O   V
    (Marieke says) that Saskia a book reads
    '(Marieke says) that Saskia reads/is reading a book'
  b. Saskia leest een boek
     S   V   O
     Saskia reads a book
     'Saskia is reading a book'
  c. Morgen leest Saskia een boek
     ADV   V   S   O
     tomorrow reads Saskia a book
     'Tomorrow Saskia will read a book'
  d. Een boek leest Saskia (morgen)
     O   V   S
     a book reads Saskia (tomorrow)
     '(Tomorrow) Saskia will read a book'

Poeppel and Wexler (1993) showed that Pierce's results on French could be replicated as a different phenomenon in German. Namely, the finite verb always

---

[5] See Avrutin (1997) for the use of root infinitives in adult Russian, and an attempt to relate OI's to these.

[6] He cited research on German, Dutch, English, Danish, Norwegian and Swedish. We will return to the discussion of English.

[7] A minority of V2 languages also move the verb in embedded clauses, but they are not relevant here.

[8] From Wexler et al. (2004b).

appeared in 2nd position and the OI always appeared at the end of the clause, where it was generated. Here are some Dutch examples (Weverink 1989):

(5) pappa schoenen wassen   ik pak 't op
    daddy shoes wash-INF   I pick it up
    ik ook lezen   baby slaapt
    I also read-INF   baby sleeps

This was perhaps the most stunning aspect of the discovery of OI's, namely that such disparate phenomena (*pas* placement in French, *second* versus final placement of the verb in German) were easily accommodated under the generalization. Linguistic theory had had such successes, accounting for what looked to be such distinct phenomena under more general descriptions and explanations, but language acquisition had had a much tougher time, especially in the field of inflection and clause structure, in coming up with deeper cross-linguistic generalizations. I think, probably for this reason, the study of Optional Infinitives (and its correlates) took off, and has become by far the most extensively studied topic in early (up to 3) syntax.

Early papers provided as evidence case studies, data from perhaps 1, 2 or 3 children. The generalizations were quite believable because the individual data fit such a systematic pattern. To show that the phenomenon really is quite general, though, it is important to have larger studies, with a much larger subject population. Such studies have begun to be provided. (6) shows the proportion of OI's out of all main verbs,[9] by age group from Wexler et al. (2004b) with 47 TD children, ages 1;7 to 3;7 (10–13 children in each age group).[10]

(6) **age group**   **% OIs**
    1;07–2;00   83% (126/152)
    2;01–2;06   64% (126/198)
    2;07–3;00   23% (57/253)
    3;01–3;07   7% (29/415)

In the last half of the 2nd year, there is about an 83% rate of OI's, reduced to 7% by the 1st half of the 4th year, a very large change over an 18 month period. The regular decline in OI rates is a typical result. Although it can't be decided from a cross-sectional study like this one, it's also known from longitudinal studies that the rate of finiteness increases incrementally over time in individuals, rather than in an all-or-nothing fashion. We'll discuss rates of development of finiteness and what affects them later.

Blom and Wijnen (2000) argue that at the very beginning of verb production in Dutch, there are 100% OI's. It seems very natural that this might be so. Wexler (1993) argued that finiteness rates tended toward zero as the studied population became younger, but that measuring the limiting rate at the youngest ages was difficult.

---

[9] Only main verbs, not auxiliaries and copulas are counted, because it is known that auxiliaries and copulas do not become infinitival in tensed contexts. Rather, they are omitted. We will return to the theoretical explanation of this phenomenon.

[10] We have shown the distribution of OI's by age; the paper also shows the distribution by MLU.

Many factors go into the first verbs at very young ages, including imitations, hard to discern productions and "formulaic" expressions. Even Wijnin finds some finite verbs, and tries to argue that they are formulaic, not part of the productive capacity of the child. Quite possibly this is so, but it is hard to prove.

Not much hangs in the balance on the question of whether at the "beginning" (when is that?) of development, there are 100% OI's or 95%, say. Either assumption seems compatible with almost all models.[11] This is because rates of finiteness grow somewhat continuously, and models that allow for the child's acceptance/ production of OI sentences have to be compatible with this growth in finiteness rates within an individual. If there is an extra process that a child has (say Tense Omission in the earliest model), it has to be allowed to happen less often as a child grows older. The kinds of models this paper will later argue for (maturational/growth models) will explain this process as the natural outgrowth of continuous maturational change over a certain period. Thus if it turns out that the true rate of "earliest" finiteness (say, age 1;0) was 100% the conclusion would be that the extra process always held at that age,[12] not that the child didn't know the INFL system.

The large rate of OI's in Dutch before two does show, however, that the conditions that cause the existence of OI's come from the child's brain, not from the environment. Most input to the child is fine; remember that the child hears a great proportion of simple utterances (Newport et al. 1973, 1977) so we expect many simple clauses, which will contain finite verbs only. Even complex sentences will contain root finite verbs. This argument is supported by an empirical study by Wijnen (2000) who shows that the large majority of verbs in the input to young Dutch children is finite.

So most of the verbs that children hear are finite, yet most of the verbs that the youngest children produce are non-finite. Clearly the large number of non-finite verbs does not follow from some kind of "learning" or environmental experience – only the child's linguistic system, her brain and its state, is causing this stage to exist. In fact, the existence of the OI stage is another argument for innateness, for the brain dictating the structure of grammar, not the environment, just as linguistic theory expects. (Cf: Borer and Wexler's (1987) *Triggering Problem* and Babyonyshev et al. (2001) *Argument from the Abundance of the Stimulus*.) There are large numbers of such arguments in the study of OI's; we'll touch on some of them.

Note also that surface "simplicity" cannot account for the existence of OI's. A Dutch infinitive like *werken/to work* is more complex to pronounce than the 1st singular present form *werk/work*, but children produce *werken* instead of *werk*. To my knowledge there is no evidence that surface (e.g. phonetic or morphological) simplicity is a cause in the OI effect.

---

[11] Except, perhaps for a model like Radford's (1990a, b) "no functional categories" model, in which it is assumed that the youngest children have no functional categories at all. Even in Radford's data, however, there were productions that looked as if they needed functional categories to derive forms which Radford had to find ways to explain.

[12] Or that the child hadn't learned the finite inflection at that extremely early age. The question then would be: why has the child learned the infinitival inflection but not the finite inflection? This is especially relevant in a language in which some finite forms are zero but the infinitival isn't.

Could some other kind of less "surfacy" simplicity account for the existence of such a large proportion of OI's? Perhaps, but a proposal must be given. Suppose, for example, that young children prefer structures with no movement. Then a Dutch verb, say, couldn't move to C. The result would be that the verb remained at the end of the clause. The fact that must be explained, however, is that when the verb remains at the end, it is always non-finite. So the child would be ignoring the requirement that root sentences must be finite in order to not have to carry out a movement operation. But why? Why wouldn't the child simply leave the verb at the end of the clause, but make it finite?

Such an analysis would also explain OI's in French. The child preferred to not raise the verb to T, thus leaving it in place. On the assumption that there is no other way to make the verb finite, the verb will have to be non-finite. Again, the child has to ignore the requirement that root sentences be tensed. Why shouldn't the child simply make the verb finite but not move it? Such processes occur in, for example, English. Furthermore, such a proposal would have trouble explaining why OI's exist in languages in which the verb doesn't move, for example, English. (Or the embedded clauses of Swedish). As we will see, English has OI's. Why, on this proposal? Another problem with such a proposal is that, as we will see, there are many languages that don't have OI's, yet have verb movement. On this proposal, why?

In fact, the theory that this paper will argue is the UCC, which in fact is a constraint that represents a kind of syntactic computational "simplicity." The kind of simplicity that is needed is indeed a syntactic one. However, so far as we can tell, these biological constraints on the developing system do not arise strictly from our understanding of UG. Rather, they are developmental constraints. The situation in language in this regard seems to be fairly strictly analogous to the situation in biology in general. Developmental biology attempts to understand the nature of development. But for the most part it doesn't derive the pattern of development from the nature of the fully mature system.

(7) shows the distribution of verbs in V1/V2[13] position in Dutch versus the final position in clause for finite and non-finite root verbs (that is, only OI's, non-finite verbs that should be finite (i.e. main verbs of roots), not verbs that *should* be infinitival[14]).

(7)

	V1/V2	Vfinal
Finite	1953 (99%)	11 (2%)
Non-finite	20 (1%)	606 (98%)

---

[13] V1 means the verb is in first position. Analyses of the OI stage of Germanic languages, Dutch in particular, standardly treat these as correct verb placement, as V2, with a topic-drop or other reason for omission of the first position (Wexler et al. 2004a, b). Dutch in fact does topic-drop fairly enough, so that V1 sentences do occur often. We'll discuss later Yang's (2002) claim that in fact V1 occurs in child productions because the child analyzes Dutch as a Semitic-style V1 language. This is surprising to Dutch linguists, who hear these sentences as typically Dutch for the most part.

[14] It is well-known that verbs that *should* be infinitival are produced by children correctly in the OI stage. See, for example, Lorusso, Caprin and Guasti (2005) Italian study.

There is stunning regularity in this data. It is rare, at best, for one to see data like this in cognitive development. Out of about 2,600 utterances, only 31 (about 1%) go against the prediction. The data are extremely significant in a statistical sense, i.e. there is a very strong "tendency" for word order and finiteness to correlate. But that statement, although typical of psychological research, is too weak and, not the right way to think of the result. Rather, the result is close to categorical, something like a litmus test in chemistry, distinguishing bases and acids. There is always a bit of mystery about the 1% of cases that go against the prediction, but that happens in chemistry too, dirt in the solution, mixing up the beakers, and so on. Even physics accepts as standard the concept of "experimental error." We can easily assume, till proven otherwise,[15] that the small number of errors from the prediction involve mistakes that the child makes in producing a sentence, not part of her linguistic system. Simply put, it is a fact of child Dutch that when a main finite verb is used, it is in 2nd position and when a root infinitive is used it is in final position.

Note how easy it would have been to have a less strong result. Perhaps there was only a "tendency" to correlate word order and position. Then we might have gotten a statistically significant result showing the correlation, but there would have been large numbers of cases that didn't show the correlation. This didn't happen. Alternatively, most of the utterances, finite or not, might have shown up in 2nd position. Or most of the utterances, finite or not, might have shown up in final position. Or there might have been a random distribution of word orders given the morphology of the verb. None of these very conceivable distributions, the kind expected by psychological research, were produced. Instead, we [the field] discovered a law of nature. This tells us we are on the right track. So I will add a second reason why the study of OI's took off so fast and so intensely. The first reason, already mentioned, is the deep cross-linguistic generalization, not typical of cognitive research or language acquisition research. The second is the stunning regularity and beauty of the data. Both of these together make the field look like science, like chemistry, say, as Wexler (2003) argued.

What I have said up to now about the nature of the data, I believe, is uncontroversial in the generative study of language acquisition.[16] In fact, I don't know of any non-generative work that challenges these empirical conclusions either.

An important correlate of the OI stage is the question of what the child in the OI stage knows about agreement morphology on the finite verb, e.g. how the verbal inflection depends on the person and number features of the subject. Poeppel and

---

[15] And, of course, there might be interesting differences in the patterns of errors; one suggestive possibility is that there are a higher (though still very small) proportion of errors leaving a finite verb in final position in main clauses of SOV/V2 languages than moving an infinitival verb into second position. Richer data and analyses are needed.

[16] Except perhaps for the work of Yang (2002) that has been already noted. Yang, though, doesn't disagree with the child data. Rather, he doesn't accept the standard assumption that V1 utterances in Dutch exist as a kind of topic-drop so that he thinks V1-first utterances show that the Dutch child doesn't know the word order parameters.

Wexler (1993) first argued against the standard assumption (Clahsen 1986) that young German children don't understand agreement, e.g. they don't understand that 3rd person singular *t* is 3rd person singular.[17] They made the crucial methodological move of measuring knowledge of agreement as the proportion of subjects that agreed with the finite verbal inflection (not the opposite measure – the proportion of verb inflections that agreed with the subject). This allowed the role of OI's to be taken into consideration.

To take one example of knowledge of agreement, from the same rich database of Wexler et al. (2004a, b), in (8) we see their data reporting the percentage of agreement errors (i.e. the subject doesn't agree with the finite verbal inflection) for each different present tense finite morpheme on main verbs in Dutch (*–0* is 1st singular, *t* is 2nd/3rd singular, *en* is plural (the only *en* that's counted is 2nd position *en*, i.e. finite *en*)).

(8) % of non-agreeing subject for each of 3 present tense morphemes in Dutch

MLU	-0	-t	-en	total
1	15%	0%	5%	9%
	4/27	0/9	1/22	5/58
2	5%	4%	0%	5%
	10/185	2/54	0/17	12/256
3	2%	3%	0%	2%
	6/273	2/73	0/32	8/378
4	2%	6%	0%	3%
	11/449	7/114	0/52	18/615
5	3%	15%	0%	5%
	3/97	4/26	0/14	7/137

The data are grouped in this case in terms of MLU level instead of age, but recall that all the 47 children are 1;7–3;7, pretty much equally distributed across ages, so that many children are less than 2, even more less than 2;6. This means that at none of these age levels is there a large proportion of agreement errors. The percentages are very small. There is a bit of error, but not much. Only at MLU level 1, the least developed children, are there more than 9% of errors.

There are probably a few more agreement errors than word placement errors given finiteness (where we have seen the level at about 1%); still, the rate is pretty small. For example, at MLU 2, *t* is used correctly for 2nd or 3rd singular subjects 52 out of 54 uses. The same children at the same stage use *0* correctly for 1st singular subjects 175

---

[17] Though see Hyams' (1992) analysis of Italian agreement, which argues for good knowledge. Many scholars, though, including Hyams, thought that only rich agreement languages like Italian showed this good knowledge. Poeppel and Wexler suggested that it was more far-reaching, and Wexler (1998) proposed the generalization: *Very Early Learning Of Inflection*.

out of 185 times. It is not surprising that there are a few errors. After all children do have to learn the phonetic form for each set of agreement features.[18] The small amount of comprehension evidence in this domain will be discussed later.

Similarly, Harris and Wexler (1992) showed that when the 3rd singular inflection *s* was used by an OI-stage English-speaking child, first singular subjects were almost never produced.

It is mostly generally agreed that in the OI stage there is only a small percentage of agreement errors. Given the rather extraordinary amount of knowledge of agreement patterns by OI-stage children and the essentially perfect knowledge of the finiteness/word order correlation that they exhibit, we have to ask why the requirement that root clauses be finite is so often (mostly, at the youngest ages) violated. The answer can only be the state of the child's brain/linguistic computational system. We will return to this.

1 OI and Non-OI Languages

There are many studies of many languages in the OI stage. One of the more remarkable facts about the OI stage, however, is that there are languages that do not seem to undergo the OI stage, as Wexler (1993) suggested might happen. Guasti (1993/4) was the first paper to demonstrate empirically that at least one language (Italian) does not go through an OI stage. Some languages that either show OI's or do not show OI's in the age range up to about 3 years of age given in Wexler (1998) (see references there) are:

(10) a. Languages that go through an OI stage: All Germanic languages studied to date, including Danish, Dutch, English, Faroese, Icelandic, Norwegian, Swedish, French, Irish ,Russian, Brazilian, Portuguese, and Czech. We can add Afrikaans (Cable 2005) to this list.
  b. Languages that don't go through and OI stage: Italian, Spanish, Catalan. Tamil, and Polish.[19]

Just as in the study of OI languages, the early papers provided only a few case studies, so that richer studies, with many more subjects are valuable, to show how general the effect is. Caprin and Guasti (2009) is a cross-sectional study of 59 children from 22 to 35 months of age. In age they are fairly comparable to the youngest 3 age groups in Wexler et al.'s (2004a, b) Dutch children, who are 19–36 months (see (6)), so that we have a good comparison group.

---

[18] This is too simple; distributed morphology probably makes the learning task easier, but we don't have space to discuss this issue here.
[19] Hebrew (like Czech) is an interesting mixed case, being OI in some part of the paradigm but not others. See Wexler (1998) for discussion and references.

Caprin and Guasti find that of 2,145 total verbal forms, 31 are RI's in the sense of true, "non-governed" i.e. "root" infinitives, about 1%. The number of OI's (use of infinitival inflection for main verbs) is extremely small. And Caprin and Guasti argue that even that small number is an overestimate; many of the 31 verbs on closer inspection don't look like OI's. Nevertheless, to get a fairer comparison to the Dutch data, let's only consider main verbs, comparing present indicative and "other tense" to the "infinitives", i.e. the OI's. There are 2% RI's in this data,[20] compared to 24% RI's in the Dutch children in (7).

The difference between 2% and 24%, of course, greatly underestimates the contrast in OI rates between Italian and Dutch, since the data include the later ages, in which the OI rate goes way down even in Dutch. Consider, instead, the youngest Italian group, G1, the group with the shortest MLU. Their mean age is 27.6 months. That's about the same mean age as Wexler, Schaeffer and Bol's group 2, which is 27 months.[21]

The Italian G1 kids produce 69 present indicative verbs and no "other tense." They produce two ungoverned (root) infinitives. Thus their OI rate is 2/71 < 3%. (6) shows that the Dutch kids of same age (Group 2) have a 64% OI rate. 64% versus 3% is a huge difference, by any standards.

As reasonably large population samples come in, we see that Italian OI's are vanishingly small compared to rates in other languages. We will assume (and as Caprin and Guasti continue to argue) that Italian kids don't produce OI's.

The following generalization has stood the test of time – I know of no counterexamples.

(10) *The Null-Subject/Optional Infinitive Generalization* (OI/NS) Wexler (1998) [22]: Main verbs[23] in a language go through an OI stage if and only if the language is not an INFL-licensed null-subject language.

---

[20] The calculation for Italian: The Italian kids produce 1,079 present indicative forms and 264 "other tense" forms. Adding, we get 1,343 finite forms of main verbs (not counting verbs with aux (*passato prossimo*), imperatives, past participles, gerunds or "governed" (non-root) infinitives). There are 31 RI's at best. Thus the rate of OI's for Italian is 31/(1343+31)=31/1374, approximately 2%. For Dutch, from (7) there are 626 RI's and 2,590 total verbs, making the OI rate 626/2,590=24%.

[21] In fact, Caprin and Guasti's G1 are the *slowest* (in terms of MLU) developing Italian group, so that we're comparing a slow-developing Italian group to a group of Dutch kids of the same age who aren't selected for being slow. Thus if there were no difference in how OI's develop, we'd expect *more* OI's in the Italian, since, given the mean age, it's a somewhat slow-developing group. Wexler, Schaeffer and Bol also do an analysis of OI rate in terms of MLU. As usual, we can't really compare kids cross-linguistically on the basis of MLU. MLU's measured in particular ways vary a great deal based on the particular properties of the language; this is well understood. Thus the best comparison is via age. Any more or less reasonable MLU analysis, if it could be given, would confirm the result of course.

[22] See also Sano and Hyams (1994).

[23] We say main verbs, because other properties of the OI stage (like auxiliary omission) might exist even in a null-subject language, as Wexler (1998) argues.

Italian, for example, has null-subjects, licensed by an INFL that has the property of licensing (in fact, requiring, except in special circumstances, like change of topic or emphasis) a phonetically null subject. Thus NS/OI predicts that Italian will not go through an OI stage. Dutch does not have INFL-licensed null-subjects, so its main verbs *do* go through an OI stage. All languages in (10b) are INFL-licensed null-subject languages, and all languages in (10a) are not.

We talk about "INFL-licensed" null-subject languages, because there are other kinds of null-subjects, e.g. Russian has many null-subjects, but it's not clear they are licensed in the same way as Italian null-subjects. Rather, they are often treated as discourse-based. NS/OI thus doesn't rule out OI's in Russian and, indeed, Russian does have OI's.[24]

Although modern syntax considers that whether languages are INFL-licensed null-subjects is a property of the INFL node in the language, and not a direct reflection of verbal morphology, it is known that INFL-licensed null-subject languages strongly (though not exclusively) tend to be languages that show rich agreement, i.e. in which different person/number features show different verbal morphemes that agree. English does not have rich agreement; in the present tense it only has the *–s* and *0* morphemes on the verb. Italian does have rich agreement; there are six different morphemes, one for each of the person/number combinations (1st, 2nd, 3rd person x sing, plural). Wexler (1993), already aware that Italian might not have OI's, suggested that rich agreement was correlated with lack of OI's. Which is it, rich agreement or the licensing of null-subjects? Icelandic provided the critical experiment. Icelandic does not INFL-license null-subjects, although Icelandic has rich agreement. Sigurjónsdóttir (1999) showed that the evidence for OI's in Icelandic is quite strong. We can conclude that NS/OI is the correct generalization regarding which languages go through an OI stage.

2 English

Unlike most Germanic languages, English does not mark infinitives with an audible inflection. Infinitives in English have "zero-morphology", the root takes a (phonetically) zero inflection to make the infinitive (concentrating only on the verb itself); the particle *to* is a completely different discussion, residing in INFL. We'll return to *to*. English OI's on main verbs then are mostly verbs that look like a stem with a 3rd singular subject.[25] Omission of copulas and auxiliaries (we'll later discuss these in

---

[24] The proportions of OI's in Russian are relatively small, though they exist in sufficient numbers to warrant the conclusion that Russian is an OI language (Bar-Shalom and Snyder 1997). We don't know enough about why the numbers of Russian OI's are small.

[25] Of course, OI's can exist in English with other person/number combinations. The form of the verb, however, will be identical to the finite form. The form of subject case, we'll see, will help us to see OI's in these other person/number combinations.

general) are other examples of non-finite verbs in the OI stage. *Have* and *be*, which have infinitival forms different from the root, can also provide evidence for OI's. Since aux *have* and aux and copula *be* are mainly omitted rather than showing up as infinitival (we'll discuss why), the bulk of this evidence comes from main verb, i.e. possessive *have*, which indeed shows up as infinitival *have* even when the subject is singular.

English children produce a large number of OI's, even more than Dutch children of a certain age do – we'll return to the comparison when we ask what explains quantitative difference in the expression of OI's.

3 Case and OI's

One other set of facts that has been influential in the development of models of OI's concerns the case of the subjects of OI's. Subjects of finite verbs have a special case, NOM(inative). In English, only pronouns show case-marking, e.g. *she* [NOM] versus *her* [ACC, or better, NON-NOM].[26] When children in the OI stage use a finite verb, they almost always make subject case NOM (in those languages where NOM is marked on the surface); we'll see some data soon. Clearly, children have a fine ability to learn structural case-markings. Interesting phenomena occur when an OI is used. We wouldn't expect OI children to assign NOM structurally to the subject – it takes some kind of finiteness on the verb to do that. And in fact, there is a famous type of case "error[27]" (11) in children learning English (e.g. Rispoli 1994; Valian 1991; Vainikka 1994) that puts an "Accusative" marking on the subject.

(11) a. Him fall down. (Nina, 2;3.14, File 17)
    b. Her have a big mouth. (Nina, 2;2.6, File 13)

Syntacticians distinguish between structural case and case-marking without a structural case marker. The latter is known as "default" case. We will see that, in fact, a morphological analysis allows default case to be assigned even without assuming there is such a special category. E.g. DP Answers to questions (12a) or post-copula positions (12b, c) or subjects of (non-finite, of course) exclamatives (12d) are assigned default case, there being no structural case-marker.

(12) a. Who ate the candy I left here last night? Answer: Him/*He
    b. Look, it's her/*she
    c. Who is the winner? John is him/*he
    e. **Her/***she leave for California? Never!

---

[26] To simplify, we'll ignore genitive/possessive relations and marking.
[27] We put scare quotes around "error" because we'll see that what children do isn't an error after all.

The natural assumption (Wexler 1995; Bromberg and Wexler 1995; Aldridge 1989) among others is that the child knows that in non-structural case-marked positions, default case is used, and furthermore, that the child knows the form of default case. Thus when the verb is non-finite, NOM can't be assigned and thus default case (NON-NOM in English) will be assigned. This predicts the existence of (11) in children in the OI stage. When they produce non-finite verbs, they'll assign default case.[28]

Loeb and Leonard (1991) and Schutze and Wexler (1996) showed that with finite verbs, the subjects are almost always NOM. With non-finite main verbs (OI's for Schutze and Wexler), the subject is often ACC, as we see in (11). We can think of this as the default case, what is used when the NOM assigning finite element is missing from the verb.

Here is a summary table from Schutze and Wexler:

(13)
Subject	Finite	-Finite
he + she	255	139
him + her	14	120
% non-NOM	5%	46%

$\chi^2 = 115.7, p < .000001$

So far, we understand why finite verbs almost always produce NOM subjects and why OI's allow NON-NOM subjects. Schutze and Wexler extensively discuss the following problem: Why does NOM appear so often when the subject is an OI? There seems to be no easy way to predict this fact if Tense assigns NOM and if Tense is missing from OI's. For then, we should *only* see NOM in subject position of OI's, contrary to fact.

Schutze and Wexler proposed the following solution to this problem of case of subjects of OI's. They argue that syntax actually suggests that it is *agreement* and not *tense* that assigns NOM case. They propose that the child in the OI stage omits either AGR *or* TNS.[29]

(14) Agr/Tns Omission Model (ATOM): Omit either AGR or TNS.

Schutze and Wexler propose a precise morphological model (in terms of distributed morphology) that has the following consequences. The morpheme –*s* may be inserted only when both AGR (3rd person) and TNS (present) are in the phrase-marker.

---

[28] This fact is one of many that show that the purely phonological view of OI's – that children really take them as finite, but drop-off endings – in English is on the wrong track. If OI's in English were finite, but phonetically reduced, why should they (and only they) allow what appear to be ACC subjects, i.e. forms like (11)?

[29] There is a serious question about whether both AGR *and* TNS can be omitted in the OI stage and what behavior that would lead to. For simplicity in this paper, we will assume that only one of these projections can be omitted in the OI stage.

Thus omitting either AGR or TNS will mean that *–s* may not appear, and only the "default" verbal morpheme *–0* will be inserted. Furthermore, NOM may be inserted only when AGR is present. This seems to be the simplest model that captures the facts of (adult) English.

Following ATOM, when the child omits AGR, leaving TNS, *-s* can't be inserted, so *–0* appears. This results in *her go*. When the child omits TNS, leaving AGR, again *–s* can't appear, so *–0* appears, but in this case the presence of AGR means that NOM will be assigned, generating *she go*. The optional *her/she go* pattern of the data follows. But when the verb is finite, e.g. *goes*, the existence of *–s* means that AGR is in the representation, so that the subject *must* be NOM, again the correct fact.

Major support for the idea that ACC subjects of infinitives are due to the use of default case (i.e., in Schutze and Wexler's terms, simply the child's mechanistic application of the correct morphological model of the verbal system) comes from the study of languages in which default case is NOM rather than NON-NOM or ACC. Such languages are German or Dutch. Children in those languages produce many OI's (as we have seen in detail for Dutch). Yet the subjects of those OI's are essentially always NOM, not ACC (Powers (1995) re Dutch).

3.1 Models of the OI Stage: A First Pass

There are very many more relevant analyses and facts about the OI stage, to some of which we will return. First we should consider alternative approaches. First, let's gather together in (15) some relevant facts that the models will have to account for.

(15) a. Basic OI facts, existence of OI's and correlation of finite/non-finite verbs with position (3)
 b. NS/OI
 c. Facts about the relation between case and agreement following from ATOM, i.e. default case account of subjects of OI's when AGR isn't present

The facts of the OI stage are so striking that many authors have tried to say something about them. Probably the biggest division of models involves the question about whether the phrase-marker of an OI utterance is truly non-finite in the sense that the one or more finiteness features (e.g. agreement, tense) are actually missing the feature (like the models discussed so far) or whether the OI sentences are truly finite – i.e. no finiteness feature is missing from the p-m; rather the child makes a kind of phonetic error. Let's call the former approach the "radical omission" idea and the latter the "phonetic spell-out" idea.

The original OI papers (Wexler 1990, 1992, 1993) argued for radical omission. They adopted the Tense Omission model as the implementation of this idea.

(16) Tense Omission Model of the OI stage: Optionally omit the functional projection Tense from the phrase-marker.[30]

ATOM is another example of a radical omission model, and we will soon describe other important models and compare them on empirical grounds. First, however, let's consider the possibility that radical omission is wrong. This is a natural possibility. After all, since p-m's of declarative sentences in adult grammar are generally considered to have finiteness features (perhaps in all languages, even if they don't occur on the surface in some languages[31]), perhaps we can account for the existence of OI's as a phonetic error, thereby relieving ourselves of the responsibility of worrying about why the child's grammar appears different from the adult's (though then having the problem of why the child's phonetics are different from the adult's).

The simplest idea is that children just have a very hard time learning the inflections of their language. After all, inflections are language-specific, so they have to be learned; surely, that takes time, even if children know a great deal about UG. Furthermore, inflections are often unstressed – do children even hear the inflections correctly? Could that lead to error? Let's call this the "inflection difficulty" idea.

There are many considerations that argue fairly conclusively against the "inflection difficulty" idea, and as we introduce more facts the problems only multiply. Here are some of the problems (see Wexler 1998, 2003 for extensive discussion). First, children in the OI stage do brilliantly, as we have seen, on agreement. That is, if they use a finite inflection, the subject almost always agrees with it. How could they learn the agreement patterns so well if they can't learn inflections? The problem appears to only be about replacing finite forms by non-finite forms, not about making mistakes on inflections.

Second, this conclusion might lead to a further speculation. Perhaps the children use the non-finite forms as a "default" form, perhaps as some kind of citation form, because they haven't learned or can't remember the finite form. In fact, this is what appears to go on in second language acquisition, not only for adults but also for children learning a second language who are too old for the OI stage.[32] However, it runs up against a very strong and irremediable fact – the correlational facts of the OI

---

[30] This is a descriptive statement. Much of the latter part of Wexler (1993) is devoted to attempts to derive (16) from more fundamental considerations. We will not describe those, but will take another more fundamental computational approach in later sections.

[31] See Cable (2005) for arguments that Afrikaans, a language with almost no verbal inflection goes through an OI stage, together with arguments from these developmental data that grammatical processes involving inflection operate even when the inflection is phonetically zero.

[32] See Haznedar and Schwartz (1997), Prevost and White (1999), Ionin and Wexler (2002), among many others. In other words, past a certain fairly young age, the OI stage doesn't exist.

stage (15a). If children used the non-finite form as a default for the finite form, it would appear in the positions of the finite verb. But that's exactly what doesn't happen in the OI stage.[33] Only 1% of the very large number of OI's in Dutch showed up in 2nd position, though thousands in final position. If those verbs that looked like infinitives were actually finite verbs, but with "default" (infinitival) spell-out they would appear in 2nd position, where finite verbs go. They don't appear there. No way has been proposed that captures that default idea can even come close to getting this massive and reliable empirical effect correctly. That's probably why the default idea for kids was quickly discarded. It occasionally comes back, perhaps because it is intuitively natural for adult second language learning.

Third, there are many cases where a simple phonetic error, of the type expected from children, will make the wrong prediction. One of the major reasons that the OI stage took so long to be discovered was that so much work in acquisition was driven by work on English. English has no audible infinitival ending; the bare form sounds like the nonfinite form (*take/take*). In English it has often been proposed (Brown 1973 among many others) that young children omit inflection, that is, they will make errors of omission but not of commission. That will correctly predict why e.g. *takes* becomes *take* and why children will not make agreement errors, e.g. a child won't say *I takes* (a massively correct prediction, as Harris and Wexler (1996) show). However, in most other OI languages, the errors are not purely of omission. E.g. in Dutch, the first singular present tense form is very often replaced by the infinitive, as we have seen, a *–0* ending being replaced by *–en*. This is not an error of omission. Most languages don't agree with the "only errors of omission" prescription. The particular facts about English misled the field. There is no phonetic account for why bare forms are easier for the Dutch child if they are replaced by infinitival forms.

Fourth, there are even facts in English that argue against the idea that it is a simple omission (e.g. of *s* on a verb) that accounts for the facts. Possessive *have* is an irregular main verb in the present tense (the only one?). We don't say *she haves the book*, rather *she has the book*. But there are many examples of *have* replacing *has* in the OI stage (Harris and Wexler 1996). This OI cannot be derived by omitting *–s*; that would result in unattested #*Mary ha the book*. Moreover, as soon as we hear this case of an irregular verb, it sounds right, i.e. like something that children would say. It's not a phonetic simplification; it's the substitution of a non-finite form for a finite from.

Fifth, we have the NS/OI facts (15b). We have seen how children in Italian massively do *not* produce OI's, just as children in Dutch *do* produce OI's. There is no known phonetic difficulty account of the cross-linguistic differences, so far as I know. What is the phonetic difference between Dutch and Italian that accounts for this result? Do Italian kids hear better?

---

[33] It happens in L2; that's why L2 looks so different, why it doesn't go through the OI stage, in adults and even children older than the OI-age.

Sixth, we have the case facts (15c). If, say, English-speaking children produce OI's because they are omitting *–s*, but really take the finite as finite, including the finiteness features in the p-m, why do they provide ACC case with these OI's? Well, perhaps they also have trouble learning case spell-outs, so they don't know ACC versus NOM? But then why do they only produce NOM when the verb is finite?

Aux-Omission: There is a more sophisticated version of a surface omission model that we should consider, namely an *auxiliary-omission* model, for example Boser et al. (1992). On the surface, many or most OI's look as if they might be finite sentences containing an auxiliary or modal, but the auxiliary or modal is not pronounced. In the German OI (16a), we can add a finite modal back in to obtain a grammatical sentence of German, (16b).

(16) a. Ich das Buch lesen
    I the book read [–fin]
  b. Ich will das Buch lesen
    I want the book read [–fin]
    'I want to read the book'

The idea of the aux-omission model is that the kid in the OI stage sometimes omits the aux (or presumably, modal as in (16)), thus accounting for OI's. It is another example of a model that rejects radical omission, claiming that the omission is only on the surface, that is, that the phrase-marker of the kid's utterance in (16a) actually contains the relevant finite morphemes. One might ask whether the kid's utterance in (16a) has the modal meaning of (16b) – Poeppel and Wexler (1993) argue that many OI's have finite meaning.[34] But the aux-omission model doesn't have to predict that all OI's are modals; it can take recourse to the notion that there is an Empty Dummy Modal (EDM), that is a phonetically empty, semantically dummy modal that the child uses. Essentially a phonetically empty form of the English modal *do*, as in *she does not wear hats*, where *does* has no semantic interpretation; it's just there for grammatical reasons.

The aux-omission model derives the basic OI correlation between tense morphology and verb position. There are several mis-predictions, however. Let's first consider what the models say.

First, we have to decide if the omitted element is truly an aux (though phonetically empty) or if it can it be a modal. Consider the English OI in (17a).

(17) a. Mary eat candy
   b. Mary does eat candy
   c. Mary wants to eat candy
   d. #Mary to eat candy

---

[34] The issue of the meaning of OI's, especially of whether they have to be modal, is complex. We'll return to that.

On the aux-omission model, (17a) might be derived for the child as a form of (17b), but one in which *does* is not pronounced. But why should the English-speaking OI child invoke (17b) (an otherwise ungrammatical form if there's no emphasis) to begin with? There is also no explanation of why *does* is omitted. Harris and Wexler (1996) show that grammatical *does* is actually omitted much less often by young children than inflectional tense (*s*).

Possibly (17a) comes from a sentence like (17c), in which a modal appears. To derive (17a), both the modal and *to* must be omitted. However, children in the OI stage never produce *to* with their OI's, as in (17d). It's not as if children at this age never use *to* with a verb; *to* appears with many infinitival complements. We'll return to a discussion of some empirical properties of *to* in the OI-stage.

The aux-omission model makes the wrong predictions for other OI properties. First, like other models that deny radical omission, it doesn't explain the case facts ((11), (13)). If the auxiliary/modal (or EDM) really are in the p-m, just not pronounced, the prediction is that NOM will always show up on the subjects of English OI's, contrary to fact Second, the aux-omission model doesn't tell us why NS/OI holds. Why do Dutch children omit auxiliaries and modals (or insert an EMD) but Italian children do not?

Third, and crucially, the aux-omission model mis-predicts the relation between tense and position in V2 sentences in which fronting of a non-subject has taken place (Poeppel and Wexler 1993). In a German sentence with a modal, suppose the object or another non-subject is raised into Spec,C, as in (18a).

(18) a. Den Apfel will Johann essen
the apple wants John eat [-fin]
'John wants to eat the apple'
b. #Den Apfel Johann essen (*not produced in OI stage*)
c. Johann den Apfel essen (*produced in OI stage*)

The aux-omission model predicts that the auxiliary in (18a) can be omitted, or in another version of the model, that an EDM can be inserted where the modal *will* occurs, that is in the finite position, where the aux/modal is spelled out. This results in the OI sentence (18b). A radical omission model, on the other hand, claims the finiteness features (or some of them) are missing from the p-m when an OI appears. V2 mechanics work because there are features in C that attract the verb. If the finite features are missing from C, then no verb can be attracted to C. Another way of saying this is that C will only attract a finite verb. If the finiteness features (or some of them) are missing in an OI, say, on C, then no verb can be attracted to C. This will yield OI's like (18c), with the subject *Johann* remaining in Spec,T.

However, there is a second syntactic operation that is necessary when non-subjects appear in first position, as in (18a). A phrase must be moved to Spec, C. Thus in (18a) the object *den Apfel* moves to Spec, C. If there are no (finiteness) features in C, however, no phrase can be attracted to Spec, C. Thus on a radical omission model there is no way to derive (18b), an OI with a fronted phrase in Spec, C.

The aux-omission model predicts that OI's with fronted phrases are possible productions in the OI stage, and radical omission predicts that they are not possible.

Poeppel and Wexler show that in the speech of Andreas, the 2;1 old German boy they studied, there are no fronted OI's like (18b) despite the fact that there are many fronted finite sentences (both direct object and adverb fronting). They show that the chances of obtaining this result by chance are very small. Since then, many studies (e.g. Santelmann (1995) re Swedish) have shown that in the V2 languages, fronted OI's (like (18b)) are essentially non-existent.

The non-existence of fronted OI's is an empirical argument against the aux-omission model. The fact and spirit of the model say that it's a model of non-radical omission – the features are there in the phrase-marker. It's just a question of taking a good sentence and leaving out the verb – a phonetic effect of some kind. The interaction with syntax is unexpected on this model.

The conclusion seems to be that aux-omission models wrongly predict some important facts about the OI stage. Other models include ideas involving difficulties in learning properties of verbs and tense, etc. We will extensively discuss the most developed case of one of these models later (Legate and Yang's (2007) proposal).

3.1.1 Radical Omission Models

First, however, let us turn to radical omissions models. The dominant attempts to model the stage have been radical omission models. There are a variety of radical omission models. I will describe in some detail what appear to be the two most widely adopted models and spend some time in comparing them empirically. First we'll have to see how well the models do on the basic facts of the OI stage. Then a comparison of the two models will be a vehicle by which we can describe a wide variety of other phenomena discovered about the stage.

The UCC

We have seen how the case facts argue that the original OI model, the Tense Omission model, a radical omission model, has to be replaced by the ATOM, another radical omission model that explains not only the basic correlational facts of the OI stage (15a) but also the case facts (15c). The model does not explain (15b), however. Why can't null-subject languages like Italian be governed by ATOM when children are in the OI age-range? We might also ask why the ATOM holds at all? Why can either AGR or TNS be omitted?

Wexler (1998) proposed a model invoking that *Unique Checking Constraint* that explains why ATOM or TNS can be omitted, i.e. why ATOM holds. The model then turns out to explain not only the facts that follow from ATOM (15a, c) but also NS/OI (15b[35]).

---

[35] We will return to a large variety of other facts that UCC explains.

First, we need to review some syntactic background. We make several standard assumptions. The verb and its arguments, including the subject, are generated within the verb phrase. We can specify that this is the light vP, with the light verb v selecting the subject in its specifier and a VP as its complement.[36] The sentence level functional projections AGR[37] and TNS are generated outside the vP.

Standardly it is assumed that the subject raises to an INFL projection because there is a kind of EPP feature, sometimes thought of as a D (Determiner) feature on INFL. INFL has an uninterpretable D feature; the subject DP raises to INFL, INFL's interpretable D-feature deleting the uninterpretable D-feature on INFL.

Wexler (1998) assumes that both AGR and TNS have uninterpretable D-features. When DP raises to one of them, the lower (say TNS to be precise), eliminates the D-feature on TNS, with the D-feature of DP remaining, since it is interpretable. DP then raises to AGR, eliminating AGR's uninterpretable D-feature. All this is standard, with some variation in the syntactic literature on whether there are one or two INFL projections.

Once we see that both AGR and TNS features are crucial, the intuitive idea arises that it is checking each of them that is the difficulty for the child. Wexler introduces the UCC:

(19) *Unique Checking Constraint* (on OI-age children, i.e. until about 3 years):
A DP can check only one D-feature.

Given (19), UCC can check (and eliminate) the D-feature of AGR or the D-feature of TNS, but not both. Since an uninterpretable D-feature remaining at LF (on either AGR or TNS) means that Full Interpretation (the assumption that all features that remain at LF are interpretable) fails, the derivation crashes. If nothing else is said, finite sentences, with both AGR or TNS, cannot be derived as grammatical if UCC holds.

The child's grammar's solution to this dilemma, the dilemma of not being able to express a simple proposition, is to omit either the AGR or TNS projection from the phrase-marker for the sentence. Once that happens, a converging sentence can be derived.

We should ask about the omission of AGR or TNS. How can this be possible and the child still follow the principles of syntax? The answer is interesting. It's very difficult to find a principle of syntax that requires the existence of AGR or TNS in

---

[36] For the purpose of explaining the OI facts under consideration in this section, one could assume the older VP, with the subject in its spec, ignoring the vP. We assume the vP here, not only because of its wide acceptance, and the reasons for its acceptance, but because it will be useful (perhaps necessary) later in explaining the UCC's application in the case of clitic omission, scrambling and short-form negation in Korean.

[37] Often it is argued, perhaps on Minimalist grounds, that AGR is not an independent projection. But the evidence isn't so clear, and there are approaches that project AGR independently. It's also probably possible to replicate the results I will described within a system that has only an INFL projection, both both tense and agreement features. Research along these lines would be valuable.

the phrase-marker. We always write them in, because if they're there with the rest of syntax, they predict the properties of the grammar. But why are they there? So far as I have been able to discover, or to conceive, there is nothing in syntax, minimalist or otherwise, that requires the presence of AGR or TNS. Most likely, there is an interface condition that requires their presence. Suppose that some interface condition IC is the culprit, and the child knows IC.[38]

The child constrained by UCC, with knowledge of IC, faces a dilemma – there is *no* way to derive a sentence expressing even the thematic roles of a sentence. If both projections are there, satisfying IC, then the sentence doesn't converge, in a technical sense; there are uninterpretable features at LF. On the other hand, if AGR or TNS is missing, then IC isn't satisfied.

Wexler (1998) proposes that the child picks one of the best solutions to the problem. Leave AGR and TNS in the p-m, deriving the finite sentence, thus satisfying IC, but not satisfying UCC. This derives a finite sentence. Alternatively, omit AGR or TNS, thus violating IC, but satisfying UCC. This derives an Optional Infinitive, one of two kinds, with either AGR or TNS omitted.

It seems reasonable to think that the child prefers to do the least damage to either IC or UCC, so that the child prefers to omit only one of AGR or TNS. If this is correct, then the suggestion in Schutze and Wexler (1996) that ATOM allows both AGR or TNS to be omitted, wouldn't be right. More work needs to be done on the question of whether both projections can be omitted.

Now all the properties of ATOM (15a, c) follow from UCC. We have a computational model of ATOM; a syntactic explanation of why omitting projections is possible. Radical omission is the response to UCC, a response by a child who is always subject to Full Interpretation, clearly the most crucial underlying motivation of convergence. The child's UG, like the adult's, can't tolerate features at LF that aren't interpretable. This seems pretty fundamental for a system that is basically an interpretable computational system. The most fundamental property seems to be retained, and gives us great reason to say that the OI grammar is a grammar in the human sense, although it differs a bit from the adult's. Surface differences apart, even computational differences apart, a fundamental property of the specifically human system of language remains, Full Interpretation.

What do we have to add to derive the other crucial property of the OI stage, NS/OI, the generalization (10) that a language goes through the OI stage if and only if it's a null-subject language? Nothing. As Wexler (1998) shows, NS/OI now comes for free, given the nature of the linguistic system of null-subject grammars. Null-subject languages have a crucial property that is different from the non-null-subject languages that we have been considering. Namely, in null-subject grammars, the D-feature of AGR is interpretable. After all, that's what makes them null-subject grammars. AGR has traditionally been taken as the "subject" of null-subject

---

[38] Languages like Chinese are usually thought to lack Tense and Agreement on the surface. Whether they actually lack these in a deeper sense is much less clear, and possibly the dominant linguistic view is that they don't.

languages like Italian. Since AGR expresses the subject, there is no reason for a DP in traditional subject position, and in the unmarked case there is none. In special, marked cases, for reasons of emphasis of disambiguity, a subject appears, and is thought of as a kind of clitic-doubling – the subject and the D-feature of AGR are doubles, co-referential.

This line of thought is supported by the conclusion in current studies of null-subject grammars like Italian (Barbosa 1995; Alexiadou and Anagnostopoulou 1999) that the visible subject, when it appears in an Italian sentence, does not raise to the highest inflectional position. In our terms, we can take the subject as raising to TNS but not to AGR. Since TNS has an uninterpretable D-feature, the subject DP raises to TNS to eliminate it. But the subject stops there; it doesn't raise to AGR, because the D-feature of AGR is interpretable, hence it needs no DP to eliminate an uninterpretable feature.

This account shows us why we have VSO sentences in languages like Italian – the subject is in Spec,TNS, but the verb raises all the way to AGR. When there *is* an SVO sentence in Italian, the subject is raised to a projection higher than AGR – this is a semantically, A-bar, motivated movement. This is the argument of Barbosa (1995) and Alexiadou and Anagnostopoulou (1998).

That's the nature of an Infl-licensed null-subject language. Now we intersect these results with UCC. The subject of a null-subject language will raise to TNS, eliminating its uninterpretable D-feature. AGR has an interpretable D-feature. There is no reason for the subject to raise to AGR; it stays in Spec, TNS and the finite sentence converges (no uninterpretable features at LF) with both AGR and TNS in the phrase-marker. There is no reason to violate IC; the convergence goes through with the IC-preferred projections in place.

This analysis derives NS/OI with no special assumptions, just UCC, the nature of null-subject languages and syntactic principles known to the child. The syntactic principles include Full Interpretation, which we take as very basic, and the mechanistic properties that follow from minimalist considerations, like checking, elimination of features and DP movement and its consequences.

UCC thus derives the full set of basic OI properties in (15). The fact that NS/OI, an otherwise bizarre property, falls out for free, in fact is necessary, is striking evidence for UCC and for the set of syntactic mechanisms that we have discussed. The child allows an important experiment that we couldn't have otherwise accomplished. Suppose the system allows only one checking, what happens then?

Radical omission is a property of the UCC theory, of course. The features themselves must be gone (or totally inactive, which we take to amount to the same thing in this context) from the p-m. UCC as an explanation of the OI stage is all about computation and its limitations in the young child. Presence or absence of projections is only one consideration; the nature of syntactic computation and Full Interpretation play a very strong role, just as in adult grammar. The child's system, although different in some ways from the adult's system, actually supports the nature of UG in a quite strong way. How could we derive these facts except as a slight perturbation of a particular kind on the computational system?

Truncation

The theory of "Truncation" (Rizzi 1993) is another major idea about the nature of the OI stage. Like Wexler's TNS Omission, ATOM and the UCC, Truncation is also a theory of radical omission. Rizzi explicitly accepts Wexler's (1990, 1992, 1993) arguments about the nature of the correlations (15a) in child grammar and for the (radical) omission of the TNS projection from the p-m in OI's. But he goes further. He proposes that any part of the p-m, from the CP through AGRP through TNSP can be omitted, leaving only the lower part. The crucial defining property of truncation is that if a functional projection FP is missing from the p-m, then all projections that dominate FP are also missing. Rizzi proposes (20) as a principle of UG:

(20) Root=CP

Once the root is chosen as CP, the other functional projections are all selected, so the appropriate ones appear in place, e.g. C selects AGR, what that AGRP appears under CP and so on. Rizzi then proposes that the child has one limitation that we can write as (21).

(21) *Truncation*: The child in the OI stage doesn't know that Root=CP must hold; the child can pick the head of the root arbitrarily.

Thus the child might choose CP as the root; once that is done, all the appropriate projections will appear by selection. Or the child might choose AGRP, the lower projections (TNS, VP, etc.) appearing appropriately via selection. Or the child might choose TNSP or VP. Rizzi argues that typical OI's are VP's, with the functional projections (CP, AGRP, TNSP) missing from the p-m. For Rizzi, the presence of the infinitive means that TNS is missing. Thus AGRS and CP, which appear above TNS, must be missing. Thus OI's are VP's.

Truncation is a radical omission model. It assumes a large amount of material might be omitted. It has the characteristic feature that if the head X selects YP, then if YP is omitted from the structure, then XP must also be omitted. Thus we think of the theory as "truncating" the entire top portion of the phrase-marker, leaving a phrase-marker that starts at some root phrase and has all the necessary phrase-markers that appear under that root phrase.

How does Truncation do on the basic properties of the OI Stage (15)? It predicts the existence of OI's via Truncation (TNS is missing) and the correlations of finites and word order (15a) because, like Tense Omission and ATOM, it is a radical omission theory that assumes knowledge of the basic syntactic operations and knowledge of the morphemes, etc.

How about (15c), the relations between subject case in finiteness of the verb? ATOM proposes that either AGRS or TNS are missing from an OI. The subject can appear in the specifier of the one of these two that aren't missing, e.g. AGRS if TNS is missing or TNS if AGRS is missing. For a VP analysis of OI's (Truncation), the subject would have to appear in Spec,V or in some kind of adjoined position. How does the subject ever acquire NOM case if the verb is an OI? Certainly there's nothing to assign NOM in the (VP-dominated) phrase-marker. Perhaps there's no structural case at all, but rather just default case in the VP analysis of OI's. This might work for languages that have default NOM case. For English and other languages with default NON-NOM case, the prediction would be that only NON-NOM would appear. We have seen that this isn't true for English OI's, where there is a mixture of NOM and NON-NOM for subjects of OI's.[39]

We can think of ways of overcoming this case problem by considering various orders of functional categories. Suppose AGRS assigns case, as Schutze and Wexler argue. Suppose, unlike the usual assumption, that TNS dominates AGRS. If the child chooses AGRS as the root, omitting TNS and CP, then the verb will be spelled out as infinitival (no TNS). On the other hand, AGRS appears, so that NOM can be assigned. So perhaps *him go* is a VP whereas *he go* is an AGRSP. German and Dutch would show forms like *him go* because default case is NOM, so that NOM appears even in the VP OI's. For this analysis to work, TNS must dominate AGRS in English. Allowing the hierarchy of functional categories to vary seems to be necessary in the attempt to apply Truncation to phenomena in the OI stage (Haegeman 1996).

This leaves us with (15b), NS/OI. UCC solves NS/OI for free; NS/OI must hold, given our understanding of null-subject languages, if UCC holds. It would be a problem for UCC if NS/OI didn't hold. This is a strong argument. What does Truncation say?

I know of one attempt to derive (part of) the effects of NS/OI from Truncation. Rizzi (1993) notes that in Italian infinitival verbs raise to TNS. Suppose that TNS is omitted from the structure in an OI. Rizzi assumes that it is a condition on the *infinitival verb* itself that it raise to TNS. Thus if TNS is not in the structure, this condition can't be satisfied and the derivation is ungrammatical.

One might ask how reasonable it is within current theories of syntax to assume that a condition like Rizzi proposes is possible. It's not a condition on the functional category TNS. Rather it's a condition on the "infinitival verb." What does that mean? We usually put features on the functional categories, and they attract other categories. After all, one might say that it's a condition on the finite verb in root sentences in V2 languages that it raise to C. But if CP is omitted, under Truncation, and the verb only moves to TNS, the sentence isn't ruled out. So it's not clear how this idea could be implemented in current theory.

Furthermore, Icelandic, similarly to Italian, has infinitives (of the same type) that must raise to TNS. Yet, Icelandic is an OI language, as we have seen. Rizzi's proposal would amount to the claim that the languages that don't go through the OI stage are languages in which the infinitive raises to TNS. Icelandic is a clear contradiction.

In addition, consider the following problem. Suppose an Italian OI child starts a structure with TNS, omitting CP and AGRSP. This should result in an OI, since there are no agreement features in the structure, thus no way of the morphology licensing a finite morpheme. The verb will be spelled out as an infinitive, presumably.

---

[39] French is another test case, though a bit more complicated, perhaps. NON-NOM appears in the subject position of OI's (*moi parler*). The data is rather limited, however, because OI's in French are overwhelmingly null-subject (Pierce 1992a, b).

Yet TNS is in the structure, so that the infinitive can move to TNS, Why isn't this a way of obtaining an OI in Italian?

The derivation of NS/OI seems particularly difficult for Truncation. I know of no proposals since the very brief suggestion of Rizzi (1993). Yet UCC gets it for free. This is one of the major empirical advantages of UCC over Truncation, although not the only one.

3.2 UCC Versus Truncation: Further Empirical Predictions and Tests

UCC and Truncation have been the two leading contenders as models of the OI stage. One might argue on conceptual grounds about which one is to be preferred. A defender of Truncation might say, look how simple it is, it makes a claim directly about the structures. That is, the child doesn't know *CP* = Root, so that any structure compatible with that is possible. A defender of UCC might say (as I would), in syntax today we don't think of structures as basic. Rather the computations are basic. All structures exist as the result of merge and selection. Selection is to a large extent semantically given. If the child's grammar is somehow different from the adult's, this should be reflected in the computational syntax. Structures will follow.

Rizzi has said (pc), "The 3rd year of life is all about structural simplification." Let's take that as the spirit of Truncation. In a similar manner, I would say that the 3rd year of life is all about computational simplification. It is not for nothing that Chomsky calls the syntax the "computational system" of language (CS).

These conceptual arguments help to clarify, to explain approaches. But honest assessment has to see that only empirical differences can tell us which is closer to the truth. NS/OI seems clearly to favor UCC. What properties are claimed to favor Truncation?

Since UCC predicts ATOM, for many of the empirical issues we can just look at the predictions of ATOM versus Truncation. Later we'll have to invoke the more general UCC to make the appropriate comparisons.

The major evidence that Rizzi uses to argue for truncation (as opposed to theories of the OI stage that don't require as severe an omission of material from the p-m, e.g. Tense Omission), involves negation and infinitives. Suppose negation demands a NegPhrase, and suppose that NegP appears above TP. Since NegP dominates TP, when the sentence contains negation, Truncation implies that TP must appear. This means that all sentences that show sentential negation must be finite. In short, OI's can't be negated.

This indeed is a striking prediction, a prediction not made by other models. Is it true? Rizzi gives some evidence showing that finite utterances are negated more than are infinitivals in French (see Friedemann 1993/1994). But the evidence is rather unconvincing. The classic work in OI's (Pierce 1992a, b) shows that there are large numbers of negated infinitivals in OI French. When the verb is an OI, *pas/not* almost always appears before the verb. Some examples of produced utterances of this form are in (2). The placement of *pas* with infinitivals versus finites is a classic phenomenon in the OI stage. The prediction seems to be wrong. My impression is that it has been given up on. Haegeman (1996), noting that negated infinitivals appear in the Germanic OI stage, attempts to save Truncation by suggesting that the Negation/Tense hierarchical order is parameterized, with Germanic having the opposite hierarchy than French. Of course, such a parameterization is against the spirit and results of much of modern phrase-structure analysis, which argues that semantic considerations are relevant to the order.

Another example of this type of prediction concerns questions that show wh-movement. We have already seen that Poeppel and Wexler (1993) showed that in a young German child who had lots of non-subjects in Spec, C, the verbs in these non-subject first sentences were always finite and that this phenomenon has been amply confirmed. In other words, movement to Spec, C does not take place in an OI. Rizzi concentrated on wh-movement, but the argument is more general, concerning any movement to Spec, C. Rizzi argues that this phenomenon in V2 languages is predicted in the following way. For there to be movement to Spec, C it must be the case that CP is present. If CP is present, Truncation implies that TP is present. Thus the verb is finite. In conclusion, movement of a phrase to Spec, C implies that the verb is finite. Such movement cannot take place in OI's.

This prediction, no wh-movement in OI's, does seem correct for V2 languages. It's not true for English, however, as can be seen in empirical results on a few children in Bromberg and Wexler (1995) and Roeper and Rohrbacher (1994). Children in the OI stage in English produce many sentences like *where he/him/e going*, *what he/him/e eat*, that is wh-questions with non-finite verbs (*be* omission in the first instance, non-finite main verb in the second). The subjects can be filled or empty. Here is a table from Bromberg and Wexler:

(21) Finiteness of Null and Pronominal Subjects in Adam's *Wh*-Questions

	Finite	Nonfinite
Null	2	118
Pronominal	117	131

These sentences look quite clearly as if they contain CPs but aren't finite. Rizzi agrees that the English data contradict the predictions of Truncation, and suggests that English non-finite productions in the early years are not in fact OI's, but rather perhaps simply some kind of phonetic omission. This proposal is not made on principled grounds, but in order to save the prediction of truncation. On the other hand, the striking results in (21), that show that null-subjects aren't permitted with finite wh-questions but are permitted with non-finite wh-questions show clearly that the English forms that appear to be non-finite indeed have the grammatical properties of non-finiteness. In particular, the non-finite forms license null-subjects, the finite forms don't. Moreover, the Schutze and Wexler case facts and analysis we discussed earlier also show that the non-finite productions of the child have to be taken as potentially omitting grammatical features, e.g. AGRS, because of the failure to license NOM case for the subject.

On the other hand, how do alternative models account for the facts about wh-movement and infinitivals? We have already seen the analysis of Poeppel and Wexler, that predicts the non-existence of phrases moved to Spec,C in the V2 languages because of a requirement in these languages that only a finite element in C licenses movement of a phrase into Spec, C. This requirement is needed anyway in these languages, since no phrase moves into Spec, C unless a (finite) verb has moved into C. For example, in embedded clauses in German or Dutch, where there is no movement of the verb into C, no phrase moves into Spec. So the result really comes for free.

On the other hand, what does this "for free" analysis say about English? How is it possible that English children produce a phrase in Spec, C in wh-questions when the verb is non-finite? English is called a "residual V2" language because it seems to show the V2 effect only in questions and a few related constructions. Note that topicalization without verb movement to C is fine in English; in fact that's how it's done. It's not very good to topicalize and do V2.

(22) a. Beans, they are eating
     b. *Beans are they eating
     c. Beans, I like
     d. *Beans do I like

Suppose that English doesn't have the requirement that to move a phrase into Spec, C, a finite element must be in C. This would allow for (22a, c). We then have to ask what is the requirement in English that forces movement of a finite verb (an aux or modal) into C when a wh-phrase has been moved into Spec, C.[40] Why is (23) ungrammatical?

(23)   What Mary is eating?

We won't attempt to state a precise analysis of the relevant features. Whatever the solution, we would expect that the residual nature of V2 in English (only questions, and only aux – *what eats Mary for dinner?) should have something to do with the much less stringent requirement that C be filled in English and thus with the possibility of a child's non-finite wh-questions.

As we have seen, both Truncation and ATOM appear not to have completely solved the exceptional status of wh-questions in English OI's. Both models predict their impossibility in the V2 languages, but without anything else said, both also seem to predict their non-occurrence in English, contrary to fact. It does seem fair to say that the existence of wh-questions in English OI's seems to take away an argument that CP must be missing if TP is missing (Truncation). Nevertheless, both ATOM and Truncation have a difficulty in predicting the behavior of English in this regard.

---

[40] In much recent work, topics and wh-phrases go into different positions. In order to simplify, I am ignoring such theoretical differences. They might potentially help with the current problem, if we had the right idea.

It seems fair to say that the evidence concerning the hierarchy that Truncation would like to use to argue as support is either (a) False (as in the case of the existence of French negative infinitivals) or (b) at least as naturally predicted by ATOM. Furthermore, Truncation has to make many stipulations including stipulations of variations in the order of functional categories in order to obtain results. This gives a large amount of parametric variation, a larger amount than might actually exist. Moreover, these stipulations are against the spirit of modern work in "cartography" (Cinque 1999, 2002) that suggests the hierarchy of functional categories is fixed, related to semantic considerations, not varying cross-linguistically.

We should mention briefly that the most important use of the data in (21) is not as an argument against truncation. In fact, Wexler (1998) used the data to argue strongly that in English the null-subject parameter is set correctly (non-null-subject) very early. The idea is that there are two sources of null-subjects in children. First, a non-finite verb licenses PRO, an empty subject. Thus an OI but not a finite sentence licenses PRO. Secondly, subjects may be omitted from Topic (say, Spec, CP) position if in fact there are topics. The data in (21) follow, given standard assumptions. Non-finite wh-questions (object or manner questions) can have null-subjects, because they will have PRO subjects, licensed by the non-finite verb. Finite wh-questions won't allow null-subjects because the wh-phrase in Spec, CP disallows Topics (thus no Topic-Drop) there and the finite verb won't license PRO. Italian children at this age omit plenty of subjects in finite wh-questions as Guasti has shown.

3.2.1 OI's in Embedded Sentences

The most distinctive property of truncation is that it predicts that there won't be any kind of embedded OI's. Since only the "top" of a p-m may be omitted, there is no way for an upper part (say a VP or even a CP) to be there and then for an embedded sentence to show omission. This structural notion helps to lead to the terminology of *Root* Infinitives in children – they should be the *only* kind of incorrect infinitives.

On the other hand, UCC is not a structural notion; it's computational. It says that such and such processes occur or don't occur; it doesn't matter *where* they are. Computationalist theories find the source of children's differences in mechanisms, in computations, not in parts of structures.[41]

The most obvious place to look to see which model predicts better is in embedded tensed sentences. Truncation predicts there are no infinitives replacing main verbs in embedded sentences; UCC (ATOM) predicts that there could be such. Unfortunately, children who are in the age range of the OI stage (say, roughly less than 3) produce very few embedded tensed sentences (or embedded sentences that *should*

---

[41] It's interesting given the locationalist/computationalist distinction to ask about Wexler's (1990, 1993) Tense Omission model or the ATOM. Since they relate to particular parts of a structure (TNS, AGR), perhaps they're locationalist. UCC does seem to be a departure, in concentrating on mechanisms.

be tensed).[42] I can't think of any study that actually measures whether a child who produces many OI's in matrix sentences does the same in embedded sentences. The predictive differences are clear, however, and perhaps a study will eventually be forthcoming.

Fortunately, there is a related phenomenon, however, for which there is good evidence. This involves the infinitival morpheme *to* in English, as in (25a).

(25) a. I want to go
 b. *I want go
 c. I made her smile
 d. *I made her to smile

(25b) shows that to is obligatory in the sentence. *To* is typically taken to be in INFL, it is the spell-out of non-finite INFL. Small clauses like *her smile* in *(25c)* are called "small" because INFL is missing. (25d) shows that INFL must be missing in that structure. If one has a model in which AGR and TNS are both projections, we can ask whether *to* is in AGR or TNS. For our purposes, we don't have to determine the answer to this question.

Truncation predicts that *to* will not be omitted. UCC (ATOM) predicts that it will. Whatever subject exists for the VP in the embedded clause, it will have to check against AGR and TNS. We expect *to* to be omitted given UCC.

Sentences with infinitival complements like (25a) are quite prevalent during the OI stage, so they provide a good testing ground for the varying predictions.

Roberts (1996) was the first study that I know of to consider the question of whether *to* is omitted during the OI stage. He studies Adam and Sarah from Brown's (1973) corpus. During the age ranges (somewhere in 2's) that he studies, Roberts demonstrates that Adam and Sarah are "firmly" in the OI stage. He then asks about their infinitival *to* complements. Many embedded infinitivals have *to*, but many don't. Roberts argues that it looks as if at the earliest stages, the children analyze *wanna* as a main verb (equivalent of *want*) without an infinitival marker, while at the same time omitting *to*, that is producing an OI in what should be an embedded infinitival complement.

To give an example of how much children omit *to*, the last 3 of Adam's files that Roberts analyzes show 6 uses of *to* where 97 are required, less than a 6% production

---

[42] For example, Roberts (1997) writes, "It is particularly interesting that, from the moment that subordinate clauses begin to appear in Adam's speech, several different kinds appear at the same time. There seems not to be a period n which one kind of subordinate clause is learned, then another, and so on. An exception, however, is the class of unambiguously finite complements, which appear only rarely; for example, (9c) *Go belong* (which Adam's mother interprets as *Go where it belongs*)." It's worth remarking that this one very rare clause that is interpreted as a finite utterance seems to be an embedded OI with a null-subject and a missing wh-phrase. Roberts finds a total of seven complements that should be finite in the two children that he studies; none of them are inflected. But these are too few to form a conclusion from. It is suggestive, however, of the conclusion that OI's exist in embedded clauses. As extensive a study as possible of OI's in embedded clauses that should be finite would be welcome.

in required contexts.. While she is 2;2.0, Sarah produced 1 *to* out of 15 contexts in which it required, about a 7% rate in required contexts.

These rates are somewhat less than precise because of the issue of the production of *wanna*. Here are some examples from Roberts (his (11)) of *to* omission with verbs other than *want*.[43]

(26) a. Do you want me get in (Adam 2;11.0)
    b. Do want he walk (Adam 2;11.0)
    c. Do you like come in with me (Adam 2;11.0)
    d. I going play baseball (Adam 2;11.0)
    e. I going swallow it (Adam 2;11.0)
    f. She going buy another one (Adam 2;11.0)
    g. I going drink it all up (Adam 2;11.0)
    h. Going take a wheels off (Adam 2;11.0)
    i. I going turn hot water on (Adam 2;11.0)

Sarah (2;8.25) produces *I come get you*. Independently of any issue of the reduction of *want to*, we see *to* omission in these children. Roberts concludes: "The speech of Adam and Sarah shows that these children in fact omit tense across the

---

[43] Tom Roeper (p.c.) points out that children never say *I want/don't want*, but always *I want to/I don't want to*, asking whether this is a counter-example to the conclusion that *to* is omitted by children in the OI stage. Although I don't know of any studies, this statement about child productions feels as if it may be right. If so, the question is: why isn't *to* omitted in this type of VP ellipsis even though it's omitted in non-ellipsis contexts? It seems that there is a quite likely explanation. Note that an elided VP must be governed by Tense. Small clauses (*Mary leave* in I *made Mary leave*) don't contain tense. It seems that small clauses VP's can't undergo this same VP ellipsis process.

(i) Speaker 1: John left early
(ii) Speaker 2, in response: *I saw/made Sue (i.e., cannot mean *I saw/made Sue leave early*).

There is no VP ellipsis of the VP in the small clause. Compare to the possibility of VP ellipsis in the infinitival clause.

(iii) Speaker 1: John left early
(iv) Speaker 2, in response: I want Sue to (i.e. means I want Sue to leave early)

There *is* VP ellipsis in the infinitival. Infinitival *to* is standardly assumed to occupy the head of the Tense projection; it is "infinitival" tense. So infinitival *to* (Tense), locally commands the VP and licenses VP ellipsis. In the small clause (ii), however, there is no Tense (no finite Tense, no infinitival Tense (*to*)) so Ellipsis is not allowed. All we have to assume is that the young child knows this condition on VP ellipsis, and we predict Roeper's interesting observations. If this is one the right track, we have further evidence for radical omission: omitting *to* means that the whole Tense projection is omitted, therefore disallowing VP ellipsis. (E.g., aux-omission couldn't predict such a fact, since the syntactic features (Tense) remain). Further empirical studies and theoretical analysis will be useful.

board, and do not merely truncate the initial projections of their main clauses. This observation argues strongly for the Optional Tense Hypothesis.[44]"

Norris (2000) analyzed many more children and files, considering the case of *to* deletion in both *want+[PRO clause]* constructions, like most of those we've discussed in Roberts' paper, and Exceptional Case Marking constructions, that is *want* taking an infinitival clause with a subject, that she calls *Lexical Subject [LS] clauses*. Norris analyzed 947 files, from 222 American children. (27) is Norris' (3[45]). As Norris concludes, *to-omission* is quite large, but drops off after 3;0, and to an even lower percentage after 3;4.

(27) *to-deletion in* want+*[PRO clause]: all children except Nathaniel*

Age	want+[PRO clause]	to	% *to* of total
1;3–2;0	186	68	37%
2;0–2;4	708	191	27.0%
2;4–2;8	1,308	193	14.8%
2;8–3;0	885	130	14.7%
3;0–3;4	583	26	4.5%
3;4–3;8	228	3	1.3%
3;8–4;0	166	3	1.8%
4;0–4;6	147	0	0%
4;6–5;0	124	1	0.8%
5;0–6;0	54	1	2%

Norris argues that the rates of *to-omission* seem to follow the rates of OI's in matrix clauses at about the same age. Thus *to-omission* is a phenomenon of the OI stage, trailing off as OI's trail off.

(28) shows Norris' table of *to-omission* (her (6)) when there is a lexical subject.

(28) *to-deletion in* want+*[LS clause]: all children*

Age	want+[L.S. clause]	to	% *to* of total[46]
1;3–2;0	10	6	(60%)
2;0–2;4	42	18	43%
2;4–2;8	100	25	25%
2;8–3;0	78	40	51%
3;0–3;4	255	166	65.1%
3;4–3;8	53	4	8%
3;8–4;0	53	4	8%
4;0–5;0	41	13	32%

---

[44] At the time of Roberts' writing, the ATOM and UCC had not yet been proposed, nor were the case facts yet part of the OI discussion, so the Tense Omission hypothesize was clearly the one to consider. It is of course equally clear that ATOM and the UCC are supported vis a vis Truncation.

[45] In this table, the data from one child, Nathaniel, is omitted because he seemed atypical; his to-omission extended somewhat longer than the other children. Norris also provides the data with Nathaniel included. It doesn't change much, just a bit higher percentages of to-deletion, especially at the older ages.

[46] Norris writes, "When there are not enough data points to produce a statistically significant percentage, the computed percentage is in parentheses."

With lexical subjects there is a large amount of *to-deletion* during the OI stage. At 2;8–3;0, there is 51%; at 3;0–3;4 there is 65.1%, at which time the rates of to-omission become much lower, e.g. only 8% at 3;4–3;8. Again, the rates of *to-omission* more or less track the OI stage rates.[47] Here are two examples of the use of *want* with (29a) and without (29b) *to* (from Norris' (5)).

(29) a. adam30 (3;5)
   I want Paul to play with dis.
   b. adam13 (2;9)
   want me open?

To omission with a lexical subject is particularly interesting, as there is no way it can be related to a phonetic realization or reanalysis of *want* and/or *want + to*. *To* appears after the DP. Its omission is very close to what would happen when TNS is omitted in a main clause. At 2;0–2;4, the children omit 43% of the *to* particles (TNS) that should appear after the subject of the infinitival.

Truncation has a very difficult time dealing with the phenomena of *to*-omission, because projections are supposed to delete only if all projections above them delete, clearly the case for none of the examples in these tables. ATOM predicts exactly these phenomena. It appears as if the evidence from embedded infinitival complements shows us that the computationalist rather than the locationist approach is correct.

Does UCC predict omission of *to*? Is there a double-checking of the subject in infinitivals? There is a subject in ECM (LS) infinitivals, and it has to check against functional categories. Is there both AGR and TNS in the infinitival complement? There is no reason to think there isn't, even if infinitivals in most languages don't show agreement distinctions. (They also don't show tense distinctions on the surface). I'll leave the precise technical development to another time. But I should point out that Norris has her own syntactic theory of how all this works out, which could be studied, as it relates to interesting thoughts about complementizers, and so on. We'll leave it with the conclusion that the fact and spirit of Truncation seems contradicted by phenomena in infinitival complements, whereas UCC seems to predict the phenomena.

3.3 Why Does the OI Stage Exist?

We have seen that the OI stage is one in which young children speaking many languages produce (ungrammatical) non-finite forms alongside (grammatical) finite forms, but produce these forms in the "correct" places, e.g. the finite verb in

---

[47] Norris shows that most of the late *to-omission* is from one child, Adam. Since there aren't many older children in the study, Adam counts disproportionately. Adam is often considered to have somewhat atypical, even delayed language. Norris concludes that *to* drops off before 4;0, both in *PRO* subject clauses and in *LS* clauses.

SOV/V2 languages is produced in 2nd position whereas the mistaken, root non-finite verb, is produce in final position. There is no difficulty in explaining how the children know *where* to produce each form – we only have to assume (Wexler 1998) that children are brilliant learners of (at least these aspects of) morphology and parameter values and that they know UG. That is the fairly standard assumption by now in the study of OI's. (We will return to more empiricist alternatives). On the other hand, this explanation does not tell us why the children produce OI's at all. We have argued that assuming that UCC holds of the children explains the data. The question is, why does UCC hold?

The only explanation for why UCC holds that has been offered to date is that language acquisition as more a process of language *growth* than language *learning*, as Chomsky has advocated. Although there are important aspects of learning (setting parameters, learning morphology and a lexicon, etc.), the appropriate way to look at language acquisition is as a process of growth. Of course, that's the way most biological development takes place. Since the central achievement of modern linguistic theory (generative grammar), simply stated, is the placement of language within the study of biology, we expect growth to take place in the area of language just as it does in pretty much every other area of biology. Otherwise we would have a total mystery – why is it that language, almost uniquely in the biological world, emerges at birth (at conception?) fully formed, with only a few pieces of learning to take place. In other words, linguistic theory, along with biology, *expects* that some properties of grammar develop over time as a matter of genetic influence.

Borer and Wexler (1987, 1992) first made these arguments, and they have often been restated in various ways (Babyonyshev et al. 2001; Wexler 2003). Rizzi (1993) accepts Borer and Wexler's idea of maturation to be the appropriate explanation for the OI-stage.

Although Borer and Wexler originally argued for the idea of maturation of linguistic abilities on learning-theoretic and linguistic-theoretic grounds,[48] the detailed evidence for it is by now overwhelming. See Wexler (2003) for detailed arguments and data. This evidence includes experimental evidence showing that the "learning environmental" variables that influence parts of language that *are* under strong environmental influence (e.g. vocabulary size) do not affect the development of Tense (Rice et al. 1998). Further evidence includes the study of Specific Language Impairment.

The empirical arguments advanced in Wexler (2003) were strong enough so that Chomsky (2005) wrote, that one of the "three factors that enter into the growth of language in the individual [is] ... Genetic endowment, apparently near uniform for the species, which interprets part of the environment as linguistic experience, a non-trivial task that the infant carries out reflexively, and determines the general course

---

[48] In particular, Borer and Wexler proposed the *Triggering Problem*. Why does evidence apply at one age and not an earlier age. Babyonyshev et al. (2001) called this the *Argument from the Abundance of the Stimulus*. The evidence in the case they studied was so prevalent in the input, it was very difficult to see why learning should be delayed.

of the development of the language faculty. Among the genetic elements, some may impose computational limitations but that disappear in a regular way through genetically-timed maturation. Ken Wexler and his associates have provided compelling evidence of their existence in the growth of language, thus providing empirical evidence for what Wexler calls 'Lenneberg's dream.'"

In my view, too, the data is compelling. In all sciences, conclusions are open to discussion. What isn't open to discussion, however, is that evidence matters.

Since the publication of Wexler (2003), there have been further advances in the evidentiary basis for the *growth* argument, in particular the genetic basis for the argument. First, Bishop et al. (2006) studied a large population of identical and fraternal twins with at least some language delays. They measured the children on a number of behavioral variables, include an early version of Rice and Wexler's (2001) *Test of Early Grammatical Impairment (TEGI)*, a measure of finiteness in obligatory contexts. To the extent that identical twins are more alike on a measure than are fraternal twins, behavioral genetic analysis concludes that the measure is inherited, that is, is under genetic control.[49] Against their own expectations, the authors found that not only was variation in finiteness behavior strongly inherited (i.e. under genetic control) but that the genetic source of finiteness was different than the genetic source of another inherited behavior, phonological working memory (PWM) as measured by the Non-Word Repetition task. Bishop et al., conclude, "Most crucially, this study reveals that impairments in use of verb inflections have distinctive genetic origins and cannot be explained away as secondary consequences of limitations of phonological STM [Short Term Memory]." Note that "verb inflections" is the term these authors use for "finiteness", which was what they measured.

Bishop has long argued that a "general" psychological measure, such as Phonological Working Memory, should underlie language impairment. The fact that in this paper, she and her co-authors conclude the opposite, that finiteness[50] (possibly a more general syntactic construct, one cannot tell from these results) has an independent genetic source, shows how detailed empirical evidence about language and language development can influence even "general purpose" theoreticians in psychology, against their dearest biases. Ultimately in science, the data does out. Surely linguists and psycholinguists can recognize that the growth (as opposed to the

---

[49] Of course, the measure has to be one for which it is reasonable to assume that parents don't treat identical twins more alike than they treat fraternal twins (as might be the case, for example, in clothing choice). It is hard to think of any cognitive measure that is less likely than production of finiteness (by parents) to have the wrong property, i.e. a situation whereby parents tended to use the same proportion of finite utterances with identical twins, but varied their finiteness proportions more for fraternal twins. If behavioral genetics is appropriate for *any* cognitive behavior, it is appropriate for OI's.

[50] Given our conclusions, is not finiteness that is under genetic control. Rather it is the withering away of UCC that is under genetic control. In other words, a particular computational limitation on the child's grammar dies away under genetic control.

learning) of language might be a supportable assumption – after all, the expectation that there is growth (and not only learning) is part of the very foundation of the field. There is no special conceptual reason to argue for what has been called "continuity[51]" – the assumption that a child at birth has the same linguistic capacities as an older child. Perhaps the claim of continuity (rather, rigidity, as in the footnote) is slightly simpler, since a maturational schedule has to be stated. But it goes against the overall simplicity of science, since it is surprising from a biological point of view that the foundations of linguistics sets itself in. Furthermore, a complex "learning theory", for which there is often no evidence, has to be stated. Thus it's not so clear that "continuity/rigidity" is "simpler." Certainly, linguistic theory doesn't say this, nor expect it.[52]

There is even genetic (not behavioral genetic, rather linkage) evidence concerning the development of finiteness. Falcaro et al. (2008) provide evidence that the "SLI2" gene or genes, located on a particular region of chromosome 19q, is a controlling factor in the development of past-tense marking, one of the measures of finiteness. This paper and others show that the "SLI1" gene, a controlling factor of phonological working memory, is on another chromosome completely. Given these results together with the results discussed in this paper, the field is even beginning to hone in on which gene or genes control the development of UCC. Of course, it is early days. But we see what can be attempted and quite possibly accomplished, when one takes linguistic theory and its foundations (the genetically guided growth of language) seriously together with serious analysis of child language and genetic studies. These are exciting times; the detailed quantitative and theoretical study of child language might have brought us to the point where a genetics of language is

---

[51] Wexler (1999) argued that in fact "continuity" is a misleading name for this concept. He argued that the claim that there was no genetically controlled growth of the linguistic capacity should rather be called "Rigidity." "Continuity" would better be reserved for the claim that there is a strong genetic basis to UG, with some small maturational changes in capacity as in e.g. the withering away of UCC, or (on another topic, not discussed here), the dieing away of the Full Phase Requirement (Wexler 2004).

[52] Furthermore, as Rizzi (1993) points out, if a child's UG is identical to an adult's, then linguistic theory can't learn much from acquisition, except confirmation. But if a child's UG has slight "perturbations" from UG, then child language can provide a kind of "experiment" that shows what happens under these perturbations, providing a potentially rich source of evidence for linguistic theory. There are already many examples in the literature. Consider, for example, what the OI stage tells us about the relation of case and finiteness, and default case, as in the work of Schutze and Wexler (1996). We see there that a main verb without agreement in child English can elicit the "default" non-nominative case: *her go*, whereas in child Dutch or German, the equivalent non-nominative subjects won't exist for the OI's, prevalent as these OI's are, because the default case in those languages is nominative. The English cases are quite rare in the adult, existing only in "exhortative" sentences and similar (*her/*she go to California? Never!*) but they are a well-known feature of early linguistic development in ordinary declaratives in young children in the OI stage. Thus this possibility of often leaving out an agreement feature from a phrase-marker during the OI stage, this slight "perturbation" of UG, provides a lovely source of evidence about the interaction of subject case and finiteness.

attainable. Linguistic theory (generative grammar) expects exactly this and for a long time it was the only scientific discipline that expected this relation, at least in any really clear fashion.[53]

Thus, the new genetic studies are adding further evidence to foundational thoughts in linguistic theory and detailed studies of language acquisition. This body of work leads to a pretty clear conclusion that maturation/growth/UG theories are on the right track, and that "learning" as the most fundamental cause of how and why grammar develops is not. Thus we conclude that the UCC dies away under genetic influence, just as a first set of teeth fall out under genetic influence, and a second set develops under genetic influence.

3.4 Empiricist Theories of the OI Stage

The OI stage was discovered and investigated within generative grammar oriented studies in developmental psycholinguistics, that is, a type of study that takes as fundamental the existence of grammatical representations in the adult, and asks how a child's representations develop toward an adult's. To solve particular problems, a genetically based theory of UG is assumed, along with various open possibilities (lexicon, parameter) that have to be set via learning.

Although such a view has gained strength in the last decades, and might even be "dominant" (as suggested in the Introduction to Hoekstra and Schwartz (1994)), in the study of language acquisition, another view seems never to die out. This is the empiricist view, that takes as axiomatic that there are no innate principles of language and that developing language is a long, slow, tedious process of figuring out or stamping in the environment. With the existence of a great deal of interest in the OI stage (due to the interest of the stunning data, in my view), empiricist oriented psychologists tried to reduce its interest – to say that these were simply some kind of error due to the long, slow, difficult biologically uninformed learning process. For example, Tomasello (2000) suggests that the OI stage is due to the learner hearing subjects followed by non-finite verbs in some cases (e.g. *I made Mary go*). Since *Mary go* is in the input, that is, is heard, as two contiguous words, why shouldn't the learner decide to say *Mary go*? Tomasello doesn't specify learning theories, he's not a learning theorist, but he alludes to some kinds of ideas about a kid paying attention to two words side by side. Wexler (2003) discusses Tomasello's proposals, and shows that there is no way they can work to explain the data. Here let's point out only that non-finite verbs are a small percentage of the input in general, so why should mostly non-finite output in the early child exist? Tomasello tried also to

---

[53] Biology should also have expected this result, but biology, for the most part, knew so little of language, that nothing much was said, for the most part. There were a few exceptions, but without experimental detail. Lenneberg (1967) did expect this kind of result, in a direct way. He was much influenced by Chomsky's arguments about generative grammar as well as biology. We wouldn't expect (mainstream) psychology to expect this kind of result, as its foundations are completely different, presuming an associationist, empiricist model as axiomatic.

explain Schutze and Wexler's (1996) observations that kids in the OI stage use non-NOM subjects with OI's (*her go*) but not with finite verbs (#her goes) by saying that *her go* exists in the input (*I made her go*) whereas *her goes* doesn't. As Wexler points out, the last observation is incorrect (cf: *who did you tell her goes to the store every day*)? Furthermore, and crucially, the exact same observations about which pairs of words occur in the input holds for German, yet kids in Dutch and German don't use non-NOM subjects (because, as Schutze and Wexler argue, NOM is default in Dutch and German). At the bottom of all these ideas is the extremely implausible basis for this theory – that kids as old as three (at least) simply map pairs of words they hear onto pairs or words they say, without going through any kind of cognitive computation. For more detail, see Wexler (2003).

Ideas of this sort are developed with respect to child data and applied to the OI stage in English in Pine et al. (2005), in particular as a way of "testing" the ATOM model. The basic idea is that different lexical verbs show different amount of finiteness marking during the OI stage, which is supposed to show that ATOM doesn't hold. It's hard to see what the logic is. Of course, there may be other factors that enter into amount of finiteness, but in no way does this invalidate a model that has a computational explanation of why OI's exist, why there should be differences between languages, and how many different phenomena occur or don't occur, for example, subject case and finiteness. At any rate, Pine et al. don't provide a theory, other than to say that somehow finiteness is learned as part of the verb that's heard, and responds differently to different verbs, etc. So they aren't comparing ATOM to another theory that they claim is better. At best they show there are some phenomena that ATOM doesn't predict. On the other hand, nothing in what they say can begin to explain the basic phenomena of the OI stage, for example, the word order/finiteness correlation that we shown so strongly holds. The authors don't discuss languages other than English, languages that are more fundamental to the claims made about the OI stage, since the infinitival ending is so audible, unlike English. The ideas are so vague that one suspects that no matter what the set of phenomena that were observed, the authors would have used the same set of ideas to "explain" them. If the associationist/empiricist view is an axiom, well nothing can disprove an axiom.

Instead, I would like to take some space to discuss claims that it seems to me have at their heart some properties that are quite similar to empiricist views, yet are made by scholars who accept the relevance of generative linguistics, and the actual existence of the OI stage as a representational state. Legate and Yang (2007) accept that the behavior that children produce in the OI stage reflects the state of their grammar (grammars, actually, a point to which we will return). They accept that there is a UG and parameters and that these are represented in the minds of children. So they start from a basis that seems much more compatible with other (generative) studies of the OI stage than the empiricist studies that we have briefly reviewed here. Yet their claims are like empiricist claims in that the authors assume (assert) that the process of learning some very simple piece of grammar is long, arduous, and difficult, even with a good deal of built-in knowledge. I have chosen this paper to spend a bit more detailed space on because the paper is the most worked out attempt to build a learning-theoretic account of the OI stage. Legate and Yang should be given credit for attempting to make a learning-theory model predict the properties of data that have been discovered in the developmental psycholinguistic literature. That is much more than most empiricist models, which don't attempt to deal with the central problems. In fact, by developing a (partially) implemented model along (at least partially) empiricist learning lines, the inadequacies of empiricist ideas on language learning can be highlighted in a very precise way.

Legate and Yang start from the well-known observation that languages like Chinese don't mark Tense. They propose that there is a parameter of whether or not a language marks Tense: English/French/Spanish have the *yes* value, Chinese has the *no* value. However, Legate and Yang make no proposals about whether this parameter relates to a deep property of grammar, e.g. whether in Chinese phrase-markers actually are missing Tense, or are only a lack of spelling out of Tense in the surface, with the features actually being in the structure. They write (p. 33, footnote 322), "And thus we forgo a detailed discussion on the proper, but largely orthogonal, theoretical treatment of these languages, e.g. whether [−Tense] languages have identical clausal structure and functional nodes as [+Tense] languages." But it can be argued that this question is not "orthogonal", but crucial. Whichever way the answer is given, we will see that their proposal cannot capture the data.

According to Legate and Yang children have to learn the value of this parameter, and it is a long, hard, error-ridden process. In particular, the authors assume Yang's (2002) theory of learning, which has the following general properties:

(30) a. The learner has many grammars at one time, in particular, grammars that have every combination of every parameter value. Learning the grammar means that the weights of the input grammar's parametric values are driven up very high and the other values are driven very low.
b. Grammars in the child's mind have different weights, and these weights are increased when a sentence is heard that can be generated by the grammar, and decreased when a sentence is heard that cannot be generated by the grammar.

The feasibility of such a system is clearly an issue, because the space of grammars that the child has to deal with will be huge. For example, if there are 40 binary parameters (hardly a huge number to assume), the child will have 2 to the 40th grammars in her mind, a huge number. This might easily lead to a computationally intractable problem for human capacities. I don't know any work that answers this question for this type of model.[54]

---

[54] The approach of Gibson and Wexler (1994) followed the basic strategy of Wexler and Culicover (1980) of seeing how much could be learned via a strong UG system and a simple learning system, so that the computational "learning" problem was simple. This was also in line with the ideas that introduced parameters into linguistic theory – that they helped to solve the tension between language variation and language learning by making the learning problem so simple (setting a parameter via simple data, in a simple way) given the strong UG, that the data would make the learning take place easily. Gibson and Wexler showed that even in an extremely simple three-parameter system, this vision wasn't realized, so that more structure would have to be added to the problem. To not take into account the limited abilities of the child (or even adult) in doing computations (2 to the 40 grammars to consider?) seems to miss the point of parameters. How it is "feasible" (Chomsky 1965) to set parameters, that is, to set them within human capacities regarding memory, storage, access to data and so on?

Charles Yang (pc) says that Yang (2002) does answer this question for the learning model. The variational learning model assigns a probability to each (binary) parameter, the probability that value 1 is chosen. So it looks as if the child learning *n* parameters only has to hold *n* values in mind. But a long tradition of learnability investigations argues that such a system doesn't really work. The basic problem is one of interacting parameters, as discussed in Manzini and Wexler (1987) and Wexler and Manzini (1987) for Subset Principle considerations and in Gibson and Wexler (1994) for parametric learning more generally. There may be no evidence that tells the child how to set a parameter unambiguously, independent of other parameters. The discussion (Chap. 2) of this question in Yang (2002) acknowledges the problem of non-independent parameters.[55] He adopts the notion of *signature*. Although not formally defined, a signature seems to be a sentence (I think not a *set* of sentences) that unambiguously (i.e. independent of the other parameters in the target grammar) tells the learner which value to assign to a particular parameter. This notion was previously discussed under the name of *unambiguous trigger* in Gibson and Wexler, where it was argued that such a datum was unlikely to exist, in many or most (or even all) cases.

Yang (2002) argues that there are very often signatures, i.e. unambiguous triggers. However a slight broadening of the evidence shows that his examples do not have the property of independence. In particular, the proposed signatures are not signatures. Furthermore, signatures are unlikely to exist for the cases discussed. Consider a case quite relevant to the current discussion, the Verb to Tense parameter (Yang, p. 40) (*plus* value in e.g. French), where the finite verb (*mange* in this example) raises to Tense, on the left of negation *pas*, yielding Yang's (28a) *jean ne mange pas de fromage/John doesn't eat cheese*.

Yang calls Verb to Tense an "independent" parameter. He writes that his (28a) (similarly for an adverb instead of negation) is a signature for the plus value of Verb to Tense. However, a little reflection about cross-linguistic syntax shows that this is unlikely to be the case. Suppose that a language is right-headed, that is, the sentence is SOV. Usually it is thought that Tense T in such a language also is a right-head, taking the verb phrase as a complement on the left of Tense: SOVT. If the language has Verb to Tense, then the verb moves to the *right* to adjoin to Tense. If negation is in the specifier of Tense (as much negation is taken to be, e.g. *pas* in French is usually taken to be in the spec of NegP) then negation will show up to the left of the VP: S NEG OV T. If the verb raises to Tense, it won't change the word order. Since Tense is adjacent to the verb, the word order of the "visible" parts of the sentence will be S NEG OV, the same as for Yang's (28a) in French that we have just considered. On the other hand, if the language does *not* have Verb to Tense, the word order will be exactly the same.

---

[55] The term stems, presumably, from Manzini and Wexler's and Wexler and Manzini's *Independence Principle*, which explicitly gives a formal definition of independence of parameters in order to make the Subset Principle work in the multi-parameter case.

In short, the proposed word order is *not* a signature for Verb to Tense. It only is (at best) in an SVO language. A case in point is Korean (see references in Baek and Wexler (2008)), where the word order in *short-form negation* has the negative element *an* before the verb, although Korean (an SOV language) is usually argued to have Verb to Tense.

Even if we restrict ourselves to SVO languages, where we can even take Tense to precede the VP, it is unlikely that the proposed sentence (the verb before negation) will be a signature, that is, that the verb before negation will unambiguously show that the verb raises. It is sometimes argued that negation itself can raise in some languages (e.g. Italian), so if negation is allowed to raise it may turn out that negation can precede the verb even if the verb raises to Tense, and even if there is a universal hierarchy (often doubted) that places Tense above negation.

The question of whether signatures (or unambiguous triggers, the original term from Gibson and Wexler) is an empirical question. It must be answered by seeing what parametric values of different languages are. In my view, the arguments I have previously made against the existence of unambiguous triggers still seem right. At any rate, it is important to argue from evidence for the existence of unambiguous triggers (signatures).

Yang (2002) allows that there are cases of non-independent parameters. He argues that the variational learning model handles those by simply punishing the weights of *every* parameter when a sentence in the input can't be generated, even a parameter whose particular value has been amply supported in much previous data. What is the evidence presented that such a model works? The claim is that a simulation shows that a system of ten parameters can be learned (comes to have high (close to 1) weights for value 1 and low (close to 0) weights for the zero value) after about 600,000 sentences are presented. But we don't know what the parameters were that went into the simulation, whether they were linguistic-like, whether there was independence (both within the set of 10 parameters, and more generally). This is worrying. If it takes 600,000 sentence presentations for a set of 10 parameters, we might expect some kind of exponential growth of number of presentation required with the number of parameters growing, so it might be hundreds of millions (or more) of sentences required to get close to convergence for a 40 parameter system. Furthermore, the parameters may have been chosen to display independence, a property we have just seen may (almost) never hold in natural language.

It doesn't seem to be a problem of "cleverness" of the learning system. There is something we fundamentally don't understand about parameter-setting in humans. The point of Gibson and Wexler's (1994) *Triggers* paper was to show this. The problem of the lack of existence of unambiguous triggers is the central problem. Parameters *interact*. The evidence is very ambiguous for a learner. Learning systems of the traditional kind (Yang's is extremely traditional, as he points out) aren't built to handle this kind of problem. Let me be clear: I don't think any learning system that has been proposed (the main contenders are triggers, cues, and weight-changing systems) are adequate. My own hunch (and that's about all we can have at the moment, given the lack of empirically adequate results in the field of parameter-learning) is that some kind of biological mechanism is in place, perhaps pushing some parameters to be set first, refusing to let them change when other input comes in, etc. This is vague, I completely understand. We need a breakthrough.

However, doubts aside about the parametric learning theory proposed in Yang (2002), the particular model of finiteness development discussed within that theory doesn't capture the central empirical phenomena, and that is the main point of our discussion here.

First, why does the OI stage exist? Legate and Yang attribute it to the child's having grammars both with +Tense (like English) and –Tense (like Chinese). The theory assumes that the child starts out with all values, and then increases and decreases weights as in (30). OI's are sentences that are produced with the –Tense value, that is, when the learner chooses (with probabilities determined by relative weights) to produce a sentence with the – Tense (Chinese) value.

Why does it take so long, many years, to change the –Tense value to a very low weight, so that adults produce no OI's?[56] According to Legate and Yang, this is because many sentences that a child hears in many languages, do not give unambiguous evidence for +Tense. Many verbs that the child hears are "compatible" with both a +Tense and –Tense grammar. Consider a sentence like *I go* in English. Either of two grammars[57] (parameter values) that a child has (with different weights) can analyze this sentence, either +Tense or –Tense, for there is no obvious tense morpheme.[58]

Suppose the child is learning a +Tense language. If the form is ambiguous, and if the child analyzes the sentence with the –Tense grammar (this will happen probabilistically) then the child's +Tense grammar will be "rewarded" (weights will increase) and the child's –Tense grammar will be "punished" (weights will decrease). In other words, if the child hears *I go*, there is a probability greater than zero that this will be used as evidence for the child to decide that a Chinese-style –Tense grammar is correct.

---

[56] Except exhortatives, etc., that we already discussed. Legate and Yang acknowledge that these shouldn't count; they have a very different semantics – the problem is, why adults eventually produce no OI's in more standard contexts.

[57] It's only 2 because this paper doesn't study more than this one parameter.

[58] All of Legate and Yang's arguments depend on the learner knowing whether or not a morpheme is a +Tense morpheme, e.g. that *ed* marks past tense. They don't show how this can happen despite the OI stage, but simply assume this knowledge. However, what could it mean for the learning theory to both learn *ed* as +Past and not know that the language is a +Tense language? There are many other considerations and unclarities that could possibly be answered by a simulation that put a few properties into the system to be learned. Given that the paper only presents some aspects of the computation of whether +Tense or –Tense holds, we don't know what would happen. My own theoretical hunches and long-time experience in learning theory lean me toward guessing that all this can't work, that the arguments can only be made in the absence of studying the interaction. Of course we don't know for sure until the analysis is done. We should hope that the believers in such models do an analysis of this kind. The central point of Gibson and Wexler (1994) and what made its results so widely attended to, with alternative systems attempted, was that it studied a system of linguistic parameters together, highlighting the interaction problems. Since then, learning theory has known that systems of parameters have to be studied in order to not miss the central issues. The one-parameter problem distorts the situation qualitatively, not just quantitatively.

Thus the Dutch child at around age 2 who uses 70% OI's, say, is using a Chinese-style −Tense grammar 70% of the times in productions, meaning the weight of −Tense is quite high relative to +Tense. The child alternates from +Tense to −Tense in productions, according to relative weights.

The main idea of Legate and Yang is that this model predicts that the time to learn +Tense will vary across languages according to the proportion of ambiguous Tense forms the language has, in particular, according to the proportions of ambiguous forms that appear in input to the child. They consider English, French and Spanish. They try to decide which forms that the child hears are "ambiguous," and show that English has the most ambiguous forms, followed by French, followed by Spanish. They look at child language and conclude that Spanish either doesn't have such an OI stage (as predicted by NS/OI) or one which ends extremely early (2;0), that the French OI stage ends around 2;8 and that the English OI stage ends around 3;5. This relative ordering of the length of the OI stage follows the prediction, thus, Legate and Yang claim, supporting the model.

However, the basis for deciding on the proportions of ambiguous Tense is not at all clear. Let me try to state their ideas a bit more precisely, defining the parameter so that the learning theory they offer makes sense. What is the parameter? Thinking that the +Tense value means that there is some morpheme that marks Tense, let us think of the Tense parameter as having the +value if the language has two verbal morphemes X and Y, such that for a verb V, V+X has a different tense value than V+Y. E.g. in English, take X to be *ed* and Y to be the (phonetically) 0 morpheme. Then for the verb push, push+ed is past tense and push+0 is present tense (abstracting away from 3rd singular): *I pushed, I push*.

But given this Tense parameter, when the child hears *I push* and computes it according to the −Tense value of the parameter, then the −Tense value is increased, and the +Tense value is decreased. It will be a long, slow learning process, with large numbers of errors.

The reader might think: why doesn't the child simply notice that there are two different verbal inflections *−0* and *−ed*, with different tense values (present and past) and directly conclude that the language is +Tense? Because the theory doesn't work that way.[59] Rather, the theory simply says that if the child happens to generate the sentence with one value of the parameter, then the child won't ask whether the other value can also generate it, and say, well, this doesn't give me evidence – it's ambiguous.

---

[59] Even Gibson and Wexler's (1994) *Triggers* model, which was attempting to capture what linguists meant by "simple" learning of parameters (using "triggers") said that if the child could generate a sentence, the parametric value wasn't changed. Yang's theory, however, pushes down the alternative value—thus data that is truly irrelevant can make the language learner go the wrong way. This happens a great deal – when there is ambiguous data. This is the basis for the very slow learning of the model.

How does a child know whether a sentence can be generated by a value of the Tense parameter? The child has to know (a) that a particular morpheme (perhaps phonetically empty) is a Tense morpheme or not, and what its semantic interpretation is. So far as I can tell there is no model of this learning in Legate and Yang's paper – it is simply assumed that the child has learned this. But if the child knows that two morphemes are +Tense morphemes, doesn't that mean that the child knows that the grammar shows Tense distinctions? Suppose the child knows that *ed* is +Past and that *0* is –Past, however she's learned that. According to the model under review, the child still does not infer that the language is a +Tense language. But the +Tense value simply says that there exist two morphemes like this. So the child can completely have the materials to make an inference but doesn't make the inference. Rather, the child goes through this trial-and-error process. Why?[60]

Returning to Legate and Yang's results, there is much to be said in terms of other models. We understand that Spanish won't have OI's, according to NS/OI. But there is much in the literature discussing varying rates of OI's, even for non-null-subject languages, e.g. Wexler et al. (2004a, b) comparing Dutch and English. UCC (ATOM) predicts various rates depending on the morphology of the language, but not because it is difficult to learn this morphology. Rather, given a detailed morphological model, ATOM predicts that certain finite forms will be produced correctly even if a feature is omitted. For example, in English, suppose AGReement is omitted. A past tense *ed* will still be correctly produced, because *ed* does not specify agreement. Detailed formal models are given in Schutze and Wexler for English and Wexler et al. (2004a, b) for Dutch. Applying ATOM to them, Wexler et al. show that the correct relative ordering of OI rate is predicted.

French also has many verbal forms in its paradigm that have zero marking, e.g. *je parle/I speak*, where there is a 0-morpheme for the inflection part. It is easy to imagine that omitting one of the AGR/Tense combinations will still allow the form to be produced correctly.[61] A form like *s* in English, however, depends on both Tense (present) and Agreement (3rd singular) so omitting one of these features will cause an OI. We thus expect, subject to be a more detailed working out, that French will show fewer OI's than English.

Consider another parameter, the verb raising parameter, movement of V to I. Legate and Yang point out that many sentences will be ambiguous on this point too; for example, the sentence *Jean voit Marie/John sees Mary* "obviously is consistent with both values of the parameter; in other words, the child learner will succeed

---

[60] As we discussed earlier, Hyams had proposed that the null-subject parameter took awhile to learn, and Yang (2002) attempts to explain this as the result of the trail-and-error learning model. But as we discussed (see the data in (21) and the pages following it), the evidence is strong and accepted in the developmental psycholinguistic field that very young children have the correct value of this parameter.

[61] This idea was suggested in the GALA talk in Edinburgh that Wexler (1998, 1999) was based on, although it is not in the paper. I know of no detailed morphological model in combination with ATOM that has been computed. But the idea seems clear.

regardless of whether she has selected the + or − value to analyze this sentence." They point out that when there is an adverb like *souvent/often*, the sentence will not be ambiguous: *Jean voit souvent Marie* (their (4)). In this sentence, only the + verb raising parameter value will succeed.

Legate and Yang don't discuss this example further, and don't do any learning computations for verb raising.[62] However, they calculate that most (93%) of sentences that the French child hears will be ambiguous; that is, they don't have adverbs or *pas/not*, so that it can't be determined if verb raising has taken place. If the comparison could be done, it might even turn out that there is a higher proportion of ambiguous input on this question than on the question of whether the form were + Tense or not, in French, or even in English. (It is difficult to do the comparison because, as I pointed out, we don't understand the analytical basis for classifying a verb form as showing unambiguous tense or not, contra to the case of the Verb raising parameter.) Thus Legate and Yang's theory would predict that the learning of verb raising, V to I, should be very slow, that there should be an "optional verb raising stage", a stage, in fact that takes longer to resolve, possibly than the OI stage.

But no such stage exists. Pierce (1992a, b) showed this in great detail, and her conclusions have been replicated and extended several times. The very young French child (even during the OI stage) will almost never fail to raise a finite verb. Thus the "variational" learning model, the idea that ambiguous forms will slow learning makes a wrong prediction. It is hard to see how to resolve this problem within the set of ideas given.

It is easy to see where the model has gone awry. The whole *point* of the problem of the OI stage is that the child has brilliant knowledge of parameters, e.g. the V to I parameter, or the V to C parameter.[63] These parameters are learned easily and well. The mystery is, why is *finiteness* so delayed, in contrast to knowledge of the

---

[62] Charles Yang (pc) writes, "We cite Yang 2002, which does discuss the example further, and does do the calculations. These calculations demonstrate that the age of learning of V to I is correctly predicted by the model." I have searched Yang (2002) and can't find any calculations for the learning of V to I via the variational learning model. On p. 103, Yang says that verbs preceding negation or adverbs are signatures (i.e. unambiguously, independent of all other parameters), which we have already argued they are not. He calculates on that page that sentences with verbs preceding negation or adverbs make up about 7% of the input to the French-learning child, and thus takes 7% as an empirically-derived bound on how much of such input is necessary But there is no calculation of how the Verb to I (Tense) parameter is learned, here or elsewhere in the book, so far as I can find. Even if we don't add other parameters, and thus leave the relevant sentences as "signatures" in this very restricted (one parameter) context, the point I've made in the main text holds. Namely, learning of V to I should be very slow, since whenever the child selects a 0 (no) value for V to I for the grammar on a trial (which should happen fairly often), and thus correctly parses (up to the other parameters, if they're relevant) an input sentence (93% of input sentences), the 1 (yes) value of the V to I parameter will be punished. I see no calculations in Yang (2002) that show that this is wrong.

[63] The variational learning theory would also have comparable problems explaining why V to C (for finite verbs) wouldn't also suffer from being presented with many ambiguous sentences. Consider, for example, an SVO sentence in Swedish or another mainland V2 Scandinavian language.

morphosyntactic parameters. One has to look at the *system* of parameters and UG processes to understand what is happening.

In particular, I suspect that the idea of English and Chinese differing in that there is a Tense parameter that distinguishes them would be difficult to maintain. It is understood that crucial features get spelled out differently, but it is hard to say globally that English spells out Tense. It only does that sometimes, not even in most present tense cases, and even then (*s*) as a combination, specified with agreement. It is hard to see what is fundamental about the difference in English and

---

This could be analyzed without verb movement, since the underlying word order is SVO. In fact, there seem to be counts of productions showing that the speakers of the language produce mostly SVO sentences (Wexler 1993, following p.c. from David Lightfoot). Shouldn't this slow down the setting of the +V2 value? Yet we know (Wexler 1994 and many subsequent publications in the OI literature) that this value is set very early, with almost no errors. Yang (2002 in fact argues that the V2 parameter is *not* correctly set at an early age. He points out (section 4.1.2) that many early utterances in one Dutch child are "V1", that is, the first word is the verb. He concludes from this that the child has not learned the V2 setting; rather, that V2 is competing somehow with a setting that would characterize Hebrew. But there is no reason to think that in fact the child hasn't learned that V moves to C. As pointed out in footnote 13, it is well known that Dutch shows topic-drop. If a DP is sufficiently prominent in the discourse and is in Spec, CP, then it may be omitted. It is an open empirical question whether children in the OI stage drop topics more than adults do (which wouldn't be surprising on independent grounds). Note that two of the examples that Yang cites (p. 106) provide evidence for the Topic-Drop view, since objects seem to be missing from sentences with transitive verbs (thus the direct object would be missing). These include the Dutch equivalents of *know I not* (something like *that* missing from Spec, CP) and *see I yet not* (the object of *see* appears to be missing, presumably from Spec, CP). The other two examples (*shines the sun* and *can I not run*) do not appear to be missing direct objects (on the common reading of *run*), but could easily be omitting some kind of adverbial. It would be very good to have an empirical study that determined how many of the V1 sentences could be interpreted with a fairly obvious missing element in Spec, CP. If such an analysis exists, I don't know it. At any rate, Dutch linguists have felt quite comfortable in interpreting these sentences as showing a Dutch-like ability to drop an element in Spec, CP under certain pragmatic conditions. Furthermore, and importantly, independent of the V1/V2 discussion, the major point made at the beginning of this footnote holds. The finiteness/word order correlation (even with V1/V final) can't hold in the variational learning model because when the child hears an SVO sentence, and has selected a value of no verb raising at all (e.g. something like an English value), this setting will have its weight added to. Just as Legate and Yang argue that ambiguous data leads to the OI stage, the 70% or so SVO data that a child hears in an SVO language should lead to a long period of producing sentences with objects, adverbs, etc. raised to Spec, CP (topicalized) followed by the subject followed by the finite verb, that is XP NP (subject) V pattern. We know that these hardly exist (Poeppel and Wexler 1993; Santelmann 1995 among many others). See (7) for example, where many of the 1st position NP's won't be subjects). Furthermore, since this V2 Scandinavian language will be OI for children, the model we are discussing says that the kids think that the finite (for adult) verb forms don't show tense, that is, the languages are –Tense. Presumably this means that the finite verbs (which the kids will take to be not marked by tense) will not be able to raise to V2 (this follows Legate and Yang's ideas about the word order/finiteness correlation). Thus the prediction that verbs in this language can't raise to C will be reinforced for young children. Finite verbs will have to stay in position, leading to many errors of production again, I know of no calculations of learning of V2 in this theory, but its properties don't appear to satisfy the empirical constraints.

Chinese on this score – rather the paradigms (or more likely, the lexical entries for the morphemes) differ. Now, there may be some deep syntactic understanding that says Chinese is different but the paper advances no ideas on this score.[64]

So far as I can see, the model in Legate and Yang doesn't explain the central property of the OI stage – that there is a finiteness/word order correlation. Legate and Yang are aware that the proposal *must* explain this correlation; otherwise it is simply inadequate at the start. The fundamental question is, how does the variational theory predict the finiteness/word order correlation, e.g. in an SOV/V2 language, a finite verb in 2nd position and the OI in final position? See (7) to see how robust this correlation is. They offer two possibilities. Here's what the authors say about the first possibility (p. 338): "Under our framework, a straightforward way to account for this pattern is to assume that, as a matter of UG principle, [+Tense] grammar is a necessary – though not sufficient – condition for raising the verb."[65]

What does this mean? If a child has a –Tense grammar, the verb can't be raised in that grammar.[66] But remember that the child has a mixture of + and –Tense grammars. So we have to consider both cases. And remember, crucially, that there is "ambiguous" evidence, evidence that the *child*, the *learner* considers to be ambiguous. Now, to consider whether this idea of Legate and Yang's can explain the pattern of morphology/word order correlation, we have to decide which meaning of the Tense parameter the authors have in mind, because they each predict something different. Let's consider both possibilities.

First, suppose that Chinese is radically missing Tense; there simply is no Tense in the phrase-marker. Thus when a child in the OI stage in English/French/Dutch, etc., selects a –Tense grammar, Tense is radically missing from the phrase-marker. Now consider a verb form that the child hears that is "ambiguous" for Tense, for example, *werk* in Dutch, the 1st singular present tense form of *werken/work*. When the OI stage child hears *werk* she will sometimes (according to weights) give it a –Tense analysis; that's exactly what the variational theory claims. This will increase the weight of the –Tense value and decrease the weight of the +Tense parameter. Now, let's imagine the child *producing* a sentence, trying to produce the 1st singular value of *werken*. But since the child's – Tense grammar accepted *werk* as a –Tense verb, we know that the child can produce *werk* (presumably according to weights) as a –Tense verb.

---

[64] In fact, on p. 338, the authors write, "…it would nevertheless commit us to the position that verbs do not undergo movement to Tense or similar functional nodes in [–Tense] grammars such as Chinese – which at least one of us not comfortable with." Given this consideration, it would seem that it may be only a question of how each verb is spelled out (given the inflectional features that drive movement) that is under consideration. Why then, is there a "parameter" of + or – Tense? Everytime there is variation, it doesn't mean a "parameter" has to be learned. Rather, there might be a lexicon that has to be learned. E.g., how to spell out features. It is possible that the fact that Chinese never spells out Tense, and English sometimes does is a parameter, but it would have to be argued for. What syntactic phenomena follow from the proposal?

[65] The authors (p.c. to Jill de Villiers) say that they prefer the second possibility, which we will soon discuss.

[66] We'll ignore the fact that there are languages (e.g. Italian, Icelandic) in which infinitives raise.

Thus, by the proposal they give that +Tense is necessary for verb raising, the form *werk* in this case will not raise, but will stay in final position.

This is a strong misprediction, as the work we've already reviewed shows. Finite verbs always raise, including verbs that Legate and Yang consider "ambiguous", e.g. a pure stem (consider French *parl* for another common example).[67]

Suppose that one attempted to say, no, the child *knows* that *werk has* Tense, that it would be *werken* if it were untensed, so the child will always raise *werk*. But that proposal is incompatible with the assumption that is crucial to the variational model as presented, namely the assumption that the child does *not* know that *werk must* mark +Tense. I see no way out of this contradiction.

On the other hand, suppose that the Tense parameter means only that –Tense languages don't ever *morphologically* mark Tense, that there aren't two distinctive verb inflections marking different tenses. But Tense (the features, and/or the projection, depending on the model) exists in the phrase-marker. Now consider the proposal that the finiteness/word order correlation is predicted by +Tense being necessary for verb raising. The child wants to produce the 1st singular present form of *werken*. The phrase-marker has +Tense even in a –Tense grammar. If the child chooses *werk* as the form, it will raise to C, correctly. If the child chooses *werken* as the form, it too will raise to C! Whether a form raises or not, doesn't depend on this assumption, on whether it's a + or – Tense grammar, since Tense appears in the phrase-marker in either case. This prediction is also seriously wrong; as we can see in (7) non-finite verbs essentially never raise in the OI stage.

Thus there seems to be no way, under either of the possible interpretations of the Tense parameter, that the central correlation of the OI stage, that between finiteness and word order, can be derived via this suggestion.

Now, let's turn to the second possibility the authors advance for predicting the finiteness/word order correlation in children in their framework, the possibility that they prefer (see footnote 66). They write (p. 338), "Another way of accounting for [the correlation between word order and finiteness in French children – KW] more closely follows the spirit of probabilistic and quantitative learning advanced in the present article." Basically they suggest that a child learns the correlation by observing that (p. 38) "Tense is far more likely to be inflected when the verb is high – as indicated by its position relative to negative and VP-level adverbs – than otherwise, and indeed, they very quickly learn that the probability of the former is close to 1." They do the calculations for the input to one child and show, unsurprisingly, that verbs that are unambiguously high (e.g. to the left of negation) are much more likely to have unambiguous tense than a lack of tense marking.[68]

---

[67] Furthermore, suppose that the child selects the +Tense value while producing a sentence. That means that the structure contains Tense. What form should the child use on the verb? Why not the infinitival form? After all, the child may consider the infinitival form (with an infinitival suffix) as "ambiguous" for tense marking. What in the theory says that this won't happen? I don't see any consideration, since the theory of ambiguity seems to only say that a verb is ambiguous if and only if there is no suffixal marking on it. Since the infinitive has such an inflection, it should sometimes raise (as often as finite verbs?), again strongly contrary to fact.

[68] I assume that they mean a lack of tense marking. They say, "rewards" [–Tense.]

In other words, hearing finite verbs (mostly finite aux it turns out) before *pas*, etc. is supposed to lead the child to "learn" that finite verbs appear high. This all sounds very plausible. But it's totally inconsistent with the Legate and Yang model. Plausibility isn't at issue. The classical OI model has a simple immediate explanation of the correlation of tense and verb position. The kid has learned the parameter value. It seems plausible in the classical OI model to say that verb raising in French is learned by finite verbs appearing before pas and in similar constructions. But Legate and Yang cannot treat the data as resulting from the correct setting of the verb to Tense parameter because in order to obtain the OI effect they have assumed that kids don't know whether "ambiguous" verbs are tensed or not, so that these ambiguous verbs might be treated as non-finite by the child and thus be wrong information for the learning of the verb to tense parameter, and lead to errors in the correlation of word order and finiteness. We'll explain further.

What does it mean for Legate and Yang to say that a kid learns that finite verbs are high? Which part of their model allows them to learn this? So far as I can tell, it's not something one can learn in Yang's parametric model. Yang's model has no such place for learning. How should a child search? What should a child think? What's the representation? If it's not a parameter it's not in the model, so far as I can tell, so this second idea of Legate and Yang's must be something outside the model.

Let's recall Legate and Yang's basic explanation of the OI stage. Kids don't know whether French is a +Tense or –Tense language, that is, both values have fairly high weights. So when they produce OI's it is because they have chosen for that production a –Tense grammar; that's the explicit assumption. So imagine a French child in the OI stage, one who has a fairly high weight of –Tense for French.

The child chooses a –Tense grammar sometimes. Since she thinks that *parl* could in fact be –Tense (that's the basis for much of their explanation of the OI stage in French), she produces *parl*. Now, suppose that the sentence is negative, it's got *pas* as well as *parl*. Since the child has chosen a –Tense grammar, the child who "learns" the correlation between tense and height will produce *pas parl*. This is exactly what doesn't happen. The problem with Legate and Yang's argument, of course, is that their heuristic explanation of the learning of the finiteness/word order correlation fails to take into account their own foundational assumption – that the child doesn't know during this stage whether or not the language displays Tense.

Consider yet another issue in the heuristic explanation of the correlation that Legate and Yang propose. In addition to verbs that precede negation or adverbs, they take verbs that precede the subject to be instances of "high" verbs in the input, and say that these too will help the child learn that high verbs are finite. (They count these in their Table 8 of input forms). Once again, the lack of cross-linguistic considerations lead these thoughts into trouble, if one truly wants to account for the learning of parameter values. Consider any language in which verbs don't raise to Tense but *do* raise to Complementizer (C), e.g. auxiliaries in English questions or certain Mainland Scandinavian languages in all sentences (depending on grammatical assumption, perhaps just in non-subject-first sentences). If a child learning one of these languages took Legate and Yang's heuristic proposal as the basis for learning finiteness/word order correlations, the wrong ones would be produced.

E.g. in the languages in which the verb does not raise to Tense, but does raise to C, in an embedded (thus no V2) clause with negation, the negative element precedes the verb, contra French. But Legate and Yang's proposal would have the child producing the finite verb before negation. The only way to reasonably handle these phenomena is to have the child's output depend on her current setting of the parameters. This is exactly what Legate and Yang reject by implicitly assuming for this data that only one parameter is relevant, their Tense parameter, and ignoring the question of the setting of the verb to Tense parameter.

There is no parametric explanation of the "learning" of the finiteness/word order correlation in Legate and Yang. Rather, the kids are simply assumed to use the correlation in the input data of "unambiguously" tensed forms and "high position" and "unambiguously" untensed forms and "low position" to "learn" the central fact of the OI stage But Legate and Yang do not in any way relate this to the learning of a parameter, and given our discussion, there is no way that they can. So far as I can tell, what Legate and Yang must mean is that children in the OI stage don't produce finite verbs after *pas* because they have learned the parameter value of Verb to Tense. Rather, on their view, kids learn statistical correlations and reproduce them, independent of any kind of grammar, independent of the parameters.[69] So that's the theory we're dealing with: an empiricist-style learning of statistical correlations in the input that are produced in some kind of mimicking fashion. Of course it can't work, for reasons we've discussed, including the fact that if this were the correct theory, then children wouldn't produce OI's, since they almost never hear them.

It's clear why the model fails; it doesn't understand that the developmental pattern of the morphosyntactic parameters, on the one hand, and the requirement for Tense in a structure, are completely different. That's the problem that has to be solved. To attempt to say that it's all one problem misses the essential discoveries that have been made.

One interesting feature of Legate and Yang's second idea to explain the finiteness/word order correlation under discussion here is that it makes central use of the "unambiguous" finiteness of the finite auxiliaries in French. The idea is that since these (e.g. ai/am) are "unambiguous", the child will make use of them in "learning" the correlation between finiteness and word order. This is ironic, because it is exactly this lack of ambiguity that Yang's learning model doesn't allow to be used to learn the Tense parameter. Since there are so many unambiguous auxiliaries that the child hears, why doesn't the child simply use this knowledge to quickly conclude that she is learning a +Tense grammar? The model has to find a way to not allow this to

---

[69] Legate and Yang must be aware that their explanation of this central, strong empirical result is not parametric, but rather statistical and independent of the parameter system, because they choose to give it a different explanation than their parametric explanations. In other words, Verb to Tense is *not* learned as a parameter value in their system, at least not during the OI stage. Of course, we have seen in the text that the parametric explanation predicts the data correctly and their statistical explanation doesn't.

happen, so the model says, ambiguous forms can slow down learning, since the bad value can be reinforced by hearing an ambiguous form. But why don't such ambiguous forms then slow down the learning of the verb to Tense parameter? Of course they will. Quite possibly that's why Legate and Yang don't try to solve the existence of the finiteness/word order correlation by assuming it's the result of the learning of the verb to Tense parameter; Yang's learning model would slow down the learning of this parameter, causing errors in the correlation. Possibly Legate and Yang are aware of this inconsistency and that is why they choose to treat the child's beautifully precise production of the finiteness/word order correlation not as a question of parameter learning but separately, as something statistical laid on top of the parametric theory, a statistical observation on patterns of sentences, unrelated to the grammar. Besides the fact that this is a stipulation completely out of the spirit of the learning model they are working with, it doesn't capture the data.

The treatment of the verb to Tense parameter is another instance of how the Yang model has not been tested by considering more than one parameter at a time. Legate and Yang have a slow learning of parameter value explanation of the OI stage (it's because kids learn the Tense parameter so slowly), but they never put this together with the question of the learning of the verb to Tense parameter; as I said before, neither in Legate and Yang nor in Yang's other works that we have reviewed is a computation done of the learning of two syntactic parameters at a time. So in this case, the question of why the central finding of the OI stage, namely the correlation of word order and finiteness, is tacked on as an afterthought, not as the result of the learning model being applied to the learning of the Tense and the verb to Tense parameters at the same time. If the computation were done, ti would run into the empirical problems that we have outlined.

It's worth noting that the earliest discussion of the OI stage (Wexler 1990, 1992, 1994) understood that one could speculate that learning was one candidate for a process that caused movement out of the OI stage. The first section of the paper is entitled "The Problem of *s* in English". The idea that third singular *s* could be forced in by learning was considered. But the paper argued on the basis of much data of many different kinds that this didn't seem to be what was going on. The problems raised by the "learning" analysis of the OI stage are part of the reason that OI phenomena have become so central to the study of language acquisition. The answers to the developmental problems are not psychology business as usual, some mixture of associationism, stamping in, long, arduous, hard learning. They are much more cognitive, linguistic, representational, brain-oriented.

Legate and Yang criticize maturational proposals, saying: "Biological maturation, which presumably takes place largely independent of linguistic data, is one possibility (Rizzi 1994; Wexler 1994, 1998). This proposal is not entirely satisfactory, however, as the mechanisms of biological maturation of linguistic ability are not currently well understood. Moreover, biological maturation abandons the Continuity Hypothesis, the hypothesis that children's competence system is not qualitatively different from adults, which has served well in the investigation of child language and cognitive development."

It is a very old argument against the existence of an innate UG that the biological mechanism is not known.[70] We hypothesize and argue for UG on the basis of computational level arguments. The non-existence of biological mechanism does not lead us to say that we must have a learning theory mechanism rather than an innate UG. If one accepts this inference from the best evidence for UG, then exactly the same considerations show that there is no conceptual argument against maturation.[71]

As for the second argument, well, maturation has a long tradition in the study of psychology, and there are many well-known problems of cognitive development that might benefit, and often have benefited, from a maturational argument. The term "continuity", in fact, comes from the study of language acquisition, not from cognitive development. The concept of total non-change over time in linguistic abilities might better be called "Rigidity", as Wexler (1999) suggested, and it's not clear it has served so well. The maturational hypothesis in this case, UCC, is that there is a limitation on computational abilities that dies away under genetic guidance. For many phenomena, maturation (UG-based maturation, in the sense of Borer and Wexler (1987)), has served better than Rigidity.

The authors also point out that there is variation in the production of OI's; it's not all or none even within a given child. But of course, as has been argued (e.g. Wexler 2003), maturation is not all or none. A child doesn't go from having no tooth to having a fully grown tooth instantly. Maturation is biological, and we expect some variation in development, some continuous growth. The UCC dies away over time. That is what maturational theory would expect. It's like any other maturation.

Ultimately, the argument has to be empirical. This section has considered in some detail a particular learning-theoretic account, to ask whether it is adequate to the task of explaining the OI phenomena. I would like to end on a positive note, repeating what I said at the outset of this discussion. Legate and Yang deserve credit for attempting to be more precise and linguistically detailed than other empiricist accounts of the OI stage. It's very helpful to see what kind of a theory must be invoked to slow down the learning process. The conclusion one comes to after a deep immersion in the developmental psycholinguistic literature is that the Principles

---

[70] It might even be said that the genetics of development of OI's has made more progress (though only a bit) so far, than the genetics of UG, and might be an avenue to help us discover the genetics of UG. For example, if we find the gene(s) (on chromosome 19q? (Falcaro et al. (2008)) that are responsible for the existence or withering away of UCC, we might have a link to genes that help to specify how syntactic feature-checking mechanisms work. Just speculation for now, but we can't take the lack of of a biological mechanism for UG to be an argument against its existence. Ditto for maturation.

[71] One might also point out that we have no knowledge of the biological mechanism for learning, so that UG, maturation, learning are all equal on this score. Failing any physical evidence, we must go with the best computational level explanation, which is what linguistics and psycholinguistics do as standard business.

and Parameters framework is on the right track in concluding that the learning model makes parameter-setting straightforward and relatively easy. The problem is to discover a learning theory that does exactly this.

3.5 Be-Omission

We have concentrated on OI's in main verbs, the appearance of an overt infinitival where a finite verb appears in the adult. Since the beginning of studies of the OI stage, e.g. Wexler (1993), however, it has been realized that there are other constructions that show the effects of the OI stage. In particular, the omission of auxiliaries and copulas has been taken to be OI phenomenon. "Optional Infinitive" is a name that describes perhaps the most striking phenomenon of the stage, but the phenomena that characterize the stage go considerably beyond the appearance of infinitivals where they shouldn't be.

Be is hugely omitted in the OI stage.[72] For example, in English, a study of 40 3 year-old typically developing children (Rice and Wexler 1996) showed the proportion of use of *be* in obligatory contexts as 64% in an elicitation task and 70% in spontaneous production. In German, the auxiliaries *sein (be)* and *haben (have)*, both used with the perfect tense are often omitted, leaving only the participle.

There is a total consensus in the literature that auxiliaries and copulas are often omitted in the OI stage. One other remarkable fact exists (I believe first pointed out in Wexler (1993)). Copulas and auxiliaries are often omitted but they never appear as infinitives. Although young children learning standard English will readily produce forms with *be* missing like (30a), they essentially never produce forms like (30b).

(30) a. Mary going
     b. #Mary be going[73]

---

[72] Of course, not just forms of *be* are omitted. Other auxiliaries are omitted also. In English, the major other auxiliary is *have*, used in the perfect. Since English-speaking young children (especially American children as opposed to British) hardly use the perfect during the age-range of the OI-stage, we don't have much of a chance to observe *have* omission. However, *have* omission is broadly seen in other languages, where the perfect is used as the simple past, for example, German. There has been discussion of *modal* omission also, although to my knowledge, strong and clear quantitative results on this topic aren't available.

[73] The few examples of forms like (30b) that are observed are forms where *be* is clearly a kind of main verb, not an auxiliary, sometimes meaning something like *act like*, as in, *You be Superman and I be Batman*, meaning, you act as Superman and I'll act as Batman. It doesn't mean *You are Superman and I am Batman*. Also, some readers might relate (30b) to forms that occur in some varieties of African American English. But the meanings would be quite different. (30b) in AAE relates to particular relations between tense and aspect; the form might look the same, but it's not an example of an OI.

Grammatical Computation in the Optional Infinitive Stage 107

First, let's review a small amount of data. Tables (31a–c) are from Becker (2000) as reported in Schutze (2004, his Table 2–4), for three children between 2;0 and 2;6:

(31) a. ***Be* production in finite contexts (Becker** 2000)

Child	Overt *be*	Omitted *be*	Omission rate
Nina	231	267	54%
Peter	579	286	33%
Naomi	350	189	35%

b. **Form of overt *be* in finite contexts (Becker** 2000)

Child	Finite	Infinitive
Nina	231	0
Peter	579	0
Naomi	349	1

c. **Finiteness on main verbs (Becker** 2000)

Child	Inflected	Uninflected	OI rate
Nina	56	282	83%
Peter	178	117	40%
Naomi	61	49	45%

(31a) shows the usual substantial omission rates for finite *be*, whereas (31b) shows that there is at most one (debatable in Becker's discussion) overt infinitival *be* in the same files. (31c) shows that the omission rate for finite *be* roughly parallels the omission rates for main verbs.

To show the results in a larger study of 400 children, Fig. 1 graphs data from Rice and Wexler (2001) with 50 children in each of 8 ages groups at 6 month intervals.[74] The data came from a stratified sample across the US, taking care to represent children of diverse socio-economic and geographic backgrounds with both genders equally represented. The curves of finiteness for main verbs and existence of required finite *be* seem to closely parallel each other over a 4-year range (2;0–6;11).

Wexler (1993) proposed that in forms like (30a), Tense was missing (the Tense Omission hypothesis applied to them). He further proposed that *be* is only inserted to "pick up" TNS features; it has no meaning. It follows that when there are no tense features (TNS is omitted), there will be no *be*. Thus (30a) and not (30b) is produced. This became something like the standard hypothesis of why auxiliaries are omitted; they are only there to spell out (or bind) morphosyntactic features like TNS and AGR, so that when these features aren't in the p-m (in an OI), no form of *be*, even the infinitival (30b), is produced. The idea is that if *be* isn't needed, it can't be inserted; do the least that is necessary. Wexler noted that in small clauses in the adult grammar, for example, *I made him leave*, there is no INFL in the small clause *him leave*, and thus no need to insert *be*, and thus no possibility of *be*: *I saw him (*be) leaving*. We'll call Wexler's suggestion the *pleonastic view*. The idea is that *be* is pleonastic; it has no meaning so is only inserted when necessary for the features.

---

[74] The graph in Fig. 1 was made by Carson Schutze, and produced in Schutze (2004).

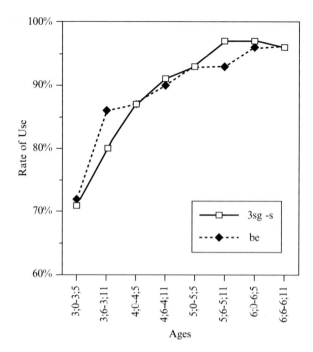

Fig. 1 Rate of production of 3rd person singular -*s* and finite *be* in obligatory contexts for samples of 50 children in each age group (Adapted from Rice and Wexler 2001)

Truncation adopted Wexler's pleonastic view also (Rizzi 1993). If an OI like (30a) is, say, a VP, then there are no TNS or AGR features for *be* to bind, and thus no need to insert *be* and thus *be* isn't inserted.

Richie Kayne (pc) pointed out to me that the pleonastic view runs into trouble. English contains sentences with infinitival *be* like (32).

(32) a. I want to be happy
 b. *I want to happy
 c. *I want happy

In (32a), *be* doesn't appear to be spelling out any TNS features in the embedded clause. Yet *be* can't be omitted. (32b) and (32c) are strongly ungrammatical. Infinitival *be* can be necessary. Why don't children produce infinitival *be* instead of deleting it?

The solution comes in a trenchant analysis by Carson Schutze entitled, *Why Nonfinite Be Is Not Omitted While Finite Be Is* (BU 1994 Proceedings). First, Schutze considers two alternative explanations of *be* omission: (a) an explanation as Wexler (1993) first proposed it, following from the *Tense Omission Hypothesis (TOH)* as opposed to (b) a theory that says *be* is omitted because it lacks meaning (the *semantic vacuity hypothesis, SVH*). Either TOH (or ATOM, of course, a more modern version, or UCC) will predict omission of finite *be*. Schutze points out that in cases where *be should* be infinitival (like (32) from his paper), TOH won't predict omission of *be* (because nonfinite *be* stands in a different relation to finiteness than finite *be* does – we'll come back to this). But SVH predicts that infinitival *be* as in (32) should be omitted in (32) according to SVH (as Schutze argues, if anything nonfinite *be* is *more* semantically vacuous than finite *be* – nonfinite *be* doesn't even display tense features). Thus SVH predicts more omission of nonfinite *be* than of finite *be*.

(33) a. Mary's gonna be nurse.
 b. He'll be coming soon.

This observation leads Schutze to study the omission of nonfinite *be*, the first such study so far as I know. He studies the productions of several children, and they yield consistent results. Here is data from one child, Anne, directly from Schutze's paper (Table 5).

(34) **Distribution of *be* forms – Anne (Theakston et al. 2000), Files 7–31 (2;0.15–2;8.24)**

Context	Form	
	Overt	Omitted
Finite	1,262	430 (21%)
Nonfinite	38	1 (3%)

Anne omits 21% of required finite *be*'s but only 3% (1 instance) of required nonfinite *be*'s. Examples of required nonfinite *be* that Anne produces are in (35):

(35) Correct production of nonfinite be
 a. they should be in here
 b. that one wants be up there?
 c. that's gonna be driver

As one reads sentences like (33), it is easy to admit that intuition would agree – it seems distinctly unchildlike to say *they should in here*. Perhaps it's an after-the-fact intuition; at any rate, the data are strikingly clear.

Here's one more table from Schutze's Table 6, from another child.

(36) **Distribution of *be* forms – Aran (Theakston et al. 2000), Files 16–34 (2;4.20–2;10.28)**

Context	From	
	Overt	Omitted
Finite	1,262	323(20%)
Nonfinite	98	0

Aran omits 20% of finite *be* and no nonfinite *be*. There are 98 instances of overt nonfinite *be*. The data are striking.

Schutze's observations of the nonexistence of omitted nonfinite *be* is a major discovery, a crucial empirical element in the puzzle of *be*-omission. Clearly, the semantic vacuity hypothesis can't explain the data; rather, the correct explanation must be some form of the Tense Omission Hypothesis. What is it? I already pointed out, Wexler's idea that *be* was only required to "pick up" tense and agreement features accounts for much of the data but isn't quite true, since nonfinite *be* exists. Even more strikingly, it cannot account for why nonfinite *be* is not omitted by the child.

Before I go on to describe Schutze's solution, we should take a moment to observe the progress of the field.. We have a puzzle at an exquisitely precise level of detail. Just the existence of the puzzle is evidence for the advance of the science.

Even better, there is a solution. Here are the central assumptions of Schutze's analysis, based on a great deal of syntactic work (see Schutze's paper for references). Much of (37) is a direct quote:

(37) a. All forms of *be* are verbs (they don't arise in INFL)
 b. The "V Requirement": Forms of *be* surface "due to a formal requirement that clauses have an element of category V; when the substantive predicate is not of that category (AP, PP, NP) *be* must step in."
 c. The V Requirement is imposed by Tense (subject to cross- linguistic variation).

Briefly applied to the English data we have been studying here, it's clear that English has the V Requirement. When Tense is in the structure, a verb must exist in the structure. When there is no other main verb, *be* must be inserted.[75] Note that these assumptions account for nonfinite *be* as well as finite *be*. Under the standard assumption that infinitival structures have (infinitival) tense, there *is* tense in infinitives, and this Tense forces a verb to exist in the structure. If there is no other main verb, *be* must exist, as in structures like (33).

Given the Tense Omission Hypothesis, the pattern of children's results now become clear. In the OI stage, Tense is often omitted. When Tense is omitted, there is no requirement for a main verb, and *be* doesn't not have to step in as the main verb, even if there is no other main verb. Thus we have *be* omission for finite *be*.

Consider now infinitival *be*. These occur in "selected" infinitivals, that is, following "modals, auxiliaries, semiauxiliaries such as *better*, *gotta*, *sposta*, main verbs like *want*, *try*, *let*, and the infinitival morpheme *to*". In each case, the item that selects the infinitival is in Tense. That is, the existence of a modal or auxiliary or semiauxiliary indicates that Tense is in the structure. In Schutze's example, *you will be the fireman*, for example, the modal *will* occupies Tense. Thus Tense exists in the structure. When Tense is in the structure, it requires a main verb. Modals and auxiliaries are not main verbs; they cannot satisfy the requirement. If no other main verb exists, then *be* must be inserted. Thus *you will the fireman* is ungrammatical because Tense (*will* is in Tense) requires that there be a verb; *be* plays that role. The child knows these requirements. Thus the child will not omit nonfinite *be*.[76]

---

[75] Small clauses like *I made him leave* are called "small" because they are assumed to have no inflectional functional categories, in particular no Tense category. Since Tense does not exist, there is no V Requirement in small clauses. Thus *be* is not required in small clauses; therefore, it doesn't exist in small clauses.

[76] Schutze points out that there might be cases where Tense is omitted in the embedded clause, and thus *be* could be omitted. E.g. in *John will be late* (the "target structure"), the child might omit Tense, and thus no *will* and no *be* would be inserted, and *John late* would surface. It would be hard to know from CHILDES data, however, if that were the proper analysis of these structures – they might arise from e.g. *John is late*. Thus the best cases are the ones Schutze studies, where there is the surface existence of Tense indicated by the modal, or by the existence of *to*. An elicitation study, though difficult, might provide data, that is, an elicitation of sentences where the most natural form would be something like *John will be late*. If the child provides *John late* to such an elicitation, it would confirm that Tense omission and *be* omission were going on.

What is the nature of this solution? There is a syntactic principle that requires that *be* be inserted whenever Tense exists. The fact that children don't omit infinitival *be* means that children in the OI stage know this syntactic principle, just as they know other relevant syntactic principles.

Interestingly, there are many languages that do not require *be* insertion in copula constructions. Schutze discusses Arabic. He points out that Benmamoun (2000) provides good evidence that Tense exists in Arabic copulas, but that there is no requirement to add a copula. (Benmamoun also argues that it isn't simply the case that the copula is null). To the extent that these conclusions are right, the requirement that Tense implies the existence of a verb must be parametric. It holds in English, but not in Arabic, for example.

To the extent that these arguments are correct, we have to take the data on English to be support for yet another instance of *VEPS* (Wexler 1998). English-speaking children know that their language requires *be* when there is tense in the structure. (Otherwise, why would they never omit infinitival *be*?) It would be good to have evidence from a language in which the alternative value of the parameter holds, e.g. Arabic. The prediction of VEPS of course is young Arabic children won't insert the copula in sentences where it isn't inserted in the adult language. If we find evidence like this in some null copula language, we will have evidence that both values of the parameter are set at very young ages. An analysis of Arabic or a similar language asking whether children incorrectly insert the copula would be valuable.

How would children set a parameter which states a yes/no answer to the question: does Tense require a verb?[77] In a language like English, they hear *be* in copulas. All the child has to note is that *be* exists in the structure, *be* seems to be a verb (fairly straight-forward given inflectional features and word order), *be* has no other contentful verbal meaning and that Tense exists in the structure. The child should then make the straight-forward computation that *be* might be a verb required by Tense. Othewise, what is its function? Similarly for the inverse for languages like Arabic. Predicative sentences with Tense exist,[78] but nothing in the sentence is a verb. Then the parameter must be set at *no – Tense does not require a verb*.

We thus have yet more evidence for young children's (as young as less than 2) knowledge of syntactic principles. And more evidence that this knowledge doesn't come from their experience of the language. Children omit finite *be* a huge amount of time, despite no model for this in the input. It is counter-input. So one might be tempted to say, well, then, it must be some kind of processing or other consideration, perhaps the *Semantic Vacuity Hypothesis*. But children' don't omit infinitival

---

[77] Schutze considers a potentially more fundamental way of deriving the cross-linguistic differences; the parameter has to do with how event variables are bound. This shouldn't make a difference in the argument here, except that there might even potentially be more evidence available to the learner about which value of the parameter is correct. The suggestions I have made here should be fairly easy and formal for the learner; thus they may be the way the parameter is set even if it relates to the binding of event variables.

[78] Assuming either that all languages have Tense in root structures, or assuming that Arabic has Tense in predicative structures because it has tense in other (verbal) structures.

be. So it can't be that. The pattern of children's linguistic behavior follows from principles; they make large errors of a very precise kind. Some non-existent input structures are produced extensively by children, others aren't. The model must explain the data. If we take the data on *be*-omission seriously (and the regularity of the data is stunning), we are left with no alternative but to assume that children know the nature of linguistic principles and the potential variants (parameters) and, as in other central cases of morphosyntactic parameters that have been studied, learn the relevant parameters early and well. The errors must follow from some kind of genetically determined specification, there is no alternative hypothesis that has been proposed, after many years of study, that can explain this type of behavior. The empirical evidence informs us that we must conclude that genetically-specified development takes place. *Be* omission provides yet one more rich area of phenomena that leads to this conclusion.

4 Some Omitted Topics

There are a large number of topics in the OI literature that we have not been able to cover. Here are some of them.

***Object phenomena*:** Most of the phenomena we have studied involve the "subject:" functional projections, agreement, tense and related processes. There are many phenomena that occur in the OI stage involving lower projections, projections involving the VP and object arguments. Some of these have been claimed to follow from the same principles which lead to the OI phenomena. Such considerations lend further support to the computational, UCC analyses, since Truncation and other structural approaches relating to the top of the phrase-marker won't be able to predict the phenomena. The phenomena include:

(a) Clitic omission. Wexler (2000) argued that the phenomenon of object clitic omission (e.g. Hamann 1997; Jakubowicz et al. 1997) followed from the UCC, so that it was another result of the "OI" stage. In fact, the UCC also predicts cross-linguistic variation in whether clitic omission occurs or not (Tsakali and Wexler 2004; Wexler et al. 2004a, b; Gavarro et al. in press).
(b) Baek and Wexler (2008) argue that well-known errors in the development of short-form negation in Korean follows from the UCC, that it's an OI-stage phenomenon.
(c) Wexler (2004) argues that the failure of young children to always scramble objects that should be scrambled (Schaeffer 2000) is the result of the UCC, so another OI-stage phenomenon.

The interpretation of OI's: Modal Meanings? It had always been understood that OI's had a range of temporal meanings, including finite meanings, present and past tense meanings, future means, and modal meanings, whereas finite verbs had only finite meanings. Hoekstra and Hyams (1998, 1999), however, claimed that OI's are strictly modal in many languages, e.g. in Dutch and German, whereas they aren't modal in English. Hyams (2007) derives this result from considerations involving events and tense in the different languages. However, the empirical result seems quite shaky.

Behrens (1993) finds non-modal OI's existing alongside modal OI's in German. Blom et al. (1998), Blom and Wijnen (2000) and Blom (2002) do the same for German.

It is difficult to determine interpretation of OI's in natural production data. Exactly what did the child mean to say? This is a much more difficult question than the form of the verb or word order. Comprehension experiments thus are very important. Schoenenberger, Pierce, Wijnen and Wexler (1995) did such an experiment on English and argue from it that there is free interpretation of the modal.

Similarly, Hyams (2007) argues that OI's fairly strictly have eventive interpretations. The empirical basis is mostly the work of Wijnen (1998). This is probably a somewhat more accurate generalization, though not completely true. Even in Hyams own work, for example, possessive *have*, a stative, non-eventive work, exists as an OI.

There is no room to give fair treatment to these unresolved questions about interpretation. My own view is that we need a great deal more research, and possibly new methods, to determine the status of claims about interpretation.

OI's in comprehension: The vast majority of research concerning OI's uses production data. It is difficult to do comprehension experiments in children at the young OI age. However, Rice et al. (1999) had young children perform grammaticality judgments on OI's, e.g. "*Mary go*", "bad agreement" sentences in which the subjects didn't agree with the verb (e.g. *I goes*) and grammatical sentences (*Mary goes*). The children accepted the OI's more than they did the bad agreement sentences but less than they did the grammatical sentences. This relative acceptance of OI's indicates that the phenomenon is not restricted to production. We might add that there is even now some beginning work on which brain regions are involved in comprehending OI's (Kovelman et al. 2009).

5 Conclusion

The discovery of the OI stage in early syntactic development has lead to a great leap in our understanding of the early development of syntax. A thriving field of research exists built around a large set of interrelated phenomena. This research is important not only for our understanding the facts of development but also for how linguistic development will relate to biology. We can look forward to continuing surprises, as we plumb the amazing ability of a child to develop language.

References

Aldridge, M. 1989. *The acquisition of INFL*. Bloomington: IULC.
Alexiadou, A., and E. Anagnostopoulou. 1998. Parametrizing AGR: Word order, V- Movement and EPP-checking. *Natural Language and Linguistic Theory* 16: 491–539.
Alexiadou, A., and E. Anagnostopoulou. 1999. Raising without infinitives and the nature of agreement. In *Proceedings of WCCFL 18*. A version of this article appeared in Dimensions of Movement.

Avrutin, S. 1997. EVENTS as units of discourse representation in root infinitives. *MIT Occasional Papers in Linguistics* 12: 65–91.

Babyonyshev, M., J. Ganger, D. Pesetsky, and K. Wexler. 2001. The maturation of grammatical principles: Evidence from Russian unaccusatives. *Linguistic Inquiry* 32: 1–44.

Baek, J., and K. Wexler. 2008. The acquisition of negation in Korean. In P. Li General ed. *Handbook of East Asian psycholinguistics, Part III*, ed. Korean Chungmin Lee, Youngjin Kim and Greg Simpson, London: Cambridge University Press.

Barbosa, P. 1995. Null subjects. PhD diss., MIT, Cambridge, MA.

Bar-Shalom, E., and W. Snyder. 1997. Root infinitives in child Russian: A comparison with Italian and Polish. In *Proceedings of the GALA '97 Conference on Language Acquisition*, ed. A. Sorace, C. Heycock, and R. Shillcock, 22–27. Edinburgh: University of Edinburgh.

Becker, M. 2000. The development of the copula in child English: The lightness of be. PhD diss., University of California, Los Angeles.

Behrens, H. 1993. *Temporal reference in German child language: Form and function of early verb use*. Doctoral dissertation, University of Amsterdam.

Benmamoun, E. 2000. *The feature structure of functional categories: An essay in comparative Arabic syntax*. New York: Oxford University Press. Beveridge, W.I.B. 1949. *The art of scientific investigation*. New York: Vintage.

Beveridge, W.I.B. 1949. The art of scientific investigation. New York: Vintage.

Bishop, D.V.M., C.V. Adams, and C.F. Norbury. 2006. Distinct genetic influences on grammar and phonological short-term memory deficits: Evidence from 6-year-old twins. *Genes, Brain and Behavior* 5: 158–169.

Blom, E. 2002. On the use and interpretation of root infinitives in early child Dutch. Ms., University of Utrecht, Utrecht, The Netherlands.

Blom, E., and F. Wijnen. 2000. 'How Dutch children's root infinitives become modal.' In: *Proceedings BUCLD* 24: 128–139.

Blom, E., F. Wijnen, and S. Gillis. 1998. Modal infinitives in the speech of Dutch mothers and their children. In *English as a human language. To honour Louis Goossens*, ed. J. Van der Auwera, F. Durieux, and L. Lejeune, 12–21. München: LINCOM Europa.

Borer, H., and K. Wexler. 1987. The maturation of syntax. In *Parameter setting*, ed. T. Roeper and E. Williams, 123–172. Dordrecht: Reidel.

Borer, H., and K. Wexler. 1992. Bi-unique relations and the maturation of grammatical principles. *National Language & Linguistic Theory* 10: 147–187.

Boser, K., B. Lust, L. Santelmann, and J. Whitman. 1992. The syntax of V-2 in early child German grammar: The strong continuity hypothesis. In *Proceedings of the Northeastern Linguistic Society* (NELS), vol. 22, 51–66.

Bromberg, H. S, and K. Wexler. 1995. Null subjects in child wh-questions. In *Papers in Language Processing and Acquisition*, ed. C. T. Schütze, J. Ganger and K. Broihier. Cambridge, MA: MIT Working Papers in Linguistics, vol. 26, 221–247.

Brown, R. 1973. *A First language: The early stages*. Cambridge, MA: Harvard University Press.

Cable, S. 2005. The optional infinitive stage in Afrikaans: Evidence for phonologically neutralized rich agreement. In *Plato's Problems: Papers on Language Acquisition*, ed. Aniiko Csirmaz, Andrea Gualmini, and Andrew Nevins. Cambridge, MA: MIT Working Papers in Linguistics.

Caprin, C., and M.T. Guasti. 2009. The acquisition of morphosyntax in Italian: A cross-sectional study *Applied Psycholinguistics* 30: 23–52.

Chomsky, N. 1965. Aspects of the Theory of Syntax. Cambridge, MA: MIT Press.

Chomsky, N. 2005. Three factors in language design. *Linguistic Inquiry* 36: 1–22.

Cinque, G. 1999. *Adverbs and functional heads: A cross-linguistic perspective*. Oxford: Oxford University Press.

Cinque, G. (ed.). 2002. *Functional structure in DP and IP: The cartography of syntactic structures*. Oxford: Oxford University Press.

Clahsen, H. 1986. Verb inflections in German child language: Acquisition of agreement markings and the functions they encode. *Linguistics* 26: 79–121.

Falcaro, M., A. Pickles, D.F. Newbury, L. Addis, E. Banfield, S.E. Fisher, A.P. Monaco, Z. Simkin, G. Conti-Ramsden, and The SLI Consortium. 2008. Genetic and phenotypic effects of phonological short term memory and grammatical morphology in specific language impairment. *Genes, Brain and Behavior* 7: 393–402.

Friedemann, M.-A. 1993/1994. The underlying position of external arguments in French: A study in adult and child grammar. *Language Acquisition* 3(3): 209–255.

Gavarro, A., V. Torrens, and K. Wexler. in press. Object clitic omission: Two language types. *Language Acquisition* 17(4): 192–219.

Gibson, E., and K. Wexler. 1994. Triggers. *Linguistic Inquiry* 24: 407–454.

Guasti, M.T. 1993/1994. Verb syntax in Italian child grammar: Finite and nonfinite verbs. *Language Acquisition*, 3: 1–40.

Haegeman, L. 1996. Root infinitives, tense and truncated structure. In *Generative perspectives on language acquisition*, ed. H. Clahsen. Amsterdam: John Benjamins.

Hamann, C. 1997. From syntax to discourse: Children's use of pronominal clitics, null arguments, infinitives and operators. Habilitationsschrift, University of Geneva, Geneva.

Harris, A., and K. Wexler. 1996. The optional-infinitive stage in child English: Evidence from negation. In *Generative perspective on language acquisition*, ed. H. Clahsen, 1–42. Philadelphia: John Benjamins.

Haznedar, B., and B. Schwartz. 1997. Are there optional infinitives in child L2 acquisition? In *BUCLD 21 Proceedings*, ed. M. Hughes and A. Greenhill, 257–268. Somerville: Cascadilla Press.

Hoekstra, T., and N. Hyams. 1998. Aspects of root infinitives. *Lingua* 106: 81–112.

Hoekstra, T., and N. Hyams. 1999. The eventivity constraint and modal reference effect in root infinitives. In *Proceedings of BUCLD*, vol. 23. Sommerville: Cascadilla Press.

Hoekstra, T., and B. Schwartz (eds.). 1994. *Language acquisition studies in generative grammar*. Amsterdam/Philadelphia: John Benjamins.

Hyams, N. 1992. Morphosyntactic development in Italian and its relevance to parameter-setting models: Comments on the paper by Pizzuto & Caselli. *Journal of Child Language* 19: 695–709.

Hyams, N. 2007. Aspectual effects on interpretation. *Language Acquisition* 14(3): 231–268.

Ionin, T., and K. Wexler. 2002. Why is "Is" easier than "s"? – Acquisition of tense/agreement morphology by child L2-English learners. *Second Language Research* 18(2): 95–136.

Jakubowicz, C., N. Muller, B. Riemer, and C. Rigaut. 1997. The case of subject and object omission in French and German. In *BUCLD 21*, eds. E. Hughes, M. Hughes, and A. Greenhill, 331–342. Somerville: Cascadilla Press.

Kovelman, I., S. Ghosh, P. O'Loughli, I. Ostrovskaya, T. Perrachione, J. Lymberis, E. Norton, S. Cosman, K. Wexler and J. Gabrieli. 2009. Optional infinitive: Evidence of how the adult brain processes grammatical errors that are typical and atypical of childhood language acquistion. Poster presented at the annual meeting of the Cognitive Neuroscience Society, San Francisco, California.

Legate, J.A., and C. Yang. 2007. Morphosyntactic learning and the development of tense. *Language Acquisition* 14(3): 315–344.

Lenneberg, E. 1967. *Biological foundations of language*. New York: Wiley.

Levow, G.-A. 1995. Tense and subject position in interrogatives and negatives in child French: Evidence for and against truncated structure. *MIT Working Papers in Linguistics (MITWPL)* 26: 281–304.

Lightbom, P. 1977. Consistency and variation in the acquisition of French. PhD diss., Columbia University, New York.

Loeb, D.F., and L.B. Leonard. 1991. Subject case marking and verb morphology in normally developing and specifically language-impaired children. *Journal of Speech and Hearing Research* 34: 340–346.

Lorusso, P., C. Caprin, and M. T. Guasti. 2005. Overt subject distribution in early Italian children. In *A supplement to the Proceedings of the 29th Annual Boston University Conference on Language Development*, eds. A. Brugos, M. R. Clark-Cotton, and S. Ha. Somerville: Cascadilla Press.

Manzini, R., and K. Wexler. 1987. Parameters, binding theory, and learnability. *Linguistic Inquiry* 18: 413–444.
Newport, E.L., L.R. Gleitman, and H. Gleitman. 1973. A study of mothers' speech and child language acquisition. *Papers and Reports on Child Language Development* 10: 111–116.
Newport, E.L., H. Gleitman, and L. Gleitman. 1977. Mother, I'd rather do it myself: Some effects and noneffects of maternal speech style. In *Talking to children: Language input and acquisition*, ed. C.E. Snow and C.A. Ferguson, 109–150. Cambridge: Cambridge University Press.
Norris, R. 2000. Acquisition of the T and C system in clausal complements. MS thesis, Massachusetts Institute of Technology, Cambridge, MA.
Pierce, A. 1992a. *Language acquisition and syntactic theory: A comparative analysis of French and English child grammars*. Dordrecht: Kluwer.
Pierce, A. 1992b. *Language acquisition and syntactic theory. A comparative study of French and English child grammars*. Dordrecht: Kluwer.
Pine, J., C. Rowland, E. Lieven, and A. Theakston. 2005. Testing the Agreement/Tense Omission Model: Why the data on children's use of non-nominative 3psg subjects count against the ATOM. *Journal of Child Language* 32: 269–289.
Poeppel, D., and K. Wexler. 1993. The full competence hypothesis of clause structure in early German. *Language* 69(1): 1–33.
Pollock, J.Y. 1989. Verb movement, universal grammar and the structure of IP. *Linguistic Inquiry* 20: 365–424.
Powers, S.M. 1995. The acquisition of pronouns in Dutch and English: The case for continuity. In *Proceedings of BUCLD 19*, 439–450. Somerville: Cascadilla.
Prevost, P., and L. White. 1999. Finiteness and variability in SLA: More evidence for missing surface inflection. In *Proceedings of the BUCLD 23*. Somerville: Cascadilla Press.
Radford, A. 1990a. *Syntactic theory and the acquisition of English syntax: The nature of early child grammars of English*. Oxford: Basil Blackwell.
Radford, A. 1990b. The syntax of nominal arguments in early child english. *Language Acquisition* 1: 195–223.
Rice, M.L., and K. Wexler. 1996. Toward tense as a clinical marker of specific language impairment in english-speaking children. *Journal or Speech and Hearing Research* 39: 1239–1257.
Rice, M.L., and K. Wexler. 2001. *Rice/Wexler test of early grammatical impairment*. San Antonio: The Psychological Corporation.
Rice, M.L., K. Wexler, and S. Hershberger. 1998. Tense over time: The longitudinal course of tense acquisition in children with specific language impairment. *Journal of Speech, Language and Hearing Research* 41: 1412–31.
Rice, M., S. Redmond, and K. Wexler. 1999. Grammaticality judgements of an extended optional infinitive grammar: Evidence from English-speaking children with specific language impairment. *JSLHR* 42: 943–961.
Rispoli, M. 1994. Pronoun case overextensions and paradigm building. *Journal of Child Language* 21: 157–172.
Rizzi, L. 1993. Some notes in linguistic theory and language development: The case of root infinitives. *Language Acquisition* 3: 371–393.
Rizzi, L. 1994. Early null subjects and root null Subjects. In *Language acquisition studies in generative grammar*, ed. T. Hoekstra and B. Schwartz. Amsterdam: Benjamins.
Roberts, T. 1997. Evidence for the optional tense hypothesis: Tense in subordinate clauses in the acquisition of English. Unpublished Ms., Massachusetts Institute of Technology, Cambridge, MA.
Roeper, T., and B. Rohrbacher. 1994. Null subjects in early child English and the theory of economy of projection, University of Pennsylvania Working Papers in Linguistics 2, 83–119.
Sano, T., and N. Hyams. 1994. Agreement, finiteness and the development of null arguments. In *Proceedings of NELS*, vol. 24. Amherst: GLSA.
Santelmann, L. 1995. The acquisition of verb second grammar in child Swedish: Continuity of universal grammar in Wh-questions, topicalization and verb raising. PhD diss., Department of Linguistics, Ohio State University, Columbus, OH.

Schaeffer, J. 2000. *The acquisition of direct object scrambling and clitic placement.* Amsterdam/Philadelphia: John Benjamins.

Schonenberger, M., A. Pierce, F. Wijnen, and K. Wexler. 1995. Accounts of root infinitives and the interpretation of root infinitives. *Geneva Generative Papers* 3(2): 47–71.

Schutze, C. 1994. Why nonfinite be is not omitted while finite be is. In Alejna Brugos, Linnea Micciulla, and Christine E. Smith) *Proceedings of the 28th Boston University Conference on Language Development*, 506-521.

Schutze, C.T. 2004. Why nonfinite be is not omitted while finite be is. In *Proceedings of the 28th Boston University Conference on Language Development*, ed. Alejna Brugos, Linnea Micciulla, and Christine E. Smith, 506–521.

Schutze, C., and K. Wexler. 1996. Subject case licensing and English root infinitives. In *Proceedings of the 20th Boston University Conference on Language Development*, 670–681. Somerville: Cascadilla.

Sigurjónsdóttir, S. 1999. Root infinitives and null subjects in early Icelandic. In *Proceedings of the 23 rd Annual Boston University Conference on Language Development*, ed. A. Greenhill, H. Littlefield, and C. Tano, 630–641. Somerville: Cascadilla.

Theakston, A., E. Lieven, J. Pine and C. Rowland. 2000. The role of performance limitations in the acquisition of 'mixed' verb argument structure at Stage I. In *New directions in language development and disorders*, eds. in M. Perkins and S. Howard, 119–128, Kluwer Academic: Plenum, New York.

Tomasello, M. 2000. Do young children have adult syntactic competence? *Cognition* 74: 209–253.

Tsakali, V., and K. Wexler. 2004. Why children omit clitics in some languages but not in others: New evidence from Greek. In *Proceedings of GALA 2003*, vol. 2, eds. J. van Kampen and S. Baauw, 493–504. Utrecht: LOT.

Vainikka, A. 1994. Case in the development of English syntax. *Language Acquisition* 3: 257–325.

Valian, V. 1991. Syntactic subjects in the early speech of American and Italian children. *Cognition* 40: 21–81.

Weverink, M. 1989. The subject in relation to inflection in child language, M.A. thesis. The Netherlands: University of Utrecht.

Wexler, K. 1990. Optional infinitives, head movement and the economy of derivations in child grammar. Paper presented at the annual meeting of the Society of Cognitive Science. Cambridge, MA: Massachusetts Institute of Technology.

Wexler, K. 1992. Optional infinitives, head movement and the economy of derivation in child grammar. Occasional paper 45. Center for Cognitive Science. Cambridge, MA: Massachusetts Institute of Technology.

Wexler, K. 1993. Optional infinitives, head movement and the economy of derivations. In *Verb movement*, ed. D. Lightfoot and N. Hornstein, 305–350. Cambridge, MA: Cambridge University Press.

Wexler, K. 1994. Optional infinitives, head movement and the economy of derivations. In *Verb Movement*, eds. D. Lightfoot, and N. Hornstein, 305–350. Cambridge, U.K: Cambridge University Press.

Wexler, K. 1995. Feature-interpretability and optionality in early child grammar. Paper presented at the Workshop on Optionality, Utrecht.

Wexler, K. 1998. Very early parameter setting and the unique checking constraint: A new explanation of the optional infinitive stage. *Lingua* 106: 23–79.

Wexler, K. 1999. Maturation and growth of grammar. In *Handbook of language acquisition*, eds. W.C. Ritchie, and T.K. Bhatia. San Diego: Academic.

Wexler, K. 2000. The development of clitics in SLI and normal development: Evidence for the unique checking constraint. In *Syntax, Morphology, and Phonology in Specific Language Impairment*, eds. C. Jakubowicz, L. Nash, and K. Wexler. Cambridge, Mass: MIT Press.

Wexler, K. 2003. Lenneberg's dream: Learning, normal language development, and specific language impairment. In *Language competence across populations: Toward a definition of specific language impairment*, eds. Y. Levy, and J. Schaeffer, 11–62. Mahwah: Lawrence Erlbaum.

Wexler, K. 2004. Theory of phasal development. *MIT Working Papers in Linguistics* 48: 159–209.

Wexler, K., and P. Culicover. 1980. *Formal principles of language acquisition*. Cambridge, MA: MIT Press.

Wexler, K., and R. Manzini. 1987. Parameters and learnability in binding theory. In *Parameter setting*, eds. T. Roeper and E. Williams, 41–76. Dordrecht: D. Reidel.

Wexler, K., A. Gavarró, and V. Torrens. 2004a. Feature checking and object clitic omission in child Catalan and Spanish. In *Romance languages and linguistic theory 2002*, ed. R. Bok-Bennema, B. Hollebrandse, B. Kampers-Manhe, and P. Sleeman, 253–269. Amsterdam: John Benjamins.

Wexler, K., J. Schaeffer, and G. Bol. 2004b. Verbal syntax and morphology in typically developing Dutch children and children with SLI: How developmental data can play an important role in morphological theory. *Syntax* 7: 148–198.

Wexler, K., J. Schaeffer, and G. Bol. 1999. Verbal Syntax and morphology in Dutch Normal and SLI Children. In *Proceedings of the 14th Annual Conference (IATL 6)*, The Israel association for theoretical linguistics, Ben Gurion University of the Negev.

Wijnen, F. 1998. The temporal interpretation of Dutch children's root infinitivals: The effect of eventivity. *First Language* 18: 379–402.

Yang, C. 2002. Knowledge and learning in natural language. New York: Oxford University Press.

Computational Models of Language Acquisition

Charles Yang

1 Introduction

All models strive to represent reality, and efforts in language research are no exception. Computational models of language acquisition must begin and end as an integral part of the empirical study of child language.

Much of language acquisition research is dedicated to accurate and insightful characterizations of child language and its developmental stages. Nevertheless, no theory of child language is complete without providing a concrete account of the mechanism responsible for the changes in the child's linguistic system during acquisition. In other words, while it is useful to establish that "the child knows A at age X but B at age X+Y", a more complete explanation will require a specification of what kind of learning model, acting on what kind of linguistic data, can facilitate the change from A to B during the time course of Y. It is often remarked in the developmental literature that children just "pick up" their language, or that children's linguistic competence is identical to the adults', or that the syntactic parameters are set correctly from very early on. Their empirical validities aside, these statements would be more compelling if an explicit theory of how the child reaches such milestones is also on offer. This is where computational models of learning, which demand a concrete algorithmic process that interacts with the input data in specific ways, can make a crucial contribution.

We will develop these themes throughout this review. Section 2 takes a look at the statistical properties of natural language, which have not received adequate attention in the study of child language. This sets the stage for the formal and empirical discussions of learning models in the rest of the chapter. Section 3 provides a

---

C. Yang (✉)
Department of Linguistics & Computer Science, University of Pennsylvania, Philadelphia, USA
e-mail: charles.yang@ling.upenn.edu

brief survey of computational learning research, the theoretical foundation of the computational approach to language acquisition, with the clarification of some persistent misunderstandings in the linguistic and psychological literature. This research highlights the necessity of a constrained space of linguistic hypotheses that must be assumed, in one form or another, by all acquisition models. Section 4 focuses on computational models that make use of distributional learning in acquisition, and underscores the pressing need to draw better connections with research in computational linguistics and natural language processing where these topics have been intensively studied. Section 5 reviews some specific models of syntactic acquisition, all of which can be framed as a problem of searching for a target in a constrained space of grammatical hypotheses. The emphasis is on the parameter setting approach, with special attention to the complexity and psychological plausibility of the models. Section 6 connects computational models with the empirical study of development across languages, a direction that deserves fuller attention in future research.

2 Data and Generalization

A hallmark of human language is its unbounded generative capacity. This is evident in child language acquisition even, and especially when children commit linguistic mistakes. Every time a child says "Don't giggle him" or "The sun is sweating me", there is a grammatical system at work that generalizes beyond the input – and it occasionally gets it wrong.

To fully recognize the necessity of generalization in language learning, it is useful to examine the statistical properties of the primary linguistic data that the child receives and the potential difficulties the child faces.[1] This type of data exploration is now quite straightforward to carry out, thanks to the availability of large scale linguistic corpora and advances in natural language processing technology. Similar problems have received considerable attention in computational linguistics, and ought to be recognized more fully in the study of language acquisition. Their relevance becomes more significant in light of recent developments in the psychological study of language acquisition.

First, the very notion of generative productivity has been challenged by the item/usage-based approach to language learning (Tomasello 1992, 2003) and linguistic theorizing (e.g., Bybee 2001; Goldberg 2003; Culicover and Jackendoff 2005). For instance, the central tenets of Construction Grammar view constructions as "stored pairings of form and function, including morphemes, words, idioms, partially

---

[1]We emphasize at the outset that the exploration of the input data only addresses part of the language acquisition problem. Linguistic studies have revealed many constraints on the syntactic system that are negative in nature, i.e., they specify the *impossible* forms of language. While theoretical formulations vary, the generalizations of island constraints, binding principles, etc. remain, and the acquisition studies of these constraints have been largely successful; see O'Grady (1997), Crain and Thornton (1998), Guasti (2002), etc. for reviews.

lexically filled and fully general linguistic patterns" and "the totality of our knowledge of language is captured by a network of constructions" (Goldberg ibid, p 219). Recent developments in lexicalized grammatical theories (Sag 2010) also reflect the commitment that constructions be defined over specific lexical items. If so, the generalization problem uncovered by computational studies (Sect. 3) becomes a moot point: the child learner only needs to memorize the constructions in the input. Second, recent work in the artificial language learning literature suggests that human learners may be quite adept at extracting statistical regularities in language (Saffran et al. 1996), thereby leading to increased interest in the distributional learning approach to language (and consequently a diminished role for domain specific and/or innate constraints as previously conceived). We return to the discussion of distributional learning in Sect. 4. The role of memorization through item/usage based learning and the accumulation of constructions, however, has been greatly exaggerated.

According to what has become known as *Zipf's law* (1949), the statistical distributions of words follow a curious pattern: relatively few words are used frequently – indeed, *very* frequently – while most words occur rarely, with many words occurring only once in even large samples of texts. More specifically, the frequency of a word tends to be approximately inversely proportional to its rank in frequency. Let f be the frequency of the word with the rank of r in a set of N words, then:

(1) $f = \dfrac{C}{r}$ where C is some constant

In the Brown corpus (Kučera and Francis 1967), for instance, the word with rank 1 is "the", which has the frequency of about 70,000, and the word with rank 2 is "of", with the frequency of about 36,000: almost exactly as Zipf's law entails (i.e., $70,000 \times 1 \approx 36,000 \times 2$). And a full 43% of words appear only once in this one million word corpus. The Zipfian characterization of word frequency can be visualized by plotting the log of word frequency against the log of word rank. By taking the log on both sides of the equation above ($\log f = \log C - \log r$), a perfect Zipfian fit would be a straight line with the slope -1. Indeed, Zipf's law has been observed in vocabulary studies across languages and genres, and the log–log slope fit is consistently in the close neighborhood of -1.0 (Baroni 2008).

The characteristic long tail of Zipfian distribution becomes more pronounced when we consider combinatorial linguistic units (Fig. 1). Take, for instance, n-grams, the simplest linguistic combination that consists of n consecutive words in a text.[2] Since there are a lot more bigrams and trigrams than words, there are consequently a lot more low frequency bigrams and trigrams in a linguistic sample (if they are attested at all), as Fig. 2 illustrates from the Brown corpus (for related studies, see Teahan 1997; Ha et al. 2002).

---

[2]For example, given the sentence "the cat chases the mouse", its bigrams ($n=2$) are "the cat", "cat chases", "chases the", and "the mouse", and its trigrams ($n=3$) are "the cat chases", "cat chases the", "chases the mouse". When $n=1$, we are just dealing with words, or unigrams.

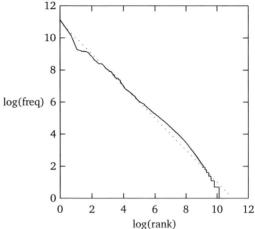

Fig. 1 Zipfian distribution of words in the Brown corpus Kučera & Francis (1967). A perfect fit has the log–log slope of −1, as indicated by the *dotted line*

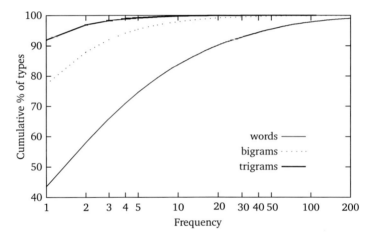

Fig. 2 The vast majority of linguistic units are rare events

Here the x-axis denotes the frequency of the units, and the y-axis denotes the cumulative % of the units that appear at that frequency or lower. For instance, there are about 43% of words that occur only once, about 58% of words that occur 1–2 times, 68% of words that occur 1–3 times, etc. The % of units that occur multiple times decreases rapidly, especially for bigrams and trigrams: approximately 91% of unique trigrams in the Brown corpus occur only once, and 96% occur once or twice.

The range of linguistic forms is so vast that no sample is large enough to capture all of its varieties even when we take language models that are more abstract than n-grams. Figure 3 plots the rank and frequency distributions of syntactic rules, in the form of context free grammars, of modern English from the Penn Treebank (Marcus et al. 1993). Since the corpus has been manually annotated with syntactic

Fig. 3 The frequency distribution of the syntactic rules in the Penn Treebank

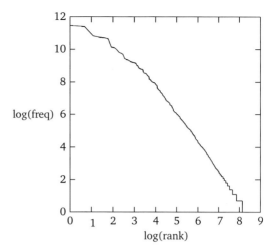

structures, it is straightforward to extract rules and tally their frequencies.[3] The most frequent rule is "PP → P NP", followed by "S → NP VP", reflecting the genre of the corpus (the Wall Street Journal): again, the Zipf-like pattern can be seen by the close approximation by a straight line on the log–log scale.

In computational linguistics, the Zipfian long tail of language has been referred to as the *sparse data problem*: the number of linguistic combinations, and thus the number of parameters for a statistical model of language, grows a great deal faster than the amount of linguistic data. These observations are not only relevant for the theory of how the child learns – like the computer, the child does not have unlimited data or infinite time – but also for *what* the child learns; see Valian et al. (2008) and Yang (2011) for extensive discussion. A central tenet of the item/usage based approach to acquisition emphasizes the storage of specific linguistic forms and constructions. Child language, especially in the early stages, is claimed to consist of specific item-based schemas, rather than a productive linguistic system as previously conceived. The lack of productivity is largely established on the basis of the lack of diversity in syntactic combinations. For instance, according to the Verb Island Hypothesis (Tomasello 1992), which forms the foundation of item/based learning, about half of the verbs and predicates in a child's language are used in one and only one constructions (e.g., with a specific object), over two thirds are used in only one or two constructions. The underlying assumption appears to be that a systematic grammar would lead to multiple construction types for all/most productively used items. But this line of reasoning fails to take the Zipfian nature of language into account. Not only do linguistic units (words, *n*-grams, phrases, rules) follow Zipf-like distribution, the combinations between linguistic units do so as well. Figure 4 presents the construction frequencies of the top 15 most

---

[3]Certain rules have been collapsed together as the Treebank frequently annotates rules involving distinct functional heads as separate rules.

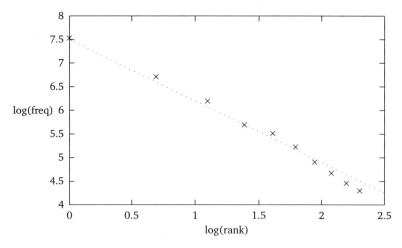

Fig. 4 Rank and frequency of verb-object constructions based on child directed English. These verbs are: *put, tell, see, want, let, give, take, show, got, ask, make, eat, like, bring* and *hear*. The frequency tallies of the top 10 most frequent constructions are 1904, 838, 501, 301, 252, 189, 137, 109, 88, and 75

frequently used transitive verbs frequencies from 1.1 million child directed English utterances from the CHILDES database (MacWhinney 2000). The frequencies of the top 10 constructions in which these verbs appear are tallied. We again observe Zipf like behavior: verbs appear in relatively few but highly frequent constructions and the diversity of attested constructions is low. The observation of verb islands is in fact characteristic of adult language; see Buttery and Korhonen (2005) for related discussion.

The Zipfian distribution of linguistic combinations means that most constructions of "pairings of form and function" will never be heard, never mind stored, and those that do appear may do so with sufficiently low frequency such that no reliable storage and use is possible. It seems, then, the role for memorization in recent approach to language and language learning must be far less significant than previously hoped (*pace* Goldberg 2003). Both the child and the computer need to generalize far beyond the input; the formal treatment of this process is the study of learnability, to which we turn presently.

3 Learnability

The formal study of learning started soon after the development of generative grammar (Chomsky 1957, 1965). Indeed, the seminal work of Gold (1967) was an attempt to formalize the problem of learning with specific reference to language and helped establish the field of computational learning theory, with important results in the 1970s and 1980s (Blum and Blum 1975; Angluin 1980; Valiant 1984). This parallels the development in the theory of statistical inference and approximation

(Vapnik and Chervonenkis 1971; Vapnik 1995), and some points of contact between these two traditions can be found (Blumer et al. 1989). In these studies, one typically partitions the problem of learning into several components: the presentation of data, the composition of the hypothesis space, the mechanism and complexity of the learning algorithm, the condition of convergence, etc. These components can be varied, producing different learning scenarios that can be studied formally.

The field of machine learning, as computational learning theory is frequently referred to, is vast and constantly evolving. Many of its applications have found their way into the study of language such as computational linguistics and natural language processing; we will return to some relevant connections in Sect. 4. Recent developments have significantly departed from the original conception of language learning; nevertheless, the mathematical foundations of learning theory remain stable, and there are important results relevant to all research in language acquisition that are worthwhile to review. It must be stressed that, in our experience, a proper understanding of the formal results involves going through the mathematical details, for which we can only provide references here.

In a typical setting of formal learnability, the learner is presented with a sequence of examples drawn from an unknown target language, which can be viewed as a set of strings composed of an alphabet. The learner's task is to learn the language after only seeing a finite number of examples (since nobody learns forever). And given the infinity of language, the learner must able to be able to generalize beyond the examples it has seen. It has long been noted that a finite number of examples are consistent with infinitely many hypotheses (Goodman 1955) and learnability research studies the conditions under which the learner can escape from this dilemma and does so in a computationally tractable fashion.

3.1 Negative Results

Pertinent to our discussion are two related but distinct frameworks of learning, both of which have developed a very large technical literature. The classic inductive inference framework of Gold (1967) generally requires the learner to converge exactly on the target language within a finite amount of time and on all the orders in which the examples are presented. The Probably Approximately Correct (PAC) framework (Valiant 1984) only requires the learner to get arbitrarily close, e.g., the distance between the conjectured grammar and the actual grammar can be made as small as possible, but it must be able to do so efficiently. The complexity of learning is defined over the size of the problem, which may consist of the size of the example (e.g., the length of the strings), the size of the hypothesis (e.g., the number of parameters or rewrite rules needed to specify a grammar), etc. In the spirit of traditional complexity theory, the efficiency condition of PAC learning requires the number of examples needed for convergence be a function that grows no faster than polynomially. The inductive inference learner in the sense of Gold (1967), by contrast, is allowed to learn for however long it wants, as long as it eventually stops at the target grammar.

Both frameworks are broad enough to allow modifications of the assumptions about the learner, the presentation of the data, the criterion for convergence, etc. In general, however, both frameworks have yielded learnability results that are overwhelmingly negative. For instance, Gold shows that when using positive data alone, only languages that have a finite number of sentences are learnable. Natural language, well known for its infinite use of finite means, lies outside of the learnable class. If negative data is allowed, all primitive recursive functions, which include context free and context sensitive languages in the Chomsky hierarchy, become learnable. Of course, given the general lack and ineffectiveness of negative evidence in language acquisition (Marcus 1993) and the cross-cultural differences in the mode of parent–child interaction (see O'Neil and Honda 2004 for review), the cognitive relevance of learning with negative data is at best questionable. When computational complexity is taken into account, as in the case of PAC learning, it has been established that virtually no language families in the Chomsky Hierarchy, e.g., finite state, context free and context sensitive languages, can be learned efficiently, even if the learner has access to both positive and negative data (Kearns and Valiant 1994).

The computational learning theory is well understood but its implications for the empirical study of language acquisition deserve careful consideration; see Osherson et al. (1985), Angluin (1992) and Niyogi (2006) for overview.

First, learnability results are very general and can be modified to accommodate a wide range of learning situations. For instance, one might object that the inductive inference learner is unfairly restricted by only having access to strings drawn from the target grammar and thereby deprived of semantic and pragmatic information. However, one could simply take the input examples to be pairs that consist of a string and its corresponding "meaning", and the language to be acquired would be a subset of the universe that is the product of the set of all possible strings and the set of all possible meanings (Niyogi 2006). The non-learnability results hold equally for these alternative conceptions of language.

Second, learnability results are usually obtained irrespective of the learning algorithm. In other words, barring major surprises in complexity theory that would impact our lives more than the model of language acquisition (e.g., the security of widely used cryptographic schemes), a negative learnability result is negative not because we have not found an algorithm that works but because no such algorithm can exist. And there is no point in trying the latest and trendiest techniques on a more powerful computer. These negative results, then, corroborate the discussion in the philosophical and linguistic literature (e.g., Goodman 1955; Chomsky 1959) that *tabula rasa* learning is impossible and that the space of hypotheses must be constrained by prior knowledge. The linguistic approach to solving the language acquisition problem is to postulate Universal Grammar (UG), a domain-specific hypothesis space with limited options of variability. While the present author works in this tradition, it is worth pointing out that the mathematical results do not show that the linguistic approach is the only way to achieve learnability. It is at least a theoretical possibility that the success of language acquisition comes from other constraining forces such as working memory, processing limitations (e.g., Elman 1990) and other, presumably domain general, factors including learning mechanisms (e.g., Hudson Kam and Newport 2005) that narrow down the search space of grammars in a non-linguistic fashion. To substantiate this possibility, however, requires the specification of exactly what these constraints are, which must also be supposed as innate, and demonstrate their effectiveness. Moreover, the importance of UG to language acquisition comes through more strongly from the empirical study of language development rather than any mathematical result (see Yang 2006 for an overview).

3.2 Positive Results

So much for the bad news: Are there positive learnability results? Yes, but they come with hefty price, and they all involve providing the learner with additional information about the properties of the grammar to be acquired.

One way to gain learnability is to restrict the class of languages with special constraints. And there are two lines of research with different starting points – often viewed as divergent – that are in fact similar in spirit. An empirical approach is taken by modern linguistic theorizing, much of which is devoted to providing a more restrictive syntactic system from the perspective of cross-linguistic studies. To the extent these are descriptively successful efforts, one can take up the question whether such theories facilitate the task of language acquisition as well; we take these questions in Sects. 5 and 6. Another, more computational approach aims to define demonstrably learnable classes of languages: the central challenge is to show that such classes are sufficient for the description of human language syntax. We review some representative results in this direction below.

While a class of all finite state languages is not learnable, Angluin (1982) proves that a subclass of finite state languages, that of *reversible* languages, is learnable. Informally, a reversible languages consists of a set of strings such that if any two strings share any "tails" (a substring that continues to the end), then they also share *all* tails. For instance, suppose that a reversible language contains "John likes pizza", "Mary likes pizza", and "John drinks tea". Since "John" and "Mary" share the same tail ("likes pizza"), they must share all continuations. Thus, "Mary drinks tea" must also be part of the language, and the learner can effectively generalize. (Sub)string substitutability is the defining characteristic of reversible languages; see Clark and Eyraud (2007) for a similar approach.

Obviously, the utility of reversible language to language acquisition is limited since natural language is beyond the descriptive powers of all finite state languages which properly include reversible language. But there may be parts of the syntactic systems that can be characterized as reversible and thus learnable. For instance, Berwick and Pilato (1987) develop a learning algorithm for the English auxiliary and noun phrase specifier systems, both of which are well known for their complexity (Pinker 1984; Jackendoff 1977). But this positive learnability result is obtained by constraining the innate space of hypotheses, which is fundamentally in the same spirit of the linguistic approach (e.g., the Principles and Parameters theory of Chomsky (1981)): the learner would have to "know" that the relevant domain of language is reversible; only then is the deployment of the learning algorithm warranted.

Another way to obtain learnability is to assume that the learner has access to some additional information about the target language. Wexler and Culicover (1980) show that if the learner has access to the surface string of a sentence as well as its underly deep structure, then a transformational grammar (Chomsky 1965) is learnable under several further constraints on the grammar and the learning strategy. Note here that the deep structure is not to be identified with "meaning", but rather a specific level of syntactic descriptions, including, for instance, the positions from which syntactic movement takes place. Having access to this information effectively limits the range of possible syntactic operations that relate the deep with the surface structure. This assumption is perhaps unrealistically strong as structures vary across languages and are therefore the target of learning as well.

A third potentially useful source of information for the learner concerns the statistical distribution of the language in question. Both the inductive inference and the PAC frameworks aim to derive learnability results in the "distribution-free" sense, that is, with no prior assumptions about the distribution from which the learning sample is drawn. This requirement produces results of greatest generality and interest but it can be relaxed as well. It has been shown (Osherson et al. 1985; Angluin 1988, among others) that if one has certain information about the distribution of the input, then the class of learnable languages is considerably enlarged. But this is a very strong assumption to make, as the estimation of the distribution of a function is generally harder than the estimation of the function itself – and it is the function itself that the child learner is trying to learn during the course of language acquisition: he is learning how to say "I am hungry", not how often "I am hungry" is said.

It appears that the positive learning results under certain statistical distributions have been misunderstood in a wide range of literature in computational linguistics (Manning and Schütz 1999), language acquisition (e.g., MacWhinney 2004) and linguistics (e.g., Abney 1996), and almost always in the context that attempts to argue for a probabilistic concept of learning and grammar rather than Gold's inductive inference framework that requires exact convergence on the target grammar. For instance, a recent volume on the probabilistic approach to language (Bod et al. 2003) remarks that "unlike categorical grammars, probabilistic grammars *are* learnable from positive evidence" and that "if the language faculty is probabilistic, the learning task is considerably more achievable" (pp 6–7, emphasis original). The source of these claims appears to be Horning (1969), which is a probabilistic instantiation of Gold's learning paradigm in a Bayesian framework. While for specific problems such as parameter setting and language development (see Sects. 5 and 6), some probabilistic algorithms are indeed superior to discrete ones, there is no evidence that probabilistic learning necessarily holds the upper hand. Indeed, it is difficult to directly compare learnability results from these frameworks, which operate under different assumptions (see Nowak et al. 2002). It is not even the case that PAC learning, which is probabilistic, admits a larger class of languages than Gold learning: for instance, finite languages, which are learnable under the Gold framework with positive evidence alone, are not learnable under the PAC framework even with both positive and negative evidence.

It is useful to provide some background for the much misunderstood work of Horning (1969). As reviewed above, context free languages are not learnable under the inductive inference or the PAC learning framework. Horning's result involves probabilistic context free grammars, which associate context free grammar rules with expansion probabilities.[4] However, once probabilities become part of the rule system, the distribution of sentences becomes very favorable to learning in the sense that Angluin (1988) describes. In a probabilistic context free grammar, the probability of a sentence is the product of the probabilities of rules involved in its derivation. It follows, then, that longer sentences are vanishingly unlikely.[5] Horning's learner can, in effect, ignore sufficiently long sentences without affecting the overall approximation to the target. Now the grammar is, in effect, *finite*, a position that few language scientists would find appealing. Finite languages, however, *are* learnable, as Gold had already shown. Furthermore, Horning's results are achievable only through exceptional computational resources. Foreshadowing much of the recent work on Bayesian models of grammar learning, some of which are reviewed in Sect. 4, Horning's algorithm works by searching through the space of probabilistic context free grammars. Not only must these grammars be available to the learner, the prior probabilities of these grammars must also be assumed. The learner calculates the posteriori probabilities of grammars given the data and selects the grammar with the highest value. The computational complexities of Bayesian models are prohibitive, as Horning noted himself. So far as we know, Horning's model has never been implemented and tested on a reasonable sample of natural language data.

To conclude this brief discussion of formal learning theory, it is necessary to remind ourselves that learnability results must be placed in a cognitive setting to contribute to language acquisition. A formal solution that yields positive results may not correspond to the psychological reality of the human learner. For example, a strong and very general result from learning theory states that only hypothesis spaces with a finite degree of complexity are learnable (Vapnik 1995). Thus, most contemporary theories of language such as the Principles & Parameters Theory (Chomsky 1981, 1995), Optimality Theory (Prince and Smolensky 1993), which admit only a finite number of possible grammars, are in principle learnable. But this space contains potentially a very large number of grammars, thus it remains a very active (and open) problem to develop computationally feasible models of learning (see Sects. 5 and 6).

Computational models of syntactic acquisition have followed similar developments. On the one hand, linguistic theories have devoted major efforts to characterize linguistic constraints to ensure that the learner only has access to a limited range of

---

[4] We put aside the issue whether (probabilistic) context free grammars are the right representation for natural language; there are well known arguments to the contrary.

[5] While this may be empirically true in a given corpus, long sentences can be perfectly grammatical and ought to be part of the learner's linguistic knowledge – and they are, as any child familiar with *The House that Jack built* and other nursery rhymes knows well.

possible languages: the principles and parameter approach in syntax (Chomsky 1981), which we review in Sects. 5 and 6, is the most prominent example of this approach. On the other hand, the learner may indeed be endowed with more powerful computational capacity than generally supposed and thus be capable of successfully exploring a less restrictive space of grammars: this approach is best represented by models of distributional learning of language, which we review below.

4 Grammar and Distributional Learning

The recent flurry of interest in the distributional information of language is frequently seen as a reaction to generative grammar, but that seems to be a misreading of history. Distributional and statistical approaches to language and language learning have roots in the structuralist tradition of American linguistics (Harris 1951) and are evident in the earliest writing on generative grammar, the *Logical Structure of Linguistic Theory* (LSLT, Chomsky 1955/1975). For instance, LSLT outlined an approach to words and categories "through the analysis of clustering... the *distribution* of a word as the set of contexts of the corpus in which it occurs, and the distributional *distance* between two words". The conception of syntactic analysis has a direct information-theoretic interpretation: "defined the best analysis as the one that minimizes information per word in the generated language of grammatical discourses". Grammars are evaluated such that "any simplification along these lines is immediately reflected in the length of the grammar"; this was later termed the Minimum Description Length principle (Rissanen 1989), now widely used in the statistical/distributional approach to language with deep similarities with the Bayesian learning framework. Perhaps best known to the contemporary audience is the suggestion that word boundaries might be defined via transitional probabilities over successive syllables, an idea implemented experimentally on artificial languages in a widely influential study (Saffran et al. 1996), which helped popularize the distributional learning approach to language and cognition. More generally, the way in which linguistic theorizing is practiced always turns on the notion of distribution, starting with the identification of phonemes in a language and ending with the broadest typological generalizations across languages. Distributional information is precisely what guides the theorist toward more compact and thus general descriptions of language. It would certainly be interesting if this process, typically carried out by trained professionals, can be operationalized by the child during the course of language acquisition.

4.1 Distribution and Syntactic Categories

A major research area in the distributional learning of language has focused on the acquisition of linguistic categories such as phonemes, words, grammatical categories. These efforts are usually those of data exploration in line with the structuralist notion of a discovery procedure: computational models are constructed to see what kind of distributional regularities can in principle be extracted from a corpus of linguistic data. Whether the human child is capable of such distributional learning, or whether the proposed model is psychologically plausible, is set aside. The statement from Mintz et al. (2002) is representative of this approach; their model of distributional learning via cluster analysis "is not to model the actual procedure a child might use, but rather to examine *the information available in children's input.*" (p 396; emphasis original).

Perhaps the most comprehensive study of distributional learning of syntactic categories is Redington et al. (1998), who present a clustering analysis for syntactic categories that formalizes earlier proposals of Maratsos and Chalkley (1980) and others. A word in the child-directed speech is represented by a context vector, which represents the identities of two immediately adjacent words to its left and right. For instance, the word "John" will be represented as "I saw at school" if it occurs in the sentence "I saw John at school". If the input also contains the sentence "I saw Bill at school", and "John" and "Bill" will have identical distributional profile which may be an indication that they belong to the same syntactic category. By contrast, if the input contains "I saw Bill eat pizza" instead, then obviously the distance between "John" and "Bill" would be farther though their distributional profiles still partially overlap through the "I saw" portion. It is important to realize that distributional similarity or even identity does not entail shared category membership (Pinker 1984): given "John drinks coffee every day" and "John drinks heavily every day", a distributional learner may incorrectly group "coffee" and "heavily" into the same category. And there are linguistic subtleties – "John is easy/eager to please" (Chomsky 1965) – that do not straightforwardly fall out of distributional analysis in the conventional sense. It is hoped that spurious generalizations of this sort can be avoided by cluster analysis if the amount of input data is sufficiently large such that informative data would overwhelm the misleading kind.

Redington et al. uses a hierarchical agglomerative clustering algorithm applied to the vector representations of words. It attempts to merge sufficiently similar words, as measured by vector distance, into groups of increasingly larger size and thereby creates a tree-like structure of categories. This algorithm is computationally expensive, as the distances between words and groups need to be calculated in pairwise fashion, and there is an enormously large number of possible groupings of words. Moreover, a decision must be made as to when to stop merging; in other words, there must be a minimum distance over which words will be forced into different categories (for otherwise every word will be placed into a same category eventually). The threshold for where to "cut" is the most critical feature of the computational model; in Redington et al.'s study, a value is hand selected to maximize the performance of the algorithm. Free parameters like this often feature in the distributional analysis of language. Other models of syntactic category learning require the researcher to specify the number of categories (e.g., Schutz 1995; Clark 2001). Similar approaches can be found in the distributional learning that makes use of parametric probability models. For instance, Vallabha et al. (2007) assume the distributions of vowel categories to be Gaussian, and the task of learning amounts to the estimation of the parameter values that characterize these Gaussian distributions. These interventions on the part of the researcher raise challenging questions about the psychological plausibility of distributional learning, as it is not obvious that the child finds the optimal parameter values.

Redington et al. (1998) and related work show that simple distributional information could be useful in the learning of syntactic categories. Indeed, they propose a useful metric for evaluating the categories discovered by the clustering algorithm that measures both the homogeneity (e.g., "Peter" and "at" should not be merged) and inclusiveness (e.g., "Peter" and "John" should) of conjectured categories. Nevertheless, it cannot be said that distributional learning, even under favorable assumptions, has provided an adequate solution for the syntactic category learning problem. The best clusters produced by the Redington et al. model scattered proper nouns across several categories and at the same time grouped wh-words and auxiliary verbs together. And these results are only obtained for the most frequent 1,000 words in their corpus of child-directed speech. Given the Zipfian distribution of natural language (Sect. 2), the remaining words are likely to be very infrequent, and there may not be sufficient data to generate their distributional vectors for clusterings.[6]

The syntactic category learning problem has been extensively researched in computational linguistics literature under the task of part-of-speech tagging. Considerable progress has been made in *supervised* learning – see also Sect. 4.2 below – where the learning model has access to a corpus where all words have been manually assigned with the correct category labels. When such data is unavailable, as is the case of child language acquisition, progress has been slower and the hand tuning of parameters to optimize performance is still the norm (Merialdo 1994; Smith and Eisner 2005; Goldwater and Griffiths 2007 among others).

4.2 Distributional Learning of Grammar

Compared to the distributional learning of syntactic categories, there is a smaller body of work on distributional learning of grammar, most of which focuses on the acquisition of auxiliary inversion in English question formation, a problem which featured prominently in the argument from the poverty of stimulus to motivate the innateness of the Principle of Structure Dependence in syntax (Chomsky 1975; Crain and Nakayama 1987; Legate and Yang 2002). We review some of these efforts

---

[6]In an interesting manipulation, Redington et al. explore the idea whether having complete knowledge of one category (e.g., nouns) contributes to the clustering of the other categories. This could correspond to some additional strategy by which the child could arrive at a syntactic category. Perhaps somewhat surprisingly, clustering quality actually diminishes. This suggests that even successful clustering of high-frequency words may not provide a sufficiently good bootstrapping device for the clustering of low frequency words. By contrast, children appear to be capable of using known syntactic categories to determine those of unknown words (Valian and Coulson 1988).

below, before turning to the research on the learning of general grammatical rules, a topic that has been extensively pursued in computational linguistics if not within the cognitive study of language.

Lewis and Elman (2001) train a simple recurrent network to discriminate grammatical strings that follow the inversion rule and those that do not (e.g., moving the first auxiliary verb such as "Is the man that tall is nice?"). However, the training data for the network are generated by a very small artificial grammar: the learner only learns from short declarative sentences containing an auxiliary verb and an inverted interrogative counterpart. Strings that conform to the grammar result in lower error terms for the network than ungrammatical ones. However, even though child-directed speech contains a large amount of questions, it remains to be seen how a network generalizes on a mixture of naturalist and diverse syntactic constructions.

Reali and Christiansen (2005) use string based models such as bigrams to capture the patterns of auxiliary inversion based on naturalistic data from child-directed speech. The model can consistently assign higher probabilities to grammatical strings than ungrammatical strings, which was interpreted as having successfully learned the correct rule of inversion. However, as Kam et al. (2008) note, this result is due to the fact that bigrams such as "who is", which appears in the grammatical string "Is the boy who is tall nice" are much more frequent than "who tall", which appears in the ungrammatical string "Is the boy who tall is nice" – a direct result of the very large number of Wh-questions in child-directed English (e.g., "who is here?"). The model performs very poorly for other cases of inversion and for languages such as Dutch where question formation does not have the accidental property of English that works in favor of the Reali & Christansen model.

Perfors et al. (2006) approach the structure dependency problem from a Bayesian learning perspective. Unlike the efforts that are designed to only discriminate between grammatical and ungrammatical strings, this work attempts to learn a grammar that could generate additional sentences. Strictly speaking, though, the Bayesian model here does not actually learn a grammar: it evaluates and selects between two grammars, a finite state grammar and a context free grammar, both of which are manually constructed by the researchers on the basis of a simplified subset of child-directed English. Much like Horning's original formulation of Bayesian learning of grammars (1969), the two grammars are assigned prior probabilities, with the smaller grammar being favored. The learning model then calculates the likelihood of the input data given a grammar, which is then multiplied with the prior probability of the grammar to obtain the posterior probability of the grammar. Thus, the grammar's size and its coverage of the data are given simultaneous consideration, and the model is able to favor the context free grammar when the input data has reached a certain level of volume and complexity.

Since the context free grammar contains rules such as "S→aux IP, IP→NP..., NP→NP CP", the principle of structure dependency is therefore already built in and the question of innateness vs. learning is moot. We thus instead focus on the Perfors et al. model in the more general context of grammar learning. The conception of learning here actually deviates from the traditional sense of grammar learning as inductive inference and is in fact conceptually more in line with the parameter setting approach to language acquisition (Sect. 5) where the learning is viewed as selecting a hypothesis out of some space of possibilities innately defined, as there are two grammars in the present case. A major concern, though, has to do with the plausibility of the learning model. While the authors "do not focus on the question of whether the learner can successfully search the space" and only study an "ideal" learner, theoretical considerations (e.g., Heckerman et al. 1995) and simulation results suggest that the enormous computational demand on the Bayesian learner may even limit its utility in practice. For instance, McClelland (2009) notes that just one part of the Bayesian learning model took 352 h, or 11 days, for a simplified subset of child-directed utterances (about 15,000 in total). This type of computing requirement, which will likely grow exponentially when scaled up to realistic samples of linguistic input, may prove taxing for the model's relevance as well as the modeler's patience.

A distinct, and potentially fruitful, line of research in the distributional learning of grammar is more directly motivated by experimental findings. The main task is to explore the utility of certain language learning processes that have been demonstrated in a controlled setting (e.g., artificial languages) in a more realistic setting see Yang (2004) for an evaluation of statistical and structural learning strategies in word segmentation. Linguists and cognitive scientists can do well to draw insights from the computational linguistics literature where the distributional learning of grammar has been extensively studied as a statistical parsing problem. First, the statistical parsing community has a set of standard databases and tasks on which performance measures can be quantified and compared, the algorithmic details are sufficient for replicability, and source code is publicly available; in the cognitive modeling of language acquisition, individual researchers tend to develop their own criteria for evaluating the learning model, often leading to widely diverging results on the same task. Second, and more important, certain ideas in the cognitive science of language have been anticipated and explored in computational linguistics, and there is no reason not to learn from these endeavors. For instance, a direction in the experimental approach to distributional learning makes use of transitional probabilities between words/categories (Saffran 2001; Thompson and Newport 2007): adjacent units that are reliably predicted are assumed to constitute part of a syntactic rule, much like the treatment of word segmentation over syllable sequences (Saffran et al. 1996). This approach is in fact subsumed by an approach to parsing that uses mutual information (Magerman and Marcus 1990). As these authors note (see also Pereira and Schabes 1992; de Marcken 1995), grouping units with high transitional probabilities very often produces incorrect grammatical rules. For instance, the Magerman-Marcus learner frequently groups nouns and prepositions into a phrase; this error stems from the fact that English nouns and prepositions are frequently adjacent, but that's only because a noun phrase is frequently adjoined by a prepositional phrase. Over the past twenty years, various remedies have been proposed to address this problem, largely by introducing more linguistically motivated structures to constrain grammar induction (de Marcken 1995; Charniak 2000; Collins 2003); it would be interesting to pursue similar lines in the experimental approach to see if human subjects can exploit these structural constraints in conjunction with distributional learning.

The task of statistical grammar induction and parsing differs considerably from child language acquisition. Statistical parsing typically takes a large set of grammatical rules (e.g., probabilistic context free grammar) and finds appropriate parameter values (e.g., expansion probabilities in a probabilistic context free grammar) on the basis of an annotated training data such as the Treebank (Marcus et al. 1993) where sentences have been manually parsed into phrase structures. The performance of the trained grammar is evaluated by measuring parsing accuracy on a new set of unanalyzed sentences, thereby obtaining some measure of generalization power of the grammar. This type of learning is referred to as supervised learning because the statistical learner in effect has a teacher that has specified the learning target (i.e., the structural description of a sentence in the form of a parse tree). The child learning a language, of course, does not "see" the structures of the sentences they hear (though it is possible that other sources of information, e.g., prosody, may provide certain cues; see Morgan and Demuth 1996); the traditional approach in both formal and empirical studies of learning generally assumes the learner to have only access to the surface string.[7] Finally, like many distributional learning models reviewed earlier, statistical parsing employs computationally intensive algorithms that are not presently known to have any psychological relevance, and thus cannot be directly taken as an appropriate model of language acquisition.

Nevertheless, statistical parsing can be viewed as a tool that explores what type of grammatical information is in principle available in and attainable from the data, and thus reveal the scope and limits of distributional learning methods. Here we give an example to illustrate how statistical parsing can inform the research in grammar learning from both theoretical and cognitive perspectives. Contemporary work on statistical grammar induction makes use of wide range of potentially useful linguistic information in the grammar formalism. For instance, an phrase "drink water" may be represented in multiple forms:

(2) a. $VP \rightarrow V\,NP$
   b. $VP \rightarrow V_{drink}\,NP$
   c. $VP \rightarrow V_{drink}\,NP_{water}$

(2a) is the most general type of context free grammar rule, whereas both (2b) and (2c) include additional lexical information: (2b) provides a lexically specific expansion rule concerning the head verb "drink", and the bilexical rule in (2c) encodes the item-specific pairing of "drink" and "water", which corresponds to notions such as lexicalized syntax which has a long tradition in syntax

---

[7]Nevertheless, supervised learning has been used extensively in computational modeling of language acquisition, often without commentary on its suitability. For instance, virtually all models in the so-called past tense debate of morphology (e.g., Rumelhart and Mcclelland 1986) and those in the phonological learning of Optimality Theory (e.g., Tesar and Smolensky 2000) assume the learner has simultaneous access to paired input–out forms (e.g., "walk $\rightarrow$ walked", "drink $\rightarrow$ drank", or /dæm/$\rightarrow$[dæ̃m], as in English vowel nasalization), though clearly the input to the child learner does not arrive in this pre-processed form. Learning the pairing is arguably the most challenging component of learning in these cases; see Chan (2008) for extensive discussion.

(e.g., Gross 1975 and many contemporary lexical theories of grammar) and sentence frames as in the psychological literature (e.g., the verb island hypothesis of Tomasello (1992)).

By using subsets of rules in (2) and evaluating parsing accuracy of the grammar thus trained, we can obtain some quantitative measure of how each type of rules, from general to specific, contributes to the grammar's ability to generalize to novel data. Bikel (2004) provides the most comprehensive study of this nature. Bilexical rules (2c), similar to the notion of sentence frames and constructions, turn out to provide virtually no gain over simpler models that only use rules of the type (2a) and (2b). Furthermore, lexicalized rules (2b) offer only modest improvement over general categorical rules (2a) alone, with which almost all of the grammar's generalization power lies. These findings are not surprising given the Zipfian nature of linguistic combinatorics (Sect. 2): lexically specific combinations are useful to keep track of only if they recur in the data but that is highly unlikely for most combinations. The fundamental challenge for language learning, distributional or otherwise, remains to be that of generalization from a small set of data.

5 Learning as Selection

The syntactic theory of parameters is usually associated with the Government and Binding theory and the subsequent development of Minimalism (Chomsky 1981, 1995). For formal considerations, however, we can extend the term to include any theory that acknowledges the finiteness of human language grammar; the task of acquisition is to select the grammar(s) used in the learner's linguistic environment from a finite albeit potentially very large set of grammars. Even learning models that use context free grammars may be construed as an instance of parameter setting: the learner is to determine the forms of expansion rules (and their probabilities in a stochastic formalism), assuming, as is the case in practice, that there is an upper bound on the number of non-terminal and terminal nodes, the length and format (e.g., Chomsky Normal Form) of rules. The Bayesian learning model reviewed earlier (Perfors et al. 2006) is similar: the learner is to choose between a finite state and a context free grammar. In all these approaches, then, the constitutive primitives of the grammar space, which can be broadly called Universal Grammar (UG), are assumed to be innately available to the learner. The sometimes heated debate in the computational models of language acquisition is not about the innateness of UG but about particular conceptions of UG, e.g., whether the learner should be characterized as a set of abstract parameters or a set of context free grammar rules. The debate is ultimately empirical, as we turn to some useful evidence from children's language development in Sect. 6. For the purpose of the present review, we focus on computational models of grammar selection more directly situated in the Principles & Parameters framework, chiefly due to the amount of empirical child language research in this tradition.

5.1 Parameter Setting

In the P&P framework, the grammar of natural language is determined by valuing a universal set of parameters. These parameters are typically binary-valued or could be stated as such. The learner's task, often referred to as *parameter setting*, is to determine the values of the parameters in her language. The original conception of parameters draws firstly from cross-linguistic comparative work. They can be viewed as a type of anchor points for dividing up the linguistic space: the interactions among them would provide coverage for a vast array of linguistic data – more "facts" captured than the number of parameters, so to speak – such that the determination of the parameter values would amount to a simplification of the learning task. The idea of learning by triggering (Chomsky 1981) could be related to the notion of imprinting in ethology: the learner is innately primed to rapidly adopt specific behavioral patterns in the environment.

An influential algorithmic formulation of triggering was developed by Gibson and Wexler (1994):

(3) At any time, the learner is identified with a grammar G, i.e., a string of 0's and 1's

  a. Upon receiving an input sentence s, analyze (e.g., parse) s with G
  b. If successful then do nothing; return to a.
  c. If failure then

    1. Randomly select a parameter value and flips its value, thus obtaining a new grammar G'
    2. Analyze s with G'
    3. If successful, then adopt G'; return to a.
    4. If failure, revert back to G; return to a.

There are several notable design features about the triggering model. First, learning is online: for each input sentence, the child considers at most two grammars before moving on to the next sentence. This is also reflected in the minimal modification of the failed grammar (1) by changing only one parameter value. These measures are taken to keep the computational cost of learning at the minimum, or at least manageable. Second, the learner only revises its hypothesis when failing to analyze an input sentence (3c), and learning is thus error-driven, reflecting the tradition both in the inductive inference framework (Gold 1967) and in other computational approaches to language learning (Wexler and Culicover 1980; Berwick 1985; Tesar and Smolensky 2000).

Unfortunately, parameter setting by triggering, both in the specific formulation of Gibson and Wexler (1994) and as a general model of language development, is known to have serious defects. We turn to the developmental issues in Sect. 6.2; the computational problems of the triggering model have been insightfully analyzed using Markov Chains (Berwick and Niyogi 1996), a suitable framework for studying all learning models that traverse through a finite space of hypotheses. Each grammar (i.e., a string of parameter values) can be identified with a state in the Markov chain. For a specific language in the environment, a directed arc is drawn from grammar A to B if the language contains sentences that would lead the learner to abandon A and adopt B according to the learning algorithm. For instance, under the restriction that failure of the current grammar results in only one parameter value change, a sentence unparsable by A but parsable by B will not lead the learner to adopt B if A and B differ by more than one parameter away. There are multiple grammars, all of which are one parameter away from A and all of which can parse a specific sentence type unparsable by A; the learner as formulated will take an uninformed random guess among this set when that sentence form is encountered in the input. In principle, one can take a (large) sample of child-directed speech from a target language, measure the frequencies of each sentence type and determine the structure and transitional probabilities of the Markov Chain that provides a complete specification of the behavior of the learning model. Convergence results can then be explored by calculating the probability of the learner reaching to the target state from certain stating states as well as the expected number of input sentences required to do so.

It is impractical to explore the learning behavior in a realistic parameter space; just 30 parameters produce a Markov Chain of 2^{30} states, far too many to manipulate computationally. Yet even smaller parameter spaces have proved problematic for the triggering model (Berwick and Niyogi 1996). The most serious problem comes from ambiguity between data and grammar. For instance, consider a child learning English, an SVO grammar, but his current hypothesis is a Japanese-like SOV grammar. Suppose the input sentence is "John likes Bill", for which the SOV grammar fails. There are multiple ways of modifying the grammar that will succeed. For example, the learner could flip the ordering of OV to VO to obtain the target. But it could also turn on the verb second parameter, which is characteristic of many Germanic languages, in effect getting the German-like grammar where the underlying word order is SOV (like Japanese) but the movement of the verb is to the second position of the matrix clause, also leading to the successful parsing of "John likes Bill". Since learning is online, the learner must make a local decision which, as the Markov formulation shows, can lead to a sequence of actions that eventually land the learner in a (non-target) state. And the learner is permanently stuck in a sink state. This type of non-convergent behavior has been confirmed in computer simulations in a sizable and linguistically motivated parameter space (Kohl 1999; Sakas and Fodor 2001).

We review two main lines of attack on the ambiguity problem in parameter setting. In Sect. 5.2, we return to the question just how severe the ambiguity problem is in a realistic space of parameters. The first focuses on how the learner may make more intelligent choices in the navigation of the parameter space. Building on the similar problem of learning the metrical stress system (Dresher and Kaye 1990), Dresher (1999) and Lightfoot (1999) propose that the learner is innately endowed with crucial piece of linguistic patterns dubbed *cues*, which can reliably determine the values of parameters they are associated with. Moreover, these cues (and thus parameters) are ordered sequentially; that is, the cue for a parameter can not be used unless the parameters before it have been set. This offers a solution to certain ambiguity problems. Consider a child learning German, a verb second grammar. The most frequent word order in German is SVO but the learner cannot conclude that her grammar is Verb Second, despite the positioning of the verb, since the pattern (obviously) is also compatible with the English type SVO grammar. However, if the learner has already established previously that the order in the verb phrase is OV, then the SVO must result from the movement of the verb and thus the string becomes an unambiguous cue.[8] Under the cue-based approach, parameter setting is essentially pre-programmed: the child simply follows the path by looking for specific patterns in the linguistic data. A very similar proposal, the idea of a parameter hierarchy (Baker 2002), largely motivated from a comparative/typological considerations, may similarly benefit the child's task for parameter setting. According to this view, the child would follow a sequence of decision that proceeds from major divisions of languages (e.g., ergativity) to minor ones (e.g., adjunct placement (Cinque 1999)). The hierarchy, like cues, is conjectured to be innate and thus solves the ambiguity problem from within. The natural question, of course, is to what extent the parameters required to describe the world's languages follow the ideal expressed in these works.

A related proposal for disentangling parametric ambiguity is suggested by Fodor (1998) and colleagues (Sakas and Fodor 2001; Fodor and Sakas 2009, in prep). Here the learner hedges its bets more intelligently than the random guess triggering learner. It avoids learning from input that is compatible with multiple hypotheses and only modifies the grammar on unambiguous data. To detect data-grammar ambiguity, Fodor proposes that the learner have access to multiple grammars to parse an input sentence. If a sentence is compatible with more than one parameter setting, then clearly it is ambiguous and the learner will ignore it and move on to the next sentence. Fodor notes that parsing a sentence gives a structural description that reveals much more about how parameters interact than the triggering learners' evaluation of a sentence as simply grammatical or ungrammatical. For example, consider again the string SVO, which is ambiguous between an SVO and non-V2 grammar (e.g., English) and a SOV and V2 grammar (e.g., German). A superficial scanning of the SVO string cannot determine, for instance, how V and O are ordered in the base position. However, a linguistically informed parser may know that the base order is determined by the location of the verb's *trace* relative to the object, when the verb has moved elsewhere. It appears that very small parameter domains (e.g., Gibson and Wexler 1994; Fodor 1998) do have unique unambiguous evidence for each grammars, though the matters are not clear in realistic parameter spaces. The feasibility of ambiguity resolution by parsing is also a concern, as one cannot realistically expect the learner to try out all, or even very many, grammars for any given sentence.

---

[8]The OV order parameter, therefore, must be set independently and prior to the V2 parameter by its own cue, e.g., a string where the object is followed by the past participle form of the verb, which indicates its base position before any movement.

An altogether different approach introduces a domain general and probabilistic learning component to language acquisition under Universal Grammar. The *variational* learning model (Yang 2002) rejects a central assumption of triggering and similar models where the learner's grammar changes depending on its success or failure in input. Rather, the learner is identified with a population of grammars whose probabilistic distribution changes in response to the input but the grammars don't, following a process first studied in the mathematical psychology literature (Bush and Mosteller 1951). Suppose that there are n (binary) parameters $\alpha_1, \alpha_2, \ldots, \alpha_n$, each parameter α_i is associated with probability p_i, which denotes the probability of α_i set to, say, the value 1. The learner is then identified with a n-dimensional vector of real numbers in $[0, 1]$ $\mathbf{P} = (p_1, p_2, \ldots, p_n)$, and it is $\mathbf{P}$ that changes during the course of learning. A specific instantiation of the variational learning model is illustrated below:

(4) a. Upon receiving an input sentence s, the learner uses $\mathbf{P}$ to probabilistically (and thus non-deterministically) generate a composite grammar G.
  b. If G can analyze s, reward all the parameter choices in G; i.e., increase/decrease p_i if α_i has been chosen the value 1/0
  c. If G fails to analyze s, punish all the parameter choices in G

Many variants of (4) are possible while maintaining the probabilistic nature of the learning model. For instance, the probability update function can be linear, sigmoid, or Hebbian, and one may also consider learners that only punish failures or only reward successes.

An obvious problem with the scheme in (4) is that it is possible for a learner to have selected the correct values of some parameters but end up punishing these because the composite grammar fails due to other parameters. For instance, for a given trial, a child learning English has chosen the Wh-movement parameter to 1, which is correct, but also happens to have chosen the wrong parameter values of OV in the verb phrase. If the sentence is a declarative SVO sentence, then obviously the composite grammar will fail. The naive learner will punish both the Wh-movement and the OV option: the latter does take the learner toward the target but the former pushes it away. Likewise, incorrect parameter values may be rewarded as the side effects of adjusting parameter probabilities en masse. A proof given by Straus (2008) shows that this naive type of parameter learning will eventually converge on the target. However, in the worse case, the convergence time can grow exponentially relative to the number of parameters.

To fully assess the plausibility of parameter setting models would require a more realistic assessment of just what the actual space of human language grammar is. We review some recent efforts below.

5.2 *Toward Feasible Parameter Setting*

As we have emphasized throughout, computational modeling is the abstract study of language acquisition; computational results, both positive and negative, can only be interpreted in the context of empirical findings. For instance, assuming the finiteness of human language grammars as suggested by most linguistic theories, the learning problem is in principle resolvable. A learner can list all of the parametric grammars in some systematic fashion and sequentially process input sentences from a target grammar. If a grammar is contradicted by a sentence, the learner will move on to the next grammar on the list. It is easy to see that the learner will eventually find the target grammar – all non-target grammars have some positive probability of being contradicted – and permanently stay there, yet no one has seriously suggested this to be a plausible model of human language acquisition. It is clear that the learner will eventually converge on the target grammar. The time it takes to do so, however, could be extraordinarily long, and the learner thus construed is essentially one that learns by guessing, and cannot be taken as a feasible model of language acquisition.

The conception of parameters is an effort to characterize the space of human language grammar to facilitate feasible language learning. The parameter is designed to connect seemingly disparate syntactic phenomena between within and across languages: to restate each traditional rewrite rule with a parameter is not a theoretical advancement. Consider a classic example from the comparative syntax literature. It is well known that English and many other language exhibit the so-called *that-trace* effect, where the extraction of the subject from a relative clause with the complementizer *that* is ungrammatical (5a). Languages such as Italian do not show the that-trace effect (5b).

(5) a. *Who$_t$ do you think that t will visit?
    b. Chi$_t$ credi che t verra a visitarci?
       who think that t will visit
       'Who do you think will visit?'

Ungrammatical examples such as (5a) would not appear in the input data; the learner, of course, cannot in general conclude that non-existent linguistic patterns are necessarily ill-formed. And this raises a paradox: how does the English learning child come to know that (5a) is ungrammatical with explicit evidence?

The comparative syntactic work from the 1970s on has established syntactic correlates of the that-trace effect. For instance, Italian, for which the that-trace effect is absent, allows free inversion of the subject, whereas English does not:

(6) a. *I think that has telephoned John.
    b. Credo che abbia telefonato Gianni.
       think that has telephoned Gianni.
       'I think that Gianni has telephoned.

Moreover, the availability of subject inversion is further correlated with the possibility of *pro-drop*, the omission of the pronouns under certain verbal agreement conditions, which can also be seen from the examples above.

While there is still debate over the theoretical details of these issues, the generalization remains that (at least) three seemingly disconnected syntactic phenomena can be unified under one choice – whether the language in question allows *pro-drop*.

If they all fall under a parameter, then the learner only has the simpler task of making one, rather than three, choices. Furthermore, the property of *pro-drop* is robustly attested in about 70% of all sentences (Bates 1976), providing the child with ample learning opportunities. By contrast, the frequencies of subject inversion and long distance Wh-questions appear considerably lower for languages that allow them, and non-existent or very rare for languages that do not, yet these structurally "deeper" properties could be obtained as a by-product of learning a grammatical pattern much closer to the surface. As long ago as Chomsky (1965), it was observed that a major requirement for a theory of grammar is the feasibility of language acquisition: "(w)e want the hypotheses compatible with fixed data to be 'scattered' in value, so that choice among them can be made relatively easily. This requirement of feasibility is the major empirical constraint on a theory, once the conditions of descriptive and explanatory adequacy are met" (61–62). From this perspective, parameters can be viewed as devices that scatter the grammar space effectively, much like a lower dimensional description of a complex function (as is familiar in the tradition of principal component analysis, for instance). In light of the Zipfian distribution of linguistic combinations (Sect. 2), parameters or similar compressive descriptive devices, appear necessary in order for the child to acquire her grammar in a few years.

The cue-based learning approach (Dresher 1999; Lightfoot 1999) and the notion of parameter hierarchy (Baker 2002) are efforts to structure the parameter space to benefit acquisition. They allow the learner to focus on one parameter at a time and the resolution of each parameter value effectively cuts the space of grammars in half. While certain special cases, such as the parametric space for metrical stress, have been shown to support this approach (Dresher and Kaye 1990), the feasibility of parameter setting, then, can be determined only by looking at some actual parameters and see if they indeed reduce the complexity of acquisition.

The probabilistic nature of the variational learning (Yang 2002) can take advantage of the parametric space in a different way. While the linguistic input consists of an abundance of ambiguity with respect to grammars, it is possible that the ambiguity problem is less severe for parameters. Specifically, many parameters may be associated with *signatures* (Yang 2002, 39). The signature for a parameter refers to sentences that are analyzable only if that parameter takes on the correct value of the target language. Conversely, if the parameter in question does not have the correct value, then the composite grammar of which the said parameter is a constituent necessarily fails. Moreover, a parameter's value is irrelevant for the success or failure of the composite grammar (see 4) if the input sentence is not a signature. Empirically, it is not difficult to find parameters with signatures. For instance, consider the verb to tense raising parameter, which places the finite verb before negation and adverbs in languages such as French and after in languages such as English:

(7) a. Jean voit *souvent* Marie.
 Jean sees *often* Marie.
 b. John *often* sees Marie.

The relative position of finite verbs and adverbs, then, would be the signature for the verb-to-tense raising parameter: when a child learning French has the parameter to the English option, it is guaranteed to fail upon seeing sentences such as (7a), whereas the English learner cannot analyze (7b) if it has selected the French option either.

In Sect. 6.2 we outline several more parameters and their signatures, which have important implications for the quantitative study of language development. If all parameters have signatures, then the variational learning model, specifically one which only rewards success, can efficiently set parameters. Suppose the learner has encountered a signature sentence s_α for a parameter α. The learner now selects a composite grammar G based on the current parameter probability vector $\mathbf{P}$ as described in (4). If the non-target value for α is selected, then G must fail, following the definition of signature – in which case the reward only learner will do nothing. If α has been selected to take on the target value, then G may either succeed or fail. It may fail because the selection of the target value for α given s_α is only a necessary but not sufficient condition for success: other parameter values may have been incorrectly chosen leading the whole grammar G to fail – in which the learner does nothing. When G succeeds and is subsequently rewarded, the target value of α is guaranteed to be rewarded. Thus, when the signature of a parameter is presented in the input, the parameter has a positive probability of moving toward the target and will eventually converge. The question, of course, is whether the existence of signatures can be expected.

There is now reason to be optimistic. In recent work, Fodor and Sakas (2009, in prep) have carried out an extensive exploration of a realistic parameter space and examined its structural properties with respect to learnability. Taking 13 linguistically important and largely uncontroversial parameters pertaining to word order variation, they constructed a space of over 3,000 "languages". Each language has on average 827 distinct syntactic patterns (e.g., subject verb object, Wh-object verb subject indirect object, etc.); there are altogether over 48,000 distinct patterns in the entire space. The data-grammar ambiguity, as long suspected, is quite high: on average, there are 53 languages compatible with each sentence. However, with respect to parameters, they find that 10 out of the 13 parameters have signatures, or what they call global triggers. The remaining three parameters have cue-like properties, that their signature will only become effective after certain other parameters have reached target values already. For the reward only variational learning, this will merely delay but will not affect convergence.

To summarize, the effort in the study of parameter setting has consistently pointed to the need for a hypothesis space favorable to the learner, which echoes the general conclusion from the mathematical study of learning. Assuming the hypothesis space *is* favorable – given Fodor & Sakas's recent exploration, and the fact that children *do* learn grammars impressively fast and accurately – there may exist a range of computational learning models that are formally successful. A cue-based learner innately endowed with the knowledge of parameters and their signatures can converge on the target by searching for specific patterns in the input. The variational learner, as just discussed, may also converge to the target but it benefits from the existence of signatures, an extensional property of the parameter space that the learner needs not have explicit knowledge of. The comparative merits and deficiencies of these models can only be revealed when we turn to the empirical study of child language acquisition.

6 Learnability and Development

The connection with language development is the aspect of computational learning that demands the most attention and remedy. Notable early efforts include Pinker (1984; see also Pinker 1979, a useful review of the inductive inference framework) and Berwick (1985). The former contains numerous observations about child language and suggestions for the computational mechanisms of language acquisition. The discussion, however, does not generally involve formal treatment though they did lead to much subsequent computational work (e.g., distributional learning reviewed earlier). Berwick's Subset Principle (1985; see also Manzini and Wexler 1987) is perhaps the first major result from learnability research to have a direct impact on language acquisition.

6.1 The Subset Principle

The Subset Principle follows from the logic of inductive inference: the hypotheses the learner entertains must be ordered in such a way that positive examples can disconfirm incorrect ones. This tends to force the smallest possible grammar to be adopted first: no other grammar compatible with the data that leads to the new grammar should be a (proper) subset of that grammar. If the learner has conjectured a grammar that is the superset of the target, the positive data alone, at least logically, will not force the learner to adopt the more restrictive grammar. The Subset Principle is not restricted to language learning and has been implicit in Gold (1967) and Angluin (1980)'s general results. Take a non-linguistic example. Suppose the learner is to learn the concept ("New England cities") from which the following examples are drawn:

(8) a. Boston, MA
    b. Providence, RI
    c. New Haven, CT
    d. Portland, ME
    e. ...

If he conjectures the hypothesis "cities in the United States", a superset of the target, then clearly no further examples such as Concord, NH or Springfield, MA can lead to its rejection.

The Subset Principle can be implemented either as a constraint on the hypothesis space or as a principle of learning that strives for the most conservative generalizations, and these efforts needn't be mutually exclusive. One of the earliest applications of the Subset Principle concerns the acquisition of grammatical subjects across languages; see Roeper and Williams (1987). The *pro-drop* grammar such as Italian and *topic-drop* grammar such as Chinese, which allow the omission but do not prohibit the presence of the subject, appear to constitute a superset to English-like grammar for which the subject is obligatory. The Subset Principle would then imply that the learner adopts the more restrict English option initially. This, however, leads to the prediction that children learning English acquire the obligatory use of subject very early, which would be the default option. But this is contradicted by the extended period of subject drop, to which we return in a moment. Upon further reflection, however, it becomes clear that the English grammar is not a subset of the pro-drop or topic-drop grammar, for obligatory subject languages are exemplified by the use of expletive subjects; in the terminology introduced earlier, (9) is the signature for the negative settings of the pro-drop and topic-drop parameters.

(9) a. There is a toy train on the floor.
　　b. There seems to be some noise in the basement.

It remains to be seen if there are any parameter for which the alternative values constitute a strict subset-superset relation.

A learner that operates by conservative generalizations, which has featured in recent linguistic and psychological theorizing (e.g., Culicover 1999; MacWhinney 2004), can be seen as an embodiment of the Subset Principle as a learning mechanism. A related strategy is the use of *indirect negative evidence* (Chomsky 1981): roughly, if the learner had conjectured an overly general hypothesis but has not observed attestations of examples that would follow that hypothesis, he may be led to retreat to a more restrictive hypothesis. It is possible to develop a Bayesian instantiation of this principle (Feldman 1997; Tenenbaum and Griffiths 2001). While these ideas may seem intuitively appealing, Fodor and Sakas (2005) observe that their implementations will likely introduce serious complications. At the very minimum, the determination of superset-subset relations between hypotheses in general involves the calculation of, and subsequent comparisons between, the extensions of grammars (i.e., the set of sentences that they can generate), which can easily become computationally intractable.

6.2 Parameters and Development

The theory of parameter offers promise for the empirical study of language development. Since the totality of grammar is capped, the child's systematic errors can be interpreted as biologically possible though non-target grammars. Hyams' pioneering work (1986) was the first major effort to make use of parameters and triggering in this regard. It is a well established fact that children acquiring English omit a large number of subjects, on average 30% of the time, during the first three years of life (Valian 1991). A small but non-trivial number of objects are omitted as well (Wang et al. 1992). It is an extremely attractive proposition to assume that children in this stage of acquisition have incorrectly set the subject parameter to pro-drop (Hyams 1986) or topic-drop (Hyams 1991; Hyams and Wexler 1993). Unfortunately, quantitative studies show that the frequencies of subject and object omissions in child English differ significantly from those in (child and adult) Italian and Chinese. Moreover, the disappearance of null subjects is gradual (Bloom 1993) rather than abrupt, as would have been predicted by the triggering model where the child resets an incorrect parameter value. Indeed, the largely gradual development of syntax would pose a challenge for the cue-based learning approach as well where the learner also makes decisive moves in the modification of its hypothesized grammar.

There remains a possibility that the mechanisms of grammar learning are not reflected at all in language development. This would be true if by the time when the child produces naturalistic speech, or by the time when experimental techniques can be applied to investigate the nature of child language, all the major aspects of the grammatical system are firmly established with respect to the target language. While this position may disappoint those engaged in the computational modeling of language, developmental researchers from a variety of perspectives have indeed made this assumption (Pinker 1984; Valian 1991; Wexler 1998, etc. though see Tomasello 1992, 2003). There is no denying that many components of child language are learned very early, a pattern that has been repeatedly observed since Brown (1973), it is also the case that young children do not talk *quite* like adults; the null subject phenomenon is just a case in point. Such errors have subsequently been interpreted as deficiencies in either the child's competence or performance system, both of which may still be in the process of biological maturation that is presumably independent of experience. However, a cross-linguistic look at language acquisition raises serious questions for these approaches. For instance, both Italian and Chinese children, from a very early stage, use subjects and objects at frequencies comparable to adults (Valian 1991; Wang et al. 1992), in sharp contrast to children learning English. It would be awkward to suggest that obligatory subject languages delay the cognitive development and maturation.

The variational learning model was designed to connect the gap between language learnability and language development. The introduction of probabilistic learning is designed on the one hand to capture the gradualness of syntactic development and on the other to preserve the utility of parameters in the explanation of non-target forms in child language, all the while providing a quantitative role for the input data in the explanation of child language. It must be acknowledged that language acquisition research in the UG-based tradition has not paid sufficient attention to the role of the input, which may in fact provide complementary evidence for the role of UG in general and the theory of parameters specifically.[9] For instance, a

---

[9]Certainly, admission that input plays a role in language acquisition – how else would the English learning child learn English and the Chinese learning child learn Chinese – does not mean that the input can account for all aspects of the child's linguistic knowledge. This point seems obvious, though the persistent failure to even assess the role of the input points to a methodological deficiency in the current practice.

very large body of literature has been developed for the Root Infinitive (RI) phenomenon (see Wexler, current volume for recent): children acquiring languages that require a tensed verb in the root clause go through a stage in which the root verb is sometimes non-finite. Theoretical accounts for RI often hypothesize qualitative differences between children's grammatical system and the target system. However, this approach faces difficulties in dealing with the gradient nature of RI: that children in the RI stage of a particular language do not exclusively use non-finite forms but rather use a mixture of finite and non-finite forms, and that the duration of RI across languages is not uniform, where morphologically "richer" languages tend to have shorter RI stages. These aspects of RI are especially amenable to a treatment under the variational learning model (Legate and Yang 2007), which focuses on the connection between the RI stage and the parameter space of possible grammars: that there are grammars (e.g., Chinese) where the root verb is not marked for tense, and these are the grammars that must be unlearned by the children. An English learning child, for instance, must rely on morphological evidence of tense marking to acquire the requirement that English root verbs must be tensed, that is, in utterances such as "I go to school", where the null but finite tense morpheme renders the verb indistinguishable from the non-finite form; such input data thus does not tell children that they are *not* acquiring a Chinese type non-tense-marking grammar. By tabulating the frequencies of tense marking verbal forms in several languages, we can relate the quantity of input evidence to the duration of the RI stage, which varies across languages:

Here we briefly summarize some quantitative evidence for parameters in syntactic acquisition.[10] For parameters with signatures (see Sect. 5.2), it is clear that those with more frequent signature evidence in the input will be learned – i.e., the probability converging to the target value – faster than those for which signature evidence is less abundant. By estimating the frequency of signatures in child-directed input, one can study the acquisition of parameters quantitatively and cross-linguistically. Table 1 summarizes the results from these investigations (see also Yang 2004); the reader is directed to the references cited in the table for the linguistic and psycholinguistic details, including the empirical evidence for the parameters and their associated signatures.

Evidence such as this not only provides support for a probabilistic model of learning that is sensitive to the quantity of linguistic input but also highlights the developmental correlates of the parameter based approach (Table 2).

The tracking of longitudinal development of syntax may also contribute to the resolutions of theoretical debates in language acquisition. For instance, it has been frequently suggested that the development of tense correlates with the use of grammatical subjects (Wexler 1998), though the accuracy of this observation has been disputed (Phillips 1995). Figure 5 (from Legate and Yang 2007) illustrates the

---

[10] We refer the reader to Yang (2002, 2006) and references cited therein for distributional evidence that children's systematic deviation from the target grammar is best explained by appealing to non-target but UG possible parametric options.

Table 1 Quantitative comparisons of the amount of unambiguous morphological evidence for tense marking and the reported duration of the RI stage in three languages

Language	% evidence for Tense	Duration of RI stage
Spanish	60.1	~2;0[a]
French	39.7	~2;8[b]
English	5.8	>3;5[c]

a. Grinstead (1994)
b. Rasetti (2003)
c. Phillips (1995)

Table 2 Statistical correlates of parameters in the input and output of language acquisition

Parameter	Target	Signature	Input frequency (%)	Acquisition
Wh fronting	English	Wh questions	25	Very early[a]
Topic drop	Chinese	Null objects[b]	12	Very early[c]
Pro drop	Italian	Null subjects in questions[b]	10	Very early[d]
Verb raising	French	Verb adverb/*pas*	7	Very early (1;8)[e]
Obligatory subject	English	Expletive subjects[b,f]	1.2	3;0[c,d]
Verb second	German/Dutch	OVS sentences[b,g]	1.2	3;0–3;2[b,h]
Scope marking	English	Long-distance questions	0.2	>4;0[i]

Very early acquisition refers to cases where children rarely, if ever, deviate from target form, which cantypically be observed as soon as they enter into multiple word stage of production (e.g., finite verb raisingin French; Pierce 1992). Later acquisition is manifested through children's systematic use of non-target butparametrically possible options

References cited:
a. Brown (1973)
b. Yang (2002)
c. Wang et al. (1992)
d. Valian (1991)
e. Pierce (1992)
f. Hyams (1986)
g. Lightfoot (1999) and Yang (2002)
h. Clahsen (1986)
i. Thornton and Crain (1994)

longitudinal developments of null subjects and RI of a Dutch child (the Hein corpus; Haegeman 1995). Note that his RI stage essentially ended at 3;0–3;1, when his usage dropped to around 5%, yet there were still about 30% of null subject sentences in his production. This suggests that the null subjects and RI are not the reflections of a single grammatical development.

The learning mechanism of the variational model is general and not limited to specific assumptions about the theory of grammar; as reviewed earlier, the quantitative formulation of how the hypothesis probabilities change adaptively in response to the input comes from the tradition of mathematical psychology (Bush and Mosteller 1951). The reward scheme is strongly similar to a wide range of machine learning algorithms such as reinforcement learning (Sutton and Barto 1998) that

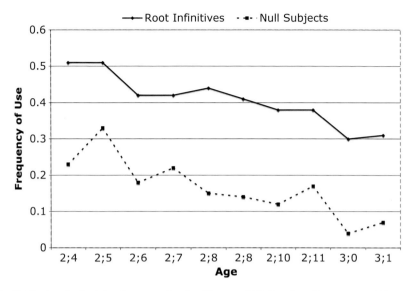

Fig. 5 The longitudinal development of null subjects and RI: data from Haegeman (1995)

have found applications in many domains and tasks. One can easily apply the learning model to other conceptions of the hypothesis space; for instance, the child's Universal Grammar may consists of a body of probabilistic context free grammar rules. Consider a small fragment below:

(10) $S \xrightarrow{\alpha}$ pronoun VP

$S \xrightarrow{\beta} VP$, where $\alpha + \beta = 1$

(10) may be viewed as a model of the distribution of pronominal subjects across languages. For English, α would be close to 1, i.e., all pronoun subjects must be present, whereas in Italian, α will be fairly small (and β large), i.e., most of pronoun subjects are omitted due to pro-drop. A probabilistic learning model – perhaps most probabilistic learning models – working on some English and Italian corpora may quickly drive α and β to the right values. Putting aside issues such as efficiency and computational complexity, one might even say that such a learning model, and the specification of the hypothesis space as a PCFG might provide a formal solution to the grammar learning problem. But it ought to be obvious that child language development poses more challenges. The overwhelming number of pronoun subjects in English will push a probabilistic learner very rapidly toward $\alpha=1$, but as we have reviewed, the actual learner of English goes through an extended stage of omitted subjects. An explicit learning model, which provides a causal connection from grammar to grammar learning, may play a crucial role in the development and evaluation of linguistic theory.

7 Conclusion

So far the task of learning a grammar, something that every five year old accomplishes effortlessly, has eluded computational brute force. As computational models become an increasingly important methodology for linguistic research, one needs to be mindful that these models must be constantly guided and constrained by the findings from the linguistic and psychological studies of child language. Modern computational learning research has produced a wealth of tools that may discover regularities and structures in data, many of which have found useful applications in natural language processing. Yet all current models of language learning still have some ways to go to match the linguistic competence of a young child. And machine learning models, which are often computationally complex and require a tremendous amount of training data, may not directly translate into suitable models of human language acquisition. Of equal importance are the trajectories of learning in machines and children: does the learning model, as the input data is processed, produce behavioral patterns consistent with the longitudinal development of grammar? Finally, the search for an acquisition theory applicable across languages should likewise be reflected in the computational approach, which must address the apparent diversity and complexity of the world's languages. Ultimately, computational models are part of a psychological theory of child language.

References

Abney, S. 1996. Statistical methods and linguistics. In *The balancing act*, ed. P. Resnick and J. Klavins, 1–26. Cambridge, MA: MIT Press.
Angluin, D. 1980. Inductive inference of formal language from positive data. *Information and Control* 45(2):117–135.
Angluin, D. 1982. Inference of reversible languages. *Journal of the ACM* 29(3):741–765.
Angluin, D. 1988. *Identifying languages from stochastic examples*. Technical Report 614. New Haven: Yale University.
Angluin, D. 1992. Computational learning theory: Survey and selected bibliography. In *Proceedings of the Twenty-Fourth Annual ACM Symposium on Theory of Computing*, Victoria, 351–369.
Baker, M. 2002. *Atoms of language*. New York: Basic Books.
Baroni, M. 2008. Distributions in text. In *Corpus linguistics: An international hanbook*, ed. A. Lüdelign and M. Kytö. Berlin: Mouton de Gruyter.
Bates, E. 1976. *Language and context: The acquisition of pragmatics*. New York: Academic Press.
Berwick, R. 1985. *The acquisition of syntactic knowledge*. Cambridge, MA: MIT Press.
Berwick, R., and S. Pilato. 1987. Learning syntax by automata induction. *Machine Learning* 2(1):9–38.
Berwick, R., and P. Niyogi. 1996. Learning from triggers. *Linguistic Inquiry* 27:605–622.
Bikel, D. 2004. Intricacies of Collins' parsing model. *Computational Linguistics* 30:479–511.
Bloom, P. 1993. Grammatical continuity in language development: The case of subjectless sentences. *Linguistic Inquiry* 24:721–34.
Blum, L., and M. Blum. 1975. Toward a mathematical theory of inductive inference. *Information and Control* 28(2):125–155.

Blumer, A., A. Ehrenfeucht, D. Haussler, and M. Warmuth. 1989. Learnability and the Vapnik-Chervonenkis dimension. *Journal of the ACM* 36(4):929–965.
Bod, R., J. Hay, and S. Jannedy. 2003. *Probabilistic linguistics*. Cambridge, MA: MIT Press.
Brill, E. 1995. Unsupervised learning of disambiguation rules for part of speech tagging. In *Proceedings of the 3rd Workshop on Very Large Corpora*, Cambridge, 1–13.
Brown, R. 1973. *A first language*. Cambridge, MA: Harvard University Press.
Bush, R., and F. Mosteller. 1951. A mathematical model for simple learning. *Psychological Review* 68:313–323.
Buttery, P., and A. Korhonen. 2005. Large-scale analysis of verb subcategorization differences between child directed speech and adult speech. In *Proceedings of the Interdisci – Plinary Workshop on the Identification and Representation of Verb Features and Verb Classes*. Saarbrucken: Saarland University.
Bybee, J. 2001. *Phonology and language use*. Cambridge: Cambridge University Press.
Chan, E. 2008. Structures and distributions in morphology learning. PhD diss., Department of Computer and Information Science, University of Pennsylvania, Philadelphia.
Charniak, E. 2000. A maximum-entropy-inspired parser. In *Proceedings of the NAACL, Association for Computational Linguistics*. Stroudsburg, PA, Seattle, 132–139.
Chomsky, N. 1955/1975. The logical structure of linguistic theory. Manuscript, Harvard/MIT. Published in 1975 by New York: Plenum.
Chomsky, N. 1957. *Syntactic structures*. Berlin/New York: Mouton.
Chomsky, N. 1959. Review of *Verbal behavior* by B. F. Skinner. *Language* 35(1):26–58.
Chomsky, N. 1965. *Aspects of the theory of syntax*. Cambridge, MA: MIT Press.
Chomsky, N. 1975. *Reflections on language*. New York: Pantheon.
Chomsky, N. 1981. *Lectures on government and binding*. Dordrecht: Foris.
Chomsky, N. 1995. *The minimalist program*. Cambridge: MIT Press.
Cinque, G. 1999. *Adverbs and functional heads*. New York: Oxford University Press.
Clahsen, H. 1986. Verbal inflections in German child language: Acquisition of agreement markings and the functions they encode. *Linguistics* 24:79–121.
Clark, A. 2001. Unsupervised language acquisition: Theory and practice. PhD thesis, University of Sussex, UK.
Clark, A., and R. Eyraud. 2007. Polynomial identification in the limit of substitutable context-free languages. *Journal of Machine Learning Research* 8:1725–1745.
Collins, M. 2003. Head-driven statistical models for natural language processing. *Computational Linguistics* 29(4):589–637.
Crain, S., and M. Nakayama. 1987. Structure dependency in grammar formation. *Language* 63:522–543.
Crain, S., and R. Thornton. 1998. *Investigations in universal grammar*. Cambridge, MA: MIT Press.
Culicover, P. 1999. *Syntactic nuts*. New York: Oxford University Press.
Culicover, P., and R. Jackendoff. 2005. *Simpler syntax*. New York: Oxford University Press.
de Marcken, C. 1995. On the unsupervised induction of phrase-structure grammar. In *Proceedings of the Third Workshop on Very Large Corpora*, Cambridge, MA, 14–26.
Dresher, E. 1999. Charting the learning path: Cues to parameter setting. *Linguistic Inquiry* 30:27–67.
Dresher, E., and J. Kaye. 1990. A computational learning model for metrical phonology. *Cognition* 34:137–195.
Elman, J. 1990. Finding structure in time. *Cognitive Science* 14:179–211.
Feldman, J. 1997. The structure of perceptual categories. *Journal of Mathematical Psychology* 41:145–170.
Fodor, J. D. 1998. Unambiguous triggers. *Linguistic Inquiry* 29:1–36.
Fodor, J. D., and W. Sakas. 2005. The subset principle in syntax. *Journal of Linguistics* 41:513–569.
Fodor, J. D., and W. Sakas. 2009. Disambiguating syntactic triggers. Paper given at workshop on input and syntactic acquisition, Irvine.

Gibson, E., and K. Wexler. 1994. Triggers. *Linguistic Inquiry* 25:355–407.
Gold, M. 1967. Language identification in the limit. *Information and Control* 10:447–74.
Goldberg, E. 2003. Constructions. *Trends in Cognitive Science* 7:219–224.
Goldwater, S., and T. Griffiths. 2007. A fully Bayesian approach to unsupervised part-of-speech tagging. In *Proceedings of the Association for Computational Linguistics*. Stroudsburg, PA.
Goodman, N. 1955. *Fact, fiction and forecast*. Cambridge, MA: Harvard University Press.
Grinstead, J. 1994. Consequences of the maturation of number morphology in Spanish and Catalan. M.A. thesis, Los Angeles: UCLA.
Gross, M. 1975. *Méthodes en syntaxe*. Paris: Hermann.
Guasti, M. T. 2002. *Language acquisition: The growth of grammar*. Cambridge, MA: MIT Press.
Ha, Le Quan, E. I. Sicilia-Garcia, J. I. Ming, and F. J. Smith. 2002. Extension of Zipf's law to words and phrases. In *Proceedings of the 19th International Conference on Computational Linguistics*, 315–320. Taipei: Howard International House.
Haegeman, L. 1995. Root infinitives, tense, and truncated structures. *Language Acquisition* 4:205–55.
Harris, Z. 1951. *Methods in structural linguistics*. Chicago: Chicago University Press.
Heckerman, D., D. Geiger, and M. Chickering. 1995. Learning Bayesian networks: The combination of knowledge and statistical data. *Machine learning* 20:197–243.
Horning, J. 1969. A study of grammatical inference. Doctoral dissertation, Department of Computer Science, Stanford University, Stanford.
Hudson Kam, C., and E. Newport. 2005. Regularizing unpredictable variation: The roles of adult and child learners in language formation and change. *Language Learning and Development* 1(2):151–195
Hyams, N. 1986. *Language acquisition and the theory of parameters*. Dordrecht: Reidel.
Hyams, N. 1991. A reanalysis of null subjects in child language. In *Theoretical issues in language acquisition: Continuity and change in development*, ed. J. Weissenborn, H. Goodluck, and T. Roeper, 249–267. Hillsdale: L. Erlbaum Associates.
Hyams, N., and K. Wexler. 1993. On the grammatical basis of null subjects in child language. *Linguistic Inquiry* 24:421–459.
Jackendoff, R. 1977. *X syntax: A study in phrase structure*. Cambridge, MA: MIT Press.
Kam, X., I. Stoyneshka, L. Tornyova, J. D. Fodor, and W. Sakas. 2008. Bigrams and the richness of the stimulus. *Cognitive Science* 32:771–787.
Kearns, M., and L. Valiant. 1994. Cryptographic limitations on learning Boolean formulae and finite automata. *Journal of the ACM* 41:67–95.
Kohl, K. 1999. An analysis of finite parameter learning in linguistic spaces. Master's thesis, Massachusetts Institute of Technology.
Kučera, H., and N. Francis. 1967. *Computational analysis of present-day English*. Providence: Brown University Press.
Legate, J. A., and C. Yang. 2002. Empirical reassessments of poverty stimulus arguments. *Linguistic Review* 19:151–162.
Legate, J. A., and C. Yang. 2007. Morphosyntactic learning and the development of tense. *Language Acquisition* 14:315–344.
Lewis, J., and J. Elman. 2001. Learnability and the statistical structure of language: Poverty of stimulus arguments revisited. In *Proceedings of the 26th Annual Boston University Conference on Language Development*, 359–370. Somerville: Cascadilla.
Lightfoot, D. 1999. *The development of language: Acquisition, change, and evolution*. Oxford: Blackwell.
MacWhinney, B. 2000. *The CHILDES project*. Mahwah: Lawrence Erlbaum.
MacWhinney, B. 2004. A multiple process solution to the logical problem of language acquisition. *Journal of Child Language* 31:883–914.
Magerman, D., and M. Marcus. 1990. Parsing a natural language using mutual information statistics. *Proceedings of the AAAI* 2:984–989.
Manning, C., and H. Schütz. 1999. *Foundations of statistical natural language processing*. Cambridge, MA: MIT Press.

Manzini, M. R., and K. Wexler. 1987. Parameters, binding theory, and learnability. *Linguistic Inquiry* 18:413–444.
Maratsos, M., and M. A. Chalkley. 1980. The internal language of childrens syntax: The ontogenesis and representation of syntactic categories. In *Childrens language*, ed. K. Nelson, vol. 2. New York: Gardner Press.
Marcus, G. 1993. Negative evidence in language acquisition. *Cognition* 46:53–85.
Marcus, M., M. Marcinkiewicz, and B. Santorini. 1993. Building a large annotated corpus of English: The Penn Treebank. *Computational Linguistics* 19:313–330.
McClelland, J. 2009. The place of modeling in cognitive science. *Topics in Cognitive Science* 1:11–38.
Merialdo, B. 1994. Tagging English text with a probabilistic model. *Computational Linguistics* 20(2):155–172.
Mintz, T., E. Newport, and T. Bever. 2002. The distributional structure of grammatical categories in speech to young children. *Cognitive Science* 26:393–424.
Morgan, J., and K. Demuth. 1996. *From signal to syntax*. Mahwah: Lawrence Erlbaum.
Niyogi, P. 2006. *The computational nature of language learning and evolution*. Cambridge, MA: MIT Press.
Nowak, M., N. Komarova, and P. Niyogi. 2002. Computational and evolutionary aspects of language. *Nature* 417:611–617.
O'Grady, W. 1997. *Syntactic development*. Chicago: University of Chicago Press.
O'Neil, W., and M. Honda. 2004. Understanding first and second language acquisition (Handbook 10). In *Awakening our languages*, ed. Lizette Peter. Santa Fe: Indigenous Language Institute.
Osherson, D., M. Stob, and S. Weinstein. 1985. *Systems that learn*. Cambridge, MA: MIT Press.
Pereira, F., and Y. Schabes. 1992. Inside–outside reestimation from partially bracketed corpora. In *Proceedings of the ACL* 1:128–135.
Perfors, A., J. Tenenbaum, and T. Regier. 2006. Poverty of the stimulus? a rational approach. In *Proceedings of the 28th Annual Conference of the Cognitive Science Society*, Vancouver.
Phillips, C. 1995. Syntax at age 2: Cross-linguistic differences. In *MIT Working Papers In Linguistics*, vol. 26, 325–382. Cambridge, MA: MITWPL.
Pierce, A. 1992. *Language acquisition and syntactic theory*. Boston: Kluwer.
Pinker, S. 1979. Formal models of language learning. *Cognition* 7(3):217–283.
Pinker, S. 1984. *Language learnability and language development*. Cambridge, MA: Harvard University Press.
Prince, A., and P. Smolensky. 1993. Optimality theory: Constraint interaction in generative grammar. Technical Report RuCCS-TR-2. New Brunswick: Rutgers University Center for Cognitive Science.
Rasetti, L. 2003. Optional categories in early French syntax: A developmental study of root infinitives and null arguments. Doctoral diss., Université de Genève, Switzerland.
Reali, F., and M. H. Christiansen. 2005. Uncovering the richness of the stimulus: Structure dependence and indirect statistical evidence. *Cognitive Science* 29:1007–1028.
Redington, M., N. Chater, and S. Finch. 1998. Distributional information: A powerful cue for acquiring syntactic categories. *Cognitive Science* 22(4):425–469.
Rissanen, J. 1989. *Stochastic complexity in statistical inquiry*. Singapore: World Scientific.
Roeper, T., and E. Williams. 1987. *Parameter setting*. Dordrecht: Kluwer.
Rumelhart, D., and J. Mcclelland. 1986. On learning the past tenses of English verbs: Implicit rules or parallel distributed processing? In *Parallel distributed processing: Explorations in the microstructure of cognition*, ed. J. McCelland, D. Rumelhart, & the PDP Research Group, 216–271. Cambridge, MA: MIT Press.
Saffran, J. 2001. The use of predictive dependencies in language learning. *Journal of Memory and Language* 44(4):493–515.
Saffran, J., R. Aslin, and E. Newport. 1996. Statistical learning by 8-month-olds. *Science* 274:1926–1928.
Sag, I. 2010. English filler-gap constructions. *Language* 86:486–545.

Sakas, W., and J. D. Fodor. 2001. Structural trigger learners. In *Parametric linguistics and learnability: A self-contained tutorial for linguists*, ed. S. Bertolo, 228–290. Oxford: Oxford University Press.
Schütz, H. 1995. Distributional part-of-speech tagging. In *Proceedings of the European Chapter of the Association for Computational Linguistics (EACL)*, University College Dublin, Belfield.
Smith, N., and J. Eisner. 2005. Contrastive estimation: Training log-linear models on unlabeled data. In *Proceedings of the Association for Computational Linguistics*, University of Michigan, Ann Arbor.
Straus, K. 2008. Validations of a probabilistic model of language learning. Ph.D. Dissertation. Department of Mathematics, Northeastern University, Boston, MA.
Sutton, R., and A. Barto. 1998. *Reinforcement learning*. Cambridge, MA: MIT Press.
Teahan, W. J. 1997. Modeling English text. DPhil thesis, University of Waikato, New Zealand.
Tenenbaum, J., and T. Griffiths. 2001. Generalization, similarity, and Bayesian inference. *Behavioral and Brain Sciences* 24:629–640.
Tesar, B., and P. Smolensky. 2000. *Learnability in optimality theory*. Cambridge, MA: MIT Press.
Thompson, S., and E. Newport. 2007. Statistical learning of syntax: The role of transitional probability. *Language Learning and Development* 3(1):1–42.
Thornton, R., and S. Crain. 1994. Successful cyclic movement. In *Language acquisition studies in generative grammar*, ed. Hoekstra, T. and B. Schwartz, 215–253. Amsterdam/Philadelphia: Johns Benjamins.
Tomasello, M. 1992. *First verbs: A case study of early grammatical development*. Cambridge, MA: Harvard University Press.
Tomasello, M. 2003. *Constructing a language*. Cambridge, MA: Harvard University Press.
Valian, V. 1991. Syntactic subjects in the early speech of American and Italian children. *Cognition* 40:21–82.
Valian, V., and Coulson, S. 1988. Anchor points in language learning: The role of marker frequency. *Journal of Memory and Language* 27:71–86.
Valian, V., S. Solt, and J. Stewart. 2008. Abstract categories or limited-scope formulae? The case of childrens determiners. *Journal of Child Language* 35:1–36.
Valiant, L. 1984. A theory of the learnable. *Communications of the ACM* 27:1134–1142.
Vallabha, G., J. McClelland, F. Pons, J. Werker, and S. Amano. 2007. Unsupervised learning of vowel categories from infant-directed speech. *Proceedings of the National Academy of Sciences* 104(33):13273–13278.
Vapnik, V. 1995. *The nature of statistical learning theory*. Berlin: Springer.
Vapnik, V., and A. Chervonenkis. 1971. On the uniform convergence of relative frequencies of events to their probabilities. *Theory of Probability and Applications* 17:264–280.
Wang, Q., D. Lillo-Martin, C. Best, and A. Levitt. 1992. Null subject vs. null object: Some evidence from the acquisition of Chinese and English. *Language Acquisition* 2:221–254.
Wexler, K. 1998. Very early parameter setting and the unique checking constraint: A new explanation of the optional infinitive stage. *Lingua* 106:23–79.
Wexler, K., and P. Culicover. 1980. *Formal principles of language acquisition*. Cambridge, MA: MIT Press.
Yang, C. 2002. *Knowledge and learning in natural language*. Oxford: Oxford University Press.
Yang, C. 2004. Universal grammar, statistics, or both. *Trends in Cognitive Sciences* 8:451–456.
Yang, C. 2006. *The infinite gift*. New York: Scribner.
Yang, C. 2011. A statistical test for grammar. In *Proceedings of the Workshop on Cognitive Modeling and Computational Linguistics*. Association for Computational Linguistics. Stroudsburg, PA.
Zipf, G. K. 1949. *Human behavior and the principle of least effort: An introduction to human ecology*. Cambridge, MA: Addison-Wesley.

The Acquisition of the Passive

Kamil Ud Deen

The passive voice is arguably the most well-studied phenomenon in all of child language. From the earliest days of the modern era, it has been noted that children appear to have difficulties with the passive, both in comprehension and production. This apparent delay in the passive has taken up enormous amounts of time at academic conferences and consumed countless pages in academic journals. But despite this sustained attention and careful scrutiny over four decades, we are only now beginning to learn that children may have knowledge of the passive at younger ages than ever thought.

This chapter surveys some of the more influential empirical studies and theories that address the apparent delay in the passive. In Sect. 1, the question of why the passive might be difficult for children to begin with is considered. Section 2 describes the early experimental studies which establish the backbone of our understanding of this delay in the passive. In Sect. 3, several highly influential theories of the delay in the passive are discussed, as well as evidence for and against these theories. The chapter closes with a review of more recent developments, all of which indicate that the delay in the acquisition of the passive may be less severe or of a different nature than previously thought.

1 Reasons for a Potential Delay

1.1 Grammatical Role Reversal

One of the earliest things children acquire is the canonical word order in their language, especially in languages that have relatively fixed orders, such as English.

K. Ud Deen (✉)
Linguistics Department, University of Hawaii, 1890 East-West Road,
Moore Hall #559, Honolulu HI 96822, USA
e-mail: kamil@hawaii.edu

Table 1 Typical grammatical and thematic relations in active and passive sentences in English

	Active			Passive		
	The dog	chased	the cat	The cat	was chased by	the dog
Grammatical role	Subject		Object	Subject		Object
Thematic role	*Agent*		*Theme*	*Theme*		*Agent*

Limiting the discussion to English for the time being, early on in development, children assign the agent thematic role to the noun phrase that precedes the verb (the subject), and the theme/patient role to the noun phrase that follows the verb (the object). There is a vast amount of naturalistic evidence for this (see, for example, Brown 1973) as well as a good amount of experimental evidence (e.g., Hirsh-Pasek et al. 1984; Hirsh-Pasek and Golinkoff 1999).

One key property of the passive voice is that this canonical relationship between word order and thematic roles is reversed. That is, in the active sentence, the typical subject of a sentence is an agent and the typical object is a theme. But in the passive, this relationship is reversed: the subject in the passive is typically the theme of an event, while the agent occurs in an oblique position within a by-phrase (Table 1).

Thus if a child has (i) acquired canonical word order in English as Subject-Verb-Object, and (ii) learned that the subject is typically the agent, then one might expect children to miscomprehend the passive. Furthermore, one might expect that the miscomprehension would occur predictably in one direction: the passive should be misunderstood as the active counterpart, but not vice versa (Bever et al. 1973).

How does this reordering of arguments occur in the adult grammar? A classic treatment of passive voice is that it derives from its active counterpart. Thus the active sentence (1a) may be thought of as the sentence from which the passive sentence (1b) originates. The manner of this derivation is typically thought to involve some form of movement (or promotion) of the object into subject position, and a corresponding movement (or demotion) of the subject into an optional by-phrase, as in (1c).

(1) a. Fido chased Felix
    b. Felix was chased by Fido
    c. Felix [e] was chased [e] by Fido

If one views the passive in this way, one has a potential answer to why the passive is so difficult for children: this additional necessary movement may be something that children do not master until relatively late in childhood, and thus the passive is necessarily delayed (see Sect. 3.1, A-Chain Deficit Hypothesis below).

1.2 Functional Similarity

The reordering of arguments in the passive does not render its core meaning significantly different from its active counterpart. A sentence like *the dog chased the cat* and *the cat was chased by the dog* are both perfectly grammatical sentences in English, and both adequately describe the very same scene. The differences in usage of these sentence types are relatively subtle: (i) the passive is typically used when one wants to de-emphasize or hide the identity of the agent, (ii) the passive can be used to place emphasis on the patient of the action, and (iii) the passive can be used to retain the topic of conversation in subject position across multiple clauses (see Celce-Murcia and Larsen-Freeman 1999), or (iv) when the speaker wishes to express a sense of adversity or distress. But ordinarily if one were to use an active or a passive sentence to describe any scene, it is unlikely to be incorrect or even lead to confusion. This fact is evident in the question of whether one should avoid passive voice (in favor of the active) in writing – a common recommendation by writing and grammar teachers. If the passive and active were not so close in meaning, this refrain would hardly be necessary (see for example, Pullum 2009, for a recent discussion of this). So because the meaning of the passive and active are essentially the same, use of the passive is rarely (if ever) obligatory. And so if children acquire active sentences early (which they do), and if they can get by perfectly well without ever using a passive, it seems natural that the passive should be a relatively late acquisition.

1.3 Frequency

The passive, while fairly frequent in written English, is significantly less frequent in the input to children than active sentences. Gordon and Chafetz (1990) performed a corpus analysis of the speech of adults to three children (Adam, Eve and Sarah; Brown 1973) from the CHILDES database (MacWhinney 2000) and found that of the 86,655 combined utterances to these three children, a total of 313 passive tokens were found, yielding a rate of passives-per-utterance of 0.36%. Thus by any metric, the passive is a very rare structure in child-directed speech in English. Furthermore, as described below, there are various important distinctions within the category of 'passive' (e.g., verbal vs. adjectival passives, long vs. short passives, neutral vs. adversity passives, etc.), and each of these subcategories occur at an even lower rate than 0.36%.

Moreover, the importance of frequency is not entirely clear. While it is an intuitive notion that rare things in the input may be harder for children to acquire, this is not always the case. For example, Brown (1973) investigated the acquisition of 14 morphemes in the speech of those same three children, Adam, Eve and Sarah. He found that while the 14 morphemes in question were acquired generally in order of most frequent to least frequent, there were other factors that mitigated this effect (e.g., semantic complexity, paradigmatic complexity, etc.). Thus while frequency may not entirely determine the time course of acquisition, it is likely a contributing factor (see Yang's discussion of Zipf's law, this volume).

An important wrinkle comes from cross-linguistic differences. While the passive is a very rare structure in child-directed speech in English, the frequency of the passive varies from language to language. In some languages, the passive is even rarer than English (predicting even later acquisition), and in other languages, the passive is more common than in English (predicting earlier acquisition). This issue will arise below in the discussion of results from Sesotho, a Bantu language in which the passive is reported to be significantly more frequent in child-directed speech than in English.

1.4 Syntactic Synonyms

Recall that one common treatment of the passive is to derive it from its active counterpart (1a–c). This kind of derivation only applies to true *verbal passives*. There exist forms in English which look deceptively like passives, but are not true verbal passives. Consider (2a), which at first blush looks like a passive without the optional by-phrase. This sentence is ambiguous between being a true verbal passive or what is called an adjectival passive. The former is what we have been discussing so far in this chapter, the analysis of which is shown in (2b). Note that 'the door' is moved from the object position, and *broken* is a passive participle. The interpretation of the true verbal passive can be thought of as a description of an event – the event of someone breaking the door.

(2) a. The door was broken
 b. [The door$_i$ [$_{AUX}$ was [$_{VP}$ broken [t$_i$]]]]   Verbal Passive
 c. [The door [$_{VP}$ was [$_{AdjP}$ broken]]]   Adjectival Passive

The second way we could think of (2a) is not as a verbal passive, but as what is called an *adjectival passive*. In this case, (2a) is a description of the state of the door, rather than a description of an event. For example, the following are all descriptions of the state of the door, with the last one being an example of an adjectival passive: 'the door was brown,', 'the door was big,' and 'the door was broken.' Thus *broken* in (2a) is an adjectival participle, and *the door* is not moved into subject position, but is base generated as the subject of the sentence. To further show that these are not verbal, there are plenty of examples in which the adjective has no verbal root: polka-dotted, four-legged, etc., as *in the shirt was polka-dotted*. The analysis of the adjectival passive is shown in (2c).

The fact that verbal passives occur alongside adjectival passives is a potential problem for children because if the child's task is to uncover the fact that passives involve movement of the object to subject position (and the subject into the by-phrase), and if some of the relevant sentences the child encounters look like passives but do not in fact involve movement, then this is a potential complication that could well add to the difficulty of the passive. And in fact, this is precisely what has been proposed in the literature on the passive (see Sect. 3.1, A-Chain Deficit Hypothesis below).

1.5 Optionality of By-phrase: Short Versus Long Passives

One property of the passive noted above is that the agent of the action occurs in a by-phrase at the end of the sentence. But this by-phrase is optional in many languages, and because the function of the passive is to de-emphasize or hide the identity of the agent, the by-phrase is often omitted. Thus a passive without the by-phrase (referred to in the literature as a 'short passive') such as 'the boy was kissed' is just as grammatical as a passive with the by-phrase (referred to as a 'long passive'), e.g., 'the boy was kissed by the girl.' This optionality could potentially be problematic for children because the agent of the action is often hidden in the passive, making the sentence potentially more difficult to interpret.

1.6 Other Complications

Finally, and more generally, there are numerous ways that the passive interfaces with other aspects of grammar which pose further complications for children. Most of the literature has focused on the passivization of an indirect object, with relatively little attention to the passivization of other arguments such as the indirect object, as in *the dog was given a cat* (although, see Roeper et al. 1981). Furthermore, what happens when the verb that is being passivized is grammatically unusual, e.g., so-called ECM verbs, as in *The boy was forced to go*? Or when a causative verb is passivized, as in *The girl was made to cry*? Moreover, middles (e.g., *bread slices easily*) are forms that are remarkably similar to passives (the sole nominal is the patient, there is an implicit agent), but there is no passive morphology. How does the child distinguish middles from passives? These complications, coupled with those mentioned above, lead to the very reasonable expectation that the passive will be acquired late by children.

Having briefly surveyed some of the reasons the passive may potentially be problematic for children, we turn now to some of the studies that documented such difficulty.

2 Early Studies of the Passive

2.1 Imitation, Comprehension and Production

The passive has been studied extensively for many decades now (e.g., Fraser et al. 1963 and Turner and Rommetveit 1967 are some of the earlier studies). One of the more influential early studies was de Villiers and de Villiers (1973), who investigated the passive using an act-out methodology, inspired and adapted from Bever et al. (1973). Children (n=33; female=18, male=15; age 19 months to 37.5 months)

Table 2 Results from de Villiers and de Villiers

Stage	# of children, ages (MLU)	Active		Passive	
		% correct	% reversed	% correct	% reversed
1	8, 19–23 months (1.06–2.99)	45.8	10.4	25.4	30
2	10, 24–27 months (1.06–3.94)	65.8	16.9	39	37.3
3	9, 28–31 months (2.24–4.16)	78.9	15.5	31.8	50.4
4	6, 32–37.5 months (2.86–4.25)	87.8	12.2	34.4	65.6

were given various toys and asked to act-out test sentences, presented in the following form: "Make the boy hit the girl"(active), and "Make the boy be hit by the girl". The children were tested in two sessions: half the children received passive prompts, then actives, and vice versa for the other half of the children. There was a 1 week gap between sessions.

The results (Table 2) show that younger, less mature children performed poorly on both the actives and the passives, responding correctly less than 50% of the time to both sentence types (the numbers do not add up to 100% because there were various other errors, discussed by de Villiers and de Villiers, but ignored here). As the children mature, their response rate on the actives climbs (to almost 90% correct in stage 4), but the response rate in the passive condition remains low, remaining around 30% correct.

Baldie (1976) extended these findings, testing 100 children aged 3;0–8;0, using three different methodologies: Imitation, picture selection (comprehension) and picture description (production). The basic finding here was that the ability to imitate passives occurs earlier (before 5;0) than the ability to comprehend passives (approximately age 6;0), which in turn occurs before the ability to produce passives (as late as 7;6).

So both de Villiers and de Villiers (1973) and Baldie (1976) found that the passive was significantly delayed relative to the active in English. This appears to be true across multiple methodologies.

2.2 Actional Versus Non-actional Passives

Maratsos et al. (1985) investigate whether verb semantics plays a role in the comprehension of passive sentences. They hypothesize that verbs that denote an action (e.g., hit, kiss, chase, etc.) will be easier for children to understand in the passive than verbs that denote an experience, or a non-action (e.g., see, hear, forget, like, etc.). Their hypothesis is based upon the observation that languages differ in terms of which verbs may participate in the passive: some languages allow the passive only with actional verbs (e.g., 'Superman was chased by Batman'), while English allows passivization of both actional and non-actional verbs (e.g., 'Superman was seen by Batman'), but not other supposedly "less asymmetrical" verbs (e.g., 'Superman was resembled by Batman', Wasow 1977).

Table 3 Percent correct responses to a picture selection task testing active and passive sentences with actional and non-actional verbs (Maratsos et al. 1985)

Age	Actional		Non-actional	
	Active	Passive	Active	Passive
4	97	85	92	34
5	99	91	96	65
7	99	92	97	62
9	100	96	99	87
11	100	99	100	99

They conducted two experiments. In experiment 1, they tested 31 children (14 four-year-olds, 17 five-year-olds) on four actional and eight non-actional verbs. They showed children some toy characters, and then presented a test sentence, followed by the question, "who did it?" E.g., "Here is Superman, and here is Batman. Ok...Superman was chased by Batman...who did it?" The children's task was to point to the character that did the event denoted by the verb.

(3) a. Superman was chased by Batman   Actional Passive
    b. Superman was seen by Batman   Non-actional Passive

One possible objection to this methodology is that it favors actional verbs – asking "who did it?" is more compatible with an actional verb than a non-actional verb. To address this concern, Maratsos et al. tested children in both the active and the passive. If the methodology favored the actional verbs, this should be apparent in both the active and the passive conditions. In the active condition, children responded correctly to 91% of actional verbs and 88% of non-actional verbs, showing that the methodology itself was not problematic for the testing of non-actional verbs.

Turning to the passive test sentences, children responded by selecting the correct referent in the actional condition 67% of the time. This was significantly higher than chance. And importantly, in the non-actional condition, children selected the correct referent only 40% of the time, a rate that is significantly lower than chance. Children thus perform significantly worse on passives of non-actional verbs than actional verbs.

In experiment 2, 80 children aged 4–11 years were tested on a picture selection task: two pictures were presented with a test sentence and children were asked to select the picture that matched the test sentence. Non-actional verbs were depicted using thought bubbles, or other visual mechanisms to indicate the non-actional meaning. The results are presented in Table 3.

Children performed essentially at ceiling with the active sentences in both actional and non-actional conditions, and the passive in the actional condition. But problems with comprehension of the passive with non-actional verbs seem to persist until age 9 years. Thus the conclusion from this study is that actional passives appear to be acquired earlier than non-actional passives.

Very similar results are found by Sudhalter and Braine (1985) who tested 50 children aged 3–6 years on an act-out task (e.g., children were shown various toy characters, heard the test sentence, and then asked to pick up the one who kissed/

called/etc. the other). Once again, the finding is that children perform significantly better on actional passives than non-actional passives (See also Gordon and Chafetz 1990 for similar findings, although they offer a verb-class-based account of these findings).

2.3 Long Versus Short Passives

A salient feature of the passive is that there is an optional *by*-phrase. Horgan (1978, using a picture description task with 54 children aged 2;0–4;2 and 180 children aged 5–13 years), found that children rarely produced long passives (i.e., with an overt agentive *by*-phrase). At early ages (younger than 6 years), only roughly 10% of all passives occurred with an overt *by*-phrase. Interestingly, Horgan reports that children often substituted *by* in the *by*-phrase with other prepositions, such as *from* or *with*. Horgan argues that children initially treat passives as stative (or adjectival) structures, and are therefore not compatible with an agentive *by*-phrase. This argument re-appears in the discussion of Borer and Wexler's A-Chain Deficit Hypothesis below.

So in sum, here are the major empirical findings from the early studies on the passive:

(a) The passive is generally delayed, with acquisition not being complete until well after age 6 years.
(b) The ability to imitate passives is acquired before the ability to comprehend passives, which in turn is acquired before the ability to produce passives.
(c) Passives occurring with non-actional verbs are significantly more problematic for children than passives occurring with actional verbs.
(d) So-called 'long' passives (with an overt *by*-phrase) are more difficult for children than short passives (with no *by*-phrase).

3 Theoretical Accounts for the Delay in the Passive

3.1 A-Chain Deficit Hypothesis

Recall that there are several potential reasons for the relative delay in the acquisition of the passive, including their rarity in the input, grammatical role reversal, the optional *by*-phrase, and the kind of predicate that is being passivized (actional, non-actional) Borer and Wexler (1987, 1992) argue that these facts can be derived from a single syntactic difference between adults and children. They claim that child grammars and adult grammars are essentially identical, with the one difference being the ability to form A-chains. They call their hypothesis the A-Chain Deficit Hypothesis (ACDH).

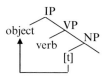

Fig. 1 Movement of the object into subject position

Under derivational theories of syntax, the passive is derived from an active counterpart by movement of the object into subject position (and the optional extra-positioning of the subject into a *by*-phrase). This movement is depicted in Fig. 1.

The movement of the object into subject position is an example of A(rgument)-Movement, since the moved element moves into an argument position (a position selected for by the verb, such as subject or object). Borer and Wexler (1987) argue that this kind of movement is not available to young children, and thus when faced with a passive sentence, children interpret the sentence as a sentence that does not contain movement, i.e., as an active sentence. Thus sentence (4a), whose syntax is indicated by the [t] which shows the position from which Superman moved, is interpreted as (4b), which has no movement notation whatsoever.

(4) a. $Superman_i$ was chased $[t_i]$ by Batman
    b. Superman chased Batman

The prediction of this theory, therefore, is that children will systematically interpret active sentences correctly, but systematically interpret passive sentences as their active counterparts, in essence ignoring the passive morphology and by-phrase. As we have seen above, from the results surveyed so far, these predictions seem to be confirmed (although see below).

Several questions remain, however. For example, how is the actional-non-actional distinction captured by this theory? How is the long versus short passive distinction captured? And how does the child ever develop the ability to make A-chains?

Let us consider the last question first. Borer and Wexler claim that A-chain formation is subject to linguistic maturation. The idea is that children are initially born without the ability to create A-chains, thereby rendering passives (and all A-chain related sentences) problematic for children. But sometime after age 5 years (an age selected on the basis of the experimental results) the ability to form A-chains matures with the concomitant ability to comprehend passives.

It is fair to say that this claim of maturation is the most controversial aspect of this theory. The notion of maturation is often thought of as a somewhat dissatisfying 'explanation', one that seems to not actually answer the question of how children develop. Positing maturation essentially ends the discussion of how development happens since maturation is not something that can be manipulated or mitigated. But it would be a mistake to dismiss this theory purely on one's dislike of the notion of maturation. The ACDH, whatever one thinks of the accompanying idea of maturation, is a remarkably insightful theory that makes clear, testable predictions. Let us turn to some of these predictions.

Prediction 1: Uniform Application of the ACHD to All Passives

Assuming maturation of the ability to form A-chains, the natural consequence is that prior to maturation, children should not be able to comprehend any passive sentences. But it has been well-documented that problems with passives appear to be limited to non-actional passives, and perhaps non-actional passives with a *by*-phrase (see discussion around Fox and Grodzinsky (1998) below). How does the ACDH account for this? Recall from Sect. 1.4 that verbal passives have syntactic synonyms in adjectival passives:

(5) a. The door was broken (by the wind)   verbal passive
    b. the door was broken (description of the state   adjectival passive
        of the door)

The adjectival passive does not require A-movement, and is therefore unaffected by the ACDH. This means that adjectival passives can be freely used by children, and that is in fact what children use both in production and in comprehension. But non-actional passives, given their semantics, are incompatible with an adjectival analysis. For example, the non-actional verb 'to hear' cannot be used in the passive in an adjectival sense, such as 'the frog was heard', meaning 'the frog was in the state of being heard.'

Given this semantic incompatibility, non-actional verbs may not occur in the adjectival passive pattern. But actional verbs may be interpreted in an adjectival manner. So when a child is tested on an actional passive, such as 'Superman was chased,' she is unable to perform A-movement, and so ordinarily would not comprehend this sentence. However, the child is able to apply an adjectival analysis to this sentence and arrive at an interpretation. So the interpretation that the child arrives at is essentially the same as a verbal passive, but it is in fact not a verbal passive, but an adjectival passive (which does not require A-movement).

But when tested on a non-actional passive, the child is still unable to analyze the sentence using A-movement. Furthermore, because the semantics of the non-actional verb are not compatible with an adjectival analysis, the adjectival passive 'escape route' is not available to the child. The child therefore is stuck. All that the child can do is to interpret the sentence according to the rest of its grammar, which is to say, interpret the non-actional passive as a non-actional active sentence. Thus what looks like comprehension of verbal passives is an illusion of syntactic synonymy – it is the adjectival passive that children are using. But this illusion only works with actional passives, since adjectival passives only occur with such actional verbs.

Furthermore, this also neatly accounts for the absence of *by*-phrases in child speech (Horgan 1978): adjectival passives cannot occur with a *by*-phrases since the presence of the *by*-phrase overtly indicates the agent of the action. Adjectival passives are specifically *not* agentive (but rather, descriptions of a state), and so *by*-phrases simply don't occur. So the ACHD, by using the idea of syntactic synonymy, accounts for two important facts about the acquisition of the passive: the relative difficulty of non-actional passives, and the absence of *by*-phrases.

Prediction 2: Uniformity of the A-Chain Deficit

The second prediction the ACDH makes is that the passive should not be the only sentence pattern affected: any pattern involving A-movement, passive or otherwise, should be problematic for children. For example, unaccusative verbs such as *arrive* and raising verbs such as *seem* are predicted to be problematic for children.[1] The next two sections address each of these predictions in turn.

Unaccusatives

Borer and Wexler (1992) make the point that if children are unable to form A-chains, this should hold across all A-chain-related constructions. One such case is that of unaccusative verbs. The analysis of a sentence such as (6a) is given in (6b), where the subject of the sentence is in fact the underlying object (Perlmutter and Postal 1984). This is in contrast to other kinds of intransitive verbs (referred to as unergative verbs) in which the overt subject is in fact the underlying subject (7a-b).[2]

(6) a. The three men arrived
    b. [The three men]$_i$ arrived [t$_i$]
(7) a. The three men talked
    b. [The three men] talked

The movement shown in (6b) is a case of A-movement, since the object is moved into the subject (an argument) position, and so should be impossible for children in the ACDH stage. Does this mean children will never produce unaccusative verbs? Perhaps. But more likely, according to Borer and Wexler (1992), communicative need is so strong that children will force a different analysis onto the string of words just so as to be able to parse a sentence. Borer and Wexler argue that children at this stage of development will analyze unaccusative verbs as unergative verbs: that is,

---

[1] Perhaps most problematic, subsequent to Borer & Wexler's proposal, the notion of the VP-internal subject (Koopman & Sportiche, 1991) was largely adopted by the field. This is problematic because movement of the subject from a VP-internal position to the subject position is clearly A-movement, and is therefore predicted to be problematic for children under the ACDH. However, the Universal Phase Hypothesis, discussed below, which updates the ACDH, does not suffer from this problem, and so this is not discussed further.

[2] There is ample evidence for this analysis, e.g., in English, unaccusatives may occur with expletive subjects, but unergatives may not (compare 'there arrived three men', and 'there talked three men'). This is because the argument in the unaccusative originates in object position, and if it stays in that position, an expletive is inserted to fill the subject position. This is not possible with unergatives, since the sole argument is already in subject position. Furthermore, verbs that take an underlying object (unaccusatives) behave like passives when it comes to the possibility of a resultative clause. For example, the passive sentence 'The floor has been swept clean' is a passive with a resultative 'clean'. Unaccusatives behave like passives in allowing resultatives, e.g., 'The river froze solid', while unergatives do not allow resultatives: 'Dora shouted hoarse' (Levin & Rappaport Hovav, 1995; see also Burzio 1986). The similarity with passive in this respect suggests that both constructions are underlyingly similar, i.e., both involve an underlying object.

they will assume that the overt subject is in fact the underlying subject, thereby avoiding the necessity for A-movement. Thus when a child says or hears a sentence like 'the three men arrived', the analysis she assumes is one in which 'the three men' is base generated in subject position, with no movement whatsoever.

Unfortunately, it is not easy to test this hypothesis in English since it is difficult to differentiate between an unaccusative and an unergative. And so no clear evidence, one way or the other, exists on this issue in English. However, other languages offer some help. Babyonyshev et al. (2001) present an interesting test case for the acquisition of unaccusatives in Russian, where there is a construction known as the Genitive of Negation (henceforth GoN). Simplifying somewhat, this is a construction in which the direct object of a verb, which ordinarily occurs with accusative case morphology (8a), may occur with genitive case morphology when the nominal is negated (8b, hence the name Genitive of Negation). In the latter case, the interpretation of the object is usually non-specific or indefinite. Crucially, the subject may never occur with genitive case, even in a negative sentence. Thus GoN applies to objects and not subjects.

(8) a. Ja   ne   polucil   pis'ma.   ACC object
        I   not   received   letter Acc.PL
        'I didn't receive the/some letters.'
    b. Ja   ne   polucil   (nikakix)   pisem.   GEN object
        I   not   received   (NEG-kind-   letter-GEN.PL
                                GEN.PL)
        'I didn't receive any letters.'

Turning now to unaccusative verbs, the argument of an unaccusative verb also participates in this case alternation of the GoN. That is, the argument of an unaccusative verb, which canonically occurs in the postverbal direct object position, may take either accusative case (9a) or genitive case (9b) in negated sentences.

(9) a. Ne   rasstajalo   ni   odnoj snez'inki.
        not   melted-NEU.SG   NEG   single-GEN.SG   snowflake-GEN.SG
        'Not a single snowflake melted.'
    b. Ne   rasstajala   snezinka.
        not   melted-FEM.sG   snowflake-NoM.sG
        'The snowflake didn't melt.'

At first glance, it is unclear what position these arguments are in. That is, are they in object position, as their postverbal position suggests? Or are they grammatical subjects (as they typically are in languages like English), only in postverbal position? Pesetsky (1982) applies a series of subject-hood tests and finds that the argument of an unaccusative verb in Russian is pronounced in its base (object) position, and is not in fact a grammatical subject . Thus Russian is different from English in that the object of the unaccusative verb in Russian is pronounced in object position, while in English it is moved to subject position and then pronounced.

But Russian is not as different from English as this evidence suggests. Babyonyshev et al. show that while it is true that the object of an unaccusative is pronounced in its base object position, it is nonetheless associated with subject position at some point in the derivation after pronunciation. This later level of representation is referred to as Logical Form, or LF, and movement at LF is often called *covert movement* (since it cannot be seen). The evidence they provide for this covert movement of the object of the unaccusative comes from properties of negation in the GoN. The details of this need not concern us,[3] but they show that the object of an unaccusative moves to subject position at a point after pronunciation. This is a welcome result since it shows that at an underlying level, languages like Russian and English behave in a similar fashion.

So in sum, the Russian unaccusative takes a single argument that is pronounced in post-verbal (object) position, but which moves to subject position after pronunciation. Furthermore, in the GoN construction, the object of an unaccusative may occur with either accusative case or with genitive case (just like other direct objects in Russian).

Babyonyshev et al. make the following predictions regarding unaccusatives in the GoN construction in child Russian. First, if children behave in an adult-like manner (i.e., the ACDH does not apply in their grammar), in negative sentences, children should produce accusative or genitive case on the object of transitive verbs (this is the GoN) as well as the object of unaccusative verbs (GoN), but nominative case on the subject of unergative verbs (since the GoN only applies to objects). But if the ACDH does apply in their grammar, then they should behave adult-like for transitive verbs (i.e., mark the object with either accusative or genitive case) and unergative verbs (mark the subject as nominative), but with unaccusatives, children should mark the argument as *nominative*. This is because the semantics of the argument of an unaccusative is more subject-like: in a sentence like *arrived three men*, 'three men' is likely the subject. Children, unable to form A-chains, misanalyze the argument as a postverbal subject instead of an object, and because the GoN only applies to direct objects, the argument cannot take genitive morphology. These predictions are summarized in Table 4 below.

Babyonyshev et al. tested 30 Russian speaking children aged 3–5 years on knowledge of this using a sentence completion task. Stories were told to the child, followed by a summary statement provided by a puppet. The puppet then

---

[3] Babyonyshev et al. show that in Russian a negative element (such as *no one*, or *nothing*) must be licensed by clausal negation. This licensing occurs when the negative element is m-commanded by negation. Important to our point, a negative argument of an unaccusative is licensed NOT when negation m-commands the object position, but only when negation m-commands the subject position. This shows that at some point in the derivation (presumably at LF), the object argument is associated with the subject position, and hence the claim that the unaccusative argument undergoes covert movement to subject position.

Table 4 Predictions made by Babyonyshev et al. (2001) for case morphology in the negative sentences in Russian

	Adult-like children	ACDH children
Object of transitive verbs	Accusative/genitive	Accusative/genitive
Subject of unergative verbs	Nominative	Nominative
Argument of unaccusative verbs	Accusative/genitive	Nominative

Table 5 Rates of genitive case morphology in GoN environments with two kinds of unaccusatives in child Russian

Sentence type	% Genitive nominal
Transitives	73
Unergatives	4
Regular unaccusative	45
Bleached unaccusative	47

provided a prompt, such as: 'I know what happened. The cat painted two houses and didn't paint …' The child's predicted response is:

(10) odnogo   velosipeda.
      single-GEN.SG   bicycle-GEN.SG
      'a single bicycle.'

Children were tested on a variety of sentence types including transitives, unergatives, and crucially, two kinds of unaccusatives: regular unaccusatives and so-called bleached-unaccusatives. The former *allow* the argument of the unaccusative to take genitive case (but accusative case is also possible, depending on whether a specific or non-specific interpretation is intended), and the latter are a class of unaccusatives which *always require* a genitive subject.

Their results reveal that children respond with a genitive nominal in the transitive condition 73% of the time, but almost never in the unergative condition. This shows that children know the GoN construction – that only objects may take genitive case under negation. Now considering unaccusatives, children respond with genitive nominals between 45% and 47% of the time – a figure that is statistically significantly below that of the transitive condition. Remember, adults treat unaccusatives identically to transitives with respect to GoN, and so the null hypothesis is that the rates in the two unaccusative conditions should be identical to that in the transitive condition, counter to fact. Babyonyshev et al. interpret this to mean that a significant proportion of the time, unaccusative verbs are analyzed as unergatives, thus lowering the rate of genitive case nominals with unaccusatives (Table 5).[4]

---

[4] The fact that the rate of supply of genitive case in the regular and the bleached unaccusative conditions are so similar is not addressed by Babyonyshev et al. except to point out that the bleached verbs occur with GoN 100% of the time in the input, and so a rate of genitive supply of 47% for the bleached unaccusatives is remarkably low.

The reason the rate is not identical to unergatives, Babyonyshev et al. argue, is that there are individual differences within the 30 children. They show that some children are essentially adult-like, and are therefore past the ACDH stage, while others are entirely within the ACDH stage, and they produce far less genitive case arguments, in line with the predictions of the ACDH.

Thus Babyonyshev et al. provide evidence that in a language in which the difference between unaccusatives and unergatives can be observed with morphological case, children appear to treat unaccusatives much like unergatives, analyzing the underlying object as a subject. Furthermore, they show that as children mature, they reanalyze unaccusatives as taking an object argument, and when they do this, they begin to alternate case marking on the object between accusative and genitive.

Additional evidence has been put forward from Korean by Lee and Wexler (2001) who observe that in Korean, children omit nominative case markers more frequently with unaccusative verbs than with other kinds of verbs. They argue this is because nominative case is assigned to a nominal in subject position; if the child is unable to move the object of the unaccusative into subject position, nominative case will not be assigned. The natural consequence is omission of case morphology.

However, Ko (2005) investigates the omission of nominative case in Korean, and finds three interesting facts. First, Korean adults, who also omit case markers occasionally, omit nominative case more often with unaccusatives than other verb types. The omission of nominative case with unaccusatives in adults is unlikely to be because of the inability to form A-chains, and so this casts doubt on the ACDH as an explanation for children. Ko goes on to show that when the other verb types (non-unaccusative) are broken down into unergatives and transitives, Korean children omit nominative case more often with unergatives than transitives, a fact that finds no explanation in the ACDH. And finally, Ko breaks the unaccusative verbs down into various subclasses (adjectival verbs, copular verbs, existential verbs, psych verbs and lexical unaccusative verbs), all of which are supposedly unaccusatives in that they involve A-movement of the object into subject position. He finds that the rates of omission vary greatly from subcategory to subcategory, suggesting that other factors are involved in the omission of nominative case morphology in child Korean. Taken together, these results shed significant doubt on the idea that nominative case morphology is omitted with unaccusative verbs because of the inability to form A-chains.

Raising

Raising verbs are a special class of verbs such as *seem,* whose analysis is given in (11a). Note that the main verb (*seem*) does not have a subject of its own, and takes as a complement a full clause. In a language like English, in which subjects are obligatory, this poses a problem for such verbs since there needs to be a way to give this verb a subject. There are two ways in which raising verbs get their subjects. The first is to insert a dummy subject into subject position, thereby satisfying the requirement for a grammatical subject. This is typically done with what is called an expletive subject, such as 'it', exemplified in (11b).

(11) a. [[e] seems [John is happy]].
   b. [It seems [John is happy]].
   c. [John seems [[t] to be happy]].

The second way is done is by stealing the subject from the lower clause. The lower clause has a subject, which it can surrender, provided it is infinitival. Infinitives are one of the few contexts in English in which a null subject is permissible. Thus the raising verb takes the subject from the lower clause, which, without a subject, must lose its finiteness in order to be grammatical. Because it is a secondary clause, it is grammatical for it to be an infinitival clause (an option not available to the main, raising verb). This satisfies all requirements of the sentence – both clauses are either infinitival, or have subjects.

As can be seen in (11c), the subject of the clause, *John*, has moved from the lower subject position to the higher subject position. Since this movement is into an Argument position, this constitutes a classic case of A-movement, and thus should be subject to the same difficulties postulated by the ACDH for the passive. More specifically, the ACDH predicts that children should not allow the raised variant of the raising predicate (11c), but should allow the expletive variant (11b). In fact, Borer and Wexler (1992) suggest that when faced with a raised subject like (12b), children will parse the sentence as best they can and assign a copular analysis to it – that is, for a sentence like *John seems to be happy*, children who lack the ability to form A-chains will interpret this sentence essentially as *John is happy*.

Becker (2006) tests 43 children aged 3–5 years on raising sentences using a Truth Value Judgment Task (TVJT) (Crain and McKee 1985). Children heard a story accompanied by pictures, and at the end the puppet offered a statement which the children were to judge as either true or false. The premise of the stories is that there is a question of whether an event is actually true or only true in appearance. For example, a white dog sees a purple light and when he stands beneath it, he looks purple. The puppet says something like 'the dog seems purple'. If the child assigns a raised structure to this, the child will accept the sentence, since it is true. But if the child is unable to raise the subject, she will interpret the sentence essentially as a copular sentence, i.e., 'the dog is purple.' The child should therefore reject the sentence on the grounds that the dog is not really purple, he just looks that way. Becker found that children essentially perform like adults – that is, they interpret the raised sentences not as copular sentences, but as true raised verbs. If the ACDH holds, this is an unexpected result, since children should not be able to raise subjects, and thus should interpret the sentences as involving a subject that is generated in the higher clause, i.e., as a copular sentence.

Hirsch et al. (2008) challenge this result, arguing that children were simply confused by the question of whether the dog (in the example above) was genuinely purple or not. They therefore replicate Becker's study, but they modify the test sentences by adding 'really' into the sentence, as in 'the dog really seems to be purple', to emphasize the distinction between reality and appearance. They test 50 children aged 3–7 years, using similar stories to Becker, testing children on a variety of sentence types, including raised and unraised sentences. They find that with the unraised sentences (e.g., 'it seems the dog is really purple'), children perform well (children

Table 6 Results from HWO's test of raised and unraised sentences

Age	Unraised	Raised
3	75	3
4	70	36
5	84	34
6	85	68
7	80	71

younger than 4 years respond correctly 70–75% of the time). However, in the raised condition, young children perform significantly worse (Table 6).

This is in contrast to results from Becker, which Hirsch et al. argue shows that when the reality-appearance factor is highlighted for children, they respond in a manner consistent with a copular analysis of raised sentences. They conclude that children are unable to perform raising, consistent with the ACDH. Moreover, recently, Choe (2011) notes various methodological flaws in the design of Hirsch et al.'s study, and after correcting these errors, she nonetheless finds that English speaking children are unable to comprehend raising sentences, thus further confirming Hirsch et al.'s contention that raising is difficult for young children.

Prediction 3: Developmental Synchrony

A third prediction made by the ACHD is that the time course of all A-chain related sentence patterns should be tightly constrained (all else being equal). That is, because A-chain formation matures at a particular point in time, the ACDH predicts that when children begin to comprehend passives appropriately, they should also begin to comprehend raising sentences, and unaccusative sentences. Thus not only does the ACDH predict patterns across seemingly disparate sentence patterns, it makes the bold prediction of synchronous development across these seemingly disparate patterns. As suggested earlier, the results of unaccusatives and raising are partially in conflict, and so this prediction is yet to be confirmed.

Prediction 4: Universal Delay of A-Chains

One further prediction made by the ACDH is that passives (and other A-chain related constructions) should be universally delayed. Because the delay in the ability to form A-chains is biologically predetermined to mature, this must be true of children in all languages in all parts of the world. Thus the ACDH makes a strong cross-linguistic prediction. Initial results seem promising. There is ample evidence that in many European languages, the passive is delayed in a similar fashion to English. But problems do seem to be emerging in the acquisition of other, non-European languages. See Sect. 3.5 for discussion.

3.2 Universal Phase Requirement

More recently, Borer and Wexler's ACDH has been replaced by the Universal Phase Requirement (Wexler 2004). In Chomsky's (1995) Minimalist Framework, the notion of phases is introduced: certain categories are designated as categories within which all syntactic functions (such as feature checking, application of AGREE, etc.) must be performed. Chomsky proposes several phase categories, including vP. A Phase can be thought of as a small domain within the sentence, within which all syntax is performed, incrementally from one phase to the next. Once all the syntactic functions are complete within the lowest phase, that phase becomes opaque to further syntactic functions (save certain positions within that category, such as the specifier of the top node). So in a sentence that has, say, two phases, syntactic processes begin in the lower phase where all checking of features is done, and once that is complete, the material within this phase is not available for any further syntactic computation. So in the higher phase, all feature checking must be completed using only the features available within that highest phase. Crucially, nothing from the lower phase may be used for the purposes of syntactic computation in the higher phase, since that lower phase has now been sealed-off from syntax, and is thus opaque to syntax.

This approach runs into problems with the passive in that the position of the underlying object is so deep within the vP phase, and the features on the subject position need access to this deep position within the sealed-off phase. In order to solve this problem, Chomsky argues that the vP phase in the passive is 'deficient': unlike normal phases, the vP in a passive it is not sealed-off to further manipulation, thus allowing the passive to proceed through derivation. So-called 'deficient' phases are also thought to occur in all of the other constructions that have traditionally been tied to the passive, e.g., unaccusatives, raising verbs, etc.

The predictions made by the UPR, therefore, are largely unchanged (except for the welcome difference that the UPR no longer predicts problems with the VP-internal subject, since no deficient phase is involved in this process) in that the phenomena that are predicted to be problematic for children remain the same: passives, unaccusatives and raising verbs. The evidence for and against these predictions has been reviewed above in relation to the ACDH.

Before we move on to the next theoretical treatment of the delay in passives, a word about the impact of the ACDH (and its sister proposal, the UPR) is in order. Whilst the theory has been highly controversial, and debates have been highly charged, there is no disputing that this theory is responsible for an enormous amount of research in our field. Because it is such a strong theory, and because it makes such striking, clear and falsifiable predictions, it has generated large amounts of interest and research. And all this work has led us to our current understanding of the passive in child language (see Sect. 4 below), as well as various refinements in methodology.

3.3 Theta-Transmission

The ACDH is a theory that capitalizes on one important component of the passive: movement of the object. Another important component of the passive is that the subject (optionally) occurs in a *by*-phrase. Fox and Grodzinsky (1998) propose that the fundamental difference between adults and children is that children lack the ability to *transmit* the external theta role to the agent in the by-phrase. They present a theoretical outline for how this system works in the adult grammar (see below), followed by some experimental evidence.

The subject of a passive optionally occurs in a *by*-phrase, but how does the subject receive its theta-role? Ordinarily, verbs assign theta roles to their arguments. But in a passive, that theta role is transmitted from the external argument (subject) position to the nominal in the by-phrase. Fox and Grodzinsky provide four examples:

(13) a. Bill was killed by Mary. (agent)
 b. The package was sent by John. (source)
 c. The letter was received by Bill. (goal)
 d. That professor is feared by all students. (experiencer)

In examples (13), we see that the interpretation of the by-phrase is not unitary, but seems to be determined by what the external argument of the verb is. So in (13a), the external argument of 'kill' is an agent, as is the by-phrase in the passive variant. In (13b), the external argument of 'send' is a source, as is the by-phrase in the passive. Etc. The conclusion is that the external theta-role of the verb is *transmitted* to the by-phrase in the passive.

There is, however, a second way that the nominal in a *by*-phrase can receive a theta role, and that is from *by* independently assigning a theta role. But importantly, when *by* assigns a theta role, the semantics of the *by*-phrase are limited to agents (14), instruments (15), or creators/possessors (16).

(14) a. The refugees were imprisoned by the government.
 b. the imprisonment of refugees by the government
(15) a. The city was destroyed by lightning.
 b. the destruction of the city by lightning
(16) a. a book/article/painting by John
 b. CK1 by Calvin Klein
(17) a. i. The package was received by John.
 ii. the receipt of the package (*by John)
 b. i. Harry was feared by John.
 ii. the fear of Harry (*by John)
 c. i. Mary was respected by John.
 ii. the respect for Mary (*by John)

Fox and Grodzinsky conclude that a *by*-phrase assigns a theta-role to an <u>affected</u> nominal only. And here is where the theory gets interesting. They point out that passivized non-actional verbs cannot assign a theta role via the *by*-phrase because non-actional verbs are intrinsically non-affecting, and thus are incompatible with an argument. Therefore the *by*-phrase mechanism to assign a theta role to the nominal in the *by*-phrase is unavailable, leaving *transmission* as the only mechanism to assign a theta-role. Fox and Grodzinsky's hypothesis is that this latter theta-role assignment option is unavailable to children, and thus non-actional passives pose a problem for children, and not actional passives.

3.3.1 Predictions of the Theta-Transmission Model

Prediction 1: Actionality

The first prediction is that actional passives will be acquired early, but non-actional passives will be acquired late. This is because non-actional verbs are the only ones which are semantically incompatible with theta-role assignment from the *by*-phrase. We have already seen that this prediction is borne out: Maratsos et al. (1985, amongst others) have found that children comprehend actional passives significantly better than non-actional passives.

Prediction 2: Interpretation of the *By*-phrase

If children are unable to transfer the theta-role in a passive, the prediction is that the *by*-phrase in a sentence such as 'the baby was hit by the lamppost' should take a locative interpretation. To my knowledge, the only study to investigate this is Pearson and Roeper (2004), who look at the different acquisition paths of locative sentences of this kind and passives in mainstream American English versus African American English. Putting aside the dialectal issue, they find that the locative interpretation of by-phrases like 'by John' in sentences like 'The book was dropped by John' emerges significantly later than the agentive reading. So children tend to interpret 'by John' more often as an agent than a location – exactly the opposite of what the Theta-Transmission Model predicts.

Prediction 3: Long Versus Short Passives

The third prediction made by this theory is that only long passives (i.e., with an overt *by*-phrase), which occur with a non-actional verb will be delayed; all other passives should be unproblematic for children. Thus not only do they predict problems with non-actional passives and with long passives, they predict an interaction effect, since it is only the semantic incompatibility of the non-actional verb with the nominal in the *by*-phrase that results in a breakdown in comprehension.

Fox and Grodzinsky provide experimental evidence for this last prediction. They tested 13 English speaking children aged 3;6–5;5 on a Truth Value Judgment Task

(Crain and McKee 1985) in which children heard a story (acted out with toy props), and at the end a puppet made a statement that was either true or false on the passive reading. Below is a sample story, and two sample test items, the Match being true with respect to the story, and the Mismatch being false.

(18)   Sample story from Fox and Grodzinsky (1998)

A koala bear finds an abandoned egg. He says, "Here is an egg. But there is no one to hatch it. How will it stay warm? I know. I will keep it warm." The koala bear hugs the egg. Then, in walks the rock star. He says, "I have a show in 10 min. I need a drum. Where can I find a drum? Here, the koala bear is holding a drum. I'll take that." The rock star grabs the egg from the koala bear. The bear protests, "Don't take that, I need to keep it warm." At this point the rock star starts running away with the egg and yells back, "It's not an egg. It is a drum, and I need it. Sorry." The koala bear screams, "I won't let you go. I will chase you until I get the egg back." And he starts chasing the rock star.

Puppet then says one of the following test items:

Match: I know what's happening. The rock star is being chased by the koala bear.
Mismatch: I know what's happening. The koala bear is being chased by the rock star.

Looking just at the mismatch test item, if the child understands the test sentence, the target answer is 'false'. But if the child understands the test sentence as an active sentence, i.e., something like 'the koala bear is chasing the rock star', then we expect the child to answer 'true'. They tested children on 24 test items using the verbs *touch, chase* (actional verbs), *hear* and *see* (non-actional verbs). They tested long and short passives, as well as *be-* versus *get-*passives.

Their results show that children performed at ceiling (100% correct) for all active control sentences (both actional and non-actional), as well as actional passives (long and short, *be-* and *get-*passives alike). When it comes to non-actional passives, children did well (although not at ceiling) on short non-actional passives (e.g., *the bear is seen*), responding correctly 86.5% of the time, but they did very poorly on long non-actional passives (e.g., *the bear was seen by the horse*), responding correctly only 46% of the time. This result, therefore, is precisely what their theory of theta-transmission predicts: problems with long non-actional passives only.

3.4   *Frequency*

As noted in Sect. 1.2, the passive is a very rare structure in child-directed speech, occurring at a rate of less than 0.5% of utterances. One possibility is that all of the above findings may very well be a function of sheer frequency. That is, the extreme rarity of passives in general means that children have less exposure to this noncanonical sentence type, and by common sense, the passive would be learned later than other more common sentence types. Furthermore, one could argue that long passives are rarer than short passives; non-actional passives are rarer than actional passives; and long non-actional passives are perhaps the rarest of all. In fact, in their corpus count of child-directed speech, Gordon and Chafetz (1990) found exactly that – actional passives are significantly more frequent than non-actional passives. Thus the frequency of these constructions may very well be related to the synchrony and order of acquisition. The problem is that these variables are confounded: the theoretical proposals discussed in 3.1–3.3 make the same predictions that the frequency account does.

Demuth (1989) points out that the rarity of passives is not universal – there are languages in which the passive occurs fairly commonly, even in child-directed speech. Demuth notes that one such language is Sesotho, a southern Bantu language spoken in the nation of Lesotho (other languages in which the passive appear to be more frequent than English include Zulu (Suzman 1987); Inuktitut (Allen and Crago 1996); K'iche' Mayan (Pye and Quixtan Poz 1988)). In Sesotho, Demuth points out, there is an independent restriction on wh-question formation in that the subject of a sentence cannot be questioned in-situ. In order to question the subject of a sentence, one must either passivize the sentence (thereby demoting the subject into the *by*-phrase, and then questioning the *by*-phrase) or relativize the subject, or form a cleft. This results in a relatively high proportion of passives in both adult-to-adult speech as well as in child-directed speech. And perhaps more importantly, this results in a large number of long passives because in many cases, the purpose of the passive is to question the underlying subject (which, in the passive, occurs in the *by*-phrase). Thus Sesotho is a language in which the frequency account may be pitted against the theoretical accounts described earlier.[5]

Demuth reports that Sesotho children acquire the passive at a remarkably young age. Demuth provides 84 hours of naturalistic data collected from four children over the course of 2 years. The speech samples were collected in the children's homes in conversations with parents, care-givers, siblings, etc. Demuth finds that at early ages (2;1–2;8) children produce relatively few passives. These passives are likely formulaically learned, as the diversity of verbs exhibited in the passive is relatively limited, and the overall frequency of passives is under 1% of verbal utterances. However, at around the age of 2;8 in the speech of two children (and a few months later for the other children), there is a spurt in the use of passives. Both the overall frequency as well as the diversity of verbs used with the passive increase. Furthermore, Demuth shows that a good proportion of the passives used by these young children are long passives. Thus Demuth concludes that the passive is acquired at around age 2;8 – years before English speaking children acquire the passive. Furthermore, this finding is clearly in conflict with the claims of the ACDH and the Theta-transmission theory (although at the time of Demuth's study, Fox and Grodzinsky were yet to publish their study).

The response to Demuth's study was mixed. Some researchers embraced the finding as a confirmation of the importance of the input. Other researchers (see, for example, Crain et al. 2009), embraced the findings as a confirmation of the continuity of child grammar with adult grammar – the fact that children, given sufficient input, are able to acquire the passive, with all of its complicated syntax and semantics,

---

[5] It should be noted that frequency is not the only factor that differentiates Sesotho from English. Passive morphology in Sesotho is a suffix on the verb, and is far less variable than in English (as described in the introduction). For examples, adjectival passives are not synonymous with verbal passives. Furthermore, middles are not marked with the passive morphology, and are therefore very distinct from passives. Thus frequency alone may not be what differentiates the time course of the acquisition of passive in Sesotho from English.

is a remarkable confirmation of the sophistication of child grammar. And yet others were not convinced by the Sesotho data. One crucial weakness with the Sesotho finding is that it comes from naturalistic data, as opposed to experimental data. All other findings in the field came from data gathered in an experimental setting. The difference between naturalistic data and experimental data is that the former is essentially a measure of a child's production abilities, while experimental data are seen as tapping knowledge that gives perhaps a better view of the child's linguistic competence. So while the Sesotho data are suggestive, it is possible that all the passive sentences the children produced were formulaically learned, and not in fact representative of the children's internal linguistic competence (although see below).

3.5 Other Languages

In the discussion of the passive in Sesotho in the previous section, it was noted that a cluster of other languages have also been studied, all of which reveal results very similar to Demuth's claim – that when the passive is relatively frequent in the input in a particular language, children at young ages are able to produce and comprehend passives in that language. But all of these studies are based upon corpora of naturalistic data, and are therefore subject to the same criticism leveled at Demuth. Nonetheless, the fact that there is now a cluster of such languages is strongly suggestive that knowledge of the passive is perhaps not beyond children in these languages.

One language that has been studied relatively intensely is Japanese. A well-known fact about Japanese passives is that there are two kinds: regular passives and adversity passives (the latter involve some kind of negative affect on the patient). Sugisaki (1999) investigates the acquisition of these two kinds of passives in Japanese and finds that adversity passives are acquired earlier than regular passives. This is important because adversity passives are typically analyzed as not involving A-movement, while full passives are analyzed as involving A-movement. So Sugisaki's conclusion from this is that the ACDH holds in that those passives that involve adversity are acquired early, thus giving the impression of early acquisition, whereas 'real' passives are not acquired until later (presumably not until after the maturation of A-chains). See Sugisaki and Otsu (Sect. 7, this volume) for more details.

Furthermore, Sugisaki suggests that Demuth's Sesotho result may be explained using a similar line of reasoning: it is possible that the majority of passives used by the Sesotho children were used with a negative affect (Demuth does not report on the affect of these utterances). If this is the case, and if the passive in Sesotho could be analyzed along the lines of a Japanese adversity passive, then the Sesotho data would be brought in line with the ACDH: the Sesotho children were simply using adversity passives at young ages, none of which require the movement of an argument into subject position. In fact Crawford (2005), in a reanalysis of the same data used by Demuth (1989), argues precisely this for Sesotho – that between 32% and 56% of the passives in the speech of two of the children in the Sesotho corpus involve a morpheme that may be an applicative morpheme, which may carry an adversity reading. See Demuth, Moloi and Machobane (2010, discussed below) for arguments against this position.

A somewhat different perspective is given in the work of Sano (2000) and Okabe and Sano (2002), who investigate the acquisition of the unaccusative and the passive using a TVJT. They find that the unaccusative appears to be acquired early, but that there is a significant delay in the passive, especially the full passive with a *ni*-phrase (the Japanese equivalent of the *by*-phrase). They further investigate the acquisition of other constructions, such as the benefactive, in which the recipient of the benefactive action can be marked by a variety of particles, including *ni*-. They find that when the benefactive is marked by *ni*-, it also is delayed, but when it is marked by one of the other particles, comprehension improves. They suggest that the apparent delay in the Japanese passive may be due to problems with the particle *ni*-, and not with any inability on the part of children (specifically, they argue against Borer and Wexler's ACDH). Moreover, the fact that unaccusatives (which involve A-chains) are acquired early suggests that ACDH must not hold in Japanese (although see Machida et al. 2004).

4 Recent Developments

It is fair to say that the consensus in the field until recently has been that at least some aspect of the passive is problematic for children. Cross-linguistic differences aside, it seemed clear that English speaking children, at the very least, find long non-actional passives particularly difficult, and that these difficulties persist well past the age of 5 years. Furthermore, this supposed difficulty has been documented across a variety of methodologies, both experimental as well as naturalistic.

Nonetheless, recent developments have shed doubt on the classic view that passives are a late acquisition. In particular, developments in the implementation of the truth value judgment task have resulted in an apparent falsification of the results from Fox and Grodzinsky (1998; as well as Maratsos et al. (1985); Sudhalter and Braine (1985), amongst many others) – that young children fail to comprehend long, non-actional passives. Furthermore, the use of newer psycholinguistic techniques (priming) have shown that while children's ability to produce passives and respond to experimental questions may be deficient, their knowledge state appears to be adult-like (Bencini and Valian 2008). And finally, follow-up experimental work by Demuth on the controversial question of passives in Sesotho appear to confirm her earlier claims that young Sesotho children have full knowledge of passives (of all kinds), and are able to not only produce passives in naturalistic conditions, but to respond appropriately in experimental conditions.

4.1 Revisions to the Protocol of the Truth Value Judgment Task

O'Brien et al. (2006) set out to replicate the results from Fox and Grodzinsky (1998), with one change to the experimental protocol. They note that the typical TVJT story used in testing the passive contains two characters, one of whom acts upon the other (in the actional verb cases). So for example, in a typical story, Superman and Batman are the protagonists, and at the end of the story, Batman chases Superman. The test passive sentence in this context would be something like 'Batman was chased by Superman' (false on the passive reading, true on the active reading). O'Brien et al. point out that one function of the passive is to deemphasize the agent/experiencer, and this is done by not producing it in subject position, but placing it in an optional *by*-phrase. The optionality of the *by*-phrase is key – why would the speaker use the *by*-phrase if the purpose of the passive is to de-emphasize the agent/experiencer? The answer that O'Brien et al. provide is that the *by*-phrase is used when there is potential confusion as to who the agent/experiencer might be. Consider a story in which Louise is trying to decide who will kiss her: Superman or Batman. They go back and forth, with the two superheroes arguing their case, and in the end, Superman kisses Louise. If the test sentence in this case were 'Louise was kissed', this may be true, but it is unclear if the speaker of the test sentence understood the story properly – there were two potential kissers, and only one was able to kiss Louise. So in this case, the use of the *by*-phrase is not only motivated, but perhaps crucial.

The point is that if a potential alternative agent/experiencer is not in the story, then the inclusion of the *by*-phrase is not properly motivated. And this infelicity may contribute to children's poor response rates in the long, non-actional condition.

O'Brien et al. test this hypothesis on 12 children aged 3;5–3;11 (mean: 3;6) and 11 children aged 4;0–4;10 (mean: 4;4) using a TVJT with a modified story in which alternative agents and experiencers were included. Below is a sample story:

(19)   Sample story from O'Brien et al. (2006) which satisfies the felicity conditions for the use of the *by*-phrase.

Experimenter:	Bart, the gorilla and the cheetah were relaxing in the jungle one day, when Bart found a bunch of bananas.
Bart:	Hey cool! Look what I found!
Gorilla:	Would you mind sharing some of those with me?
Bart:	No way dude, these are all mine, all mine! Hee, hee. If you want some you're going to have to chase me.
Cheetah:	I could chase him, but I'm not all that fond of bananas.
Gorilla:	Well bananas are my favorite, so watch out Bart, here I come!!! (Gorilla chases Bart).
Experimenter:	Gobu, can you tell me something about that story?
Gobu:	Well, let me see. In that story the gorilla was chased by Bart.

They tested the verbs *see, like* and *hug* as well. Overall, they found that children comprehended actional passives extremely well (even the 3 year olds comprehended actional verbs at a rate of almost 90%). Furthermore, both the 3 year olds and the 4 year olds comprehended long non-actional passives at a remarkably high rate, correctly responding between 82% and just over 90%, respectively.

To be certain that the change they made to the felicity conditions of the passive are responsible for this increased comprehension rate, they replicated the Fox and Grodzinsky's protocol in which the alternative agent/experiencer was not present, hoping to see a corresponding fall in correct response rates. And as predicted, they obtained diminished correct responses: 3 year olds correctly responded to non-actional passives at just over 60%, and actional passives were slightly worse.

The conclusion from these experiments, therefore, is that children appear to be able to comprehend long, non-actional passives at a remarkably early age: as young as 3;6. This is far younger than has been found before, and this finding essentially refutes the notion that child grammar is different from adult grammar. This result is therefore very problematic for the ACDH, the UPR and the Theta Transmission models outlined above.

4.2 Priming

Priming is a process whereby the presentation of one stimulus (called the prime) allows faster and more accurate reaction to a second, related stimulus (called the target). For example, Rayner and Posnansky (1978) tested native English speakers on a picture-word interference task. Participants were asked to listen to a word (the prime) and then label a picture as quickly as possible. When the prime matched the picture or if the prime was phonologically similar to the label of the picture, participants labeled the picture quickly and accurately. But when the prime was unrelated (both semantically and phonologically), reaction time and accuracy fell. This is taken as evidence that the prime can facilitate or inhibit processing of language. Bock (1986) takes this one step further in showing that syntactic patterns can prime as well (known as *Structural Priming*). Crucially, it is assumed that in order for something to be primed, it must constitute some level of knowledge on the part of the participant. If not, then there should be no reason for the prime to have any effect on the participant. Thus structural priming can be taken as evidence for knowledge of a particular sentential pattern, such as the passive.

Bencini and Valian (2008) make use of this procedure and test 53 English speaking children aged 2;11–3;6 (mean:3;2) on the passive.[6] Participants were broken into an active group and a passive group. Each child heard a sentence (passive or active) that described a picture, e.g., the spoon stirs the coffee, the coffee is stirred by the spoon. The child then saw a different picture (e.g., a picture of a knife cutting an orange) and was asked to describe it. They could respond either in the active or the passive. There was also a 'No Prime' condition in which children were just shown the first picture, and then asked to describe the second picture. This was to see if the first picture somehow influenced children in their description of the second picture.

The rationale of this experiment is straightforward: if the passive is primable, then when primed by a passive sentence in the first picture, children should show a tendency to describe the second picture with a passive sentence. And if this occurs,

---

[6] Similar results have been obtained using a more intensive protocol, where children are trained on one kind of passive and are then able to generalize on the basis of that training (see, for example, de Villiers (1980); Brooks and Tomasello (1999)). Here, just a single prime is provided (no training), and is therefore a measure of the child's knowledge state.

the conclusion is that children have knowledge of the passive (otherwise, the prime should have no effect).

The results showed that in the No Prime condition, children never used the passive to describe the second picture. So their preference (independent of any prime) was to describe the pictures using active sentences. When the prime was an active sentence, the second picture was described using the passive only 2% of the time. But when the prime was a passive sentence, the second picture was described using a passive between 11% and 16% (depending on the choice of two scoring methods). Both results are statistically significant, indicating that priming has taken place.

Bencini and Valian's result shows that children as young as 3;2 have knowledge of the passive. Some caveats are in order. First, the observed priming effect held only when the sentences used inanimate subjects and objects (as in the sentences above). For reversible animate sentences, the effect was weak, and did not approach significance. Second, the test items did not include non-actional verbs – precisely the class of verbs that are hypothesized to be problematic for children. But the result is nonetheless important because it provides evidence that the basic passive pattern is intact and available in English speaking children as young as age 3;2. Furthermore, it employs a technique that can be used on fairly young children, leaving open the possibility that non-actional verbs may be tested in the future.

4.3 *Mandarin and Cantonese*

Mandarin and Cantonese are two recognized varieties of Chinese, although they are significantly different from each other. The passive in Cantonese is much like the passive in Mandarin, except that in the former, the equivalent of the 'by' phrase is obligatory in every passive sentence. In Mandarin, on the other hand, the passive may be optionally omitted, much like English and most other languages.

In Mandarin, Xu and Yang (2008) find that the passive is delayed in much the same way as in English.[7] However, Lau and Deen (in prep.) investigate the acquisition of the passive in young Cantonese speaking children. They first investigate the frequency of the passive in child directed Cantonese in the Hong Kong Child Cantonese Language Corpus (CANCORP, Lee and Wong (1998)), available at the Child Language Data Exchange System (CHILDES) database (MacWhinney 2000). Data from eight children were included, and the results show that of the 128,401 child-directed utterances in the corpus, there were three tokens of passive (a passive utterance rate of 0.00002%). Furthermore, of the 62,410 child utterances in the corpus, there were no tokens of the passive found. So the passive is remarkably rare in child-directed Cantonese and completely absent from the speech of Cantonese children (at least in this large database).

---

[7] Although see Xu (2010) who finds that when the protocol employed by O'Brien et al. (2006) is used, Mandarin speaking children appear to understand actional and non-actional passives quite well.

Children's knowledge was tested using a picture selection task, much like that used by Maratsos et al. (1985) and Demuth, Moloi and Machobane (2010, see below). Children were shown two pictures and a puppet uttered a statement, either in the passive or the active, with an equal number of filler items interspersed. Children were tasked with selecting the picture that best matched the puppet's utterance. 14 3-year-olds (mean age 3;5) and 12 4-year-olds (mean age 4;6) were tested on 8 passive utterances (and an equal number of actives), half of which were actional verbs and the other half were non-actional verbs.

Surprisingly, unlike English children, Cantonese children performed well on the task. Children in both age groups responded correctly more than 70% of the time to the actional passives (which is significantly above chance). Furthermore, children performed well with the non-actional passives, responding correctly just under 70% of the time (also significantly above chance). This finding is in contrast to results from English.

The explanation Lau and Deen put forward is that the obligatory presence of the 'by'-phrase in Cantonese makes the passive in this language a single, uniform category, unlike the passive in languages like English. Thus both the rarity of the structure, and the potential complexity posed by the long-short distinction are mitigated by the obligatory presence of the by-phrase. This result, once again, comports with neither the ACHD nor the Theta Transmission Model.

4.4 Sesotho Passives Revisited

The Sesotho data and the claims that sprang from them have been highly controversial and subject to great criticism, most notably that the data are purely naturalistic. Recently, Demuth, Moloi and Machobane (2010; in press, DMM henceforth) address this issue with a series of experiments testing young Sesotho speaking children on their knowledge of various kinds of passives.

DMM conduct three experiments testing 16 Sesotho speaking children aged 2;11–3;5 (mean 3;1), as well as 10 adult controls. Experiment 1 is a two-choice picture selection task. Following O'Brien et al. (2006), DMM include in their pictures three characters instead of two: two primary characters and the third character is the potential alternative agent/experiencer. They test six actional verbs (fasten/tie, cut hair, wipe, bite, carry on back, teach) and six non-actional verbs (see, look for, expel, like, leave behind, and help), all familiar to the children. After a warm-up period, children were shown two pictures and asked, for example, to 'point to the picture where the girl is being carried by the boy.'

Overall, the children were significantly better at comprehending active sentences (82%) than passive sentences (73%). Children were also marginally significantly better at actional verbs (active and passive, 82%) than non-actional verbs (active and passive, 72%), but the interaction of verb type and passive/active was not significant. Furthermore, and crucially, the difference between actional passives (77%) and non-actional passives (69%) was not significant, and comprehension of non-actional passives was significantly above chance.

While these results are strongly indicative of comprehension of the non-actional passives, the fact that non-actional passives are comprehended at a relatively low 69% is somewhat problematic. However, DMM report that the results from adults mirror those of the children in many respects. Adults, like children, perform better on actional passives (99%) than non-actional passives (89%). DMM suggest that the fact that adults also perform (relatively) poorly on non-actional passives shows that the decreased rate of correct responses for both adults and children on the non-actional passives is due to the problem of depicting non-actional verbs in pictures – creating pictures that effectively depict scenes of helping and leaving behind, and liking, etc. is not as easy as creating pictures of actional verbs, and so some difficulties of interpretation may arise from this fact alone.

Experiment 2 is an elicited production task targeting 12 verbs, 6 positively affected and 6 negatively affected. The reason for this split is that various researchers have claimed that so-called adversity passives in languages like Japanese do not involve A-Movement (e.g., Sugisaki 1999). As such, if Sesotho children were to produce large numbers of passives (in apparent contradiction of the ACDH and the UPR), it is possible that all such passives are negatively affected (like the adversity passives in Japanese), and therefore NOT contra the ACDH and UPR.

Children were shown pictures, and each picture was described (e.g., this is kissing). They were then asked either agent-focused or patient-focused questions to elicit actives and passives, respectively. For example, in a picture of a girl kissing a boy (with the mother watching on), the agent-focused question of 'what is the girl doing?' would target an active response, and the patient-focused question of 'what is happening to the boy?' would target a passive response.

Overall, 95% of agent-focused questions resulted in an active response and 98% of patient-focused questions resulted in a passive response. Furthermore, there was no difference in response rate with respect to positive versus negatively affected verbs, thus disproving the claim that Sesotho children's passives are essentially adversity passives across the boards.

In Experiment 3, DMM test whether children generalize the passive pattern to novel verbs. They created two novel Sesotho verbs and paired each with a novel toy that performed a novel action (e.g., a toy with a trap door, where the agent pulled a string and the patient fell through). The child was first taught the novel verb "This is to Verb". The child was then introduced to the new toy, and modeled a test sentence eight times, all in the same frame (active or passive). For example, the experimenter would say, "Now look! The boy is Verb-ing the girl. Look, he's Verb-ing the girl again. Now look – this time the girl is Verb-ing the boy. Let's do it again. Look, the girl is Verb-ing the boy. Now I'll do it. Look, I'm Verb-ing the girl. Do you want to do it now? Look, you're Verb-ing the girl!", etc. Then the experimenter turned to the second novel verb and the second novel toy and the same procedure was repeated, but with the verb used in the opposite frame. The order of presentation of frame was counterbalanced.

At this point, the experimenter returned to the first toy, reminded the child of the toy and the novel verb, and encouraged the child to play with the toy. As the child did this, the experimenter asked questions designed to elicit the opposite frame to that of the training. For example, if the verb had been introduced with the passive, then the experimenter asked agent-focused questions, such as "What is the girl doing?", and vice versa.

All 16 children successfully generalized the passive from the active (95%), and the active from the passive (99%). Of the sentences generalized from the active to the passive, 65% occurred with a full *by*-phrase.

Overall then, DMM is a resounding response to the criticism aimed at Demuth (1989), with results that seem to verify the original claim that Sesotho children as young as 3;2 have significant (if not entirely adult-like) knowledge of the passive. This happens to correlate with high frequency rates in the input, but it also matches the other more recent empirical results discussed above from other methods such as the modified TVJT of O'Brien et al. (2006), the structural priming study from Bencini and Valian (2008), and the uniform by-phrase results from Cantonese (Lau and Deen in prep).

5 Conclusion

For many decades, all indications were that the passive is a late acquisition – not acquired by children until well after age 5 years. This early conclusion in the field has been an important one for our field. It has generated a great deal of work, both in English and in a wide variety of languages. It spawned dozens of research projects around the world and has led to further discovery about other aspects of language and the study of its acquisition that would not have come about were it not for this endeavor. And all this research into the passive has ultimately led us to the current understanding that perhaps children acquire the passive significantly earlier than previously thought. This has several practical and theoretical implications.

Practical Implications: We conclude that in designing a TVJT (or any other experimental protocol), the discourse context and other pragmatic and contextual factors are not just important, they are critical to the success of the experiment. We also conclude that cross-linguistic work is not only useful, but it can be crucial in the discovery of the true nature of child language. And we conclude that with the advancement of new techniques and new theories, our understanding of both the facts and their interpretation may very well change.

Theoretical Implications: Recall that the ACDH and the Theta-Transmission Model are theories that propose parts of Universal Grammar do not operate in the child grammar as they do in the adult grammar. Our current understanding of the passive, that it may in fact be acquired early by children, might be interpreted in a somewhat stronger way: Universal Grammar provides children with the same grammatical tools that adults have, from birth, with nothing maturing or absent. As such, nothing really needs to be acquired for children (with respect to the grammar) to comprehend the passive. Rather, children's grammatical knowledge is fully intact, but their failure in experiments can be attributed to other, non-grammatical factors (see, for example, Crain et al. (2009), for discussion of this very point). These other factors, such as immature pragmatic and discourse knowledge, interfere with the interpretation of the passive, and once such factors are controlled for, experimenters are able to reveal the underlying grammatical knowledge. As such, the 40 years endeavor that is the study of the passive has resulted in a validation of the theory of Universal Grammar in that children appear to have knowledge of this complex, rare, diverse grammatical pattern, and this knowledge is present in children at the youngest testable ages (younger than age 3 years).

References

Allen, S.E.M., and M.B. Crago. 1996. Early passive acquisition in Inuktitut. *Journal of Child Language* 23(1): 129–155.
Babyonyshev, M., J. Ganger, D. Pesetsky, and K. Wexler. 2001. The maturation of grammatical principles: Evidence from Russian unaccusatives. *Linguistic Inquiry* 32(1): 1–44.
Baldie, B.J. 1976. The acquisition of the passive voice. *Journal of Child Language* 3: 331–349.
Becker, M. 2006. There began to be a learnability puzzle. *Linguistic Inquiry* 37(3): 441–456.
Bencini, G.M.L., and V. Valian. 2008. Abstract sentence representation in 3-year-olds: Evidence from comprehension and production. *Journal of Memory and Language* 59: 97–113.
Bever, T.G., M. Garrett, and R. Hurtig. 1973. The interaction of perceptual processes and ambiguous sentences. *Memory and Cognition* 1: 277–286.
Bock, J.K. 1986. Syntactic persistence in language production. *Cognitive Psychology* 18: 355–387.
Borer, H., and K. Wexler. 1987. The maturation of syntax. In *Parameter setting*, ed. T. Roeper and E. Williams, 123–172. Dordrecht: Reidel.
Borer, H., and K. Wexler. 1992. Bi-unique relations and the maturation of grammatical principles. *Natural Language and Linguistic Theory* 10: 147–189.
Brooks, P., and M. Tomasello. 1999. How young children constrain their argument structure constructions. *Language* 75: 720–738.
Brown, R. 1973. *A first language: The early stages*. Cambridge, MA: Harvard University Press.
Burzio, L. 1986. *Italian syntax*. Dordrecht: Reidel.
Celce-Murcia, M. and D. Larsen-Freeman. 1999. The grammar book: An ESL/EFL teacher's course. Boston, MA: Heinle and Heinle Publishing Company.
Choe, J.S. 2011. What seems to be real may be Illusory: Acquisition of raising with an experiencer. In *Proceedings to the 35th Annual Boston University Conference on Language Development*, ed. N. Danis, K. Mesh, and H. Sung, 110–118. Somerville, MA: Cascadilla Press.
Chomsky, N. 1995. *The minimalist program*. Cambridge, MA: MIT Press.
Crain, S., and C. McKee. 1985. Acquisition of structural restrictions on anaphora. In *Proceedings of the North Eastern Linguistic Society*, vol. 16, 94–110. University of Massachusetts, Amherst.
Crain, S., R. Thornton, and K. Murasugi. 2009. Capturing the evasive passive. *Language Acquisition* 16(2): 123–133.
Crawford, J. 2005. An adversity passive analysis of early Sesotho passives: Reanalyzing a counterexample to maturation. In Online Supplement to the *Proceedings of the 29th Boston University Conference on Language Development*, eds. A. Brugos, M.R. Clark-Cotton and S. Ha. Somerville: Cascadilla Press.
de Villiers, J. 1980. The process of rule-learning in child speech- a new look. In *Child language*, vol. 2, ed. K. Nelson. New York: Gardner Press.
de Villiers, J., and P. de Villiers. 1973. Development of the use of word order in comprehension. *Journal of Psycholinguistic Research* 2: 331–341.
Demuth, K. 1989. Maturation and the acquisition of Sesotho passive. *Language* 65: 56–80.
Demuth, K., F. Moloi, and M. Machobane. 2010. Three-year-olds' comprehension, production, and generalization of Sesotho passives. *Cognition*, 115, 238–251.
Fox, D., and Y. Grodzinsky. 1998. Children's passive: A view from the by-phrase. *Linguistic Inquiry* 29: 311–332.

Fraser, C., U. Bellugi, and R. Brown. 1963. Control of grammar in imitation, comprehension, and production. *Journal of Verbal Learning and Verbal Behavior* 2: 121–135.
Gordon, P., and J. Chafetz. 1990. Verb-based versus class-based accounts of actionality effects in children's comprehension of passives. *Cognition* 36: 227–254.
Hirsch, C., R. Orfitelli, and K. Wexler. 2008. The acquisition of raising reconsidered. Paper presented at the Conference on Generative Approaches to Language Acquisition, Barcelona.
Hirsh-Pasek, K., and R. Golinkoff. 1999. *How babies talk: The magic and mystery of language acquisition*. New York: Dutton/Penguin.
Hirsh-Pasek, K., R. Golinkoff, and L. Gordon. 1984. Word order comprehension in a new paradigm: Did Big Bird Tickle Cookie Monster? Paper presented at the Boston University Conference on Language Development. New York: Dutton/Penguin.
Horgan, D. 1978. The development of the full passive. *Journal of Child Language* 5: 65–80.
Ko, I. 2005. Nominative case-marker omission and A-chain deficit in child language acquisition of Korean. In *University of Hawaii Working Papers in Linguistics*, ed. A. Schutz, vol. 36(9), Honolulu: UHWPL.
Koopman, H., and D. Sportiche. 1991. The position of subjects. *Lingua*, 85.1, 211–258.
Lau, F., and K. Deen, in review. Early acquisition of the passive in Cantonese. Manuscript in review.
Lee, H., and K. Wexler. 2001. Nominative case omission and unaccusatives in Korean acquisition. Selected papers from the International Conference of Korean Linguistics, 12: 263–79.
Lee, T., and C. Wong. 1998. CANCORP: the Hong Kong Cantonese Child Language Corpus, *Cahiers de Linguistique Asie Orientale*, 27(2): 211–228.
Levin, B., and M. Rappaport Hovav. 1995. *Unaccusativity: At the syntax-lexical semantics interface*, Linguistic inquiry monograph, vol. 26. Cambridge, MA: MIT Press.
Machida, N., S. Miyagawa, and K. Wexler. 2004. A-chain maturation re-examined: Why Japanese children perform better on full unaccusatives than on passives, ms. In *MIT Working Papers in Linguistics: Plato's problem. Papers in language acquisition*, 48, eds. Csiramz, Aniko, A. Gualmini and A. Nevins, 91–112. Cambridge, MA.
MacWhinney, B. 2000. *The CHILDES project: Tools for analyzing talk*, 3rd ed. Mahwah: Lawrence Erlbaum Associates.
Maratsos, M.P., D. Fox, J. Becker, and M.A. Chalkley. 1985. Semantic restrictions on children's passives. *Cognition* 19: 167–191.
O'Brien, K., E. Grolla, and D. Lillo-Martin. 2006. Long passives are understood by young children. In *Proceedings from the 30th Boston University Conference on Language Development*, ed. D. Bamman, T. Magnitskaia, and C. Saller, 441–451. Somerville: Cascadilla Press.
Okabe, R., and T. Sano. 2002. The acquisition of implicit arguments in Japanese and related matters. In *Proceedings to the 26th Annual Boston University Conference on Language Development*, eds. Skarabela, Barbora, S. Fish, and Anna H.-J. Do, 485–499. Somerville, MA: Cascadilla Press.
Pearson, B., and T. Roeper. 2004. Learnability and triggers: Obligatory versus optional triggers for the passive in two dialects of English and in language impairment. In *The Proceedings of the 28th Annual Boston University Conference on Language Development*, eds. A. Brugos, L. Micciulla, and C. Smith, 447–460. Somerville, MA: Cascadilla Press.
Perlmutter, D., and P. Postal. 1984. The 1-advancement exclusiveness hypothesis. In *Studies in relational grammar*, 2nd ed, ed. D. Perlmutter and C. Rosen, 81–126. Chicago: University of Chicago Press.
Pesetsky, D. 1982. Paths and categories. Unpublished Doctoral dissertation. MIT: Cambridge, MA.
Pullum, G. 2009. 50 Years of stupid grammar advice. *The Chronicle Review*, 55(32): B15.
Pye, C., and P. Quixtan Poz. 1988. Precocious passives (and Antipassives) in Quiché Mayan. Papers and reports on child language development, Stanford, 27.71–80.
Rayner, K., and C.J. Posnansky. 1978. Stages of processing in word identification. *Journal of Experimental Psychology: General* 107: 64–80.
Roeper, T., S. Lapointe, J. Bing, and S. Tavakolian. 1981. In *Language acquisition and linguistic theory*, ed. S. Tavakolian, 35–58. Cambridge, MA: MIT Press.

Sano, T. 2000. Issues on unaccusatives and passives in the acquisition of Japanese. In *Proceedings of the Tokyo Conference on Psycholinguistics*, vol. 1, 1–21. Tokyo: Hituzi Shobo.

Sudhalter, V., and M. Braine. 1985. How does comprehension of passives develop? A comparison of actional and experiential verbs. *Journal of Child Language* 12: 455–470.

Sugisaki, K. 1999. Developmental issues in the acquisition of Japanese unaccusatives and passives. In *Proceedings of the 23rd Annual Boston University Conference on Language Development*, ed. A. Greenhill, H. Littlefield, and C. Tano, 668–683. Somerville, MA: Cascadilla Press.

Suzman, S. 1987. Passives and prototypes in Zulu children's speech. *African Studies* 46: 241–254.

Turner, E., and R. Rommetveit. 1967. Experimental manipulation of the production of active and passive voice in children. *Language and Speech* 10: 169–180.

Wasow, T. 1977. Transformations and the Lexicon. In *Formal Syntax.*, eds. Peter W. Culicover, T. Wasow, and A. Akmajian. New York: Academic Press.

Wexler, K. 2004. Theory of phasal development: Perfection in child grammar. In *MIT Working Papers in Linguistics 48: Plato's Problems: Papers on Language Acquisition*, eds. A. Csirmaz, A. Gualmini, and A. Nevins, 159–209. Cambridge, MA.

Xu, T. 2010. Are chinese children's passives delayed? In *Proceedings to the Tokyo Conference on Psycholinguistics*, ed. Y. Otsu, 269–289. Tokyo: Hituzi Syobo.

Xu, T., and X. Yang. 2008. Children's acquisition of passives in Chinese. In *The Proceedings of the Ninth Tokyo Conference on Psycholinguistics*, ed. Y. Otsu. Tokyo: Hituzi Syobo.

The Acquisition Path for Wh-Questions

Tom Roeper and Jill de Villiers

1 Introduction

The topic of wh-questions has been central in language acquisition because it has been pivotal in linguistic theory itself. Rare and intricate sentences—across all known grammars—revealed that wh-extraction was sharply limited by structural "barriers" to movement. Refinement of these questions has progressed from Ross's (1967, 1986) first Island constraints to the Barriers work (Chomsky 1977, 1981) to Chomsky's recent Strong Minimalist Thesis (2005, 2008a). The critical claims are about *what does not happen,* for which no direct empirical evidence can arise. Hence no empirical learning procedure could conceivably work to learn "barriers". Our perspective is the traditional one: what kinds of innate constraints does a child bring to the acquisition problem and what principles of grammar are on view? A modern extension of that perspective comes from the question: how do innate principles of grammar create an interface with other domains of mind?

What should an acquisition theory look like? One primary question is about the Initial State: is there a set of Default representations with which a child begins? From there, questions arise about the mechanisms whereby the child constructs a grammar across many domains, or modules. Given UG considerations, we can argue that the child seeks to restrict how much information he assimilates at each step, namely:

T. Roeper (✉)
Linguistics Department, 226 South College, University of Massachusetts at Amherst,
150 Hicks Way, Amherst, MA, USA
e-mail: roeper@linguist.umass.edu

J. de Villiers
Departments of Psychology and Philosophy, Smith College, Bass Hall 401,
Northampton, MA, USA
e-mail: jdevilli@smith.edu

The Modular Interface Constraint: a child first represents a new construction in a single module.

We take the classic notions of syntax-internal modules to include at least a Movement module, a Case module, a Binding module, and a Thematic role module, the boundaries of which are still open to discussion. Therefore we predict acquisition will be governed by a broad constraint that favors single modules over modular interaction. Where can we see an example of this order in acquisition? A classic case is the contrast between A-movement (e.g. passive) in (1), and A-bar-movement (wh-) in (2). They differ both in landing sites—A-movement goes to subject-position and A-bar movement to an element in the CP system- and in Case.[1] In English, A-movement <u>precedes</u> case-assignment, while wh-movement follows it, so wh-movement shows the same case in both positions and can be analyzed in a single module, the movement module:

(1) A-movement:
  passive: John saw me/ I was seen by John
(2) A-bar movement:
  wh-movement: I saw what/what did I see

In the same vein, the prediction is that Topicalization, as A-bar movement, could be acquired very early, precisely because it shows no impact of case-marking change:

(3) I like him → him I like[2]

If there is no interaction with another module, then the application of the rule is transparent on the surface of the grammar, and that would make it is easier to acquire.[3] It has in fact often been claimed that children grasp Topicalization very quickly (Gruber 1967; Grinstead 2004). In contrast, the acquisition of A-movement is delayed (Borer and Wexler 1992; see Deen, this volume). Though case is mastered early in English, mastering the passive must entail representing the impact of both modules of movement and case, which are not morphologically independent. Were that not the case, we would expect a stage in English where the child says:

(4) *me was pushed

---

[1] Tornyova and Valian (2009) point to the impact of morphology and other dimensions in their cross-linguistic comparison of inversion in English and Bulgarian. We argue that there is a specific mechanism whereby modules are integrated which must be articulated. The general idea that other factors influence the acquisition path does not provide the mechanism whereby information across modules is integrated, which is crucial to understanding the acquisition differences in cross-linguistic variation.

[2] WH-movement also has complex historical interactions with case-assignment, but appears to be moving toward independence: complete loss of –m in <u>whom</u> in favor of <u>who</u>.

[3] Interesting new complications arise when we consider modular interactions in other languages, where for example, case might appear on wh questions.

but this has never been reported. Therefore children at an early stage in English either analyze the subject as unmoved, and therefore receiving nominative cause, or they immediately grasp that A-movement precedes case marking.

Take a more directly relevant case in the acquisition of wh-questions. One task of a child is to identify the lexical properties of wh-words. The wh-words enter English in roughly the order: *what* and *where*, then *how*, *when*, *where* and later *why*, and last, *which* or *whose*. One can ask: Does this occur before or after the words are linked to *movement* chains? In fact, children may not complete lexical analysis before they link wh-words to movement chains. They appear to recognize Question Force in a moved position—seeing it within a single module—before they work out how they differ from each other in meaning. Evidence shows that wh-words are confused (*how* and *why*) long after they first analyze them within the movement module, as expected under our constraint. This is most evident in languages with rich case systems, like German where dative, accusative, and genitive are distinct, but wh-words and movement appear before case is mastered.

Moreover children recognize movement chains before they fully grasp the logical properties of *sets* and *exhaustivity* with question words (see discussion below)—which enter into a Logical Form module. The process of integration is what the description of the acquisition mechanism must capture. In what follows, we will illustrate this concept of modular complexity for both Discourse linking and Logical form.

Full wh-acquisition introduces many questions often linked to the unusual semantics of wh-questions. Let us outline roughly what must be acquired with an eye toward cross-linguistic variation. (Occasional special terminology introduced here is described in the sections below and defined in more detail as needed).

1. The **lexical** properties of wh-words. Some are arguments, required by the verb (*what, who, where*) and some are adjuncts (*how, when, why, where*) which freely relate to any verb. There is also internal morphology that must be identified: a wh-morpheme may

    (a) Attach to other morphemes (what = wh + that, where = wh + there, when = wh + then).
    (b) Show case-assignment overtly (who/whom/whose—and others in other languages)

2. The **semantic** properties of wh-words

    (a) They refer to a <u>set</u>
    (b) The set must be exhaustive (who committed the crime)
    (c) Multiple wh-words enter into Pairing relations (who bought what)

3. The **movement** properties of wh-words, varying across languages:

    (a) They may not move overtly, just at Logical form.
    (b) They may allow or disallow Long-distance movement altogether
    who did John say Bill claimed Mary invited__
    (c) Partial Movement may occur where the wh-question moves only partway: What did John say Bill claimed <u>who</u> Mary invited (German, Romani, many others)

(d) Pied-piping may occur where more than a wh-word is moved to the front:
Which car from Brazil did Bill want to buy___?

4. **Multiple** wh-words may or may not move together or obey Superiority:

(a) Superiority: a condition that blocks one wh-word from moving over another, limiting their ordering:
"*what did who buy"
(b) Multiple Wh-Fronting (Bulgarian, Serbo-Croatian)
"who what where did he put it"

Each of these features of wh-movement could, in principle, emerge independently or be decided independently, and the order of decisions could be fixed by UG or be subject to the nature of the input. If we can identify linked decisions, parameters, or chains of implication, they will simplify the acquisition task.

The literature from the last 30 years is voluminous, and so we focus here on major issues. Our goal will be to connect the current data and theory in those domains where a theoretically reasonable acquisition story can be told, and to point out promising avenues for future work. The chapter is divided into three major sub-topics:

(a) Wh-questions as movement rules within a single clause, entailing debates about the scope of the formal generalizations the child makes and whether the underlying structures are adult-like.
(b) The logical properties of wh-questions, and semantic properties of sets, exhaustivity and scope.
(c) Long distance movement, principled restrictions and barriers to movement, and interfaces with semantics and pragmatics (including the Strong Minimalist Thesis from Chomsky 2008).

2 Movement Rules

2.1 *Landing Site*

In modern revisions of linguistic theory (Chomsky 1995) elements (including *wh*-forms) are said to *move* because they contain a set of features that are attracted to a certain "landing site" in the linguistic structure matching those features. Considering languages that exhibit overt wh-movement, a *direct* question moves to a landing site at the front of the sentence. The label for the position in the phrase into which it moves is the "CP" or Complementizer Phrase. Each clause in a sentence has the potential for such a position, although it is not always occupied. In (3), the CP position is marked for a *direct question feature*, which the *wh*-word must match:

(5) What did the boy buy ____?
$_{CP}$ [wh + direct Q]   [wh + direct Q]

The Acquisition Path for Wh-Questions

In those languages that exhibit wh-movement, young children produce initial wh- almost immediately. The first use of wh-question force may be with fixed phrases like *"what dat"* or *"whazzat."* However even with very limited syntax spontaneous expressions occur like:

(6) English: (Roeper and Rohrbacher 1994; MacWhinney 2000)
where go?
what hit?
what watch huh?
where go bye bye?
where zip it, huh?
where waving?

German: from Spinner and J. Grinstead (2006):
was das denn?
what that then
"What's that, then?"
Wo ist?
Where is
"Where is (it)?"
Wo sind die Ringe?
"Where are the rings?"

French: from Zuckerman (2000)
Comment tu as fait ça ? (Fronting)
how you have done that
"How did you do that?"
Qu'est-ce que tu as fait?
what is it that you have done
"What did you do?"

In Indonesian wh-in-situ, or no overt wh-movement, is the norm in the adult language. It is evident very early in children (from Cole et al. 2001):

(7) Minum *apa* ya? HIZ-27
drink what yes

[Experimenter asks child what he wants to drink; child reflects]
"What will I drink?"
Bikin *apa* ya? HIZ-32
make what yes

[Child playing with crayons, wonders what to draw]
"What should I make?"
Mana taronya? HIZ-31
where put-ASSOC
[Child carrying a chair, wondering where to put it]

"Where should I put it?"

Consider, however, that although in situ wh- is fairly common in adult French (*il va ou*—he went where), children do not necessarily use in situ wh-questions at the start (Zuckerman 2000; Plunkett 1992). In French, inversion is required if the wh-word is fronted, but children begin with an initial wh-word and without inversion, that is, they produce questions starkly at odds with the input (Zuckerman 2000). The difference between true wh-in-situ languages and those with wh-movement is thus evident from the beginning. Clearly some kind of parameter has been set from the input, but still children can ignore parts of the input. Therefore the child's analysis is not complete.

What should the analysis of these early wh-questions be? They could be the result of movement, or simply Merged, like any other word selected from the lexicon, in keeping with an important UG hypothesis:

Merge is preferred over Move.

Rizzi (1997) has proposed an elaborated sequence of nodes on the left periphery for adults which (a) may not all be universal, and (b) may involve a number of acquisition steps, some of them possibly parameterized, distinguishing Force (e.g. Imperative, Question), Topicalization, and Focus phenomena. Certainly the earliest wh-questions have Question Force, but that is not necessarily sufficient to fix the structure. It is clear that if the nodes are not all universal, then the child has a substantial challenge in determining the sequence and labeling of each node of the left periphery.

What else do we know about the left periphery in child grammar? Spinner and Grinstead (2006) make the interesting argument that three quite different forms: overt subjects, topicalized objects, and wh-questions co-occur in the acquisition of Spanish, but emerge at different points in German. Why should this be so? Spinner and Grinstead make the theoretical assumption that overt subjects are in a discourse-sensitive part of the left periphery in Spanish, a pro-drop language, so all of these phenomena in Spanish entail a position in the left periphery (8a). But German (8b) is a non-pro-drop language, and since its overt subjects are not discourse dependent, they are not in the CP. In consequence they appear independently of, and before, wh-questions in acquisition.

(8) (a) Spanish: Topic/CP
    Topic
    Wh-
    Subj
  (b) German: Topic/CP Spec-IP
    Topic   subj
    Wh

But is this Topic/CP node in the left periphery already the same as the adult CP? In the theoretical literature, the "fine structure of the left periphery" is regarded as a pre-existing structure that includes a division of the functions of the Complementizer Phrase into landing sites for questions (Force), Topics, and Focus as different from one another, but not all are present or playing the same role in every language. Therefore although the full array may be part of UG, the child must select nodes relevant to his language. It would be natural for the child to refine the structure as new information arises. One possibility suggested by the discussion above is that the child begins with a proto-CP, and it undergoes an actual process of Splitting as suggested by Hollebrandse and Roeper (1998) to end up with a distinct series of nodes with different functions. In other words, the historical terms "Split-IP" and "Split-CP" may define actual acquisition processes. Unfortunately these fascinating questions suffer from the mismatch between an elaborate theory and minimal data. The child's early utterances are so attenuated that these claims are highly theory-dependent. Still this roadblock may not be fatal. If we look to the next step, we can reason back to the claim that, whatever that first node holds, it may not be the adult CP.

Traditionally questions entail agreement between the auxiliary and the head, under Spec-Head Agreement (Rizzi 1991), but we will discuss an alternative motivation below. This agreement gives rise to auxiliary movement from I to C:

(9) What can he juggle?

Without spec-head agreement, auxiliary movement is not required.

(10) *What he can juggle?

Note that this occurs when there is no question force as in exclamatives:

(11) What things he can juggle!

However, (10) is what children often produce, with clear question force. This could be analyzed under the assumption that the child's Proto-CP has a C node, but not a full Spec-Head representation that forces Agreement:

(12) Where daddy is going?
 What mommy can do?
 Why me can't do that?

(Brown 1973; Tornyova and Valian 2009)

If the child lacked a full Spec-Head projection, we predict that (10) would occur.[4] The joint theoretical observations that Merge is a primitive operation and that the Left-periphery varies across languages make it plausible under Minimalism that the child would begin with Merge. So let us make an acquisition claim at this point similar to de Villiers (1991):

A child shifts from merging the wh-word to fill a C node to fully articulating a CP with a Spec position.[5] Some background on subject-auxiliary inversion in acquisition is necessary before advancing the argument on behalf of this claim.

---

[4] In fact, Lasnik and Saito (1992) proposed a C without a Spec as a way to explain various barrier phenomena.

[5] Children do have structure-dependent rules for aux inversion, as Crain and Nakayama (1987) have shown quite definitively. They invert full NP's like "*the boy who is here*" and not simply the first auxiliary "is the boy who is here happy" and not with the "closest" auxiliary. Their claim is that the operation of auxiliary inversion is structure-dependent as young as age 3 years. Nevertheless because it is a local operation and a limited set of auxiliaries are involved, it can be acquired with lexical restrictions, where either auxiliaries or their semantics may be restricted, especially before the age of three.

2.2 Auxiliary Movement in Questions

The first question to be considered is whether auxiliary inversion is learned all at once or in a piecemeal or lexical fashion. Lexical sensitivity in acquisition has been argued from many quarters (Tomasello 2003), even within the generative framework (Roeper 1993; Roeper and de Villiers 1994; Borer and Wexler 1992 among others). Linguistic theory under Bare Phrase Structure maintains that individual lexical items project one item in (13) (push) as the label of the node when they Merge. "Push" can take *wagon* or any noun as its complement.

(13)   push
        /   \
      push   wagon

The higher node is replaced by V as more elements fit the pattern. This is essentially identical to recent lexicalist claims of Rowland and Pine (2000), except insofar as they argue that lexical extensions are the full explanation. But for generative approaches, the extensive array of lexical exceptions (for children as well as adults) *complicate,* rather than *facilitate* the child's grasp of the generative rule. Ultimately, and traditionally, the lexicon carries lexical exceptions that *violate* the productive rule. Therefore the child must be sure *not* to generalize them. The fact of lexical exceptions makes it more remarkable that a child ever decides to promote a general rule.

Ultimately, something forces the child to see beyond the extensive variation to just the right principle of inversion that applies to any NP AUX string to make a question. But what forces the child to see it? The answer is not clear, but the interaction of modules may play a role here. If the child were to just project a pair of independent frames:

(14) NP Aux
     Aux NP

that would fail to capture Number Agreement that obtains between them. Since the construction interacts with the Number-Agreement system, a different linguistic module, we have the variants:

(15) Is he
     Are they

and these link to:

(16) He is
     They are

If children have to solve both of these problems, the system becomes much simpler if the operations are performed in this order:

Number Agreement
Subject-Auxiliary Inversion

This is another version of our argument that constructions which involve two modules are a greater challenge than constructions whose analysis is transparent within a single module. The solution to the interaction of these modules depends upon both the recognition of two general rules and their ordering.

This ordering, which affects languages with richer agreement more than English, must be kept separate from an additional form of lexical uncertainty which is frequent in English: Main verb inversion (like V2 in German) which applies to *be* in English (and *have* and *be* in some British English) supports the hypothesis that inversion might involve the Main Verb:

(17) Are you here?

Have you any money?

American English has moved toward isolating the SAI to pure auxiliaries by introducing *do*-support with main verb *have*:

(18) Do you have any money?

Predictably children assume the construction is limited to auxiliaries, and may briefly produce forms like (19):

(19) Do it be here[6]?

Such children must then do a further reanalysis and put *be* back into an exceptional class of Main Verb inversion in English with respect to the Inversion rule, although it participates in the modular ordering of Agreement before Inversion. Thus it is misleading to call it "auxiliary inversion" when it involves Main verb "*be*" as well.

2.3 *Auxiliary Inversion and Building a CP*

How can these properties of auxiliary inversion help us to determine the nature of the child's CP? Consider that a robust fact about language acquisition is that English children fail to perform subject-auxiliary inversion in wh-questions long after they perform the same operation in yes/no questions (Tyack and Ingram 1977; Erreich 1984; de Villiers 1991):

(20) Can I sing

What I can sing

One might have predicted that the inversion operation in yes/no questions would extend immediately to wh-questions. The discrepancy in inversion between the two types of questions calls for a theoretical explanation. If we follow the proposal above that the initial merge involves only C, i.e. that there is

---

[6] This is also found in African-American English with habitual *be*.

one C position, but no Spec position, it means only one position is available. This predicts exactly that one can have auxiliaries in this first position or wh-questions, but not both.

However, whether the auxiliary is absent or in uninverted position in wh-questions is empirically complex,[7] with the weight of data now in favor of the auxiliary being mostly *absent* in wh-questions before appearing in inverted position (Stromswold 1990; Rowland and Pine 2000). In other words, if the auxiliary is present at all in a question, it is likely to be inverted. It could be that if inversion is called for, but grammatically impossible for the child, then the child avoids the auxiliary altogether. So failure to include the auxiliary could itself be a response to a child's sense of structural conflict: they hear questions with inversion, but their grammar is missing a position for it. Since they know that an uninverted auxiliary (what he can do) is also not target-consistent, a "conservative" move[8] would be to avoid producing sentences with auxiliaries or main verb BE.[9]

Individual variation is also unmistakable. Stromswold (1990) reports an average inversion rate of 93% for children in wh-questions, though individual children's rates range from 60.1% to 99.3%. In addition, sometimes there can be quite a long period of unstable development, with the adult rate of 100% inversion not becoming fixed until at least age 5. First, we consider the evidence that children build a full CP to house the wh-word and the auxiliary in C. Then we consider the thorny question of lexical variation versus productivity, both in the wh-words and in the auxiliaries that invert.

Suppose the critical step in subject aux inversion is the realization of a full CP with a Spec node. What could trigger it? De Villiers (1991) discovered a possible

---

[7] Brown (1973) pointed to a specific case where the child Adam produced a large number of *why* and *why not* questions that appeared to be immediately appended to declaratives his mother had just uttered:

Mother	Adam
You bent that game	Why me bent that game?
He was playing a little tune	Why he play little tune?
You can't dance.	Why not me can't dance?
I don't see any	Why not you see any?

Brown interpreted these as a transformational rule applied in discourse, onto the base sentence supplied by Adam's mother. Several others have noticed this phenomenon, and given it a different interpretation, focusing on the special case of *why* (Thornton 2007; de Villiers 1991). This account fits the notion that children have a simple version of Merge available to them.

[8] This is in the sense of conservativity which Snyder (2007) has carefully documented. It is not clear how to account for this phenomenon, but a theory of Multiple Grammars where a child has grammars that are in conflict might lead in this direction (Roeper, 2000).

[9] Syntax is not the end of the story. Possible semantic motivation for inversion must be considered as a further factor. See Roeper (2007, 2009) and de Villiers (2010) for evolving work on the role of propositions in this domain.

trigger. There is a developmental correlation between the appearance of inverted auxiliaries in wh-questions and subordinated indirect questions:

(21) John asked what he can do
     What can he do

de Villiers (1991) argued that the appearance of the wh-word in medial position coincides with its analysis as part of CP, subcategorized and lexically governed by a particular verb in the matrix sentence. In modern terms, verb subcategorization must project into a new clausal Phase, which is marked by a Phase-Edge position, namely the Spec of CP.

The subcategorization across a Phase boundary provides the trigger that the appropriate position for the question feature is in Spec of CP, rather than in a lower inaccessible Topic position. One consequence of this re-analysis is that it makes available the C-position into which the auxiliary can move, because Wh- is in Spec of CP, hence the appearance of inversion in the matrix clause thereafter.

If the higher verb *ask* lexically projects a wh-feature into the next clause, UG requires that it goes onto the Spec of CP in the subordinate clause because only the SPEC (Edge) position is a landing site for movement, and the feature must be satisfied by Movement not Merge. Therefore we argue that Indirect Questions serve as a good SPEC trigger:

(22) ask [CP Spec- C [IP NP AUX …
                        →   +wh
      [CP   Spec   C   [IP   NP   Aux   Verb ____
                   can←=========
         what ←===============

Thus the triggering of SPEC-CP by the projection of the wh-feature by Inheritance further creates a Spec-Head Agreement requirement that forces inversion in simple clauses as well.[10] Our earlier hypothesis that initial Merge involved a Proto-CP, without the structure to participate in Wh-Aux agreement is now supported because we have seen how it can be re-analyzed in the next step.

Lexical factors are a potential influence. Wh-words and auxiliaries retain lexical variations into adulthood (e.g. dialects that allow "might could", *how come* has no inversion: how come he can sing? (Conroy, 2005; Fitzpatrick, 2005). If children start with lexical definitions to prevent overgeneralizations, then the lexical variation continues to be a source of obscuring the generative generalization.

In fact de Villiers' (1991) demonstration of a striking coincidence between the first evidence of inverted auxiliaries for main wh-questions, and the emergence of embedded questions occurred with the *same* wh-word. The coincidence was always most apparent for *why* questions, but follow up analyses looking at *what, when, where* and *how* revealed the same general trend. Interestingly, the coincidences were

---

[10] Note that exclamatives also have non-inversion (what he can do in 1 h!) which means that it is only when a Q-feature is involved that Agreement is called for.

lexically specific: for Adam, inversions appear at quite different points for *what, how* and *why,* and the order of those developments was mirrored in the order of the development of embeddings of those questions. Caution is needed here, because the spread-out nature of the development could be an artifact of the frequency of the wh-forms compounded by sampling (Snyder 2007). It is conceivable that with a richer statistical analysis, the development might prove not to be so lexically specific. That is, the change to Spec-CP might in fact be immediately productive, but because the wh-questions differ in frequency, they appearance of inversion and subordination occurs at different time points. This would be a good research question to pursue further.

A second vital factor that needs to be considered in explaining the slow emergence of complete aux-inversion in wh-questions is the nature of the verb that subcategorizes for the CP. There is huge variation in English and cross-linguistically in the type of CP that any given verb permits, so this is clearly a subcategorization that requires lexical learning (de Villiers 1991; Felser 2004). If the child permits a Spec-CP under one verb (*ask*), there is no guarantee that this would be true for another verb (*wonder*), and so the result would be variability in development not only across wh-words, but across verbs. It follows that matrix clause inversion would have to depend for each child on when they recognized lexically specific subordination for a set of critical verbs (*ask, tell, wonder, say, know, think about* which take indirect questions, unlike *think, believe* which do not). This lexical variation in the adult language naturally predicts the individual variation found in the acquisition path.

Thirdly, consider a further impact of lexical specificity that needs more clarification. It is clear that a child may produce a limited kind of wh-aux combination, at the start, as in the case of the contraction *"what's"*. Such cases might represent misanalyses of the wh-word, so the child's whole output needs to be analyzed as in Brown's (1973) examples from Adam. How widespread might this be? Could the child develop a whole set of routinized forms *"whatc'n"* (what can), *"where's"*, *"whydoes"*? In a study of 12 young English-speaking children's spontaneous speech, analyses of their errors in wh-questions suggested piecemeal acquisition of the inversion rule for different *auxiliaries*, not all-at-once acquisition of the movement rule (Rowland et al. 2005). It must be noted that the children were under age 3 years. These authors argue that a great many of the early wh-questions were formulaic, such as *"what's …"* or *"where's …"* with a contracted copula or auxiliary that may not be analyzed as a separate element at this stage. Non-inversion errors were extremely rare, only about 1.7% of all the wh-questions produced. Other errors, also rare, include cases where the auxiliary is doubled:

(23)   What did he can see?

These latter errors more often occur with a copy of the same auxiliary in both positions:

(24)   What did he did see?

and these questions have been taken by generative linguists as evidence of a movement rule that has not deleted the copy from its original position (Hurford 1975).

However Rowland et al. see in such questions the mark of formulaic, piecemeal learning, in which fragments of two sentence types have been combined.

Those who have argued on behalf of a more lexical/construction grammar in young children (e.g. Tomasello 2003, Ambridge et al 2006) would argue that this kind of patterning is exactly what would and does occur, in contrast to UG accounts in which children would not make concatenations that lack grammatical justification. Lexically specific subcategorizations make sense grammatically, but fusing any two elements that co-occur frequently would not be expected under UG.

Nevertheless, the lack of lexical diversity is a problem to be reckoned with in explaining the early stages of subject-aux inversion. The phenomenon cannot be a reflection only of the more restricted set of things children want to talk about, because it would fail to explain why particular auxiliaries are used but stay uninverted in wh-questions. A grammatical explanation is in order.

So why are individual auxiliaries inverted or not at different rates, with the same wh-word (Rowland et al 2005)? It seems necessary to do the kind of fine-grained analysis of each auxiliary in yes/no questions and wh-questions in each child, to see if a child had mastered that auxiliary inversion for yes/no questions but not for wh. This has not been established, though Rowland et al write:

> The differences cannot be attributed to the child having failed to learn the lexical forms. All the Manchester corpus children except Ruth produced a number of examples of copula are, auxiliary are, and auxiliary have in their speech by Stage III and were capable of producing correct utterances with these forms in other structures at the same time as they produced substantial numbers of wh-question errors.

If that proves to be the case, which is likely given the differential rates reported, then the argument about the joint requirements of different modules might need further expansion.

The child has to integrate three things:

(a) that this lexical item can invert in English
(b) that agreement, if needed, must be ordered before inversion
(c) that there is a spec-CP and therefore a place in C for the aux in a wh-question

It appears that these three demands place an extra burden on the grammar of wh questions in English, with the defaults being either:

(i) Good agreement but no inversion (a and b without c)
Or
(ii) Inversion but possibly nonagreement (a and c without b)[11]

In French, Zuckerman (2000) explored the acquisition of particular wh-words and their structures using an elicitation task, unfortunately with older children so

---

[11] We must also account for the fact that many English dialects around the world have exactly this kind of non-inversion, from African-American English to Singaporean English, to Trinidadian, to South African Black English (quite obviously not derived from each other). At some point, those who speak Mainstream English receive enough individual inversions with all wh-words to eliminate the variation.

the extension to the pattern of development is only speculative but interesting. As mentioned, there was a disparity between the children's preferences for different kinds of structures and those of their parents. In fact Wh-elements that received more Fronting responses from adults, received less Fronting from children, and wh-elements that received more in-situ responses from adults received fewer in-situ from children. Zuckerman argues that the input is only an indirect influence in moving children through hypothetical stages: first in-situ, then fronted without inversion, then inversion, and that these stages occur independently for each wh-word. As in English, there are lexical restrictions in French e.g. *pourquoi* (why) is never found in situ.

In stark contrast to English, in children acquiring Romance languages, there is no individual variation in subject-aux inversion: children in several languages show a 100% adult-like inversion rate from their very first production of wh-questions (Goodall 2004). This pattern has been attested in Catalan (Serrat and Capdevila 2001), European Portuguese (Soares 2003), Italian (Guasti 2000), and Spanish (Pérez-Leroux and Dalious 1998; Serrat and Capdevila 2001). Why might this be so?

It is controversial in the adult theories of Romance as to where an *overt* subject resides in the structure. In Spanish, Italian, European Portuguese and Catalan the wh form is adjacent to the verb, and the subject cannot intervene between auxiliary and verb:

(25) a. Che cosa ha detto Maria? [Italian]
       what has said Maria
       "What did Maria say?"
    b. Onde foi a Maria? [European Portuguese]
       where went the Maria
       "Where did Maria go?"
    c. Què farà en Joan? [Catalan]
       what do the Joan
       "What will Joan do?"
    d. Adónde fue María? [Spanish]
       where went Maria
       "Where did María go?"

There are several accounts of where the subject might be in wh-questions in Romance, but Perez-Leroux and Dalois make a good case that the subject in Spanish, at least, remains VP internal, and does not raise to spec-AGR.[12] The verb raises to IP, but does not move further. This also accounts for why "inversion" also appears, in embedded questions as well as matrix wh questions at least in some dialects of Spanish (Pérez-Leroux and Dalious 1998) because it is really not inversion, but base-generated . It is then not surprising that children acquiring Spanish show no problems with the ordering of verb and subject in questions, because apparent "inversion" involves no extra movement.

---

[12] There are continuing unresolved problems, such as Case assignment.

In German, all verbs move to C even in declaratives, therefore again, we see no failure of inversion. Notably we find V2 ("inversion") with both main verbs and auxiliaries as in the examples cited, such as[13]:

(26) Where is (it)?
Wo sind die Ringe?
"Where are the rings?"

(27) Was ma(chst) du?
What do you?
"What are you doing?"

German allows wh and Topic in Spec CP, and Main Verb in C, thus the categories are more general from the outset allowing the children to represent them unambiguously from the input without splitting the CP. Since all declaratives have the same requirement of verb movement, no non-inversion stage occurs for wh-questions. A similar result is found for Bulgarian, again with no apparent delay in auxiliary/verb inversion (Tornyova and Valian 2009).

Thus the refined concept of the CP is matched by refined cross-linguistic comparisons. This is an important joint success of acquisition and linguistic theory. These cross-linguistic results stand in contrast to the constructionist picture of acquisition in which lexical patterns are gradually amassed by the child on the basis of the frequency of their co-occurrence. These children make early language particular decisions that involve not only the Head Parameter but such properties as V2, swiftly implicating many other steps, including auxiliary movement and overt subject movement. Discourse and Focus factors are relevant to the decisions in German and Spanish (Spinner and Grinstead 2006). The lexical particularity of specific wh-words in English (how come *you can sing*) and Italian (*perche*) (Thornton 2007), and the homophony of the most frequent auxiliaries and main verbs in English, understandably delay the recognition that subject-auxiliary inversion in English is fully productive.

2.4 Structural Approaches to Subject-Object Asymmetry

We turn now from subject-aux inversion to how wh-expressions move to the CP-domain. There has been ongoing debate in the theoretical literature about whether invisible movement from IP to CP is obligatory for adults for subject questions (*who came?*). A prediction from Economy of Derivation and Merge-over-Move is that:

Children acquire non-movement structures before movement structures which therefore predicts that subject questions would emerge before object questions.

---

[13] See Roeper (1972) for a specific comparative production test showing V2 in German at a time when there is no inversion in English.

Since it is difficult to find linguistic evidence for the movement of subjects outside of their original IP position to CP, the order of acquisition offers unique perspective on the question. If the child has no CP at all, or changes nothing about the structure of the sentence, it is possible to produce an apparently well-formed subject question:

(28) Who ate the cake?

In contrast, an object question requires a syntactic slot of some sort at the front of the sentence to house the moved wh-word and potentially also the auxiliary or do- support:

(29) What did she eat?

If we assume that the child has a CP from the early stages, and moves the subject wh-word into it, then subject wh-questions should still be easier than object wh-questions because of (a) the shorter distance that they move and (b) no requirement of auxiliary movement or do-support.

In terms of comprehension, similar claims can be made that object questions require more processing than subject questions. From a parsing perspective, the distance of movement is further from object position to CP, than from subject position. The parsing perspective is partly captured within linguistic theory itself via the concepts of Shortest Move (a reflection of the Minimal Link condition and economy) and coincides with predictions under Relativized Minimality (see also Jakubowicz 2011). Therefore object questions in English might be more demanding in their syntactic requirements than subject positions. It is clearly an interesting question to ask whether there is any asymmetry in the acquisition of subject versus object questions. O'Grady (1997) predicted an asymmetry in development as a consequence of the syntactic 'distance' between the wh filler and its gap. According to this syntactic distance hypothesis, the differential difficulty is related to the length of the A-bar chain involved.

In what follows we will consider evidence from several sources: early comprehension and production of matrix clauses, and then performance with more complex two clause sentences that attempt to isolate where the child faces a challenge.

2.5 Asymmetry in Matrix Questions

How soon do children understand subject and object questions in simple sentences? Early work on 3-year-olds tested in studies by Ervin-Tripp (1970) and Tyack and Ingram (1977) suggested that children of that age were unable to correctly answer either subject- (Ervin-Tripp 1970) or object- (Tyack and Ingram 1977) questions. Some early experimental comprehension studies with preschool children report that object wh-questions are misunderstood more often than subject-wh-questions (Ervin-Tripp 1970; Tyack and Ingram 1977; but see Cairns and Hsu 1978). More recent work has tried to minimize task demands, by measuring eyegaze in even younger children.

The earliest ages at which comprehension has been explored by this method are 13, 15, and 20 month olds in a study by Seidl et al. (2003). Toddlers were seated in an eyetracker allowing the investigators to track looking direction at two objects, following a short animation in which one object hit another e.g. an apple hit a set of keys. Objects had names that would likely be familiar even to the youngest subjects. The study compared e.g.

(30) a. Subject-question: "What hit the apple?"
b. Object-question: "What did the apple hit?"
c. Where-question: "Where is the apple?"

The findings were that by 20 months, toddlers could respond appropriately to simple subject-, object-, and where-questions. That is, there were statistical differences in their eyegaze to the right versus the wrong object. Moving even younger, 15-month-olds looked appropriately for simple subject- and where- questions, but not for object-questions. So 15-month olds showed the predicted asymmetry between object and subject questions. The 13-month-olds were unable to respond appropriately to any of the question types. This study suggests that comprehension of object-questions emerges between 15 and 20 months.

These results suggest an asymmetry of a subtle kind, operating in comprehension to privilege subject questions over object questions even before any overt evidence of questions is likely in the children's speech. The possibility is that there is a shift in grammar happening between 15 and 20 months, presumably very early parameter setting of Head Direction, and assuming knowledge of canonical argument frames for the verb. But it is at least conceivable that the necessary grammar is already formed at 15 months, and the change is in processing resources (Santelmann and Jusczyk 1997) Though very important and suggestive, we may still need other indices than eyegaze to unpack what is going on in the grammars of young children. For example, we cannot be sure that the wh-word was even understood as a question. Substituting X for the wh-word would entail a similar preferential looking pattern, if say X was a topic:

(31) X hit the apple
X did the apple hit
X is the apple

The prediction is that young children would also show difficulty with a true topicalization like "X the apple hit". The experiment really has a logically prior condition in which the wh word and the question force is eliminated and the question about movement asymmetry is addressed with topicalization.

The research on children's *production* of subject versus object questions is mixed, with different results depending on the age of the children and the subtlety of the analysis conducted. Cross-linguistic evidence is necessary to fully explore the factors responsible.

Some early work on wh-questions reported earlier emergence of object (*what*) or predicate questions (*where*) than subject questions (Klima and Bellugi 1966). However Stromswold (1990) was among the first to explore this issue in a large-scale way, using longitudinal samples of speech from 12 English-speaking children in CHILDES. Surprisingly, she found that object questions were found to be acquired at the same age or earlier than subject questions for simple sentences, and both appeared between age 2–3 years. Nonetheless, she argued that if one takes the base frequency in the adult language into account, one could argue that objects are earlier than subjects because subject questions are much rarer in the input (see also Coopmans et al. 2001)

Studies of production in experimental formats attempted to motivate each type to equalize frequency considerations. Here it is generally found that English speaking children produce more well-formed subject wh -questions than well-formed object wh-questions in elicited speech (Ervin-Tripp 1970; Wilhelm and Hanna 1992; Yoshinaga 1996; Friedmann et al. 2009). Cross-linguistically, in languages such as Hebrew (Friedmann et al. 2009), French (e.g. Jakubowicz and Gutierrez 2007) and Italian (Guasti 1996; de Vincenzi et al. 1999), subject questions were found to be easier for children to produce than object questions in experimental conditions. In a study of older children with grammatical SLI, Van der Lely and Battell (2003) found that object questions presented particular difficulties for these children with language delay. In an elicited production task using a Clue type detective game, children with SLI produced forms such as the following, suggesting serious problems with object wh- movement, in particular with gap filling and tense:

(32) a. *Who did Mr Green saw somebody?
 b. *Which did Mrs Peacock like jewellery?
(33) a. *What cat Mrs White stroked?
 b. *What did she spotted in the library?

In a follow–up study (van der Lely et al. 2011) on judgment of ungrammatical wh-questions with older children and adolescents with grammatical SLI, an asymmetry was found with subject questions more accurately judged for *which* and *who* questions but not for *what* questions. Friedmann and Novogrodsky (2011) report that subject questions are significantly easier to comprehend in older children with grammatical SLI who speak Hebrew.

2.6 *Intervention Effects*

Could it be, not the fact of movement or the distance involved, but the content of moved objects that causes this problem? Much of linguistic theory has focused on "intervention" effects that block movement of one element over another

(Belletti and Rizzi 2010), as in Barriers to wh-movement, to which we turn below. However recent acquisition work suggests that a much deeper principle may be involved. The fundamental finding first observed for the passive voice by Postal (1971) is that an NP that moves or crosses over another NP sharing some features, in particular animacy, results in a kind of interference effect[14]:

(34)   * ?I was kissed by myself.

Animacy identity does not bother adults in parsing a clefted passive such as:

(35)   It was the girl the boy liked t.

But for children and aphasics, almost any shared features cause a block or sharply reduce acceptability. It seems that moving the NP *the girl* over the NP *the boy* is difficult. We will now review some of the approaches with these broad facts in mind.

Grillo (2008) argued that this cross-over effect was critical for passives, and others have found it to be critical for Principle B sentences, object–clefts and object questions (Friedmann et al. 2009) However, exactly which features create this clash and how it should be formulated at different levels of grammar remains an important and open question.

In wh-movement, a related concept was articulated by Rizzi (1991) as Relativized MInimality where a specific Spec-Head Agreement mechanism was used which blocked Adjuncts from moving over Adjuncts or Arguments over Arguments. The core idea remains, but the conditioning effects become very subtle. For example, Negation blocks long-distance movement of Manner in a sentence like:

(36)   ?How didn't John say that Bill played baseball

and the explanation is that both are "adjuncts", so *how* mistakenly undergoes AGREEMENT in the Neg phrase which stops further movement.[15]

One approach, exploiting the Spec-Head Agreement notion, has been developed by Guasti et al. (2011) following the work of Franck et al. (2006). They found in an elicited production task with 4–5 year olds that the object questions were considerably easier if the two DPs (the subject and the object) were differentiated for animacy features. They proposed that the difficulties children experience in the production of wh- object questions arise because the object copy takes on the features of AGR-S, i.e. interferes with the Agree relation between the postverbal subject and the verb (see the paper for the technical details).

---

[14] Baker et al. (1989) sought to assimilate the notion to Principle B, since disjoint reference applies to implicit arguments as well, and they suggested that *–ed* could be construed as a pronoun.

I was helped → someone helped me and not I helped myself.

However children acquire the disjoint reference restriction on passives by 3–4 years, long before they stop making principle B errors, so it appears to be something deeper than pronominal coreference.

[15] But the effect is not strong for adults and, again, if one puts Focal stress on *didn't*, it seems to improve the sentence by making it no longer fully identical.

The possibility of intervention effects between two like NPs has been most thoroughly explored recently in the domain of comprehension, but its characterization is an open issue. Friedmann et al. (2009) propose to locate the difficulty with object wh-questions in the structural similarity between the object and the intervening subject. That is, because both subject and object share the feature [+NP], object wh-questions (38) are difficult to produce and to understand.

(37) Who saw the man?
(38) Who did the man see?

Although *who* could be generic, they found that a block is even more likely for questions such as *which boy* where both subject and object are marked for definiteness (via *the* and *which*) again indicating that the notion of "similarity" or "identity" is, at times, being construed even more subtly:

(39) Which boy did the man see?

The research has found that both typically developing children and those with SLI evidence especial difficulty with the object-which questions because of the presence of the intervening, referential NP. They argue that this reflects the process of assigning thematic roles to NP's under cross-over (see also Friedmann and Costa (2010) on a similar effect in European Portuguese).

2.7 Asymmetries in Long Distance Wh-Questions

A test domain for these claims arises in long distance (LD) wh-movement. Is subject wh-extraction (40) easier than object extraction (41)?

(40) Who did you see __ play baseball
(41) What did you see someone play __

An adult speaker of English finds both easy to say and understand.

In LD movement, object-movement is clearly further than subject movement and object questions should therefore be more difficult to parse. But if Intervention effects hold the key rather than distance, the predictions turns out differently. A close look at the movement path reveals a special and striking fact about object LD movement: the object must move over two subjects. However, in long distance movement of a subject, the subject itself must also move over another subject:

(42) what did you think John made __
  ←obj===subj===subj======
  who   do you think ___ made a cake
  ←subj===subj=====

Therefore if we extend the Intervention concept in a logical way to include not just features such as +NP and animacy, but also particular grammatical relations, we find precisely that it is the Subject, not the Object, which causes a conflict for subject LD questions, even though the LD object passes over *two* other NP's. This illustrates the "relativized" notion perfectly with different levels of grammar and different stages responding to various levels of similarity that are open to syntactic representation. The theory of Agreement articulated originally by Kayne (2000) and utilized by Guasti and Rizzi (2002) specifically distinguishes Object-Agreement from Subject-agreement and therefore the grammatical relation concepts are already written into the Feature system that undergoes agreement.

How do the data look so far? The acquisition evidence is tantalizing but contradictory. Stromswold (1995) in her study of spontaneous production in English investigated the emergence of long-distance questions in complex sentences,

(43) Who did she say she liked ____

and the results are very clear: *object* questions emerged first in speech. All children asked at least one long distance object question (mean age 2;10), but only one child asked a long distance subject question (at 5;0).[16] It is possible that there is an asymmetry of opportunity in spontaneous speech, so elicited production studies try to equalize opportunity to see if there is still an asymmetry. Jakubowicz and Strik (2008) did an elicited production study in French and Dutch, with 4 year olds, 6 year olds and adults, targeting long distance movement. In French, it was clear that LD object questions were most frequent and LD subject questions least frequent in all groups, particularly in the adult and the 6 year old groups. However, LD questions of both types were rare in Dutch, as children adopted a Copying strategy instead (see below). When they did occur, there was no sign of a preference in Dutch for LD object questions over subject questions. If anything, children produced more LD subject cases, but the LD questions represent a small residue relative to the preference for Copying.

There are some contradictory data from Philip et al. on long distance question understanding. They tested the structural distance hypothesis using Dutch, which allows an ambiguity in long distance wh-question sentences such as in (44a) which has either a subject (44b) or object (44c) interpretation:

(44) a. Wie zei je dat de beer natspoot?
          who said you that the bear squirted
      b. Wie zei je dat [t [de beer natspoot]] (S-WH)
                           S   O   V
      c. Wie zei je dat [de beer [t natspoot]] (O-WH)
                           S   O   V

Because Dutch allows scrambling of definite references, "de beer" could be the subject or object of the lower clause, and therefore "wie" could be linked to the object or the subject trace. The examples are matched for changes in canonical word

---

[16] To date we can find no studies of spontaneous LD questions in other languages, clearly an important lacuna in the literature, though they will undoubtedly be rare.

order, and both require the animate question *wie* (*who*). Thus any differences in preference for subject versus object interpretation could not be due to the confounds of SVO order or a preference for animate references for *wie*. They used a truth-value judgment task with 4–7 year old Dutch children and adult speakers. The *syntactic distance hypothesis* that they explored made the prediction that Dutch children would prefer an S-WH analysis of (44a), and that O-WH interpretation would be dispreferred due to its greater processing difficulty because of the extra distance. They predicted that Dutch adults, in contrast, would be equally likely to interpret it as a subject or object question, as they are no longer constrained by syntactic distance.

Dutch adults showed no difference in the allowability of these options in a Truth value judgment task, however children were more likely to accept the subject than the object interpretation. Philip et al. take this as evidence that children show an effect of structural distance in parsing wh-questions. They argue that, "It seems that it is a universal property of language processing that the further a *wh*-expression is removed from its gap the more difficult it is to process *wh*-movement. The effects of this difficulty are so pronounced in preschool children's performance that they even can be detected with off-line techniques".

An interesting further issue arises when we consider the Partial Movement option which will be a focus of our concern below. Younger speakers are prone in their errors to produce Partial Movement questions, in which the wh- word appears in the medial position. We have an extended discussion of this acquisition phenomenon in the next section, but we can ask in advance of that discussion, is there more of a tendency to produce partial movement for subject than for object questions? The asymmetry would follow under the assumption that Partial Movement does not involve any further movement for subjects, therefore no Intervention occurs. That is, partial movement is a way of avoiding LD movement and the special intervention difficulties for subject questions.

Relevant evidence exists on three languages to date: English, French and Dutch, but unfortunately the results vary across the languages. The data on English come from a small sample of children (14) studied by Thornton (1991) in an ingenious elicitation task designed to get the 3–5 year olds to produce long distance questions such as:

(45) Who do you think really is in the can?

A small number of PM questions were produced, with a what scope marker and a medial question, but a larger number were copying cases such as:

(46) Who do you think who's in there, really really really? (Amber 4;6).

For both types of constructions, the strategy was more common (about twice as often) for subject questions than object questions, though only a subset of the children did it at all.

As mentioned, Jakubowicz and Strik (2008) studied the long distance subject, object and adjunct questions obtained from French and Dutch speakers aged 4, 6 and adult, who produced "other" responses that included both Partial Movement and Copying. For French, the asymmetry holds: Partial Movement questions were more frequently produced by children in the case of subjects than for objects. In fact there were none for object questions. The nontarget construction was more productive for subject questions (see (47a)), though it also appears in the case of adjunct *where* and adjunct *why* questions (see (47b) and (47c) respectively) e.g.

(47) a. **Qu'est-ce que** Billy a dit **qui** boit de l'eau? 28
   what is it that Billy has said who drinks water
   'Who did Billy say is drinking water?'
   b. **Qu'est-ce que** Lala a dit **où** le poisson nage?
   what is it that Lala has said where the fish swims
   'Where did Lala say that the fish is swimming?'
   c. **Qu'est-ce que** Lala a dit **pourquoi** Grenouille part?
   what is it that Lala has said why Frog leaves
   'Why did Lala say that Frog is leaving?'

Thus the hypothesis about a difficulty with long distance subject questions continues to receive support for French and English.

But once again, Dutch changes the picture. The Dutch children did not show a greater tendency to produce either PM or Copying for subject versus object questions. Note that the exceptions (Jakubowicz and Strik 2008; Coopmans et al. 2001) to the generalization being explored, namely that LD subject questions are harder than LD object questions, are for Dutch. Why might Dutch be exceptional? Dutch allows scrambling of the NPs as well as wh-copying, and is analyzed as an SOV language, unlike English and French. Perhaps scrambling within the subordinate clause precedes wh-movement, but adds an extra level of complexity to the object questions, making them harder to comprehend. But why is production also different? The impact of these factors on Intervention remain for further work—perhaps in other languages—to disentangle. In Sect. 3.3 where Superiority phenomena are discussed, we encounter a possibility that might reconcile the Dutch findings.

We began by asking whether matrix subject questions were easier than object questions, and the data seem to confirm that for English at least. However long distance movement of subject and object gives rise to competing explanations in terms of parsing: distance versus intervention effects predict different orders of difficulty. More research is needed in this domain.

3 Quantificational Properties of Wh-Questions

3.1 Pairing

The acquisition path for wh-questions entails semantic complexity that is entangled with the syntax. The semantics falls into sharp relief because there are sentences as in (48):

(48) Who ate what?

which are simple to parse, well within a child's memory ability, but require the child to coordinate three semantic ingredients. First, a single wh-word requires reference to a <u>set</u>. Thus the sentence *who came* requires an answer with a <u>set,</u> not an individual (though often it is a set of one) which is secondly, <u>exhaustive</u>: no relevant *eater* can be omitted. (48) has yet a third requirement: <u>pairing</u>. The exhaustive sets of *who* and *what* must be pairwise linked. The child's experience of such sentences is minimal—they are virtually absent in the CHILDES database: a total of five examples have been found by Grebenyova (2006a) in the entire English database.[17] The impoverished input makes this a perfect domain in which to look for UG-coordinated abstract capacities. What is the acquisition path for these properties? An attractive hypothesis from a Full Competence model would be:

All wh- properties are immediately triggered with the Question-feature.

If so, these semantic properties—reference to a set, exhaustivity and pairing—should appear as soon as a child begins to ask questions, perhaps as soon as the wh-word engages the Force node in CP, if we treat it cartographically as in Rizzi (1997). In fact there is evidence that some children are able to provide paired and exhaustive answers to questions at the age of 3 years (de Villiers and Roeper 1993). This suggests that the Q-feature does engage hypotheses about other wh- properties. Nevertheless, of critical importance is the fact that half the children at least recognize the question force of wh-words but *not* the exhaustiveness or pairing, giving instead what we call a "singleton" response (detailed below, see Schulz and Roeper 2011). So the Force property of wh-words appears to be a feature independent of the exhaustive set and pairing properties.

How could this be captured? Currently evolving theories posit an <u>Information Structure</u>, part of which is <u>Logical Form (LF)</u>. Logical Form is involved with still higher projections above the syntactically visible CP. If children have the CP for a Q-feature, but LF representations are unfixed, then they could recognize Question force without the other properties. Quantifier scope relations are generally captured by invisible movement operations to the front of the sentence at LF.

Information Structure captures the fact that Intonational Focus, Discourse-linking, Propositional commitments *and* Scope phenomena must interact. Information Structure is difficult to clearly incorporate in our reasoning because it is theoretically in flux (Krifka 2007), but it is clear that Focus, Presuppositions, and Implicatures are factors which must be built into the acquisition mechanism.

There are two hypotheses here to test. First, there is the hypothesis that the properties of sets, exhaustive sets and pairing are under separate control and could appear at different times in acquisition. For instance, the Q-feature could be a syntactic feature on wh while the Exhaustivity property could belong to Information Structure and thus they could take separate acquisition paths. Kratzer (2009a, b) has suggested that exhaustivity could be a Default pragmatic property, while Zimmerman

---

[17] Roeper corpus has two imperfect examples, each of which carries pairing:

"whose bed is who" [comment on Goldilocks] 4 years
"which foot is which foot" [=which foot is which] 5 years]

(2010) has suggested that it could be an implicature. If properties of constructions like paired-wh do not appear altogether, then that would support those theories that claim that different dimensions of grammar are engaged.

The second hypothesis is that properties in common to quantifiers and wh might co-occur, being governed by the same module. In fact, there is suggestive direct evidence for a connection in acquisition between quantification with wh-words and typical quantifiers (*every*). Strauss et al. (2006) has shown that the same children who make exhaustivity errors on sentences like *who bought what* also tend to exhibit quantifier "spreading" (see Philip chapter) for sentences like *every dog has a bone*. That is, they have not yet acquired the right properties of either wh or *every* as a quantifier, under one hypothesis. If both forms are suddenly acquired together, it could suggest a common "exhaustivity" feature that is realized on *every* and wh. Evidence for that latter coincidence is not yet established (but see Schulz and Roeper 2011).

3.2 Pragmatic Background

To capture the subtle, microscopic steps in the acquisition path, we must begin with a careful look at the pragmatic environment. For the majority of questions, a single ("singleton") answer is appropriate e.g. when the set consists of one item:

(49) What are you reading?
    The newspaper.

In some non-wh-question contexts a multiple answer is called for by pragmatics (perhaps the Gricean maxim of quantity):

(50) Is someone at the door?
    Yes, Bob, Mary, and Sally.

A paired answer is not ungrammatical with a single wh-question, though it may be more than is required:

(51) What are your students reading?
    John is reading Moby Dick, and Bill is reading Jane Austen, and....

Consider a question in court like "Who was in the car the night of the murder?" It would lead to a charge of perjury if you mention just one person when there were three. "Who is sitting where?" requires person-by-person answers even if it might pragmatically seem adequate to say, "They are all on chairs". Note however that even here, contextual restrictions have to be recognized. If we say: "what is in the icebox?" we mean "what (to eat)" and not "drawers, paint, and cold air". Thus a pragmatic *accommodation* is needed.

The critical point is that no matter what the context is, for adults:

(a) wh-words require a set reading and
(b) "wh- verb wh-" expressions require paired readings.

How does the set property emerge? As mentioned, several experiments have shown that initially, both typically-developing children and those with language delay provide singleton answers in contexts where adults provide multiple answers (see Finneran 1993; de Villiers and Roeper 1993; Schulz and Roeper 2011). In environments where there is a strong bias for adults to give an exhaustive set, children persist in providing a singleton answer. For example, in Roeper et al. (2007), a picture was presented of a number of girls, and the question asked,

(52) Who is wearing a sweater?

The adult answer would be to point to the three girls who are wearing sweaters. However, young children often point to only a single instance of a girl wearing a sweater. Disordered children stay in the singleton stage much longer. One response from a child was particularly revealing, "I don't know which one to choose" which indicates that the child was pragmatically aware that several girls fit the description, but took the *who*-question as a request for a single person.[18]

This path from singleton to exhaustivity has been replicated in many European languages (Schulz 2010a) in part via work from the COST[19] project, which has shown that children in 11 out of 12 languages move from singleton to exhaustive readings in a common manner. Yet Schulz (2010a) shows cross-linguistic differences which reveal how contexts which inherently call for pairing can be enhanced by explicit markers. In a language like German the presence of an exhaustivity marker *alles* (*all*) encourages children to provide the exhaustive answer, and appears to trigger the knowledge that wh-words without *alles* are exhaustive as well. Children who fail to see wer-*alles* as exhaustive fail without exception to see *wer* as exhaustive, signaling that some link must exist (Schulz 2010a). A similar difference emerges between Bulgarian and Polish: Bulgarian has a plurality marker in the wh-word that seems to trigger early exhaustivity, but Polish children lag well behind (Gavarró et al. 2010), providing only 40–60% exhaustive answers at age 5.

While an explicit marker like *all* can apparently enhance the speed of a child's recognition of a covert feature on another word, what stands out is the uniformity across the languages in the realization of a sophisticated notion like pairing. One would expect that large variations in morphology, word-order, case and Focus movement across languages would cloak comparisons in obscurity. A result of this kind must have architectural implications. In a broad sense it supports modularity: while carrying Force and quantification features, wh-pairing must proceed fundamentally independent of case-marking, agreement, and lexical variation in wh-morphology in the child's hypothesis space. Otherwise the acquisition path for wh-pairing in

---

[18] It is often suggested that the verb-agreement suggests a singular referent:
who is
However the same experiment was carried out by Bart Hollebrandse in Dutch where plural verbs are allowed (cf who are) and children persisted in giving singleton answers.

[19] A European Union Project on cross-linguistic analyses of disorders and dialects run by Uli Sauerland.

The Acquisition Path for Wh-Questions

each language would be entangled in how the children realize, for instance, case-marking on wh-words in languages where it is very rich.

An interface question arises here. Is there a relationship between linguistic exhaustivity and the cognitive operation of "being complete"? A natural hypothesis—particularly if one takes a cognitive view—is that children will proceed from a singleton reference to a <u>plural</u> reference, and finally move to an exhaustive reference. That is, given five out of six girls are wearing a sweater, children first point to just one, later to say three of the five and only gradually point to the exhaustive set. But that does not happen: children move from a singleton answer to an exhaustive answer, suggesting that a specific feature is triggered. Less than 2% of children ever point to more than one, but less than an exhaustive answer (i.e. an insufficient plural) (Schulz 2010a; Roeper et al 2007). The complete shift is what we expect if a specific property or Feature is triggered.[20]

Pairing shows a similar path. Children begin with either singleton, single pair or single set (all objects or all subjects) answers. They exhibit exhaustive pairing reliably by 4½ (though again, this achievement is systematically delayed for children with language disorders (Finneran 1993; Schulz 2010a, b) and shows cross-language variation (Schulz 2010a).

(53) Who ate what?
 Correct answer: "Daddy ate the apple and baby ate the banana"
 Wrong answers: "apple and banana"
  "Daddy ate the apple"

Notice that the phenomenon of pairing requires c-command in syntax, in that the subject wh-must dominate the object or adjunct wh-s. When the wh-words do not c-command each other, as in conjunction, the pairing is broken (Krifka 2001). Note the contrast where (54a) allows *how* and *what* lists and (54b) requires pairing:

(54) (a) How and what did Bill sing
 (b) How did Bill sing what[21]

Ideally, then, experimentation needs to show that different answers are elicited when coordination occurs. This would provide solid evidence that linguistic structure is involved.

---

[20] Our discussion leaves many questions open. One question (see Heizmann-Dodd (in preparation)) is whether there is a single acquisition path for exhaustivity, uniting performance in wh questions, quantifiers, and cleft sentences). She has shown that cleft sentences like:

(a) "It was the bush that sprouted up" followed by a question "Is that right?"
in comparison to:

(b) "The bush sprouted up" followed by "Is that right?"
 are exhaustive for adults ("No the tree did too" for (a) not (b)).

[21] Schulz and Roeper (2011) tested the conjunction "who ate and what" in which pairing should be broken, but it was observed in many children's answers. However further pilot evidence (Frattoli 2010) suggests that conjunction can break pairing if sentence-initial ellipsis is present : as in "How and what did Bill sing". If this can be substantiated, then children are sensitive to the c-command constraint that one wh- word must dominate another to engage obligatory pairing.

We can also ask: How far does pairing go? Schulz (2010a, b) boldly pushed the question even further beyond the daily experience of children, looking at pairing across three wh-words:

(55) Who gave what to whom[22]

[grandma gave toy to child, the man gave a bone to the dog, the mother gave a bucket to the girl]

Children aged 5 quite easily extended the pairing requirement beyond two, though there were more errors than with only two.

In sum, a number of formal properties are isolated by a close examination of acquisition and the introduction of cross-linguistic perspectives. We are able to separate the acquisition of sets, exhaustivity, and pairing. The modularity of the wh-Operator system is suggested by the relatively few effects of cross-linguistic variation in case-marking, word-order and the like.[23]

3.3 Superiority

The acquisition of the phenomenon of superiority provides a splendid example of complex language-specific data that a child masters with little help because examples in the input data are extremely rare (the "sparse data problem" discussed by Yang (2011)). Therefore abstract parameters in UG must play a critical role but these are far from worked out. The central contrast, found in English is:

(56) who bought what
    *what did who buy [compare: what did Bill buy]

However, not all languages show this difference, including German. What kind of variation in multiple Wh-s is revealed by a cross-linguistic comparison? A language may or may not:

(a) allow multiple wh- (English does, Italian does not)
(b) allow multiple wh-fronting (English does not, Bulgarian and Polish do)
(c) allow an intervenor between fronted wh-words (Polish)
(d) allow Single Pair readings (Japanese, Singhalese (Hagstrom 1998))
(e) allow overt movement at all (Chinese does not, so any pairs would be in-situ)

---

[22] It is not the case that all instances of 3-term wh-words elicit pairing. Under Multiple Wh-Fronting in Slavic, Gavarro shows that it is not obligatory. A variety of fronting phenomena allow pairing to be optional in Slavic—which means it is a pragmatic option, unforced by the grammar—see Bošković (1997, 2000, 2002) and others for discussion.

[23] A number of pertinent L2 studies have been undertaken on LD questions in English. See Hawkins (2005) who discusses the claim that L1 Transfer with [+uninterpretable] features does not occur, and Yusa (1999) for discussion in terms of the transfer of Multiple Spec capability across languages. Schulz (2004) shows that the basic phenomenon of spontaneous Partial Movement is robustly found in many L2 languages (see also Strik 2009).

The Acquisition Path for Wh-Questions

Each of these phenomena deserves investigation in acquisition. In English, which-questions like (57) allow superiority violations (Pesetsky 2000), and the claim is that it is because such questions are directly Discourse-linked, (D- linked), and therefore can be licensed from a Discourse referent and need not be fully reconstructed in their site of origin.

(57) Look at the boys. Which boys do which girls like t?

Children must have knowledge of divisions between linguistic modules to prevent them from being misled by *apparent* superiority violations, such as in D-linking. A variety of theories have sought to explain superiority effects in terms of semantics or pragmatics, but we will argue in what follows that a core syntactic factor—economy—provides the best explanation. However, that entails providing an explanation for linguistic variation.

The question we ask is: Is superiority essentially syntactic or semantic from an acquisition perspective? Weissenborn, de Villiers and Roeper (1996) undertook a cross-linguistic study with identical stories and materials which asked whether 4 year olds in English obeyed superiority and those in German did not. The participants were 17 English children and 21 German children (4–6 years). The method was designed to elicit double wh-questions that might reveal obedience to Superiority or not.

One experimenter played the role of a bird puppet, and the children were told that the puppet decided everything that should happen with a set of toys. So the child had to ask the puppet what to do with the toys each time by completing the question begun by the experimenter. There were occasions designed for pairing among *who*, *what*, *where*, *when* and *how* questions.

(58) So we need to know <u>who</u> is gonna sleep, and we need to know <u>where</u> they're gonna sleep. So we have two things to ask the puppet, but we can ask only ONE question, so let's try:
"Who…." (would result in obedience to superiority : who sleeps where?)
Or on another occasion:
"Where…" (would result in a violation of superiority in some situations: where is who gonna sleep?)

A total of 45 "double questions" of the type:

(59) Who can wear what?

were produced by the 17 children, and only one of these violated Superiority (notably using the discourse-sensitive *"which"*):

(60) "When is which gonna use the bathtub?"

Clearly, English speaking children resisted Superiority violations, often turning the question around to obey the constraint (one child actually said, "It's better if I start").

In a follow up on a very large scale in the testing of the DELV assessment test, we provided two occasions for the production of double wh-questions, one with the correct lead-in question in terms of superiority and one with no lead-in. Only the older children (age 7 and up) in this very diverse sample were able to produce double wh-questions, but when they did produce them, they obeyed superiority almost without fail. Out of 623 "double wh-questions" produced from children aged 4–10 years on two items, the exceptions to Superiority are just the ones in (61):

(61) What are which kids are wearing?
Which hat belongs to who?
Which hat is which kid wearing?
Which hat belongs to which?
Which hat belongs to who?
Which hat is which kid wearing?

But all these apparent violations involve *which*. The evidence suggests that Superiority is robustly obeyed in English speaking children.

3.3.1 Absence of Superiority in German

In contrast, the German-speaking children in Weissenborn et al (1996) gave different results. Fourteen of the twenty-one children clearly allowed double questions in 42/112 answers. Of these over a third (15/42) were superiority "violations", including two-argument cases e.g.

(62) "was kann wer spielen"
what can who play?
As well as adjunct- argument cases e.g.
"wo soll wer schlafen"
(where should who sleep),

The German children allow superiority violations in identical contexts to those in which English children do not.

These results provide a unique perspective from which to view a variety of proposals about Superiority of different types. All semantic proposals link superiority to quantification and LF.[24] Whatever the details of various LF theories, they lead to the hypothesis that children will acquire Superiority at the same point at which

---

[24] For example Higginbotham and May (1981) argue that:

Free scope exists if both quantifiers are at the same node at LF (Absorption)
who bought what → [what, who] [t buy t]

Under their assumptions, if one element is not in CP then something they define as Absorption – which allows either element to have wide scope—cannot work and pairing cannot be generated. In the following the who remains inside the VP and does not move to LF (which is not consistent with other theories):

who bought what→ [who$_x$, what$_y$ [t$_x$ buy t$_y$]]
[$_{CP}$what$_1$ did [t [$_{VP}$ who buy t]]

similar LF scope phenomena are mastered. However, evidence is accumulating on quantifiers, negation, and other phenomena (see Philip (this volume) and Musolino (this volume) to show that children have problems with scope assignment up until around age 6 years or later.)[25] What then explains the early acquisition of superiority in English and its absence in German?

First we should consider an account of German proposed by Grohmann (2002) that in German, apparent superiority violations involve D-linking, so that the German version of *what did who say* cannot be uttered out of the blue. If so, German superiority "violations" resemble the D-linked cases of *which* in English:

(63) The boys and girls all came. Which boys do which girls like?

However, since our experiment was discourse-identical in both languages, this approach cannot predict that 4-year-old children would exhibit a contrast across English and German. Why would English children not generate "*what did who buy*" as D-linked as well? Although Discourse-linking in German may have merit as an explanation for adults, we argue instead that the fact of early acquisition favors an account based on syntax.

Other theories argue for a syntactic basis for superiority, namely the Minimal Link Condition, including Chomsky (1995) and Cheng and Rooryck (2000). They argue that superiority is a byproduct of <u>economy of representation</u> calling for a shorter distance movement. To put it briefly, *what* has further to move in [<u>what [did who buy t</u>] than *who* has to move in [who [t bought what]]. If children have a grasp of syntax, then we can predict that they would observe this constraint early on.

Yet such theories do not account for German without a further twist because it looks like a pure distance requirement would rule out Object before Subject in German as well. Ferguson and Groat (1994) revised the definition of distance to capture German:

Distance is measured in terms of Constituent Boundaries crossed.

We can translate that claim into modern theory by proposing that Boundaries=Phases. (Note that we have not provided a full technical account, as that would depend upon how the inner structure of VP is represented in Phase theory.) But their solution depends upon a further step: the idea that the Head Parameter governs more than the object. They assign a different structure to the German VP, which we can call the Extended Head Parameter:

The subject and object are <u>both</u> inside the VP.

If we assume <u>economy of representation</u> in terms of the number of <u>Phase boundaries</u> like VP, each form moves the same distance to CP in German:

(64) a. [$_{CP}$ wer [hat [$_{VP}$ <u>t was</u> gekauft]] = who has what bought
 b. [$_{CP}$ was [hat [$_{VP}$ <u>wer t</u> gekauft]] = what has who bought

---

[25] Notoriously adult judgments are also often quite weak, see Reinhart (2006).

To repeat, if both subject and object wh- chains originate in the same Phase, the distance moved is the same and therefore no economy difference is present, thus no superiority violation occurs.

If again, the OV/VO Head Parameter includes the position of the subject, then the asymmetry between English and German is available at the point at which children set the Head parameter. It follows that the superiority contrast between English and German will be evident to children with no direct evidence, simply on the basis of economy of derivation. There is evidence that the Head parameter is set very early (Roeper 1972; Wexler 2011). Whether or not the Extended Head Parameter (suggested by Ferguson and Groat) is likewise immediately available at that point is a matter of future investigation. Recall that Dutch- an SOV language- was the exception to the intervention effects that predicted subject questions would be harder than object questions. It is possible that the proposal here might explain the discrepancies in those results. And in what follows, from rather different perspectives, we will provide further evidence that the notion of Phase is pivotal in the acquisition process.[26]

3.3.2 Superiority in Slavic and Multiple-Fronting Languages

Now we can confront an important new question: what happens to Superiority in Multiple wh Fronting languages like Russian, Bulgarian and Polish? Rojina (2004) and Grebenyova (2006a, b) explored the acquisition of multiple fronting for Russian. Grebenyova showed that multiple interrogatives are very rare in the input (in her study of Varvara's CHILDES database, for the age range 1;7–2;11, there was one multiple interrogative sentence in the adult input). Yet in two elicitation tasks with English and Russian preschoolers (aged 3.5–6.5) she obtained multiple interrogatives from young children almost as often as adults. The only difference was that the Russian children left one of the wh words in situ, rather than move it to Focus as in adult Russian (see below). However adult Russian apparently does not have any ordering restriction on the multiple wh forms: no superiority restrictions apply.

Taking into account some recent work on Bulgarian and Polish may lead to a re-consideration of a broader set of factors. In these languages, the two wh-words are both moved to the front of the sentence. Yet Bulgarian obeys superiority in this ordering, whereas Polish does not. However, despite surface appearances of similarity, the languages are argued to differ in the landing sites of the two whs. Rudin (1988) first observed that Bulgarian wh- interrogatives form a unique constituent in the left periphery of the clause, while Polish allows for intervening material (e.g. clitics, adverbials, parentheticals) to occur between the wh constituents. Romanian patterns like Bulgarian, while the Polish-type pattern is found in Russian, Czech and

---

[26] The VP-internal subject hypothesis must be refined to capture these claims. Minimalist theory allows a language specific variation in the projection of features to nodes which would have to be properly restated.

Serbo-Croatian. In later work, Bošković (1997, 2002) argues for two mechanisms of 'wh-fronting':

(i) pure (syntactic) wh-movement (to Spec,CP to check the u[+wh] feature of C°), and
(ii) focus movement ('non-wh-fronting'; licensed by the [+focus] feature of C° or Foc° and due to the inherent focus feature of wh-s).
(iii) involves no change in meaning. Gavarró et al. (2010) argued that in Bulgarian all wh constituents move to Int(errogative)P. This Interrogative head operates under a "Attract closest" constraint, resulting in strict Superiority because of obedience to economy, or shortest move. They provide evidence that in Polish only the *first* wh- moves to the spec of this Interrogative head. The *remaining* wh- constituents are moved to a different Head, suggested in Gavarrö et al to be Focus, as in Bošković (2002).

<u>Wh-movement</u> (to Spec,CP): C° bears an u[+wh] feature and via *Attract Closest* of Chomsky (1995) assures that WH_1 moves first to check this feature, hence *Superiority effects observed*.
<u>Focus movement</u> (to Spec,CP or some lower FocP forced by the [*attract-all-focus*] feature of C°/Foc°)[27]: *not sensitive to Superiority*: it does not matter in which order wh-phrases will check their inherent focus features and check the attract-all-focus feature of the attractor (the same number of maximal projections is crossed).

Gavarrö et al. 2009

As a result, Polish shows a different syntactic pattern in its multiple wh-fronting: the grammar permits intervening elements to appear after the first wh- constituent, between the Interrogative and Focus heads. In terms of Superiority, the effects are more limited than in Bulgarian: Superiority effects are obtained between the first and second wh, but not between wh2 and subsequent questions.

Gavarró et al. (2010) report the results of a repetition task with 3–5 year old Polish and Bulgarian-speaking children. They gave the children single and multiple wh-questions to repeat, and included some that were ill-formed in one of the languages, for example, with intervening material or Superiority "violations" (note that these would not count as problems in adult Polish), or in situ wh (disallowed in both). The results revealed awareness of the language-specific properties of multiple wh interrogatives: The Bulgarian children avoided intervening constituents (by omitting them) and Superiority violations (also by omitting constituents, sometimes reversing them). The Polish children allowed intervening constituents and although they sometimes omitted one of the wh-words, they did not reverse the order of wh-questions. Both groups corrected some in-situ wh- constituents by fronting them.

What can we conclude? The cross-linguistic variation itself—in a very rare phenomenon—points toward very early articulation of both different nodes and different feature content of these nodes, leading to different kinds of obedience to

---

[27] Since Chomsky (1995) it is believed that one and the same head can attract a particular feature more than once.

Superiority. We have suggested that they exhibit parameter-like linking based on the Head parameter the first step of which may be set early (Wexler 2011) While many details remain to be worked out, the central contrast is that the appearance of exhaustive pairing is constant across all of these languages, while obedience to Superiority shows a wide variety of language-specific variation. For instance, Multiple-Wh-fronting languages move to Focus as well as CP. The principle of Superiority appears to be a UG universal that shows its presence in rare data despite apparent counter-examples (D-linking).

The facts across languages strongly suggest that children must follow an acquisition path that allows demarcation of different modules of the grammar in order to guarantee learnability. The child must not be misled by discourse-linking into thinking superiority violations are acceptable. How to conceive of the path of acquisition with interacting modules that engage discourse as a part of Information Structure is an important task on the acquisition theory agenda.

4 Barrier Theory and the Strong Minimalist Thesis

4.1 Long Distance Movement

One of the most active areas of research in wh-questions is concerned with islands (Ross 1967, 1986) or barriers to movement (Chomsky 1986), for example from two clause sentences. This work takes on special significance in acquisition because it promises to reveal what children know without being taught, namely, some abstract properties of Universal Grammar (de Villiers 1996).

We assume that in a multi-clause sentence like (65), the wh-form moves through all intermediate possible landing sites, namely the CP at the front of each clause, but fails to stop if its features are not perfectly matched. If a landing site is not "open," the movement cannot advance. In (65), there is an open CP (CP_2) in the "bought" clause, but there is no matching feature, so the wh-word advances to CP_1, where it does match the feature.

(65) What did the boy say   he bought ____?
      [CP_1 [Wh + direct Q]   [CP_2]]

By contrast, an indirect question in (66) will move to a CP position with the right features to host an indirect question:

(66) John learned   how to play baseball
      [CP_1 learn   [CP_2: +indirect Q]]
           + indirect Q ==========→

The *how* stays below in CP_2 because the word *learn* "projects" a possible indirect question in the CP of the following (lower) clause. That is, the verb has as part of its lexical entry the possibility that it can take an embedded or indirect question.

The Acquisition Path for Wh-Questions

Example (66) is an indirect question and the how in (66) is not actually answered, unlike a real question (67),

(67) How did John learn to play baseball?

Finally, long distance movement is not always permitted in the adult grammar. Consider the following context: a woman buys a car on Monday, using her lottery winnings. On Saturday she calls her brother to tell him all about the lucky break she got. If the question were:

(68) When did the woman say she bought the car?

The question is potentially ambiguous: either Monday (when she bought it) or Saturday (when she told her brother). However, if the sentence includes a wh-word in the middle, or "medial" complementizer position, CP_2, as in (69),

(69) <u>When</u> did she say <u>how</u> she bought the car?
    $[CP_1 (+ Q)]$ $[CP_2 (+\text{indirect } Q)]$

The long distance interpretation of the wh-question *when*, namely "when she bought the car" (Monday) is now unavailable because its path through the landing site in the intermediate or medial CP, is blocked by the complementizer *how*. The lower clause is called an "island" (Ross 1967), and the elements in it "cannot get out of the island." The principle is that the path, namely each CP, must be open at every point for long distance movement to be allowed. In the case of an island sentence, the short distance reading is still possible, namely the one in which the wh-word originates next to the verb *say*, i.e. "when she said it" (Saturday).

Islands for movement formed the heart of theoretical work for 25 years and, eventually, spawned the concept of Phase. Evidence for islands was itself abstract or defined by "absence": movement rules, such as wh-movement, do not permit extraction from islands. Islands include relative clauses and other complex NPs, indirect questions, or more generally, complements with a wh-word (*when does John know how to sing t), and adjunct clauses (*what did John drink milk after eating t).

Children obey these never-articulated constraints.[28] Experimentation clearly supports the classic argument that UG places boundaries on grammatical interpretations. Young children are presented with questions following stories that provide potential and plausible answers for both interpretations, essentially, pragmatically inviting

---

[28] Violations occur, but very rarely, and those that do may be based on echo-focus (Partee, pc):

"what do dogs sweat through their___"

Errors are virtually unattested in typically developing children (but see Wilson and Peters (1988) for an unusual case from a blind child). These cases call for an explanation as well. One possibility is that they are based on Focus from a previous sentence:

"people sweat through their SKIN"

with a kind of phonological Focus-based Radical Reconstruction allowing syntactic violations (see discussion of Bulgarian and copying below, as we argued above).

violations. The earliest such study was that of Otsu (1981), who looked at children's answers to wh-questions containing relative clause barriers. Otsu tested whether preschool children would allow a wh-question to come from inside a relative clause. His stories were designed to make the blocked interpretation salient, for example:

(70) This boy is painting a picture of a bird with a blue brush.
The bird has long wings with pink feathers.
Question: What did the boy paint a bird that had long wings with?

Adults can only get the reading "a blue brush." The answer "pink feathers," would require the what-question to move from inside the relative clause, "the bird that had long wings." Otsu's 4–6 year olds did respect the relative clause barrier, though the performance was not perfect until children gave other proof that they could comprehend relative clauses. In later work with relative clauses, de Villiers and Roeper (1995) used adjunct questions instead of arguments, and their 3- to 5-year-old subjects were very good at avoiding long distance readings with relative clauses. However, in a larger sample of children, the barrier of relative clauses was not as strong as the barrier of wh-complements (almost 20% errors compared to <10%: de Villiers et al. 2008), a fact that still deserves further exploration.[29]

In another early study, de Villiers et al. (1990) compared 3–6 year olds' answers to a variety of different forms of adjunct and argument questions, with either no medial wh, argument wh, or adjunct wh. Children as young as age three and a half allowed long distance movement of wh-questions. They heard stories followed by ambiguous questions that permitted the children a choice between two interpretations of the site of the wh-trace. For example, the following short story ((71), accompanied by pictures for the children) was used to set the stage of the ambiguous question in 72:

(71) Story: This little girl went shopping one afternoon, but she was late getting home. She decided to take a short way home across a wire fence, but she ripped her dress. That night when she was in bed, she told her mom, "I ripped my dress this afternoon."

(72) Question: When did she say she ripped her dress?

The two possible interpretations of the question are reflected in the story: Is *when* connected as an adjunct to say, or as an adjunct to *rip*?:

(a) When$_i$ did she say [trace$_i$] she ripped her dress? (at night)
OR
(b) When$_i$ did she say she ripped her dress [trace$_i$]?(that afternoon)

---

[29] One approach to these facts might come from considering Extraposition. If the relative clause is extraposed, as in:

a woman came in [who wore a mink coat]
The relative is now attached to the topmost CP, but it has escaped the NP-island. Therefore its barrier status is weaker. If the child performed extraposition automatically it would be outside an object NP as well: [the bird] [that flew with long wings t].

The 3- to 6-year-old children in the study readily provided either answer to questions like (72), suggesting that they do permit long distance movement. de Villiers, et al (1990) tested whether the same children would block LD interpretations in the presence of a medial wh complementizer. Consider question (73) with a medial adjunct

(73) <u>When</u> did she say <u>how</u> she ripped her dress?
     [CP Q when]   [CP2 indirect Q how]

Here the answer "that afternoon" is blocked. The initial small study confirmed that 3–6 year old children obeyed these barriers to LD movement. In a follow up study, de Villiers and Roeper (1995) tested a small group of children throughout a preschool year every 3 or 4 months, and again found that barriers were obeyed. Vainikka and Roeper (1995) showed that children obeyed barriers even when the barrier was completely invisible, choosing an answer that was depicted in a picture but never mentioned. The barrier was invisible because it involved an Operator linked to a hidden relative clause:

(74)   The boy bought the lemonade [Op to drink t].

The NP *the lemonade* is the object of both *buy* and *drink*. The derivation links the *lemonade* is to a hidden Operator in a purpose clause inside the NP which behaves like a relative clause:

(75)   [bought the lemonade which was to drink]

and therefore does not allow an adjunct *where* to be extracted from it:

(76)   "The boy wanted to drink lemonade under a tree"
        [picture of boy buying lemonade at a stand]
        Where did he buy [it OP to drink t]] t   → lemonade stand (where-buy),
                                                                          *under a tree (where-drink)

The conclusion is inescapable: children allowed movement across clauses only when appropriate in UG. However, the theories behind the linguistic phenomena continue to evolve.

Rizzi (1991) pointed out that there are important distinctions between movement possibilities for adjunct versus argument questions. Argument questions (*who, what*) circumvent barriers and allow movement more easily than adjuncts (*how, when, where, why*). When one compares the long distance movement possibilities of different questions, this distinction becomes significant. Compare the adjunct question in (77a) with the argument question in (77b) where we can see exactly that a non-obligatory adjunct will block long-distance movement of an adjunct-wh, while the obligatory argument-wh is not blocked:

(77) (a) <u>When</u> did Mary ask how to help?
       (b) <u>Who</u> did Mary ask how to help?

The answer to (77a) is unambiguous: the question is about when Mary asked the question, not when to help, that is it is acceptable under the reading where the trace is in the first clause. But given some reflection, the answer to (77b), is ambiguous: it could be asking who Mary asked, or it could be asking who she wanted to help. In (77b) the long distance reading of *who* is possible. The wh-word seems to have moved long distance despite the intervening how question.[30]

4.2 Relativized Minimality and the Argument/Adjunct Distinction

A variety of theories can explain these phenomena but the core contrast between adjuncts and arguments is captured by Rizzi's theory of Relativized Minimality, the precursor to the intervention concept we discussed above.

(78) In a configuration: X....Y....Zn
    X cannot govern Z if a closer governor of the same type is available.
    Types = Argument (what, who) or Adjunct (where, why, how)

Since in (77a) the *how* is closer to the <u>trace</u> than *when,* it blocks the proper government of when. However, in (77b) the *who* is the closest *argument* to the <u>trace</u> and the intervening adjunct (a different type) does not block it. Children's responses indicate clear knowledge of this distinction (de Villiers et al. 1990, 2008).

In related work, Goodluck et al. (1992) found children did not allow extraction out of entire clauses that are adjuncts (e.g. temporal adverb clauses), and other adjuncts have also been explored (see de Villiers et al. 2008).

In general, the results reveal extraordinary conformity to barriers, even in large-scale studies of typically developing children, and even in children with language delay (de Villiers et al 2008). The basic results on similar structures have been confirmed in German and French (Weissenborn et al. 1995), Dutch, Italian, Spanish and Greek (Baauw 2002; Leftheris 1991), and Arabic (Abdulkarim and Roeper 1997; Abdulkarim 2001) (for an early review see de Villiers & Roeper 1993).

There are several fascinating questions that remain unanswered in this literature. For instance, what happens in a language with no wh-movement, like Chinese or Japanese? Do children still show resistance to interpretation of wh-questions from inside an island? (See Otsu and Sugiyaki (this volume) for discussion of Asian grammars.)

Perhaps most bewildering of all, but overlooked at the time, is the fact that long distance interpretation was so popular a choice for children, though not for adults.

---

[30] Even though their explanation in the current frameworks is less clear, these facts still stand.

In general, 4 year olds in the absence of a barrier provide long distance answers about 70% of the time, the opposite of the adult preference for a short distance construal. This fact revealed the striking difference between no-barrier and barrier sentences (where long distance responses were less than 10%). But the strong preference for LD movement seemed to violate our expectations of natural economy: why would children prefer long movement to short? Why is the lower clause the preferred origin of the wh-question?

Two decades later we see the result as a clue to deeper UG principles and to a second robust finding, namely, the fact that children often prefer to answer the medial question in a question such as:

(79) When did she say how she ripped her dress?

For example, children might answer this by saying "the fence tore it", that is, answering the medial *how*. This type of answer is curious because it has no basis in adult English, but it is permissible in other languages. As we shall see, the explanation ultimately goes to the heart of modern Phase theory.

4.3 Phase Theory, Spontaneous Partial Movement and Interpretation

The option for more local movement, resulting in a medial direct question in a sentence, exists in some dialects of German and other languages such as Hindi and Romani (McDaniel 1989; McDaniel et al. 1995). Recent reports have distinguished several varieties in the world's languages and there are some important recent analyses of the adult data (Dayal 2000; Abdulkarim 2001; Fanselow 2005; Schultz 2004; Oiry and Demirdache 2006). In these languages, a lower-clause wh-question word moves only to the medial CP where it has the status of a real question and is pronounced. Thus its movement is locally constrained. Such constructions are called Partial movement (that is, the wh movement is only to the first or embedded CP) and they occur in languages that also allow in-situ wh-words (Fanselow 2005). They are marked by a second wh-word in front, usually identical. In fact, identical copies sometimes occur almost unnoticed in English:

(80) HOW did you say how you were able to fix your bike?

Most people answer how-you-fixed it (with a screwdriver), not how you said it (very loud).

Across languages, there are several varieties of constructions that have medial wh-words serving as direct questions (Fanselow 2005 for an overview). In the extreme, there is Simple Partial Movement, that is cases with no marking in the top clause except perhaps an invisible Q marker for Force that is indicated by intonation. SPM always co-exists in languages that also have full wh-movement and wh-in-situ. The example below in (81) is from Slave (Fanselow), but this form is common in Malay languages (Cole and Hermon 1998):

(81) a. Raymond [Jane judeni ri yili] kodhisho
Raymond Jane where FOC 3-be 3-know
b. Raymond [judeni Ri Jane yili] kodhishi
"where does Raymond know that Jane is"

More common is a medial wh with an initial overt Q particle or wh-question word that tends to be the most unmarked form in the language, such as *was* in German (Partial Movement) (Fanselow 2005):

(82) WAS glaubst du Wen Irina t liebt what believe you
Who-acc Irina loves "who do you believe that Irina loves?"

And still more common is Copying, in which the medial question word is echoed in form by the initial question word as in German and Frisian (Fanselow 2005):

(83) Wo denkst du wo sie wohnt
Where/what think you where she lives
"Where do you think she lives"

The jury is still out as to the relationship among these forms, and why the varieties occur. Some theorists lump them into one category, and others consider the differences significant. Hiemstra (1986) suggests what is shared and what is different across the constructions.[31] She argues (as do others) that wh-movement is always the movement of a wh-feature. But languages vary as to what needs to be "pied-piped" when the wh-feature moves. In long distance wh-movement constructions, the whole feature matrix, including the phonetic matrix, of the wh-phrase is moved. Other languages may allow nothing except the wh-feature to move, in which case it must be spelled out in the landing site. It will be usually phonetically realized by the most unmarked wh expression of the language: *was* in German, *wat* in Frisian, *kyaa* in Hindi, etc.

4.3.1 Wh-Copying and Indirect Dependency

Finally, there is the possibility of featural pied-piping in which person-number features of the wh-phrase are also moved: the feature complexes copied upwards like [wh, 3rd sg., acc] will then be spelled out as the corresponding wh-words. This

---

[31] Under Feature theory it is not clear what motivates two movements if every movement requires checking off a feature. Schulz (2004) suggests that movement to medial wh- satisfies a Focus feature, not a question feature. Were it a real indirect-Q feature it would be immune to movement under Rizzi's notion of Criterial Freezing (2006), which blocks extraction from a classic indirect question:

*who do you wonder__went

If movement to a Criterial position occurs, satisfying the indirect Q, then no further movement is possible. (See Rizzi (2006) for a full explanation.)

gives rise to the Copy Construction. However, wh-copying is ungrammatical with complex wh-phrases: the copying seems to be restricted to pronominal features (Chomsky 1981) and cannot carry sufficient feature information to realize morphologically a complex Wh-phrase like *which boy* (Thornton 1991).

(84) Wh-Copying: Complex (PP) Wh-Phrase:
*Miti welchen Jungen glaubst du mit welchen Jungen Hans spricht?
"With which boy do you think with which boy Hans talks?"

A further dimension of theoretical interest is the analysis of these forms as either "direct dependency," in which the lower clause is subcategorized by the top verb, or " indirect dependency," in which the lower clause is essentially an adjunct or a separate sentence like (Dayal 1994, 2000):

(85) What did you say—where are we going tonight?

We will attend to the fact that the different types occur in children learning different languages to different degrees, a fact that requires some explanation. In addition, we believe that the best evidence is for a direct dependency analysis in the case of the child's grammars, but it is still an open question as we shall see.

Throughout the work on comprehension of complex questions, we originally intended the medial question (e.g. *what* in (86)) in our stimulus sentences to be merely the "barrier" to long distance movement of the *how*. But children answered the medial, to our surprise.

(86) How did she say what she bought?
Adult answer: "She whispered it"
Child answer: "Cake"

Furthermore, although the error is common at 3 and 4 years of age, it persists until children are 6 or 7, and even longer for children with language disorders (de Villiers et al. 2008). We recognized the error as a reflection in children's grammars of what McDaniel had pointed out as Partial Movement in several languages (de Villiers et al. 1990). The medial answer has been found in six languages (de Villiers and Roeper 1993), and prominently, in L2 acquisition by Asian, French, and Basque learners (See Schultz 2006; Liceras 2010; Guttierrez 2005).

As discussed earlier, Thornton (1991) found production data in an elicitation paradigm suggesting that children adopted these alternate grammars. The majority of questions of this sort matched the medial-Wh questions and the initial Wh-phrases, as illustrated in (87):

(87) Who do you think who is in the box?
What do you think what Cookie Monster likes.

Two children who asked medial-Wh questions also asked questions in which the Wh-phrases did not match, as shown in (88):

(88) What do you think who jumped over the fence?

So Copying was more common that Partial movement, and no Simple Partial Movement was observed.

Yet children in different languages use one or more of these types to different degrees. For example, as well as Partial movement, Simple Partial Movement (no overt initial wh) occurs in French-speaking children (Oiry and Demirdache 2006):

(89) Tu crois quoi qui est caché dans l'sac ? Oiry (2002)
you believe what C-that is hidden in the-bag
'What do you think is hidden in the bag?'

They argue that there is a non-lexical Q morpheme in French that licenses both wh-in-situ—be it in the child or the adult grammar—and partial wh-movement in the child grammar. But other forms are also observed in French with the form *Qu'est-ce que*;

(90) Qu'est-ce que tu crois qu'est-ce caché dans le sac ? Oiry (2002)
what-is-it-that you believe what-is-it hidden in the bag
'What do you think that is hidden in the bag?'

Qu'est-ce que tu penses qu'est-ce que j'aime lire ? Strik (2008)
what-is-it-that you think what-is-it-that I like read
'What do you think that I like to read?'

Qu'est-ce que is exclusively a matrix question, and cannot occur in the medial position as an indirect question in adult French.

Oiry and Demirdache argue that children who produce these forms have a grammar that allows essentially juxtaposition and coindexing of two matrix questions at the initial stage. They make an analogy between this and the "indirect dependency" analysis of Hindi in Dayal (1994, 2000). In Hindi, the in-situ wh-phrases each move at LF to the specifier position of the CP dominating them, yielding two local wh-dependencies. The connection between the two clauses is established indirectly by coindexing the matrix wh-phrase and the subordinate wh-question. In French L1, Oiry and Demirdache see reflections in overt syntax of this strategy at an early stage.

Oiry & Demirdache propose a developmental sequence for French in which children's grammars progress from

"1. an indirect dependency stage which involves simultaneous local covert or overt movement of an argument wh-phrase in both the matrix and the subordinate clause;
2. a direct dependency stage involving local wh-movement to the subordinate Spec CP—licensed by an expletive Q morpheme in the matrix; and
3. a long movement stage which involves either overt or covert movement of an embedded wh-phrase to the matrix Spec CP."

This account is quite natural under the view that new material is initially subject to (a) Merge over Move and High Attachment.(Adjoined at the Root). The new merged structure now entails that the wh-word c-commands the rest of the clause and the child to seek the creation of an internal merge relation and a covert movement analysis becomes possible. In other words, the wh-connection shifts from a co-indexing to a movement representation.

4.3.2 Evidence for Movement

How can we tell if the relation is one of movement or co-indexing? Abdulkarim (2001) showed in a subtle experiment that movement must be involved. We know that negation is a barrier to adjunct movement. If there is covert movement in these copied forms, then the presence of intervening negation should force a short-distance answer. Abdulkarim used examples like:

(91) (a) why did she say why she slept
     (b) why didn't she say why she slept

Children from ages 3–5 strongly preferred the long distance reading for (a) and the short distance reading for (b). This provided dramatic proof that movement is involved.

Furthermore, how much is moved—how much is "pied-piped" along—is also a source of variation in languages, but some occurs in production as Thornton (1991) has shown. In Thornton's study, the children seemed to resist wh-copying of complex wh-forms, though a couple were recorded:

(92) Ben 3;11
     <u>What one</u> do they think <u>what one</u> has the big marble?
     Katie B. 4;4
     <u>What ones</u> did they guess of these guys <u>what ones</u> they kicked in the leg?

Notably, these copies occur only with Tensed clauses—this fact will figure significantly in our proposals about how to capture children's grammars.

Children who produce these copied structures also judge them to be grammatical in judgment tasks (McDaniel et al. 1995). So spontaneous production, comprehension and judgment evidence all demonstrate the child's attraction towards a non-target grammar reflecting Partial movement. Such findings have been reported in children in several other languages both in comprehension (Weissenborn et al. 1995; Leftheris 1991) and in elicited production (Oiry 2008; Jakubowicz and Strik 2008 and Strik 2009). We conclude:

Children adopt a partial movement option in their productions in the preschool years.

The evidence provides strong, spontaneous support for cyclic syntactic movement and the psychological reality of invisible chains. In sum we have found not only evidence for cyclic chains in the acquisition data, but evidence on five varieties:

Co-indexing: what (do you think?)....who did it (indirect dependency)
Copying: what did he say what...?
Simple Partial movement: Invisible Op.........wh
Pied-Piping: which animal did he say which animal
Partial Movement: How..........what......

The data is not fine-grained enough for us to see if all children pass through distinct stages—or how far they vary across languages—but they all occur as spontaneous behavior even when not in the target language. Collectively, they show that not only the chains, but the content of chains [trace, copy, wh-expletive] are represented in the child grammar.

One fact remains to be explained: comprehension—interpretation—reflects these options longer than production. The interpretation we will now argue engages the interface properties of Phase theory.

4.3.3 Interpretation: Child Evidence for Grammar's Primary Interface

What governs the interpretive consequences of partial movement? Is the medial answer by children identical in meaning to the adult semantics of partial movement? A tantalizing asymmetry remains: the preference for the medial interpretation remains longer than partial movement in production.

To address these questions, we need to return to first principles. What mechanism exactly blocks movement? Barrier theory is open to many technical representations. How can children know a property of UG which, to the average person, seems so arcane? And yet the most abstract principles, like gravity, are never obvious on the surface of phenomena. We shall argue that an explanation emerges from a different angle, involving the interface of Phase theory with semantics. The child's interpretation follows from a principle that dictates locality for both syntactic chains and semantics.

Until recently in syntactic theory, "islands" to movement were the constraints that needed to be explained, and long distance movement was considered the normal condition. However, in the most recent versions of Minimalist Theory (SMT; Chomsky 2007), a new concept has emerged for what were regarded as "islands" to movement, now called a "Phase." Chomsky argues that under ideal circumstances, the syntactic component transfers its contents to the phonological and interpretive components of the language system one "phase" at a time:

> There are Transfer operations: one hands the Syntactic Object (SO) already constructed to the phonological component, which maps it to the Sensori-Motor interface ("Spell-Out"); the other hands SO to the semantic component, which maps it to the Conceptual-Intentional interface. Call these SOs phases. Thus Strong Minimalist Thesis entails that computation of expressions must be restricted to a single cyclic/compositional process with phases. In the best case, the phases will be the same for both Transfer operations. To my knowledge, there is no compelling evidence to the contrary. Let us assume, then, that the best-case conclusion can be sustained. It is also natural to expect that along with Transfer, all other operations will also apply at the phase level.

This may seem like a highly technical claim, but at bottom it is very intuitive and opens a new vista of explanation and motivation for the acquisition path. It explicitly argues that the semantic interpretation occurs cyclically. Thus in the ideal scenario, a wh-word will move to the Head of a Phase, and be pronounced

The Acquisition Path for Wh-Questions

and <u>interpreted</u> there.[32] But then the basic fact of wh-displacement across a clause boundary (in English) is in competition with the more general principle of "locality," namely, completing the operation within the clause, or more precisely, the Phase. In an English 2-clause sentence, as in (93), the wh-word moves to the front of the sentence, to CP_1, and leaves an unpronounced trace at CP_2.

(93) [CP_1 What did John say [CP_2 trace he bought trace]]

Nevertheless the SMT now asserts that the ideal grammar would prefer to <u>move</u>, <u>pronounce</u>, and <u>interpret</u> a wh-word at the boundary of the first Phase, namely the subordinate CP, not the matrix CP or sentence initial position where English speakers pronounce it. Therefore the child should interpret the *what* at the first Phase boundary where it delivers the meaning *what-bought*, i.e. what was actually bought, and not *what-said-bought*. This is exactly what happens. However, there is an additional semantic and pragmatic step in that we, and the child, answer a question by connecting the semantic meaning [he bought something+Q feature, and possibly a set of possible alternative answers] to the world.

The SMT thus leads us to expect an <u>interpretation</u> of the intermediate wh-word. Interpretation of the lower clause is called for whenever the IP Phase Edge is met, and indeed *how* should be interpreted in the lower, not the upper clause in (94).

(94) When did John say [how he played baseball]?

Children would answer how-he-played, not how-he-said.

The idea that producing overt medial wh-words is linked to a parallel interpretation preference receives direct support in the work of Oiry (2008). She found that exactly those French children who in production added a lower copy also interpreted the medial question with respect to only the lower clause.

But there is a further discovery in acquisition, and that will involve further theoretical steps, many of which are at the edge of contemporary theory. Children interpret not only <u>overt wh-</u> words, but traces as well as connected only to the lower verb:

(95) [she bought a cake but said she bought paper towels]
"what did she say [t she bought t]?"

The error here is that children answer with the "truth" *what she bought ("paper towels")*, not *what she said she bought (a birthday cake)*. (see especially de Villiers 1999, 2005; de Villiers and Pyers 2002).

In other word, the child is led into two errors in a language like English: direct questions as overt medial wh-words, and interpretation of a trace inside the lower

---

[32] This is a simplification of the discussion. Under the view that the Phase-Head is processed in the next Phase, then the wh-word would not be a part of the lower Phase. Under a notion of "inheritance", it could be. We believe that these issues should be resolved with attention to the acquisition data. See Hornstein et al. (2005), and Boeckx (2008).

clause with no scope from the first clause. How does the grammar recover? How do we account for this unusual interpretation of a trace—quite different from adults? Does it reflect a natural step in UG inasmuch as it occurs "spontaneously" without adult examples of any kind?

The steps or triggers for this process of change are still speculative, though we know it seems to occur between 4 and 7 years (de Villiers and Pyers 2002; de Villiers et al. 2008). A theory of acquisition that accommodates interfaces must incorporate the impact of semantic and pragmatic properties. In keeping with Chomsky's early remark (1976) that acquisition is consistent with "triggering experience", the experience involves the semantics and the pragmatics as well. By considering these properties, we are led to an account of the child and adult grammar that captures several lines of reasoning at the edge of current syntax (Chomsky 2005, 2008).

To summarize briefly: the SMT captures a UG linguistic default, namely, Interpret at each Phase. From there it leads to an important pragmatic step; it leads to the child's interpretation of the wh-word within the lower clause and an interpretation of the semantics in the world. We take it as a natural concomitant to semantics that the child will seek a pragmatic interpretation as well, that is, to link the meaning to context. This forces a factive or a "true" answer, which is exactly what children produce. Speaker-factivity arises in the adult language in many contexts as well with particular (factive) verbs and adjectives (Kiparsky and Kiparsky 1970; de Cuba 2006):

(96) John was surprised that Bill played baseball.
      John revealed that Mary was dead.

You cannot reveal something that is not true.[33]

It has been argued by some that adults retain a factive reading as well for Partial Movement constructions (Herburger 1994): that in a sentence,

(97) was hat er gesagt was er gekauft hat
      "What did he say what he bought"

it is only possible to ask a question when what he said he bought was what he actually bought. If true, how does a subordinate clause get its property of non-factivity, or opacity?[34] Put differently, this tight constraint would seem to make LD movement itself impossible. It is clear that verbs subcategorize not only whether they take a CP at all, but also for what its properties are with respect to the tense (finite, nonfinite or subjunctive). So the higher verb can prevent, by projection of critical features

---

[33] This is not to overlook the fact that in real discourse, almost anything can be cancelled.
    John revealed his promotion with great fanfare, and then it turned out not to be true.
    John saw his mother in the kitchen, but it turned out it was someone else.
    Nevertheless factive clauses must be seen as true propositions because they function as presuppositions for later discourse.

[34] These are widely discussed in philosophy as "opaque contexts" because the truth of the lower clause is not from the speaker's perspective.

onto the lower CP, the immediate phase-interpretation of a clause. Until the child recognizes the projected (inherited) feature on the lower CP, we argue that it must be interpreted.

4.4 Tense, Propositionality and Point of View

How and where exactly does the grammar project propositions? Tense, or finiteness, is the domain in which truth or assertion seems to operate. For example, Klein (2006) discusses the notion of finiteness or FIN as follows:

"FIN carries (at least) two distinct meaning components:

1. The tense component: it marks past, in contrast to present or future;
2. It marks that an assertion with respect to whatever is said is made—in contrast to the possibility that no such assertion is made."

It is the TENSE marker that commits the sentence to being a proposition, as was recognized in early labels: "Tensed-S Propositional Island" or more recently "Phases are propositional" (Chomsky 2007: 107). Pesetsky and Torrego (2001) and Chomsky (1995) have all argued that the Tense marker must covertly move to the CP, that is, in languages where there is not overt V2 movement. We propose a further purpose for this covert movement, that the Tense carries a feature for Point of View which is responsible for making the clause opaque.

While research on Point of View has traditionally been linked to indexicals (*I, you*) and locatives (*here, there*), it can be extended to marking Subject (not speaker) perspectives on opaque domains by putting a PoV marker into the CP of the lower clause (and a Default Speaker PoV in the matrix clause) as argued by Hollebrandse and Roeper (1998); Hollebrandse (2000); Speas (2004), Kratzer (2002) and de Villiers (2005).

Following the literature that links Tense and the Propositional Islands, and Klein on the notion that Tense carries Assertion, we argue that the Tense node also carries a POV feature which must be in agreement with the PoV element in the CP. Building on the claim that Tense moves to CP covertly, we now argue that it has both a syntactic and a semantic motivation if PoV shift is involved, following the spirit of the SMT. That is, the PoV feature on Tense carries a default Speaker value unless and until it is moved to the CP where it is "re-valued" by the PoV because of the lexical properties of the higher verb projection. The upper verb imposes its PoV on the lower proposition:

wonder   => Spec- C
+Ind Q   +IndQ
+Subj-PoV   +SubjPoV

In such opaque environments, stated technically, the higher verb forces the lower CP and TP to "inherit" its projections, which includes complementizer, indirect Q marker, and PoV (speaker or subject).

When the TENSE marker moves to the CP, then at the CP it can be in agreement (Spec-Head) with a PoV marker projected by the higher verb, which is linked to the matrix subject—a topic which we articulate further below. This approaches captures grammatically at least part of the phenomenon of opacity.

This view that some form of Agreement must occur between the CP and the IP (see also Klein 2006) constitutes a further acquisition step for the child, and one that is apparently not immediately made. In the absence of that agreement, the child assumes the Speaker's Point of View on the assertion, rather than the matrix Subject's Point of View. As a result, it is factive, or a true assertion as far as the speaker is able to claim. True subordination of the clause occurs when there is an agreement between the CP and IP, that allows the matrix Subject's Point of View onto the clause, hence it allows lies, mistakes, false beliefs:

(98) She said she saw a UFO.

Consider then the wh-movement derivation of the long distance question in the adult grammar:

(99) $_{CP}$ [What did $_{TP}$ [t she say $_{CP}$[t $_{TP}$ [t she saw t]]]]

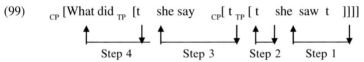

Step 4   Step 3   Step 2   Step 1

(100) Stage of derivation:
    (i)   She said [[she saw what?]]
    (ii) She said [[what she saw]]
    (iii) She said [what [she saw]]
    (iv) What she [[said she saw]]
    (v) What did she [[say she saw]]

In step 1, the wh-question moves to the edge of the IP Phase, perhaps into Topic position, where it retains its original full copy meaning.[35] with a Default Speaker-PoV. In step 2, it moves to the next Phase, namely CP, and it must have an open PoV value to take on the subject PoV in the CP. In step 2, however, the wh inherits the PoV of the subject from the verb *say*, so that the answer to the question is no longer just what was *seen* but what she said she *saw*. In step 3, it moves to the edge of the sentence to the second Topic position, then in step 4 it moves to spec-CP of the matrix clause, where is it pronounced as a wh-question. (de Villiers and Roeper 2010).

Why do children interpret the wh-word in the lower clause? A recent line of research on movement (Miyagawa 2006; Sauerland and Elbourne 2003) has identified <u>Total Reconstruction.</u> The idea is that a kind of movement exists which occurs at only Phonetic Form or PF. From the hearer's point of view, Total Reconstruction

---

[35] Topic position is most likely given the existence of wh- in exclamatives such as

What nice clothes you are wearing!
Notably, they do not entail inversion, so the wh is not in spec-CP.

means reconstructing the word in its original position. But this Total reconstruction at PF is blind to semantic and syntactic effects. Normally, an interpretation is contingent not just on where an element started out in the phrase marker, but also on its final position. A moved constituent derives part of its meaning from its new position.[36]

In Total Reconstruction, the wh-element is completely reconstructed to the place where it started out. Thus the child who hears:

(101)   What did she say [t she bought t]

reconstructs:

(102)   ? she said [what she bought]

and then

(103)   she said she bought what

In this way, the interpretation depends only on its original position in the lower clause. Then when it moves to the edge of the first phase, it gets an interpretation solely within that Phase. Adult wh-movement entails interpretation at both the original and the landing sites, i.e. both PF and LF (Logical Form) changes.

The possibility is that the child begins with Total Reconstruction in wh-movement, although it eventually occurs only in scrambling, binding, and echo environments in the adult grammar.[37] Miyagawa (2006) argues that Total Reconstruction fills a logical gap in the paradigm of movement operations: there ought to be the possibility of movement after interpretation. If that is true, then we can expect that it could occur spontaneously in children. It now fits the claim above: if a child can analyze a new sentence as involving a shift in only one module, then it is transparent and preferred.

In sum, if a child can analyze a wh-sentence as PF movement, no change in interpretation is possible or necessary: restore an element to its previous position with no change in meaning. Consequently the child interprets:

(104)   what did she say [CP t [IP [what] she bought t

with the meaning of *what* entirely in the lower clause. Why could adults not do the same? What blocks adults from reconstructing a Speaker-factive interpretation of the wh-clause?

Now let us trace the derivation carefully again. The wh-word moves to the Lower CP which, for adults, has acquired the upper-clause PoV:

(105)   (what does)John$_1$ thinks [CP what [IP what [IP Bill did t]
                               PoV$_1$ PoV-sp (adult)   PoV-sp (child)

---

[36] An example is binding:
   Which picture of Bill did he like? [Bill=he or someone else]
   He liked which picture of Bill [he=someone else]
   where Bill is higher than he only after movement has occurred.

[37] Thanks to S. Cable for suggesting this possibility to us.

For the child, under pure reconstruction, no change in meaning occurs. The adult must shift PoV if the lower CP has inherited information from the word *think*. Therefore in English the adult cannot perform pure reconstruction anymore, while the child can.[38] When children acquire the PoV projection from the verb, they become adults and block pure reconstruction.

We have argued that when the Tense moves to CP, it carries a PoV Feature. What happens if there is no Tense node, for instance, as is arguably true for infinitives? Here we make a sharp acquisition prediction. If the construction has no Tense, such as an infinitive, then it will also carry no PoV shift. Therefore we should find that children do not produce errors on wh-extraction from infinitives. This is exactly what seems to occur.

(106)   What did Mary want to buy?

Children have no difficulty with (106) even though opacity and a possible truth-contrast remains: what she actually bought may not be what she *wanted* to buy. The same children at 3 years old children who do not mistake *what she did buy* for *what she wanted to buy* do mistake *what she bought* for *what she said she bought* (de Villiers 2005).[39]

This underscores the syntactic nature of the acquisition path: it is specifically the derivational path of the syntactic chain, not simply a contrast between reality and what a sentence expresses which the child must master. In sum, we have argued that the CP can carry a Subject-PoV, linked to Tense, which produces opacity in the realm of truth. The child's grammar must incorporate the PoV feature onto the subordinating CP, and also form an Agree relation to the Tense of the lower clause. We correctly predicted that infinitives, lacking a Tense, would not force a clash, though more targeted research is necessary.

In conclusion, we have seen that the acquisition evidence uniquely highlights the power of the Strong Minimalist Thesis, itself the first and strongest interface claim in minimalism.

5 Conclusion

The domain of wh-questions provides an illustration of the expectation that subtle acquisition data can provide unique evidence of core, but empirically obscure, properties of grammar.

We have reviewed three major areas of wh-question acquisition, relating to the movement rules in simple sentences, the logical properties of wh, and the barriers

---

[38] See Fox (1999) for the role of interpretation of intermediate traces.

[39] But see Perner et al. (2003) for an explanation in terms of the different conceptual development of desires and beliefs. Though this is undoubtedly a factor, there remains a contribution of the syntax of these expressions, even in German *that* clauses with *want* (see de Villiers 2004).

that constrain movement across clauses. Here we summarize the major points from each domain, and point to the unanswered questions.

1. Landing Site: is the landing site the same for adults as it is for children, in spec-CP? We have argued that given the nature of cross-linguistic variation in such nodes as Focus and Topic, it is not likely that the child at age two can fully determine the structure of the left periphery.
2. Lexical specificity: English data suggests considerable lexical variation in wh and auxiliary, justified by the uncertainties of the adult language. However cross-linguistic data contradicts the lexicalist position that the forms will be learned piecemeal: the lexical variability complicates acquisition, which makes it more difficult to recognize the productive UG principles.
3. Principles of economy: we have argued for (a) Single Module principle for acquisition, and provided evidence for (b) Merge over Move, and (c) Length of derivation, and (d) Total Reconstruction as both guiding and constraining acquisition. The Superiority phenomena are interestingly nuanced across languages and deserve further exploration in a greater range of languages to figure out which parameters need to be set first.
4. Interpretation: We have argued that (a) the emergence of quantification (reflected in exhaustivity in wh-words) is not immediate, and (b) the interpretive character of the SMT overconstrains the first stage of long-distance movement. The question of whether exhaustivity is reflected in quantifiers (every, each) and wh-words needs to be elaborated in light of other domains of exhaustivity (cleft sentences) and implicatures.

Overall, Barriers to long distance rules have been a fixture of linguistic theorizing in theoretical linguistics for decades, and they have proved an extremely fruitful analytic instrument for child grammar. Instead of focusing on the surprising obedience to barriers at a young age, we took a deeper look at the mechanism and argued that the child's grammar may be constrained by an idealization of the Strong Minimalist Thesis as an interface principle that combines syntax, phonology and semantics. The hypothesis that each Phase should be shipped off to interpretation leads to a unique and surprising prediction about acquisition. We put forward the theory that the child allows Total Reconstruction, essentially linking the initial wh-word to its trace in the lower clause from which it does not then escape before it is interpreted there. This, we argue, explains the pervasive facts of partial movement as a preferred option for child grammar, and children's initial inability to construe opaque complements as having a different Point of View than the speaker.

In the process, we have made a number of general claims that deserve exploration in other acquisition domains, each of which is a reflection of theoretical principles. We began with the Interface constraint, that children prefer represent a construction in a single module, to explain the possibility that children might begin with a merged Topic. We suggested that the acquisition process obeys constraint: Merge over Move. Finally we argue that Transfer occurs one Phase at a time in the child's grammar, following the SMT, giving an interpretive perspective on why partial movement exists in child language. The implications of these go beyond wh-questions, and may lead to challenges from exciting research in the next decade.

In our estimation, Wh-movement provides an unparalleled domain for examining UG, the implications of UG for acquisition, and for emerging perspectives on interfaces.

References

Abdulkarim, L. 2001. Complex wh-questions and universal grammars: new evidence from the acquisition of negative barriers. Unpublished PhD thesis, University of Massachusetts, Amherst.
Abdulkarim, L., and T. Roeper. 1997. Negative islands in language acquisition. In *Gala Proceedings*. Edinburgh: University of Edinburgh.
Ambridge, B., C.F. Rowland, A.L. Theakston, and M. Tomasello. 2006. Comparing different accounts of inversion errors in children's non-subject *wh*-questions: 'What experimental data can tell us?'. *Journal of Child Language* 33: 519–557.
Baauw, S. 2002. *Grammatical features and the acquisition of reference: A comparative study of Dutch and Spanish*, Outstanding Dissertations in Linguistics. New York/London: Routledge.
Baker, M.K., Johnson, and I. Roberts. 1989. Passive arguments raised. *Linguistic Inquiry* 20: 219–251.
Belletti, A., and L. Rizzi. 2010. Ways of avoiding intervention: Some thoughts on the development of object relatives, passive and control. In *A poor input*, ed. R. Berwick, R. Grammars, and M. Platelli-Palmerini. Oxford: Oxford University Press.
Boeckx, C. 2008. *Bare syntax*. Oxford: Oxford University Press.
Borer, H., and K. Wexler. 1992. Bi-unique relations and the maturation of grammatical principles. *Natural Language and Linguistic Theory* 10: 147–187.
Bošković, Ž. 1997. Fronting wh-phrases in Serbo-Croatian. In *Formal approaches to Slavic linguistics: The Indiana meeting*, vol. 6, ed. S. Franks and M. Lindseth, 86–107. Ann Arbor: MIT Press.
Bošković, Ž. 2000. Sometimes in [Spec CP], sometimes in Situ. In *Step by step: Essays on minimalist syntax*, ed. H. Lasnik, R. Martin, D. Michaels, and J. Uriagereka, 53–88. Cambridge, MA: MIT Press.
Bošković, Ž. 2002. On multiple wh-fronting. *Linguistic Inquiry* 33: 351–383.
Brown, R. 1973. *A first language: The early stages*. Cambridge, MA: Harvard University Press.
Cairns, H., and J.R. Hsu. 1978. Who, why, when, and how: A developmental study. *Journal of Child Language* 5: 477–488.
Cheng, L.L.S., and J. Rooryck. 2000. Licensing *wh*-in-situ. *Syntax* 3: 1–19.
Chomsky, N. 1976. *Reflections on language*. New York: Praeger.
Chomsky, N. 1977. On wh-movement. In *Formal syntax*, ed. A. Akmajian, P.W. Culicover, and T. Wasow, 71–132. New York: Academic.
Chomsky, N. 1981. *Lectures on government and binding*. Dordrecht: Foris.
Chomsky, N. 1986. *Barriers*. Cambridge, MA: MIT Press.
Chomsky, N. 1995. *The minimalist program*. Cambridge, MA: MIT Press.
Chomsky, N. 2005. Three factors in language design. *Linguistic Inquiry* 36: 1–22.
Chomsky, N. 2007. On phases. In *Foundational issues in linguistic theory*, ed. R. Freidin, C. Otero, and M.L. Zubizarreta. Cambridge, MA: MIT Press.
Chomsky, N. 2008. Approaching UG from below. In *Interfaces + Recursion = Language: Chomsky's minimalism and the view from syntax-semantics studies in generative grammar*, vol. 89, ed. H. Gärtner and U. Sauerland. Boston/Berlin: Mouton de Gruyter.

Cole, P., and G. Hermon. 1998. The typology of wh-movement: Wh-questions in Malay. *Syntax* 1: 221–258.
Cole, P., D. Gil, G. Hermon, and U. Tadmor. 2001. The acquisition of in-situ wh-questions and wh-indefinites in Jakarta Indonesian. In *Proceedings of the 25th Annual Boston University Conference on Language Development*, ed. A.H.J. Do, L. Domínguez, and A. Johansen, 169–179. Cambridge, MA: Cascadilla Press.
Conroy, A. 2005. The semantics of how come: A look at how factivity does it all. University of Maryland Working Papers.
Coopmans, P., W. van Atteveldt, and M. van der Meer. 2001. Subject-object asymmetry in child comprehension of wh-questions. In *Proceedings of the 25th Annual Boston University Conference on Language Development*, ed. A.H.J. Do, L. Domínguez, and A. Johansen. Boston: Cascadilla Press.
Crain, S., and M. Nakayama. 1987. Structure dependence in grammar formation. *Language* 63: 522–543.
Dayal, V. 1994. Scope marking as indirect wh-dependency. *Natural Language Semantics* 2: 137–170.
Dayal, V. 2000. Scope marking: Cross-linguistic variation in indirect dependency. In *Wh-scope marking*, ed. U. Lutz, G. Muller, and A. Von Stechow, 157–193. Amsterdam: John Benjamins.
de Cuba. 2006. The adjunction prohibition and extraction. In *Non-Factive CPs Proceedings of the 25th West Coast Conference on Formal Linguistics*, ed. D. Baumer, D. Montero, and M. Scanlon, 123–131. Somerville: Cascadilla Proceedings Project.
de Villiers, J.G. 1991. Why questions? In *The acquisition of wh*, ed. B. Plunkett and T. Maxfield. Amherst: UMOP.
de Villiers, J.G. 1996. Defining the open and closed program for acquisition: The case of wh-questions. In *Towards a genetics of language*, ed. M. Rice. Hillsdale: Lawrence Erlbaum.
de Villiers, J.G. 1999. On acquiring the structural representations for false complements. In *New perspectives on language acquisition*, ed. B. Hollebrandse. Amherst: UMOP.
de Villiers, J.G. 2004. Getting complements on your mental state verbs. In *Proceedings of 2003 GALA Conference*, ed. S. Baauw and J. van Kampen, 13–26. Utrecht: LOT.
de Villiers, J.G. 2005. Can language acquisition give children a point of view? In *Why language matters for theory of mind*, ed. J. Astington and J. Baird. New York: Oxford University Press.
de Villiers, J.G. 2010. On building up a sufficient representation for belief: Tense, point of view and wh-movement. In *Language Acquisition and Development: Proceedings of Gala 2009*, ed. A. Castro, J. Costa, M. Lobo, and F. Pratas. Newcastle: Cambridge Scholars Press.
de Villiers, J.G., and J. Pyers. 2002. Complements to cognition: A longitudinal study of the relationship between complex syntax and false-belief-understanding. *Cognitive Development* 17: 1037–1060.
de Villiers, J.G., and T. Roeper. 1993. The emergence of bound variable structures. In *Knowledge and language: Orwell's problem and Plato's problem*, ed. W. Abraham and E. Reuland. Dordrecht: Kluwer Academic.
de Villiers, J.G., and T. Roeper. 1995. Relative clauses are barriers to wh-Movement for young children. *Journal of Child Language* 22: 389–404.
de Villiers, J.G., and T. Roeper. 1996. Questions after stories: Supplying context and removing it as a variable. In *Methodology in child language research*, ed. D. McDaniel, H. Cairns, and C. McKee. Hillsdale: Erlbaum.
de Villiers, J., T. Roeper, and A. Vainikka. 1990. The acquisition of long–distance rules. In *Language processing and language acquisition*, ed. L. Frazier and J. de Villiers, 257–297. Boston: Kluwer.
de Villiers, J.G., T. Roeper, L. Bland-Stewart, and B. Pearson. 2008. Answering hard questions: wh-movement across dialects and disorder. *Applied Psycholinguistics* 29: 67–103.
de Villiers, J.G., P.A. de Villiers, and T. Roeper. 2010. Wh-questions: Moving beyond the first phase. *Lingua* 121: 3.

de Vincenzi, M., L.S. Arduino, L. Ciccarelli, and R. Job. 1999. Parsing strategies in children comprehension of interrogative sentences. In *European Conference on Cognitive Science: Conference Proceedings*, ed. S. Bagnara, 301–308. Rome: Instituto di Psicologia del CNR.
Erreich, A. 1984. Learning how to ask: Patterns of inversion in yes-no and wh-questions. *Journal of Child Language* II: 579–592.
Ervin-Tripp, S. 1970. Discourse agreement: How children answer questions. In *Cognition and the development of language*, ed. J.R. Hayes, 79–106. New York: Wiley.
Fanselow, G. 2005. Partial wh-movement. In *The Blackwell companion to syntax*, vol. 3, ed. M. Everaert and H. van Riemsdijk. Oxford: Oxford University Press.
Felser, C. 2004. Wh-copying, phases, and successive cyclicity. *Lingua* 114: 543–574.
Ferguson, K.S., and E. Groat. 1994. *Defining "Shortest Move" GLOW presentation*. Cambridge, MA: Harvard University Press.
Finneran, D. A. 1993. Bound variable knowledge in language disordered children. Unpublished Master's thesis, University of Massachusetts, Amherst.
Fitzpatrick, J. 2005. The whys and how comes of presupposition and NPI licensing in questions. In *Proceedings of the West Coast Conference on Formal Linguistics 24*. Vancouver: Simon Fraser University.
Fox, D. 1999. Reconstruction, variable binding, and the interpretation of chains. *Linguistic Inquiry* 30: 157–196.
Franck, J., U.H. Frauenfelder, G. Lassi, and L. Rizzi. 2006. Agreement and movement: A syntactic analysis of attraction. *Cognition* 101: 173–216.
Frattoli, C. 2010. *How and why in questions*. Amherst: University of Massachusetts.
Friedmann, N., and J. Costa. 2010. The child heard a coordinated sentence and wondered: On children's difficulty in understanding coordination and relative clauses with crossing dependencies. *Lingua* 120(6): 1502–1515.
Friedmann, N., and R. Novogrodsky. 2011. Which questions are most difficult to understand?: The comprehension of Wh questions in three subtypes of SLI. *Lingua* 121(3): 367–382.
Friedmann, N., A. Belletti, and L. Rizzi. 2009. Relativized relatives: Types of intervention in the acquisition of A-bar dependencies. *Lingua* 119: 67–88.
Gavarró, A., W. Lewandowski, and A. Markova. 2010. An approach to multiple interrogatives in child Bulgarian and Polish. In *Language Acquisition and Development Proceedings of GALA 2009*, ed. A. Castro, J. Costa, M. Lobo, and F. Pratas. Newcastle: Cambridge Scholars Press.
Goodall, G. 2004. The Limits of Syntax in Inversion. Paper presented at the Chicago Linguistic Society.
Goodluck, H., M. Foley, and J. Sedivy. 1992. Adjunct islands and acquisition. In *Island constraints*, ed. H. Goodluck and M. Rochemont, 181–194. Dordrecht: Kluwer.
Grebenyova, L. 2006a. Multiple interrogatives in child Russian. In *Proceedings of the 30th annual Boston University Conference on Language Development*, eds. D. Bamman, T. Magnitskaia and C. Zaller, 225–236. Cambridge, Ma: Cascadilla Press.
Grebenyova, L. 2006b. Multiple interrogatives: Syntax, semantics and learnability. Doctoral diss., University of Maryland.
Grillo, N. 2008. *Generalized minimality*. Utrecht: LOT.
Grinstead, J. 2004. Subjects and interface delay in child Spanish and Catalan. *Language* 80: 40–72.
Grohmann, K.K. 2002. Some concepts and consequences of discourse-restricted quantification. In *Proceedings of SCIL10. MIT Working Papers in Linguistics 37*, ed. M. Feist, S. Fix, J. Hay, and J. Moore. Cambridge, MA: MIT Press.
Gruber, J. 1967. Topicalization in child language. *Foundations of Language* 3: 37–65.
Guasti, M.T. 1996. The acquisition of Italian interrogatives. In *Generative perspectives on language acquisition*, ed. H. Clashen. Amsterdam: John Benjamins.
Guasti, M.T. 2000. An excursion into interrogatives in early English and Italian. In *The acquisition of syntax: Studies in comparative developmental linguistics*, ed. M.-A. Friedermann and L. Rizzi, 105–128. Harlow: Longman.

Guasti, M.T., and L. Rizzi. 2002. Agr and tense as distinctive syntactic projections: Evidence from acquisition. In *The cartography of syntactic structures*, ed. G. Cinque. New York: Oxford University Press.

Guasti, M., C. Branchini, and F. Arosio. 2011. Interference in the production of Italian subject and object wh questions. *Applied Psycholinguistics*, 1–39.

Guttierrez, M. J. 2005. The acquisition of English LD wh-questions by Basque/Spanish bilingual subjects in a school context. PhD diss., University of the Basque Country.

Hagstrom, P. 1998. Syntax and semantics of questions. PhD diss., MIT.

Hawkins, R. 2005. Second language acquisition and universal grammar review. *Language* 813: 754–757.

Heizmann-Dodd, T. (in preparation) *Dissertation on exhaustivity*. Department of Linguistics, University of Massachusetts, Amherst.

Herburger, E. 1994. A semantic difference between full and partial wh-movement in German. Paper presented at the Linguistic Society of America Conference, Boston.

Hiemstra, I. 1986. Some aspects of wh-questions in Frisian. *NOWELE* 8: 97–110.

Higginbotham, J., and R. May. 1981. Questions, quantifiers and crossing. *The Linguistic Review* 1: 41–79.

Hollebrandse, B. 2000. The acquisition of sequence of tense. PhD diss., University of Massachusetts, Amherst.

Hollebrandse, B., and T. Roeper. 1998. *Point of view operators, features and a theory of barriers*. University of Pennsylvania Linguistics Colloquium.

Hornstein, N., J. Nunes, and K.K. Grohmann. 2005. *Understanding minimalism*. Oxford: Cambridge University Press.

Hurford, J.R. 1975. A child and the English question formation rule. *Journal of Child Language* 2: 299–301.

Jakubowicz, C. 2011. Measuring derivational complexity: New evidence from typically developing and SLI learners of L1 French. *Lingua* 121(3): 339–351.

Jakubowicz, C., and J. Gutierrez. 2007. Elicited production and comprehension of root wh-questions in French and Basque. Presentation at the COST meeting on Cross Linguistically Robust Stages of Children's Linguistic Performance, Berlin.

Jakubowicz, C., and N. Strik. 2008. Scope-marking strategies in the acquisition of long distance Wh-questions in French and Dutch. *Language and Speech* 51: 10.

Kayne, R. 2000. *Parameters and universals*. Oxford/New York: Oxford University Press.

Kiparsky, P., and C. Kiparsky. 1970. Fact. In *Progress in linguistics*, ed. M. Bierwisch and K. Heidolph. The Hague: Mouton.

Klein, W. 2006. On Finiteness. In *Semantics meets acquisition*, ed. V. van Geenhoven. Dordrecht: Kluwer.

Klima, E., and U. Bellugi. 1966. Syntactic regularities in the speech of children. In *Psycholinguistic papers*, ed. J. Lyons and R. Wales, 183–208. Edinburgh: Edinburgh University Press.

Kratzer, A. 2002. *Impersonals and Logophoricity Semantics Archive*.

Kratzer, A. 2009a. Pragmatic Strengthening for Free DFGS lecture, Groningen.

Kratzer, A. 2009b. Situations in natural language semantics. In *The Stanford encyclopedia of philosophy*, ed. E. Zalta. Stanford: CSLI.

Krifka, M. 2001. Quantifying into question acts. *Natural Language Semantics* 9: 1–40.

Krifka, M. 2007. Basic notions of information structure. In *Interdisciplinary studies of information structure*, vol. 6, ed. C. Fery and M. Krifka. Potsdam: Universitätsverlag Potsdam.

Lasnik, H., and M. Saito. 1992. *Move-alpha conditions on its application and output*. Cambridge, MA: MIT Press.

Leftheris, K. 1991. Learning to interpret wh-movement in modern Greek. Honors thesis, Smith College, Northampton, MA.

Liceras, J. 2010. *Talk on partial movement and copying in L2*. Amherst: University of Massachusetts.

MacWhinney, B. 2000. The CHILDES project: Tools for analyzing talk, vol 2: The database 3rd ed. Mahwah: Lawrence Erlbaum Associates.

McDaniel, D. 1989. Partial and multiple *wh*-movement. *Natural Language & Linguistic Theory* 7: 565–604.
McDaniel, D., B. Chiu, and T. Maxfield. 1995. Parameters for wh-movement types: Evidence from child language. *Natural Language & Linguistic Theory* 13: 709–753.
Miyagawa, S. 2006. EPP and semantically vacuous scrambling. In *The free word order phenomenon: Its syntactic sources and diversity*, ed. J. Sabel and M. Saito, 181–220. Berlin: Mouton de Gruyter.
O'Grady, W. 1997. *Syntactic development*. Chicago: University of Chicago Press.
Oiry, M. 2002. Acquisition des Questions à Longue Distance. Master's thesis, University of Nantes.
Oiry, M. 2008. L'acquisition des questions à Longue Distance par des enfants de langue maternelle française. Stratégies à dependance directe versus indirecte et questions alternatives. Unpublished thesis, University of Nantes.
Oiry, M., and H. Demirdache. 2006. Evidence from L1 acquisition for the syntax of wh-scope marking in French, Manuscript, University of Nantes.
Otsu, Y. 1981. Universal grammar and syntactic development in children: Toward a theory of syntactic development. Unpublished doctoral diss., Massachusetts Institute of Technology.
Pérez-Leroux, A.T., and J. Dalious. 1998. The acquisition of Spanish interrogative inversion. *Hispanic Linguistics* 10: 84–114.
Perner, J., M. Sprung, P. Zauner, and H. Haider. 2003. 'Want That' is understood well before 'Say That', 'Think That', and 'False Belief': A test of de Villiers' linguistic determinism on German-speaking children. *Child Development* 74: 179–188.
Pesetsky, D. 2000. *Phrasal movement and its kin*, Linguistic inquiry monographs, vol. 37. Cambridge/London: MIT Press.
Pesetsky, D., and E. Torrego. 2001. T-to-C movement: Causes and consequences. In *Ken Hale: A life on language*, ed. M. Kenstowicz. Cambridge, MA: MIT Press.
Plunkett, B. 1992. Continuity and the landing site for wh-movement. In *Bangor Research Papers in Linguistics*, 4, 53–77. Bangor University, Wales.
Postal, P. 1971. *Cross-over phenomena*. Cambridge, MA: MIT Press.
Reinhart, T. 2006. *Interface strategies*. Cambridge, MA: MIT Press.
Rizzi, L. 1991. *Relativized minimality*. Cambridge, MA: MIT Press.
Rizzi, L. 1997. The fine structure of the left periphery. In *Elements of grammar: Handbook of generative syntax*, ed. L. Haegeman, 281–331. Dordrecht: Kluwer Academic.
Rizzi, L. 2006. On the form of chains: Criterial positions and ECP effects. In *Wh-movement: Moving on*, ed. L. Cheng and N. Corver, 97–133. Cambridge, MA: MIT Press.
Roeper, T. 1972. Approaches to the acquisition of German. PhD diss., Harvard University.
Roeper, T. 1993. How the least effort concept applies to language acquisition. In *Knowledge and language: Orwell's problem and Plato's problem*, ed. W. Abraham and E. Reuland. Dordrecht: Kluwer Academic.
Roeper, T. 2000. Universal bilingualism. *Bilingual Language Cognition* 2: 169–186.
Roeper, T. 2007. *The prism of grammar*. Cambridge, MA: MIT Press.
Roeper, T. 2009. *Vacate phase: The strong minimalist thesis and subject-aux inversion*, University of Massachusetts.
Roeper, T. Personal corpus of Roeper M. and Roeper, T.
Roeper, T., and J.G. de Villiers. 1994. Lexical links in the Wh-chain. In *Syntactic theory and first language acquisition: Cross linguistic perspectives*, Binding, dependencies and learnability, vol. II, ed. B. Lust, G. Hermon, and J. Kornfilt. Hillsdale: Lawrence Erlbaum Associates.
Roeper, T., and B. Rohrbacher. 1994. Null subjects in early child english and the theory of economy of projection. In *University of Pennsylvania working papers in linguistics*, vol. 2, ed. C. Hamann and S. Powers, 83–119. Dordrecht: Kluwer Academic.
Roeper, T., P. Schulz, B. Pearson, and I. Reckling. 2007. From singleton to exhaustive: the acquisition of wh-. In *Proceedings of the 3rd Conference on the Semantics of Underrepresented Languages in the Americas SULA: University of Massachusetts Occasional Papers in Linguistics*, ed. M. Becker, and A. McKenzie, 33, 87–10. Amherst: University of Massachusetts.
Rojina, N. 2004. The acquisition of wh-questions in Russian. In *Nordlyd 32, Tromso Working Papers in Language Acquisition*, vol. 1, ed. K. Bentzen, 68–87.

Ross, J. 1967. Constraints on variables in syntax. Doctoral diss., MIT, Cambridge, MA.
Ross, J. R. 1986 Infinite syntax! Ablex, Norwood.
Rowland, C., and J. Pine. 2000. Subject-auxiliary inversion errors and wh-question acquisition: 'What do children know?'. *Journal of Child Language* 27: 157–181.
Rowland, C., J. Pine, E. Lieven, and A. Theakston. 2005. The incidence of error in young children's Wh-questions. *Journal of Speech and Hearing Research* 48: 384–404.
Rudin, C. 1988. On multiple questions and multiple wh-fronting. *Natural Language & Linguistic Theory* 6: 445–501.
Santelmann, L.M., and P.W. Jusczyk. 1997. What discontinuous dependencies reveal about the size of the learner's processing window. In *Proceedings of the 21st Annual Boston University Conference on Language Development*. Brookline: Cascadilla.
Sauerland, U., and P. Elbourne. 2003. Total reconstruction. PF-movement and derivational order. *Linguistic Inquiry* 33: 283–319.
Schulz, P. 2003. Factivity: Its nature and acquisition. Tübingen: Max Niemeyer Verlag. Linguistische Arbeiten 480. [Rezension: Hollebrandse, B. 2002. GLOT International, 6: 9/10, 304–306.].
Schulz, P. 2010a. Who answered what to whom? On childrens' understanding of exhaustive questions. In *COSTA33*, London.
Schulz, P. 2010b. Some notes on semantics and SLI. In *GALA 2009*, Lisbon.
Schulz, P., and T. Roeper. 2011. Acquisition of exhaustivity in wh-questions: A semantic dimension of SLI? In *Specific Language Impairment SLI. Across Languages: Properties and Possible loci*, ed. P. Schulz and N. Friedmann, 383–407. Special Issue of Lingua, 121: 3.
Schultz, B. 2004. A Minimalist account of partial wh-movement. In *Proceedings 2004: Selected papers from the eighth college-wide conference for students in Languages, Linguistics, and Literature*, eds. L. Clarito and T. McKamey. Honolulu, HI: University of Hawaii Press.
Schultz, B. 2006. Wh-scope marking in German-English and Japanese-English interlanguage grammars: An investigation of clustering syntactic properties. In *Proceedings of the inaugural GALANA conference*, eds. K. U. Deen, J. Nomura, B. Schulz and B. D. Schwartz. Storrs: UConnWPL.
Seidl, A., G. Hollich, and P. Juzcsyk. 2003. Early understanding of subject and object Wh-questions. *Infancy* 43: 423–436.
Serrat, E., and M. Capdevila. 2001. La adquisición de la interrogación: Las interrogativas parciales en catalán y castellano. *Infancia y Aprendizaje* 93: 3–17.
Snyder, W. 2007. *Child language: The parametric approach*. Oxford: Oxford University Press.
Soares, C. 2003. The C-domain and the acquisition of European Portuguese: The case of wh questions. *Probus* 15: 147–176.
Speas, M. 2004. Evidentiality, logophoricity and the syntactic representation of pragmatic features. *Lingua* 114(3): 255–276.
Spinner, P., and J. Grinstead. 2006. Subjects, topicalizations and Wh- questions in child german and southern romance selected. In *Proceedings of the 9th Hispanic Linguistics Symposium*, ed. Nuria Sagarra and Toribio Almeida Jacqueline, 241–251. Somerville: Cascadilla Proceedings Project.
Strauss, U., T. Roeper, B. Pearson, J. de Villiers, and H. Seymour. 2006. Acquisition of universality in wh-questions. Manuscript, University of Massachusetts, Amherst
Strik, N. 2008. Syntaxe et acquisition de phrases interrogatives en francais et nederlandes Une etude contrastive. Diss., Paris 8.
Strik, N. 2009. *Derivational contrasts in Dutch and French*, Linguistics in the Netherlands. Amsterdam: John Benjamins.
Stromswold, K. 1990. Learnability and the acquisition of auxiliaries. Unpublished PhD diss., MIT.
Stromswold, K. 1995. The acquisition of subject and object wh-questions. *Language Acquisition* 4: 548–994.
Thornton, R. 1991. Adventures in long distance moving: The acquisition of wh-questions. Unpublished doctoral diss., University of Connecticut.
Thornton, R. 2007. Why continuity. *Natural Language & Linguistic Theory* 26: 107–146.
Tomasello, M. 2003. *Constructing a language: A usage-based theory of language acquisition*. Cambridge, MA: Harvard University Press.

Tornyova, L., and V. Valian. 2009. The role of cross-linguistic variation in the acquisition of auxiliary inversion in Wh-questions. In *Proceedings of the 3rd Conference on Generative Approaches to Language Acquisition North America GALANA 2008*, ed. J. Crawford et al., 282–290. Somerville: Cascadilla Proceedings Project.

Tyack, D., and D. Ingram. 1977. Children's production and comprehension of questions. *Journal of Child Language* 4: 211–224.

Vainikka, A., and T. Roeper. 1995. Abstract operators in early acquisition. *Linguistic Review* 12: 275–310.

van der Lely, H.K.J., and J. Battell. 2003. Wh-movement in children with grammatical SLI: A test of the RDDR Hypothesis. *Language* 79(1): 153–181.

van der Lely, H., M. Jones, and C. Marshall. 2011. Who did Buzz see someone? Grammaticality judgement of wh-questions in typically developing children and children with Grammatical-SLI. *Lingua*. 1213: 408–422.

Weissenborn, J., T. Roeper, and J. de Villiers. 1995. *Wh*-acquisition in French and German. *Recherches Linguistiques* 24: 125–155.

Weissenborn, J., J. de Villiers, and T. Roeper. 1996. Superiority differences between German and English in Acquisition. Paper presented at conference on What Language Acquisition Can Tell Linguistic Theory, Utrecht.

Wexler, K. 2011. Grammatical computation in the optional infinitive stage. In *Handbook of Generative Approaches to Language Acquisition*, ed. Jill de Villiers. Dordrecht: Springer.

Wilhelm, A., and K. Hanna. 1992. On the acquisition of *WH*-questions. *Calgary Working Papers in Linquistics* 15: 89–98.

Wilson, B., and A.M. Peters. 1988. What are you cookin' on a hot?: A three-year-old blind child's "violation' of universal constraints on constituent movement. *Language* 64: 249–273.

Yang, C. 2011. Computational models of language acquisition. In *Handbook of Generative Approaches to Language Acquisition*, ed. Jill de Villiers. Dordrecht: Springer.

Yoshinaga, N. 1996. Wh questions: A comparative study of their form and acquisition in English and Japanese. PhD diss., University of Hawaii at Manoa.

Yusa, N. 1999. Multiple specifiers and Wh-island effects in L2 acquisition. In *The development of second language grammars: a generative approach*, ed. E.C. Klein and G. Martohardjono. Amsterdam: John Benjamins.

Zimmerman, M. 2010. Quantifying question particles and the non-exhaustiveness of wh-questions. Manuscript, Potsdam University, Postdam.

Zuckerman, S. 2000. The acquisition of "Optional" movement. Groningen diss., University of Groningen.

Binding and Coreference: Views from Child Language

Cornelia Hamann

1 Introduction

1.1 The Interaction of Theoretical and Empirical Research

The interpretative properties of pronominal systems have been the focus of attention in theoretical and empirical investigations for several decades now. Research has focused on the description of such systems in different languages aiming to establish the universals and the differences. At the same time, the interpretation of pronouns served as one of the most quoted arguments for the poverty of the stimulus, which led to a fruitful interaction of theoretical developments and empirical research on the acquisition of pronominal systems.

Soon after the formulation of the Binding Theory in the *Lectures on Government and Binding* (Chomsky 1981) constraining the interpretation of anaphors/reflexives (Principle A), pronouns (Principle B), and of lexical noun phrases (Principle C), research on young children's comprehension of these elements was intensified. Jakubowicz (1984, 1989), Wexler and Chien (1985), and Crain and McKee (1985) showed that English speaking children almost always do well when interpreting pronouns and lexical nominal expressions in sentences like *He washed Luke Skywalker* or reflexives in sentences such as *Luke Skywalker washed himself*. However, in sentences such as *Luke Skywalker washed him* children interpreted pronouns correctly in only about half of the cases allowing the pronoun to refer to Luke Skywalker in the other half. Since then it has been widely accepted that there is a difficulty with Principle B, which was called the "Delay of Principle B Effect – DPBE".

C. Hamann (✉)
Carl von Ossietzky Universität Oldenburg Fakultät III, Institut für Fremdsprachenphilologien, Seminar für Anglistik/Amerikanistik D-26111, Oldenburg, Germany
e-mail: cornelia.hamann@uni-oldenburg.de

Children's difficulty with pronouns as opposed to reflexives and referential expressions posed a serious problem since the structural constraints in all three cases involve essentially the same mechanisms, c-command and a locality constraint. How could children show knowledge of the constraints in sentences with reflexives and at the same time not know them in a sentence with a pronoun? The phenomenon was all the more puzzling as English children do well with pronouns in production, so that it seemed problematic to assume that the feature specification of pronouns is not mastered.

When Chien and Wexler (1990) reported on their Experiment 4, the problem appeared to be solved: with the picture version of a Truth Value Judgment Task, Experiment 4 showed that children only rarely interpreted sentences such as *Every bear is touching her* as every bear touching herself, whereas they were only about 50% successful with sentences such as *Mama Bear is touching her*. This result indicated that children indeed know Principle B: in case of a "misapplication" a quantified antecedent allows only a bound variable reading of the pronoun. Since this reading was not assigned, the principle had been applied correctly.

For acquisition, the result meant that Principle B is in fact acquired at the same time as the other two principles and what remained to be shown was which factors mask its application. Chien and Wexler (1990) and others suggested that a pragmatic principle (disallowing a pronoun to corefer with an antecedent in most contexts) has not yet been acquired, whereas Grodzinsky and Reinhart (1993) pointed to processing limitations aiming for a unified account of the difficulties shown by children and patients with agrammatic aphasia. The result of Chien and Wexler's (1990) Experiment 4 has since been replicated in other languages, so that the label DPBE seems inappropriate. Arguments for abandoning the term have also been supplied in recent research focusing on the asymmetry in comprehension and production found in Dutch and English (Hendriks and Spenader 2006; de Villiers et al. 2006) or on cross-linguistic research with aphasic patients. Therefore the term DPBE has been replaced by the term "Pronoun Interpretation Problem – PIP", see also Baauw and Cuetos (2003).

During the first decade of intensive research on binding, theoretical research was stimulated by the possibilities emerging from acquisition results, namely that there may be two mechanisms establishing the reference of anaphoric elements, bound variable and coreference, and by the division of labor between syntactic and pragmatic constraints suggested by this. On the empirical level, a pragmatic or processing explanation was challenged by cross-linguistic results. Using the same experimental paradigm for both languages, McKee (1992) corroborated Chien and Wexler's result for English, but showed that Italian children of the same age do not show a PIP. The same holds for French and Spanish, see Jakubowicz (1989), Hamann et al. (1997), Hamann (2002), Baauw et al. (1997), Baauw (2000, 2002); McKee (1992) argued that the pragmatics of pronouns is the same cross-linguistically and that processing limitations should be equal in children of the same age. Therefore the early mastery of pronoun interpretation in Romance languages must be due to the fact that they are clitics. Since Romance clitics occur high in the clause and are referentially deficient in ways that Germanic pronouns are not, structural/derivational accounts of the good performance of Romance children were suggested (McKee 1992; Baauw 2000; Baauw and Cuetos 2003). However, pragmatic explanations have also been proposed (Avrutin and Wexler 1992; Hamann 2002; Hendriks et al. 2007).

Many cross-linguistic investigations of pronoun interpretation also addressed ECM-constructions as in *The girl sees her dance*. These constructions are of theoretical interest because different versions of the Binding Principles make different predictions. Under certain formulations of "local domain" the pronoun falls under principle B in the Standard Theory, whereas the Reflexivity Framework predicts that Principle B does not apply here, and coreference is ruled out through a general condition on chain formation. An experiment run by Philip and Coopmans (1996) showed not much difference in simple and ECM constructions in English but a clear difference in Dutch. Interestingly, also Romance children (and agrammatics) show a PIP in ECM constructions (Hamann et al. 1997; Baauw et al. 1997; Baauw and Cuetos 2003). Again, two basically different lines of argumentation have been employed in order to explain this effect. Researchers focusing on the syntactic side are Philip and Coopmans (1996), Baauw (2000), Baauw and Cuetos (2003), whereas Hamann (2002) favors a pragmatic account that can be uniformly applied to the different contexts.

So the interesting questions concerning acquisition of pronominal systems are: In which circumstances can a production/comprehension asymmetry be observed? What masks children's knowledge in the case of Germanic pronouns? Why does the PIP not show up in languages that have clitic pronouns of the Romance type? Why is the PIP stronger in ECM contexts than in simple sentences in some languages? Why does the PIP show up only in ECM contexts in Romance languages? Why can the PIP be observed also in agrammatic patients in languages where children show it? Another question always accompanying the empirical research is which of the current versions of the binding theory the results support.

Recently, studies have focused on problems raised by the earlier results and their different explanations. If it plays a role that Germanic pronouns are ambiguous in that weak and strong pronouns coincide in form, then it is expected that in languages that separate the forms, the strong forms will show the PIP whereas the weak or clitic forms will not. Varlakosta (2000) and Baauw and Cuetos (2003) address this problem with different results. Moreover, in languages having a pronoun system very similar to English or Dutch, it is expected that children will show the PIP, but the surprising results of two recent studies on German (Ruigendijk 2008; Hamann and Ruigendijk 2009) show that German children behave like French or Spanish children in simple and ECM contexts.

One way of dealing with the problems of binding theory is integrating syntax and pragmatics into one rule system as was proposed by Burzio (1998) and has been further developed in Optimality Theory, see Fischer (2004). Focusing on the asymmetry in comprehension and production found in Dutch and English, where production is more or less intact, Hendriks and Spenader (2006) and de Villiers et al. (2006) suggest such accounts for child language. Hendriks et al. (2007) couch their analysis in a bidirectional Optimality framework using a constraint ranking for the hearer and a possibly different one for the speaker (see Jäger 2002). The idea is that in comprehension children neglect the corrective speaker's perspective when matching a form to a meaning, while only the speaker's perspective matters and no correction in ranking is needed in production. This account remains speculative as to why children cannot do bidirectional ranking. Since Theory of Mind is long acquired, as de Villiers et al. (2006) point out, an appeal to processing limitations comes to mind. Optimality Theory accounts thus allow integrating a rather classic syntactic analysis with well discussed pragmatic notions and processing ideas in order to explain asymmetries in comprehension and production.[1]

In other recent studies, the results obtained in earlier experiments, the basis for much theorizing, were criticized for methodological reasons. Especially the asymmetry found for quantified and lexical antecedents has been called into question in a careful analysis by Elbourne (2005). His analysis aims to show that this asymmetry is an artifact of the experimental method. Therefore, Elbourne (2005) concludes, there is no evidence in English that Principle B is acquired. Conroy et al (2009) demonstrate the opposite: If the factors singled out as problematic by Elbourne (2005) are properly controlled for, then children show knowledge of Principle B in simple sentences. Other studies pointing to the production/comprehension problem and using controlled context conditions also contribute to this discussion (see de Villiers et al. 2006). Finally, a recent study by Verbuk and Roeper (2010) concentrates on the question of how children can assign the relevant referentiality features to the pronominal elements they find in their language given that not all languages have a simple distinction into pronouns and reflexives and given that there is ambiguous input in English. This approach is in the tradition of accounting for cross-linguistic variation through parameters that differ with respect to the feature specification of certain lexical items. In this case the task is to select the specific lexical items that are reflexives/anaphors and pronouns and to determine their domain.

1.2 Aim and Structure of the Article

This article concentrates on the developments and problems of the theoretical framework and on questions arising from the cross-linguistic acquisition results on pronoun interpretation in different constructions. Section 2 is focused on theoretical considerations: the Standard Binding theory (Sect. 2.1) and its problems (Sect. 2.2), the distinction of reference assignment through a bound variable configuration and through coreference (Sect. 2.3), the typology of anaphors and the cross-linguistic

---

[1] de Villiers et al. (2006) point to a principled problem inherent in the fexibility: whenever constraints are added to accommodate data this demonstrates a certain arbitrariness of the approach, see the ease with which Hendriks and Spenader (2006) change Fischer's (2004) theoretically motivated constraint system in order to make it predictive of child data.

variation in the types of anaphors (Sect. 2.4) as well as newer theoretical developments (Sect. 2.5). The article then addresses the acquisition results in detail, discussing the classical results on the asymmetries of pronouns and reflexives or of pronouns with lexical and quantified antecedents as well as the accounts given at the time in Sect. 3. Section 4 addresses the findings on ECM constructions and their explanations. More cross-linguistic results will be examined in Sect. 5 dealing with Romance languages, but also with new results from Modern Greek and German. Section 6 introduces the recent criticism as to the methodological problems in earlier experiments and shows how this critical work has already influenced approaches to acquisition. The conclusion gives a summary and outlines a possibility to integrate recent findings on acquisition with findings on agrammatic patients.

2 Theoretical Background

2.1 The Standard Binding Theory

The basic observation about pronominal elements is that they are different from other nominal elements such as names or definite descriptions (lexical DPs) in that they are referentially deficient. They are anaphoric elements receiving their ultimate interpretation through their antecedent. The interpretation of such elements therefore turns on the identification of their antecedent. Here the feature specification of the pronominal element (person, number, gender, case) plays a decisive role. Additionally, the traditional distinction of pronominal elements into reflexives and pronouns captures two fundamental possibilities of antecedent identification: the antecedent can be within the clause or it can be a salient element in the discourse. The interpretations of reflexives, pronouns and referring expressions are shown in (1a,b,c) using the conventions of formal semantics and the GB framework: coindexed terms are interpreted as referring to the same individual and contraindexed terms usually refer to different individuals since it holds that if the index of A is different from the index of B, then neither can be the antecedent of the other.[2]

(1) a. John$_i$ saw himself$_i$/*himself$_j$/*herself$_i$
   b. John$_i$ saw him$_j$/*him$_i$
   c. John$_i$ /he$_i$ saw John$_{j/*i}$

If the examples in (1a,b,c) look straight forward, the examples in (2a,b,c,d) show that it is not easy to determine in which cases a pronoun (and a referential expression) can or cannot corefer with a possible antecedent. Reinhart (1983) showed that notions of linearity are irrelevant and introduced a structural relationship, the notion of c-command.

---

[2] See Heim (1993), Hamann (2002) on the relationship of indices and the variables of formal semantics.

(2) a. John_i says that he_i is tired
   b. *He_i says that John_i is tired
   c. When he_i was arrested, John_i was with his wife
   d. The people who know him_i well say that John_i is very intelligent

C-command is defined as given in (3), and the kind of referential identity achieved through coindexation in c-command relations is called (syntactic) binding; see (4) for the definition.

(3) x c-commands y iff x does not contain y and the first branching node dominating x also dominates y

(4) x binds y iff x c-commands and is coindexed with y

In the examples (1a,b) a certain complementarity of reflexives (called anaphors in GB-theory) and pronouns appears, also noticeable in (5a,b,c). It also appears that anaphors have an antecedent within the clause, whereas pronouns do not. Investigating examples like (5a,b,c), it emerges that the relevant notion is not the clause, but a local domain that nevertheless allows some distance between the coindexed elements (see the ungrammaticality of (5d)).

(5) a. John hated Mary_i's pictures of herself_i
   b. John_i hated Mary's pictures of him_i
   c. *John hated Mary_i's pictures of her_i
   d. *John_i hated pictures of him_i

Given the definitions in (3) and (4) and the fact that locality plays a role, possible antecedents for the different types of nominal expressions as illustrated in (1), (2) and (5) have been constrained in the **Standard Binding Theory** (Chomsky 1981) spelled out in (6).

(6) a. **Principle A**: An anaphor is bound in a local domain.
   b. **Principle B**: A pronoun is free in a local domain.
   c. **Principle C**: An R-expression is free.

The notion of the "local domain of x" is usually made precise as the **governing category** of x.[3] See Chomsky (1981), Manzini and Wexler (1987), Reuland and Everaert (2000) for a discussion.

The principles given in (6) successfully describe "recurrent patterns in the languages of the world" (Reuland and Everaert 2000: 641) and capture the basic complementarity of pronouns and reflexives. So they provide a good enough working model of the referential properties of pronominal elements, even though it was clear from the beginning that there were problems with these purely syntactic constraints on interpretation.

---

[3]This is usually defined as the minimal category containing x, a governor of x and a SUBJECT (accessible to x).

2.2 Problems with the Standard Binding Theory

Already Ross (1982) pointed out that in English sentences like (7) the pronoun and the reflexive are not in complementary distribution but are both licit in a situation where the gun is near James Bond. Postulating that Principle B constrains only semantic co-arguments of a predicate, not adjuncts, solves this problem. This has consequences for sentences like (8), however, where Max and the pronoun are not semantic co-arguments. So the co-indexation in (8) and in other Exceptional Case Marking (ECM) constructions must be ruled out by a constraint different from Principle B.

(7) James Bond noticed the gun near him/himself.
(8) * Max_i heard him_i criticised.

More problems emerge in the discussion of so-called picture noun anaphors (Pollard and Sag 1992; Reinhart and Reuland 1993) which freely take non-local antecedents as exemplified in (9). This type of anaphor appears to be exempt from the binding constraints, so that Reinhart and Reuland (1993) call the type of anaphor in (9) "logophoric" because it has to do with point of view or perspective. The same observation about the impact of point of view and emphasis has been made for other contexts in which anaphors are free in their local domain as in (10). Reuland and Everaert (2000: 643) and the authors quoted there provide a detailed discussion of this problem.

(9) $John_i$ remembered that Aunt Sally had kept a picture of $himself_i$ in the attic.
(10) There were three linguists in the room apart from myself.

Another possibility to deal with the questions raised by the examples (7), (8), (9) and (10) is outlined in Levinson (2000) and Verbuk and Roeper (2010). In their accounts, scalar implicatures and discourse context regulate the possible interpretations (see also Sect. 2.3). Similar mechanisms relying on a markedness scale for pronominal expressions are built into the constraint rankings suggested in OT treatments of binding.

Other problematic contexts are the ones in (11a,b) and (12) where pronouns have the same referent as a local antecedent. Such contexts have been extensively discussed by Evans (1980), Grodzinsky and Reinhart (1993), by Heim (1993) and Reinhart (2004), who develop an explicit, rigorous formal semantic/pragmatic system for such cases.

(11) a. If everyone hates $Oscar_i$, then $Oscar_i$ hates him_i/*$himself_i$.
     b. I dreamt I was Mel Gibson and kissed me/*myself.
(12) A: Is that speaker Zelda? – B: She must be. She praises her to the sky.

2.3 Binding vs. Coreference

Since the examples (11a,b) and (12) exemplify contexts where pronouns can have the same referents as their antecedents, one way of dealing with the problem is to assume that there are two mechanisms resulting in a mapping to the same referent, coindexation (which in a c-command configuration means binding) or coreference. Coreference can arise because in semantics it is the index of a nominal expression to which an individual is assigned as its interpretation. So, departing from the assumption of disjoint reference in such cases, the same individual could be accidentally assigned as referent to two different indices. Note that Principle B is not violated in such cases, since different indices have been marked on the pronoun and the antecedent.

These two different mechanisms had been discussed already by Sag (1976), Williams (1977), Evans (1980), and Higginbotham (1983) in connection with possessive pronouns in cases of VP-ellipsis like (13). In (13) the pronoun can refer to Al or to somebody else outside the sentence. Even if one disregards a discourse referent, the sentence is ambiguous due to the ellipsis in the second conjunct. It has the reading in (13a) where Bill also loves Al's sister (strict reading) and the reading in (13b) where Bill loves his own sister (sloppy reading). In (13b) the pronouns are coindexed with an antecedent leading to a binding relation for each pronoun In (13a) the referent of the pronoun has been fixed and happens to be the same in both cases – a mechanism which is also necessary in case the referent is a person salient in the discourse. Clearly, the interpretation (13a) involves a form of coreference (or linking – Higginbotham 1983).

(13) Al loves his sister and Bill does too
   a. Al$_i$ loves his$_i$ sister and Bill$_j$ loves his$_i$ sister too
   b. Al$_i$ loves his$_i$ sister and Bill$_j$ loves his$_j$ sister too

Under the assumption that there are two mechanisms, rules are required that allow coreference in some contexts, force coreference precisely in the contexts of examples (11a,b) or (12) and rule it out in run of the mill contexts. Such rules restricting contexts are not constraining syntax but are pragmatic in nature. Their introduction therefore marks a break with the standard binding theory in assigning part of the work to syntax and part of the work to pragmatics, an approach which has been taken further in accounts integrating syntactic and pragmatic constraints into one (Optimality) constraint hierarchy (Burzio 1998; Fischer 2004) or in claims that all the work should be left to pragmatics, see Levinson (1987, 2000).

Chien and Wexler (1990) introduced one such pragmatic rule, their Rule P, given as (14). Rule P does not attempt to define the contexts, but is nevertheless a pragmatic rule.

(14) Contraindexed NPs are noncoreferential unless the context explicitly forces coreference.

Another rule which can be interpreted as pragmatic in origin, namely as a special case of Grice's Quantity maxim is the coreference rule proposed by Grodzinsky and Reinhart (1993), here paraphrased (and simplified) as (15). The rule essentially says that a pronoun cannot be used if replacing the pronoun with a reflexive leads to the same interpretation.

(15) **Rule I: Intrasentential Coreference**
    α cannot corefer with β if an indistinguishable interpretation can be generated by replacing α with a variable bound by the trace of β.

Rule I and the variant introduced by Heim (1993) (for discussion see Hamann 2002) allows coreference in (11a,b). If the pronoun were replaced by a reflexive in (11a), then a different interpretation would ensue, namely "If everyone hates Oscar then Oscar hates himself". Whereas (11a) can be used to explain the rule of universal instantiation, the latter cannot – because the inference now is about self-hating, not about hating Oscar. The same reasoning applies to (11b), the dream is about Mel Gibson kissing the speaker, not about Mel Gibson kissing himself. Heim (1993) identifies these contexts as those where "structured meaning matters" so that the use of a pronoun is a licit expression of coreference. In contrast, in a run of the mill context as in (1a), coreference of the pronoun and the antecedent is excluded because a coreferential reading could not be distinguished from the reading obtained by replacing the pronoun with a reflexive.

Verbuk and Roeper (2010) also demonstrate how coreference and disjoint reference readings can be derived. They follow Levinson (2000) in using the Horn scale <reflexive, pronoun> where the reflexive is encoding the stronger dependency. This Horn scale allows deriving Rule I as a special scalar implicature. Once a child has acquired the properties of the different elements of the pronominal system found in her ambient language and discovered a certain complementarity, then the Horn scale can be established, identifying the reflexive as the element stronger in referential dependency and, at the same time, Principle B can be assumed to be operative in the language. In normal Principle B contexts the Q-maxim allows to calculate that the stronger term, the reflexive, should have been used if coreference had been intended. Since the pronoun has been used, it can be concluded that disjoint reference is meant. In the cases where pronouns allow coreference, this implicature has to be cancelled. Verbuk and Roeper (2010) following Ward (1983), point out that an open proposition must be computed in order to allow cancellation. In the case of (11a) this is *x hates Oscar*. Because of the open proposition the Q-maxim is cancelled and instead an I-implicature based on informativeness is calculated. Verbuk and Roeper (2010) formulate a Discourse Condition on Exceptional Coreference Contexts given in (16). In this condition the open proposition is the crucial factor in forcing coreference in contexts like (11a,b), whereas in contexts like (7) or (9) and (10) coreference is possible, but not forced because no open proposition has to be computed. In such cases, the context may fix the referent as part of the common ground for speaker and hearer or it may not have fixed the referent. In the former situation, using the reflexive would change the meaning and thus coreference is possible, whereas in the latter case, disjoint reference is forced by the Q-implicatures since the stronger anaphor has not been used (see Verbuk and Roeper 2010: 58).

(16) Discourse Condition on Exceptional Coreference Contexts

A pronoun and a non-quantificational antecedent that c-commands it must corefer if the Common Ground contains an Open Proposition that fixes the referent of the pronoun to the same referent as that of the c-commanding antecedent.

So far, nothing has been said about the mechanism allowing coreference in (12). For such identity debate contexts, Heim (1993) points to the fact that the identification of the referent is mediated by the sense (intention) of the definite description. So we have the name, Zelda, which gives access to the identification of the individual we know as Zelda, and we have "the speaker", which identifies Zelda in one of her roles. In this particular example there is also a deictic component (*that*) identifying the speaker in the situation through a pointing gesture. Heim (1993) uses the term "guise" for this phenomenon and allows coreference of contraindexed pronouns and antecedents if the pronoun and the antecedent are identified via different guises, here "the speaker" and "Zelda". A modification of the coreference rule such that it takes into account guises will explain (12). Note that "guise" often involves the well-known "intension" involved in such famous examples as (17). Here coreference is asserted and this is not a tautology because the same referent is presented in two guises. "Guises" also arise, however, through direct reference assignment in the case of names or through deixis, the pointing gesture used to identify referents.

(17) The morning star is the evening star

Summing up, we have identified two contexts where accidental coreference is the rule: One is a context where structured meaning matters and the other is a context where different guises are under debate. Presumably, these are the contexts which "force coreference" in Rule P from Chien and Wexler (1990). Note here that the structured meaning cases in (11a,b) in Heim's (1993) model do not involve different guises, but can be derived straightforwardly from Rule I. In Verbuk and Roeper's account, the identity contexts involve an open proposition, a question under discussion, present in the situational context, and so (16) forces coreference also in such a case.

The problem cases discussed so far led to a distinction of the cases of bound anaphora, which fall under binding theory, and cases of coreference, which can be allowed or excluded by pragmatic rules. Clearly, the interpretation of pronominal elements is not only regulated by the structural binding principles: for pronominals the identification of coreference and disjoint reference is subject to pragmatic computations.

2.4 *Reflexivity and the Typology of Anaphors*

More problems emerged when cross-linguistic investigation showed that many languages do not have clean-cut pronominal systems: pronouns on one side and anaphors on the other (Zribi-Hertz 1989). Some languages, e.g. Dutch and German have a tri-partite system with pronouns and two distinct kinds of anaphors, *zich* and *zichself* (Reinhart and Reuland 1993). In other languages, e.g. Frisian (Reuland 1994), Old and Middle English (Faltz 1985; Van Gelderen 2000), elements that are clearly pronouns do double duty as reflexives. They can be used in contexts where Dutch uses the pronoun or *zich*. Still other languages (Norwegian, Icelandic) have elements that are clearly anaphoric but are not necessarily locally bound, note especially the extensive discussion of the Icelandic long-distance anaphor *sig*, first described by Thráinsson (1976). Some of these problems can be addressed by postulating a parameterization. This can be made explicit by parameterizing the domain of an anaphor as suggested by Manzini and Wexler (1987), or through the feature specification of certain lexical elements in binding "parameters" as suggested by Elbourne (2005) for Frisian and older stages of English and further developed by Verbuk and Roeper (2010).

The Reflexivity framework proposed by Reinhart and Reuland (1993), and developed in Reuland and Everaert (2000), Reuland (2001, 2011) separates coreference from the cases of bound anaphora and integrates the idea of markedness in a typology of anaphors. In these accounts two components are responsible for the distribution of pronouns and anaphors: reflexivization, as the marked option, is defined over predicates and the configurational effects normally derived from the Binding Principles are obtained via chain formation. The reformulation of the binding principles in terms of reflexivity and reflexive marking as in (19) in turn relies on a typology of anaphoric expressions replacing the simple distinction into pronouns and anaphors. Nominal expressions are partitioned into three or four classes by the properties [SELF] and [R], where the property [SELF] describes the ability to reflexivize the predicate and the property [R] captures referential independence (Reinhart and Reuland 1993). In earlier versions of the Reflexivity framework only the first three types of pronominal elements given in (18) are listed, in Reuland (2008) we additionally find the type PRON/SELF relevant for Modern Greek.

(18)

	SELF (English) *himself*	SE (Dutch *zich*)	PRON	PRON/SELF
Reflexivizing function	+	–	–	+
R(eferential independence)	–	–	+	+

(19) **Condition A**: a reflexive-marked syntactic predicate must be interpreted reflexively.

Condition B: a reflexive semantic predicate must be reflexive-marked.

Reflexive marking can be achieved in the lexicon (inherently reflexive predicates like *shave* and *wash*), by adding a *-self* suffix as in the case of English, or by choosing the lexically reflexive marked pronoun as in the case of *zich* in Dutch and *se* in French, see (20) for a definition. The definitions of syntactic and semantic predicates are given in (21), here following Reuland and Everaert (2000).

(20) a. **A predicate is reflexive** iff at least two of its arguments are coindexed
 b. **A predicate (formed of P) is reflexive marked** iff either P is lexically reflexive with respect to an indexed argument, or one of P's indexed arguments is a SELF-anaphor.

(21) a. The syntactic predicate of (a head) P is P, all its syntactic arguments, and an external argument of P (subject). The syntactic argument of P are the projections assigned theta-role or Case by P.
   b. The semantic predicate of P is P and its arguments at the relevant semantic level.

The conditions (19) and the definitions (20) and (21) talk explicitly only about coindexing and its interpretation. However, Condition B has much the same effect as the standard Principle B. It works only by exclusion and does not apply if the semantic argument of a predicate is not the pronoun but a clause as in (8). Therefore Condition B is restricted to semantic predicates, whereas Condition A concerns syntactic predicates. In order to rule out (8), the other ingredient of this theory, chain formation is appealed to. (22) gives the definition of an A-chain used by Reinhart and Reuland (1993), see also the modifications in Reuland and Everaert (2000).

(22) Any sequence of coindexation that is headed by an A-position and satisfies antecedent government is an A-chain (Reinhart and Reuland 1993: 693,4).

This definition subsumes trace-tailed coindexations (movement chains) and chains arising through coindexation for purposes of interpretation/reflexivization. In fact, it integrates both types of chains and treats a sequence of indices arising through a combination of movement and interpretative coindexation as an A-chain.[4] The crucial condition on such general chains is formulated in (23).

(23) **General Condition on A-chains**
A maximal A-chain $(\alpha_1,....,\alpha_n)$ contains exactly one link – α_1 - that is both + referential [+R] and Case-marked. (Reinhart and Reuland 1993: 696)

Expressions that are [+R] carry a "full specification for φ-features and structural case" (Reinhart and Reuland 1993: 697). That this is only a necessary condition for referentiality not a sufficient one, however, can be demonstrated by English *himself* and *him* which have the same φ- and case features. The pronoun is [+R], however, the anaphor is [–R]. It is generally held that [–R] expressions are "referentially defective...which entails that they cannot be used as demonstratives, referring to some entity in the world" (Reinhart and Reuland 1993: 658).

Coming back to example (8) and the problem of how to exclude it if Condition B only applies to semantic predicates, we see that it is the classification of English *him* as [+R] together with the Chain Condition that disallows coindexation. Coindexation of *him* and *Max* would violate the Chain condition since two elements would be specified as [+R]. Note that the general conditions on chain formation include the configurational information so important for the standard binding theory, namely

---

[4] See Chomsky (1981) and many others for arguments that these two types of coindexations do not have the same properties.

that one of the coindexed elements c-commands the other one. In this manner a major ingredient of the binding theory can be reduced to general properties of the computational system.

2.5 Binding Theory, Minimalism and Other Recent Developments

The modifications of the binding theory discussed so far have introduced a pragmatic component and have derived the basic structural constraint operative in the principles from more general constraints on chains. More radical changes are necessary, however, if the new approach to the nature of syntactic computations outlined in the *Minimalist Program* (Chomsky 1995) is to be applied. Without going into the details here, it is argued that the Binding Principles are not well-formedness conditions that apply at S-Structure/Spell-Out but are interface conditions holding at the LF interface. So Chomsky (1995: 211) proposes a "very simple interpretive version of binding theory". With D being the "relevant" local domain, the new formulation is given in (24):

(24) A. If α is an anaphor, interpret it as coreferential with a c-commanding phrase in D.
 B. If α is a pronominal, interpret it as disjoint from every c-commanding phrase in D.
 C. If α is an r-expression, interpret it as disjoint from every c-commanding phrase

It is clear that these principles, even though they are now interface conditions, do not integrate some of the insights discussed here. The possibility of accidental coreference is ignored together with the typology of anaphors obvious in languages that do not have a bipartite system like English. Another major change is that in the computational system indices can be abandoned, which is a welcome consequence for Chomsky. Indices are semantic in nature in that they encode the assignment of referents, and removing them from the computational system is another step towards the "autonomy of syntax", a desirable aim, at least in Chomsky's program.

The unfortunate consequence is that the (referential) relations they express must be replaced "by a structural account of the relation they annotate" Chomsky (1995: 217, footnote 53). It is at this point that former simplicity is replaced by not very intuitive, complex construction. Reuland and Everaert (2000: 666) propose to construct the relation stepwise through the existing morpho-syntactic relations: "an object anaphor is linked to the verb and the verb's inflectional system by structural Case, the verb is linked to its functional system, and the functional V-system is linked to the subject." Another conceivable approach to indices closer connected to exploring the "relation they annotate", see above, would be to define Agree relations via the features [+/− reflexivising] and [+/− referential] which hold in the usual structural configurations. See Reuland (2011) for developments of such approaches.

But see also Szabolcsi (2001) and Beghelli and Stowell (1997) who discuss the referentiality feature and a Referentiality Phrase in an attempt to eliminate the operation of quantifier raising. This treatment suggests that such a feature is necessary for other reasons anyway and exploring it for binding relations might turn out to be quite straightforward.

Apart from these difficulties and the remaining problems with accidental coreference, types of anaphors etc., shifting the binding conditions to the interpretative interface has a certain appeal.[5] It enables a new division of labor: conditions can apply at the lexical level, at the syntactic level and at the interfaces. So the necessary pragmatic rules can be easily conceived as interface conditions at the next level: the semantic-pragmatic interface. This shift also forces a new look at the interaction of conditions working at different levels.

Research on the interaction of different types of constraints with the notion of economy of derivation (and processing) have led to the assumption that it is cheaper to be able to treat a phenomenon, here encoding a dependency, in the narrow syntax than having to use an interface rule which brings into play other cognitive domains. Reuland (2001) proposes that derivation in narrow syntax is more economical than derivation at logical syntax, which in turn is more economical than having to integrate contextual factors from discourse. Extending this to situational context, which under this account is even harder to integrate into the derivation, yields the hierarchy (25) for referential identification (adapted from Grillo 2008: 48).

(25) Level   Operation
      Narrow Syntax   feature checking (chain formation)
      Semantics (logical syntax)   bound variable
      Discourse context   coreference
      Non-linguistic context   deixis

The effect of the economy hierarchy is that certain types of dependencies are possible only if no cheaper derivation is available. So bound variable chains, which involve cross-modular operations, are more costly than chains established through feature checking at narrow syntax, and establishing coreference, which necessarily involves the discourse level is more costly still. Note that this hierarchy, Burzio's (1998) constraint on *Referential Economy* and the Horn scale employed by Verbuk and Roeper (2010) derive very similar effects. In the adult grammar a sentence with a pronoun cannot (in a normal context) indicate coreference since in that case syntactic binding, i.e. a reflexive, would be preferred because it is the cheaper option. For explaining acquisition facts, it has to be assumed that the hierarchy is not in place yet. In particular, narrow syntax is not the cheapest option for the child, perhaps because full automatization or the step from the particular to the general is

---

[5] Heim and Kratzer (1998: 127) do not follow this view and explicitly treat the binding conditions as purely syntactic. Verbuk and Roeper (2010) also argue that they are syntactic because they refer to syntactic entities: the local domain or the minimal clause.

not achieved yet. This means that the use of a pronoun does not necessarily imply disjoint reference since the use of a reflexive might not be cheaper for the child.[6] Such approaches to the economy of derivation can be tied in remarkably well with the idea of different classes of features instrumental in defining constraints on chain formation in narrow syntax, especially recent refinements of Relativized Minimality (Rizzi 1990, 2004). Since reflexivity could be derived by head-movement (see Reuland 2011) and Romance clitic pronouns are involved in both types of chains (Hamann 2002) such restrictions, resting on a distinction of argumental, quantificational, modifying and topic-features might be interacting with the hierarchy sketched above.

As to the acquisition of the Binding Principles, theoretical advances developed from a detailed examination of problem cases have influenced empirical research not only in hypothesis formation but also in experimental designs and, naturally, in the interpretation of the results. Especially the distinction of binding and coreference and the development of the reflexivity framework have proved fruitful for acquisition research.

3 Children's Problems with Pronouns

3.1 The Pronoun/Reflexive Asymmetry

Wexler and Chien (1985) and Chien and Wexler (1990) showed that English children give adult responses to sentences containing reflexives in 80–90% of the cases between the age of 5;6–6;6. Performance on sentences with pronouns were much worse, however, showing close to chance performance in many cases. This asymmetry has been replicated for English and other languages in many studies (Deutsch et al. 1986; Grimshaw and Rosen 1990; McDaniel et al. 1990; Sigurjónsdóttir and Hyams 1992; Avrutin and Wexler 1992). Only Kaufmann's (1988) results indicated that children are about as good with pronouns as with reflexives.

Chien and Wexler (1990) give an overview over a series of experiments showing that English children respect locality constraints and know c-command. Interestingly, their experiments demonstrate a slow acquisition of anaphors and Principle A: looking at the experiments 1–3, only 13% local readings are assigned to the anaphors at age 2;6–3;0 and there is a steady increase till at age 6;0–6;6 children choose the local antecedent in 89.4% of the cases. In the same experiments, the interpretation of pronouns was only 64% adult like at the age of 6;0–6;6, giving rise to the misnomer DPBE as discussed above.

---

[6]However, even if the approaches arrive at similar outcomes for the simple cases, differences in predictions might arise for cases like (11) and (12); see Verbuk and Roeper (2010) and their discussion of Reinhart (2004).

Possible explanations were that children may not have yet determined the local domain for pronouns (see McKee 1992) or, advocated by Chien and Wexler themselves, that they have not mastered a pragmatic principle that governs coreference and so is relevant for pronouns, not for reflexives. This lead to a different set of experiments probing for the effects of accidental coreference.

3.2 The Quantified Antecedent/Simple Antecedent Asymmetry

As has been sketched in the introduction important issues are related to Chien and Wexler's (1990) finding that there is an asymmetry in children's mastery of contexts with lexical antecedents and with quantified antecedents: the claim that pronominal reference is regulated by two mechanisms, syntactic binding and pragmatic coreference, and the claim that the binding principles are all three mastered at the same time. So we will give some space to the original experiment.

In their Experiment 4, Chien and Wexler (1990) tested sentences with reflexives and pronouns paired either with a lexical antecedent or with a quantified antecedent as given in (26a,b,c,d). The distinction of (26c) and (26d) is especially important because quantified antecedents do not allow accidental coreference. Quantifiers are non-referential elements and so cannot enter into a coreference relation with pronouns. In the case of coindexation the quantifier automatically binds the pronoun on the semantic level so that reflexive interpretations always indicate violations of Principle B.

Chien and Wexler (1990) used the picture version of a Truth Value Judgment Task, also called Picture Verification Task. Children were shown a picture either depicting the situation where, e.g., the subject(s) touch(es) someone else or her/themselves, and they heard a sentence which described the picture correctly (match condition) or incorrectly (non-match condition) uttered by a puppet who is looking at the picture with the child. The child's task is to tell whether the puppet is right or wrong about the situation in the picture.

(26) a. Mama Bear is touching herself   name-reflexive
     b. Every bear is touching herself   quantifier- reflexive
     c. Mama Bear is touching her   name-pronouns
     d. Every bear is touching her   quantifier –pronoun.

Chien and Wexler (1990) obtained the following results. At around 5 years of age, children interpret quantifiers correctly and at that time they do not have problems with the name-reflexive nor with the quantifier-reflexive conditions, even though there always is a slightly lower success rate for non-match conditions. For the name-pronoun conditions, it turned out that in the match condition even 2–3 year-olds interpret the pronoun as referring to a person outside the clause in 90% of the cases. The difficulty lies in the non-match conditions where the pronoun is interpreted as coreferring with the subject in 70% of the cases at 4 years of age, in 50% of the cases at age 5–6 and at 25% at 6–7. In contrast to these results on name-pronoun sentences, children gave perfect judgments for the quantifier-pronoun condition in the matching cases and gave correct "no"-responses to the non-match condition about 84% of the time between 5 and 6 years of age. Concentrating on the fifth year of life we get a contrast of 50% correct responses in the non-match condition for pronouns with lexical antecedents, 84% correct responses in the non-match conditions for pronouns with quantified antecedents and nearly perfect responses for reflexives.

These results and their explanation via a pragmatic rule (see 2.3, (14,15)) that has not yet been acquired by children fit in very well with the theoretical developments of the time and were corroborated in several experiments for English with different experimental paradigms. Among these studies are Philip and Coopmans (1996) also using a Picture Verification Task, McDaniel et al. (1990) and McDaniel and Maxfield (1992) using a Grammaticality Judgment Task, and studies using the story version of the TVJT such as Avrutin and Thornton (1994), Matsuoka (1997) and Thornton and Wexler (1999). Thornton (1990) and Boster (1991) used a TVJT and distinguished a coreference context from a bound variable context through the use of constructions with Wh-movement as in (27). They thus avoided the problem of a possibly late acquisition of quantifiers.

(27) Bert and Huckleberry Hound scratched them.
    I know who scratched them – Bert and Huckleberry Hound.

Boster (1991) in her Experiment 1 found 96% correct interpretation of the Wh-contexts vs. 62% correct interpretation of simple contexts for children 4;6–6;0 years old, and Thornton (1990) reports 92% correct interpretation of the Wh-contexts vs. 51% correct interpretation of the simple contexts by children between 3;7 and 4;8 years of age.

In contrast to these studies, some experiments did not find any asymmetry in the interpretation of pronouns with quantified and lexical antecedents. Studies on English that find about equal performance in both contexts are Kaufmann (1988) (90% and 87% correct for name-pronoun and quantifier-pronoun respectively), Lombardi and Sarma (1989) (45% and 51%), Boster (1991) Experiment 2 (62% vs. 58%), Utakis (1995) (63% and 60%). Note that Kaufmann (1988) finds a reasonably good performance in both contexts whereas the other studies show about chance performance.

Conroy et al. (2009) provide a very useful table summing up these different results according to experimental paradigm. Their Table 2 also gives information about results on languages other than English. Interestingly, Avrutin and Wexler (1992) find an asymmetry for Russian (48% and 83% correct) in contexts with Wh-binding, whereas they do not find it with the quantifier corresponding to *every* (48% vs. 59%). Likewise Hestvik and Philip (1999) do not find an asymmetry for Norwegian (91% and 97% correct), whereas Philip and Coopmans (1996) establish a small but significant difference for Dutch (36% vs. 53% correct). Though Dutch children show about chance performance in the quantified antecedent condition, their performance is significantly worse in simple contexts. Note again, that Kaufmann (1988) and Hestvik and Philip (1999) basically find mastery of pronoun interpretation, whereas the other two studies find chance performance or below chance.

It comes to mind that in experiments where performance is good on the simple cases, any asymmetry might be masked by a ceiling effect. In particular, this concerns the experiments on clitic languages: an asymmetry is not predicted since Jakubowicz (1989) and McKee (1992) established that Romance children do not have a PIP.

For completeness of the discussion on the quantifier asymmetry, however, some comments on experiments with French and Spanish children are given here. Hamann et al. (1997) and Baauw et al. (1997) used exactly the same kind of material for French and Spanish as Philip and Coopmans (1996) had used for Dutch and English. Hamann et al. found that 4 year-olds were 78% correct in simple non-matching contexts vs. 70% correct in non-matching contexts with quantified antecedents; 5 year-olds were 100% vs. 88% correct and 6–7 year-olds were 100% vs. 94% correct. Compared to overall almost-adult performance, they consistently find more problems in quantified non-matching contexts, but no significant differences. Baauw et al. (1997) report 90% mastery on both conditions for children with a mean age of 5;6, which almost exactly replicates the results on French. Since McKee (1992) also reports 90% adult performance in simple contexts, the results on French and Spanish were predicted by any account that sees the reason for the early mastery in Italian in some special property of clitic pronouns. Many accounts on clitics have in effect claimed that clitic pronouns do not allow coreference – which exempts them from the PIP.[7]

Recently, the experiments and results showing the quantifier/simple asymmetry have been criticized (see Elbourne 2005; Conroy et al. 2009, and Sects. 6.1 and 6.2 here) so that it is an open question whether there is a PIP or not. Nevertheless, I would like to outline the accounts offered.

3.3 Explaining the PIP

Whereas the reflexive/pronoun asymmetry showed that there is a PIP, the quantified antecedent asymmetry indicated that children have problems with pronouns only in contexts where accidental coreference is possible, presumably because they have not yet acquired the rule that excludes coreference in such contexts (Chien and Wexler 1990, here (14)). An alternative explanation claims that children's processing limitations do not allow a full computation of the relevant constraint (Grodzinsky and Reinhart 1993, (15)).

The account proposed in Grodzinsky and Reinhart (1993) assumes that children know Principle B and the Coreference Rule I, but that their processing capacity does not suffice to compute the two interpretations and compare them. A processing account of the PIP is attractive because the difficulties are not only observed in

---

[7]This is the account that Hestvik and Philip (1999) also offer for Norwegian since Norwegian pronouns move like clitics at LF.

language acquisition but also in language impairment and loss (see Grodzinsky and Reinhart 1993; Avrutin 2004; Baauw and Cuetos 2003 on agrammatic aphasia, and van der Lely and Stollwerck 1997 on SLI).

A different account of the PIP was developed by Thornton and Wexler (1999). After Heim (1993) had elaborated Reinhart's Rule I and introduced guises in order to explain the identity debate contexts, Avrutin (1994), Hamann (2002) and Thornton and Wexler (1999) employed this notion to explain the PIP. Hamann (2002) following Grimshaw and Rosen (1990) and very similar to Avrutin (1994, 1999), assumes that children can anchor strong pronouns in the situational context, hence might allow deictic identification through pointing as a guise for the pronoun.[8] This differs from the guise of the possible antecedent DP and so allows coreference. Thornton and Wexler (1999) develop Heim's proposal into the stronger claim that children overextend guise creation. Since different guises make coreference readings possible, this explains the PIP. In their interpretation of Heim (1993, 1998), Thornton and Wexler (1999) make the generalization that different guises are created in cases like (12) as well as cases like (11a,b), whereas only the former are the case where Heim (1993) explicitly discusses different guises. So, they argue, what children do not know is which contexts restrict guise creation.

Recently, Verbuk and Roeper (2010) have criticized both the above explanations. They argue that a processing account relying on the derivation and comparison of two representations cannot hold, since children compute two representations and compare them in many cases where scalar implicatures are involved as e.g. the choice of *some* over *all*. They refer to an experiment by Papafragou (2002) who showed that 5;3-year-old children correctly compute scalar implicatures based on the <*all, some*> scale 77.5% of the time. So, Verbuk and Roeper conclude, children are well able to compare two interpretations at the age at which they still show the PIP. The argument is relativized by Verbuk and Roeper by also pointing out that in general children perform poorly in tasks where the implicature arises through an underinformative statement. This is the case for computing the implicature on exclusivity for the use of *or* as shown by Chierchia et al. (2001) and Gualmini et al. (2001). Chance performance was also found for implicatures of modal verbs and quantifiers by Noveck (2001). Likewise, Papafragou (2002) finds that 5-year-old children compute the non-completion implicature for aspectual verbs like *start* and *begin* only one third of the time. On the other hand, the same study showed that these children performed above chance if the sentence contained the term *half*. Papafragou and Musolino (2003) present similar findings: 5-year-olds perform below chance on <*some, all*> and on <*start, finish*>, but do pretty well on a scale based on numerals. So children may do poorly on some scales, but they can handle other scales pretty well. When Papafragou and Musolino extend their study such that they first train children to pay attention to

---

[8]Note that this deictic guise or interpretation of the pronoun always involves pointing and is radically different from what Conroy et al. call the deictic interpretation of a pronoun.

what is the expectation in the given context and also provide more context so that this expectation is salient for the child, it turns out that children do much better in rejecting the less informative statement and that they give the right reasons for doing so.

The conclusion that can be drawn from these experiments is that children can do some implicatures pretty well, especially when they are given enough context to realize that the speaker's statement has not met the expectation. So what it boils down to is that children have to compute an open proposition (the question under discussion) for implicatures[9] and that this might be the difficulty. In any case, the argument put forward by Verbuk and Roeper needs corroboration by more empirical research. At this point, it is impossible to decide whether children cannot compute the alternative for processing reasons, whether they cannot do so because they cannot construct the open proposition, or whether they cannot do so because they lack the speaker's perspective, the possibility offered by Hendriks and Spenader (2006).

Regarding extended guise creation, Verbuk and Roeper (2010) show that children give random answers in critical contexts like (11a,b) and (12). Though some of the experimental conditions may be problematic for other reasons,[10] the experiment shows that children have difficulties in such contexts, which Verbuk and Roeper interpret as showing that children certainly do not overextend guise creation, rather they seem to have difficulties creating the elaborate guises necessary in such contexts.[11]

Apart from such criticism of specific accounts, it remains relatively uncontroversial that the manifestations of the PIP observed in different experiments must be related to the coreference relation. However, another asymmetry, that between simple sentences and ECM sentences with pronouns, indicated that other theoretical proposals should be explored in so far as additional factors may be involved.

---

[9]See also Gualmini and Meroni (2009), who suggest that the difficulty can be located in accommodating a "Question under discussion" for the derivation of an underinformative implicature.

[10]In one of the stories Bill, Mary and Jane want to draw somebody. They get paper and crayons and then Bill draws Mary and Mary draws Bill. The story ends with the sentences: "Nobody drew Jane. So Jane drew her". Here the following problem may arise: If nobody drew Jane, then a child may find it confusing that Jane drew her – nobody did. The problem is that the quantifier in the intended interpretation ranges only over the two protagonists mentioned in the last part of the story. The child might interpret it as ranging over all the protagonists including Jane.

[11]Note here, that under a strict reading of Heim (1993), guise creation is not the crucial point in (11a), so that the criticism may be valid for Thornton and Wexler's (1999) version but does not touch the original account. Note also that, Avrutin (1994, 1999) and Hamann (1997, 2002) may escape the criticism because they do not assume that children will always be able to create the guises required in complicated contexts, they refer specifically to the simple possibility of deictic anchoring which can provide the guise for the pronoun. Such non-adult deictic anchorage is evident in other areas of child speech as well, e.g. tense.

4 Reflexivity and the Effects of the Chain Condition

Following Reinhart and Reuland's (1993) different perspective on the binding principles, which turns on the fact that different languages may have different sets of anaphoric expressions and as a consequence different syntactic contrasts, acquisition research reoriented to the idea that "the acquisition of pronominal anaphora can be accounted for purely in terms of the acquisition of specific lexical features", as stated in Philip and Coopmans (1996). This kind of approach is already suggested by Chien and Wexler (1990) for the developmental profile of Principle A, which suggests a slow acquisition of the lexical properties of reflexives (see Sect. 3.1 here), and is pursued very successfully in the paper by Verbuk and Roeper (2010). At the same time it is clear that decisive data on how different sets of anaphoric expressions can be acquired will best come from comparative studies.

4.1 Reflexivity and Types of Verbs: The Case of Dutch

Focusing on Dutch, which has a tripartite anaphoric system, see (18), Sigurjónsdóttir and Coopmans (1996) report that 5-to-6 year old children show adult performance in simple principle B sentences only 17% of the time, whereas they interpret the anaphor *zichself* correctly about 80% of the time. The reflexive/pronoun asymmetry is therefore unusually pronounced in Dutch.

Using the reflexivity framework, the above authors assumed that Dutch children have problems identifying pronouns as referentially independent so that the Chain Condition will not constrain pronoun use as it does for adults. To provide evidence that the Chain Condition is not applied in an adult-like manner by Dutch children, Sigurjónsdóttir and Coopmans (1996) compared inherently reflexive verbs and transitive verbs. This contrast can provide evidence because in this framework only the Chain Condition can rule out the use of a pronoun with inherently reflexive verbs as in (28b), whereas for regular transitive verbs both Condition B, as formulated in (19), and the Chain Condition (23) apply.

(28) a. Fred$_i$ schaamde zich$_i$
Fred shamed self
'Fred was ashamed (of himself)'
b. *Fred$_i$ schaamde hem$_i$
Fred shamed him
Fred was ashamed

By Condition A in (19), an inherently reflexive predicate must be interpreted reflexively which is the case in both (28a) and (28b) indicated by coindexation. The verb is inherently reflexive which implies that it is reflexive marked, so Condition B is fulfilled in (28b). (28b) is ruled out by the Chain Condition, however.

When Sigurjónsdóttir and Coopmans (1996) found that children do better with transitive verbs like *aaien* 'stroke' than with verbs like *wassen* 'wash' that also have an inherently reflexive reading, they concluded that children establish a chain in cases like (28b). This implies that in child grammar the pronoun is not specified as referential: only elements specified as [−R] allow a chain.

4.2 The Chain Condition and the Asymmetry in ECM and Simple Sentences

Pursuing this line of argumentation other contexts were investigated, in particular ECM cases, see (8). Recall that in such constructions the pronoun is not a semantic co-argument of the verb, so that Condition B does not apply and only the Chain Condition rules out coindexation. Accidental coreference can apply as always in cases of contraindexation.

The experiments typically were Picture Verification Tasks, which considerably narrowed the range of testable ECM constructions. So the pictures for testing children's performance in ECM cases usually include a mirror where the protagonists can do both, see each other and themselves, and the embedding verb is *see*.[12] Typical test sentences are given in (29a,b).

(29) a. The girl sees her dance.
 b. The mom sees her blow bubbles.

Using such materials, Philip and Coopmans (1996) tested English and Dutch children and found a very clear ECM effect for Dutch, though not for English.

Table 1 shows the results of the conditions in which adults would answer "No". The data indicate that Dutch children have persistent and exacerbated problems in ECM-constructions till the age of 8 years, an age when they reach chance performance in simple cases.

As an explanation Philip and Coopmans (1996) propose that there is a feature underspecification for pronouns that allows coindexation without violating the Chain Condition. They suggest that the underspecified feature is the Case feature, arguing that in the Dutch case system structural and non-structural case are "overtly indistinguishable". If Dutch pronouns are underspecified in this manner, this explains the below chance performance in ECM cases and the difference found for inherently reflexive and transitive verbs.

---

[12] A careful discussion of the problems of this experimental set-up can be found in Hamann (2002) who ran a control experiment showing that French children have no trouble in determining who can see whom in a mirror and do very well when there is a mirror and the simple Priniple B sentence (i). So it can be excluded that using mirror images added a conceptual difficulty for children. See also Coopmans and Philip (2000) and Baauw and Cuetos (2003) on this point.

(i) La maman la voit.
The mom her sees

Table 1 Correct adult no-responses to simple and ECM sentences with pronouns in Dutch and English (from Philip and Coopmans 1996)

Construction	English	Dutch	Dutch	Dutch
	6 year olds (%)	4–6 year olds (%)	7 year olds (%)	8 year olds (%)
The girl dries her	32	36	55	50
The girl sees her dance	33	10	16	38

If problems with Rule I (or P) are responsible for chance performance in simple contexts in English, then Dutch children face a double difficulty: problems with Rule I and underspecification of pronouns. They can wrongly categorize the pronoun as [−R], which allows establishing a chain, similar to reflexives. They can also occasionally categorize the pronoun as [+R], in which case they might allow coreference because of Rule I problems. This double difficulty may explain their below chance performance in simple contexts (see Table 1) and the persistence of the problem.

Note that Verbuk and Roeper (2010) in a very similar manner explain the chance performance of English children not directly through a problem with the application of Rule I but through an underspecification of the referentiality feature on pronouns, which effectively blocks the derivation of implicatures such as Rule I. If some kind of chain condition can be integrated into their account, this underspecification could also explain the bad performance in ECM sentences. The OT-account proposed by Hendriks and Spenader (2006), however, does not predict different performance in ECM and simple sentences. It is quite possible, of course, that some constraint could be added to the relevant hierarchy, which, properly ranked, gives the desired result. Such speculation is beyond this paper, however.

5 More Asymmetries: Languages with Clitic Pronouns

One of the most striking asymmetries established in cross-linguistic research on binding concerns the contrast in children's performance on pronoun interpretation in English and Dutch on the one hand and in Romance languages on the other hand. For research on binding this means in particular that any account of the PIP for English must also explain why the effect does not occur in languages with clitic pronouns. So different suggestions have been made in order to pin-point the specific property of clitics that must be responsible for their early mastery.

5.1 Formal Properties of Pronominal Clitics

In the Romance languages pronominal clitics differ from lexical nominal expressions and from full pronominals in that clitics cannot be used in isolation, cannot receive focal stress, cannot be conjoined, cannot be modified, or be separated from the verb (see Kayne 1975). Pronominal clitics fill a special head position in the highest part of the clausal functional structure.[13] So one of their striking properties is that they are nominal arguments[14] occurring in a head position of the verbal functional domain.

There are different approaches to account for this property. In base insertion accounts (Borer 1984; Sportiche 1996) complement clitics fill a dedicated head (Sportiche's "clitic voice") licensing a *pro* inserted in complement position so that the chain connecting the argumental *pro* and the clitic head captures their mixed status. Alternatively, complement clitics are assumed to be generated in complement position and move to a functional head high in the clausal functional structure (Belletti 1999; Burzio 1986; Kayne 1975, 1991; Rizzi 1978, 1982). In French and other languages with participle agreement, a complement clitic must be identifiable as a DP (an argument) at least till the Agr Participle Phrase, where it passes through the specifier. During the last links of the chain, however, only the head of this DP moves, see Belletti (1999). She also argues that Romance complement clitics have a strong case feature that needs checking and so forces overt movement.

The properties that clitics cannot be used in isolation and cannot receive focal stress go together with the observation that clitics cannot be used deictically with only a pointing gesture and no further discourse anchorage. So it has often been observed that clitics totally depend on discourse and their antecedent to receive an interpretation. Hamann (2002) argued that clitics must take on the guise of their DP antecedent so that similarities to Principle C might be observed. Note that in Principle C sentences disjoint reference readings can be suspended under certain conversational conditions as in the following dialogue: *A:Have you met the director? Does your sister know her? – B. with a smile: Oh, yes, my sister knows the director quite well. In fact, she is the director.* Hamann (2002: 106) discusses similar examples for clitics and also accepts arguments from Cardinaletti and Starke (2000) who demonstrate that clitics can be used demonstratively/deictically or with stress in specially constructed contexts. Hamann (2002) therefore concludes that accidental coreference for clitics is not categorically excluded, it is "just harder to get" than for English style pronouns (Hamann 2002: 103).

In any case, a clitic or a weak pronoun seems to be referentially deficient in a sense that full pronouns are not and so they need more context to define their guise or referent than a full pronoun or a full DP. This referential deficiency and strong identification of the clitic with its discourse antecedent has been captured by some accounts in the claim that clitics are always "bound" (see Baauw et al. 1997), an intuitive term including D-linking. Making precise this intuition, Delfitto (2002) has provided an account where clitics are variables bound by the

---

[13] The possible exception are French subject clitics, for which different analyses have been proposed.

[14] Clitic chains show A-chain properties, see Rizzi (1986).

λ-operator. For "binding" to a discourse antecedent, the left dislocation structures used for topicalization in Romance languages serve as a model. The clitic is bound by an empty topic as in (30a,b), see Baauw and Cuetos (2003: 233) who analyze clitic constructions as "hidden clitic-left dislocation structures". Since empty topics must be discourse identified, the clitic can never introduce new information in the form of a new referent and thus deictic use (in the sense of pointing) is excluded.

(30) a. [$_{topic}$ ec]$_i$ Juan la$_i$ vio en casa
          ec$_i$ John her$_i$ sees in the house
      b. [λy (Juan vio y en casa)] (ec)

Note that in this account clitics cannot enter into accidental coreference relations because they are always bound variables. However, this idea turns on the possibility of using clitics in contexts like (11a), repeated in French as (31). If exceptional coreference is possible for a clitic in such contexts, then any account that strictly excludes coreference needs to be extended in ways which can explain (11a), see Hamann (2002) for an attempt. Unfortunately, judgments are not unanimous. Most, but not all, native speakers of French accept (31), and a version with strong pronouns does not immediately come to mind. Some Spanish speakers seem to accept the Spanish version of this sentence whereas others reject it, see Baauw and Cuetos (2003).

(31) Tout le monde aime Oscar. Marie l'aime, Chantal l'aime et Oscar l'aime.
      Everybody loves Oscar. Marie loves him, Chantal loves him and Oscar loves him.

5.2 Experiments on Binding in Clitic Languages

Given their referential deficiency and their high position in the functional structure of the clause, Romance clitics manifest many differences from English pronouns. So it should not have been very surprising that only very young children in Romance languages showed a "delay of principle B" whereas 5-to-6 year-olds show mastery.

The earliest binding experiments, Jakubowicz (1984, 1989), showed in an Act-Out and a Picture Matching task that French children's performance is good already around the age of 4 years: At age 3;6–4;0 children performed 78% adult-like in (32b) and at age 4;7–5;0 children are 98% correct in (32a), 78% correct in (32b) and 75% correct in (32c). Jakubowicz (1989) also tested children's production of subject and object clitics and found a substantial delay of object clitics in production with respect to subject clitics (see also Hamann et al. 1996). Subsequently, McKee (1992) showed near perfect performance on both reflexives and clitic pronouns by Italian children at the age of 4 years.

(32)　　**age group**　　　　　　　　　　　　　　　3.0.–3.5　3.6–4.0　4,7–5.0
　　　a.　Nounours dit que Kiki se brosse　　　　　96%　　97%　　98%
　　　　　Teddy bear says that Kiki brushes himself
　　　b.　Nounours dit que Kiki le peigne　　　　　60%　　78%　　78%
　　　　　Teddy bear says that Kiki brushes him
　　　c.　chaque Schroumpfette veut que
　　　　　Marie la brosse　　　　　　　　　　　　60%　　75%　　75%
　　　　　Every Smurfette wants that Marie brushes her

More recently, in an experiment testing 99 French speaking children between the ages of 4;0 and 6;0 both in production and in comprehension Zesiger et al. (2010) found that children have more difficulty with complement clitics than with reflexive clitics both in comprehension and production. For the comprehension experiment a Picture Verification Task with photographs was used (TVJT using pictures) testing complement clitics and reflexive clitics in simple sentences as given in (33a,b).

(33) a. Papa le couvre
　　　　Papa him covers
　　　　'Daddy covers him'
　　　b. Papa se couvre.
　　　　Papa self covers
　　　　'Daddy covers himself'

In the match conditions children were perfect for both reflexives and complement clitics. In the binding mismatch conditions, however, the authors found a small but significant difference throughout the age range under investigation. The children rejected mismatches in condition A contexts at ceiling (99.3%) already at age 4;0, but rejected such mismatches in condition B contexts between 87.5% at age 4;0 and 93.8% at age 6;0. Since the difference is so small compared to studies investigating the same contexts in English or Dutch, the authors conclude that their results confirm the sharp dissociation between languages with clitics and without clitics. They offer an analysis where complement clitics, but not reflexives, cross the subject chain during derivation. This is a factor that can explain the larger difference found for production and therefore might also be responsible for the small one in comprehension (Zesiger et al. 2010, but see also Sects. 5.1 and 5.3 and the discussion about rudimentary guise creation in footnote 19).

5.3　*Accounting for the Absence of a PIP*

Explanations for the good performance on clitic pronouns and the asymmetry found for clitic and non-clitic languages are basically twofold, structural or pragmatic, where the pragmatic observations are often derived from structural or lexical properties of clitics.

McKee (1992) referred to the higher position of the clitic and proposed that this high position made it clear for the child that the "local domain" for the pronominal clitic must be the clause, the IP, whereas English children could for a time assume the VP to be the "local domain". This account has been criticized for many reasons, the most important one being that it must assume the VP external subject hypothesis. Otherwise the subject trace in the VP would provide a potential binder for the pronoun and English children should do well. See Avrutin and Wexler (1992) for a discussion, also Hamann (2002) or Baauw and Cuetos (2003) who argue that in the case of English agrammatics this would imply that they lose grammatical knowledge. This criticism does not mean that other structural accounts might not fare better, see Baauw and Cuetos (2003), who assume that clitics are bound variables and can therefore not show accidental coreference.

Avrutin and Wexler (1992) and Avrutin (1994) pursued the pragmatic road outlined in Chien and Wexler (1990). They point out that clitics are referentially deficient and therefore do not (usually) corefer. Avrutin (1994) formally derives coreference through the existence of two guises, see also Heim (1993), and argues that pronouns can introduce extra guises only if they can refer deictically. The idea simply is that deixis in its sense of pointing always introduces the guise of the entity or person pointed at – the physical presence. This possibility is also involved in the identity debate in example (12). The identity question is about whether the situationally identified referent of the pronoun is the person named Zelda. Situational, deictic reference therefore often provides one of the guises in such examples. As also discussed in Sect. 3.3, the idea then is that children might assume that such deictic reference is always available, even in contexts where this is not the case. This would allow the creation of two different guises, deixis for the pronoun and the NP-description for the possible antecedent, and thus allow coreference just as in the identity debate about Zelda. Whereas Romance strong pronouns allow deictic reference, Romance clitics do not – unless we consider the contexts discussed in Sect. 5.1. As a consequence, clitics cannot enter into accidental coreference relations, a statement which should again be taken with the proviso that examples like (31) are acceptable for many, but not all speakers.

This proposal is problematic in that it predicts that any pronominal form that cannot be used deictically will be exempt from coreference. Cross-linguistically, this means that Dutch and German children should perform better on weak pronouns in their reduced forms than on strong pronouns. Turned around, it also means that children from a clitic language should perform worse on structurally similar sentences with strong pronouns.

Cardinaletti and Starke (1995) suggested another view on the problem in proposing the deficiency hierarchy: clitic < weak pronoun < strong pronoun. That deficient pronouns do not allow coreference is derived through the assumption that they lack a referential restriction. Romance children, they argue, are confronted with two clearly different forms, clitics and strong pronouns occupying different positions and having different properties. Since children never misplace clitics in production, they clearly know that clitics are heads, and hence are deficient in lacking the outer DP shells. English pronouns, however, are ambiguous in form between weak and strong uses. Cardinaletti and Starke (1995, 2000) also introduce an Avoid Structure Principle requiring that the deficient form be chosen whenever this is possible. This means that strong pronouns are licensed only through focus or some other licensing context. Transferred to English this implies that in a sentence like (34a) in the absence of stress, the adult will interpret the pronoun as weak and so not allow coreference. The child, however, will have difficulties resolving the ambiguity and will sometimes allow coreference. The clear prediction is that children should do better in sentences with *it*, which Cardinaletti and Starke (1995) identify as the only English weak pronoun. So (34b) should show better pronoun resolution than (34a).

(34)   a. John sees him
       b. The snake saw it.

The predicted asymmetries of weak and strong pronouns have been systematically investigated only in very few studies and the results are rather contradictory. A pilot experiment conducted by Cardinaletti and Starke (1995) confirmed their prediction. However, Baauw and Cuetos (2003: 229) report on an experiment showing that the performance of Dutch children is the same on weak and strong pronouns, namely around chance. Equal performance was also found in a pilot experiment for German by Hamann and Ruigendijk (2009), with the interesting twist, that pronouns in complement position (ambiguous) and in the so called Wackernagel position next to the complementizer or V2-verb (unambiguously weak) were both fully mastered, see Sect. 5.5. Baauw et al. (1997) report that Italian children allow coreference with strong pronouns. However, Varlakosta (2000) and Varlakosto and Dullaart (2001) show that Greek children allow coreference neither with clitics nor with strong pronouns in contexts where adults do not allow it.

More recently, another explanation of the clitic/non-clitic asymmetry has been suggested by Verbuk and Roeper (2010). As in Cardinaletti and Starke (1995), the crucial factor is seen in ambiguities. Cardinaletti and Starke assumed that a lexical ambiguity keeps the child from identifying the contexts where strong pronouns are excluded leading a child from a Germanic language to overdo coreference. Verbuk and Roeper (2010) point out that English children faced with sentences like (7), (9) and (10) need some time and more evidence to decide on the referential properties of pronouns and the special status of adjuncts.

I repeat (7) here for convenience. In clitic languages only strong pronouns can be used in such contexts.[15] Therefore no lexical ambiguity interferes and children from a clitic language are much faster in determining the referential properties of pronominal elements. See Reuland (2001) for similar arguments.

(7)   James Bond noticed the gun near him/himself.

---

[15] (i) Jean a mis le ballon derrière lui (*le)/ J'ai mis le ballon derrière moi (*me)
     John placed the ball behind HIM (*m)/ I put the ball behind ME (*me - clitic)
  (ii) Il y'avait sept linguistes dans la salle sans (*me) compter moi-meme
     there were seven linguists in the class without counting (*me-clitic) myself.

5.4 Clitics and the PIP in ECM-Constructions

Neither the structural account of McKee (1992) nor the different versions of the deficiency account discussed so far can offer an explanation for another result which was established for French by Hamann et al. (1997) and for Spanish by Baauw et al. (1997) (fully documented in Baauw 2000, 2002). This is the observation that French and Spanish children show a PIP in ECM or clitic-climbing constructions.

Using the same materials and experimental paradigm as Philip and Coopmans (1996) Hamann et al. (1997) ran the classical binding tasks as given in (35) and (36) in French. They extended the experiment to cases resembling ECM and involving clitic climbing, given in (37).[16] They found that in ECM cases with pronouns performance is only about 60% adult like.

(35) a. La fille la seche   nearly adult
the girl is drying her off
b. La fille se seche   fully adult
the girl is drying herself off
(36) Chaque fille la seche   fully adult
every/each girl is drying her off
(37) a. La fille la voit danser   60% adult like
the girl sees her dance
b. La fille se voit danser   nearly adult
the girl sees herself dance

Practically the same percentages were found for Spanish (Baauw et al. 1997; Baauw 2000, 2002). Baauw and Cuetos (2003) find a special problem with the ECM construction also for Spanish agrammatics, who rejected coreference in 79% of the simple sentences with clitic pronouns, but only in 21% of the ECM/clitic-climbing cases.

Following Philip and Coopman's explanation for this effect in Dutch, Baauw and colleagues assume that only Reinhart and Reuland's (1993) Chain Condition is operative in contexts such as (37) so that chance performance in this context can be explained by the assumption that children sometimes classify complement clitics as [−R].[17] Since referentiality depends on the presence of the φ-features and case, several of these features have been discussed as the source of deficiency.

Cardinaletti and Starke (1995) suggested that clitic and weak pronouns are unspecified for the feature [human], which they have to pick up from the antecedent to become referential. Baauw et al. (1997) follow this reasoning in speculating that it is the [human] feature that remains unspecified and so leads children to sometimes

---
[16] Such sentences show "clitic climbing" (reminiscent of Postal's (1974) raise subject-to-object) because the object clitic from the lower clause climbs to the higher clause.

[17] Note that technical difficulties might arise since it must be explained how these [−R] elements can end up in high functional positions in the clause, establishing a chain with *pro* or trace in complement position.

analyze clitics as [−R]. Baauw and Cuetos (2003), following suggestions by Reuland (2001), argue that the number feature may be underspecified.

There is one basic problem with these accounts addressed in Hamann (2002) and in Baauw and Cuetos (2003). Hamann (2002) pointed out that it is surprising that this kind of underspecification only occurs in clitic climbing cases but not in simple sentences. Note that this problem does not concern the Dutch case where difficulties that might be due to such an underspecification are evident also in the simple case. It is acute only in clitic languages where practically no errors are found in the simple case. Hamann (2002) suggested that children get ample evidence that clitics move and never are tails of argumental chains so that underspecification of referentiality should be excluded. Baauw and Cuetos (2003) assume that children mostly assign the correct [+R] specification, in which case accidental coreference is excluded for clitics and the Chain Condition is applied faultlessly.

What remains to be shown is which factors make children erase a feature in clitic-climbing contexts but only rarely or not at all in simple cases. The fact that agrammatics also show these problems and that Italian SLI children have production problems in clitic climbing cases points to a processing account involving the syntactic complexity of the ECM construction.[18] Aiming for a unified account, Hamann (2002) suggested a pragmatic account of the ECM/clitic climbing cases. As discussed in Sect. 5.1, she assumes that coreference for clitics is not strictly excluded, but hard to get: strongly constructed contexts allow deictic use and the exceptional coreference context (31) may also allow the use of a clitic. Deictic reference for clitics in normal contexts is excluded because in such contexts their relationship to a salient discourse topic amounts to discourse binding. Creating coreference with the help of a deictic guise is therefore practically impossible. This explains the good performance of children in simple contexts.[19]

For ECM/clitic climbing cases, however, Hamann (2002) points out that two guises are made available and prominent by the construction. In (37) there is the guise defined by the discourse (*there is a girl and a mom*), which is "mom", and there is the guise offered by the embedded clause, "the dancer" which in turn is different from the guise "the girl". Similar to Avrutin (1994), Hamann (2002) then argues that these different guises allow accidental coreference for the child whereas it is excluded by Rule I for the adult.[20]

---

[18]Baauw and Cuetos (2003) demonstrate that children do not have difficulties with other types of embeddings with non-overt subjects such as control constructions. ECM constructions, however, are arguably more complex than these as their old name "Raise-Subject-to-Object" (Postal 1974) suggests.

[19]Note that the assumption that coreference is not categorically excluded for clitics could also explain the results found by Zesiger et al. (2010): French children show better performance on reflexives than on clitic pronouns. The difference is not remarkable but significant and could represent the few cases where French children allow coreference.

[20]This account leads Hamann (2002) to predict that German children should do better on unambiguously weak pronouns in the Wackernagel position than on pronouns in complement position. The data of Hamann and Ruigendijk 2009 do not confirm the prediction, see Sect. 5.5.

5.5 The Case of German

Interestingly enough, German may be a test case for some of these predictions, but had not been investigated up to very recently. Given that German pronouns are ambiguous as to a strong and weak paradigm and do not exhibit properties of Romance-type clitics, the null hypothesis is that German children should not behave much differently from Dutch or English children. This is indeed the explicit prediction found in Hamann (2002) and Hendriks et al. (2007). So Ruigendijk (2008) started from the hypothesis that German children should show non-adult interpretations in simple sentences with pronouns, aggravated in ECM constructions. Using a Picture Choice Task, Ruigendijk found that German children between 4 and 6 years of age are 94% correct on simple sentences with reflexives and 95.1% correct with pronouns, mirroring the perfect performance of French or Spanish children. Like Romance children, German children are also 95.5% adult like in ECM cases with reflexives, but only 77.3% adult like in ECM cases with pronouns.

Ruigendijk (2008) explores this very surprising result by pursuing two questions: (a) is there a property of German pronouns which could establish a parallel to clitic languages and (b) is there a property of German which distinguishes it from Dutch and English. Taking up the discussion in Hamann (2002), Ruigendijk speculates that a property reminiscent of clitics is that German weak pronouns can occur in the so called Wackernagel position which is a position high in the left periphery of the clause; see (38a,b) for the high position and (39a,b) for the low position. As to a difference between Dutch and English, following Reuland (2001), she points to the differences in (40a,b,c), which also establish another parallel to clitic languages: in German no ambiguities as to referentiality of pronouns can arise.

(38) a. …, dass ihn/'n der Junge gesehen hat
      that him/'m the boy seen has
      that the boy saw him
   b. Sieht ihn/'n der Junge?
      Sees him/'m the boy?
      Does he boy see him?
(39) a. …, dass der Junge ihn/?'n gesehen hat
      that the boy him/?'m seen has
      that the boy saw him
   b. Sieht der Junge ihn/?'n ?
      Sees the boy him/?'m
      Does the boy see him
(40) a. Der Mann$_i$ legt das Buch neben sich$_i$/*ihn$_i$
   b. Der man$_i$ legt het boek naast zich$_i$/hem$_i$ neer
   c. The man$_i$ puts the book next to himself$_i$/him$_j$.

Table 2 Cross-linguistic results on pronoun interpretation in principle B environments, Chain Condition contexts, and comparing strong and weak positions or forms (percentage of adult responses of children between 4 and 6 years of age)

Language	Experiment	Lexical antecedent (%)	Quantified antecedent (%)	Chain condition	Strong/weak
Dutch	Sigurjónsdóttir and Coopmans (1996)	17	–	–	–
	Philip and Coopmans (1996)	33	53	ECM: 10%	
	Baauw and Cuetos (2003)	–	–	–	50% vs. 50%
English	Chien and Wexler (1990)	50	80	–	
	McKee (1992)	50	–	–	
	Conroy et al. (2009)	89	86	–	
Russian	Avrutin and Wexler (1992)	48	83	–	48% vs. 66% (not signif.)
Norwegian	Hestvik and Philip (1999/2000)	90	99	Anti-subject Contexts 39%	–
German	Hamann and Ruigendijk (2009)	94	–	ECM Low 60% High 30%	95% vs. 95% Both:low
Italian	McKee (1992)	90	–	–	–
French	Jakubowicz (1989)	80	80	–	–
	Hamann et al. (1997)	90	80	ECM: 51%	–
Spanish	Baauw et al. (1997)	90	90	ECM: 64% Mean age: 5:6	–
Greek	Varlakosta (2000)	95	–	–	87% vs. 95%

An experiment conducted with a Picture Verification task by Hamann and Ruigendijk (2009) systematically contrasted simple and ECM sentences with the pronoun in complement position with sentences where the pronoun is in the Wackernagel position. This experiment corroborated that German children show early mastery of pronouns (98%) and reflexives (98%) in simple sentences and performed significantly worse in ECM constructions. However, there was no effect of the position of the pronoun since 4–5-year-old children performed at chance in both positions. The youngest children showed a significant effect, unexpectedly performing worse on the ECM sentences with the pronoun in the high position. The latter result demonstrates that the high position of pronouns available in German does not aid children.

In order to keep track of some of the findings discussed here, Table 2 gives an overview over experiments conducted in different languages examining crucial constructions.

6 Recent Developments

6.1 Do Children Really Know Principle B?

Grimshaw and Rosen (1990) very early pointed out that the generally low performance on simple pronoun sentences could be due to the experimental set up. They observed that the poverty or absence of a discourse context in the Picture Verification task could lead children to override the syntactic requirements or ignore the prosodic information in order to be able to anchor the pronoun to an antecedent at all. They also pointed out that such a coreferential reading is always possible if the pronoun is stressed, i.e. strong, and hence contrastive or deictic, so that overriding syntax by pragmatics is motivated by sentences well in the child's experience. In the same vein Elbourne (2005) sets out to demonstrate that in effect the asymmetry found in quantified and simple contexts is an artifact of the experimental method. This criticism concerns Chien and Wexler's (1990) Experiment 4 but also experiments using the story variant of the TVJT so the argument is not only that there is practically no context but also that there is the wrong kind of context.

Elbourne (2005) shows that in most cases the experimental set up did not give highest salience to a possible antecedent in the discourse, or even provided more salience for the local antecedent in the simple condition whereas no such salience was given to the local antecedent in the quantified condition. He concludes that children assign reference to pronouns following Salience or Relevance. Conroy et al. (2009) going through the same experiments in a very similar manner, additionally point out that in the crucial non-match conditions often the Condition of Plausible Denial is not fulfilled (see Crain and Thornton 1998). Elbourne (2005) also analyzes the Picture Verification variants, especially the pictures for the quantifier-pronoun conditions in Chien and Wexler's (1990) Experiment 4. He points out that the non-match condition for (26d) is an image of three little bears and Goldilocks where the three bears are much smaller than Goldilocks and are hard to identify as little female bears.[21] If they are not immediately identifiable as female, then it would be easy to say "No" for the child in this situation – for the wrong reason.

Note that this criticism does not immediately carry over to the Picture Verification task used by Philip and Coopmans (1996) and also Hamann and Ruigendijk (2009). All the participants are easily recognizable as female (mothers, grandmothers, girls etc.) and the only difference in size is conventionalized so that one can distinguish the adults from the children. Still, Conroy et al. (2009) dismiss all Picture Verification tasks on the grounds that "we know relatively little about how the specifics of a static picture create a context that can guide a child's interpretation of a pronoun" (ms, p. 27). This claim is forgetting that the pictures are presented together with verbal lead-ins often in a game situation introducing the participants, the action and normally mentioning the antecedent of the pronoun last suggesting the last mentioned DP as the antecedent.

The discouraging conclusion Elbourne (2005) reaches in his discussion is that there probably is no quantified/simple antecedent asymmetry: Some of the earlier studies did not find this asymmetry (see Sect. 3.2) and it might have been an experimental artifact in the other ones. This leads to the far-reaching conclusion that there is no evidence for the mastery of Principle B. Taken together with the evidence from older stages of English and modern Frisian (see Sect. 2.4) this leads Elbourne (2005) to speak of a parameter for pronouns.

6.2 Do Children Have a Problem with Pronouns at All?

Several recent studies have taken up the challenge posed by Elbourne's (2005) conclusion and his criticism of experimental methods. As to the first point, it is here that the observed asymmetry in production and comprehension becomes relevant as several studies have pointed out. If children are good at pronoun production, then they clearly master Principle B.

This was first pointed out by Bloom et al. (1994), who studied the spontaneous production of English children and compared it to known results on comprehension. The problem with this study is, however, that it is based mostly on the occurrence of the speaker oriented pronouns *I, me, my*, for which identification of the referent through a salient discourse antecedent is irrelevant. De Villiers et al. (2006) provide an experimental comparison using third person pronouns and find that production of pronouns is significantly better than comprehension even when the antecedent is made relevant in the context. Similar results were obtained for Dutch by Hendricks et al. (2006).

To complicate matters, cross-linguistic research does not unanimously show better production of pronouns. In French the asymmetry rather goes in the opposite

---

[21] Many seminar discussions on this point have shown that even adults have difficulties identifying the little bows the girl bears wear.

direction. Comprehension precedes production as numerous studies on the production and comprehension of complement clitics have shown, see e.g. Jakubowicz (1989) and Zesiger et al. (2010). Note that the production problem here is not so much the use of a reflexive but the omission of the complement clitic or the use of a lexical DP, which is usually attributed to the complexity of the clitic-construction. In a study of Hebrew (which has the PIP) and German (which does not), Ruigendijk and Friedman (2009) concentrate on reflexive contexts to establish whether children will use pronouns in such contexts. These, they argue, provide the real test for non-mastery of Principle B and the production/comprehension asymmetry. They find no asymmetry, neither in German nor in Hebrew.

Most of the work done on this asymmetry shows that controlling context conditions seems to make the gap between production and comprehension smaller (see de Villiers et al. 2006 or Spenader et al. 2009), which brings us back to Elbourne's second contribution to the discussion of the PIP, his criticism of the early experimental conditions. In experiments by de Villiers et al. (2006) and Spenader et al. (2009) the context setting lead-ins are manipulated in controlled ways targeting factors like relevance and topic-hood. De Villiers et al. (2006) contrasted the paradigm in (41) with the paradigm used by Jakubowicz (1984) and Chien and Wexler (1990) given in (42).

(41) Here is a mom and a girl. The mom dries her.
(42) Mama Bear says that Baby Bear washes her.

In (42) the antecedent is highly relevant and de Villiers et al. (2006) obtain better results in comprehension and production in the conditions using paradigm (42) than in those using the paradigm exemplified in (41). They also suggest that clearly identifying the topic through mentioning only one antecedent not two should likewise help children in interpreting pronouns. Such an experiment has now been conducted by Spenader et al. (2009) confirming the prediction. It can be concluded that given the right kind of context children can interpret pronouns quite well, even though a difference in production remains. It is also evident that systematic experimental research is needed to pin down the exact context conditions which help English and Dutch children.

Conroy et al. (2009) is a contribution to this kind of systematic research. When all the context setting factors are properly controlled, they argue, English children show early mastery of simple sentences and prefer what they call a "deictic" interpretation defined as "the interpretations in which a pronoun lacks an intrasentential antecedent" (p. 7). In Conroy et al.'s (2009) experiments no asymmetry with quantified and simple sentences can be observed when both readings are made equally salient and there is a proper Condition of Plausible Denial. When they deliberately violate these conditions in their third experiment, they promptly obtain the asymmetry. Interestingly however, de Villiers et al. (2006) also tested pronoun conditions with quantified antecedents and found that they were better mastered than conditions with simple antecedents across paradigms. This shows that Conroy et al.'s findings as well as Elbourne's claims might have to be reevaluated given more systematic research on the context conditions that facilitate interpretation for children.

If we follow Conroy et al.'s reasoning for the moment, controlling the context in specific ways makes the quantifier asymmetry disappear because children do well in the name condition. However, this also makes the PIP disappear. This in itself is an important result, especially as Elbourne (2005) and Conroy et al. (2009) speculate that the asymmetry and the PIP are only expected under those theories of binding which differentiate coreference and variable binding (Reinhart 2004, 2006; Heim 1993). They also point out that the asymmetry is unexpected in accounts deriving Principle C as a special case of Principle B as Reinhart and Heim do, given that children do well on the interpretation of lexical DPs.

However, there are several things left unexplained in Conroy et al.'s article: Why don't adults need the same kind of elaborate context in order to exclude local antecedents in simple sentences with pronouns? Why do the same kind of experiments also find an asymmetry concerning the interpretation of reflexives and pronouns? Why do these experiments show a development in the interpretation of reflexives and pronouns (Chien and Wexler 1990; Jakubowicz 1989; Philip and Coopmans 1996)? Why is there a construction, the ECM construction, which is even more difficult for children than simple sentences with pronouns? Why can the same experimental material using a paradigm very much like (41) produce different results in different languages showing early mastery in Romance languages and in German, but not in Dutch and English (see Sects. 3.2 and 5.4)?

Conroy et al. (2009) answer the last question (with respect to clitic languages only) by following Baauw and Cuetos (2003) in pointing out that Romance clitics do not allow accidental coreference. So – despite their earlier speculation to the contrary – this notion must play a role in the interpretation of pronouns. Since the theoretical considerations we have outlined in Sect. 2.3. overwhelmingly indicate the need for a division of labor of syntactic and pragmatic constraints, it seems to have been a very fruitful scientific accident that the PIP emerged in certain experiments alongside with an asymmetry concerning reflexives and quantified antecedents and it may, after all, not have been an accident, as de Villiers et al.'s (2006) results seem to indicate.

Though the older experiments might not have optimally tapped into children's grammatical knowledge, they did highlight an area of difficulty for children and raised the question of what is special about the discourse requirements for pronouns in some languages, but not in others. The new results reopen the discussion, however, and make innovative approaches possible.

6.3 How to Set a "Pronoun Parameter"

Verbuk and Roeper (2010) pursue the idea that lexical, syntactic and pragmatic knowledge interact during development. They follow Elbourne (2005) in his assumption that Principle B could be parameterized and must be acquired. The English child's task is to establish that pronouns are in syntactic opposition to reflexives even though there is conflicting evidence.

Given the subset principle, the assumption is that children start with fine grained lexical distinctions of pronouns and reflexives including features such as Point of View, physical, intentional, etc. At this stage parameters do not apply and pronouns are ambiguous between pronouns and reflexives, which Verbuk and Roeper (2010) call the Middle English or Frisian stage. So children will be guided by pragmatic relevance (as shown by Elbourne) and disjoint reference and coreference readings appear at chance level in both, simple principle B contexts and exceptional coreference contexts (see (11) and (12)).

In the second stage children construct the scale<reflexive, pronoun>, which enables them to instantiate principle B. In order to arrive at this scale, children have to generalize from all the possible features distinguishing pronouns and reflexives and come to realize that pronouns and reflexives, though identical in their features in most respects, crucially differ with respect to referential dependence: "reflexives differ from pronouns in terms of being necessarily referentially dependent", p. 58. Once a rule has been established that reflexives are used instead of coreferential objects, a contrast can be established for pronouns through exposure to specific contexts. Crucially, the restriction on reflexive objects is established by reference to the syntactic category of VP. Hence, adjuncts do not fall under this restriction.

Having ordered the elements in a scale of referential dependency, children will compute disjoint reference in simple Principle B sentences but not yet in exceptional coreference contexts. In order to differentiate between these contexts, the child needs to compute an open proposition. As was discussed in Sect. 2.3, a Q-implicature can be computed as soon as a scale of referential dependency is established (provided the child has the processing capacity to compare two meanings, see also Sect. 3.3). For exceptional coreference this implicature has to be cancelled. Cancellation is forced by the open proposition implicit in the context (for (11a) this open proposition is *x hates Oscar*). Since exceptional coreference contexts are rare in the input and the child is confused by ambiguous contexts such as (7), (9) and (10), the prediction is that adult performance will be delayed. The child will assign disjoint reference in accordance with principle B and a Q-implicature such as Rule I. In order to perform adult-like, the child has to realize that an open proposition has to be extracted from the context so that informativeness implicatures can overrule the quantity implicature.

Since Verbuk and Roeper (2010) assume that Principle B is learned, they have to offer an explanation for the production/comprehension asymmetry, which is usually taken to show early mastery of the grammatical principle. They assume that once the scale is established, production will be unproblematic. However, an earlier child grammar, the Frisian grammar, will be activated in comprehension in order to accommodate the task sentence as a true utterance by the speaker.

Though the account does not specifically refer to the PIP with respect to reflexives, it outlines a story where reflexives have to be firmly established before pronouns are categorized in comparison. This can predict the observed delay of pronoun interpretation with respect to reflexives. As was outlined in Sect. 5.3, the account also predicts an asymmetry in comparison to Romance languages and given the discussion in Sect. 5.5, the same asymmetry for German. However, like most of the other accounts based on the pragmatics of pronouns, it might run into difficulties with respect to ECM sentences – unless some kind of chain condition can be integrated (see also Sect. 4.2).

7 Conclusion

In this article I have given an overview of more than two decades of research focusing on relevant and controversial results on the acquisition of pronominal reference. I have tried to highlight the interaction of theoretical advances and empirical results, especially with respect to the notion of coreference and the notion of reflexivity. Summing up the facts and phenomena is not as easy now, however, as it might have been 5 or 8 years ago.

So let me start with what was accepted knowledge at the turn of the millennium. The important observations then were that children acquiring English or other Germanic (and Slavic) languages did well in sentences with reflexives and even in pronoun sentences with quantified potential antecedents, but at the same time had difficulties with pronouns in simple sentences. In contrast, children from Romance languages did show no such pronoun problem. These observations indicated the importance of cross-linguistic investigation, since language specific constructions can often serve as test cases for the division of labor of syntax and pragmatics (see Avrutin and Wexler 1992; Sigurjonsdottir and Coopman 1994; Hestvik and Philip 1997). So any explanation advanced for the PIP needed to account for the better performance on reflexives, on pronouns with quantified antecedents, and on clitics. Explanations usually pointed to the possibility of coreference in certain configurations but not in others and suggested that the pragmatic conditions for excluding coreference are not yet acquired. Other accounts claimed that computing the pragmatics overtaxed the processing capacities.

Further studies added other observations needing an explanation. One is the fact that agrammatics show a PIP in those languages or constructions where children show a PIP. Another observation is that a PIP often surfaces in ECM constructions even when there is no such difficulty in simple sentences with pronouns. And yet another one is the asymmetry in production and comprehension in certain languages.

Trying to account for all of these phenomena is not trivial. Studies integrating results on agrammatism usually suggest a processing explanation of the PIP roughly along the lines of Grodzinsky and Reinhart (1993): processing breaks down because a coreference condition has to be computed. Including the ECM-constructions needed additional assumptions in most accounts, namely that pronouns can be underspecified as to the referentiality feature, an assumption that needs to be motivated if the underspecification manifests itself only in ECM-constructions.

This state of affairs was called into question by Elbourne (2005), who examined the experimental methods of previous experiments. Elbourne (2005) concluded that there is indeed a big problem with pronouns that does not go away with quantified antecedents. In contrast, de Villiers et al. (2006) showed that – given the right kind of discourse context – English children get better and Conroy et al. (2009) claimed that they master simple pronoun sentences from early on. Though problems remain with these accounts (see Sects. 6.2 and 6.3), they might have helped to identify the sort of discourse conditions that enable children to compute the intended reading. An example of such discourse conditions is the "question under discussion" or open proposition which – when properly introduced – facilitates the computation of implicatures (Gualmini and Meroni 2009). Another crucial factor for pronouns is the presence of a relevant antecedent (de Villiers et al. 2006) or the introduction and control of an unambiguous discourse topic as shown by Spenader et al. (2009). From this perspective, these recent studies seem to indicate that the original pragmatic explanation of the PIP was on the right track, and more studies on the ways in which discourse can help with pronoun resolution are necessary in order to advance our understanding of the syntax-discourse interface.

Another merit of the recent studies is to take very seriously the cross-linguistic variation found in the properties and types of anaphora in different languages. This reopens the developmental perspective by indicating that the referential properties of language specific reflexive and pronominal elements must be acquired. However, if this kind of feature acquisition, which is made difficult in some cases by ambiguous input, is the reason for the PIP in children, then it is at first sight difficult to explain why agrammatics show the same problems.

Let me conclude with some speculation as to a possible solution to this dilemma inspired by Grillo's (2008) account of agrammatism. Grillo assumes that due to the time course of processing, features that occur later in the derivation are most vulnerable. This mostly concerns features of the Left Periphery, the syntactic side of the syntax-discourse interface, and thus does not seem to apply to referentiality, which is traditionally defined via the φ-features and case. So one possibility would be to investigate not referentiality but topic-hood, which plays a role in some accounts. However, a referentiality feature might well be involved as some accounts of quantification postulate a referentiality feature and a Referential Phrase as a functional projection high in the clause, see Beghelli and Stowell (1997) and the discussion in Sect. 2.5. If this kind of referentiality feature is involved in pronoun resolution and is indeed a feature of the Left Periphery it might be vulnerable in agrammatism, especially in constructions involving a high processing load as in ECM-constructions. For children, this feature is hard to assign to specific elements if there is ambiguous evidence as in English, and it is vulnerable in complex constructions. Given all the currents and countercurrents in older and recent research and the surprising new results for English and other languages, many questions remain unanswered or have been reopened inviting theoretical discussion as well as further empirical research with as wide a variety of methods as possible. In my opinion, the most promising avenues of research are the further investigation of discourse conditions and the examination of referentiality and topic-hood in connection with the clitic/weak/strong distinctions for pronouns.

References

Avrutin, S. 1994. Psycholinguistic investigations in the theory of reference. Doctorial diss., Massachusetts Institute of Technology, Cambridge, MA.
Avrutin, S. 1999. *Development of the syntax-discourse interface*. Dordrecht: Kluwer.
Avrutin, S. 2004. Optionality in child and aphasic speech. *Lingue e Linguaggio* 1: 67–93.
Avrutin, S., and K. Wexler. 1992. Development of Principle B in Russian: Coindexation at LF and coreference. *Language Acquisition* 2: 259–306.
Avrutin, S., and R. Thornton. 1994. Distributivity and binding in child grammar. *Linguistic Inquiry*, 25 (1): 167–171.
Baauw, S. 2000. Grammatical features and the acquisition of reference. A comparative study of Dutch and Spanish. Doctoral diss., Utrecht University, Utrecht, the Netherlands.
Baauw, S. 2002. Grammatical features and the acquisition of reference. A comparative study of Dutch and Spanish' GLOT International 6, 2/3: 65–71.
Baauw, S., and F. Cuetos. 2003. The interpretation of pronouns in Spanish language acquisition and breakdown: Evidence for the "Principle B Delay" as a Non-Unitary Phenomenon. *Language Acquisition* 11: 219–275.
Baauw, S., L. Escobar, and W. Philip. 1997. A delay of Principle B-Effect in Spanish speaking children: The role of lexical feature acquisition. In *GALA 1997*, ed. A. Sorace, C. Heycock, and R. Shillock, 16–21. Edinburgh: HCRC.
Beghelli, F., and T. Stowell. 1997. Distributivity and negation: the syntax of *each* and *every*. In *Ways of scope taking*, ed. A. Szabolsci, 71–109. Dordrecht: Kluwer.
Belletti, A. 1999. Italian/Romance Clitics: Structure and derivation. In *Clitics in the languages of Europe*, ed. H. van Riemsdijk, 543–579. Berlin: Mouton – de Gruyter.
Bloom, P., A. Barss, J. Nicol, and L. Conway, L. 1994. Children's knowledge of binding and coreference: Evidence from spontaneous speech. *Language* 70: 53–71.
Borer, H. 1984. *Parametric syntax*. Dordrecht: Foris.
Boster, C. T. 1991. Children's failure to obey Principle B: Syntactic problem or lexical error? Ms., University of Connecticut, Storrs.
Burzio, L. 1986. *Italian syntax*. Dordrecht: Reidel.
Burzio, L. 1998. Anaphora and soft constraints. In *Is the best good enough. Optimality and competition in syntax*, ed. P. Barbosa, D. Fox, P. Hagstrom, M. McGinnis, and D. Pesetsky, 93–113. Cambridge, MA: MIT Press.
Cardinaletti, A., and M. Starke. 1995. The tripartition of pronouns and its acquisition: Principle B puzzles are ambiguity problems. In *NELS 25*, ed. J. Beckman, 1–12. Philadelphia: University of Pennysylvania.
Cardinaletti, A., and M. Starke. 2000. An overview of the grammar of clitics. In *The acquisition of scrambling and cliticization*, ed. S. Powers and C. Hamann, 165–186. Dordrecht: Kluwer.
Chien, Y.-C., and K. Wexler. 1990. Children's knowledge of locality conditions in binding as evidence for the modularity of syntax and pragmatics. *Language Acquisition* 1: 225–295.
Chierchia, G., S. Crain, M.T. Guasti, A. Gualmini, and L. Meroni. 2001. The acquisition of disjunction: evidence for a grammatical view of scalar implicature. In *Proceedings of BUCLD 25*, ed. A. Do, L. Dominguez, and A. Johansen, 157–168. Somerville: Cascadilla Press.
Chomsky, N. 1981. *Lectures on government and binding*. Dordrecht: Foris.
Chomsky, N. 1995. *The minimalist program*. Cambridge, MA: MIT Press.
Conroy, A., E. Takahashi, J. Lidz, and C. Phillips. 2009. Equal treatment for all antecedents: How children succeed with Principle B. *Linguistic Inquiry* 40: 446–486.
Coopmans, P., and W. Philip. 2000. Notes on the January experiment. Ms., Utrecht University, Utrecht.
Crain, S., and C. McKee. 1985. Acquisition of structural restrictions on anaphora. In *NELS 16*, ed. S. Berman, J.W. Choe, and J. McDonough, 94–110. Amherst: University of Massachusetts, GLSA.

Crain, S., and R. Thornton. 1998. *Investigations in universal grammar: A guide to experiments on the acquisition of syntax and semantics.* Cambridge, MA: MIT Press.

De Villiers, J., J. Cahillane, and E. Altreuter. 2006. What can production reveal about principle B? In *Proceedings of the Inaugural Conference on Generative Approaches to Language Acquisition-North America (GALANA)*, ed. K.U. Deen, J. Nomura, B. Schulz, and B. Schwartz, 89–100. Honolulu: University of Connecticut Occasional Papers in Linguistics 4.

Delfitto, D. 2002. On the semantics of pronominal clitics and some of its consequences. *Catalan Journal of Linguistics* 1: 41–69.

Deutsch, W., C. Koster, and J. Koster. 1986. What can we learn from children's errors in understanding anaphora? *Linguistics* 24: 203–225.

Elbourne, P. 2005. On the acquisition of Principle B. *Linguistic Inquiry* 36: 333–365.

Evans, G. 1980. Pronouns. *Linguistic Inquiry* 11: 337–362.

Faltz, L.M. 1985. *Reflexivization: A study in universal syntax.* New York: Garland.

Fischer, S. 2004. Optimal binding. *Natural Language & Linguistic Theory* 22: 481–526.

Grillo, A. 2008. Generalized minimality. Syntactic underspecification in Broca's aphasia. Doctoral diss., Utrecht, the Netherlands and University of Siena, Sienna, Italy.

Grimshaw, J., and S. Rosen. 1990. Knowledge and obedience: The developmental status of the binding theory. *Linguistic Inquiry* 21: 187–222.

Grodzinsky, Y., and T. Reinhart. 1993. The innateness of binding and coreference. *Linguistic Inquiry* 24: 69–102.

Gualmini, A., and L. Meroni. 2009. Scalar implicatures in child language: Cost and compliance. Presentation at GALA, Lisbon, September 2009.

Gualmini, A., S. Crain, L. Meroni, G. Chierchia, and M.-T. Guasti. 2001. At the semantics/pragmatics interface in child language. In *Proceedings of Semantics and Linguistic Theory XI.* Ithaca: CLC Publications, Department of Linguistics, Cornell University.

Hamann, C. 1997. From syntax to discourse. Children's use of pronominal clitics, null subjects, infinitives and operators. Habilitation thesis, University of Tübingen, Tübingen, Germany.

Hamann, C. 2002. *From syntax to discourse.* Dordrecht: Kluwer.

Hamann, C., and E. Ruigendijk. 2009. The German pronoun puzzle. Presentation given at the 2nd NWLK (North West Linguistics Colloquium), Bremen.

Hamann, C., L. Rizzi, and U. Frauenfelder. 1996. The acquisition of subject and object clitics in French. In *Generative perspectives on language acquisition*, ed. H. Clahsen, 309–334. Amsterdam: Benjamins.

Hamann, C., O. Kowalski, and W. Philip. 1997. The French 'Delay of Principle B' Effect. In *BUCLD 21*, ed. E. Hughes, M. Hughes, and A. Greenhill, 205–219. Somerville: Cascadilla Press.

Heim, I. 1993. Anaphora and semantic interpretation. SfS-Report-07-93. Tübingen: University of Tübingen.

Heim, I. 1998. Anaphora and semantic interpretation. In *The Interpretative Tract*, ed. U. Sauerland and O. Percus, MIT Working Papers in Linguistics, vol. 25, 205–246. Cambridge, MA: MIT, Department of Linguistics and Philosophy, MITWPL.

Heim, I., and A. Kratzer. 1998. *Semantics in generative grammar.* Oxford: Blackwell.

Hendriks, P., and J. Spenader. 2006. When production precedes comprehension: an optimization approach to the acquisition of pronouns. *Language Acquisition* 13: 319–348.

Hendriks, P., Siekman I., Smits E.-J., and J. Spenader. 2007. Pronouns in competition: Predicting acquisition delays cross-linguistically. In *ZAS Papers in Linguistics*, vol. 48 (Intersentential Pronominal Reference in Child and Adult Language. Proceedings of the Conference on Intersentential Pronominal Reference in Child and Adult Language), eds. D. Bittner and N. Gagarina, 75–101.

Hestvik, A., and W. Phillip. 1997. Reflexivity, anti-subject orientation and language acquisition. *Proceedings of NELS* 27: 171–185.

Hestvik, A., and W. Philip. 1999/2000. Binding and coreference in Norwegian child language. *Language Acquisition* 8: 171–235.

Higginbotham, J. 1983. Logical form, binding, and nominals. *Linguistic Inquiry* 14: 395–420.

Jäger, G. 2002. Some notes on the formal properties of bidirectional optimality theory. *Journal of Logic, Language and Information* 11: 427–451.
Jakubowicz, C. 1984. On markedness and binding principles. In *Proceedings of NELS 14*, ed. C. Jones and P. Sells, 154–182. Amherst: University of Massachusetts, GLSA.
Jakubowicz, C. 1989. Linguistic theory and language acquisition facts: Reformulation, maturation or invariance of binding principles. Paper presented at Knowledge and Language, Groningen, May 1989.
Kaufmann, D. 1988. Grammatical and cognitive interactions in the study of children's knowledge of binding theory and reference relations. Doctoral diss., Temple University, Philadelphia.
Kayne, R. 1975. *French syntax*. Cambridge, MA: MIT Press.
Kayne, R. 1991. Romance clitics, verb movement and PRO. *Linguistic Inquiry* 22: 647–686.
Levinson, S. 1987. Pragmatics and the grammar of anaphora. *Journal of Linguistics* 23: 379–434.
Levinson, S. 2000. *Presumptive meanings: The theory of generalized conversational implicature*. Cambridge, MA: MIT Press.
Lombardi, L., and J. Sarma. 1989. Against the bound variable hypothesis of the acquisition of Principle B. Paper presented at the annual meeting of the Linguistic Society of America, Washington, DC.
Manzini, R., and K. Wexler. 1987. Parameters, binding theory, and learnability. *Linguistic Inquiry* 18: 413–444.
Matsuoka, K. 1997. Binding conditions in young children's grammar: Interpretation of pronouns inside conjoined NPs. *Language Acquisition* 6: 37–48.
McDaniel, D., and T. Maxfield. 1992. Principle B and contrastive stress. *Language Acquisition* 2: 337–358.
McDaniel, D., H. Cairns, and J. Hsu. 1990. Binding principles in the grammars of young children. *Language Acquisition* 1: 121–139.
McKee, C. 1992. A comparison of pronouns and anaphors in Italian and English acquisition. *Language Acquisition* 2: 21–54.
Noveck, I.A. 2001. When children are more logical than adults: experimental investigations of scalar implicature. *Cognition* 78: 165–188.
Papafragou, A. 2002. Scalar implicatures in language acquisition: Some evidence from Modern Greek. In *Proceedings from the 38th Annual Meeting of the Chicago Linguistics Society*. Chicago: University of Chicago Press.
Papafragou, A., and J. Musolino. 2003. Scalar implicatures: Experiments at the semantics-pragmatics interface. *Cognition* 86: 253–282.
Philip, W., and P. Coopmans. 1996. The role of lexical feature acquisition in the development of pronominal anaphora. In *Amsterdam series on child language development*, vol. 5, ed. W. Philip and F. Wijnen. Amsterdam: Institute of General Linguistics at the University of Amsterdam.
Pollard, C., and I. Sag. 1992. Anaphors in English and the scope of the binding theory. *Linguistic Inquiry* 23: 261–305.
Postal, P. 1974. *On raising*. Cambridge, MA: MIT Press.
Reinhart, T. 1983. *Anaphora and semantic interpretation*. London: Croom Helm.
Reinhart, T. 2004. Processing or pragmatics? Explaining the coreference delay. In *The processing and acquisition of reference*, ed. T. Gibson and N. Perlmutter. Cambridge, MA: MIT Press.
Reinhart, T. 2006. *Interface strategies*. Cambridge, MA: MIT Press.
Reinhart, T., and E. Reuland. 1993. Reflexivity. *Linguistic Inquiry* 24: 675–720.
Reuland, E. 1994. Commentary: The non-homogeneity of Condition B and related issues. In *Syntactic theory and first language acquisition: Cross-linguistic perspectives*, Binding, dependencies and learnability, vol. 2, ed. B. Lust, G. Hermon, and J. Kornfilt, 227–246. Hillsdale: Erlbaum.
Reuland, E. 2001. Primitives of binding. *Linguistic Inquiry* 32: 439–492.
Reuland, E. 2008. Anaphoric dependencies: How are they encoded? Towards a derivation-based typology. Ms., OTS, Utrecht University, Utrecht, the Netherlands.
Reuland, E. 2011. *Anaphora and Language Design*. Cambridge, MA: MIT Press.

Reuland, E., and M. Everaert. 2000. Deconstructing binding. In *Contemporary syntactic theory*, ed. M. Baltin and C. Collins, 634–670. Oxford: Blackwell.
Rizzi, L. 1978. A restructuring rule in Italian syntax. In *Recent transformational studies in European language*, ed. S.J. Keyser, 113–158. Cambridge, MA: MIT Press.
Rizzi, L. 1982. *Issues in Italian syntax*. Dordrecht: Foris.
Rizzi, L. 1986. On the status of subject clitics in romance. In *Studies in romance linguistics*, ed. O. Jaeggli and C. Silva-Corvalan, 391–419. Dordrecht: Foris.
Rizzi, L. 1990. *Relativized minimality*. Cambridge, MA: MIT Press.
Rizzi, L. 2004. Locality and the left periphery. In *Structure and beyond*, ed. A. Belletti, 223–251. New York: Oxford University Press.
Ross, J.R. 1982. Pronoun Deleting Processes in German. Paper presented at the annual meeting of the Linguistic Society of America, San Diego, California.
Ruigendijk, E. 2008. Reference assignment in German Preschool Children. In *Proceedings of GALA 2007*, ed. A. Gavarró and J. Freitas, 370–380. Cambridge: Cambridge Scholars.
Ruigendijk, E., N. Friedmann, R. Novogrodsky, and N. Balaban. 2009. *Symmetry in comprehension and production of pronouns: A comparison of German and Hebrew*. Presented in GALA 2009, Lisbon, Portugal.
Sag, I. 1976. Deletion and logical form. Doctoral diss., University of Maryland, College Park.
Sigurjónsdóttir, S., and P. Coopmans. 1996. The acquisition of anaphoric relations in Dutch. In *Amsterdam Series on Child Language Development, ASCLD 5*. Amsterdam: Instituut Algemene Taalwetenschap 68.
Sigurjónsdóttir, S., and N. Hyams. 1992. Reflexivization and logophoricity: Evidence from the acquisition of Icelandic. *Language Acquisition* 2: 359–413.
Spenader, J., E.-J. Smits, and P. Hendriks. 2009. Coherent discourse solves the pronoun interpretation problem. *Journal of Child Language* 36: 23–52.
Sportiche, D. 1996. Clitic constructions. In *Phrase structure and the Lexicon*, ed. J.J. Rooryck and L. Zaring, 213–276. Dordrecht: Kluwer.
Szabolcsi, A. 2001. The syntax of scope. In *The handbook of contemporary syntactic theory*, ed. M. Baltin and C. Collins, 607–633. Oxford: Blackwell.
Thornton, R. 1990. Adventures in long-distance moving: The acquisition of complex wh-questions. Doctoral diss., University of Connecticut, Storrs.
Thornton, R., and K. Wexler. 1999. *Principle B, VP-ellipsis, and interpretation in child grammar*. Cambridge, MA: MIT Press.
Thráinsson, H. 1976. Reflexives and subjunctives in Icelandic. In *Proceedings of the Sixth Annual Meeting of NELS*, L'Association linguistique de Montreal, Université de Montreal, Montreal, Quebec, 225–239.
Utakis, S. 1995. Quantification and definiteness in child grammar. Doctoral diss., CUNY, New York.
Van der Lely, H., and L. Stollwerck. 1997. Binding theory and specifically language impaired children. *Cognition* 62: 245–290.
Van Gelderen, E. 2000. *A history of English reflexive pronouns: Person, self, and interpretability*. Amsterdam: Benjamins.
Varlakosta, S. 2000. Lack of clitic-pronoun distinctions in the acquisition of Principle B in child Greek. In *Proceedings of the 24th Annual Boston University Conference on Language Development*, ed. S.C. Howell, S. Fish, and T. Keith-Lucas, 738–748. Somerville: Cascadilla Press.
Varlakosto, S., and J. Dullaart. 2001. The acquisition of pronominal reference by Greek-Dutch bilingual children: Evidence for early grammar differentiation and autonomous development in bilingual first language acquisition. In *Proceedings of the 25th Annual Boston University Conference on Language Development*, ed. A.H.-J. Do, L. Dominguez, and A. Johansen, 780–791. Somerville: Cascadilla Press.
Verbuk, A., and T. Roeper. 2010. How pragmatics and syntax make Principle B acquirable. *Language Acquisition* 17: 51–65.

Ward, G. 1983. On Nonreflexive Pronouns in Reflexive Environments. *Penn review of Linguistics 7*, 12–19.
Wexler, K., and Y-C. Chien. 1985. The development of lexical anaphors and pronouns. Papers and Reports on Child Language Development (PRCLD), Stanford University, 138–149.
William, E. 1977. Discourse and logical form. *Linguistic Inquiry* 8: 101–139.
Zesiger, P., L. Chillier-Zesiger, M. Arabatzi, L. Baranzini, S. Cronel-Ohayon, J. Franck, H.-U. Frauenfelder, C. Hamann, and L. Rizzi. 2010. The acquisition of pronouns by French children. A parallel study of production and comprehension. *Applied Psycholinguistics* 31: 571–603.
Zribi-Hertz, A. 1989. Anaphor binding and narrative point of view: English reflexive pronouns in sentence and discourse. *Language* 65: 695–727.

Universal Grammar and the Acquisition of Japanese Syntax

Koji Sugisaki and Yukio Otsu

1 Introduction

Every normal child acquires his or her native language in just a few years. The acquired knowledge of our native language, which is called *grammar* or *I-language* (Chomsky 1986), contains many abstract properties that children could not have learned from a "general-purpose learning mechanism" and the input data they receive after birth. For example, both of the Japanese sentences in (1) are interpreted as *yes/no* questions, even though they differ in whether the embedded clause is introduced by a declarative complementizer *to* or by a question particle *ka*.

(1) a. Taro-wa [Hanako-ga ringo-o katta to] iimashita ka?
Taro-Top Hanako-Nom apple-Acc bought C said Q
'Did Taro say that Hanako bought apples?'
b. Taro-wa [Hanako-ga ringo-o katta ka] iimashita ka?
Taro-Top Hanako-Nom apple-Acc bought Q said Q
'Did Taro say whether Hanako bought apples?'

When exposed to these sentences, Japanese-learning children may plausibly form the generalization that the difference between *to* and *ka* does not have any effect on the type of answers required by these questions. Such a generalization is never part of the grammar that adult native speakers of Japanese have, however: every adult native speaker can tell that the example in (2a) and the one in (2b) are completely different in that the former is a *wh*-question while the latter is a *yes/no* question.

K. Sugisaki (✉)
Mie University, Tsu, Mie, Japan
e-mail: sugisaki@human.mie-u.ac.jp

Y. Otsu
Linguistics, Keio University, Kanagawa-ken, Japan Minato, Tokyo, Japan
e-mail: oyukio@sfc.keio.ac.jp

(2) a. Taro-wa   [Hanako-ga   nani-o   katta   to]   iimashita ka?
       Taro-Top   Hanako-Nom   what-Acc   bought   C   said   Q
       'What did Taro say that Hanako bought?'
   b. Taro-wa   [Hanako-ga   nani-o   katta   ka]   iimashita ka?
       Taro-Top   Hanako-Nom   what-Acc   bought   Q   said   Q
       'Did Taro say what Hanako bought?'

The contrast between (1) and (2) suggests that there is a significant gap between the input data and the acquired knowledge of language, a gap which the "general-purpose learning mechanism" would not be able to bridge. A question then arises as to why children are able to acquire the core portion of their linguistic knowledge despite the fact that relevant experience available to them is severely limited (i.e. under the "poverty of the stimulus" situation). This question is referred to as "Plato's problem" (e.g. Chomsky 1986) or as "the logical problem of language acquisition" (e.g. Baker and McCarthy 1981; Hornstein and Lightfoot 1981).

A modern linguistic theory known as *generative grammar* proposes the nativist solution to Plato's problem: Children are innately endowed, as part of the human genome, with "Universal Grammar" (UG), which establishes the boundary conditions on what counts as a possible human language. Under this view, knowledge of our native language is acquired through the interaction between biologically predetermined UG and the linguistic experience children take in. If this acquisitional scenario is on the right track, we can expect that the core portion of the grammar is acquired fairly early, since the innate UG constrains the course of acquisition from the beginning of life and hence children do not have to learn much from the experience.

In this chapter, we review several studies on the acquisition of Japanese that directly evaluate the validity of the acquisitional scenario just mentioned. Since Japanese has various syntactic characteristics that are not observed in Germanic or Romance languages, the investigation of its acquisition process can be especially valuable to determine the plausibility of the above scenario. This chapter is quite limited at least in the following two respects, however. First, the discussion focuses only on children's knowledge of syntax. Second, little discussion is dedicated to the acquisition of Japanese from a cross-linguistic perspective. Those readers who are interested in the acquisition of other areas of Japanese are referred to Clancy (1985) and Goro (2007), and those who wish to know about the relationship between child Japanese and language variation are referred to Murasugi and Sugisaki (2008).

2 Basic Word Order and Scrambling in Child Japanese

2.1 Basic Word Order in Child Japanese

It is widely known that in Japanese, word order is flexible. For example, both Subject-Object-Verb (SOV) and English-like SVO are possible for a simple transitive sentence.

(3) a. SOV: Taro-ga   sushi-o   tabeta yo.
           Taro-Nom   sushi-Acc   ate   Excl (amation)
           'Taro ate sushi.'
    b. SVO: Taro-ga   tabeta   yo,   sushi-o.
           Taro-Nom   ate   Excl   sushi-Acc

Yet, such SVO sentences exhibit various syntactic restrictions that do not apply to SOV order (Tanaka 2001). First, SVO order cannot appear in embedded contexts.

(4) a. Hanako-ga   [Taro-ga   sushi-o   tabeta   to]   omotteiru.
        Hanako-Nom   Taro-Nom   sushi-Acc   ate   C   think
        'Hanako thinks that Taro ate sushi.'
    b.* Hanako-ga   [Taro-ga   tabeta,   sushi-o   to] omotteiru.
        Hanako-Nom   Taro-Nom   ate   sushi-Acc C   think

Second, idiom chunks that consist of a verb and an object lose their idiomatic interpretation when the object is located after the verb.

(5) a. Taro-ga   hara-o   tateta   yo.
        Taro-Nom   stomach-Acc   set up   Excl
        'Taro got upset.'
    b.* Taro-ga   tateta   yo,   hara-o.
        Taro-Nom   set up   Excl   stomach-Acc

Third, the SVO order is incompatible with direct-object *wh*-questions.

(6) a. Taro-ga   nani-o   tabeta   (no)[1]?
        Taro-Nom   what-Acc   ate   Q
        'What did Taro eat?'
    b.* Taro-ga   tabeta   (no),   nani-o?
        Taro-Nom   ate   Q   what-Acc

The contrasts exhibited in (4)–(6) show that SVO order in Japanese is far more restricted in its use than SOV. The existence of these restrictions on SVO sentences suggests that this is a marked order, derived in some way from the SOV order, which has more freedom and hence can be considered as the basic order. In other words, the contrasts illustrated in (4)–(6) indicate that Japanese is an SOV language.[2]

Japanese-learning children around the age of 2;5 (years;months) sometimes produce utterances that contain VO order, as illustrated in (7).

---

[1] The Q(uestion)-particle *no* can be omitted when the sentence is pronounced with an appropriate questioning intonation. See Yoshida and Yoshida (1997) and Ko (2005) for detailed discussion of the Q-particle drop phenomenon.

[2] The syntactic derivation of SVO sentences in Japanese is now under heated discussion. See Tanaka (2001), Takita (2009), and the references cited there.

Table 1 Corpora analyzed

Child	Age (years; months.days)	Number of child utterances	Collected by
Aki	2;6.15–3;0.0	12,415	Miyata (2004a)
Ryo	2;4.25–3;0.30	5,901	Miyata (2004b)
Tai	1;9.3–3;1.29	29,980	Miyata (2004c)
Jun	2;3.23–3;0.1	22,444	Ishii (2004)

Table 2 Results of the transcript analysis

	Aki		Ryo		Tai		Jun	
	(S)OV	(S)VO	(S)OV	(S)VO	(S)OV	(S)VO	(S)OV	(S)VO
Total number of utterances	518	38	252	43	1120	50	754	120
Number of direct-object *wh*-questions	185	0	40	0	70	1	140	0
% of direct-object *wh*-questions	38.7	0	15.9	0	6.3	2	18.6	0

(7) a. Yomoo,   koko.
       read   this part
       'Let's read this part.'   (Aki, 2;7: Miyata 2004a)
    b. Akete,   kore.
       open   this
       'Open this.'   (Ryo 2;5: Miyata 2004b)
    c. Morattekita, kore.
       got   this
       '(I) got this.'   (Tai 2;2: Miyata 2004c)
    d. Tabenaino,   nanimo.
       eat-Neg   anything
       '(You) don't eat anything'   (Jun 2;6: Ishii 2004)

In light of these utterances involving English-like VO order, Sugisaki (2008) addressed the question of whether Japanese-learning children in fact know that SOV is the basic order and hence obey one of the key syntactic restrictions illustrated in (6) from the earliest observable stage. Four longitudinal corpora for Japanese from the CHILDES database (MacWhinney 2000) were analyzed, which provided a total sample of more than 70,000 lines of child speech. The corpora analyzed in that study are summarized in Table 1, and the results are shown in Table 2. All four children showed a clear contrast between (S)OV and (S)VO sentences: both VO sentences and direct-object *wh*-questions occurred reasonably often, but there was only a single (apparent) example of an object *wh*-question with VO order. These findings suggest that young Japanese-learning children already know that Japanese is an SOV language, and that VO sentences have the same syntactic basis as they have for adults.

2.2 Scrambling in Child Japanese

In addition to the alternation between SOV and SVO orders illustrated in (3), Japanese also permits the alternation between SOV and OSV orders. Theoretical studies of Japanese provide a number of arguments that OSV order is derived from SOV order via movement of the object NP to the sentence-initial position (see e.g. Saito 1985). This movement operation is called "scrambling", following Ross (1967).

(8) a. SOV: Hanako-ga   ano hon-o   katta.
           Hanako-Nom   that book-Acc   bought
           'Hanako bought that book.'
    b. OSV: Ano hon-o   Hanako-ga   katta.
           that book-Acc Hanako-Nom   bought

One piece of evidence for the movement analysis of OSV sentences is based on the phenomenon of Q(uantifier)-float (Kuroda 1980). As exemplified in (9b), a numeral quantifier in Japanese cannot be related to an NP across another NP argument: The numeral quantifier that modifies the subject cannot be separated from the subject by an intervening object.

(9) a.   Igirisuzin-ga   san-nin   utide-no   kozuti-o   katta.
         Englishman-Nom   3-people   striking-Gen   mallet-Acc bought
         'Three Englishmen bought (the) mallet of luck.'
    b. * Igirisuzin-ga   utide-no   kozuti-o   san-nin   katta.
         Englishman-Nom   striking-Gen mallet-Acc   3-people   bought

In contrast, however, the object NP in the sentence-initial position can be separated from its numeral quantifier by an intervening subject, as illustrated by the grammatical sentence in (10b).

(10) a. Utide-no   kozuti-o   futatu   Igirisuzin-ga   katta.
        striking-Gen   mallet-Acc   2-objects   Englishman-Nom   bought
        'An Englishman bought two mallets of luck.'
     b. Utide-no   kozuti-o   Igirisuzin-ga   futatu   katta.
        striking-Gen   mallet-Acc   Englishman-Nom 2-objects   bought

The contrast between (9b) and (10b) can be accounted for if we assume that the basic word order in Japanese is SOV and that the OSV order is derived from SOV via movement operation: The object NP is adjacent to its quantifier before it undergoes movement to the sentence-initial position.

Experimental studies conducted in the late 1970s (Hayashibe 1975; Sano 1977) investigated whether Japanese-speaking children can successfully interpret scrambled order as in (8b). The task for children was acting-out: Children were asked to act out what the test sentence meant by manipulating toy animals placed in front of them.

The results of these studies demonstrated that there is a group of children, sometimes up to five years old, who have difficulties in interpreting OSV sentences. Those children typically tend to take the first NP as the Agent of the action denoted by the verb, and the second NP as the Theme. These results had generally been considered to indicate that scrambling is acquired fairly late, even as late as children's fifth year.

The experimental study by Otsu (1994a), however, demonstrated that the purported difficulty children have when comprehending scrambled sentences is an experimental artifact. Building on the observation by Masunaga (1983), Otsu pointed out that the scrambled NP must have been established as a discourse topic in order to make the use of scrambled sentences natural. In the previous studies, stimulus sentences were given without any discourse context as illustrated in (11), which made the sentence sound awkward. If we add a context sentence as in (12), the use of scrambled sentence becomes perfectly natural.

(11) Ahirusan-o   kamesan-ga   osimashita.
     duck-Acc   turtle-Nom   pushed
     'A/The duck pushed a/the turtle.'

(12) Kooen-ni   ahirusan-ga   imashita.
     park-in   duck-Nom   was
     Sono ahirusan-o kamesan-ga   osimashita.
     the duck-Acc   turtle-Nom   pushed
     'There was a duck in a park. A turtle pushed the duck.'

In Otsu (1994a), children in the experimental group were presented each test sentence with another sentence designed to establish the first NP of the test sentence as the discourse topic, as exemplified in (12). On the other hand, children in the control group received test sentences without any discourse context, as in the previous studies. As summarized in Table 3, the results obtained from 24 three- and four-year-olds revealed that the children in the experimental group had virtually no difficulty in interpreting scrambled sentences, while many children in the control group exhibited the same error pattern as in the previous experiments. These findings suggest that children's errors observed in the previous studies are nothing more than an experimental artifact, and that the knowledge of scrambling is already in the grammar of Japanese-speaking three-year-olds.

Sano (2007) further demonstrated that children's OSV sentences do in fact involve a movement operation. His experiment examined children's interpretation of SOV and OSV sentences involving a numeral quantifier illustrated in (13).

(13) a. Sono   kuma-ga   buta-o   nihiki   kosutteru   yo.
        the   bear-Nom   pig-Acc   two   brushing   Excl
        '*Two of the bears are brushing a pig. / ^{OK}The bear is brushing two pigs.'
     b. Sono   kuma-o   buta-ga   nihiki   kosutteru   yo.
        the   bear-Acc   pig-Nom   two   brushing   Excl
        'Two of the bears, a pig is brushing.'

Table 3 Results of the experiment by Otsu (1994a)

	Number of correct responses	% of correct responses
Experimental Group	54 / 60	90%
Control Group	33 / 60	55%

As we have seen in (9) and (10), while the numeral quantifier that modifies the subject NP cannot be separated from that NP by an intervening object, the one that modifies the object NP in the sentence-initial position can be separated from its numeral quantifier by an intervening subject, since the object NP and the associated quantifier are adjacent to each other before that NP undergoes movement. By examining children's interpretation of sentences as in (13) with a Truth-Value Judgment Task (Crain and Thornton 1998), Sano (2007) revealed that children have exactly the same knowledge as adults with respect to Q-float in Japanese: while 4- and 5-year-olds rejected the association between the floated quantifier and the subject NP in Subject-Object-Quantifier-Verb sentences as in (13a) more than 90% of the time, they correctly permitted the association between the floated quantifier and the object NP in Object-Subject-Quantifier-Verb sentences as in (13b) more than 80% of the time. These findings suggest that movement is in fact involved in the derivation of OSV sentences even in child Japanese.

To summarize, the studies by Sugisaki (2008), Otsu (1994a), and Sano (2007) reviewed in this section point to the conclusion that Japanese-speaking children have adult-like knowledge of the basic order (SOV) and of the derived orders (SVO and OSV) from the early stages of acquisition.[3] Such a finding is not surprising at all in view of the assumption that language acquisition is guided by innate UG, and hence children need not learn much in order to be able to handle various word orders permitted in the target language.

3 Configurationality of Child Japanese

In the early 1980s, the property of flexible word order in Japanese discussed in the previous section was considered to be a reflex of its nonconfigurationality (e.g. Farmer 1980; Hale 1980, 1983): Unlike configurational languages like English which have the typical hierarchical structure of the subject NP separated from the VP (as in (14a)), nonconfigurational languages like Japanese and Warlpiri lack the VP node, so that they are associated with a flat structure, with all phrases being directly dominated by the S node (as in (14b)). Since all phrases have a symmetrical relation with a verb in nonconfigurational languages, they are free to occur in any order without disturbing the meaning of the sentence.

---

[3] However, the word-order alternation in ditransitive sentences seems to pose some difficulty to Japanese-speaking children. See Sugisaki and Isobe (2001) for relevant discussion.

(14) a. Configurational Languages b. Nonconfigurational Languages

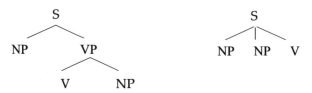

Yet, the seminal study by Saito (1985) provided a number of arguments for the existence of a VP node in Japanese, which gave rise to the movement analysis of Japanese OSV sentences. One of these arguments is based on the subject/object asymmetry in pronominal coreference.

(15) a.* Kare$_i$-ga [Mary-ga John$_i$-ni okutta tegami]-o mada
         he-Nom   Mary-Nom John-to   sent   letter-Acc yet
         yonde   inai (koto)
         read   not fact
         'He has not read the letter Mary sent to John.'
     b. [John$_i$-kara okane-o   moratta   hito]-ga   kare$_i$-o
         John-from   money-Acc   received person-Nom   he-Acc
         suisenshita   (koto)
         recommended   fact
         'The person who received money from him recommended John.'

The example in (15a) does not permit coreferential interpretation due to Condition C of the binding theory (Chomsky 1981: 188): the pronominal subject *kare* c-commands the coindexed r-expression *John* contained in the object NP. If Japanese lacks VP, the object NP should also c-command the subject NP, and hence the sentence in (15b) should also lead to a violation of Condition C, contrary to fact. The grammaticality of (15b) suggests that Japanese has VP and hence is a configurational language like English.

In light of the finding that Japanese is just as configurational as English, an acquisitional question arises as to whether the phrase structure of Japanese-speaking children is hierarchically organized in the same way as the adult phrase structure.

Otsu (1994b) addressed this question by investigating children's knowledge of the Case-Marker Drop (CMD) phenomenon. In colloquial speech, Case markers can sometimes drop. Yet, as the examples in (16) suggest, CMD is not free: It obeys a structural condition given in (17) (Takezawa 1987: 126).

(16) a.   Taro-ga   sono   hon-o   katta.
          Taro-Nom   the   book-Acc   bought
          'Taro bought the book.'
     b.   Taro-ga   sono hon-Ø   katta.
     c.* Taro-Ø   sono hon-o   katta.
     d.* Sono hon-o   Taro- Ø   katta.
     e.* Sono hon-Ø   Taro-ga   katta.

(17) When an NP is adjacent to and c-commanded by V, the Case marker attached to it can drop.

In (16b), the NP *sono hon* is adjacent to and c-commanded by the verb *katta*, and hence its accusative Case marker can drop. In (16c), the subject NP *Taro* is outside VP and thus is not c-commanded by *katta*, which makes CMD impossible. The same account applies to (16d). In (16e), the scrambled object *sono hon* is outside VP and is not c-commanded by *katta*. Hence, CMD cannot take place.

Otsu (1994b) attempted to show that Japanese-speaking three- and four-year-olds obey the structural condition on CMD in (17), thereby showing in turn that children's grammar generates configurational structures with a VP node.

In one of his two experiments, Otsu interviewed 20 children with a sentence-completion task. Each child was shown a picture of someone involved in some action, e.g. a mother eating a watermelon. The experimenter gave the following instruction to the child: "Can you tell me about this picture? First, can you begin with X?" X in the instruction is either the word corresponding to the Agent or the Theme of the action denoted by the verb of the sentence that the child is to produce. No Case marker is added to X, as shown by the example in (18).

(18) Kono   e-nituite   ohanashisite   kureru?
     this   picture-about   tell   can-you
     Mazu,   *okaasan*-de   hazimete   ne?
     first   *okaasan*-with   begin   please
     'Can you tell me about this picture? First, can you begin with *okaasan*?'

If the instruction is as in (18), (19) is the set of possible and impossible answers. When X in the instruction is the Theme, e.g. *suika* 'watermelon,' (20) is the set of possible and impossible answers.

(19) a. Okaasan-ga   suika-o   tabeteiru.
         mother-Nom   watermelon-Acc   eating
         'Mother is eating a watermelon.'
     b. Okaasan-ga   suika-Ø   tabeteiru.
     c. Okaasan-ga   tabeteiru.
     d.* Okaasan-Ø   tabeteiru.
     e.* Okaasan-Ø   suika-o   tabeteiru.
     f.* Okaasan-Ø   suika-Ø   tabeteiru.
(20) a. Suika-o   okaasan-ga   tabeteiru.
         watermelon-Acc mother-Nom   eating
         'Mother is eating a watermelon.'
     b.* Suika-o   okaasan-Ø   tabeteiru.
     c. Suika-o   tabeteiru.
     d. Suika-Ø   tabeteiru.
     e.* Suika-Ø   okaasan-ga   tabeteiru.
     f.* Suika-Ø   okaasan-Ø   tabeteiru.

Table 4 Results of the experiment by Otsu (1994b)

(19)						(20)					
a	b	c	d	e	f	a	b	c	d	e	f
33%	50%	17%	0%	0%	0%	0%	42%	0%	23%	35%	0%	0%

The results are summarized in Table 4: children exhibited no single violation of the constraint in (17). These results, showing that children at least at the age of three obey (17), indicate that children's grammar generates hierarchically-organized phrase structure, which in turn demonstrates that child Japanese is just as configurational as adult Japanese.

Sugisaki (2010) provides a new piece of evidence for the configurationality of child Japanese, based on children's knowledge concerning the distribution of the formal noun *koto*. As illustrated in (21) and (22), *koto* is attached to a human noun without adding any semantic content. The insertion of *koto* can apply either to an accusative NP as in (21b) or to a nominative NP as in (21b). Crucially, however, this *koto*-insertion obeys a structural restriction: *koto* can be associated with a NP in the direct object position, but not with a NP in the subject position, as shown by the ungrammaticality of (21c) and (22c). This distribution of *koto* can be accounted for if we assume that (i) Japanese is configurational and has a VP node, and that (ii) *koto* can be attached only to the NP in the sister of V.

(21) a.   Taro-ga   Hanako-o   aisiteiru.
        Taro-Nom   Hanako-Acc   love
        'Taro loves Hanako.'
    b.   Taro-ga   Hanako-no-koto-o   aisiteiru.
        Taro-Nom   Hanako-Gen-fact-Acc   love
    c. * Taro-no-koto-ga   Hanako-o   aisiteiru.
        Taro-Gen-fact-Nom   Hanako-Acc   love

(22) a.   Taro-ga   Hanako-ga   sukida.
        Taro-Nom   Hanako-Nom   like
        'Taro likes Hanako.'
    b.   Taro-ga   Hanako-no-koto-ga   sukida.
        Taro-Nom   Hanako-Gen-fact-Nom   like
    c. * Taro-no-koto-ga   Hanako-ga   sukida.
        Taro-Gen-fact-Nom   Hanako-Nom   like

Sugisaki (2010) conducted an experiment with 18 Japanese-speaking children (ranging in age from 4;02 to 6;08) to determine whether they already have the knowledge about the structural restriction on *koto*. In the experiment, each child was presented with a short story accompanied by a picture, and after each story, the child was asked to answer one of the questions with or without *koto*. The sample story and sample test sentences are given in (23) and (24), respectively.

(23) Sample Story:
An elephant, a baby chick, and a panda are having their favorite pizza. They are very good friends, but the elephant likes the baby chick the most, and the baby chick likes the panda the most.

(24) a. <u>Hiyokochan-ga</u>   ichiban   sukina-no-wa   dare   kana?
       baby chick-Nom   the-first   like-C-Top   who   Q
       'Who is it that the baby chick likes the most?'
       or 'Who is it that likes the baby chick the most?'
   b. <u>Hiyokochan-no-koto-ga</u> ichiban   sukina-no-wa   dare   kana?
       baby chick-Gen-fact-Nom   the-first like-C-Top   who   Q
       'Who is it that likes the baby chick the most?'
       *'Who is it that the baby chick likes the most?'

Since both the subject and the object arguments of the predicate *sukida* 'like' are marked with Nominative as illustrated in (22), the underlined nominative NP in the cleft sentence in (24a) is ambiguous between the subject NP and the object NP. In contrast, the corresponding NP in (24b) is accompanied with *koto*, and hence this NP can only be interpreted as the direct object of the predicate in the adult Japanese.

The results are summarized in Table 5. When presented with a structurally ambiguous sentence as in (24a), children showed a strong tendency to interpret the nominative NP as the subject. In contrast, when presented with a sentence involving a nominative NP with *koto* as in (24b), children consistently interpreted that NP as the object. These results suggest that Japanese-speaking preschoolers know that *koto* can attach only to the NP in the sister of V, which in turn indicates that configurational structure is already in children's grammar.

To summarize this section, there is overwhelming evidence that the grammar of Japanese-speaking preschool children generates configurational structures. This is

Table 5 Results of the experiment by Sugisaki (2010)

	Nominative NP without *koto* (%)	Nominative NP with *koto* (%)
Interpreted as the Subject	83.3	11.1
Interpreted as the Object	16.7	88.9

consistent with the view that UG plays a significant role in the acquisition of Japanese, guiding Japanese-speaking children to form hierarchically-organized phrase structure from the beginning.

4 Locality Constraints on In-situ *Wh*-Phrases in Child Japanese

In addition to the property of free word order, one of the most prominent properties of Japanese that distinguishes this language from those such as English is that *wh*-phrases may be left in-situ, as illustrated in (25):

(25) Taro-wa [Hanako-ga nani-o katta to] omoimashita ka?
 Taro-Top Hanako-Nom what-Acc bought C thought Q
 'What did Taro think that Hanako bought?'

These in-situ *wh*-phrases obey some of the island constraints that restrict overt *wh*-movements in languages like English.[4] For example, as observed by Watanabe (1992), Japanese *wh*-in-situ exhibits *wh*-island effects: the *wh*-phrase *nani-o* 'what' in an interrogative complement clause in (26) is prevented from taking the matrix scope, and the example is ungrammatical as a *wh*-question, as well as its English translation.

(26) * Taro-wa [Hanako-ga nani-o katta ka] siritagatteimasu ka?
 Taro-Top Hanako-Nom what-Acc bought Q know-want Q
 '*What does Taro want to know whether Hanako bought?'

In addition, as discussed in detail by Lasnik and Saito (1992), the adjunct *wh*-phrase *naze* 'why' is constrained by a variety of islands, including an adjunct island (see also Huang 1982). Thus, the example in (27) is ungrammatical, which can be subsumed under the ungrammaticality of the English translation if we adopt the assumption that *naze* undergoes *wh*-movement in the component that never feeds the phonology (the LF component).

(27) * Taro-wa [Hanako-ga naze sono hon-o yonde kara]
 Taro-Top Hanako-Nom why that book-Acc read after
 dekakemashita ka?
 went-out Q
 '*Why did Taro go out [after Hanako read that book *t*]?'

---

[4]See e.g. Richards (2008) for detailed discussion.

If these island constraints directly reflect properties of UG, we can expect that Japanese-speaking children obey these constraints as soon as they become able to use relevant lexical items and structures. Otsu (2007) demonstrated that this is actually the case with the *wh*-island constraint. His experiment tested 20 three-year-olds and 20 four-year-olds, using a judgment task. In this experiment, one experimenter told a story to a child and to a puppet manipulated by another experimenter. After the story, the experimenter asked some questions to the puppet, and the puppet gave his answers. The task for the child was to judge whether each of these answers provided by the puppet was appropriate to the corresponding question. The story and the crucial test sentences are given in (28) and (29).

(28) Experimental Story:
Taro and Hanako were watching TV together in the living room. Their mother came home, and brought them snacks. And she asked Taro, "Taro, who's your favorite?" Taro replied, "Of course, I like Doraemon." Mother asked Hanako, "And you?" Hanako likes Nobita, but felt a bit shy and replied, "That's a secret."

(29) Test Sentences:
a. *Experimenter:*
Hanako-wa   [dare-ga   suki   ka]   iimashita   ka?
Hanako-Top   who-Nom   like   Q   said   Q
'Did Hanako say who she likes?'
Puppet: Iie.   "No."
b. *Experimenter:*
Taro-wa   [dare-ga   suki   to]   iimashita   ka?
Taro-Top   who-Nom   like   C   said   Q
'Who did Taro say that he likes?'
Puppet: Hai.   "Yes."

If children already have knowledge of the *wh*-island constraint, they should be able to distinguish between (29a) and (29b): The *wh*-phrase in the former should be unable to take the matrix scope due to the constraint and hence the sentence should be interpreted as a *yes/no* question, while the *wh*-phrase in the latter is in a declarative complement clause and should take the matrix scope, which makes the sentence a *wh*-question. Hence, children should judge the puppet's answer as correct for (29a) but as inappropriate for (29b). The results were as expected, as summarized in Table 6. These results succinctly show that Japanese-speaking children as young as three obey one of the constraints that restrict in-situ *wh*-phrases.

In contrast to Otsu (2007) who investigated children's interpretation of questions involving an argument *wh*-phrase, Sugisaki (2009) examined children's knowledge of the questions with the adjunct *wh*-phrase *naze* 'why'. As already illustrated in (27), *naze* is not allowed to appear inside an adjunct clause. Sugisaki's experiment

Table 6 Results of the experiment by Otsu (2007)

	Number of correct responses	% of correct responses
(29a)	38 / 40	95%
(29b)	37 / 40	92%

was an attempt to demonstrate that this constraint on *naze* is also part of the grammar of Japanese-speaking preschool children.

The subjects were 37 Japanese-speaking children, ranging in age from 3;10 to 6;05 (mean age: 5;1). In each trial, a child was told a story, which was accompanied by a series of pictures presented on a laptop computer. At the end of each story, a puppet posed a question about the story to the child. The task for the child was to answer these questions. One of the target trials is presented in (30). After this story, the puppet asked the questions given in (31).

(30) Sample Experimental Story:
This is a story about a small frog and his mother. When the mother came back home from shopping for dinner, she found her son's baseball equipment at the front door. Since she had seen her son's stuff, the mother thought that her small frog had already come back home. She thought that he had come back because he had gotten very hungry.

The small frog was sitting at the dining table. He said, "I played baseball a lot today, and I am very hungry. Can I have my dinner right now?" His mother told him, "You must have got very dirty, so you should take a bath before dinner." The frog went to the bath, and cleaned himself up. After the bath, the frog enjoyed the wonderful dinner his mother had made for him.

(31) Sample Test Sentence:
Naze   gohan-o   taberu   maeni   kaerusan-wa   ofuro-ni
why   meal-Acc   eat   before   frog-Top   bath-in
hairimashita ka?
entered   Q

The question in (31) is potentially ambiguous with respect to the structural position of *naze*, as shown in (32).

(32) a. *Naze* is in the matrix clause:
    Naze   [gohan-o   taberu   maeni]   kaerusan-wa   ofuro-ni
    why   meal-Acc   eat   before   frog-Top   bath-in
    hairimashita   ka?
    entered   Q
  b. *Naze* is in the adjunct clause:
    [Naze   gohan-o   taberu   maeni]   kaerusan-wa   ofuro-ni
    why   meal-Acc   eat   before   frog-Top   bath-in
    hairimashita   ka?
    entered   Q

In (32a), *naze* is an element of the matrix clause and is associated with the VP headed by *taberu* 'eat', while in (32b), *naze* is contained in the adjunct *before*-clause and is associated with the VP headed by *hairu* 'enter'. Even though the sentence in (31) is potentially ambiguous between these two structures, the latter representation is excluded by the constraint that *naze* cannot appear inside an adjunct clause. Hence, if Japanese-speaking children have this constraint as part of their grammar, they should interpret the sentence in (31) only as a question asking the reason why the frog took a bath, and not as a question asking the reason why the frog had the dinner. Given the story in (30), we expect that children should answer "Because the frog got very dirty," and not "Because he was very hungry."

The results revealed that Japanese-speaking children are completely adult-like: When presented sentences like (31), children always interpreted *naze* as an element of the matrix clause, and answered "Because the frog got very dirty" 98.6% of the time (73 out of 74 trials). These results strongly suggest that the locality constraint on *naze* directly reflects properties of UG, thus requiring no experience to emerge.

To summarize this section, we reviewed studies on the acquisition of locality constraints on in-situ *wh*-phrases in Japanese. Previous studies on the acquisition of English convincingly demonstrated the early mastery of locality constraints on overt *wh*-movement. For example, Otsu (1981) revealed that English-speaking children have knowledge of the complex NP constraint (Ross 1967), by showing that children exclude overt *wh*-movement from a relative clause as in (33).

(33) * What is Jane drawing a monkey [that is drinking milk with *t*]?

Similarly, de Villiers et al. (1990) showed that long-distance *wh*-movement in child English obeys the *wh*-island constraint: They found that, when presented the sentence in (34), children associate the *wh*-phrase *how* with the matrix verb *ask*, not with the verb *paint* in the embedded infinitival *wh*-clause.

(34) How did the girl ask [who to paint]?

The results from the acquisition of Japanese, a *wh*-in-situ language, corroborate the findings of these previous studies on overt *wh*-movement in English, and lend strong support to the assumption that UG-related properties constrain the course of acquisition from the beginning.

5 Structure Dependence in Child Japanese

In Japanese, as well as in other natural languages, the structure-dependent notion of c-command, which is allegedly provided by innate UG, plays a fundamental role in a variety of linguistic phenomena. For example, the role of c-command in Japanese can be observed in the contrast between Case markers and Postpositions with respect to Q-float.

(35) a.   Gakusei-ga   3-nin   kuruma-de   kita.
            students-Nom   3-Cl   car-in   came
            'Three students came in cars.'
    b. * Gakusei-ga   kuruma-de   3-dai   kita.
            students-Nom   car-in   3-Cl   came
            'Students came in three cars.'

According to Miyagawa (1989: 30), in order for a floated numeral quantifier to successfully modify a NP, the quantifier and the associated NP must c-command each other. In (35a), this constraint is satisfied, given that a Case-marker is cliticized onto the NP and hence the relation of mutual c-command is established between the NP and the numeral quantifier, as shown in (36a). In contrast, in (35b), this mutual c-command constraint is violated, since the modified NP is embedded within a PP and hence the modified NP within PP does not c-command the numeral quantifier, as shown in (36b).

(36)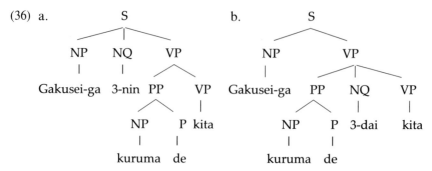

The association of in-situ *wh*-phrases and the Q-particle also relies on the structural notion of c-command. The interpretive contrast between (37a) and (37b) illustrates this point: While the former is interpreted as a *yes/no* question, the latter is interpreted as a *wh*-question. This contrast suggests that in the former, the *wh*-phrase is associated with the embedded Q-marker and hence takes the embedded scope, while in the latter, the *wh*-phrase is associated with the matrix Q-marker and hence takes the matrix scope. The observation that the *wh*-phrase in (37b) cannot take the embedded scope is attributed to the fact that the Q-marker in the embedded clause does not c-command the *wh*-phrase located in the matrix clause (Harada 1972).

(37) a. Hanako-wa   Taro-ni   [kaigi-ga   dokode   aru   ka]
       Hanako-Top Taro-Dat   meeting-Nom   where   be-held Q_1
       kikimashita ka?
       asked Q_2
       'Did Hanako ask Taro where the meeting would be held?'
  b. Hanako-wa   dokode   Taro-ni   [kaigi-ga   aru   ka]
      Hanako-Top   where   Taro-Dat   meeting-Nom   be-held Q_1
      kikimashita ka?
      asked Q_2
      'Where did Hanako ask Taro whether the meeting would be held?'

Otsu (1994c) investigated Japanese-speaking children's adherence to c-command by making use of the contrast illustrated in (35). Five three-year-olds and five four-year-olds were tested with an acting-out task. Children were presented sentences as in (38), and were asked to act out what the sentences mean, by using five toy giraffes and five toy lions placed in front of them.

(38) a. [$_{NP}$ Kirinsan-ga]   san-biki   pro   ositeimasu.
        girraffe-Nom   three-Cl   is-pushing
        'Three giraffes are pushing someone.'
  b. pro   [$_{PP}$ [$_{NP}$ Kirinsan]   [$_P$ kara]]   san-biki   tyuu-o   moratteimasu.
            giraffe   from   three-Cl   kiss-Acc   is-standing
        'Three (unspecified animals) received a kiss from a/the giraffe(s).'

The results showed that children do not make mistakes when interpreting sentences in (38): children chose as the *Agent of pushing* three giraffes for (38a), and chose as the *Recipient of kiss* three lions for (38b). These results show that Japanese-speaking three-year-olds have the constraint on floated numeral quantifier that crucially makes use of the structural notion of c-command.

Sugisaki (2007a) also demonstrated that Japanese-speaking children rely on c-command, by testing children's comprehension of questions as in (37). The actual test sentences used are given in (39).

Table 7 Results of the experiment by Sugisaki (2007a)

Sentences like (39a)	Interpreted as a *wh*-question	10%	(5/50)
	Interpreted as a *yes/no*-question	78%	(39/50)
Sentences like (39b)	Interpreted as a *wh*-question	88%	(44/50)
	Interpreted as a *yes/no*-question	10%	(5/50)

(39) a. Otoosan-wa   dokode   penginsan-ga   sakkaa-o   shitekita   ka
       father-Top   where   penguin-Nom   soccer-Acc played Q_1
       kiki-mashi-ta ka?
       asked Q_2
       'Did the father ask where the penguin played soccer?'
    b. Otoosan-wa   dokode   penginsan-ni   sakkaa-o   shitekita   ka
       father-Top   where   penguin-Dat   soccer-Acc played Q_1
       kiki-mashi-ta ka?
       asked Q_2
       'Where did the father ask the penguin whether (he) played soccer?'

The only difference between these two sentences is the Case marker attached to the noun *penguin*. In (39a), that noun is accompanied by a nominative Case marker and hence is the subject of the embedded clause, and the adjunct *wh*-phrase *dokode* preceding that NP can belong either to the matrix clause or to the embedded clause. Thus, the sentence is structurally ambiguous and has both an interpretation as a *yes/no*-question and an interpretation as a *wh*-question. In contrast, the noun *penguin* in (39b) is accompanied by a dative Case marker, and hence is an argument of the matrix verb 'ask'. Thus, the adjunct *wh*-phrase preceding that NP is unambiguously located in the matrix clause. If children have the knowledge that the *wh*-phrase in (39b) is not c-commanded by the embedded Q-marker, they should interpret this sentence only as a *wh*-question, just like adults.

The subjects were 25 children, ranging in age from 3(years);7(months) to 6;4 (mean age 4;9). Each subject was presented with two target trials, one warm-up, and one filler trial. In each trial, a child was told a story, which was accompanied by a series of pictures. At the end of each story, a puppet posed questions about the story to the child. These questions had the form of (39a) or (39b). The task for the child was to answer them.

The results are summarized in Table 7. Even though children showed a strong tendency to interpret examples like (39a) as *yes/no*-questions, they correctly assigned *wh*-question interpretation to sentences like (39b) about 90% of the time. These results corroborate the findings by Otsu (1994c) and add another piece of evidence for children's sensitivity to abstract structural relations.

6 *Zibun* Binding in Child Japanese

Zibun in Japanese shares some properties with *–self* in English, and hence is considered to be a reflexive anaphor (see e.g. Aikawa 1999). For example, *zibun* must have its antecedent in the same sentence: The example in (40) is acceptable when *zibun* refers to Taro, but is ungrammatical when it refers to someone else not mentioned in the sentence.

(40) Taro_1-ga $\text{zibun}_{1/*2}$-no   kao-o   kaita.
     Taro-Nom   self-Gen   face-Acc   drew
     'Taro drew his own face.'

Universal Grammar and the Acquisition of Japanese Syntax

Zibun also behaves like *–self* in that it must be c-commanded by its antecedent, as illustrated in (41).

(41) Taro$_1$-no   otooto$_2$-ga   zibun$_{*1/2}$-no   kao-o   kaita.
      Taro-Gen   brother-Nom   self-Gen   face-Acc drew
      'Taro's brother drew his own face.'

However, *zibun* has at least two properties that distinguish it from English *–self*. First, as illustrated in (42a), *zibun* has the "subject orientation" (SO): Its antecedent must be a subject, while *–self* in English does not have such a restriction. Second, *zibun* can be bound by a "long-distance" antecedent (LD-binding): The antecedent of *zibun* can be in a higher clause, as shown in (43a).

(42) a. Taro$_1$-ga   Ken$_2$-ni   zibun$_{1/*2}$-nituite   hanasita.
         Taro-Nom   Ken-Dat   self-about   told
         'Taro told Ken about himself.'
     b. John$_1$ talked to Bill$_2$ about himself$_{1/2}$.

(43) a. Taro$_1$-ga   [Ken$_1$-ga   zibun$_{1/2}$-o   hometa   to]   itta.
         Taro-Nom   Ken-Nom   self-Acc   praised   C   said
         'Taro said that Ken praised himself.'
     b. Taro$_1$ said that Ken$_2$ praised himself$_{*1/2}$.

The c-command requirement on the antecedent of *zibun* follows from Condition A of the binding theory (Chomsky 1981: 188), under the assumption that *zibun* is a reflexive anaphor. Furthermore, according to Katada (1991), the SO and LD-binding properties of *zibun* both follow from the assumption that *zibun* is an Operator that successively raises to VP at LF. Then, from an acquisitional point of view, children do not have much to learn to acquire the major properties of *zibun*, and hence the early emergence of these properties is expected.

Otsu (1997) conducted an experiment with 45 Japanese-speaking children ranging in age between three and five, to determine whether they could interpret sentences containing *zibun* in an adult-like way. The task was Truth-Value Judgment. Two dolls, Taro (a boy) and Hanako (a girl), are placed behind a screen on the table, and thus they are invisible to the child. Grover is introduced on the same side of the screen as the child, and hence he also cannot see Taro and Hanako. There is an experimenter on the other side of the screen, who is the only one who can see what happens on that side.

Taro and Hanako then perform a certain action. Then the experimenter on that side whispers to the child what they did, using a sentence involving *zibun*. And the same experimenter asks Grover to guess what they did. Grover then says his guess, using a sentence which does not involve *zibun* but contains names like Taro or Hanako. The task for the child is to give Grover a cookie if his guess is right, and a rag if it is wrong.

The first session of the experiment examined children's knowledge of the SO property, with sentences as in (44):

(44) Taro-ga   Hanako-ni   zibun-no   e-o   miseta.
      Taro-Nom   Hanako-Dat   self-Gen   picture-Acc   showed
      'Taro showed Hanako a picture of himself.'

The child who was whispered this sentence is expected to give Grover a cookie if Grover says that what Taro showed to Hanako was Taro's picture, but is expected to give him a rag if he says that what Taro showed to Hanako was Hanako's picture. The results showed that 12 three-year-olds, 14 four-year-olds, and 15 five-year-olds were able to understand the experimental procedure, and that all of these subjects except one three-year-old responded in an adult-like fashion.

The second session of the experiment investigated whether children obey the c-command requirement on the antecedent of *zibun*, using sentences like (45):

(45) Taro-no   otooto-ga   Hanako-ni   zibun-no   e-o   miseta.
     Taro-Gen   brother-Nom   Hanako-Dat   self-Gen   picture-Acc   showed
     'Taro's brother showed Hanako a picture of himself.'

The results revealed that, except for one three-year-old and one four-year-old, all the children correctly interpreted the test sentences.

The last session of the experiment tested children's understanding of the LD-binding property of *zibun*, with sentences involving an embedded clause as in (46):

(46) $Taro_1$-wa   [$Akira_2$-ga $Hanako_3$-ni $zibun_{1/2/*3}$-no
     Taro-Top   Akira-Nom   Hanako-Dat   self-Gen
     e-o   miseta   to]   omotta
     picture-Acc   showed   C   thought
     'Taro thought that Akira showed Hanako a picture of himself.'

Given the lengthy nature of test sentences, a smaller number of younger subjects (5 three-year-olds, 11 four-year-olds, and 15 five-year-olds) were able to participate, which was presumably due to the limited processing capacity of younger children. However, among those who were able to participate, almost all (4 three-year-olds, 10 four-year-olds, and 15 five-year-olds) responded in an adult-like fashion.

The above results by Otsu (1997) showed that children as young as three have already acquired major properties of *zibun*, such as SO, LD-binding, and the c-command requirement on its antecedent. These results are consistent with the view that these properties of *zibun* are largely determined by UG, thus requiring little experience to emerge.

Murasugi and Kawamura (2005) used *zibun* to demonstrate that children's OSV sentences are derived from SOV via movement. The test sentences in their experiment are exemplified in (47):

(47) a. SOV:
        $Ahiru-ga_1$ usi-o   [$zibun-no_1$ niwa-de]   oikaketa.
        duck-Nom   cow-Acc   self-Gen   garden-at   chased
        'The duck chased the cow at the garden of himself.'
     b. OSV:
        $Usi-o_1$ [$zibun-no_2$ niwa-de $]_3$ $ahiru-ga_2$ $t_1\, t_3$ oikaketa.
        cow-Acc   self-Gen   garden-at   duck-Nom   chased
        'The cow, at the garden of himself, the duck chased.'

In (47a), *zibun* is c-commanded and hence is bound by the subject NP *ahiru-ga*. In (47b), this requirement is satisfied before the movement of the object NP: The anaphor is properly licensed in its initial position. Using an acting-out task, Murasugi and Kawamura demonstrated that even three-year-olds can correctly interpret OSV sentences with *zibun*. This finding provides further support to the claim by Otsu (1994a) and Sano (2007) discussed in Sect. 2 that knowledge of scrambling is already in the grammar of young Japanese-speaking children.

7 Passives in Child Japanese

Japanese permits at least two major types of passives. One of them is the *direct passive* exemplified in (48), which corresponds to the English BE passive both structurally and functionally. In this construction, the passive morpheme *-rare* is attached to the verb stem, and the object NP of the active sentence appears in the subject position bearing nominative Case. The subject NP of the active optionally appears as a PP with *ni* 'by'. The other major type of passive is the *indirect passive* illustrated in (49) and in (50), which can be created not only from a transitive verb but also from an intransitive verb. As in direct passives, the passive morpheme *-rare* is attached to the verb stem, and the subject of the active appears in a PP headed by *ni* 'by'. However, in indirect passives, an additional argument appears as the surface subject, and this NP is interpreted as being adversely affected by the state of affairs expressed in the rest of the clause. For this reason, the indirect passive is often called the *adversity passive*.

(48) a. Active Transitive:
   Taro-ga   Hanako-o   osita.
   Taro-Nom   Hanako-Acc   pushed
   'Taro pushed Hanako.'
   b. Direct Passive:
   Hanako-ga   Taro-ni   os-are-ta.
   Hanako-Nom   Taro-by   push-Pass-Past
   'Hanako was pushed by Taro.'

(49) a. Active Intransitive:
   Ame-ga   hutta.
   rain-Nom   fell
   'It rained.'
   b. Indirect Passive:
   Taro-ga   ame-ni   hur-are-ta.
   Taro-Nom   rain-by   fall-Pass-Past
   'Taro was adversely affected by rain.'

(50) a. Active Transitive:
  Taro-ga   kuruma-o   ketta.
  Taro-Nom   car-Acc   kicked
  'Taro kicked a car.'
 b. Indirect Passive:
  Hanako-ga   Taro-ni   kuruma-o   ker-are-ta.
  Hanako-Nom Taro-by   car-Acc   kick-Pass-Past
  'Hanako was adversely affected by Taro's kicking a/her car.'

One of the important structural differences between these two types of passives lies in the formation of an A-chain between subject and object positions. Miyagawa (1989) observes that Q-float is possible from the surface subject of a direct passive, but not from that of an indirect passive, as shown by the examples (51) and (52), which suggests that direct passives, but not indirect passives, involve A-movement of the NP from object to subject position.

(51) *Direct Passive*:
  Yuube,   kuruma-ga   [$_{VP}$ doroboo-ni ni-dai   nusum-are-ta.]
  last night   car-Nom   thief-by   2-Cl   steal-Pass-Past
  'Last night, two cars were stolen by the thief.'

(52) *Indirect Passive*:
  *Kodomo-ga   [$_{VP}$ ame-ni   futari   fur-are-ta.]
  children-Nom   rain-by   2-Cl   fall-Pass-Past
  'Two children were rained on.'

Sugisaki (1999) and Minai (2000) conducted an experiment to determine whether Japanese-speaking children can successfully interpret these two types of passives. Using a picture-selection task, these studies revealed that Japanese-speaking four- and five-year-olds have much difficulty in interpreting direct passives as in (48b), and that indirect passives as in (49b) are easier to comprehend for these children than direct passives. Sugisaki and Minai attributed the delayed acquisition of direct passives to the A-chain maturation hypothesis proposed by Borer and Wexler (1987), which says that young children do not have the ability to form A-chains, and that this ability is maturationally controlled and hence does not emerge until the age of five or so.

Otsu (2000), however, pointed out that there is an important pragmatic factor that needs to be controlled in the experiment on children's comprehension of Japanese passives. Kuroda (1979) pointed out that both indirect and direct passives bear the connotation of adversity (more accurately, affectivity), and that the source of such affectivity lies in *ni* 'by.' To support this claim, Kuroda observes that, when preceded by a story which is written from John's point of view, the direct passive with *ni* (*ni*-passive) in (53a) is more appropriate than the direct passive with *niyotte* (*niyotte*-passive) in (53b), which is a more 'objective' description.

(53) a. *ni*-passive:

    John-wa   moosukoside   ki-o   usinau   tokoro-o
    John-Top   almost   mind-Acc lose   place-Acc
    Bill-<u>ni</u>   tasuke-rare-ta
    Bill-by   rescue-Pass-Past
    'John was rescued by Bill when he was about to lose consciousness.'

  b. *niyotte*-passive:

    John-wa   moosukoside   ki-o   usinau   tokoro-o
    John-Top   almost   mind-Acc lose   place-Acc
    Bill-<u>niyotte</u> tasuke-rare-ta
    Bill-by   rescue-Pass-Past

Building on Kuroda's (1979) observation, Otsu (2000) reasoned that if Japanese passives carry a sense of the surface subject being adversely affected, it is necessary for children to know that there is a "mind" being adversely affected on the part of the person or animal that is referred to by the surface subject. Then, there is a possibility that Japanese-speaking children have difficulty in interpreting passives due to the fact that they lack a theory of mind. In order to evaluate this possibility, Otsu (2000) examined children's interpretation of passive sentences as in (54) in which the children themselves were being adversely affected.

(54) a. direct passive:

    (Boku-ga)   Hanako-ni   os-are-ta.
    I-Nom   Hanako-by   push-Pass-Past
    'I was pushed by Hanako.'

  b. indirect passive:

    (Boku-ga)   ame-ni   hur-are-ta.
    I-Nom   rain-by   fall-Pass-Past
    'I was adversely affected by rain.'

Since the comprehension of these sentences only require young children to have an awareness of the existence of their own mind, and not someone else's, it is expected that even young children can understand these passives.

The subjects were 15 3-year-olds and 15 4-year-olds. The interpretation of 12 direct passives, 12 indirect passives, and 12 active sentences were tested, with a Truth-Value Judgment Task. These sentences were divided into two types, Type A and Type B: In Type A sentences, the subject NP referred to someone else, not the experimental subject, while in Type B sentences, the subject NP referred to the experimental subject herself.

The results are summarized in Table 8. The results from Type B sentences suggest that Japanese-speaking children can correctly comprehend both direct and indirect passives, once appropriate experimental care is taken. These results, in addition,

Table 8 Results of the experiment by Otsu (2000) (% Correct)

		3-year-olds (%)	4-year-olds (%)
Type A	Direct passive	43	61
	Indirect passive	61	68
	Active	85	94
Type B	Direct passive	80	89
	Indirect passive	87	91
	Active	89	95

show that sentence grammar (which is responsible for the derivation of passives) and pragmatic knowledge constitute independent knowledge modules, and that the former develops earlier than the latter, with the help of innately-given UG.

8 Conclusion

In this chapter, we reviewed studies on the acquisition of Japanese syntax that have a direct bearing on the "logical problem of language acquisition." Japanese has many syntactic phenomena that are not shared by languages like English, such as free word order, floated numeral quantifiers, Case-markers, *wh*-in-situ, subject-oriented anaphor, direct and indirect passives, and so on. The studies on child Japanese reviewed in this chapter demonstrated that the abstract grammatical properties related to these phenomena do exist already in the early grammar of Japanese-speaking children, which in turn strongly indicates that innate UG plays an important role in the acquisition of Japanese syntax, guiding children in what to look for and where to go.

As mentioned in the introduction, there are many other important studies on child Japanese that have not been discussed here, especially those related to parameter-setting in child Japanese (see e.g. Goro and Akiba 2004; Isobe 2003; Murasugi 1991; Murasugi and Sugisaki 2008; Sugisaki 2007b). The wide variety of studies conducted on child Japanese, however, suggests that the remark by Otsu (1999: 396) that "we are still very far from getting a coherent picture of the development of Japanese grammar as a whole" is now becoming outdated. There is no doubt that the findings concerning child Japanese not only constitute an important basis for the existence of biologically-predetermined UG, but also play a significant role in constructing a theory of language acquisition.

References

Aikawa, T. 1999. Reflexives. In *The handbook of Japanese linguistics*, ed. N. Tsujimura, 154–190. Oxford: Blackwell.
Baker, C.L., and J. McCarthy (eds.). 1981. *The logical problem of language acquisition*. Cambridge, MA: MIT Press.

Borer, H. and K. Wexler. 1987. The maturation of syntax. In *Parameter setting*, eds T. Roeper, and W. Edwin, 123–172. Dordrecht: D. Reidel.
Chomsky, N. 1981. *Lectures on Government and binding*. Dordrecht: Foris.
Chomsky, N. 1986. *Knowledge of language: Its nature, origin, and use*. New York: Praeger.
Clancy, P.M. 1985. The acquisition of Japanese. In *The crosslinguistic study of language acquisition*, vol. 1, ed. D.I. Slobin, 373–524. Hillsdale: Lawrence Erlbaum Associates.
Crain, S., and R. Thornton. 1998. *Investigations in universal grammar: A guide to experiments on the acquisition of syntax and semantics*. Cambridge, MA: MIT Press.
de Villiers, J., T. Roeper, and A. Vainikka. 1990. The acquisition of long-distance rules. In *Language processing and language acquisition*, eds. F. Lyn, and J. de Villiers, 257–297. Dordrecht: Kluwer.
Farmer, A.K. 1980. On the interaction of morphology and syntax. Doctoral diss., Cambridge, MA: MIT.
Goro, T. 2007. Language-specific constraints on scope interpretation in first language acquisition. Doctoral diss., University of Maryland, College Park.
Goro, T., and A. Sachie. 2004. Japanese disjunction and the acquisition of positive polarity. In *Proceedings of the Fifth Tokyo Conference on Psycholinguistics*, ed. Y. Otsu, 137–161. Tokyo: Hituzi Syobo.
Hale, K. 1980. Remarks on Japanese phrase structure: Comments on the papers on Japanese syntax. In *MIT Working Papers in Linguistics* 2, eds. Y. Otsu, and A. Farmer, 185–203. Cambridge, MA: MIT Working Papers in Linguistics.
Hale, K. 1983. Warlpiri and the grammar of non-configurational languages. *Natural Language & Linguistic Theory* 1: 5–47.
Harada, K.I. 1972. Constraints on WH-Q binding. *Studies in Descriptive and Applied Linguistics* 5: 180–206.
Hayashibe, H. 1975. Word order and particles: A developmental study in Japanese. *Descriptive and Applied Linguistics* 8: 1–18.
Hornstein, N., and D. Lightfoot (eds.). 1981. *Explanations in linguistics: The logical problem of language acquisition*. London: Longman.
Huang, C.-T. James. 1982. Logical relations in Chinese and the theory of grammar. Doctoral diss., MIT, Cambridge, MA.
Ishii, T. 2004. *Japanese: Ishii corpus*, Pittsburgh, PA.: TalkBank 1-59642-054-5.
Isobe, M. 2003. Head-internal relative clauses in child Japanese. In *Proceedings of the 27th Annual Boston University Conference on Language Development*, ed. Beachley, B. 358–369. Somerville: Cascadilla Press.
Katada, F. 1991. The LF representation of anaphors. *Linguistic Inquiry* 22: 287–314.
Ko, H. 2005. Syntax of why-in-situ: Merge into [Spec, CP] in the overt syntax. *Natural Language & Linguistic Theory* 23: 867–916.
Kuroda, S.-Y. 1979. On Japanese passives. In *Explorations in linguistics: Papers in honor of Kazuko Inoue*, eds. G. Bedell, E. Kobayashi, and M. Muraki, 305–347. Tokyo: Kenkyusha.
Kuroda, S.-Y. 1980. Bun no koozoo (the structure of sentence). In *Niti-Eigo Hikaku Kouza 2: Bunpou [Lectures of Japanese-English Comparative Studies 2: Grammar]*, ed. T. Kunihiro, 23–61. Tokyo: Taishukan.
Lasnik, H., and M. Saito. 1992. *Move α: Conditions on its applications and output*. Cambridge, MA: MIT Press.
MacWhinney, B. 2000. *The CHILDES project: Tools for analyzing talk*. Mahwah: Lawrence Erlbaum.
Masunaga, K. 1983. Bridging. In *Proceedings of the XIIIth International Congress of Linguistics*, eds. H. Shiro and I. Kazuko, 455–460. Tokyo: Proceedings Publishing Committee.
Minai, U. 2000. The acquisition of Japanese passives. In *Japanese/Korean linguisitcs 9*, eds. M. Nakayama, and C.J. Quinn Jr., 339–350. Stanford: CSLI Publications.
Miyagawa, S. 1989. *Structure and case marking in Japanese*. San Diego: Academic Press.
Miyata, S. 2004a. *Japanese: Aki Corpus*. Pittsburgh: TalkBank. 1-59642-055-3.
Miyata, S. 2004b. *Japanese: Ryo Corpus*. Pittsburgh: TalkBank. 1-59642-056-1.

Miyata, S. 2004c. *Japanese: Tai Corpus*. Pittsburgh: TalkBank. 1-59642-057-X.
Murasugi, K. 1991. Noun phrases in Japanese and English: A study in syntax, learnability and acquisition. Doctoral diss., University of Connecticut, Storrs.
Murasugi, K., and T. Kawamura. 2005. On the acquisition of scrambling in Japanese. In *The free word order phenomenon: Its syntactic sources and diversity*, eds. J. Sabel, and M. Saito, 221–242. Berlin: Mouton de Gruyter.
Murasugi, K., and K. Sugisaki. 2008. The acquisition of Japanese syntax. In *The Oxford handbook of Japanese linguistics*, eds. S. Miyagawa, and M. Saito, 250–286. New York: Oxford University Press.
Otsu, Y. 1981. Universal grammar and syntactic development in children: Toward a theory of syntactic development. Doctoral diss., MIT, Cambridge, MA.
Otsu, Y. 1994a. Early acquisition of scrambling in Japanese. In *Language acquisition studies in generative grammar*, eds. T. Hoekstra, and B.D. Schwartz, 253–264. Amsterdam: John Benjamins.
Otsu, Y. 1994b. Case-marking particles and phrase structure in early Japanese. In *Syntactic theory and first language acquisition: Cross-linguistic perspectives*, eds. B. Lust, M. Suner, and J. Whitman, 159–169. Hillsdale: Lawrence Erlbaum Associates.
Otsu, Y. 1994c. Notes on the structural distinction between case markers and postpositions in the acquisition of Japanese grammar. In *Synchronic and diachronic approaches to language*, eds. Chiba, S. et al. Tokyo: Liber Press.
Otsu, Y. 1997. *Zibun* Futatabi [*Zibun* Revisited]. In *Ninchi/Gengo no Seiritsu: Ningen no Kokoro no Hattatsu [Emergence of cognition and language: Development of human mind]*, ed. P. Committee, 113–122. Tokyo: Kuba Pro.
Otsu, Y. 1999. First language acquisition. In *The handbook of Japanese linguistics*, ed. N. Tsujimura, 378–397. Oxford: Blackwell.
Otsu, Y. 2000. A preliminary report on the independence of sentence grammar and pragmatic knowledge: The case of the Japanese passive – a developmental perspective. *Keio Studies in Theoretical Linguistics* 2: 161–170.
Otsu, Y. 2007. *Wh*-island in child Japanese. Paper presented at Workshop on Language, Mind and the Brain, Keio University.
Richards, N. 2008. Wh-questions. In *The Oxford handbook of Japanese linguistics*, eds. S. Miyagawa, and M. Saito, 348–371. New York: Oxford University Press.
Ross, J.R. 1967. Constraints on variables in syntax. Doctoral diss., MIT, Cambridge, MA.
Saito, M. 1985. Some asymmetries in Japanese and their theoretical implications. Doctoral diss., MIT, Cambridge, MA.
Sano, K. 1977. An experimental study on the acquisition of Japanese simple sentences and cleft sentences. *Descriptive and Applied Linguistics* 10: 213–233.
Sano, T. 2007. Early acquisition of copy & movement in a Japanese OSV sentence. In *A Supplement to the Proceedings of the 31st Boston University Conference on Language Development*, eds. H. Caunt-Nulton, S. Kulatilake, and I. Woo. http://www.bu.edu/linguistics/BUCLD/supp31.html.
Sugisaki, K. 1999. Japanese passives in acquisition. In *Cranberry Linguistics: University of Connecticut Working Papers in Linguistics* 10, eds. D. Braze, K. Hiramatsu, and Y. Kudo, 145–156. Cambridge, MA: MIT Working Papers in Linguistics.
Sugisaki, K. 2007a. Structure dependence in child Japanese. Paper presented at GLOW in Asia VI, The Chinese University of Hong Kong, Shatin, December 27–29, 2007.
Sugisaki, K. 2007b. The configurationality parameter in the minimalist program: A view from child Japanese. In *Proceedings of the 31st Annual Boston University Conference on Language Development*, eds. H. Caunt-Nulton, S. Kulatilake, and I. Woo, 597–608. Somerville: Cascadilla Press.
Sugisaki, K. 2008. Early acquisition of basic word order in Japanese. *Language Acquisition* 15: 183–191.
Sugisaki, K. 2009. LF *wh*-movement and its locality constraint in child Japanese. Ms., Mie University.

Sugisaki, K. 2010. Configurational structure in child Japanese: New evidence. Poster presented at the 4th Generative Approaches to Language Acquisition North America (GALANA 4), University of Toronto, Toronto.
Sugisaki, K., and I. Miwa. What can child Japanese tell us about the syntax of scrambling? In *Proceedings of the 20th West Coast Conference on Formal Linguistics*, eds. M. Karine and L.A. Barel, 538–551. Somerville: Cascadilla Press.
Takezawa, K. 1987. A configurational approach to case marking in Japanese. Doctoral diss., University of Washington, Seattle.
Takita, K. 2009. Argument ellipsis in Japanese right dislocation. In *Japanese/Korean linguistics* 18, eds. M. Marcel den Dikken, and W. McClure. Stanford: CSLI Publications.
Tanaka, H. 2001. Right-dislocation as scrambling. *Journal of Linguistics* 37: 551–579.
Watanabe, A. 1992. Subjacency and S-structure movement of *wh*-in-situ. *Journal of East Asian Linguistics* 1: 255–291.
Yoshida, K., and T. Yoshida. 1997. Question marker drop in Japanese. *International Christian University Language Research Bulletin* 11: 37–54.

Studying Language Acquisition Through the Prism of Isomorphism

Julien Musolino

1 Introduction

A topic that has received an enormous amount of attention on the part of scholars interested natural language semantics is the phenomenon of linguistic quantification. Over the last decade, a growing number of studies on the acquisition of semantics have focused on the way children interpret sentences containing quantified NPs and negation (Musolino 1998, 2006a, b; Musolino et al. 2000; Lidz and Musolino 2002, 2005; Musolino and Lidz 2003, 2006; Musolino and Gualmini 2004; Gualmini 2004, 2008; Gualmini et al. 2008; Krämer 2000; Noveck et al. 2007; Gennari and MacDonald 2005/2006; O'Grady 2008; Conroy 2008; among others). Much of this work grows out of an observation by Musolino (1998) that preschoolers, unlike adults, display a strong preference for the interpretation of such sentences that corresponds to the surface syntactic position of the quantificational elements involved. Consider for example, the sentence in (1) which contains the quantified NP *Every horse* and negation. On one reading, (1) can be paraphrased as meaning that every horse is such that it did not jump over the fence; in other words, none of the horses jumped, (1a). Alternatively, (1) can be paraphrased as meaning that not all the horses jumped over the fence, (1b).

(1) Every horse didn't jump over the fence

   (a) None of the horses jumped over the fence
   (b) Not all the horses jumped over the fence

Musolino's (1998) observation is that children, unlike adults, display a marked tendency to assign sentences like (1), interpretation (1a). This is what Musolino

---

J. Musolino (✉)
Psychology Department, Rutgers University, Busch Campus 152 Frelinghuysen Road, Piscataway, NJ 08854-8020, USA
e-mail: julienm@ruccs.rutgers.edu

(1998) called the Observation of Isomorphism (OI).[1] While the original, grammatical explanation of OI has now been abandoned by all investigators working on this topic, including Musolino and collaborators, the facts themselves are still in need of an explanation. That is, one needs to account for why we find such robust and systematic differences in the way preschoolers and adults resolve scope ambiguities involving QNPs and negation.

One idea, inspired by research in the field of sentence processing, is that the resolution of quantifier-negation ambiguities involves an initial commitment to surface scope which is much more difficult for children to revise away from than it is for adults (Musolino and Lidz 2003, 2006). This idea, in turn, calls for a rapprochement between the fields of language development and language processing, and has given rise to new work exploring the roots of isomorphism in adults (e.g., Conroy 2008) as well as the role played by priming in the development of this comprehension process (e.g., Viau et al. 2010).

A radically different idea was recently proposed by Gualmini and colleagues who, in doing so, make three important claims (Gualmini 2008; Gualmini et al. 2008). The first comes in the form of a new theoretical model of scope ambiguity resolution called the Question-Answer-Requirement (QAR) which views OI as a pragmatic epiphenomenon. The second is that there is no place in our theories for anything like OI, be it a descriptive generalization as in Musolino (1998), or one of the factors contributing to scope ambiguity resolution, as in Musolino and Lidz (2003, 2006). The third is that as a consequence of the demise of the notion of isomorphism, broader conclusions reached on the basis of OI have to be reconsidered.

In this chapter, I aim to accomplish two goals. The first is to review the main developments in this research area, paying particular attention to the evolution of the notion of isomorphism itself. This will provide readers with a map of the empirical and theoretical terrain and give them an overview of the developments in this area over the last 10 years. My second, more important goal, is to argue that isomorphism is best and most productively understood as a research program. In doing so, I will show that the notion of isomorphism can be used as a prism to illuminate much broader issues in domains such as language acquisition, linguistic theory, learnability theory, experimental methodology, and the development of sentence processing and pragmatic abilities. An important and positive consequence of this view is that, contrary to recent claims about its demise, Isomorphism continues to provide a productive platform where new work on a variety of issues and topics of interest to linguists, psycholinguists, and developmental psychologists continues to be produced and to create new links between the different areas involved.

The discussion is organized as follows. Section 2 lays out the basic facts and observations that gave rise to the body of work discussed in this chapter, and in particular, Musolino's (1998) Observation of Isomorphism and the original,

---

[1] In fact, as explained in more detail in Sect. 2, (1a) corresponds to an *isomorphic* interpretation of (1); that is, an interpretation where the scope relation between *every horse* and negation can be directly read off of their surface syntactic position.

grammatical account of OI. Section 3 traces the evolution of OI and chronicles the demise of the grammatical view, Sect. 3.1, and the rise of the garden-path, and QAR approaches to OI, Sects. 3.2 and 3.3 respectively. In Sect. 4, I provide a critical assessment of the QAR approach to OI, and in Sect. 5, I show that Isomorphism is best and most productively understood as a research program, illustrating some of its implications for broader issues of concern to linguists, psycholinguists, and developmental psychologists.

2 Navigating Negative Quantificational Space

This section introduces the phenomenon of quantifier-negation interaction, Sect. 2.1, as well as the developmental effect, based on this phenomenon, that will serve as our prism, namely Musolino's (1998) Observation of Isomorphism (OI), Sect. 2.2. Section 2.3 reviews the grammatical account of OI originally proposed by Musolino (1998) and Musolino et al. (2000).

2.1 *Quantifier-Negation Interaction*

To begin, let us consider the linguistic phenomenon that led to Musolino (1998) to uncover OI, namely the interaction of quantified NPs (QNPs) (e.g., *every horse*, *some boys*) and negation. As a first step, let us begin by introducing the notion of scope – a key theoretical concept – by using a simple mathematical analogy. Consider the expressions in (2) and (3):

(2) $2 \times (3+5) = 16$
(3) $(2 \times 3) + 5 = 11$

The scope of 2x (the number 2 followed by the multiplication sign) can be thought of as its domain of application. So in (2), (3 + 5) falls within the scope of 2x. By contrast, in (3), 3 falls within the scope of 2x whereas 5 falls outside of its scope. Finally, notice that different scope relations give rise to different results once the expressions are computed.

We can now turn to the concept of scope as it applies to language by considering the examples in (4) which all contain a QNP and negation.

(4) a. Every horse did<u>n't</u> jump over the fence.
     b. The Smurf did<u>n't</u> buy every orange.
     c. Donald did<u>n't</u> find two guys.
     d. Some girls wo<u>n't</u> ride on the merry-go-round.
     e. The detective did<u>n't</u> find some guys.

First, notice that (4a) is ambiguous. On one reading, it can be paraphrased as meaning that every horse is such that it did not jump over the fence. In other words, none of them did. In this case, the QNP *every horse* is interpreted outside the scope of negation (abbreviated every>not). Following Musolino (1998) and Musolino et al. (2000), I will call this an *isomorphic* interpretation because in this case semantic scope (i.e., the way the QNP and negation are interpreted with respect to each other) can be directly read off the surface syntactic position (defined in terms of overt c-command relations) between the quantificational elements involved. Alternatively, (4a) can be paraphrased as meaning that not every horse jumped over the fence; i.e. some did but others didn't. Here, the every horse is interpreted within the scope of negation (abbreviated not>every). I will call this a *non-isomorphic* interpretation because in this case, semantic scope does not coincide with the overt syntactic position of the QNP and negation.[2]

Notice that not every sentence containing negation and a universally quantified NP gives rise to the kind of ambiguity just described. To be sure, (4b), which finds the QNP in object position allows only a reading where *every orange* is interpreted within the scope of negation (not>every), an isomorphic interpretation. However, replace the universally quantified object in (4b) with a numerically quantified one, as in (4c), and the ambiguity is restored. Indeed, (4c) can either be paraphrased as meaning that it is not the case that Donald found two guys (not>two), an isomorphic interpretation, or, alternatively, that there are two specific guys that Donald didn't find (two>not), a non-isomorphic interpretation.

Returning to example (4a), we can now see that the availability of a non-isomorphic interpretation is a function of the lexical nature of the subject QNP. That is, while (4a), which contains a universally quantified NP, is clearly ambiguous, (4d), which contains an existentially quantified subject, is not. The most natural interpretation of (4d) is one on which it can be paraphrased as meaning that there are some girls who didn't ride on the merry-go-round (some>not), an isomorphic interpretation. Finally, the fact that QNPs like *some N* and *every N* give rise to different interpretive patterns when they occur as the subject of a negative statement also holds when they occur in object position. To witness, recall that (4b), which contains a universally quantified object, must receive an isomorphic interpretation. By contrast, (4e), where the QNP *some N* occurs in object position, must receive a non-isomorphic interpretation. In other words, (4e) can only be paraphrased as meaning that there are some guys that the detective didn't find (some>not), a non-isomorphic interpretation, and not as meaning that the detective didn't find anybody (not>some), an isomorphic interpretation.

Let us take stock. We have seen that sentences containing QNPs and negation give rise to isomorphic and non-isomorphic interpretations. Moreover, non-isomorphic interpretations are sometimes obligatory, sometimes optional, and

---

[2] It has been suggested to me that whether negation appears in contracted or uncontracted form may affect the ambiguity pattern (Norbert Hornstein, p.c. for cases like *Every horse didn't jump over the fence*, and Tom Roeper, p.c., for cases like *The Smurf didn't buy every orange*). However, I am not aware of any experimental evidence bearing on this issue.

sometimes unavailable. Finally, the availability of such interpretations depends on at least two factors: the lexical nature of the QNPs involved as well as their syntactic position. Given the complex mapping between form and meaning at play here, it is natural for someone interested in the acquisition of semantics to wonder how children manage to navigate this interpretive maze and arrive at the correct generalizations regarding the facts described above.

2.2 The Observation of Isomorphism

The considerations discussed above led Musolino (1998) to systematically assess the way preschoolers and adult speakers of English interpret sentences containing QNPs and negation in a series of psycholinguistic experiments using the Truth Value Judgment Task methodology (TVJT). The logic of the experimental approach developed by Musolino (1998) was to create situations that could be described using the sentences in (4) and in which each target sentence was true on one reading and false on the other. Participants' acceptance/rejection of the target sentences, along with appropriate justifications, was then taken as a measure of which reading they were accessing (isomorphic or non-isomorphic). To make things more concrete, let us consider a typical scenario used to test participants' interpretation of sentences (4a, b). Beginning with the former, imagine a situation in which three horses decide to practice jumping over various obstacles, and two of those horses end up jumping over a fence (picture 1). A puppet then describes the situation by saying: "Every horse didn't jump over the fence, am I right?". If one were to interpret the puppet's statement as meaning that none of the horses jumped over the fence (every > not), an isomorphic reading, then one ought to reject that statement on the grounds that two of the horses did jump over the fence. On the other hand, if the target sentence is interpreted to mean that not all of the horses jumped over the fence (not > every), a non-isomorphic reading, then one ought to accept it because it is indeed true that not every horse jumped over the fence; two did but one didn't.

The logic of the stories used to assess participants' interpretation of sentences containing a universally quantified NP in object position is the same. Consider for example a situation in which a Smurf decides to go to the grocery store to buy some fruit. There he sees some apples and oranges, and he decides to buy one of the three oranges (picture 2). The puppet then describes the situation by saying: "The Smurf didn't buy every orange, am I right?" As before, interpreting the target sentence to mean that the Smurf bought none of the oranges (every > not), a non-isomorphic interpretation in this case, should lead to rejection of the puppet's statement because the Smurf did buy one of the oranges. By contrast, interpreting the target sentence to mean that not all of the oranges were bought by the Smurf (not > every), an isomorphic reading, should lead one to accept the puppet's statement because the Smurf bought one of the three oranges, but not the other two.

Picture 1
'Every horse didn't jump over the fence'

Picture 2
'The Smurf didn't buy every orange'

Not > every = True
Every > not = False

Not > every = True
Every > not = False

When tested under the conditions described above, both preschoolers and adults easily accessed the isomorphic interpretation of sentences like *The Smurf didn't buy every orange* (i.e., not>every), and both groups correctly explain that the puppet is right because the Smurf only bought one of the three oranges. More surprising is children's responses to sentences like *Every horse didn't jump over the fence*. Here, adult participants almost always accept the puppet's statements on the grounds that only two of the three horses made it over the fence (see picture 1), clearly accessing the isomorphic interpretation of the target sentence (not>every). By contract, preschoolers in the same situation systematically reject the puppet's statement, because, as the children explained, two horses did jump over the fence. Thus, whereas adults can easily access the non-isomorphic interpretation of sentences like *Every horse didn't jump over the fence*, preschoolers systematically access the isomorphic interpretation.

In fact, the pattern just described generalizes to all the cases of quantifier-negation interaction described in (4). This is what Musolino (1998) called the Observation of Isomorphism (OI) (see Table 1). In a nutshell, OI captures the observation that children systematically compute semantic scope on the basis of overt syntactic scope. Musolino et al. (2000), following Musolino (1998), define OI as follows:

The observation of Isomorphism
Unlike adults, young children systematically interpret negation and quantified NPs on the basis of their position in overt syntax.

Since Musolino (1998), OI has been replicated by different investigators, in languages such as English (Musolino and Lidz 2006; Conroy 2008; Gualmini 2004; Conroy et al. 2009), French (Noveck et al. 2007), Kannada (Lidz and Musolino 2002, 2005/2006), and Korean (Han et al. 2007).

Table 1 The observation of Isomorphism

Sentence type	Children	Adults
<u>Every horse</u> did<u>n't</u> jump over the fence	every > not	not > every
The Smurf did<u>n't</u> buy <u>every orange</u>	not > every	not > every
<u>Some horses</u> wo<u>n't</u> jump over the fence	some > not	some > not
The detective did<u>n't</u> find <u>some guys</u>	not > some	some > not
Cookie Monster did<u>n't</u> eat <u>two slices of pizza</u>	not > two	not > two
		two > not

2.3 *Isomorphism as a Grammatical Epiphenomenon*

The Observation of Isomorphism, and, more generally, the existence of any systematic difference in the linguistic behavior of children and adults, raise a number of questions that we will discuss throughout this chapter. Among them is the question of what causes children to behave isomorphically in the first place. Musolino (1998) offered an account of the causal question based on the idea that preschoolers and adults have different grammars when it comes to the phenomenon under consideration. Specifically, Musolino proposed that preschoolers find themselves at a developmental stage where their computational system cannot yet generate linguistic representations that correspond to non-isomorphic interpretations, hence their necessarily isomorphic behavior.

Importantly however, Musolino (1998) regarded isomorphism as an *epiphenomenon*; an emerging property arising from the interaction of deeper linguistic principles.[3] The linguistic principles in question are the subset condition (Berwick 1985; Wexler and Manzini 1987; Crain and Thornton 1998) and the typology of QNPs. The basic idea regarding QNPs is that they come in two flavors. The first kind, Type 1 QNPs, rely on a single mechanism for purposes of scope-taking, grammatical movement (i.e., A-movement in Horsntein's 1995 system), and they are always interpreted isomorphically with respect to negation. So for example, an object QNP of Type 1 will always be interpreted within the scope of negation because AgrO, the position to which it would move, is hierarchically lower than NegP. Thus, the object QP will always occur within the c-command domain of negation, and it will therefore be interpreted within its scope. By contrast, the second kind, Type II QNPs, have an additional, non-movement-based mechanism at their disposal (Hornstein 1984, 1995; Reinhart 1995, 1997). What this means is that Type II QNPs can

---

[3]The following quote from Musolino (1998) illustrates this important point: "There would be a simple way to capture the observation of isomorphism: take isomorphism at face value and invoke it as a primitive learning principle. Call it 'the Principle of Isomorphism'... My purpose in this section is to argue that this is *not* the right way to proceed however ...My contention, therefore, is that isomorphism in the acquisition of QNP-Neg interaction is *epiphenomenal* [my emphasis]. It should be regarded as an *emergent property* [my emphasis] arising from the interplay between properties of QNPs and learnability considerations." (p. 149)

be interpreted in positions that are different from their surface syntactic position –i.e., non-isomorphically – by a mechanism that does not yield the typical signature of syntactic movement (e.g., locality effects). For example, in Reinhart's (1995) system, Type II QNPs can be interpreted as choice functions. Thus, Type I QNPs have a subset of the options available to Type II QNPs, thereby creating the familiar subset/superset configuration required for the operation of the subset principle which, on this account, would then compel children to initially hypothesize that all QNPs are of type 1. And since Type 1 QNPs never give rise to non-isomorphic interpretations, children's isomorphic behavior follows straightforwardly.

In fact, the account outlined above works for all the cases in (1), expect for sentences like *Every horse didn't jump over the fence*. Here, the key observation is that while such sentences are ambiguous in English, and give rise to a isomorphic and a non-isomorphic interpretation, they are unambiguous in Chinese, and only give rise to an isomorphic interpretation (every > not). Following the logic discussed above, Musolino hypothesized that English-speaking preschoolers go through a Chinese-speaking phase during which they initially treat such sentences as unambiguous and assign them only an isomorphic interpretation.

3 Shades of Isomorphism: Grammar, Parsing and Pragmatics

In this section, I review developments that followed the formulation of OI and the grammatical account introduced above. I first show, in Sect. 3.1, that there are now good reasons to believe that the grammatical account should be abandoned. In Sect. 3.2, I turn to an alternative account of the facts uncovered by Musolino (1998) known as the garden-path account (Musolino and Lidz 2003/2006). Finally, in Sect. 3.3, I introduce a competing account of OI proposed by Gualmini and colleagues (Gualmini et al. 2008), called the Question-Answer-Requirement (QAR).

3.1 Against the Grammatical View of Isomorphism

As work on Isomorphism progressed beyond the original studies described in the previous section, and new results began to appear, it soon became apparent that Musolino's (1998) grammatical account could not be maintained. Two mutually reinforcing sets of findings lead to this conclusion. The first is that under certain experimental conditions, children can be shown to access non-isomorphic interpretations at or near adult-like levels. The second is that the isomorphism effect can be induced in adults, who undoubtedly have mature grammars.

Beginning with adults, Musolino and Lidz (2003) showed that the isomorphism effect seen in children in the case of sentences like (5) (Musolino 1998; Lidz and Musolino 2002) could also be observed in mature speakers in the case of sentences like:

(5) Cookie Monster didn't eat two slices of pizza.
(6) Two frogs didn't jump over the rock.

In both cases, participants were tested in two conditions: an Isomorphic condition, in which the isomorphic readings of the sentences are true and the non-isomorphic readings are false, and a Non-isomorphic condition is which the isomorphic readings are false and the non-isomorphic readings are true. These design features are implemented in the same way for both sentence types. In the Isomorphic condition, the action described by the verb was performed only with respect to one of two objects (or performed by only one of two characters) whereas in the Non-isomorphic condition, the total number of objects is four instead of two, and the action is performed with respect to only two of them (or performed by only two out of four characters).

So for example, in the isomorphic condition corresponding to (5), Cookie Monster ate only one of two slices of pizza which makes the isomorphic reading (not>two) true since it is indeed not the case that Cookie Monster ate two slices of pizza, and the non-isomorphic reading (two>not) false since it is not true that there are two slices of pizza that Cookie Monster didn't eat. In the non-isomorphic condition, Cookie Monster eats two out of four slices of pizza which makes the isomorphic reading (not>two) false, since Cookie Monster ate exactly two slices of pizza, and the non-isomorphic reading (two>not) true, since there are indeed two slices of pizza that Cookie Monster didn't eat.

Under those conditions, Lidz and Musolino (2002) showed that adult speakers of English accept the puppet statements equally often in the Isomorphic and the Non-isomorphic condition corresponding to sentences like (5) (97% and 93% acceptance rate, respectively), demonstrating that they can easily access either interpretation. Children, however, display a strong preference for the Isomorphic interpretation, manifested by a significantly lower acceptance rate in the non-isomorphic condition (where the non-isomorphic reading is true) compared to the isomorphic condition (where the isomorphic reading is true) (33% vs. 81% acceptance rate, respectively). When asked to justify their negative answers in the non-isomorphic condition, children explain that the puppet is wrong by invoking the fact that the isomorphic reading is false.

Musolino and Lidz (2003) showed that the isomorphic pattern observed in preschoolers in the case of sentences like (5) can be induced in adults when they are asked to interpret sentences like (6). Following the experimental logic outlined above, adult speakers of English were tested in two conditions. In the Isomorphic condition, four frogs tried jumping over a rock, and only two succeeded, thus making the isomorphic reading (two>not) true, since there are indeed two frogs that failed to jump over the rock, and the non-isomorphic reading (not>two) false, since there are exactly two frogs that jumped over the rock. In the non-isomorphic condition, which involved only two frogs and where one managed to jump over the rock but the other didn't, the truth values of the two readings are reversed. This time, the isomorphic reading (two>not) is false, because only one frog – and not two – failed to jump over the rock, and the non-isomorphic reading (not>two) is true because it is indeed the case that the number of frogs that managed to jump over the rock is not two (since only one frog managed to do so).

What Musolino and Lidz (2003) found here is that adults always accepted the puppet's statements in the Isomorphic condition, thereby easily accessing the isomorphic interpretation of sentences like (6), but that they overwhelmingly rejected the same sentences in the non-isomorphic condition. When asked to explain their negative answers in the non-isomorphic condition, adults explained that the puppet was wrong because the isomorphic interpretation of the sentences was false. In sum, adults failed to access the non-isomorphic interpretations – which were true in this case – and instead accessed the isomorphic readings – where were false in this case. Thus, the Isomorphism effect, originally reported to manifest itself in the behavior of preschoolers, can also be induced in mature speakers of English. This general approach – 'turning adults into children' – has also been documented by Conroy (2008) in the case of sentences like *Every horse didn't jump over the fence*.

The second line of evidence bearing on the grammatical account comes from studies which show the opposite effect, namely that under certain experimental conditions, children can be shown to behave in a more adult-like fashion. In this regard, Musolino (2000) and then Musolino and Lidz (2006)[4] reported that certain contextual manipulations lead to a significant reduction in isomorphic behavior on the part of children. Specifically, Musolino showed that preschoolers systematically accessed the isomorphic interpretation of (7a) (every>not), replicating the original finding, but that they were significantly more likely to access the non-isomorphic interpretation of sentences like (7b) (not>every), which were used to describe a situation in which three horses initially all jumped over a log, and only two of them subsequently made it over a fence.

(7) a. Every horse didn't jump over the fence
 b. Every horse jumped over the log, but/and every horse didn't jump over the fence.

In a similar vein, Gualmini (2004) manipulated the felicity of the contexts in which negative sentences were used. The key insight exploited by Gualmini is that in order for negation to be used felicitously, it must point to a discrepancy between an expected outcome and the actual outcome of a situation (Wason 1972); a requirement that young children have been shown to be sensitive to (de Villiers and Helen 1975). So for example, Gualmini used sentences like (8a, b) to describe a situation

---

[4] Musolino (2000) was in fact the first to report that certain contextual manipulations can lead to a significant reduction of the isomorphism effect, and to therefore conclude that the grammatical account of Musolino (1998) had to be abandoned. The results presented by Musolino (2000) were later published as Musolino and Lidz (2006).

in which a Troll was expected to deliver four pizzas, but because he lost two on his way, only managed to deliver the remaining two.

(8) a. The Troll didn't deliver some pizzas.
    b. The Troll didn't lose some pizzas.

In this case, both sentences are false on an isomorphic interpretation (not > some), because it is not true that the Troll delivered or lost none of the pizzas: the two that were lost were obviously not delivered, and the two that were delivered were not lost. On the other hand, the sentences are true on a non-isomorphic interpretation (some > not) because there are indeed some pizzas that were not delivered – the two that were lost – or lost – the two that were delivered. Thus, (8a, b) only differ in how felicitous they are in Gualmini's pizza story. (8a) is felicitous because the Troll was expected to *deliver* the pizzas, but (8b) is not, because the Troll's task was not to *lose* the pizzas. What Gualmini found here is that preschoolers were much more likely to accept the non-isomorphic interpretation of the felicitous examples, (8a), than the infelicitous ones, (8b).

In sum, the contextual manipulations described above in the Musolino (2000), Musolino and Lidz (2006) and Gualmini (2004) studies led children to behave in a more adult-like fashion in their ability to access non-isomorphic interpretations, a fact which is hard to reconcile with Musolino's (1998) grammatical account of Isomorphism. Taken together, the evidence that adults can be turned into children, and that children can be turned into adults cast serious doubt on the validity of Musolino's (1998) grammatical account of Isomorphism, and it is now generally agreed that the answer to what I called the causal question lies elsewhere.

3.2 *Isomorphism as a Garden-Path Effect*

The developments reviewed in the previous section entail that we should shift the focus of our inquiry from the study of grammatical development to the study of ambiguity resolution. Indeed, if preschoolers, like adults, have grammars that allow them to generate both isomorphic and non-isomorphic interpretations, then the key question is now to try to understand why these two populations differ in the way they resolve quantifier-negation ambiguities. In light of the demise of the grammatical account, OI can now be recast as the observation that preschoolers, unlike adults, have a tendency to resolve quantifier-negation ambiguities isomorphically. Why should this be?

One idea, inspired by research in the field of sentence processing, is that the resolution of quantifier-negation ambiguities involves an initial commitment to surface scope which is much more difficult for children to revise away from than it is for adults (e.g., Musolino and Lidz 2003, 2006): a sort of Kindergarten-path effect, to borrow Trueswell et al.'s (1999) catchy phrasing. Notice that this approach relies on two crucial assumptions: that surface scope has a privileged status in that it tends to be initially favored by the parser, and that preschoolers are not yet as efficient as adults when it comes to revising initial parsing commitments. A review of the literature indicates that there is good evidence supporting both of these assumptions.

Regarding the special status of surface scope, the evidence available points to the conclusion that isomorphic interpretations of sentences containing multiple quantified expressions are theoretically, psychologically, and statistically privileged. To begin, current theoretical models of quantificational interactions view scope-shift – the operation that yields non-isomorphic interpretations – as a computationally costly operation (e.g., Fox 2000; Reinhart 2006). Moreover, Reinhart (2006) argues that this cost has measurable psychological consequences when it comes to the interpretation of quantified sentences.

This conclusion is supported by numerous psycholinguistic studies on this topic, using both off-line and online measures (e.g., VanLehn 1978; Gillen 1991; Kurtzman and MacDonald 1993; Pica and Snyder 1995; Tunstall 1998; Anderson 2004). For example, Tunstall's (1998) Principle of Scope Interpretation (PSI) is based on the notion that default relative scoping is determined by surface c-command relations, and her condition on general processing economy treats isomorphism between surface syntactic scope and semantic scope as a default condition to be departed from at cost and only when such departure is motivated by other factors. Anderson (2004) arrives at the same conclusions, and recasts Fox's (2000) grammatical principle of scope economy as a parsing principle according to which inverse-scope configurations are dispreferred because they are computationally more costly than surface scope interpretations.

Finally, isomorphic interpretations are also privileged in the sense that they seem to be statistically much more frequent than non-isomorphic ones. This bias was documented in a corpus analysis that examined children and adults' patterns of use of sentences containing quantified NPs and negation performed by Gennari and MacDonald (2005/2006). Since the parser is sensitive to such distributional cues in making initial commitments to a given interpretation in the course of language comprehension, these statistical patterns give us one more reason to believe that isomorphic interpretations will be favored by the parser early on.

The second assumption made by the kindergarten-path approach is that preschoolers are not as efficient at revising initial parsing commitments as mature speakers. This conclusion, as in the previous case, is also supported by independent evidence. In a landmark study, Trueswell et al. (1999) showed that preschoolers demonstrated little to no ability to revise initial parsing commitments involved in sentences containing temporarily ambiguous prepositional phrases (e.g., *Put the frog on the napkin in the box*). Summarizing what we have learned about the way preschoolers process language in real time over the last decade, Snedeker (2009) arrives at the same conclusion.

Thus, the kindergarten path approach to children's isomorphic behavior is compatible with what we know about how quantifier scope ambiguities are resolved, as well as how children process language in real time. Importantly, on this view, the kind of preference for surface scope that we have been discussing is one of many interacting factors that contributes to the interpretation of a sentence. Moreover, such a preference only represents a probabilistic tendency, which means that its effects can be mitigated – if not outright eliminated – by other, interacting factors. For example, one of the many factors that is known for its role in alleviating garden-path effects is contextual information (e.g., Crain and Steedman 1985; Altman and Steedman 1988; Tanenhaus et al. 1995, among many others). On this view, it is not surprising to find that when certain contextual features are manipulated, as in the studies by Musolino (2000), Musolino and Lidz (2006), and Gualmini (2004) discussed in the previous section, children's isomorphic behavior is significantly reduced.

On the original account proposed by Musolino (1998) and Musolino et al. (2000), OI was treated as a descriptive generalization, and the notion of Isomorphism itself was regarded as an epiphenomenon: an emerging property arising from the interaction of deeper grammatical principles. An interesting consequence of the demise of the grammatical view is that the notion of isomorphism, once regarded as a mere artifact, now lies at the heart of the garden-path approach. To be perfectly clear though, this does not mean that there is an 'Isomorphic principle' which predicts that the interpretation selected by children will always be the isomorphic one. Rather, in accordance with much recent work on language processing, isomorphism – qua the tendency to rely on surface scope – is regarded as one of the multiple factors that conspire to determine a final interpretation, which may of course ultimately differ from the isomorphic one.

3.3 *Isomorphism as a Pragmatic Epiphenomenon*

Building on the work of Gualmini (2004) discussed in the previous section, Gualmini and colleagues (Gualmini 2008; Gualmini et al. 2008) developed a radically different account of children's non-adult preferences which views OI as a pragmatic epiphenomenon. On this view, called the Question-Answer Requirement (QAR), the 'illusion of isomorphism' follows from a general pragmatic requirement that dictates which interpretation of an ambiguous sentence children (and adults) select, *regardless of the syntactic structure of that sentence*. Specifically, QAR rests on the assumption that a sentence is always understood as an answer to a question. The interpretation that children (and adults) select, in turn, must be a good answer to a Question under Discussion (QUD) (i.e., the salient question available in the context of a TVJT). An answer qualifies as a 'good answer' to a Yes/No question if it entails either the Yes or the No answer to that question. Finally, when both readings of an ambiguous sentence constitute good answers to the QUD, children (and adults) select a reading on the basis of the Principle of Charity according to which they will give a 'yes' answer whenever this is possible.

To illustrate the operation of QAR, let us return to Gualmini's (2004) 'pizza story' discussed in the previous section. Recall that in that story, a Troll has to deliver four pizzas, but he ends up losing two of them. In the end therefore, the Troll delivers only two pizzas. Consider (9) and (10) as descriptions of what happened in the pizza story. Recall that both sentences are false on an isomorphic interpretation (not>some), because it is not true that the Troll delivered or lost none of the pizzas: the two that were lost were obviously not delivered, and the two that were delivered were not lost. On the other hand, the sentences are both true on a non-isomorphic interpretation (some>not) because there are indeed some pizzas that were not delivered – the two that were lost – or lost – the two that were delivered.

(9) The Troll didn't deliver some pizzas.

    (a) It is not the case that the Troll delivered some pizzas = the Troll didn't deliver any pizzas (FALSE)

    (b) There are some pizzas that the Troll didn't deliver (TRUE)

(10) The Troll didn't lose some pizzas

    (a) It is not the case that the Troll lost some pizzas = The Troll didn't lose any pizzas (FALSE)

    (b) There are some pizzas that the Troll didn't lose (TRUE)

Since it is made clear in the context of the story that the Troll has to deliver all the pizzas, Gualmini et al. (2008) take (11) to be the relevant QUD.

(11) Will the Troll deliver all the pizzas?

To illustrate the mechanics of the QAR, consider the target sentence in (9) uttered as a description of the pizza story. In this case, both readings of (9) are good answers to the QUD in (11). To see why, notice that (9a), which can be paraphrased as meaning that Troll didn't deliver any of the pizzas, clearly entails a negative answer to the question of whether the Troll has delivered all the pizzas. Similarly, (9b), which can be paraphrased as meaning that there are some pizzas that were not delivered, also entails a negative answer to the QUD in (11). In this case, since both interpretations of the target sentence constitute good answers to the QUD, the final arbiter is the principle of charity which compels children to select the interpretation that is true in the context under consideration, namely the non-isomorphic interpretation in (9b). Thus, the QAR predicts that children will interpret (9) non-isomorphically, as is indeed the case in the study conducted by Gualmini (2004).

Let us now turn to the example in (10). According to Gualmini et al. (2008), the wide scope reading of (10), (7b), does not constitute a good answer to (11) because the fact that there are some pizzas that the Troll didn't lose (which is equivalent to saying that there are some pizzas that the troll delivered) does not entail that the Troll either delivered or failed to deliver all the pizzas. On the other hand, the narrow scope reading of (10), (10a), does constitute a good answer to (11) since saying that the Troll didn't lose any of the pizzas is equivalent to saying that he delivered them all. Thus, the QAR correctly predicts that children should display a preference for the narrow scope interpretation of (10), (10a), since only it constitutes a good answer to the QUD in (11).

At this point, it is important to observe that the narrow scope reading of (10) also happens to be the isomorphic interpretation of (10). The pivotal difference between the garden-path approach to isomorphism and the QAR should now be clear: whereas isomorphism takes children's scope preferences to be a direct consequence of the surface syntactic position of the quantificational elements involved, QAR does not assign any privileged status to surface c-command relations – or syntactic structure more generally – and thus treats isomorphism as an epiphenomenon.

In order to test the predictions of QAR, and compare the results to the set of sentences tested by Musolino (1998), Gualmini et al. (2008) investigated children's (and adults') interpretation of sentences like (12–14).

(12) a. Some pizzas were not delivered.
b. Some pizzas were not lost.
(13) The Troll didn't deliver two pizzas.
(14) Every letter wasn't delivered.

For sentences like (12), these authors report the same pattern of results as the ones where the QNP occurs in object position, i.e. (9–10). That is, children overwhelmingly accept sentences like (12a) on the reading where some takes wide scope over negation, whereas in the case of sentences like (12b), children accept the same reading much less often. In other words, the same pattern of results obtains whether the QNPs occur in subject or object position, not what one would expect on the garden-path theory of isomorphism according to Gualmini et al. (2008). Finally, these authors report that in the experiments they ran to assess children's interpretation of sentences like (13–14), using stories modeled after Gualmini's (2004) pizza story, preschoolers overwhelmingly accepted the target sentences on their non-isomorphic interpretations, unlike what had been previously reported in the literature (e.g., Musolino 1998; Lidz and Musolino 2002; Musolino and Lidz 2006).[5]

In addition to offering a new account of children's interpretation of quantifier-negation ambiguities, Gualmini (2008) makes two important, additional claims. The first is that we should abandon the notion of isomorphism altogether, be it a descriptive generalization, as in Musolino (1998), or one of the factors contributing to children's behavior, as in Musolino and Lidz (2003, 2006), and, consequently, that broader conclusions based on the notion of Isomorphism have to be reconsidered. The following two quotes from Gualmini (2008) illustrate these points:

> We argue that the observation of Isomorphism has no place in our theory of child language. In particular, we highlight the theoretical and empirical shortcomings of current theories which attribute a privileged role to surface scope in children's parsing (e.g., Musolino and Lidz 2006). Furthermore, we show that the Observation of Isomorphism cannot even be invoked to describe children's non-adult behavior ... (p. 1158)
>
> Having argued that there is no reason to assume that surface scope interpretations have a privileged status in children's grammar, it is important to consider what consequences can be drawn. This amounts to re-examining the consequences that have been drawn on the basis of the incorrect hypothesis that children display a preference for surface scope interpretations. In particular, we consider how Isomorphism has been brought to bear on experimental methodology, the role of the input for language acquisition, learnability and the time-course of parsing. (p. 1172)

---

[5]In the next section, I discuss possible reasons for this discrepancy.

The spirit of this approach is aptly captured by the title of Gualmini's (2008) article, 'The rise and fall of Isomorphism'. In the next section, I turn to an evaluation of the QAR.

4 Assessing the QAR

We all agree that the context in which ambiguous sentences are presented plays an important role in determining which interpretation children (and adults) eventually select. Thus, in trying to formalize the role played by contextual factors, Gualmini and colleagues are definitely on to something important. Another desirable feature of the QAR – which is an improvement over the garden-path approach – is that Gualmini's model actually makes predictions regarding when one should expect children to behave isomorphically and when one should not. Finally, the QAR forces us to look at old puzzles in new ways. For example, work by Krämer (2000) revealed a pattern in Dutch-speaking children which is the opposite of the one originally described by Musolino (1998). That is, children, unlike adults, were found to behave non-isomorphically in their interpretation of sentences containing indefinite QNPs and negation. As pointed out by Gualmini, the QAR approach offers a new way to make sense of this apparently contradictory set of results (Unsworth and Gualmini 2008). Based on the ideas developed in the QAR approach, these authors propose that the behavior of Dutch and English-speaking children, while superficially paradoxical, can in fact be explained in the same way: in both cases, children select the interpretation that answers the relevant QUDs. Let me now turn to Gualmini's three claims, namely (a) that the QAR is all we need to explain the relevant set of facts, (b) that there is no place in our theory of child language for the notion of isomorphism, and (c) that the consequences that have been drawn on the basis of OI must be reconsidered. Let us begin with (b). Here, it is now clear that OI cannot be invoked as a descriptive generalization of the relevant set of facts, for the obvious reason that we have learned since Musolino (1998) that children do not always behave isomorphically when it comes to interpreting sentences containing quantified NPs and negation. The best we can say now is that children *sometimes* behave isomorphically.

However, the QAR approach takes this conclusion one step further in claiming that reliance on surface scope should not even be considered as one of the factors involved in the comprehension process, regardless of which interpretation is ultimately selected. To quote Gualmini:

> Given that children can access either interpretation of a scopally ambiguous sentence, assuming that children have little or no ability to revise their initial commitment, the reasonable conclusion to draw is that inverse scope may be the first interpretation entertained by children's parsers. As far as the interpretive component of the parser is concerned there is no reason to assume that surface scope interpretations have a privileged status. (p. 1174)

However, what is known about this topic points to a different conclusion regarding the status of surface scope. Indeed, recall from our previous discussion that surface scope interpretations are theoretically, psychologically, and statistically privileged. So there are indeed good reasons to believe that surface scope interpretations are privileged as far as the parser is concerned (see Tunstall 1998; Anderson 2004;

and Conroy 2008 for a review of the relevant facts as well as new experimental evidence). Moreover, one of Anderson's (2004) conclusions is that the cost associated with the computation of inverse scope is also measurable in contexts that support the inverse scope interpretation, and, more strikingly, even when the sentence is unambiguous and only allows an inverse scope reading.

Now of course, quantifier-negation ambiguities in child language may be a totally different beast and challenge everything we know about scope ambiguity resolution and parsing. But this should certainly not be the default assumption, and given what is known, the burden of proof would seem to fall on those claiming that we should take a radical departure from our present state of understanding. Of course, this issue can be settled empirically, for example by collecting online data to determine the incremental signature of the comprehension process in this specific case; a research effort that we are currently undertaking. At any rate, until we know more about how quantifier-negation ambiguities are resolved in real time (by children and adults), we should keep an open mind about the potential factors involved.

Let us now consider (a), namely the claim that the QAR is all we need to account for the relevant set of facts. In this regard, Gualmini (2008) concludes that "despite the concerns raised by Musolino and Lidz (2003), the empirical coverage of the QAR theory is remarkable." However, a closer inspection of the account proposed by Gualmini and colleagues reveals that the overall case for the QAR remains to be made. The main reason for this state of affairs lies in the way proponents of the QAR have chosen, at least so far, to test their ideas. Given that the QAR makes very clear predictions, there would be an easy way to proceed: design a controlled set of studies aimed at directly testing the predictions of the QAR. Instead, the authors chose a different path which relies in large part on post-hoc speculation and questionable experimental methodology. Consequently, all we can say for sure is that context matters, a conclusion that all parties to this debate have been in agreement about for a while now. Whether context actually matters *in the way the QAR predicts* remains an open question. But even if it did, there is now growing evidence that an account like the QAR is only one piece of the isomorphic puzzle.

Let us first consider what would seem to be a straightforward way to test the predictions of the QAR. Recall from our previous discussion (Sect. 3.3) that a key question for the QAR has to do with trying to decide, for any given story, what the relevant Question under Discussion (QUD) should be. Given the mechanics described in Sect. 3.3, this step is crucial. Indeed, recall that the nature of the lexical items contained in the QUD determines the relevant entailment patterns, and thus, which of the two readings of an ambiguous sentence constitutes a 'good answer'. What this means is that the QAR is exquisitely sensitive to the kind of expressions contained in QUDs, since different verbs, quantifiers, etc. give rise to different entailment patterns.

So to build a strong case, it would be preferable to not have to guess, post-hoc, what the QUD might have been. An easy way to circumvent this problem, as pointed out by Musolino and Lidz (2003), and acknowledged by Gualmini et al. (2008),[6]

---

[6] Indeed, Gualmini et al. (2008) remark that "… the particular way in which the story is told is not the only way to make explicit the Question under Discussion. An obvious possibility would be for the experimenter to ask the question explicitly of the puppet at the end of the story" (p. 214).

would be to make the QUD explicit, which would allow experimenters to carefully control and manipulate their content. The next step would be to test children in different conditions, including a baseline condition, so as to show that manipulating stories/QUDs according to the predictions of the QAR indeed has the desired effects. The baseline condition could be one of the stories used by Musolino (1998) to document the Isomorphic effect in the first place. Critical conditions would contain explicit QUDs predicted to lead children to behave isomorphically or non-isomorphically. And of course, this should be systematically done for the various constructions tested by Musolino (1998). To the extent that children were found behave according to the predictions of the QAR under those conditions, one would have solid evidence supporting the account proposed by Gualmini and colleagues.

However, this is not how proponents of the QAR proceeded. In their main published study on this topic, Gualmini et al. (2008) present three experiments designed to test the predictions of the QAR by assessing the way children and adults interpret the sentences in (15–16). In those experiments, however, the QUDs are never made explicit and are always reconstructed post-hoc, baseline conditions are not used, critical factors such as age of the child participants and target materials are not controlled for, and in spite of these serious problems and confounds, Gualmini et al. (2008) reach their conclusion by comparing results across studies conducted by different authors.

(15) a. The Troll didn't deliver two pizzas.
b. Every letter wasn't delivered.

(16) a. Some pizzas were not delivered
b. Some pizzas were not lost.

For example, these authors presented children with sentences like *Every letter wasn't delivered* in the context of a story in which the main character delivered only three of the four letters he was supposed to deliver. In the end, therefore, the isomorphic reading (every>not) is false, because three letters were delivered, and the non-isomorphic reading (not>every) is true, because not all the letters were delivered. In this case, the QAR predicts, according to Gualmini et al. (2008), that children should select the non-isomorphic interpretation (not>every), and these authors report that the preschoolers they tested did so 80% of the time; a rate that is much higher than the one reported in previous studies (e.g., Musolino 1998; Musolino and Lidz 2006). These results, the authors conclude, provide evidence for the QAR.

What is there to complain about? If the devil is in the details, this is precisely what is wrong here. So let's take a closer look at the details. The first problem is that the authors only guessed, post-hoc, what the relevant QUD was, which allows them to select precisely what they needed for the account to go through. We'll see when we consider their next experiment how much of a problem this is. The second problem is that the age of the children that Gualmini et al. (2008) tested is very different from that of the children tested in the other two studies that these authors compare their results to in order to make their claim, namely Musolino (1998) and Musolino and Lidz (2006). Indeed, the children tested by Gualmini et al. were between the ages of 3;0 and 5;11 (mean age=4;8) whereas the children tested by Musolino

(1998) and Musolino and Lidz (2006) were between the ages of 4;0 and 7;3 (mean age = 5;11), and 5;0 and 5;11 (mean age = 5;4), respectively. So the children tested by Gualmini et al. were on average about a year younger than the ones tested in previous studies and the range differed by up to two years. Such differences are crucial in light of results reported by Conroy et al. (2009) who show that while 5-year-olds tested on sentences like *Every N didn't VP* do behave isomorphically, as reported in previous studies, 4-year-olds do not. Instead, the younger children in Conroy et al. (2009) did not behave differently from adults and were found to accept non-isomorphic interpretations 81% of the time, which is almost identical to the 80% rate of acceptance reported by Gualmini et al. (2008).[7] What this means, of course, is that Gualmini et al.'s results could be due to age and have nothing to do with the QAR.

A third problem is that the materials Gualmini et al. (2008) used in their experiment differ from the ones used in previous studies in that they contain passive sentences instead of active ones (e.g., *Every letter wasn't delivered* vs. *Every horse didn't jump over the fence*) as well as a different choice of predicates, two factors known to affect comprehension in the psycholinguistic literature, including the literature on scope ambiguity. This brings us to a fourth, related problem, namely the fact that Gualmini et al., in spite of the obvious confounds just mentioned (i.e., different ages and materials), did not report using any baseline or control conditions against which to assess performance in their experimental condition. In the end, therefore, there is simply no way of knowing what caused children's high acceptance rates, and therefore, such results cannot be taken as evidence supporting the QAR.

Let us now consider Gualmini et al.'s (2008) second experiment, designed to test sentences like *The Troll didn't deliver two pizzas* (12a). Here these authors conjecture, post-hoc, that the relevant QUD is *Did the Troll deliver all the pizzas*, presumably because the Troll's job was to deliver the pizzas. Given this QUD, Gualmini and al. point out that only the non-isomorphic reading of (12a), (two > not), represents a 'good answer'. Indeed, saying that there are two pizzas that the Troll didn't deliver entails a no answer to the question of whether the Troll delivered all the pizzas. In this case, Gualmini et al. (2008) report that the group of children they tested accepted the target sentences on their non-isomorphic interpretation 75% of the time, again a higher percentage compared to the ones reported in previous studies (e.g., Lidz and Musolino 2002), hence the conclusion that these results provide support for the QAR.

The problem here is that it is not clear at all that children's elevated acceptance rate is due to the QAR. To see this, consider the study by Lidz and Musolino (2002), designed to test children's interpretation of sentences like *The detective didn't find two guys*. In the relevant condition, such sentences were used in the context of a story where a detective, Donald, and four of his friends play hide-and-seek.

---

[7] In the analysis proposed by Conroy, Lidz, and Musolino (2009), this U-shaped developmental trajectory is argued to derive from the development of parsing mechanisms that generate multiple interpretations of an ambiguous sentence as well as processes involved in selecting or revising among these alternatives.

In the end, Donald manages to find two of his friends, but he fails to find the other two. Thus, in this context, the non-isomorphic reading, (two>not) is true, because there are indeed two friends that Donald didn't find, and the isomorphic reading, (not>two), is false, because Donald found exactly two of his friends. Given that the story was about hide-and-seek, and that Donald was therefore expected to try to find all of his friends, it would make sense, following Gualmini et al.'s (2008) reasoning, to assume that the relevant QUD, like in their pizza story, would be something like *Did Donald find all of his friends?*.

The problem should now be clear: the QAR would predict in this case too that children should show a marked preference for the non-isomorphic interpretation of sentences like *The detective didn't find two guys* for precisely the reasons discussed by Gualmini et al. (2008) in the context of their pizza story. But this is not what happened. Here, children displayed a strong preference for the isomorphic interpretation instead, and only accepted the non-isomorphic interpretation a third of the time. One could argue that if taken at face value, the data reported by Lidz and Musolino (2002) falsify the QAR, or at least demonstrate that it is not a sufficient condition on scope interpretation. A proponent of the QAR might reply that perhaps the QUD in Lidz and Musolino's (2002) detective story was different from the one mentioned above. But who's to decide and on what basis? This highlights a fundamental problem for the QAR as currently tested: in order to assess the predictions of this new model, one cannot go about guessing what the QUDs might have been, in one's own experiments as well as those of others, when it would be easy to make those questions explicit and remove the need to rely on post-hoc speculation. Finally, Gualmini et al.'s (2008) third experiment designed to test children's interpretation of sentences containing *some* in subject position, as in (13), suffers from some of the same problems. Their results go in one direction but results reported by Musolino (1998) go in the opposite direction, leading Gualmini et al. to speculate that perhaps the stories used by Musolino didn't "readily suggest a specific question that could only be addressed by the inverse scope interpretation …" (p. 226).

In sum, what seems to be clear is that children can access both isomorphic and non-isomorphic interpretations of scopally ambiguous sentences, and that the context in which these sentences are presented matters. For all the reasons discussed above, whether the context matters in the way described by the QAR remains an open question. Moreover, there is now growing evidence that even if the QAR was one of the factors involved in determining which interpretation children ultimately select, it would not be the only factor.

Let me now briefly discuss the results of two studies that point in this direction. The first was conducted by Musolino and Gualmini (2004) who tested children's interpretation of sentences like (17).

(17) a. The Smurf caught all the cats but she didn't catch two birds
     b. The Smurf didn't catch two of the birds

These sentences were tested in the same kinds of contexts which should have given rise to the same QUDs. Therefore, children should have accessed the same interpretation in both cases, presumably the non-isomorphic interpretation if we follow Gualmini et al.'s (2008) logic. However, what Musolino and Gualmini (2004) found is that children interpreted (17a) isomorphically, replicating Lidz and Musolino's (2002) results, but that they interpreted (17b) non-isomorphically. This shows that the presence of a partitive construction is enough to push children away from their isomorphic tendencies, a fact that seems to have little to do with felicity, context, or QUDs. What this demonstrates is that the QAR cannot be the only factor at play here, and that lexical factors may be an important part of the isomorphic equation, a conclusion that is hardly surprising in light of what we have learned about sentence processing over the last 20 years.

A similar conclusion was reached by Viau et al. (2010) who investigated the role of priming in the interpretation of scopally ambiguous sentences. Focusing on the case of sentences like *Every horse didn't jump over the fence*, these authors showed that the non-isomorphic interpretation of such sentences can be primed in ways that are inexplicable on the QAR. In one of their experiments, Viau et al. tested children in two conditions: a baseline condition and a priming condition. In both conditions, context was held constant and sentences were used in stories that have been found to elicit isomorphic responses from children. So by Gualmini et al.'s (2008) standards, those contexts must have given rise to QUDs for which only the isomorphic reading of the target sentences were good answers. In the baseline condition, children heard two blocks of three stories followed by target sentences like *Every horse didn't jump over the fence*. Not surprisingly, in both blocks, children behave isomorphically. In the priming condition, children also heard two blocks of three stories for which the contexts were identical to the ones in the baseline condition. In the first block, the stories were described by statements like *Not every horse jumped over the fence*, which are unambiguous and must receive a non-isomorphic interpretation. Those were the primes. In the second block, following the primes, children heard sentences like *Every horse didn't jump over the fence* in contexts found to elicit isomorphic interpretations in the baseline condition. However, children assigned those sentences non-isomorphic interpretations significantly more often compared to the baseline condition, demonstrating that such readings can be primed by structural factors that have nothing to do with context, felicity or the QAR. The fact that non-isomorphic readings can be primed entails that the language processor must be involved (Branigan 2007; Viau et al. 2010), and thus that QAR cannot be the whole story.

5 Isomorphism as a Research Program

Throughout this chapter, the notion of Isomorphism has played a central role in our discussion of the phenomena under consideration. In this section, I would like to take a closer look at this notion and ask: what exactly is Isomorphism? This question, I would like to argue, like the sentences we've been dealing with here, can be construed in two ways: narrowly and broadly. When narrowly construed, the question of what Isomorphism is amounts to asking whether isomorphism between syntactic and semantic structure plays any descriptive or causal role in our understanding of the way children (and adults) interpret scopally ambiguous sentences containing QNPs and negation. By contrast, the broad construal, hitherto not explicitly formulated, is what has been implicitly driving the work of Musolino and colleagues, as well as others, since Musolino's (1998) original formulation of OI. On this construal, Isomorphism is best understood as a research program. Let me first briefly consider the narrow view, and then turn to the broader interpretation to which the rest of this section is devoted.

I should begin by pointing out that the notion of Isomorphism, as narrowly construed, has undergone a number of transformations since Musolino (1998), and currently represents the main point of contention between the garden-path and the QAR approaches to OI discussed earlier. Recall that the term Isomorphism was initially used by Musolino (1998) as a descriptive label and viewed as a grammatical epiphenomenon. The demise of the grammatical account, in turn, implicitly propelled isomorphism to the front seat where this notion – qua tendency to rely on surface syntactic scope – came to be viewed as one of the causal factors at play in the way children and adults resolve scopally ambiguous sentences containing QNPs and negation (e.g., Musolino and Lidz 2003, 2006). With the advent of the QAR, Isomorphism was demoted to its earlier status of an epiphenomenon, albeit a pragmatic one this time, instead of a grammatical one. Thus, when Gualmini (2008) announced the end of Isomorphism – prematurely as we saw in Sect. 4 – he primarily attacked the narrow view, although he also clearly argued that the consequences of Isomorphism for experimental methodology, learnability, as well as the development of language processing abilities had to be reconsidered as well.

While some of the points offered by Gualmini (2008) are indeed well–taken,[8] as acknowledged in Sect. 4, his general approach fails to consider Isomorphism more broadly and realize that over the last decade the observation described by Musolino (1998) has led to a productive research program. Although research programs are usually discussed in the context of mathematics and the physical sciences (e.g., Hunt 1991), they nevertheless represent an important part of the scientific process for many disciplines, as discussed for example by Boeckx (2006) for linguistics and demonstrated by Pinker's (1999) words and rules approach. Focusing on the case of the German mathematician David Hilbert and what came to be known as Hilbert's program, Boeckx explains that "Hilbert proposed a set of guidelines, sketched a project …More than the task of a single individual, it was like a manifesto, a call for papers, a large scale project …" (p. 87).

In developing his methodology of research programs, the philosopher of science Imre Lakatos identified two key properties that are relevant in the present context (Lakatos 1970). The first is that research programs revolve around a 'core' which

---

[8] Another point made by Gualmini with which I agree is that the approach discussed in Musolino and Lidz (2006) which tries to relate preschoolers' isomorphic behavior in the case of sentences like *Every horse didn't jump over the fence* to their difficulty with scalar implicature (e.g., Noveck, 2001; Papafragou and Musolino, 2003) is problematic.

has a logico-empirical character and is viewed as being irrefutable. In the case at hand, the core would be the empirical observation that, under certain experimental conditions, preschoolers differ from adults in the way they interpret sentences containing QNPs and negation, an observation that has now been replicated many times, and thus cannot be refuted. Another important property of research programs is that are not evaluated in terms of right or wrong. Instead, programs are regarded as either fertile or sterile, or 'progressive' and 'degenerative' to use Lakatos' own terminology. To quote Boeckx again "progressive programs generate new families of questions, create new problems and conflicts, which they may or may not solve, but which might have gone unnoticed without the crucial change in perspective which programs typically generate" (p. 90).

Viewed as a research program built around a 'core' developmental observation, Isomorphism seems to possess the hallmarks of a progressive one. Indeed, over the last decade, the body of work addressing the phenomena uncovered by Musolino (1998) and its broader implications has grown, spawning new studies and establishing new links between different research areas. In trying to organize these developments, I find it useful to think about them as falling in four categories: (a) implications for models of language acquisition, (b) rapprochement between different research areas, (c) implications for linguistic theory, and (d) reconsideration of prior assumptions. In the remainder of this section, I discuss these developments by reviewing key studies in each of these four categories.

Beginning with (a), recall that the results of Musolino's (1998) study were initially taken as evidence supporting a Chomskyan/UG model of language acquisition. To quote Musolino (1998), "To the extent that this goal is achieved, the present investigation emphasizes the role played by the theory of Universal Grammar and language learnability in helping us understand language development and its biological basis" (p. 2). With the demise of the grammatical account, claims regarding implications of OI for UG-based models lost steam. At the same time, other researchers interested in the isomorphic puzzle offered different accounts of the facts uncovered by Musolino (1998). For example, Gennari and MacDonald (2005/2006) proposed a constraint-based account of quantifier scope interpretation in children inspired by recent models of language production and comprehension in adults. They key difference between Musolino's (1998) original account and the one proposed by Gennari and MacDonald is that children's non-adult behavior is regarded as reflecting their sensitivity to distributional patterns of language use rather than the operation of UG-constrained parameters.

Notice that the garden-path approach to OI discussed in Sect. 3.2 is in principle compatible with Gennari and MacDonald's constraint-satisfaction account. Yet a different account of OI was offered by O'Grady (2008) who proposed what he called a 'processor-based emergentist' account of the facts. The main idea underlying O'Grady's account is very similar in spirit to Reinhart (2006), Tunstall (1998), and Anderson (2004) in that it views non-isomorphic interpretations as computationally costly from the point of view of the parser. Again, this account doesn't seem too different from Musolino and Lidz's (2003, 2006) garden-path approach (see Sect. 3.2). A key difference between O'Grady's (2008) account and the one proposed by Gennari and MacDonald (2005/2006) is that on the emergentist view, the frequency of certain sentences in the input, or certain sentence-interpretation pairings, is a consequence of children's interpretive preferences rather than their cause. In other words, certain interpretations are difficult, and sentences with those interpretations are rare, because of the way the parser is designed to operate.

Parsing considerations, in turn, lead us to (b), the idea that Isomorphism – qua research program – calls for a rapprochement between the fields of language development and language processing. In a 1998 review article on ambiguity in sentence processing, Gerry Altmann raised the following as an outstanding question: Do children process ambiguous sentences in qualitatively the same way as adults do? (p. 151). Since then a growing body of work on children's real time language comprehension has emerged, directly bearing on Altmann's question (Trueswell et al. 1999; Snedeker and Trueswell 2004; Snedeker and Yuan 2008; Huang and Snedeker, in press; among others). What this work reveals is that by and large, preschoolers process language the way adults do. In both cases comprehension is incremental in the sense that listeners do not wait until the end of a sentence to generate hypotheses about its meaning, and like adults, children use multiple sources of information to constrain parsing and converge on the most likely analysis of an unfolding sentence.

However, there are also important differences between the two populations. Snedeker (2009) summarizes the situation as follows: "Preschoolers and adults are different in some respects: children make poorer use of context, are slower to inhibit competing alternatives, and have difficulty revising their interpretation in light of conflicting evidence. One is tempted to conclude that changes in language processing during the school years largely reflect the development of control processes." In this regard, work on Isomorphism – which is about how children resolve scopal ambiguities – can be very informative and add to this growing body of work. For one thing, the facts that we discussed throughout this chapter fit well with the overall picture described by Snedeker, and thus allow us to broaden the empirical basis upon which claims regarding the development of sentence processing abilities can be evaluated. An important question that remains to be directly addressed in the case of Isomorphism is the extent to which the computational costs associated with non-isomorphic interpretations already reported to affect real time comprehension in adults (e.g., Tunstall 1998; Anderson 2004), can also be measured in children, thereby lending support to the garden-path approach to OI discussed in Sect. 3.2.

In sum, a phenomenon that was initially believed to represent a case of grammatical development, explained in terms of parameter setting and the subset principle, turned out to offer, as more results surfaced, a window onto the developing language comprehension system. In the process, old views were abandoned, and new questions and ideas emerged – e.g., the garden-path approach, the QAR – as links between the area of language development and language processing began to crystallize. As mentioned earlier, this shift in perspective also gave rise to work exploring the roots of Isomorphism in adults, Conroy (2008), and the role played by priming in the development of this comprehension process (Viau, Lidz, and Musolino 2010).

Let us now consider (c), the implications of Isomorphism for linguistic theory. The main idea that I would like to illustrate here is that Isomorphism can be used as a tool to shed light on a number of issues of theoretical interest to linguists as well as developmental psychologists. To begin, consider the question of why children behaved isomorphically in Musolino's (1998) study. As pointed out by Musolino (1998), this observation is compatible with the fact that children rely on the linear arrangement between QNPs and negation to determine their relative interpretation. To be sure, subject NPs precede negation in English and object NPs follow it, which may account for why children tend to interpret subjects outside the scope of negation and objects within its scope. The rule here would be something like: material that follows negation is interpreted within its scope. Another possibility, of course, is that children pay attention to surface c-command relations. In this case, the rule would be: material that falls in the surface c-command domain of negation is interpreted within its scope. However, notice that since objects, but not subjects, are c-commanded by negation in the surface string, an account of children behavior in terms of c-command or linear order makes the same predictions.

In order to tease apart the effects of linear order and c-command, Lidz and Musolino (2002) tested preschoolers in two languages: English and Kannada (Dravidian).[9] Kannada represents an ideal testing case for the issue at hand because sentences like *Cookie Monster didn't eat two slices of pizza* are ambiguous in this language in the same way that they are in English, but because Kannada is an SOV language, linear order and c-command relations, at least as far as objects and negation are concerned, are not confounded. Thus, whereas in English objects both follow and are c-commanded by negation, in Kannada, objects are c-commanded by negation, but they precede it. What this means is that to the extent that Kannada-speaking 4-year-olds, like their English-speaking counterparts, display a preference for one of the two readings of sentences like *Cookie Monster didn't eat two slices of pizza*, an account of that preference in terms of an overreliance on surface c-command relations predicts that we should find the same pattern as in English – because c-command relations between the object and negation are the same in both languages – whereas an account of children's preference in terms of an overreliance on linear order, predicts opposite patterns in the two languages because objects follow negation in English but they precede it in Kannada.

What Lidz and Musolino (2002) found is that Kannada-speaking 4-year-olds do indeed display a significant preference for one of the two readings of ambiguous sentences like *Cookie Monster didn't eat two slices of pizza* but, more importantly, that the patterns are identical in Kannada and English. This result, in turn, demonstrates that preschoolers' preferences are constrained by surface c-command relations, and not linear order. Notice that this conclusion holds, regardless of what causes children to differ from adults. Thus, Lidz and Musolino (2002) used the kind of systematic difference between children and adults uncovered by Musolino (1998)

---

[9] For a similar approach involving different linguistic phenomena, see Solan (1983) and Crain et al. (2002).

as a way to find evidence in children's linguistic representations for the hierarchical structure and the abstract relations defined over these structures (i.e., c-command) that linguists take to be at the heart of our grammatical knowledge.

In a similar vein, Lidz and Musolino (2005/2006) used the kind of behavior reported by Musolino (1998) to shed some light on the theory of indefinites. Such theories vary with respect to whether these NPs can be treated as quantificational (Chung and Ladusaw 2004; Diesing 1992; Fodor and Sag 1982; Heim 1982; Kamp 1981; Kratzer 1995; van Geenhoven 1995). These considerations introduce a potential complication regarding the interpretation of Lidz and Musolino's (2002) conclusion that 4-year-olds have difficulty accessing the wide scope interpretation of numerically quantified NPs – indefinites – in sentences like *Cookie Monster didn't eat two slices of pizza*. The possibility explored by Lidz and Musolino is that children treat numerically quantified NPs as quantificational and that they have a bias to interpret quantified NPs in general isomorphically. An alternative interpretation is that children disprefer non-isomorphic interpretations in this case because they treat indefinites as individual variables bound by VP-internal existential closure, i.e., as non-quantificational.

To tease apart these two hypotheses, Lidz and Musolino (2005/2006) tested preschoolers on their interpretation of sentences containing numerically quantified NPs in subject position, e.g., *Two butterfly didn't go to the city*. On the non-quantificational analysis, children should treat indefinite subjects the way they treat indefinite objects and interpret both within the scope of negation. By contract, on the quantificational analysis, one would expect interpretation to vary as a function of syntactic position. What Lidz and Musolino (2005/2006) found is that the latter conclusion is supported by the data, suggesting that indefinites can be quantificational for children, and presumably for adults as well. In a similar vein, Han, Lidz, and Musolino (2007) used the way preschoolers and adults interpret sentences containing QNPs and negation to shed some light on the question of whether Korean is a verb-raising language.

Finally turning to (d), the research program that grew out of Musolino's (1998) study has also led to a reconsideration of prior assumptions in the areas of experimental methodology and learnability theory. Regarding the latter, a core principle of Crain and Thornton's (1998) Modularity Matching Model is a learnability constraint called the Semantic Subset Principle (SSP). In a nutshell, the SSP guides children in the acquisition of semantics by ensuring that they do not fall prey to the learnability traps associated with ambiguous sentences whose readings asymmetrically entail one another. The SSP predicts that children will learn the meaning of such sentences in a piecemeal fashion, starting with the entailing reading, and adding the entailed reading on the basis of subsequent evidence from the input. A textbook example of such a sentence is one like *Every horse didn't jump over the fence* where the isomorphic reading, (every > not) asymmetrically entails the non-isomorphic reading (not > every).[10]

---

[10] Indeed, if it is true that none of the horses jumped over the fence, it necessarily follows that not all of them did.

A consequence of this fact is that the way children interpret sentences containing QNPs and negation directly bears on the predictions of the SSP. Trying to work out these predictions, in turn, naturally leads to a systematic evaluation of the logical basis of the SSP as well as its empirical coverage. This is yet another case where isomorphism as a research program forces us to ask new questions and reconsider old assumptions. In doing so, Musolino (2006a, b) offered a detailed evaluation of the SSP and concluded that its logic and current implementation were flawed and that the empirical evidence supporting such a putative constraint was in fact nonexistent. Interestingly, Gualmini (2008) takes issue with this conclusion on the grounds that the isomorphic pattern reported by Musolino (1998) does not represent an accurate picture of the data now available, and therefore that there is no real threat to the SSP. What Musolino (2006) showed, however, is that the problems faced by the SSP run much deeper and that in all probability semantic subset problems of the type discussed by Crain and Thornton do not exist in the first place. Moreover, even if they did, none of the facts currently available in the area of quantifier-negation interaction, regardless of how one wants to characterize them, support a constraint like the SSP in any way. Furthermore, it is worth pointing out that Gualmini himself has also embraced the general conclusion reached by Musolino (2006), namely that we do not need the SSP (Gualmini and Schwarz 2009).[11]

To end this section, let us now consider some of the methodological implications of Isomorphism (as a research program) for another central piece of Crain and Thornton's methodology, namely the Truth Value Judgment Task. There has been a perception in the field, no doubt reinforced by some of Crain and Thornton's impressive results, but also by specific claims these authors made, that the TVJK is in a way bulletproof and guarantees results that cannot be attributed to performance factors. To be sure, Crain and Thornton confidently assert that preschoolers are extremely charitable creatures, and that the TVJT all but guarantees that one will uncover unfiltered grammatical knowledge, as can be seen in the two quotes below:

> In our experience with children, we have been able to identify several factors that conspire to determine which reading of an ambiguous sentence is selected ... First, children pick the reading that makes an ambiguous sentence true in the context ... the assumption is that children want the puppet to say things that are true. That is, the child prefers to say "yes" if possible. (p. 211)
>
> [The TVJT is] relatively free from the influence of performance factors ... Even when children's behavior differs from that of adults, ... the responses can be confidently attributed to linguistic knowledge and not to performance factors. (p. 4)

It is worth pointing out that these very considerations led Musolino (1998) and then Musolino et al. (2000) to reject a performance account of children's non-adult behavior regarding the interpretation of ambiguous sentences containing QNPs and negation, and to favor instead the competence account discussed in Sect. 2.3. In the case of sentences like *Every horse didn't jump over the fence*, the reasoning was that

---

[11] Gualmini and Schwarz's argument is that children can exploit non-truth-conditional evidence or evidence from sentences containing downward entailing expressions, thereby solving the putative learnability problems identified by Crain and Thornton (1998) without recourse to the SSP.

adults have a preference for the non-isomorphic reading, (not>every), and that in the relevant experiment (see Sect. 2.2), that reading was true in the context of the story that children heard. Thus, given the assumptions illustrated in Crain and Thornton's quotes, if children possessed the right grammar, they would certainly have accepted such sentences when tested with the TVJT. The fact that they didn't invites is in large part what led Musolino et al. (2000) to conclude that children must not possess an adult-like grammar. Clearly what we have learned since Musolino's (1998) original results leads to a different conclusion, and underscores the fact that overconfidence in one's own methodology can lead to erroneous interpretations of developmental patterns, as discussed in more detail in Musolino and Lidz (2006).

6 Concluding Remarks

In the preface to *Words and Rules*, Steven Pinker tells us that his book tries to illuminate the nature of language and mind by focusing on a particular phenomenon and examining it from every angle imaginable. My goal is this chapter has been more modest, but the approach I have chosen is the same. I picked a specific topic within the acquisition of semantics and focused on what might at first glance look like an arcane generalization about the way preschoolers interpret sentences containing QNPs and negation. But as Pinker reminds us, seeing the world in a grain of sand is often the way of science. Thus, building on Musolino's (1998) original observation, I have shown that examining the way children handle quantificational interactions can illuminate much broader issues in domains such as linguistic theory, learnability theory, language development, experimental methodology, and the development of sentence processing and pragmatic abilities. Indeed, construed as a research program, Isomorphism provides a productive platform where new work on a variety of issues and topics of interest to linguists, psycholinguists, and developmental psychologists continues to be produced and to create new links between the different areas involved. As discussed earlier, there is currently a debate regarding whether reliance on surface scope has its place as a legitimate factor in our theories of language acquisition – the narrow notion of Isomorphism – but whatever the answer to this question turns out to be, one can expect that it will have little impact on the overall enterprise, just like the demise of the grammatical account proposed by Musolino (1998) and Musolino et al. (2000) didn't put an end to work on Isomorphism. In the end, what matters is not that we always find the right answers, but that we continue to try to ask interesting questions.

References

Altmann, G.T.M., and Steedman, M. 1988. Interaction with context during human sentence processing. *Cognition* 30: 191–238.
Anderson, C. 2004. The structure and real-time comprehension of quantifier scope ambiguity. Doctoral diss., Northwestern University, Evanston.

Berwick, R. 1985. *The acquisition of syntactic knowledge*. Cambridge, MA: MIT Press.
Boeckx, C. 2006. *Linguistic minimalism: Origins, methods, concepts, and aims*. New York: Oxford University Press.
Branigan, H. 2007. *Syntactic priming*. Language and Linguistics Compass 1(1–2): 1–16
Chung, S., and W. Ladusaw. 2004. *Restriction and saturation*. Cambridge, Massachusetts: MIT Press.
Conroy, A., J. Lidz, and J. Musolino. 2009. The fleeting isomorphism effect, *Language Acquisition* 16(2): 106–117.
Conroy, A. 2008. The role of verification strategies in semantic ambiguity resolution in children and adults. Doctoral diss., University of Maryland, College Park. Unpublished manuscript.
Crain, S., and M. Steedman 1985. On not being led up the garden path: The use of context by the psychological syntax processor. In Natural language parsing: Psychological, computational, and theoretical perspectives, eds. D.R. Dowty, L. Kartunnen, and A.M. Zwicky. Cambridge: Cambridge University Press.
Crain, S., and R. Thornton. 1998. *Investigations into universal grammar: A guide to experiments on the acquisition of syntax and semantics*. Cambridge, MA: MIT Press.
Crain, S., A. Gardner, A. Gualmini, and B. Rabbin. 2002. Children's command of negation. In *Proceedings of the Third Tokyo Conference on Psycholinguistics*, 71–95. Tokyo: Hituzi Publishing Company.
de Villiers, J., and T.F. Helen 1975. *Some facts one simply cannot deny*. Journal of Child Language 2: 279–286.
Diesing, M. 1992. *Indefinites*. Cambridge, Mass.: MIT Press.
Fodor, J.D., and I. Sag. 1982. "Referential and quantificational indefinites," *Linguistics and Philosophy* 5: 355–398.
Fox, D. 2000. *Economy and semantic interpretation*. Cambridge, MA: MIT Press.
Gennari, S., and M. MacDonald. 2005/2006. Acquisition of negation and quantification: Insights from adult production and comprehension. *Language Acquisition* 13(2): 125–168.
Gillen, K. 1991. The comprehension of doubly quantified sentences. Doctoral diss., University of Durham, Durham.
Gualmini, A. 2004. Some knowledge children don't lack. *Linguistics* 42(5): 957–982.
Gualmini, A. 2008. The rise and fall of Isomorphism. *Lingua* 118: 1158–1176.
Gualmini, A., S. Hulsey, V. Hacquard, and D. Fox. 2008. *The question-answer requirement for scope assignment*. Natural Language Semantics 16: 205–237.
Gualmini, A., and B. Schwarz. 2009. Solving Learnability Problems in the Acquisition of Semantics. *Journal of Semantics* 26: 185–215.
Han, C.H., J. Lidz, and J. Musolino. 2007. *Verb-raising and grammar competition in Korean: Evidence from negation and quantifier scope*. Linguistic Inquiry 38(1): 1–47.
Heim, I. 1982. *The Semantics of definite and indefinite noun phrases*. PhD thesis, University of Massachusetts, Amherst, GLSA, Dept. of Linguistics, South College, UMASS, Amherst MA 01003.
Hornstein, N. 1984. *Logic as grammar*. Cambridge, MA: The MIT Press.
Hornstein, N. 1995. *Logical form: From GB to minimalism*. Cambridge, MA: Blackwell.
Huang, Y., and J. Snedeker. (in press). *Cascading activation across levels of representation in children's lexical processing*. To appear in Journal of Child Language.
Hunt, S.D. 1991. Modern marketing theory: Critical issues in the philosophy of marketing science, Cincinnati, OH: South-Western.
Kamp, H. 1981. *A theory of truth and semantic representation*. Reprinted in Truth, interpretation, and information, eds. J. Groenendijk, et al. Dordrecht: Foris .
Krämer, I. 2000. Interpreting indefinites. PhD diss., Utrecht University, Utrecht.
Kratzer, A. 1995. "Stage and individual level predicates". In *The Generic Book*, eds. G. Carlson, and F. Pelletier. University of Chicago Press, Chicago.
Kurtzman, H., and M. MacDonald. 1993. Resolution of quantifier scope ambiguities'. *Cognition* 48: 243–279.

Lakatos, I. 1970. *Criticism and the growth of knowledge*. Cambridge: Cambridge University Press.
Lidz, J., and J. Musolino. 2002. Children's command of quantification. *Cognition* 84(2): 113–154.
Lidz, J., and J. Musolino. 2005/2006. On the quantificational status of indefinites: The view from child language. *Language Acquisition* 13(2): 73–102.
Musolino, J. 1998. Universal grammar and the acquisition of semantic knowledge: An experimental investigation of quantifier-negation interactions in English. Doctoral diss., University of Maryland, College Park.
Musolino, J. 2000. Universal quantification and the competence/performance distinction. Paper presented at the 25th Annual Boston University Conference on Language Development, Boston.
Musolino, J., and Lidz, J. 2003. The scope of Isomorphism: Turning adults into children', *Language Acquisition* 11(4): 277–291.
Musolino, J. 2006a. On the semantics of the subset principle. *Language Learning and Development* 2(3): 195–218.
Musolino, J. 2006b. *Structure and meaning in the acquisition of scope*. Dordrecht: Springer.
Musolino, J., and A. Gualmini. 2004. The role of partivity in child language. *Language Acquisition* 12(1): 97–107.
Musolino, J., and J. Lidz. 2003. The Scope of Isomorphisim: Turning adults into children. *Language Acquisition* 11(4): 277–291.
Musolino, J., and J. Lidz. 2006. Why children aren't universally successful with quantification. *Linguistics* 44(4): 817–852.
Musolino, J., S. Crain, and R. Thornton. 2000. Navigating negative quantificational space. *Linguistics* 38(1): 1–32.
Noveck, I. 2001. When children are more logical than adults: Experimental investigations of scalar implicature. *Cognition* 78: 165–188.
Noveck, I., R. Guelminger, N. Georgieff, and N. Labruyere. 2007. *What autism can reveal about every ... not sentences*. Journal of Semantics 24: 73–90.
O'Grady, W. 2008. Does emergentism have a chance? Paper presented at the Proceedings of the 32nd Annual Boston University Conference on Language Development, Somerville.
Papafragou, A., and J. Musolino. 2003. Scalar implicatures: Experiments at the syntax semantics interface. *Cognition* 78: 165–188.
Pica, P., and Snyder, W. 1995. "Weak crossover, scope, and agreement in a minimalist framework." In *Proceedings of the West Coast Conference on Formal Linguistics XIII*, eds. R. Aranovich et al. Stanford, CA: CSLI.
Pinker, S. 1999. *Words and rules: The ingredients of language*. New York: Basic Books.
Reinhart, T. 1995. *Interface strategies*. OTS Working Papers, TL-95-002. Utrecht: University of Utrecht.
Reinhart, T. 1997. Quantifier scope: How labor is divided between QR and choice functions. *Linguistics and Philosophy* 20: 335–397.
Reinhart, T. 2006. Scope shift with numeral indefinites – syntax or processing? In *Non-definiteness and plurality*, Linguistik Aktuell/Linguistics Today Series, ed. S. Vogeleer and L. Tasmowski, 291–311. Amsterdam/Philadelphia: John Benjamins.
Snedeker, J., and J. Trueswell. 2004. The developing constraints on parsing decisions: The role of lexical-biases and referential scenes in child and adult sentence processing. *Cognitive Psychology* 49(3): 238–299.
Snedeker, J. 2009. Smart, fast, and out of control: Language comprehension in preschoolers. Talk given at the Linguistics Department, University of Maryland, March 06.
Snedeker, J., and S. Yuan. 2008. Effects of prosodic and lexical constraints on parsing in young children (and adults). *Journal of Memory and Language* 58(2): 574–608.
Solan, L. 1983. *Pronominal reference*, D. Reidel, Dordrecht.
Tanenhaus, et al. 1995. Integration of visual and linguistic information in spoken language comprehension. *Science* 268: 1632–1634.
Trueswell, J.C., I.A. Sekerina, N. Hill, and M. Logrip. 1999. The Kindergarten path effect: Studying on-line sentence processing in young children. *Cognition* 73: 89–134.

Tunstall, S.L. 1998. The interpretation of quantifiers: Semantics and processing. Doctoral diss., University of Massachusetts, Amherst.
van Geenhoven, V. 1995. "Semantic incorporation: A uniform semantics for West Greenlandic noun incorporation and German bare plural configurations". In *Papers from the 31st Regional Meeting of the Chicago Linguistic Society*, eds. A. Dainora, R. Hemphill, B. Luka, B. Need, and S. Pargman. University of Chicago, Chicago: University of Chicago: University of Chicago: University of Chicago: University of Chicago.
VanLehn, K.A. 1978. Determining the scope of English quantifiers. Technical report, AI-TR-483. Artificial Intelligence Laboratory, Massachusetts Institute of Technology, Cambridge, MA.
Viau, J., J. Lidz, and J. Musolino. 2010. Priming of abstract logical representations in 4-year-olds. *Language Acquisition* 17(1): 26–50.
Wason, P. 1972. In real life negatives are false. *Logique et Analyse* 15: 17–38.
Wexler, K., and Manzini, M. Rita. 1987. *Parameters and learnability in binding theory*. In Parameter Setting eds. T. Roeper, and E. Williams, 41–76. Dordrecht: Reidel.

Acquiring Knowledge of Universal Quantification

William Philip

1 Introduction

Because of its complex properties, universal quantification has always intrigued linguists, philosophers, and cognitive scientists, especially those interested in first language acquisition (L1A). The complexity would appear to present a substantial challenge to the child language learner – a seemingly insurmountable challenge without the help of Universal Grammar (UG) or some other innate cognitive principles or mechanisms that guide and facilitate L1A by severely restricting the L1 learner's hypothesis space.[1]

The first objective of this paper is to examine what the L1A of universal quantification must consist in by analyzing the components of this knowledge and considering in each case whether or not its acquisition presents a logical problem, i.e. whether or not it could in principle be derived from the positive evidence by means of general learning mechanisms. Here we will focus on two key questions, namely (i) How does the child acquire knowledge of the logical operation that underlies the core meaning of universal quantifiers, and (ii) How does she come to know the linguistic constraints on this operation that shape the actual semantic value and syntactic properties of universal quantifiers? The analysis, together with a brief review of some relevant empirical observations, will lead to the general conclusion that much of the knowledge of universal quantification is innately specified and is fully acquired by the age of 4, if not earlier.

---

[1] Henceforth the term "UG" will be used to refer to innate knowledge of two hypothetical types: (i) that which only applies to linguistic cognition and (ii) that which applies to both linguistic and nonlinguistic cognition. The existence of the former can be questioned (Chomsky 2004; Tomasello 2003), but it is unclear at this point how the issue can be resolved empirically.

W. Philip (✉)
Linguistics, University of Utrecht, Utrecht, The Netherlands
e-mail: W.C.H.Philip@uu.nl

The second objective of this paper is to examine a particular child comprehension error which appears to challenge an innateness hypothesis regarding universal quantification. This error, which will here be referred to as EXHAUSTIVE PAIRING (EP), is typically found in the comprehension performance of 4- and 5-year-olds, a relatively late age. After reviewing what EP consists in and some accounts of it in the literature, a new account will be proposed and tested in three off-line experiments.

2 Logical and Psychological Problems

The logical operation that underlies the semantic value of a universal quantifier is independent of its lexical meaning since, as we will see, it can also be expressed by sentences that do not contain a universal quantifier. Likewise, the linguistic constraints that restrict the truth-conditional and discourse-sensitive meaning of universal quantifiers also apply to other types of linguistic expressions. Our first task, then, is to tease apart these aspects of the meaning of universal quantifiers and consider, in each case, whether or not the knowledge in question could in principle be learned from the positive input without the aid of UG.

One factor that will surely initially delay the emergence, or at least the manifestation, of knowledge of universal quantification is simply the problem of identifying those grammatical morphemes of the target language that are universal quantifiers. This mapping problem is not trivial. First of all, as indicated in parentheses on the right in (1), universal quantifiers (underlined) can occur in a variety of syntactic positions even within the same language.[2]

(1) a. *Every/each (*all) dog is licking a cat.* (determiner)
 b. *All (*each/*every) the dogs are licking a cat.* (predeterminer)
 c. *The dogs are each/all (*every) licking a cat.* (preverbal)
 d. *The dogs are licking two cats each (*every/*all)* (postnominal)

They are even bound morphemes in some languages, e.g. Straits Salish (Jelinek 1995). The free variation here suggests that UG does not restrict the syntactic category of universal quantifiers. In particular, it evidently does not tell the child that they must be determiners. Some languages appear to have no determiner universal quantifiers, e.g. Japanese (Kobuchi-Philip 2003). Moreover, even if it were true that all languages had universal quantifiers that were determiners—as Barwise and Cooper (1981: 179) proposed—this would not entail that all universal quantifiers must be determiners.

---

[2] Even if *each* and *all* in (1c) are underlyingly determiners (Sportiche 1988, cf. Bobaljik 1998), *all* in (1b) clearly is not. Moreover, some languages have universal quantifiers that cannot occur in determiner position, e.g. Dutch *allemaal* 'all' (Doetjes 1997).

In addition, UG does not tell the child that universal quantifiers only express distributive universal quantification over objects. Consider the various other types of universal quantification illustrated in (2a-d).

(2) a. *The dogs have all (*each) gathered around a cat.*   (cf. **A dog has gathered.*)
   b. *That dog is all (*each) dirty.*   (cf. *It is completely dirty.*)
   c. *That water is all (*each) dirty.*   (cf. *It is completely dirty.*)
   d. *That silly dog is always licking a cat (whenever I see him).*
   e. *She is going to give birth any (#every/#each) minute.*

In (1b) and (1c) above, English *all* quantifies over objects, attributing to each one individually a certain property, but in (2a) it asserts that every member of a set of objects belongs to a group, a group which has the property of gathering around a cat (e.g. Landmon 2000). In (2b-c), *all* does not quantify over discrete individuals but rather over undefined parts of an object (2b) and undefined portions of a substance (2c), a vague kind of universal quantification that is also expressed by the adverb *completely* (Higginbotham 1995; cf. Labov 1984). In (2d), *all* is part of a morphologically complex adverb quantifier that quantifies over individual events or situations rather than objects (Schwarzschild 1989; de Swart 1991). Finally, consider the ill-formedness of (2e) when *each* or *every* is substituted for *any*. This shows that the English universal quantifiers *every* and *each* cannot function as "wideners" in the sense of Kadmon and Landman (1993). However, UG does not inform the child of this restriction since universal quantifiers can have the same function as free-choice *any* in many languages, e.g. Dutch (Philip 2002).

Even if we restrict our attention to quantification over objects, there is yet another difficulty, since in some languages some universal quantifiers give rise to scopal ambiguity in some sentences containing other scope-bearing expressions, but this does not happen in all contexts, nor with all universal quantifiers, nor in all languages. For example, English adults readily assign a "surface scope" reading to (3a), making it true if one dog licked all the cats, but they can alternatively assign an "inverse scope reading", whereby (3a) is also true if each cat was licked by a different dog (Kurtzman and MacDonald 1993). In contrast, *all* does not give rise to scope ambiguity in (3b), nor does *each* in (3c). Moreover, except as a highly marked option, none of the sentence types in (3) can have an inverse scope reading in Chinese or Japanese (Huang 1982; Hoji 1985; Aoun and Li 1993), nor in Dutch (vanden Wyngaerd 1992; Philip 2004c).

(3) a. *A dog has licked each cat.*   (surface scope or inverse scope)
   b. *A dog has licked all the cats.*   (only surface scope)
   c. *Santa Claus gave a child each present.*   (only surface scope)

The language-internal and cross-linguistic variation here suggests that UG may also provide very little guidance about constraints on quantifier scope ambiguity. At the very least the child will have to learn from the input the setting of some parameter that makes scopal ambiguity impossible (or possible), and learn that this setting applies to some universal quantifiers but not others. Thus, even for the child who has correctly identified the universal quantifiers of her target language there still remains a complex task of determining what kind of meaning each may be used to express, to say nothing of learning subtle lexical idiosyncrasies.[3]

However, the situation is even worse. Not only is there a potentially highly complex one-to-many mapping between a given universal quantifier and the types of universal quantification that it may express, there is also a one-to-many mapping between a given type of universal quantification and the types of sentences that can be used to express it. Consider the logical equivalence of (4a) and (4b). Both sentences have the same truth conditions, expressing distributive universal quantification over objects, but (4b) does not contain a universal quantifier.

(4) a. <u>Every</u> *dog is licking a cat.*
    b. *It is <u>not</u> the case that <u>there</u> is a dog who is <u>not</u> licking a cat.*

The mapping problem is indeed daunting, and this is precisely because UG offers little or no guidance. However, the mapping problem does not concern the L1A of basic knowledge. This is because, quite generally, mapping presupposes knowing what needs to be mapped. Only after knowledge of the logical operation of the universal quantifier has been acquired can the child try to identify those basic expressions of her target language that expresses this meaning. The real question, then, is how the child comes to acquire this basic meaning in the first place. Is it necessary to assume that UG teaches the child this meaning? Is this logical operation a "substantive universal" of UG?

The equivalence in (4) above has some bearing on this question. Evidently, it is not necessary for knowledge of the logical operation of universal quantification to be innately specified in order for it to be acquired. It could in principle be derived from knowledge of propositional negation and knowledge of the basic syntactic-semantic operation that makes compositional meaning possible. That is, if a language learner has enough linguistic knowledge to produce sentences like *There is a dog who is not licking a cat* and also sentences like *It is not the case that there is a dog who is licking a cat,* then he or she would also in principle be able to produce a sentence like (4b), thereby accidentally discovering the logical operation of universal quantification. The point here is not that knowledge of this operation is actually acquired this way, by accident and with no the help from UG, but rather that its acquisition is not a logical problem.

On the other hand, the absence of a logical problem does not entail that a given principle is not part of UG. Arguably, the primary role of much of UG is not to make L1A possible but rather to make it fast and efficient by finessing learning problems that, because of their complexity, would present a "psychological problem" for L1A. However, if a principle is encoded in UG only because this speeds up its L1A, then

---

[3]E.g. English *all* and *every* (but not *each*) presuppose greater-than-two plurality: *Tom extended each leg* (#*every*/#*all*) vs. *The cat extended every leg/all its legs* (cf. Vendler 1967).

this principle ought to be accessible to the child from the onset of L1A (as claimed by the Strong Continuity Hypothesis, e.g. Pinker 1984; Crain 1991). In sum, theoretical considerations lead one to expect the logical operation of universal quantification to be fully acquired very early.

This expectation is met. Universal quantifiers first appear in child speech around the age of two in sentences like *Milk all gone* and *apple all gone* (Brooks and Sekerina 2005/2006: 178). This is only vague quantification over parts of objects and portions of substances, but it is universal quantification nonetheless. It is unclear why this type of universal quantification should show up first, long before universal quantification over objects. One possible explanation is that sentences containing vague quantification over non-discrete parts or portions are easier to verify than sentences containing quantification over objects (Brooks and Sekerina 2005/2006).[4] In any case, the experimental literature shows that at least by the age of four, children are also fully capable of adult comprehension of sentences containing universal quantification over objects (Smith 1979; Hanlon 1981; Brooks and Braine 1996, inter alia.). In sum, knowledge of the logical operation of universal quantification is fully acquired as early as two and all forms of this operation appear to have fully emerged at least by age four.

Knowledge of the logical operation is not the only thing that needs to be acquired, though. To correctly understand a sentence like (6a), the child must also come to know the linguistic constraints on this logical operation.

(6) a. *Every friendly dog is licking a cat.*
 b. *Every object is a friendly dog licking a cat.*

First, she must come to know that the domain of quantification of a universal quantifier is always restricted, i.e. that a sentence like (6a) cannot have the same truth conditions as, say, (6b). This is knowledge of the principle of CONSERVATIVITY (Barwise and Cooper 1981; van Benthem 1986; Keenan and Stavi 1986; Westerståhl 1989, inter alia.): a universal quantifier always "lives on" some set of individuals. This principle applies as much to adverb quantifiers like *always*, which quantify over events or situations, as to determiner quantifiers like *every*, which quantify over objects (Schwarzschild 1989; de Swart 1991). However, when there is quantification over events there need not be any SEMANTIC RESTRICTION, i.e. a restriction provided by the denotation of a linguistic form. In (7a), which does have a semantic restriction (boldfaced), quantification is restricted to the set of events that occur in a certain living room. In (7b) there happens to be no phrase that can function as a semantic restriction, so a PRAGMATIC RESTRICTION (such as indicated in parentheses) is supplied by inferences about the discourse context. The principle of conservativity is always obeyed, if not semantically then pragmatically.

---

[4] One can determine at a glance whether or not a dog is completely wet (taking only salient visible parts to be relevant). In contrast, in order to determine whether or not every dog is wet, one must be able to individually check each member of a contextually relevant set of dogs.

(7) a. *A friendly dog is <u>always</u> licking a cat **in the living room**.*
    b. *A dog is <u>always</u> licking a cat.* ('whenever I go into the living room')

With English determiner, predeterminer, and postnominal quantifiers, conservativity is obeyed in two ways. First, the meaning of the noun phrase (NP) in construction with the quantifier must be used as a semantic restriction. Thus, *friendly dog* in (6a) above restricts the domain of *every* to a set of dogs that are friendly. In addition, the domain of quantification must always also be further restricted pragmatically to a presupposed subset of the objects denoted by the semantic restriction, i.e. to those objects that are relevant in a given discourse context. This is what is sometimes referred to as the "witness set" or "domain presupposition" (e.g. Barwise and Cooper 1981; van Fintel 1994; Szabolcsi 1997). It is what prevents (8a) from having the same truth conditions as a sentence like (8b). It is also what prevents a sentence like (8c) from being taken as false when the speaker is not naked (cf. Labov 1984:48–49).

(8) a. *<u>Every</u> dog is licking a cat.*
    b. *Every real or imaginary dog is licking a cat.*
    c. *I left <u>all</u> my clothes at home.*

The child needs to know the principle of conservativity in order to correctly understand sentences like (7), (8a), and (8c). However, she also needs to know this principle in order to correctly understand sentences like (9a), which only contain existential quantifiers. By restricting the domain of quantification to a presupposed set of contextually relevant objects, conservativity prevents (9a) from having the same vacuous meaning as (9b).[5]

(9) a. *There is a dog licking a cat.*
    b. *Among all real or imaginary dogs, there is a dog licking a cat.*

Conservativity is a very general principle. It does not just apply to universal quantifiers like *always* and *each*, and indefinites such as in (9a), but also to definite determiners (Lewis 1979), reciprocal verbal affixes (Dalrymple et al. 1995), and many other semantic operators. In light of its ubiquity and the fundamental role it plays in effective communication, it seems highly unlikely that the principle of conservativity could be derived from the positive evidence. Since its L1A appears to present a severe logical problem, we may safely assume that it is innately specified.

Let us return now to the more problematic case of the semantic instantiation of conservativity, i.e. the obligatory semantic restriction that is found with universal quantifiers such as those in (10).

(10) a. *A dog has licked <u>every</u>/each **cat**.*
     b. *A dog has licked <u>all</u> the **cats**.*
     c. *The **dogs** have <u>all/each</u> licked a cat.*

---

[5] (9b) is necessarily true, since in some imaginary world a dog is licking a cat; (8b) is necessarily false, since even in the actual world some dogs are not licking a cat. Conservativity helps police the informativeness of language by ruling out pointless assertions of this sort.

All the quantifiers here have obligatory semantic restrictions (boldfaced), but *all* is not a determiner in (10b), and arguably neither are *all* or *each* in (10c), since they occupy the syntactic position of an adverb. In (10b), *all* is a modifier of some kind contained within a nominal expression, which also contains the NP it is construed with the determiner for this NP. Following Kobuchi-Philip (2007), let us use the descriptive term "DP-local" to refer to such quantifiers. *Every* and *each* in (10a) are also DP-local, though in this case they themselves are the determiner heads of the DPs (determiner phrases) in question (cf. *each the cat, *every the cat). In contrast, *all* and *each* in (10c) are "VP-local" universal quantifiers. They occur in the canonical position (for English) of a large class of adverbs, and they can be analyzed as functioning semantically like adverbs as well, i.e. as VP modifiers (Dowty and Brodie 1984; Kobuchi-Philip 2007). Evidently, the requirement that DP-local and VP-local universal quantifiers have a semantic restriction is not triggered by their syntactic position, but rather by the circumstance that they quantify over objects. Consistent with this hypotheses, adverb quantifiers like *always*, which are also VP-local, do not have to have a semantic restriction because they quantify over events rather than objects.

What the child must come to know, then, is that when there is universal quantification over objects, the quantifier obligatorily has a semantic restriction. More precisely, she must acquire knowledge of three requirements that apply to such a quantifier: (i) it must have a semantic restriction provided by the denotation of an NP; (ii) only one NP can have this function; and (iii) this NP must always be identified by some rule. In English (perhaps in all languages), syntax is used to identify the NP in question. The descriptive generalization for English is that there are two rules: (i) for an DP-local quantifier, the NP in construction with it provides its semantic restriction, as in (10a) and (10b); and (ii) for a VP-local quantifier, the NP in grammatical subject position provides its semantic restriction, as in (10c).[6]

These are the two rules for English, but not for all languages. Consider the Japanese and Dutch sentences in (11a) and (11b), respectively. In both cases, a VP-local universal quantifier can be construed either with the subject NP (meaning 11c) or the object NP (meaning 11d).

(11) a. *Gakko de wa gakusei ga   minna hon wo yonda*
       school at TOP boy   NOM all   book ACC read
    b. *Op school hebben de jongens de boeken allemaal gelezen.*
       at school have   the boys   the books   all   read
    c. 'At school all the boys have read the books.'
    d. 'At school the boys have read all the books.'

In light of its contrast with English, this free variation in Dutch and Japanese raises the possibility that the actual rules selecting the NP that supplies the semantic restriction may be language-specific pieces of knowledge that do not derive from

---

[6] *All* in a sentence like *The dog licked them all* and *each* in (1d) (cf. Safir and Stowell 1987) are two additional types of NP-local universal quantifier (both very marked in English).

UG. Of course, the apparent differences in the way NP-local and VP-local quantifiers obtain their semantic restriction and the cross-linguistic variation observed with the latter can be analyzed in terms of UG parameters. However, the simpler hypothesis is that the rules in question are learned from the positive evidence in the same way as idioms and constructions are learned, i.e. without the help of UG (cf. Culicover 1999). Before we examine this hypothesis about the rules, though, let us first consider the more basic question of how the child acquires knowledge of the three basic requirements that apply to universal quantifiers quantifying over objects. How does she come to know that such quantifiers must have a semantic restriction provided by one and only one NP and that this NP must always be identified by some (syntactic) rule.[7]

Let us consider first the requirement that some NP or other must provide the semantic restriction. Suppose a child did not know this constraint and hypothesized incorrectly that in a sentence like (12a) none of the NPs provided a semantic restriction. For this child conservativity would be satisfied only by restricting the domain of quantification pragmatically (as often happens with adverb universal quantifiers like *always*). The hypothetical child would assign to (12a) a meaning such as (12b) or (12c).

(12) a. *Every dog is licking a cat.*
 b. *Every relevant event is one in which a dog is licking cat.*
 c. *Every relevant object is a dog licking a cat.*

The child who took (12a) to mean the same thing as (12b) or (12c) would need to learn somehow that this was not the correct adult interpretation. Unfortunately, this would be impossible. Neither positive nor negative evidence would be able to conclusively rule out her false initial hypothesis. If she ever noticed that adults considered (12a) true when she considered it false, this observation would not force her to abandon the analysis in (12b) or (12c) because she could simply conclude that she had not pragmatically restricted the domain of quantification in an adult-like fashion. Likewise, direct and indirect negative evidence could always be taken as having bearing on how the pragmatic restriction was defined rather than the semantic analysis of the sentence. We seem to be driven to the conclusion, then, that UG must teach the child to expect an NP to provide the semantic restriction. Without UG, L1A of this constraint would be a logical problem.

The next question is how the child comes to know that only one NP may provide the semantic restriction. How does she learn that a sentence like (13a) cannot mean the same thing as a sentence like (13b)?[8]

---

[7] The child must also learn that some quantifiers, e.g. English *each* and *every*, can only quantify over objects, but this appears to be an idiosyncratic lexical property since the constraint does not apply to *all* (recall 2b-c above) nor to numeral quantifiers denoting large numbers: *Four thousand ships have passed through this lock* can also be true if, say, only 1,000 ships passing through the lock but did so on 4,000 different occasions (Krifka 1990).

[8] Unselectively binding both the object and the subject NP would yield such a meaning: $Dx,y(x \in \mathbf{dog}\ \&\ y \in \mathbf{cat})\ \exists e[\mathbf{lick}(x,y,e)]$, e ranging over minimal events (cf. Heim 1982).

(13) a. _Each_ dog has licked a cat.
    b. _Each_ dog has licked _each_ cat.

If a child initially hypothesized that the only meaning (13a) had was that expressed by (13b), correcting this would be no problem, not even a psychological one. Simply noticing that an adult can use (13a) to truthfully describe a situation in which two dogs each lick only one cat would be sufficient. However, if the child thought that (13a) optionally had the same meaning as (13b), this incorrect hypothesis would be much harder to unlearn since only indirect negative evidence in the sense of Chomsky (1981: 9) could correct it. This does not make it a logical problem, though, only a psychological one. First of all, whether learning by indirect negative evidence is best described by connectionism or theoretical linguistics,[9] the hypothesis that it plays a role in L1A is well-motivated on independent grounds. There are many subset problems that children do somehow overcome, e.g. semantic over-extensions in lexical acquisition. Second, the input to the child does in fact contain some direct negative evidence as to meaning (Brown and Hanlon 1970; Hirsh-Pasek et al. 1984; Demetras et al. 1986; Bohannon and Stanowicz 1988).[10] The hypothetical child could find that she was always contradicted by adults when she took her nonadult interpretive option. Thus, if UG tells the child that the semantic restriction is supplied by just one NP, it is only because this speeds up the L1A of this piece of knowledge, not because its L1A would be impossible otherwise.

There is one remaining piece of semantic knowledge that the child must acquire in order to properly understand sentences containing universal quantification over objects. Even if she knows that only one NP must be used as a semantic restriction, she must also come to know that for each type of universal quantifier the semantic restriction is always provided by an NP identified by some grammatical rule. That this is crucial may be seen from the ungrammaticality of the meanings for the sentences in parentheses in (14) in which the quantifier incorrectly takes the boldfaced NP as its semantic restriction. How does the English child come to know that the subject NP must always provide the semantic restriction for a VP-local universal quantifier in a sentence such as (14c), but that it can never have this function for NP-local quantifiers in sentences such as in (14a-b)?

---

[9] In a connectionist model, disuse of an incorrectly hypothesized grammatical option progressively weakens the weights of the connections supporting this option until it eventually completely disappears. In the Optimality-Theoretical L1A model of Tesar and Smolensky (1998), in addition to the corrective effect of positive evidence, the failure to observe an initially hypothesized option causes a reordering of the ranking of constraints such that the option is excluded.

[10] The cited studies all report observations of adults directly correcting false child statements. E.g. while pointing at a car, the child says "That's a nice house" and the adult replies "It's not a house, dear; it's a car." While it is well-established that negative evidence plays no significant role in the L1A of grammatical form (e.g. Morgan and Travis 1989; Marcus 1993), the possible role of negative semantic evidence has never been systematically investigated.

(14) a. *A dog has licked every/each **cat**.* (cf. *The **dogs** have licked each cat.*)
b. *A dog has licked all the **cats**.* (cf. **The **dogs** have licked all a cat.*)
c. *The **dogs** have all/each licked a cat.* (cf. **A dog has all/each licked the **cats***)

If the child initially hypothesized that any NP in the sentence could in principle provide the semantic restriction for a universal quantifier quantifying over objects, it would be very hard for her to unlearn this optionality. As in the case of the "one NP only" constraint, only indirect negative evidence could correct the false initial hypothesis. Since without UG the child would face a difficult learning problem, it is reasonable to suppose that UG provides guidance here as well, in order to speed up L1A. More precisely, it seems necessary to assume that UG tells the child that, for any universal quantifier that quantifies over objects, there must be some grammatical rule or other which always selects an NP in a specific syntactic position as the source of its semantic restriction. However, it is not necessary for UG to spell out exactly what the rules in question are by supplying parameters that need to be set. This is because the actual rules can straightforwardly be learned as constructions from positive evidence. For example, suppose the child initially incorrectly hypothesized that the subject NP must always provide the semantic restriction for *all*. The positive evidence of hearing an adult produce a sentence like (14b) would show her immediately that this was a false hypothesis, even before she attempted to determine the truth-value of the sentence, since she would have expected (14b) to be an ungrammatical form due to the singularity of *a dog*. Conversely, observing that an adult can produce a sentence like (14c) would show her that the object NP does not provide the semantic restriction for a VP-local quantifier. Finally, observing that an adult can use (14a) to truthfully describe a situation in which only one dog does any cat-licking would correct such a false initial hypothesis about the semantic restriction for *each* or *every*.

In sum, for theoretical reasons, it seems likely that UG does provide substantial guidance in the L1A of constraints imposing a semantic restriction on universal quantifiers that quantify over objects, but there would also appear to be some knowledge that the child must figure out on her own. In particular, it is possible that the actual rules for syntactically identifying the NP that provides the semantic restriction simply have to be learned. This would not slow things down very much, since the rules in question would be easy to figure out from the positive evidence. It is no wonder, then, that by the age of four children appear to have fully acquired all the syntactic and semantic knowledge they need for adult comprehension of universally quantified sentences. Most of this knowledge is innately specified and, because its purpose is to accelerate L1A, it is available from the onset.

3 The Troublesome Observation

From the large body of experimental literature on the topic, which goes back to Inhelder and Piaget (1958), there is abundant evidence that by the age of four, if not earlier, children know the adult meaning of universal quantifiers and usually use them correctly under ordinary conditions of use. As I once put it, "if the question is whether

Fig. 1 Exhaustive pairing under the EO condition

or not preschool children can in principle construct adult-like representations of universally quantified sentences, then clearly the answer is 'yes'" (Philip 1995:24). However, much of the same body of experimental literature also suggests that even as late as 6;0 (in some studies at even older ages) many children lack "maximal competence" with universal quantifier in the sense that they do not show adult-like comprehension performance at all times and under all conditions (Philip 2004a). In particular, in certain experimental contexts they often show a bizarre comprehension error variously referred to as "exhaustive pairing", "over-exhaustive search", "symmetrical interpretation", or "quantifier spreading" (e.g. Inhelder and Piaget 1958, 1964; Donaldson and Lloyd 1974; Donaldson and McGarrigle 1974; Bucci 1978; Freeman et al. 1982; Freeman 1985; Freeman and Sepahzad 1987; Freeman and Schreiner 1988; Philip and Aurelio 1991; Philip and Takahashi 1991; Takahashi 1991; Philip 1995, 1996; Crain et al. 1996; Drozd 1996a, 1996b; Brinkmann et al. 1996; Drozd and van Loosbroek 1999; Philip and Lynch 2000; Kang 2001; Drozd 2001; Kang 2001; Brooks and Sekerina 2005/2006; Drozd and van Loosbroek 1999, 2006, inter alia.). For example, with a truth-value judgment (TVJ) task in which the child judges the guesses of a puppet about pictures that are visible to the child but not the puppet, preschool children often show exhaustive pairing (EP) under an EXTRA OBJECT (EO) condition such as shown in Fig. 1.

The test sentence *Each dog is licking a cat* is true because each object in the context of the quantified type (the three dogs) does indeed have the property denoted by the predicate in the nuclear scope of the quantifier (is licking a cat). The extra object (the cat in the tree) is irrelevant. However, for the child showing EP this extra object does seem to be relevant. If the puppet asks her why its guess was wrong, she typically justifies her judgment of falsity either by referring to the extra cat in the tree who is not being licked by a dog, or by explaining that there are not enough dogs for its statement to be true. Although EP can in principle occur with adults as well under this type of experimental condition (e.g. Brooks and Sekerina 2005/2006), it occurs significantly more frequently with children.[11] Clearly, this needs to be explained.

---

[11] Under an EO condition, adult agrammatic aphasics show EP as often as preschool children (Saddy 1990; Philip and Avrutin 1998).

Research suggests that EP is not significantly affected by varying aspects of the TVJ paradigm. It does not appear to matter whether the test sentence is presented by an adult (e.g. Philip and Aurelio 1991) or by a puppet (e.g. Crain et al. 1996), or by a doll with a hidden speaker controlled by a researcher not visible to the child (Donaldson and Lloyd 1974). Nor does it matter whether the test sentence is a declarative sentence (e.g. Philip 1995) or a yes/no question (e.g. Takahashi 1991). EP seems just as likely to occur when a context like that in Fig. 1 is acted out by a researcher with props or toys (e.g. Donaldson and Lloyd 1974) as when it is statically portrayed by a single picture (e.g. Philip and Takahashi 1991) or by a series of pictures depicting scenes of a story (e.g. Philip and Lynch 2000). It also readily occurs when the dependent variable is a nonverbal response (Donaldson and Lloyd 1974) and when the puppet is rewarded or punished for the correctness of its guesses (e.g. Takahashi 1991). In addition, the EP error does not seem to be eliminated by satisfying the "condition of plausible dissent" of Crain et al. (1996), although there is some evidence that this may reduce the likelihood of it occurring. According to these authors, in off-line experiments young children can have difficulty fully accessing the truth conditions of a test sentence and consequently may find it somewhat infelicitous in the sense that they must make inferences about its meaning. This can be remedied, they argue, by showing the child a context in which the test sentence would be false under an adult reading before testing the child's comprehension of this sentence. For example, if one of the dogs in the condition illustrated in Fig. 1 had not wanted to lick a cat at an earlier point in a story that ended with that scene, the condition of plausible dissent would have been satisfied. This is because at that earlier point in the story when the dog had not wanted to lick a cat, the test sentence *Each dog is licking a cat* was false.[12] According to Crain et al., when an L1A experiment includes this kind of priming of the adult semantic interpretation, the EP error will not occur. When this felicity condition is not satisfied, the authors argue, the child experiences a kind of presupposition failure which leads to an accommodation that results in an ER response. The experimental findings of Crain et al. support this hypothesis; however, these findings can be questioned on methodological grounds and their hypothesis on both empirical and theoretical grounds (Philip 1996; Gordon 1998; Drozd and van Loosbroek 1999; Philip and Lynch 2000; Geurts 2000, 2003; Drozd 2004; Philip 2004a; Brooks and Sekerina 2005/2006). Most telling, subsequent research has failed to replicate Crain et al.'s experimental findings: EP has been observed in several studies that satisfy the condition of plausible dissent, albeit often more weakly than in those that do not (e.g. Brinkmann et al. 1996; Drozd and van Loosbroek 1999, 2006; Philip and Lynch 2000; Drozd 2001), and it has not been observed with certain sentence types in studies that do not satisfy this felicity condition (e.g. Boster and Crain 1993; Philip 1995). In sum, the

---

[12] Crain et al. also propose that a TVJ experiment should include satisfaction of a "condition of plausible assent", i.e. that the child should be shown a context that verifies the test sentence under an adult-grammatical reading. However, this does not apply to the EP error, which is a nonadult-like judgement of falsity, but rather to nonadult-like judgments of truth.

evidence that EP is purely an artifact of the way in which the TVJ task is designed is extremely weak. Varying the design may affect the frequency of EP observations, but it does not seem to eliminate the phenomenon completely. Moreover, EP is not only found with the TVJ task; it has also been observed with act-out tasks (e.g. Bucci 1978; Chien and Wexler 1989) and picture selection tasks (e.g. Brooks and Sekerina 2005/2006).

The existence of EP in children's comprehension performance appears to reflect either (i) the incomplete emergence of some aspect of adult competence that plays a crucial role in the interpretation of universally quantified sentences or (ii) the "shallow processing" of such sentences by children due to the immaturity of working memory or some other "horizontal faculty" (in the sense of Fodor 1983). Let us call the first hypothesis the EMERGENCE HYPOTHESIS and the second the SHALLOW PROCESSING HYPOTHESIS. According to the emergence hypothesis, EP in children is caused by a child state of knowledge that differs qualitatively from that of the adult. The child has only "partial knowledge" (Elman et al. 1996) of that piece of adult knowledge that prevents EP from occurring with adults. According to the shallow processing hypothesis, EP is caused by a cognitive limitation. The child has fully acquired all the knowledge of universal quantification that adults have, only she cannot always make use of this knowledge as effectively as the adult can.

It is hard to determine which of these two approaches is on the right track. The claim of the emergence hypothesis does not entail that the hypothetical partially missing information is acquired accidentally by general learning mechanisms. Although partially absent at a certain stage of development, it may be predestined to fully emerge at a later stage, either through genetically controlled maturation in the sense of Borer and Wexler (1987) or through the eventual completion of a long-lasting interaction of genetic and environmental factors. An example of the latter is the way in which the cardinality principle of counting is acquired. Knowledge of this principle does not fully emerge until around age four and only after a year or so of lexical development and practice counting objects with a few numerals that have been acquired (Sarnecka and Carey 2008).

The problem with both the emergence and the shallow processing hypotheses is that neither actually predicts when EP is or is not likely to occur. The emergence hypothesis does not specify exactly what piece of knowledge is partially missing, nor does it describe any causal relation between the hypothetically partial absent knowledge and the occurrence of EP under an EO condition such as in Fig. 1. Incomplete acquisition may be necessary, but it is not clear how it could be sufficient. The same can be said of the shallow processing hypothesis. It offers no precise description of what cognitive limitation is hypothetically involved, nor does it explain why shallow processing should yield EP rather some other type of nonadult-like performance.

Below I will propose a more precise emergence hypothesis that makes testable predictions about when EP is and is not likely to occur, and present three experiments with Dutch children which test some of these predictions. However, we first need to have a closer look at the EP error itself and other possibly related child comprehension errors with universal quantifiers.

4 Exhaustive Pairing and Other Errors

When EP was first discovered, it was not taken to be a linguistic phenomenon. Inhelder and Piaget (1958, 1964) considered it another piece of evidence that logical competence develops in stages. Other researchers suggested that EP was caused by a complete failure to use grammar to process a universally quantified sentence, or that it derived from a failure of attention to the linguistic input. For example, Bucci (1978: 59) hypothesized that EP arises when the child encodes a universally quantified sentence as "an unordered set of substantive words without hierarchical structure," and Donaldson and Lloyd (1974: 82–83) suggested that (in a TVJ experiment) "the child derives from the experimenter's words a notion of the kind of question he is to consider; but he derives the precise question that he does consider from his own encoding of the physical array." As noted in Philip (1995: 28–41), the principal problem with these and other nonlinguistic proposals is that they have difficulty accounting for the observation that children who show EP under an EO condition such as illustrated in Fig. 1 above suddenly stop doing so when different types of sentences are matched with the same visual input. Consider the experimental findings for Japanese children summarized in Table 1. These are taken from a repeated-measure, within-subjects study reported in Philip (1995) in which sentences containing either predicate type A or predicate type B were presented in trials of EO conditions that used exactly the same picture type. (Table 1 shows only the results for children whose only error was EP with predicate type A.)

For these children, EP responses occurred just as frequently with each of the two quantifiers that were tested but disappeared completely for both with sentences containing predicate type B. Philip (1995) also reports significant inhibition of EP with test sentences like *Each is dog dancing* and *Dogs are licking cats*. The interaction with sentence type here seems to call for a linguistic analysis. For this reason, many researchers have attempted to account for the EP error within the framework of theoretical linguistics.

It should be noted that EP is not the only kind of nonadult-like comprehension performance that young children may show with universally quantified sentences in TVJ experiments. Two other errors that have also been observed are the PERFECTIONIST RESPONSE, a.k.a. "exhaustive response"(Philip 1995), and UNDER-EXHAUSTIVE SEARCH (Freeman et al. 1982; Drozd 2001). The perfectionist response (PR) is an incorrect judgment of falsity caused by the presence of an object that is not denoted by any NP in the test sentence. It can be observed under the PRC1 and PRC2 conditions schematically represented in Fig. 2, where arrows stand for the depiction of a licking relation. The under-exhaustive search (US) error is a nonadult-like judgment of truth under a condition such as USC1 or USC2 in Fig. 2.

It may be that the PR and the US errors are somehow related to EP. However, any hypothesis that a single factor is solely responsible for all three types of error faces an empirical problem insofar as it claims that PR and US are just as likely to occur as EP. As Donaldson and Lloyd (1974: 81–74) and others have noted, EP is by far

Table 1 EP responses with Japanese children whose only error was EP in study matching different sentence types with same EO picture type

Predicate type	Sentence type (2 trials per quantifier type, 4 trials per predicate type)	Mean percentage EP responses
A	*Otokonoko wa <u>donokomo</u> uma ni noteiru?* Boy TOP every horse on riding *Otokonoko wa <u>minna</u> uma ni noteiru?* Boy TOP all horse on riding 'Is every boy riding a horse?'	61%
B	*Otokonoko wa <u>donokomo</u> uma ni noru no ga suki?* Boy TOP every horse on ride COMP NOM like *Otokonoko wa <u>minna</u> uma ni noru no ga suki?* Boy TOP all horse on ride COMP NOM like 'Does every boy like riding a horse?'	0%

Note: N = 7; mean age 4;11; contrasts between *donokomo* and *minna* not significant (sign tests); contrasts between A and B highly significant (*t*-test, p < 0.01)

PRC1	PRC2	USC1	USC2
CAT CAT CAT ↑ ↑ ↑ DOG DOG PONY	CAT CAT ↑ ↑ DOG DOG PONY	CAT CAT ↑ ↑ DOG DOG DOG	CAT CAT BIRD ↑ ↑ ↑ DOG DOG DOG

Note. With *Each dog is licking a cat*, PR = judgement of falsity under PRC1 or PRC2, US = judgement of truth under USC1 or USC2

Fig. 2 Schematic representation of conditions allowing PR and US errors

the most common error that preschool children make with universal quantifiers under experimental conditions. Consider the results summarized in Table 2 of 12 cross-linguistic TVJ studies. These were different studies but they all used the same methodology of a puppet making guesses about hidden pictures and used translations of the same or very similar materials. They all included at least three different trials of a version of the EO condition that also allowed a PR error by including an unmentioned object in the picture as well (e.g. a girl under the tree in Fig. 1). They also always included a PRC1 condition and either a USC1 or USC2 condition or both. Table 2 shows the percentages of children in each language group that showed each type of response pattern under these three conditions.[13]

As can be seen from the bottom row of Table 2, roughly 1/3 of the 500 children who participated in these studies showed no error other than EP and almost 40% of

---

[13] This abstracts away from individual variation in the frequency of EP, PR and US errors, which was considerable. The English and Japanese studies, from Philip (1995), generally included more than three trials of each condition. The Dutch, French, Spanish, and Norwegian data come from filler items in the pronoun studies of, respectively, Philip and Coopmans (1996), Hamann and Philip (1997), Baauw and Cuetos (2004), and Hestvik and Philip (1999/2000).

Table 2 Percentages of children showing each possible EP/PR/US error pattern in cross-linguistic TVJ experiments using same or similar methodology and materials

Language	n	Ave age	No error	EP Only	EP+US	EP+PR	EP+US+PR	US only	PR only	US+PR	Quantifier tested
English (6 studies)	223	4;7	10%	33%	3%	39%	5%	8%	0%	2%	*Every* floated *all*
Japanese (2 studies)	53	5;1	17%	28%	8%	17%	9%	19%	0%	2%	*donokomo minna*
Dutch	93	6;6	40%	40%	8%	8%	1%	3%	0%	0%	*ieder*
French	40	5;9	17%	23%	17%	13%	2%	25%	3%	0	*chaque*
Spanish	45	5;6	33%	22%	13%	2%	5%	25%	0%	0%	*cada*
Norwegian	46	6;2	17%	26%	6%	0	8%	39%	2%	2%	*hver*
all 12 studies	500	5;3	20%	31%	7%	22%	5%	14%	0.5%	0.5%	

Note. Except for *minna* 'all', the non-English quantifiers tested are all obligatorily distributive in the adult grammar, i.e. analogous to English *each* and *every*

the 400 who showed any errors at all were children who only showed the EP error. This asymmetrical distribution suggests that the PR and US errors may be unrelated to EP. Moreover, while a child showing the US error or the PR error may simply be failing to attend carefully to the test sentence and responding on the basis of a response strategy rather than linguistic knowledge, it is hard to see how the performance of the child who only shows EP (henceforth the EP CHILD) could be accounted for in such terms. The US error may simply be another instance of the notorious affirmative response strategy (Slobin 1991; Chien and Wexler 1990; Grimshaw and Rosen 1990; McKee 1992; Crain et al. 1996; Gordon 1998, inter alia.) resulting from shallow processing concomitant with a failure to pay attention . In support of this hypothesis, note that the frequency of US errors can be artificially increased simply by ordering a block of experimental conditions testing *some* before a block of experimental conditions testing *all* (Smith 1979:443–445). The PR error could also be a set perceptual response (Mehler and Carey 1967) arising from correct judgments of falsity under control conditions in experiments that include several trials of test and control conditions. (This raises a methodological issue we return to below.) In contrast, the error of the EP child cannot be caused by an affirmative response bias, since it is a judgment of falsity, and does not look like the effect of a negative response strategy either, since this child gives correct affirmative responses under PRC conditions. In addition, if asked, the EP child always gives a reason for judging the puppet's statement false. Subjects under the influence of a response bias typically cannot do this because their response has not been the product of any judgment. In sum, there is reason to believe that the only child error that really needs an explanation is the EP error. Hypotheses about what causes this error may actually be weakened, rather than strengthened, by the claim that they also explain other mistakes that children can make.

5 Explaining Exhaustive Pairing

The upshot of the discussion so far is that we seem to be left with no explanation of EP. No wonder that some researchers have concluded that it must be an experimental artifact. However, there is one aspect of adult performance with universally quantified sentences that has not yet been considered. This is the way in which pragmatic restriction of the domain of quantification is defined. Many investigators have suggested, in one way or another, that the EP results from children pragmatically restricting the domain of quantification in a nonadult-like manner (Freeman, Sinha and Stedmon1982, Philip 1995; Drozd 1996a, b, 2001 Geurts 2000; Geurts 2003; Drozd and van Loosbroek 2006, inter alia.). Of these accounts of EP, the one that makes the most correct predictions to date about when EP is or is not likely to occur is the EVENT QUANTIFICATIONAL ACCOUNT of Philip (1995) (see also Philip and Avrutin 1998; Philip 2004b). This proposal is an emergence hypothesis. It suggests that EP children lack a piece of adult knowledge, and that adults showing EP are using an earlier avatar of linguistic competence. According to the Event

Quantificational Account, preschool children show EP significantly more often than adults because significantly more often than adults they mis-apply to determiner universal quantifiers like *each* the kind of event-quantificational semantics that is correctly applied to adverb quantifiers like *always*. They are obeying the principle of conservativity purely by means of pragmatic restriction and restricting the domain of quantification in such a way that the universally quantified sentence has maximally falsifiable truth conditions consistent with its lexical content. The principal objection to this hypothesis is that, as was noted above, the use of event quantification to define pragmatic restriction for a quantifier like *each* or *every* leads to an intractable learnability problem (see also Crain et al. 1996). In addition, all the correct predictions of the Event Quantificational Account crucially depend on an ad hoc assumption about how the pragmatically restricted domain of quantification is defined by the child or adult showing EP. This reduces the account to a mere description of the facts.

The other family of proposals that attribute EP to problems defining pragmatic restriction are essentially performance hypotheses. For example, Drozd and van Loosbroek (2006) propose that, because the cost of processing the adult pragmatic restriction can be prohibitively high for the child, in the absence of contextual support she is sometimes unable to pragmatically restrict the domain of quantification in the way intended by adults and instead, relying heavily on information from her visual perception of the context, constructs a nonadult-like pragmatic restriction. Unlike the event quantificational account, these proposals do not attempt to predict variations in the frequency of EP determined by manipulations of the linguistic input. Their greatest weakness, though, is that they claim to explain the underlying cause of all child errors, so they fail to capture the observed asymmetries in the distribution of the three different types of errors. However, this family of proposals does make one general prediction that can be experimentally tested. They predict that EP will be significantly inhibited with discourse contexts that support an adult definition of pragmatic restriction. This prediction has been borne out in several studies (e.g. Freeman et al. 1982; Philip and Lynch 2000; Drozd and van Loosbroek 2006). The problem, however, is that the observation that children perform in a more adult-like manner under experimental conditions that support adult-like pragmatic restriction does not necessarily show that a performance factor prevents them from doing so under other conditions. Since the observed adult-like performance crucially depends on an artificial manipulation of contextual factors, it can be argued that it is precisely the highly adult-like performance resulting from this manipulation that is artifactual (cf. Slobin 1991). Without an explanation of how the hypothesized cognitive limitation is causally related to EP, the observation that children often show EP under experimental conditions which rarely elicit EP from an adult remains prima facie evidence that they lack some piece of knowledge that the adult has.

To see what this missing piece of information might be, we need to examine more closely how adults pragmatically restrict the domain of quantification of universal quantifiers. First, for completeness, let us review the role played by lexical semantics. Due to their basic meaning, all universal quantifiers presuppose plurality; for example, the sentences in (15a-b) presuppose (15b).

(15) a. *All* the dogs are licking a cat.
   b. *Each/every* dog is licking a cat.
   c. There is more than one dog in the context.

However, the EP child clearly is well aware of this lexical presupposition, since if she thought that sentences like (15a-b) could be true even if only a single dog was licking a cat she would never show EP under an EO condition. The problem, rather, concerns identifying which objects in the context should be taken as relevant. Consider how an adult handles this task in the case of a hypothetical situation such as (16). Suppose here that Sue is in the living room and can see two cartoon dogs on TV that are each licking a different cartoon cat, and also two real dogs and some real cats that are sleeping on the floor. Bob is in the kitchen, so he cannot see what is happening, but Sue believes he is aware that there are real cats and dogs on the floor and cartoon ones on TV.

(16) Bob: *Are the dogs each licking a cat?*
   Sue: *Which ones do you mean? The ones on TV or the ones on the floor?*

A presupposition failure has occurred with Sue. She cannot determine the intended truth conditions of Bob's question without first determining which dogs he has in mind. The correct answer is "yes" if he means the cartoon dogs, "no" if he means the real dogs. In (16), Sue postpones defining the pragmatic restriction of *each* and asks for information that will allow her to do so as Bob intends. More typically, though, the adult will attempt to infer what is intended, i.e. attempt to "accommodate the speaker" (Lewis 1979).

Consider next the adult exchange in (17). Here suppose that Tom and Sue are at a race track waiting for the start of a horse race which has been delayed because one of the jockeys has not yet come out onto the track. Tom is blind, so he asks Sue what is happening.

(17) Tom: *What's holding things up? Isn't each jockey on his horse?*
   Sue: *No. One horse doesn't have a jockey.*

Note that the way Sue has interpreted the Tom's universally quantified sentence looks very similar to a EP error. Sue has accommodated by including an unseen object (the missing jockey) in the pragmatic restriction of *each jockey*. However, this is not a case of EP. It is a perfectly well-formed and normal use of a universal quantifier. The difference between the adult performance in (17) and the child EP error under the EO condition is that the adult pragmatic restriction is not based purely on visual information. Rather, the adult also makes use of his or her knowledge of the way the world normally works (and the belief that the interlocutor shares this knowledge). Because adult world knowledge includes the knowledge that in a horse race each horse normally has a jockey, Sue adds an unseen fourth jockey to the set of contextually relevant objects. The adult also makes use of world knowledge when determining the pragmatic restriction of *each dog* in the EO condition in Fig. 1. However, here world knowledge tells the adult that dogs are not normally paired up symmetrically with cats, so no invisible fourth dog is added to the set of contextually relevant objects. The child showing EP evidently does not make use of adult world knowledge to define the pragmatic restriction. However, why does she add an unseen fourth dog to the pragmatically restricted domain of quantification? What makes her imagine the existence of an additional relevant dog? If she can do this, why does she not also imagine an additional unseen cat that it is being licked by the additional unseen dog, and thus find the test sentence to be true?

The PRAGMATIC ACCOUNT of EP that I will now outline hypothesizes that EP is caused by three factors when it occurs with children. The first factor is the absence or incomplete acquisition of an innately specified principle that constrains the way adults define the pragmatic restriction for a universal quantifier. The second is the over-use by children of a default principle which has the same function as the one they lack. This is also assumed to be a UG principle but one that is more primitive and that emerges much earlier. The third factor is a perceptual mechanism which causes an unseen extra agent to become salient under an EO condition due to a near symmetrical pairing of agents and objects. The unseen agent becomes salient because its absence spoils the "good figure" of a symmetrical pairing of agents and objects that would obtain if it were present. Finally, the difference between EP with children and EP with adults is that whereas the former is partially caused by the incomplete emergence of a piece of knowledge, that latter is partially caused by a failure to access this piece of knowledge due to a shortage of processing resources. With normal adults, this is only a transitory shortage, occurring rarely and only when some other procedure is making heavy demands on the available resources. With agrammatic aphasic adults, who show EP as frequently as preschool children, there is a constant shortage of processing resources due to the brain lesion, and consequently the piece of knowledge that prevents EP is generally as unavailable as it is for the normal child.

The first factor affecting child performance, according to this hypothesis, is incomplete emergence/partial access of a UG principle that constrains adult pragmatic restriction by requiring the use of world knowledge for this purpose. This hypothesized NORMAL WORLD CONSTRAINT (NWC) may be quasi-formally described as shown in (18). Here, x ranges over objects (perceived or imagined) and s over situation types of any size (stored in long term memory); C is the set of objects in the context and R the set of relevant objects; NORM is the set of situation types which normally occur in the world, i.e. types of situations that frequently have occurred and that therefore are expected to re-occur in the normal course of events; PART(x,s) simply means "x is part of a situation type s".

(18) Normal World Constraint (NWC)
$\forall x \in C[R(x) \rightarrow \exists s[PART(x,s) \& NORM(s)]$
'If an object is contextually relevant, then there is a normal situation that it is part of.'

The NWC is hypothesized to be UG principle in the sense that it is predestined to emerge as a consequence of the interaction of genetic and environmental factors; however, it is also hypothesized to emerge late and only after a prolonged period of interaction between already acquired knowledge and an external environmental factor, namely the pressure to streamline communication with others and reduce the need for excessive accommodation. There are many ways to satisfy the pragmatic instantiation of conservativity; not all are useful for quickly identifying the speaker-intended meaning. The NWC provides a strategy that is more useful than other logically possible ones. It increases the likelihood that the listener and the speaker will have similar conceptions of the common ground of a discourse because people tend to agree about what kinds of situations normally occur in a given context.

The second factor underlying EP is the reliance on another hypothesized innate constraint on how pragmatic restrictions may be defined. Let us call this the SALIENT OBJECT STRATEGY (SOS); it can be quasi-formally described as shown in (19). Here S is the set of salient objects, i.e. objects in the context that attention naturally focuses on.

(19) Salient Object Strategy (SOS)
$\forall x \in C[R(x) \rightarrow S(x)]$
'If an object is contextually relevant, then it is salient.'

The SOS is hypothesized to be a UG principle as well, and exactly the same type of mechanism as the NWC. It reduces the need for accommodation by providing a strategy for defining pragmatic restriction. It is able to do this because objects that are perceptually salient for one person tend to be perceptually salient for others in the vicinity. Thus, like the NWC, the SOS helps the speaker and the listener have the same conception of the common ground of a discourse. However, it is hypothesized to emerge earlier than the NWC (and to eventually be largely replaced by the NWC).

The third factor hypothesized to underlie EP, both for children and adults, is a perceptual mechanism that causes objects that spoil a symmetrical pattern to become salient. To see that this pattern-recognition mechanism exists, consider the box in Fig. 3 and mentally connect each letter A with the letter B below it. It will be noted that attention is drawn to the space under the second letter A from the right. Where is the missing letter B? It has become salient because of it conspicuous absence. The claim, then, is that the cognitive mechanism responsible for this effect is precisely what causes the child or adult showing EP to imagine the existence of an unseen object.

Having outlined the Pragmatic Account of EP (henceforth PA), let us now consider its predictions. First, recall that the EP child shows fully adult-like performance under the PR and US conditions, repeated for convenience in Fig. 4.

The PA straightforwardly captures the observation that the EP child shows no errors under the PRC1 condition because the presence of the pony licking the third cat prevents an unseen third dog from becoming salient. Consequently, the child only takes the two visible dogs to be relevant and correctly judges the test sentence to be true. Adult-like judgments of truth are also predicted for the PRC2 condition because the EP child knows that the NP *dog* semantically restricts the domain of quantification. Since no pragmatically defined subset of this set can include a pony, she correctly takes the pony to be irrelevant, which also makes irrelevant any imagined third cat that would be licked by this pony if it were present. Adult performance is correctly predicted to occur under the USC1 condition because, although the near symmetry of the visual array makes a missing cat salient, its absence only

Fig. 3 Near symmetry perception test

A	A	A	A
B	B		B

PRC1	PRC2	USC1	USC2
CAT CAT CAT ↑ ↑ ↑ DOG DOG PONY	CAT CAT ↑ ↑ DOG DOG PONY	CAT CAT ↑ ↑ DOG DOG DOG	CAT CAT BIRD ↑ ↑ ↑ DOG DOG DOG

Note. Test sentence = *Each dog is licking a cat.*

Fig. 4 Schematic representation of the PR and US conditions

strengthens the child's correct perception that the test sentence must be false, since she knows that the quantifier is quantifying over dogs, not cats. Likewise, an adult judgment of falsity is correctly predicted for USC2 because the child (like an adult) has no reason to suppose the dog licking the bird should be excluded from the pragmatic restriction.

The PA can also straightforwardly capture the observation that EP is eliminated in an EO context with sentences like *Every dog likes licking a cat* (see Table 1). In this study of Philip (1995), the visible dogs were depicted as smiling and the child was told that this was because they liked to lick cats. The reason why EP did not occur, then, is simply because there is no way to verify whether an unseen extra dog does or does not like something when the only clue to their mental state is a facial expression that you cannot see. Consequently, the children correctly inferred that the imaginary dog must be irrelevant. Finally, the PA also captures the observation that EP is inhibited under an EO condition with sentences like *Dogs are licking cats* and *Every dog is sleeping*. With the former sentence type, the inclusion of an unseen dog in the pragmatic restriction cannot lead to a judgment of falsity simply because there is no universal quantifier in the test sentence in the first place. With the latter, once again the impossibility of determining whether or not an unseen object has the property denoted by the predicate in the nuclear scope of the quantifier leads to the correct conclusion that this imaginary object is irrelevant.

It was noted above that several studies have shown that the frequency of EP errors can be significantly inhibited by manipulating contextual factors in such a way that an adult pragmatic restriction of the domain of quantification is encouraged (e.g. Crain et al. 1996; Philip and Lynch 2000; Drozd and van Loosbroek 2006). Like all accounts of EP that attribute it to problems with pragmatic restriction, the PA correctly predicts this as well. However, it also predicts that the frequency of EP errors can be significantly increased by manipulating contextual factors in the opposite direction, i.e. such that they encourage the perception of a relevant unseen object. This will be tested in one of the TVJ experiments presented below by contrasting performance under two special versions of the EO condition, i.e. the CONSPICUOUS EXTRA OBJECT (CEO) condition and the INCONSPICUOUS EXTRA OBJECT (IEO) condition. In the CEO condition the context is linguistically and visually designed to increase the salience of an additional, relevant imaginary agent by emphasizing the presence of an extra object that spoils a symmetrical pairing of agents and objects. In the IEO condition just the opposite is done.

The other two TVJ experiments will test the predictions made by the PA for the two sentence types illustrated in (20b) and (20c), both presented in a CEO context.

(20) a. *Each dog is licking a cat.*
  b. *Each dog is a cat-licker.*
  c. *Each dog is smaller than a cat.*

The PA predicts that with CEO contexts EP will occur just as often with a sentence like (20b) as with a sentence like (20a). Here, if the CEO context makes an unseen dog salient and hence relevant to the EP child, her observation that he is not present licking the fourth cat will be evidence to her that he is not a cat-licker. However, since he is a relevant, it is not true that all the dogs are cat-lickers. In contrast, the PA predicts that with CEO contexts EP will occur significantly less often with a sentence like (20c) than with a sentence like (20a). This is because it is impossible to determine whether or not an imaginary dog is bigger or smaller than any of the visible cats. Consequently, the child will conclude that the imaginary additional dog made salient by the CEO context must be irrelevant despite his salience.

There is another reason for testing the two sentence-types in (20b-c). Contrary predictions for both sentence types are made by the most successful rival account of EP. The Event Quantificational Account (henceforth EQA) of Philip (1995) predicts that EP will be significantly inhibited with sentences like (20b) and that it will occur just as often with sentences like (20c) as with sentences like (20a). According to the EQA, the child who shows this error with sentences like (20a) will not be able to do so with sentences like (20b) because the predicate *be a cat-licker* is not a stage-level predicate and therefore lacks an event variable (cf. Kratzer 1989). This forces the child to abandon an event quantificational semantic analysis, which is a necessary condition for EP, and switch to adult-like quantification over objects. In contrast, the EQA predicts that the EP will occur just as often with sentences like (20c) as with sentences like (20a) because both have stage-level predicates, whose event variable makes the error possible.

6 Three Dutch Experiments

The three TVJ experiments presented in this section each have unique secondary design features and use different filler items but all employ the same methodology and have the same basic design. All three focus on the EP child by excluding child subjects who showed PR or US errors under control conditions. The results of the experiments are discussed in subsection 6.4.

6.1 Experiment I

Experiment I tests the prediction of the PA that the EP child will show the EP error significantly more often under a CEO condition than under an IEO condition.

Table 3 Participants of experiment I

Age and experimental groups		n mean	# boys	# girls	Mean age	Age range
Younger children	CEO group	21	9	12	5;2	4;3–5;9
	IEO group	24	6	18	5;2	4;4–5;9
Older children	CEO group	20	12	8	6;5	5;10–7;7
	IEO group	23	12	11	6;6	5;10–7;8
Child CEO group (younger + older)		41	21	20	5;9	4;3–7;7
Child IEO group (younger + older)		47	18	29	5;9	4;4–7;8
Adult CEO group		16	7	9	44	10–67

6.1.1 Participants

Experiment I was presented to 16 Dutch adults and to 166 Dutch children drawn from five different primary schools in or near Utrecht, the Netherlands. 32 of the children were excluded for failing to meet a basic inclusion criterion referred to as the ATTENTION FILTER and another 46 for failing to meet a second inclusion criterion referred to as the TARGET POPULATION FILTER (see below). The 88 children included in the study were divided into two age groups, YOUNGER CHILDREN and OLDER CHILDREN, and the members of each age group were randomly distributed across two experimental groups, the CEO GROUP and the IEO GROUP (see below). The age and gender statistics of all the experimental groups are summarized in Table 3. Eighty-four of the children were monolingual Dutch speakers. Four of the older children were Dutch-dominant successive bilinguals, with Moroccan Arabic their native language; two were included in a CEO group, the other two in an IEO group. The adults, who were only tested under the CEO condition, were all native speakers of Dutch with no background in linguistics.

6.1.2 Design

The experiment had a two-factor between-subjects design. The two levels of the principal factor were the two experimental groups that the children were randomly assigned to. The 41 children assigned to the CEO group were presented a set of materials that included the CEO condition but not the IEO condition, while the 47 children assigned to the IEO group received a materials set containing IEO but not CEO. The prediction of the PA is that for both child age groups a significantly greater number of children in the CEO group will give the EP response than will children in the IEO group.

The second between-subjects factor was age, with the three levels (i) younger children, (ii) older children, and (iii) adults. This variable was included simply to further corroborate the empirical claim that children are more likely to show EP errors than adults and to explore the possibility of a developmental difference between younger and older children.

Experiment I examined EP in a new way by including the unusual design feature of giving each child and adult subject only one opportunity to show EP or not under either a single trial of the CEO condition or a single trial of the IEO condition. This single-measure design was used to minimize possible CARRY OVER EFFECTS (a.k.a. "learning effects", "practice effects", "ordering effects", "set perceptual responses"). A carry-over effect occurs when the response under one trial of a given experimental condition is influenced by a response under a prior trial of the same condition. When it occurs, a carry over effect artificially inflates the number of ungrammatical or grammatical responses for a given experimental condition and invalidates all statistical inference (which is based on the assumption that each trial is a completely independent measure). This is a very real concern in the case of experimental research on children's comprehension of universally quantified sentences because in prior experiments using a repeated-measure design carry over effects have in fact been observed (e.g. Smith 1979:443–445; Philip 1995:109).

Finally, another important design feature of Experiment I was its two inclusion criteria, the attention filter and the target population filter. The attention filter was designed to screen out children who may have had some difficulty paying attention or mastering the experimental task. This was achieved by including among the filler items eight puppet guesses that were obviously true (OT items) and eight puppet guesses that were obviously false (OF items) and excluding all children who found more than two of the OT items false or more than two of the OF items true. The target population filter was designed to screen out children who showed PR or US errors. This was achieved by including in the materials one trial each of the PRC2 and the USC1 conditions (see Fig. 5 below). Any child who failed to judge the PRC2 item to be true or who failed to judge the USC1 item to be false was excluded.

6.1.3 Materials

The materials for Experiment I were two booklets which resembled children's picturebooks. Each contained several picture-stories, some consisting of a simple situation depicted by a single picture and others consisting of several pictures depicting key scenes of a story. The pictures were 21×14 cm, hand-drawn, color drawings. Generally, the pictures were placed horizontally in the top half of the right-hand page of a pair of facing pages while the story-teller's script, printed in 20 or 25 point font, was on the left-hand page.

The materials booklet for the CEO group was identical to that used with the IEO group except that the last picture-story was the HORSES STORY containing the CEO condition while for IEO group the last picture-story was the GIRLS STORY containing IEO. Prior to this test story, there were ten short filler stories, each with its own set of protagonists. Most of these stories were pilot materials for other experiments. None of them contained universally quantified sentences as part of the linguistic input. They were presented in a fixed order in both materials booklets and contained 11 puppet guesses which were true for an adult, pseudo randomly interspersed with12 guesses that were false for an adult. Eight of these true puppet guesses were different trials of the OT control condition used for the attention filter, and eight of the false puppet guesses were the OF items used for this inclusion criterion. One of

Fig. 5 PRC2 and USC1 conditions for experiment I

the filler stories preceding the test story contained both the PRC2 and USC1 control conditions. This story is shown in Fig. 5.

The pictures and text for the Horses Story and the Girls Story are shown in Figs. 6 and 7, with the text translated into English. In the actual materials, the horses in the Horses Story were always depicted in color while all other figures were colorless black-and-white drawings. The only exception to this was that the hat of "the boy with the yellow hat" was colored yellow. In the Girls Story, the girls were depicted in color while the horses were black-and-white drawings. The second picture of each story was placed on the left-hand page in the materials booklet. The right-hand page facing this showed both the third and last pictures, the former placed directly above the latter. This arrangement made it possible for the child to look back at the last three pictures of the story when she was judging the truth-value of the test sentence.

As can be seen from Figs. 6 and 7, several different contextual factors have been manipulated to encourage an EP response under the CEO condition and, conversely, to discourage such a response under the IEO condition. Aside from the use of color, the horses are drawn large in the Horses Story but small in the Girls story. The extra horse is drawn extra large and placed in the foreground in the Horses Story, while it is a tiny object in the background in the Girls story. The Horses Story is told from the horses' point of view, the Girls Story from the girls' point of view. In addition, note that in the first scene of each story the puppet asks a couple of clarification questions which the story-teller prompts the child to answer. In the Horses Story, the puppet asks how many horses there are and what they look like, but does not mention the girls. In the Girls Story, he asks how many girls there are and what they are wearing, but does not mention the horses. This made the IEO condition in the Girls Story very similar to the "Show Me Condition" of Drozd and van Loosbroek (2006), since in answering the puppet's clarification questions the child produces a verbal description of the adult domain presupposition. Finally, note also that both test conditions satisfied the felicity conditions of Crain et al. (1996), since there is a point in the story (the second picture) when the test sentence is false under an adult reading.

Acquiring Knowledge of Universal Quantification

STORY-TELLER *This is a story about a bunch of horses. One day they were in a field eating grass....*[Puppet interrupts to ask how many horses and what they look like; child answers]*...Suddenly three boys appear at the edge of the field. The yellow horse with spots says, "Oh no! Boys! I bet they're going to try to ride us."*	
STORY-TELLER *And that's what the boys try to do. The brown horse and the black horse get caught and have to give a boy a ride, but the white horse and the yellow one with spots run away so the boy with a yellow hat doesn't get to ride a horse.*	
STORY-TELLER *Then the white horse is also caught by one of the boys....*	
STORY-TELLER *And now the boy with the yellow hat is riding a horse. The yellow horse with spots is happy because he doesn't have to carry any boy. Okay, Drakkie. Can you tell us something about this story?* PUPPET *Easy.* **Each boy is riding a horse.** CHILD *Not the yellow one with spots.*	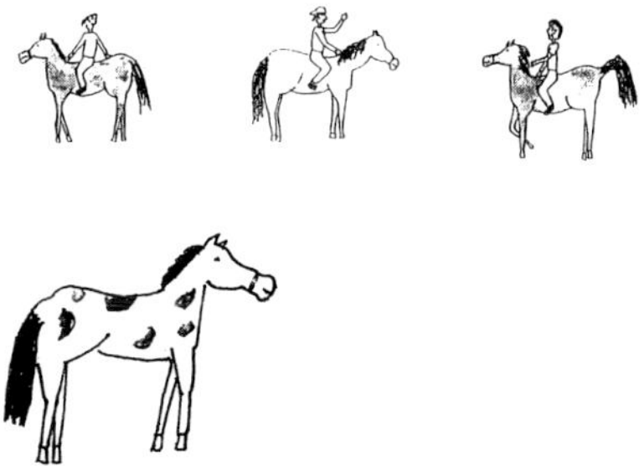

Fig. 6 Horses story (CEO condition)

378 W. Philip

STORY-TELLER *This is a story about a some girls. One day they were taking a walk in the country side....*[Puppet interrupts to ask how many girls and what they look like; child answers]...*After a while the girls find some horses. The girl with the yellow hat says, "Look! Horse! Let's try to ride them."*	
STORY-TELLER *And that's what the girls try to do. The girl with the red sweater catches a horse and she gets a ride, and so does the girl with the blue pants, but the girl with the yellow hat can't catch a horse so she doesn't get to ride one.*	
STORY-TELLER *Then the girl with the red sweater catches another horse....*	
STORY-TELLER *Now the girl with the yellow hat is riding a horse. Okay, Drakkie. Make a guess. Tell us something that's happening in this story.* PUPPET *Sure.* **Each girl is riding a horse.** CHILD *That's right.* (adult response)	

Fig. 7 Girls story (IEO condition)

The Dutch sentence used as the test sentence for the CEO condition was *Iedere jongen rijdt op een paard* 'Each boy is riding a horse', the same sentence which was used for the PRC2 condition. The Dutch sentence for the IEO condition was *Ieder meisje rijdt op een paard* 'Each girl is riding a horse'.[14]

6.1.4 Procedure

The experiment was run at the school that the children were attending. It was preceded by an instruction and warm-up session carried out as a group activity in the classroom "circle time" at the start of the school day. Here the two research assistants running the experiment explained to the children that the puppet had come to play a guessing game with them in which the puppet had to listen to the stories without looking at the pictures that went with them and try to make correct guesses about things that he could not see. The children's job, they were told, was to look at the pictures and tell the puppet if his guesses were right or wrong. This was demonstrated and practiced a few times with the children as a group, using props and warm-up pictures. To make it clear that the puppet could in principle make an incorrect guess, in the warm-up activity two of his guesses were false and two were correct.

The experiment was then presented to the children individually in a quiet area, such as a teachers' room or an unused classroom, with each child randomly assigned to the CEO group or the IEO group. During the experiment, the experimenter playing the role of the story-teller sat at a table next to the child and held the materials booklet up vertically with the pages facing herself and the child. The child sat to the right of the story-teller, so that the left hand page of the materials book that contained the pictures would be directly in her line of vision. The other experimenter, who manipulated and spoke for a puppet dragon named Drakkie, sat on the other side of the table, opposite the child and the story-teller. The story-teller read each story out loud once, presenting the pictures that accompanied each scene as the story unfolded and pointing to the objects in each picture as they were mentioned. The story-teller never repeated any part of the story. At the end of each story, and in the case of some filler stories in the middle of it, the story-teller asked the puppet to make a guess about a picture. With some of the filler stories the story-teller gave the puppet a hint, and sometimes she elicited a second guess from the puppet immediately after his first guess (e.g. the filler story containing PRC2 and USC1). This was not done for the test conditions, however. When the puppet made a guess, the story-teller

---

[14] The Dutch quantifiers *ieder(e)* in Experiments I and III and *elk(e)* in Experiment II are both obligatorily distributive (like English *each*, Vendler 1967). Unlike *every*, they do not presuppose a domain of quantification of greater-than-two cardinality; unlike both *each* and *every*, they both can have a meaning similar to English free-choice *any* in certain linguistic contexts (Philip 2002), none of which occur in the Experiments I, II or III. When they are DP-local, *ieder(e)* and *elk(e)* must agree in noun class with the NP providing their semantic restriction: e.g. *elke jongen, elk meisje* vs. **elk jongen, *elke meisje* (Booij 2002).

would say nothing and avoided eye contact with the child until after she had completed her response. Sometimes the story-teller would then give the puppet a word of encouragement by saying "good job" if the child had found his guess to be true or "too bad" if she had judged it false. The puppet expressed joy at making a correct guess, and disappointment when he failed to do so. However, the child was not asked to reward or punish the puppet, as is done in some versions of the TVJ paradigm (see Gordon 1998). With regard to the puppet's clarification questions in the first scene of the test stories, here the story-teller said to the child *Go ahead. Tell him*. Generally, this was enough to prompt the child to answer but if she hesitated the story-teller helped her get started by saying something like *Shall we count them? Let's see. One, two...Can you finish?* and *Shall we tell him what their colors are? Let's see. One is brown, one is yellow and has spots...Can you finish?.*

The experimenter manipulating the puppet recorded the child's responses on an answer sheet that also included the puppet's lines. Judgments of falsity under the CEO and IEO conditions were coded as EP responses whether or not the child spontaneously explained her judgment by alluding to the extra horse or to the insufficient number of boys or girls. Neither the puppet nor the story-teller ever asked the child to justify her judgments. Clear judgments of truth were coded as adult-like responses. If the child's response was unclear or obviously caused by a failure to interpret the pictures as intended, this was also coded as an adult-like response.[15]

The experiment was carried out by four pairs of research assistants, each a Dutch native speaker trained in the experimental methodology of the study. Natural prosody was used at all times, both by the story-teller and the puppet. For the adult control subjects, the puppet was not used. Instead, the experiment was run by a single experimenter who also delivered the puppet's lines as yes/no test questions about the stories. The adults were told that they were control subjects for an experiment with children.

6.1.5 Results

All the children included in the sample responded clearly and without hesitation to the test sentences of the CEO, IEO, PRC2 and USC1 conditions, giving either a clear judgment of truth or a clear judgment of falsity. The few children who gave unclear responses or who gave a negative response caused by a mis-coding of the picture were all among those excluded by the attention and target populati on filters. The numbers of subjects in each age and experimental group showing EP errors under the CEO or IEO test conditions are shown in Table 4, along with average percentages of adult-like responses under the OT and OF control conditions.

---

[15] E.g. a response like "Wrong, because that is a girl" with the child pointing at a boy.

Acquiring Knowledge of Universal Quantification

Table 4 Results of experiment I adult-like responses under OT/OF and EP errors under CEO and IEO

Groups		n	Mean percent adult-like responses over 8 trials		Number subjects and percent of group giving EP responses	
			OT	OF	# subjects	% of group
Younger children	CEO group	21	94%	94%	9	43%
	IEO group	24	92%	96%	2	8%
Older children	CEO group	20	96%	99%	5	25%
	IEO group	23	95%	97%	1	4%
Child CEO group		41	95%	97%	14	34%
Child IEO group		47	94%	96%	3	6%
Adult CEO group		16	97%	99%	1	6%

Kruskal-Wallis tests with H adjusted for ties show that under the CEO condition the performance of the 16 adults differed significantly from that of the 41 children as a whole ($p \leq 0.0332$) and even more so from that of the 21 younger children ($p \leq 0.0143$) but not from that of the 20 older children ($p \leq 0.1391$). The contrast between the CEO and the IEO groups was highly significant for the older children ($p \leq 0.0079$) and almost significant for the younger children ($p \leq 0.0540$). Collapsing the two child age groups, performance of the 41 children tested on the CEO condition differed with high significance from that of the 47 tested on the IEO condition ($p \leq 0.0011$).

6.2 Experiment II

Experiment II tested the PA's prediction that under a CEO condition the EP child will show EP just as often with sentences like (22) as with sentences like (21). In contrast, the EQA predicts a significant inhibition of EP responses with sentences like (22). The Dutch sentences in (21) and (22) are the two tokens of these two sentence types that were used in this study.

(21) a. *Elke hond likte een kat.*
each dog licked a cat
'Each dog licked a cat.'
b. *Elke stofzuiger heeft een muis opgezogen.*
each dust-suck-er has a mouse up-sucked
'Each vacuum cleaner has sucked up a mouse.'

(22) a. *Elke hond was een kattenlikker.*
each dog was a cat-PL-lick-er
'Each dog was a cat-licker.'
b. *Elke stofzuiger was een muisenopzuiger.*
each vacuum was a mouse-PL-up-suck-er
'Each vacuum cleaner was a mice-sucker-upper.'

Table 5 Participants of experiment II

	n	# boys	# girls	Mean age	Age range
Younger children	24	11	13	5;6	4;10–5;11
Older children	18	11	7	6;5	6;1–;11
Sixth graders	9	2	7	11;9	10;11–13;2
Adults	21	9	11	34	22–64

6.2.1 Participants

Experiment II was presented to 21 Dutch adults and to 89 Dutch children drawn from three primary schools in Utrecht. Two of the children were excluded by the attention filter of this experiment and another 36 by its target population filter. The 51 children included in the study were divided into three age groups: younger children, older children, and a group that will be referred to as the SIXTH GRADERS. The sixth graders were in their last year of primary school, "*groep* 8" in the Dutch primary school system. The age and gender statistics of the age groups are shown in Table 5. All of the children were monolingual Dutch speakers. All of the adults were native speakers of Dutch with no background in linguistics. None of the participants of Experiment II had participated in Experiment I.

6.2.2 Design

Experiment II had a four-level between-subjects variable of age, which had the same secondary purpose as the age variable of Experiment I, and a two-level within-subjects variable of predicate type testing a prediction of the PA (and the contrary prediction of the EQA). Each participant was tested on only one trial of a TRANS1 condition, which consisted of one or the other of the test sentences in (21) presented in a CEO context, and on only one trial of a NOM condition, where one or the other of the test sentences in (22) was presented in a CEO context. To reduce the likelihood of carry-over effects, the trials of the TRANS1 and NOM conditions were presented in different test stories, the CATS STORY and the MICE STORY (see below), which were placed at opposite ends of the experiment, separated by several filler stories. In addition, to counterbalance possible carry-over effects, two different sets of materials were constructed for each experimental group. One subgroup received a set in which the trial of TRANS1 occurred at the beginning of the experiment and the trial of NOM at the end. The other received a set in which the trial of NOM came first and the trial of TRANS1 at the end.

Like Experiment I, Experiment II used an attention filter and a target population filter to exclude inattentive children and children showing PR or US errors. However, these inclusion criteria were defined a bit more stringently and used slightly different control items. The attention filter was based on performance with three OT and six OF items. Any child showing incorrect judgments on more than one trial of OT

Acquiring Knowledge of Universal Quantification

> STORY-TELLER
> *There are some birds, some turtles, some flags, and there's a cat. Okay, Drakkie. Make a guess.*
> PUPPET
> ***Each bird is standing on a turtle.***
> STORY-TELLER
> *Good job, Drakkie. Try again.*
> PUPPET
> ***Each bird is holding a flag.***

Fig. 8 PRC1 and USC1 conditions of experiment II

or on more than one trial of OF was excluded from the study. The target population filter used one trial of PRC1 (rather than PRC2), one trial of USC1, and two trials of a new USC condition which will be called USC3 (see below). To be included in the study a subject had to show adult performance with all four items.

6.2.3 Materials and Procedure

Experiment II began with a filler story containing one trial each of the PRC1 and USC1 conditions shown in Fig. 8.

The next picture-story was the Cats Story. This was the first test story of the experiment and it contained the first trial of the USC3 and, at the end, a trial of either TRANS1 or NOM. After the Cats Story, there were new four filler stories containing ten false filler items randomly interspersed with ten true filler items. As in the previous experiments, the filler stories were pilot materials for other experiments that did not include universal quantifiers in their linguistic input. Among the filler puppet guesses, there were three OT items and six OF items. These were of the same type as the OT and OF items used in the previous two experiments. The seventh and last story of the experiment was second test story, containing a second trial of USC3 and a trial of either TRANS1 or NOM. This was the Mice Story shown in Fig. 9. In the actual materials, the mice were the only colored objects in the pictures. Unlike Experiment I, only the final picture was visible to the child when she was judging the test sentence for the TRANS1 or NOM conditions.

The Cats Story had exactly the same structure as the Mice Story. Its final picture is the one used to illustrate the EO condition in Fig. 1 above. (The story-teller lines for the Cats Story are not those shown in Fig. 1.) In the actual materials, the cats were the only objects drawn in color.

Two different sets of materials were made for each experimental group, which the participants were randomly assigned to. In one set, the Cats Story at the beginning of the experiment contained a trial of TRANS1 with (21a) as its test sentence while the Mice Story at the end contained a trial of NOM with (22b) as its test

STORY-TELLER *Once upon a time four "rainbow mice" were on a table. One was red, one was blue, one was yellow, one was white. That's why we call them "rainbow mice", because they are different colors.....* [picture on right shown at this point] *....Suddenly a bunch of robot vacuum cleaners came into the room and began to suck everything up.*	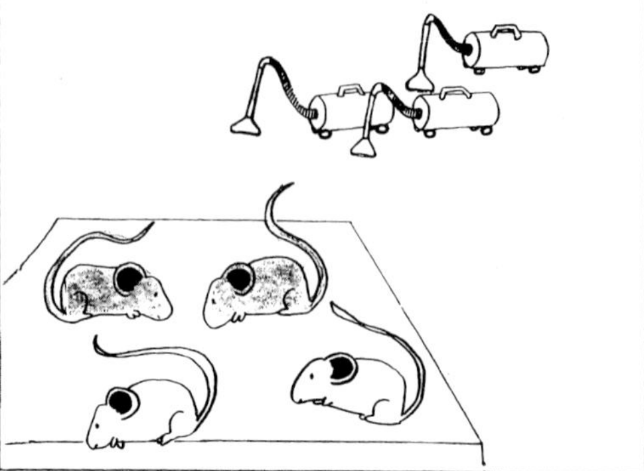
STORY-TELLER *The red mouse and the blue mouse jumped off the table to go take a look. "Don't do that!" said the yellow mouse, "You'll get sucked up!" But they didn't listen to him and, sure enough, that is exactly what happened.* **PUPPET** *Wait a minute. I'm confused.* **Did each vacuum cleaner suck up a mouse?** (= USC) [child answers] *So, only 2 mice got sucked up?* [child answers]	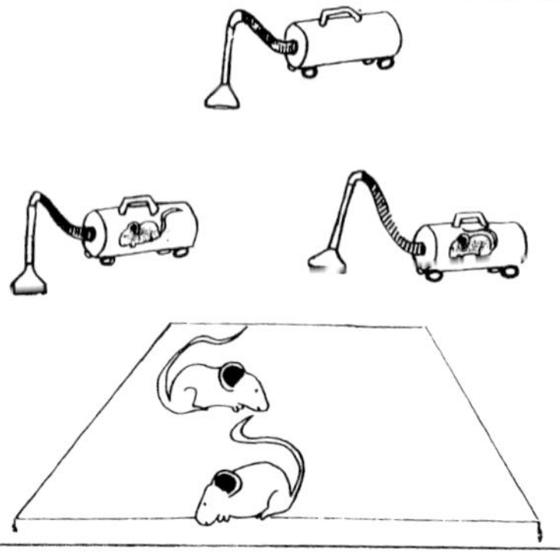
STORY-TELLER *Then the white mouse also jumped off the table to go look at the vacuum cleaners and he got sucked up too. But the yellow mouse stayed on the table and that's why he did not get sucked up. Okay, Drakkie. Make a guess.* **PUPPET** *Each vacuum cleaner sucked up a mouse.* (TRANS) *Each vacuum cleaner was a mouse-sucker-upper.* (NOM)	

Fig. 9 The mice story

sentence. In the other set, the Cats Story at the beginning contained a trial of NOM using (22a) as its test sentence while the Mice Story at the end contained a trial of TRANS1 with (21b) as its test sentence. Both sets contained the same filler items arranged in the same order.

All aspects of the procedure for Experiment II were the same as for Experiment I except that, if the children judged the test sentence to be false, the puppet asked the

Table 6 Results of experiment II adult responses under OT/OF and EP errors under TRANS1 and NOM

| | | | | Showing exhaustive pairing | | | |
| | | Average percent adult-like responses | | With TRANS1 *each dog is licking a cat* | | With NOM *each dog is a cat-licker* | |
Age group	n	OT	OF	# subjects	% of group	# subjects	% of group
Younger	24	97%	99%	14	58%	10	58%
Older	18	94%	100%	8	44%	6	44%
Sixth graders	9	100%	100%	0	0%	0	0%
Adults	21	98%	98%	1	5%	0	5%

child why his guess was wrong. A child judgment of falsity was coded as an instance of EP only if she justified this judgment by referring to the extra object or by commenting that were not enough objects of the quantified type to make the sentence true. The adult procedure was used with the sixth graders. Experiment II was carried out by a team of Dutch native speaker research assistants who had not participated in Experiment I.

6.2.4 Results

Under the test conditions, all subjects included in the sample gave either clear judgments of falsity or clear judgments of truth. The few children giving unclear responses or incorrect responses caused by a mis-coding of the visual input had been excluded by the attention or population filters. The numbers of children and adults showing EP under the TRANS1 and NOM conditions are shown in Table 6 by age group, along with average percentages of adult-like performance under the OT and OF conditions.

There were no significant contrasts between TRANS1 and NOM for any age group, nor for any pooling of age groups. Focusing on performance under TRANS1, Kruskal-Wallis tests with H not adjusted for ties show no significant contrast between the younger and the older children, nor between the sixth graders and the adults, but did find a highly significant contrast between the younger and older children pooled together as one age group and the sixth graders and the adults pooled together as another ($p \leq 0.0000$).

6.3 *Experiment III*

Experiment III tested the PA = s prediction that EP would be inhibited by a comparative predicate like *be smaller than a horse* (and the contrary prediction of the EQA).

Table 7 Participants of experiment III

Age group	n	# boys	# girls	Mean age	Age range
Younger children	33	17	16	5;4	4;3–5;10
Older children	14	7	7	6;3	6;0–6;9
All children	47	24	23	5;7	4;3–6;9
Adults	22	10	12	20	17–22

6.3.1 Participants

Sixty-eight Dutch children drawn from two primary schools in Utrecht and 22 Dutch native speaker adults participated in Experiment III. 21 of these children were excluded by inclusion criteria similar to those used in Experiments I and II, five by an attention filter and 16 by a target population filter. As in Experiment I, the subjects included in the experiment were divided into three age groups: younger children, older children, and adults. The age and gender statistics of these groups are given in Table 7. All these participants were monolingual Dutch native speakers, none of whom had participated in Experiment I or II. The adults were college students who had no formal education in linguistics.

6.3.2 Design

Experiment III had two secondary between-subjects variables and one primary within-subjects variable. The within-subjects variable tested the prediction of the PA by presenting each participant one trial of a COMP condition, whose test sentence contained a comparative predicate, immediately after one trial of a TRANS2 condition, which used the same test sentence as the CEO condition of Experiment I. The first between-subjects factor was age, with the three levels being younger children, older children, and adults. This had the same purpose as in the age variables in Experiments I and II. The second between-subjects variable explored the possibility that the presence in the test sentence of a personal pronoun bound by the quantifier might interact with EP. One experimental group received a set of materials in which the test sentences of the TRANS2 and COMP conditions included such a bound-variable pronoun. For the other group, the test sentences contained a singular indefinite direct object, just as in Experiments I and II.

Like the previous experiments, Experiment III included only a single trial of each test condition. However, unlike Experiment II, possible carry over effects were deliberately controlled in only one direction. The ordering of the materials made a carry over effect from COMP to TRANS2 impossible but possible from TRANS2 to COMP. This allowed the findings for TRANS2 to be directly compared with those of Experiment I for the CEO condition. In addition it made it harder for the prediction of the PA to be borne out, since if an EP response elicited under TRANS2 carried over to COMP this would artificially inflate falsifying evidence.

Like Experiments I and II, Experiment III used an attention filter and a target population filter in an attempt to include in the sample only EP children and children showing perfectly adult-like performance. The attention filter was slightly different from that of the other two experiments (again because different filler stories were used). To be included in Experiment III, a child had to give correct adult-like responses with two out of the three OT items that were used as well as with two out of the three OF items. The target population filter was the same as that of Experiment I except that PRC2 and USC1 were contained in different filler stories.

6.3.3 Materials and Procedure

The ordering of the materials of Experiment III was very similar to that of Experiment I, with the test stories coming at the end after several filler stories. Different filler stories were used, and there were only eight of them. All together, the filler stories included eight puppet guesses that were correct for an adult, randomly interspersed with six that were incorrect. Of these 14 filler items, three were used as OT items, three as OF items, one as PRC2, and one as a USC1. Unlike Experiments I and II, the PRC2 and USC1 items were presented in isolation, in different stories separated by a few filler items. The target input sentence for PRC2 was *Iedere dier is de plantjes water aan het geven* 'Each animal is watering the plants'; for USC1 it was *Iedere olifant is nat gespoten* 'Each elephant was drenched'.

The TRANS2 and COMP test conditions were both contained in a single test story, which was the Horses Story of Experiment I. Thus, one version of TRANS2 was identical to the CEO condition of Experiment I, the other differed only in that the test sentence contained a bound-variable pronoun. At the end of the story the puppet first presented the test sentence for TRANS2 and then immediately gave a second guess which was test sentence for COMP. The two versions of each sentence type are shown in (23) and (24).

(23) a. *Iedere jongen rijdt op een paard.* (TRANS2 = CEO of Experiment I)
'Each boy is riding on a horse.'
b. *Iedere jongen is kleiner dan een paard.* (COMP)
'Each boy is smaller than a horse.'

(24) a. *Iedere jongen rijdt op zijn paard.* (TRANS2)
'Each boy is riding on his horse.'
b. *Iedere jongen is kleiner dan zijn paard.* (COMP)
'Each boy is smaller than his horse.'

There were two sets of materials containing the same stories arranged in the same order but with one set using (23) as the test sentences for TRANS and COMP and the other using (24). For each age group, the participants were randomly assigned to two experimental groups, each receiving one of the two sets of materials.

Table 8 Results of experiment III EP errors under TRANS2 and COMP

Age group	n	TRANS2 *each boy is riding a/his horse*		COMP *each boy is smaller than a/his horse*	
		# subjects	% of group	# subjects	% of group
Younger children	33	9	27%	1	3%
Older children	14	3	21%	0	0%
All children	47	12	26%	1	2%
Adults	22	3	14%	0	0%

All aspects of the procedure for Experiment III were the same as for Experiment II. Experiment III was carried out by two teams of Dutch native speaker research assistants, none of whom had participated in Experiments I or II.

6.3.4 Results

As in Experiments II, all the children included in the study gave clear responses under the test conditions. Performance under the OT and OF control conditions was highly adult-like for all, with both the younger and older children showing adult-like performance 97% of the time with the OT items (adults 99%) and 81% of the time with OF (adults 100%). The percentages and numbers of subjects in each age group that showed EP under TRANS2 and COMP are shown in Table 8.

Kruskal-Wallis tests with H adjusted for ties show there to be no significant main or interactive effects of experimental group – those tested on (23) vs. those tested on (24) – and no significant contrasts between the younger and older children. Sign tests show that EP occurred significantly more often with TRANS2 than with COMP for the 33 younger children ($p \leq 0.0078$) and for the 47 children as a whole ($p \leq 0.0010$), but not for the older children ($p \leq 0.2500$), nor for the 22 adults ($p \leq 0.2500$).

6.4 Discussion of the Results of Experiments I, II, and III

The inclusion criteria used in these three experiments had the effect that virtually only two types of children were included in the samples: children showing perfect adult performance and children whose only error was EP. The principal finding of Experiment I was that, for children of these two types, the manipulation of contextual factors in the CEO and IEO conditions had a very significant effect on EP. It occurred with 34% of the children tested on the CEO condition but with only 6% of those tested on the IEO condition. This finding bears out a prediction of the PA, and also that of all accounts of EP that attribute this error to nonadult-like pragmatic restriction of the domain of quantification.

The principal finding of Experiment II was that EP was not inhibited in the least with nominal predicates like *be a cat-licker*, contrary to a prediction of the EQA but just as expected by the PA. A second finding of this experiment was that EP did not occur with the sixth graders. This new observation suggests that at least by the age of 12 children attain maximal competence in defining the pragmatic restriction of a universal quantifier in an adult-like manner.

The principal finding of Experiment III was that EP errors occurred significantly less often under the COMP condition than under the TRANS2 condition, despite the possibility of an artificial inflation of EP responses under COMP due to a carry-over effect from TRANS2. Though 26% of the children showed EP under TRANS2, only 2% did so under COMP. This is just as predicted by the PA (and another false prediction for the EQA). Another finding of Experiment III was that the presence of a bound-variable pronoun in the test sentence (*Every boy is riding* his *horse*) had no effect whatsoever on EP.

Experiments I-III also showed (once again) that adults can in principle show EP under an EO condition. All together 59 adults participated in one or another of these experiments. Five of them (12%) gave an EP response under a EO condition designed to encourage EP.

Before concluding this section, there are two methodological points that merit some discussion. First, it will have been noted that the three experiments presented here do not control for the "language-as-fixed-effect fallacy" (Coleman 1964; Clark 1973). One cannot generalize from the findings of Experiments I-III alone because their test conditions collectively tested only three transitive sentences, one with the predicate 'ride', one with the predicate 'lick', and one with the predicate 'suck up'. This is true; however, there is no need to demonstrate that EP occurs with all sorts of transitive predicates (and in all sorts of languages) since prior research has already robustly demonstrated that it does. What is needed, rather, is some hard evidence that this prior research gives us an accurate picture of the degree to which children show EP under an EO condition. This is not clear because (i) in at least one prior study using an EO condition the EP error was not observed at all (Crain et al. 1996) and (ii) virtually all prior research used a repeated-measure design, thereby introducing an uncontrolled variable, namely possible carry over effects. The new kind of data gathered by Experiments I-III address this issue. First, in light of the findings of Experiment I, it seems likely that one of the main reasons why Crain et al. found such highly adult-like performance was because their experimental condition was formally comparable to the IEO condition of Experiment I. Second, the findings of Experiments I-III are consistent with the general finding of the cross-linguistic studies summarized in Table 2 above. Recall that 31% of the 500 children examined in these studies only showed the EP error. Experiments I-III presented an EO condition (CEO or TRANS1) to 130 children (excluding the sixth graders). Given only one opportunity to do so, 37% of these children (48/130) showed the EP error. The empirical generalization appears to be that, when they are attentive (i.e. do not showing PR or US errors), preschool children are likely to show EP errors under an EO condition roughly one third of the time (whereas adults do so only about one tenth of the time).

The tentative empirical generalization just noted has bearing on a second methodological issue. It suggests that when greater frequencies are observed in repeated-measure experiments using an EO condition this may be because a carry-over effect from the first trial the EO condition is artificially inflating the total number of EP errors observed. This can clearly be seen (and is explicitly noted) in the first experiment of Philip (1995), where EP responses also occur quite often even with sentences like *Every dog is waving* and *Dogs are riding ponies*. In sum, the real problem for L1A research on universal quantifiers may be a "too-many-trials-enhancing-an-effect fallacy." The widespread practice of using several trials of an experimental condition in order to be able to draw statistical inferences from relatively small samples may be self-defeating. Although motivated by a valid practical concern, it may be seriously compromising the usefulness of experimental research.

7 Conclusion and General Discussion

One of the main goals of this paper was been to disentangle those aspects of adult knowledge of universal quantification that are innately known and acquired early from those that are innately known but acquired late, and from those that are not innately known but rather must be learned from the positive evidence without the help of UG. One general conclusion we seem tentatively able to draw in this regard is that it is possible that UG governs the L1A of universal quantification in a much more indirect and minimal way than is commonly assumed in theoretical linguistics. A second general observation is that much of UG does not solve any logical problem for the L1A of universal quantification but rather exists only because it solves a psychological problem, i.e. because it speeds things up.

References

Aoun, J., and Y.A. Li. 1993. *Syntax of scope*. Cambridge, MA: MIT Press.
Baauw, S., and F. Cuetos. 2004. The interpretation of pronouns in Spanish language acquisition and breakdown. *Language Acquisition* 11(4): 219–275.
Barwise, J., and R. Cooper. 1981. Generalized quantifiers and natural language. *Linguistics and Philosophy* 4: 159–219.
Bobaljik, J.D. 1998. Floating quantifiers: Handle with care. *Glot International* 3–6: 3–10.
Bohannon, J.N., and L. Stanowicz. 1988. The issue of negative evidence: Adult responses to children's language errors. *Developmental Psychology* 24: 684–689.
Booij, G. 2002. *The morphology of Dutch*. Oxford: Oxford University Press.
Borer, H., and K. Wexler. 1987. The maturation of syntax. In *Parameter setting and language acquisition*, ed. T. Roeper and E. Williams, 123–172. Dordrecht: Reidel.
Boster, C.T., and S. Crain. 1993. On children's understanding of every and or. Paper presented at Early Cognition and the Transition to Language, conference at the center for Cognitive Science, University of Texas, Austin.

Brinkmann, U., K.F. Drozd, and I. Krämer. 1996. Physical individuation as a prerequisite for children's symmetrical readings. In *Proceedings of the 20th Annual Boston University Conference on Language Development*, ed. A. Stringfellow, D. Cahana-Amitay, E. Hughes, and A. Zubowski, 99–110. Somerville: Cascadilla Press.

Brooks, J.P., and M. Braine. 1996. What do children know about the universal quantifiers 'all' and 'each'? *Cognition* 60: 235–268.

Brooks, J.P., and I. Sekerina. 2005/2006. Shortcuts to quantifier interpretation in children and adults. *Language Acquisition* 13: 177–206.

Brown, R., and C. Hanlon. 1970. Derivational complexity and order of acquisition in child speech. In *Cognition and the development of language*, ed. J.R. Hayes, 11–53. New York: Wiley.

Bucci, W. 1978. The interpretation of universal affirmative propositions: A developmental study. *Cognition* 6: 55–77.

Chien, Y.-C., and K. Wexler. 1989. Children's knowledge of relative scope in Chinese. Paper presented at the 1989 Child Language Research Forum, Stanford.

Chien, Y.-C., and K. Wexler. 1990. Children's knowledge of locality conditions in binding as evidence for the modularity of syntax and pragmatics. *Language Acquisition* 1: 225–295.

Chomsky, N. 1981. *Lectures on government and binding*. Dordrecht: Foris.

Chomsky, N. 2004. Beyond explanatory adequacy. In *Structures and beyond: The cartography of syntactic structures*, vol. 3, ed. A. Belletti, 104–131. Oxford: Oxford University press.

Clark, H.H. 1973. The language-as-fixed-effect fallacy: A critique of language statistics in psychological research. *Journal of Verbal Learning and Verbal Behavior* 12: 335–359.

Coleman, E.B. 1964. Generalizing to a language population. *Psychological Reports* 14: 219–226.

Crain, S. 1991. Language acquisition in the absence of experience. *The Behavioral and Brain Sciences* 14: 597–612.

Crain, S., R. Thornton, C. Boster, L. Conway, D. Lillo-Martin, and E. Woodams. 1996. Quantification without qualification. *Language Acquisition* 5: 83–153.

Culicover, P.W. 1999. *Syntactic nuts: Hard cases, syntactic theory, and language acquisition*. Oxford: Oxford University Press.

Dalrymple, M., M. Kanazawa, S. Mchombo, and S. Peters. 1995. What do reciprocals mean? In *Proceedings of SALT IV*, Cornell Working Papers in Linguistics, Cornell, Ithaca.

de Swart, H.E. 1991. Adverbs of quantification: A generalized quantifier approach. Doctoral diss., University of Groningen, The Netherlands.

Demetras, M.J., K.N. Post, and C.E. Snow. 1986. Feedback to first language learners: The role of repetitions and clarification questions. *Journal of Child Language* 13: 275–292.

Doetjes, J. 1997. Quantifiers and selection: On the distribution of quantifying expressions in french, Dutch and English. Doctoral diss., Leiden University, The Netherlands.

Donaldson, M., and P. Lloyd. 1974. Sentences and situations: Children's judgments of match and mismatch. In *Current problems in psycholinguistics*, ed. F. Bresson, 73–86. Paris: Centre National de la Recherche Scientifique.

Donaldson, M.A., and J. McGarrigle. 1974. Some clues to the nature of semantic development. *Journal of Child Language* 1: 185–194.

Dowty, D., and B. Brodie. 1984. The semantics of 'floated' quantifiers in a transformationless grammar. In *Proceedings of the West Coast Conference on FormalLinguistics 4*, Stanford.

Drozd, K.F. 1996a. On the sources of children's misinterpretations of quantified sentences. In *Amsterdam series on child language development*, vol. 6, ed. W. Philip and F. Wijnen, 173–210. Amsterdam: University of Amsterdam.

Drozd, K.F. 1996b. Quantifier interpretation errors as errors of distributive scope. In *Proceedings of the 20th Annual Boston University Conference on Language Development*, 177–188. Somerville: Cascadilla Press.

Drozd, K.F. 2001. Children's weak interpretations of universally quantified sentences. In *Conceptual development and language acquisition*, ed. M. Bowerman and S.C. Levinson, 340–376. Cambridge: Cambridge University Press.

Drozd, K.F. 2004. Investigations in universal grammar. *Journal of Child Language* 32: 431–457.

Drozd, K.F., and E. van Loosbroek. 1999. Weak quantification, plausible dissent, and the development of children's pragmatic knowledge. In *Proceedings of the 23rd Annual Boston University Conference on Language Development*, 184–195. Somerville: Cascadilla Press.

Drozd, K.F., and E. van Loosbroek. 2006. The effect of context on children's interpretations of universally quantified sentences. In *Semantics meets acquisition*, ed. V. Van Geenhoven. Dordrecht: Kluwer.

Elman, J.L., E.A. Bates, M.H. Johnson, A. Karmiloff-Smith, D. Parisi, and K. Plunkett. 1996. *Rethinking innateness: A connectionist perspective on development*. Cambridge, MA: MIT Press.

Fodor, J.A. 1983. *Modularity of mind*. Cambridge, MA: MIT Press.

Freeman, H.H. 1985. Reasonable errors in basic reasoning. *Educational Psychology* 5: 239–249.

Freeman, H.H., and K. Schreiner. 1988. Complementary error patterns in collective and individuating judgements: Their semantic basis in 6-year-olds. *British Journal of Developmental Psychology* 6: 341–350.

Freeman, H.H., and M. Sepahzad. 1987. Competence of young children who fail to make correct deduction. *British Journal of Developmental Psychology* 5: 275–286.

Freeman, N.H., C.G. Sinha, and J.A. Stedmon. 1982. All the cars? which cars? from word meaning to discourse analysis. In *Children thinking through language*, ed. M. Beveridge, 52–74. London: Edward Arnold.

Geurts, B. 2000. Review of Crain and Thornton 1998. *Linguistics and Philosophy* 23: 523–532.

Geurts, B. 2003. Quantifying kids. *Language Acquisition* 11: 197–218.

Gordon, P. 1998. The truth-value judgement task. In *Methods for assessing children syntax*, ed. D. McDaniel et al., 211–232. Cambridge, MA: MIT Press.

Grimshaw, J., and S. Rosen. 1990. Knowledge and obedience: The developmental status of the binding theory. *Linguistic Inquiry* 21: 187–222.

Hamann, C.O., and W. Philip. 1997. The French 'delay of principle B' effect. In *Proceedings of the 21st Annual Boston University Conference on Language Development*, Cascadilla.

Hanlon, C. 1981. The emergence of set-relational quantifiers in early childhood. In *Child language: An international perspective*, ed. P.S. Dale and D. Ingram. Baltimore: University Park Press.

Heim, I. 1982. The semantics of definite and indefinite noun phrases. Doctoral diss., University of Massachusetts at Amherst, Amherst.

Hestvik, A., and W. Philip. 1999/2000. Binding and coreference in Norwegian child language. *Language Acquisition* 8: 171–235.

Higginbotham, J. 1995. Mass and count quantifiers. In *Quantification in natural languages*, ed. E. Bach et al., 383–419. Dordrecht: Kluwer.

Hirsh-Pasek, K., R. Treiman, and M. Schneiderman. 1984. Brown & Hanlon revisited: Mothers' sensitivity to ungrammatical forms. *Journal of Child Language* 11: 81–88.

Hoji, H. 1985 Logical form constraints and configurational structures in Japanese. Doctoral diss., University of Washington, Seattle.

Huang, J. 1982. Logical relations in Chinese and the theory of grammar. Doctoral diss., MIT, Cambridge, MA.

Inhelder, B., and J. Piaget. 1958. *The early growth of logical thinking from childhood to adolescence*. New York: Basic Books.

Inhelder, B., and J. Piaget. 1964. *The early growth of logic in the child*. London: Routledge.

Jelinek, E. 1995. Quantification in straits Salish. In *Quantification in natural languages*, ed. E. Bach et al., 487–540. Dordrecht: Kluwer.

Kadmon, N., and F. Landman. 1993. Any. *Linguistics and Philosophy* 16: 353–422.

Kang, H.-K. 2001. Quantifier spreading: Linguistic and pragmatic considerations. *Lingua* 111: 591–627.

Keenan, E., and J. Stavi. 1986. A semantic characterization of natural language determiners. *Linguistics and Philosophy* 9: 253–326.

Kobuchi-Philip, M. 2003. Distributivity and the Japanese floating numeral quantifier. PhD diss., CUNY Graduate Center.

Kobuchi-Philip, M. 2007. Individual-denoting classifiers. *Natural Language Semantics* 15: 95–130.
Kratzer, A. 1989. Stage-level and individual-level predicates, In Papers on Quantification, NSF grant BNS 8(1999) report, UMass at Amherst, Amherst.
Krifka, M. 1990. Four thousand ships passed through the lock. *Linguistics and Philosophy* 12: 487–520.
Kurtzman, H.S., and M.C. MacDonald. 1993. Resolution of quantifier scope ambiguities. *Cognition* 48: 243–279.
Labov, W. 1984. Intensity. In *Meaning, form, and use in context: Linguistic applications*, ed. D. Schriffin. Washington, DC: Georgetown University Press.
Landmon, F. 2000. *Events and plurality*. Dordrecht: Kluwer.
Lewis, D. 1979. Score keeping in a language game. *Journal of Philosophical Logic* 8: 339–359.
Marcus, G.F. 1993. Negative evidence in language acquisition. *Cognition* 46: 51–80.
McKee, C. 1992. A comparison of pronouns and anaphors in Italian and English acquisition. *Language* 2: 21–54.
Mehler, J., and P. Carey. 1967. Role of surface and base structure in the perception of sentences. *Journal of Verbal Learning and Verbal Behavior* 6: 335–338.
Morgan, J.L., and L.L. Travis. 1989. Limits on negative evidence in language input. *Journal of Child Language* 16: 531–552.
Philip, W. 1995. Event quantification in the acquisition of universal quantification. Doctoral diss., University of Massachusetts at Amherst.
Philip, W. 1996. The event quantificational account and a denial of an implausible infelicity in children's comprehension of universal quantification. In *Proceedings of the 20th Annual Boston University Conference on Language Development*, 564–575. Somerville: Cascadilla Press.
Philip, W. 2002. Dutch teenagers' SLA of English *any*. In *Linguistics in the Netherlands 2002*, ed. H. Broekhuis and P. Fikkert, 129–138. Amsterdam: Benjamins.
Philip, W. 2004a. Clarity of purpose in L1 acquisition research: A response to Ken Drozd's 'learnability and linguistic performance. *Journal of Child Language* 42(2): 496–499.
Philip, W. 2004b. Two theories of exhaustive pairing. Ms., UiL-OTS, Utrecht University, Utrecht
Philip, W. 2004c. Pragmatic control of specificity and scope: Evidence from Dutch L1A. In ed. Maier, E., C. Bary, and J. Huitink, 271–280. Papers presented at the 9th Sinn und Bedeutung. Nijmegen Centre of Semantics, Nijmegen.
Philip, W., and E. Lynch. 2000. Felicity, relevance, and acquisition of the grammar of every and only. In *Proceedings of the 24th Annual Boston University Conference on Language Development*, Somerville: Cascadilla Press.
Philip, W. and S. Aurelio. 1991. Quantifier spreading: Pilot study of preschoolers' *Every*. In Maxfield and Plunkett.
Philip, W., and S. Avrutin. 1998. Quantification in agrammatic aphasia. In *The interpretive tract: MIT working papers in linguistics 25*, ed. U. Sauerland and O. Percus, 63–72. Cambridge, MA: MIT Press.
Philip, W., and P. Coopmans. 1996. The double Dutch delay of principle B. In *Proceedings of the 20th Annual BU Conference on Language Development*, ed. A. Stringfellow, D. Cahana-Amitay, E. Hughes, and A. Zukowski, 576–587. Somerville: Cascadilla Press.
Philip, W., and M. Takahashi. 1991. Quantifier spreading in the acquisition of *Every*. In Maxfield and Plunkett, 283–301.
Pinker, S. 1984. *Language learnability and language development*. Cambridge, MA: MIT Press.
Saddy, J.D. 1990. Investigations into grammatical knowledge. Doctoral diss., MIT.
Safir, K., and T. Stowell. 1987. Binominal *each*. Proceedings of NELS 18: 426–450.
Sarnecka, B.W., and S. Carey. 2008. How counting represents number: What children must learn and when they learn it. *Cognition* 108: 662–674.
Schwarzschild, R. 1989. Adverbs of quantification as generalized quantifiers. In *Proceedings of the North Eastern Linguistics Society*, vol. 19, 390–404. Amherst: GLSA.
Slobin, D.I. 1991. Can crain constrain the constraints? *The Behavioral and Brain Sciences* 14: 633–634.

Smith, C.L. 1979. Children's understanding of natural language hierarchies. *Journal of Experimental Psychology* 27: 437–458.

Sportiche, D. 1988. A theory of floating quantifiers and its corrollaries for constituent structure. *Linguistic Inquiry* 19: 425–449.

Szabolcsi, A. 1997. *Ways of scope taking*. Dordrecht: Kluwer.

Takahashi, M. 1991. Children's interpretation of sentences containing *Every*. In *Papers in the Acquisition of WH*, ed. T.L. Maxfield and B. Plunkett, 303–323. Amherst: GLSA.

Tesar, B., and P. Smolensky. 1998. Learnability in optimality theory. *Linguistics Inquiry* 29: 229–268.

Tomasello, M. 2003. *Constructing a language: A usage-based theory of language acquisition*. Cambridge, MA: Harvard University Press.

van Benthem, J. 1986. *Essays in logical semantics*. Dordrecht: Reidel.

vanden Wyngaerd, G. 1992. Een reviewer zal elk abstract nalezen. *Tabu* 22–1: 65–74.

Vendler, Z. 1967. *Linguistics in philosophy*. Ithaca: Cornell University Press.

von Fintel, K. 1994. Restrictions on quantifier domains. Doctoral diss., University of Massachusetts at Amherst, Amherst.

Westerståhl, D. 1989. Quantifiers in formal and natural languages. In *Handbook of philosophic logic*, vol. IV, ed. D. Gabby and F. Guenther, 1–131. Dordrecht: Reidel.

Index

A

Abdulkarim, L., 231
Accommodation, 213, 362, 371
A-chain, 8, 18, 54, 156, 158, 162–171, 177, 178, 258, 270, 312
A-chain deficit, 54, 156, 158, 162–171
Acquisition, 1, 13, 54, 119, 155, 189, 247, 291, 319, 351
Adversity passives, 157, 177, 183, 311
Afrikaans, 56, 63, 69
Agrammatic aphasia, 248, 265
Agrammatics, 248, 249, 251, 265, 273, 275, 276, 284, 285, 361, 370
Agreement, 13, 20, 22, 27, 29, 41, 56, 61–63, 65, 67–70, 74, 75, 78, 86, 89, 97, 99, 109, 112, 113, 141, 195–197, 199, 201, 207, 209, 214, 235, 236, 270, 335
Agr/Tns omission model (ATOM), 53, 67–69, 73, 75, 77, 79, 81–83, 85, 86, 91, 97, 108
Alexiadou, A., 76
Allen, S., 33, 42, 43, 45, 46
Altmann, G.T.M., 342
A-movement, 54, 164–166, 169, 170, 177, 183, 190, 191, 312, 325
Anagnostopoulou, E., 76
Anaphor, 9, 36, 247, 250–253, 255–261, 267, 285, 308, 309, 311, 314
Anderson, C., 330, 334, 335, 341
Angluin, D., 126–129, 144
Aoun, J., 353
Arabic, 26, 111, 226, 374
Argument-chain,
Asymmetries in acquisition, 9, 208–211, 251
ATOM. *See* Agr/Tns omission model
Attention filter, 374, 375, 382, 386, 387

Auxiliary movement, 195–197, 203, 204
Auxiliary omission model, 71
Avrutin, S., 57, 261, 263, 265, 266, 273, 276

B

Baauw, S., 248, 249, 264, 268, 271, 273–278, 282, 365
Babyonyshev, M., 13, 59, 87, 166–169
Baek, J., 112
Baldie, B.J., 160
Barbosa, P., 76
Barrier, 189, 192, 195, 207, 222–240
Barwise, J., 352
Basic word order/word order, 2, 54, 55, 61, 63, 77, 91, 93, 94, 99–104, 111, 113, 138, 139, 143, 155, 156, 214, 216, 292–297, 302, 314
Bates, E., 18, 29
Battell, J., 206
Bayesian learning, 130, 133, 134, 136
Becker, M., 107, 170, 171
Beghelli, F., 260, 285
Behrens, H., 113
Bel, A., 29
Belletti, A., 270
Bellugi, U., 13
Bencini, G.M.L., 180, 181, 184
Benmamoun, E., 111
Be-omission, 53, 106–112
Berwick, R.C., 17
Bever, T.G., 159
Bidirectional optimality, 249
Bikel, D., 136
Binding principles, 9, 120, 249, 256, 257, 259, 261, 262, 267

Blom, E., 113
Blom, L., 13, 16, 25, 30–32, 34, 35, 40, 42, 44, 46
Bloom, P., 280
Bobaljik, J.D., 352
Bock, J.K., 180
Boeckx, C., 3, 340, 341
Bohannon, J.N., 359
Booij, G., 379
Borer, H., 18, 54, 87, 162, 163, 165, 170, 172, 312, 363
Boser, K., 71
Bošković, Ž., 221
Boster, C.T., 263
Brazilian Portuguese, 26, 63
Bromberg, H., 19, 23
Bromberg, H.S., 80
Brown, R., 13, 16, 23, 36, 43, 83, 146, 148, 157, 198, 200, 359
Bucci, W., 364
Bulgarian, 190, 192, 203, 214, 216, 220, 221, 223
Burzio, L., 249, 260, 270
Buttery, P., 124

C
Cable, S., 56, 69
Cantonese, 181, 182, 184
Caprin, C., 60, 63, 64
Cardinaletti, A., 270, 273–275
Cardinality principle, 363
Carey, P., 367
Carey, S., 363
Carry-over effect, 375, 382, 389, 390
Case, 2, 13, 53, 126, 157, 190, 247, 298, 322, 351
Catalan, 29, 63, 202
C-command, 9, 215, 230, 248, 251, 252, 254, 255, 259, 261, 298, 299, 306–311, 322, 325, 330, 332, 343, 344
Chafetz, J., 157, 175
Chain condition, 258, 267–269, 275, 276, 278, 284
Chalkley, A., 131
Chan, E., 135
Cheng, L.L.S., 219
Chien, Y.C., 9, 247, 248, 254, 256, 261, 262, 267, 273, 278, 279, 281, 363, 367
Chierchia, G., 265
Choe, J.S., 171
Chomsky hierarchy, 126

Chomsky, N., 2–4, 9, 13, 14, 22, 40, 44, 128, 142, 172, 219, 221, 232, 234, 235, 252, 259, 359
Christiansen, M.H., 133
Clahsen, H., 19, 35, 148
Clancy, P., 41, 45, 46
Clancy, P.M., 292
Clark, A., 127
Clark, R., 21
Clitic-climbing, 275, 276
Clitics, 9, 34, 74, 76, 112, 220, 248, 249, 261, 264, 269–277, 281, 282, 284, 285
Competing grammars, 5, 20–23
Computational complexity, 136, 149
Condition of plausible dissent, 362
Configurationality, 297–302
Connectionism, 359
Conroy, A., 250, 263, 264, 278–282, 285, 319, 328, 335, 337, 342
Conservativity, 198, 355, 356, 358, 368, 371
Constraint on movement, 190
Cooper, R., 352
Coopmans, P., 249, 263, 264, 267–269, 275, 278, 280, 282
Copying, 209–211, 228–231
Coreference, 247–285
Covert movement, 167, 230–235
CP, 22, 25, 26, 57, 77–82, 99, 133, 190, 192, 194, 195, 197–204, 212, 218, 219, 221–225, 227, 230, 233–239
Crain, S., 37, 120, 148, 219, 221, 232, 234, 235, 247, 325, 344–346, 355, 361, 362, 367, 368, 372, 376, 389
Crawford, J., 177
Crisma, P., 19
Cross-over, 207, 208
Crousaz, D., 26
Cuetos, F., 365
Culicover, P.W., 21, 128, 358
Czech, 63, 220

D
Dalrymple, M., 356
Danish, 15, 16, 20, 23–25, 27, 29, 31, 45, 57, 63
Dayal, V., 230
Default case, 66–68, 78, 89
de Haan, G., 25
Delay of principle B effect (DPBE), 9, 247, 248, 261
Delfitto, D., 270
Demetras, M.J., 359
Demuth, K., 176–178, 182, 184

Index

den Besten, H., 25
Determiner, 14, 35, 46, 74, 352, 355–357, 368
de Villiers, J.G., 159, 160, 189, 247, 291, 319
Diary drop, 27–29, 35, 37, 45, 46
Diesing, M., 344
Discourse, 4, 5, 17, 20, 25, 30, 33, 40–43, 45, 46, 65, 99, 130, 184, 191, 194, 198, 203, 212, 217, 219, 222, 234, 251, 253–255, 260, 271, 276, 279, 280, 282, 285, 296, 352, 355, 356, 368, 371
Discourse Condition on Exceptional Coreference Contexts, 255
Discourse-linking, 212, 219, 222
Distributional learning, 120, 121, 130–136, 144
Distributive/collective reading (of universal quantifiers), 353, 354
Doetjes, J., 352
Domain presupposition, 356, 376
Donaldson, M.A., 364
Dowty, D., 357
DPBE. *See* Delay of principle B effect
DP-local, 357, 379
Dresher, E., 138
Drozd, K.F., 14, 361, 362, 364, 367, 368, 376
Du Bois, J., 42, 44, 46
Dutch, 11, 19, 53, 133, 209, 248, 334, 352

E

Economy, 2, 203, 204, 217, 219–221, 227, 239, 260, 261, 330
ECM. *See* Exceptional case marking
Eisenberg, Z., 18, 19, 29
Elbourne, P., 250, 257, 279–282, 284
Elman, J.L., 133
Emergence hypothesis, 363, 367
Empiricist theories, 90–106
EQA. *See* Event quantificational account
Ervin-Tripp, S., 36, 204
Evans, G., 253, 254
Event quantification, 11, 367, 368, 373
Event quantificational account (EQA), 367, 368, 373, 381, 382, 385, 389
Everaert, M., 252, 257
Exceptional case marking (ECM), 85, 86, 159, 249, 251, 253, 266, 268, 269, 275–277, 279, 282, 284, 285

Exhaustive pairing, 11, 215, 222, 352, 361, 364–373
Exhaustive response, 364
Extra object (EO) condition, 361, 363–365, 369, 370, 372, 383, 389, 390

F

Falcaro, M., 89
Farmer, A.K., 297
Faroese, 63
Felix, S., 17
Ferguson, K.S., 219
Fischer, S., 249, 250
Fodor, J.A., 363
Fodor, J.D., 20, 139, 143, 145, 344
Force, 26, 81, 104, 110, 126, 131, 144, 150, 159, 165, 191, 193–196, 199, 205, 212, 214, 216, 221, 227, 231, 234, 235, 238, 254– 256, 260, 270, 283, 334, 345, 358, 373
Fox, D., 173–175, 178, 179, 330
Francis, N., 122
Franck, J., 207
Fraser, C., 13, 36
Freeman, H.H., 361, 364, 367, 368
Freeman, N.H., 367
French, 15, 16, 19, 20, 24, 25, 27–29, 34, 41, 54, 55, 57, 58, 60, 63, 78–80, 82, 92, 96– 98, 102, 142, 143, 148, 193, 194, 201, 202, 206, 209–211, 226, 229, 230, 233, 248, 249, 257, 264, 268, 270–272, 275–277, 280, 324, 365
Frequency, 18, 20–22, 25, 28–32, 121– 124, 132, 147, 157, 158, 175–177, 181, 184, 200, 203, 206, 342, 363, 365, 367, 368, 372
Frisian, 228, 256, 257, 280, 283

G

Gavarró, A., 29, 221
Genetics of SLI, 89
Gennari, S., 319, 330, 341, 342
Gerken, L., 25, 31, 33
German, 7, 16, 55, 134, 191, 248, 292, 340
Gibson, E., 21, 92–96, 137
Gillen, K., 330
Gold, M., 124–126, 128, 129
Goodluck, H., 226
Gordon, P., 157, 175
Goro, T., 292
Governing category, 252
Grebenyova, L., 212, 220

Greek, 226, 251, 254, 274
Greenfield, P., 15, 41
Grillo, A., 285
Grillo, N., 207
Grimshaw, J., 261, 265, 279
Grinstead, J., 148, 194
Grodzinsky, Y., 9, 173–175, 178, 179, 248, 253, 254, 264, 284
Grohmann, K.K., 219
Gualmini, A., 265, 266, 319, 320, 324, 326, 328, 329, 331–340, 345
Guasti, M.T., 19, 24, 60, 63, 64, 82, 120, 207, 209
Guasti, T., 13
Guerriero, A., 42, 45
Guilfoyle, E., 20, 23, 24
Guise, 5, 9, 256, 265, 266, 270, 272, 273, 276
Gürkanli, O., 45, 46

H

Haan, D., 25
Haegeman, L., 19, 25, 27, 28, 145
Hamann, C.O., 16, 19, 20, 23, 24, 27, 29, 31, 34, 45, 247, 365
Han, C.H., 344
Hanlon, C., 355, 359
Hawkins, R., 216
Haznedar, B., 69
Head movement, 54, 261
Head parameter, 7, 203, 219, 220, 222
Hebrew, 63, 99, 206, 281
Heim, I., 253, 255, 256, 265, 266, 273, 282, 344
Heizmann-Dodd, T., 215
Hendriks, P., 249, 266, 269, 277
Hestvik, A., 263, 278, 284, 365
Hiemstra, I, 228
Higginbotham, J., 218, 254
Hindi, 227, 228, 230
Hirsch, C., 170, 171
Hirsh-Pasek, K., 359
Hoekstra, T., 24, 25, 41, 90, 112
Hollebrandse, B., 195, 214, 235
Horgan, D., 162
Horning, J., 128, 129
Horn scale, 255, 260
Hornstein, N., 233
Huang, C., 20, 40
Huang, Y., 342
Hughes, M., 33, 42, 43, 45
Hyams, N., 13, 15–17, 19–21, 23–25, 28, 30–33, 35, 37, 40–46, 55, 62, 64, 97, 112, 113, 145, 148

I

Icelandic, 63, 65, 78, 100, 256, 257
Imitation, 15, 31–37, 40, 59, 159, 160
Imperatives, 36–39, 64, 194
Implicature, 9, 212, 239, 253, 255, 265, 266, 269, 283, 285, 340
Indefinites, 166, 334, 344, 356, 386
Inductive inference, 125, 126, 128, 129, 133, 137, 144
INFL licensed, 64, 65, 76
Information structure, 4, 15, 30, 40–46, 212, 222
Ingham, R., 20, 23
Ingram, D., 204
Inhelder, B., 360, 364
Interface, 3–5, 8–10, 75, 159, 189, 192, 215, 232–235, 238–240, 259, 260, 285
Intervention, 132, 206–208, 210, 211, 220, 226
Inverse scope, 330, 334, 335, 353, 3338
Ionin, T., 69
Irish, 63
Ishii, T., 292
Isobe, M., 314
Italian, 15–22, 24, 26, 27, 29, 31, 32, 35, 40–46, 53, 55, 60, 62–65, 70, 72, 73, 76, 78, 79, 82, 94, 100, 141, 145, 146, 149, 202, 203, 206, 216, 226, 248, 264, 271, 276
Item/usage based learning, 120, 121, 123
I-to-C movement, 195

J

Jaeggli, O., 20
Jakubowicz, C., 34, 112, 209, 210, 231, 247, 248, 264, 271, 278, 281, 282
Japanese, 8, 20, 138, 216, 226, 291, 352
Jelinek, E., 352

K

Kam, X., 133
Katada, F., 309
Kaufmann, D., 261, 263
Kayne, R., 3, 7, 209
Kenstowicz, M., 26
Kim, Y.J, 20, 25
Kindergarten path effect, 329
Klein, S.M, 17
Klein, W., 235
Klima, E., 13
Kobuchi-Philip, M., 357

Ko, H., 293
Ko, I., 169
Korhonen, A., 124
Koster, J., 25
Krämer, I., 23, 24, 334
Kratzer, A., 212, 235, 344, 373
Krifka, M., 358
Kucera, H., 122
Kuroda, S.Y., 312, 313
Kurtzman, H.S., 330

L

Lakatos, I., 340, 341
Language-as-fixed-effect fallacy, 389
Lasnik, H., 195, 302
Learnability, 2, 3, 6, 7, 17, 93, 124–129, 143–149, 222, 320, 325, 330, 340, 341, 344, 346, 368
Lebeaux, D., 20
Lee, H., 169
Lee, T., 181
Left periphery, 4, 26, 194, 195, 220, 239, 277, 285
Legate, J.A., 6, 91, 92, 95–105
Leonard, L.B., 67
Levinson, S., 253–255
Levow, G.A., 19, 55
Lewis, J., 133
Lexicalist, 196, 239
Lidz, J., 319, 320, 324, 326, 329, 330, 333, 335–344, 346
Lightfoot, D., 138, 148
Lillo-Martin, D., 17, 40
Lloyd, P., 364
Loeb, D.F., 67
Logical problem of language acquisition, 14, 17, 292, 314
Long-distance movement, 191, 207, 225, 239
Longitudinal development, 147–150
Lorusso, P., 18, 29, 60
Lust, B., 36

M

MacDonald, M.C., 319, 330, 341, 342
Machobane, M., 177, 182
MacWhinney, B., 43, 193
Magerman, D., 134
Malay, 228
Mandarin, 181, 182
Manzini, R., 93, 252, 257
Mapping problem, 352, 354

Maratsos, M.P., 131, 160, 161, 174, 178, 182
Marcus, M., 134
Masunaga, K., 296
Matsuoka, K., 263
Maturation, 6, 8, 15, 18, 26, 47, 53, 59, 87–90, 104, 105, 146, 163, 164, 177, 312, 363
Maxfiel, T., 263
McClelland, J., 134
McDaniel, D., 229, 261, 263
McKee, C., 37, 247
Meroni, L., 266
Methodology, 10, 37, 150, 159, 161, 172, 320, 323, 333, 335, 340, 344–346, 365, 373, 380
Minai, U., 312
Minimalism, 4, 36, 195, 238, 259–261
Mintz, T., 131
Miyagawa, S., 306, 312
Mlu, 31, 32, 34, 35, 44, 45, 58, 62, 64
Modal meanings, 71, 112
Module, 2–4, 8, 10, 189–191, 196, 197, 201, 213, 217, 221, 222, 237, 239, 314
Moloi, F., 177, 182
Morphological uniformity, 5, 19, 20, 35, 41
Musolino, J., 319

N

Negation, 10, 13, 14, 74, 79, 80, 93, 94, 98, 101–103, 112, 142, 166–168, 207, 219, 231, 319–325, 328, 330, 333–335, 340, 341, 343–346, 354
Negative element, 94, 103, 167
Negative evidence, 3, 28, 126, 129, 145, 358–360
Niyogi, P., 126
Normal world constraint, 370
Norris, R., 85, 86
Norwegian, 57, 63, 256, 263, 264, 365
Noveck, I.A., 265
Null subjects, 5, 14–47, 53, 64, 65, 73, 75, 76, 78, 80, 82, 83, 97, 146, 148, 149, 170
Null subjects (English), 15, 16, 20, 24, 41, 170

O

O'Brien, K., 178, 179, 181, 182, 184
O'Grady, W., 23, 24, 120, 204, 341
Oiry, M., 230
Okabe, R., 178
Optimality theory, 129, 135, 249

Optional infinitive (OI), 5, 53–113
Orfitelli, R., 15, 37
Osherson, D., 126
Otsu, Y., 224, 291
Output omission model (OOM), 30–32
Over-exhaustive search, 361

P

PA. *See* Pragmatic account
PAC learning. See Probably approximately correct learning
Pairing, 11, 135, 191, 211–218, 222, 352, 361, 364–367, 370, 373, 385
Papafragou, A., 265, 340
Parameter
  missetting, 15–30
  setting, 3, 5, 6, 14–16, 20, 21, 23, 27, 36, 46, 87, 94, 106, 120, 128, 133, 136–140, 142, 143, 205, 314, 342
Parsing, 10, 21, 134–136, 138, 139, 204, 207, 210, 211, 326, 330, 333, 335, 342
Partial knowledge, 363
Passive, 8, 54, 155, 190, 311, 337
Pearson, B., 174
Perfectionist response (PR), 364
Performance, 4, 5, 8, 9, 15, 25, 27, 29, 32, 35–39, 46, 131, 132, 134, 135, 146, 204, 210, 215, 224, 249, 261, 263–265, 267–269, 271, 272, 274, 277, 279, 283, 284, 337, 345, 352, 361, 363, 364, 367–369, 371, 372, 381, 383, 385, 387–389
Perfors, A., 133
Perner, J., 238
Pesetsky, D., 166, 235
Phase, 8, 36, 220, 223, 227–240, 326
Philip, B., 364
Philip, W., 263, 278, 284, 365, 367, 372, 373, 390
Phillips, C., 23, 24, 148
Piaget, J., 360, 364
Pica, P., 330
Picture verification, 262, 263, 268, 272, 279, 280
Pierce, A., 13, 14, 25, 54, 55, 57, 98, 113, 148
Pine, E., 196, 198
Pine, J., 91, 196
PIP. *See* Pronoun interpretation problem
Pinker, S., 17, 144, 340, 346, 355
Plato's problem, 9, 292
Plausible denial, 279, 281
Plunkett, K., 16, 20, 23, 24, 27, 29, 31, 34, 45

Poeppel, D., 13, 23–25, 57, 61, 62, 71, 73, 80, 81
Point of view, 4, 8, 89, 235–240, 283, 309, 312, 341, 376
Pollock, J.Y., 54
Portuguese, 18, 19, 26, 29, 63, 202, 208
Posnansky, C.J., 180
Postal, P., 207
Poverty of the stimulus, 132, 247, 292
Pragmatic account (PA), 40, 249, 276, 370, 371
Pragmatic restriction, 355, 358, 367–372, 388, 389
Pragmatics, 4, 9, 192, 213, 217, 234, 248, 249, 254, 279, 284, 326–334
Presupposition failure, 362, 369
Priming, 178, 180–181, 184, 320, 339, 342, 362
Principle A., 247, 252, 261, 267
Principle B., 9, 247–250, 252, 253, 255, 258, 262, 264, 267, 271, 278–283
Principle C., 247, 252, 270, 282
Probably approximately correct (PAC) learning, 125, 126, 128, 129
Pro-drop, 5, 15–22, 24, 25, 27, 29, 32, 34, 35, 42, 141, 142, 145, 146, 149, 194
Production-comprehension asymmetry, 249, 281, 283
Pronoun interpretation problem (PIP), 248

Q

Quantification, 10, 11, 213, 214, 218, 239, 285, 319, 351–390
Quantified antecedents, 9, 248, 251, 262–264, 278, 281, 282, 284, 285
Quantifier float, 295, 297, 306, 312
Quantifier scope ambiguity, 353
Quantifier spreading, 213, 361
Question answer requirement, 10, 320, 326, 331
Question-under-discussion (QUD), 256, 266, 285, 331, 335

R

Radford, A., 35, 59
Raising, 16, 76, 97–102, 142, 143, 148, 165, 169–172, 260, 344
Rasetti, L., 20, 24, 27, 28, 148
Rayner, K., 180
Reali, F., 133
Reconstruction, 223, 236–239
Redington, M., 132

Referential economy, 260
Referentiality, 250, 258, 260, 269, 275–277, 284, 285
Reflexives, 9, 247, 250–252, 261, 262, 267, 269, 271, 272, 276, 279, 282–284
Reflexivity framework, 249, 257, 261, 267
Reinhart, T., 216, 248, 251, 253, 254, 257, 258, 264, 265, 267, 275, 282, 284, 325, 326, 341
Relativized minimality, 204, 207, 226–227, 261
Relevance, 4, 5, 91, 120, 126, 134, 135, 279, 281, 283
Response strategy, 367
Reuland, E., 252, 257–260, 267, 274–277
Rice, M.L., 88, 107, 113
Richards, N., 302
Rizzi, L., 5, 6, 16, 17, 24–29, 40, 41, 46, 77–80, 87, 89, 194, 212, 225, 226, 228
Roberts, I., 21
Roberts, T., 83–85
Roeper, T., 1, 3, 9, 19, 21, 23, 27, 28, 41, 80, 84, 145, 174, 189, 225, 291
Rohrbacher, B., 19, 23, 41, 80
Rojina, N., 220
Role of input, 146, 333
Romance, 202, 248, 249, 251, 261, 264, 269–271, 273, 277, 282–284, 292
Romani, 191, 220, 227
Rooryck, J., 219
Root clause, 5, 19, 24, 26, 28, 56, 57, 63, 147
Root infinitive, 23, 26, 41, 55–57, 61, 64, 82, 147, 149
Root subject drop parameter, 25–30
Rosen, S., 261, 265, 279, 367
Ross, J.R., 189, 253, 295
Rowland, C., 196, 201
Rudin, C., 198
Ruigendijk, E., 277–281
Rule I., 255, 256, 264, 265, 269, 276, 283
Rule P., 9, 254, 256

S

Saddy, J.D., 361
Safir, K., 19
Sag, I., 253, 254, 344
Saito, M., 195, 298, 302
Sakas, W., 143, 145
Salient Object Strategy (SOS), 371
Sano, T., 20, 23, 24, 28, 64, 178, 295–297, 311

Sans, Y.C., 29
Sauerland, U., 214
Schaeffer, J., 64
Schlonsky, U., 26
Schroeder, H., 45, 46
Schultz, B., 227
Schulz, P., 214, 216, 228
Schutze, C.T., 13, 67, 68, 75, 78, 89, 91, 97, 107–111
Schwartz, B., 69, 90
Schwarzschild, R., 353, 355
Scope, 10, 135, 145, 192, 210, 212, 218, 219, 234, 302, 303, 307, 320–322, 324, 325, 329–335, 337, 338, 340, 341, 343, 344, 346, 353, 361, 372
Scrambling, 209, 211, 237, 292–297, 311
Seidl, A., 205
Semantic restriction, 11, 355–360, 379
Semantics, 5, 9, 55, 95, 160, 164, 167, 173, 176, 191, 192, 195, 211, 217, 232, 234, 239, 251, 254, 260, 319, 323, 344, 346, 368
Semantic subset principle (SSP), 344
Serbo-Croatian, 192, 221
Serratrice, L., 18, 29, 42, 45
Sesotho, 158, 176–178, 182–184
Shallow processing, 363, 367
Signature, 7, 93, 94, 142, 143, 145, 147, 148, 326, 355
Sigurjónsdóttir, S., 65, 261, 267, 268, 278
Simplicity, 3, 59, 60, 67, 89, 259
Slave, 228
SLI. *See* Specific language impairment
Smith, J., 15, 41
Snedeker, J., 330, 342
Snow, C., 43
Snyder, W., 198, 330
Sorace, A., 40, 42
Spanish, 15, 16, 29, 63, 92, 96, 97, 148, 194, 202, 203, 226, 248, 249, 264, 271, 275, 277, 278, 366
Speas, M., 235
Spec-head agreement, 195, 199, 207, 236
Specific language impairment (SLI), 87
Spenader, J., 249, 266, 269, 281, 285
Spinner, P., 193, 194
SSP. *See* Semantic subset principle
Standard binding theory, 250–254, 258
Starke, M., 270, 273–275
Statistical learning, 103, 135
Stowell, T., 357
Straus, K., 140
Strauss, U., 213
Strik, N., 209, 210, 231

Stromswold, K., 14, 198, 206, 209
Strong continuity hypothesis, 355
Strong minimalist thesis, 189, 192, 222–240
Strong pronouns, 249, 265, 271, 273, 274
Structural case, 66, 67, 258, 259, 268
Structure dependence, 132, 306–308
Subject-auxiliary inversion, 8, 195–197, 203
Subject-object asymmetry, 20, 33, 41, 203–204
Subset principle, 5, 10, 17, 26, 28, 93, 144–145, 283, 326, 342, 344
Sudhalter, V., 161, 178
Sugisaki, K., 177, 291
Superiority, 5, 192, 211, 216–222, 239
Surface scope, 320, 329–331, 333, 334, 346, 353
Symmetrical interpretation, 361
Syntactic categories, 130–132
Syntactic distance, 204, 210
Szabolcsi, A., 260

T
Takita, K., 293
Tamil, 63
Tanaka, H., 293
Tanenhaus, M., 331
Target population filter, 374, 375, 382, 383, 386, 387
Tense, 5, 13, 53, 135, 206, 266
Tense omission model, 68, 69, 73
Tense parameter, 93, 96–104
Tense-phrase, 100, 101
Tesar, B., 359
Test of early grammatical impairment (TEGI), 88
Thematic role reversal, 156
Theta-transmission, 173–176, 184
Thornton, R., 120, 148, 229, 231, 263, 265, 266, 325, 344–346
Thráinsson, H., 257
Thrasher, R., 27
Tomasello, M., 90, 146
Topicalization, 22, 23, 25, 29, 81, 190, 194, 205, 271
Topic drop, 20–22, 24, 26, 27, 29, 33–35, 40, 41, 60, 61, 82, 99, 145, 146, 148
Topic-hood, 281, 285
Tornyova, L., 190
Triggering, 18, 21, 59, 87, 137–140, 145, 146, 199, 234
Trochaic, 33, 34

Trueswell, J.C., 329, 330
Truncation, 5, 6, 24–30, 53, 77–83, 85, 86, 108, 112
Truth value judgment (TVJ), 10, 37, 170, 174, 178, 210, 248, 262, 297, 309, 313, 323, 345, 361
Tuijman, K., 25
Tunstall, S.L., 330, 341
Tyack, D., 23, 204

U
Ud Deen, K., 155
UG. *See* Universal grammer
Unaccusatives, 165–169, 171, 172, 178
Unambiguous trigger, 6, 93, 94
Under-exhaustive search, 364
Uninterpretable features, 75, 76, 216
Unique checking constraint, 6, 53, 73, 74
Universal grammar (UG), 1, 5, 14, 126, 140, 149, 184, 291–314, 341, 351
Universal phase requirement, 172
Utakis, S., 263

V
V2, 7, 8, 21, 24, 25, 27, 29, 57, 60, 61, 72, 73, 78, 80, 81, 87, 98–100, 103, 139, 197, 203, 235, 274
Vainikka, A., 225
Valian, V., 18–20, 23, 25, 27–34, 36, 38, 40, 42, 43, 123, 148, 180, 181, 184, 190
Vallabha, G., 131
Van der Lely, H.K.J., 206, 265
Van Gelderen, E., 256
van Loosbroek, E., 368, 376
Variational learning, 93, 94, 98, 99, 141, 143, 144, 147, 148
Varlakosta, S., 249, 274, 278
Varlakosto, S., 274
Verbuk, 250, 253, 255–257, 260, 265–267, 269, 274, 282, 283
Verbuk, A., 9
Verrips, M., 13, 25
Viau, J., 339
Villiers, J.D., 1
VP-local, 357–360
VP modifier, 357

W
Wang, Q., 19, 20, 22, 23, 25, 148
Watanabe, A., 302

Weak pronouns, 273, 275–277
Weissenborn, J., 13, 19, 23, 25, 27, 28, 217, 218
Westergaard, M., 7
Weverink, M., 24
Wexler, K., 9, 13, 18–21, 23–25, 30–33, 35, 40, 42–46, 53, 56–58, 61–65, 67, 69, 71–78, 80–82, 87, 89–97, 105–109, 112, 113, 128, 137, 162, 163, 165, 169, 170, 172, 252, 257, 312
Wh-in-situ, 10, 193, 194, 228, 230, 302, 306, 314
Wh-island, 302, 303, 305
White, L., 17
Wh-movement, 54, 80, 81, 141, 190, 192–194, 207, 208, 210, 211, 221, 223, 226–228, 230, 236, 237, 240, 263, 303, 306, 307
Why-questions, 199, 211
Williams, E., 3, 145
Wong, C., 181

X

Xo chains, 54
Xu, T., 181

Y

Yang, C., 3, 6, 21–23, 25, 27, 29, 33, 35, 60, 61, 91–105, 119, 123, 134, 147, 148, 216
Yang, X., 181
Yoshida, K., 293
Yoshida, T., 293
Yoshinaga, N., 206
Yusa, N., 216

Z

Zesiger, P., 272, 276, 281
zibun/anaphor, 308, 309, 311
Zimmerman, M., 212
Zipf, G.K., 121, 123, 124
Zipf's law, 121, 158
Zuckerman, S., 193, 201, 202

Printed by Books on Demand, Germany